Fourth Edition

Public Law

Fourth Edition

Paul Reid
Advocate, Ampersand

W. GREEN

THOMSON REUTERS

First Edition	2003 by Jane Munro
Second Edition	2007 by Jane Munro
Third Edition	2015 by Paul Reid
Fourth Edition	2020 by Paul Reid

Published in 2020 by Thomson Reuters, trading as W. Green, Atholl Exchange, 6 Canning Street, Edinburgh, EH3 8EG. Registered in England & Wales, Company No.1679046. Registered Office and address for service: 5 Canada Square, Canary Wharf, London, E14 5AQ.

For further information on our products and services, visit
http://www.sweetandmaxwell.co.uk/wgreen

Typeset by Letterpart Limited, Caterham on the Hill, Surrey, CR3 5XL.

Printed and bound in Great Britain by CPI Group (UK) Ltd, Croydon, CR0 4YY.

A CIP catalogue record of this book is available from the British Library.

ISBN (print): 978-0-414-06052-4

ISBN (print & e-book bundle): 978-0-414-08127-7

ISBN (e-book): 978-0-414-08128-4

Preface

"The great advantage of teaching constitutional law", I was assured back in 2004 when I first accepted a post as a part-time tutor at Edinburgh University, "is that nothing really changes so prepare once and your notes will last 20 years."

That particular piece of advice has not aged well. As Jane Smith noted in her preface to the previous edition, it is not that long ago that constitutional law could be readily mistaken for constitutional history. During the first two decades of this century, that idea has been swept away. It is too soon to tell what history will make of the events of the last few years (a constitutional flash in the pan or a watershed in the understanding of our constitution?), but it has been a fairly surreal time in which to be a constitutional lawyer. Dusty and dry topics of the constitution (the Royal Prerogative in respect of international obligations and the power to prorogue Parliament) have become leading news and the subject of general debate. The constitution is recalibrating to take account of the United Kingdom's departure from the European Union, at the behest of the result of a referendum (which, for the first time, produced an outcome that nobody in a position of power appeared to have properly contemplated or prepared for). All of that, taken with a vocal and well represented nationalist government in Edinburgh, has at times appeared to test the constitution to its very limits. So whatever aspirations I may have had for this edition being a relatively straightforward update of the previous one lay in tatters. That is reflected in this edition appearing several years later than first planned (or, as my ever-patient editors may say, promised). Structurally, the most significant change is the division of "judicial review" into two chapters: one on principles and practice and the other concerning the grounds of judicial review. Hopefully that part of the text should thus become more accessible, in particular to practitioners. Otherwise, the text has been revised to take account of material changes since the last edition.

Every effort has been made to reflect events arising out of the 2016 referendum and the United Kingdom's subsequent departure from the European Union in an objective and apolitical way. Some comment upon, but restricted I hope to the legal consequences of, events is necessary to properly explain and critique what has happened. But nothing should be taken as expressing an opinion one way or another on the underlying merits of the "Brexit" debate. Otherwise, every effort has been made to state the law as at 31 January 2020, subject to two qualifications. First, as usual, such subsequent developments as it was possible to take into account are reflected in the text (but no account has been taken of the legislative, and other, response to coronavirus). Second, the legislative arrangements for leaving the European Union are discussed in Ch.10 and those include the effect of the implementation period. But where EU law was relevant, for example, to the competences of the Scottish Parliament and the Scottish Government, the text proceeds on the assumption that the implementation period has ended and "retained EU law" now serves as the limitation on devolved competence.

Again, thanks are due to a number of people. Much of the text, and the overall structure, of the book originally prepared by Jane Smith remains and I am grateful to her for allowing me to revise what was her book. Feedback on the third edition from various colleagues, both at the Faculty of Advocates and the University of Edinburgh, persuaded me that undertaking a fourth edition was worthwhile and I am grateful for that encouragement. Likewise, I appreciated the many expressions of sympathy for (and, with hindsight at least, the many more of amusement at) my plight as yet another constitutional storm broke over the last few years. In the course of working on this text, I have benefitted from discussions with many of my colleagues at the Faculty on the various topics and themes covered by the book. In particular, John MacGregor and Daniel Byrne (both of Axiom Advocates) have helped with much of my thinking on what is now Ch.14 on judicial review procedure. Special mention is again due for Dr Daniel Carr (University of Edinburgh) who has been the source of much encouragement, many a reference or authority that may otherwise have gone unnoticed and who has spent many hours discussing, and consequently improving, various points made throughout the text. And my current devils (who by the time this is published will have started upon their respective careers at the Scottish Bar), Euan Scott and Victoria Arnott, have each gone above and beyond in reviewing draft chapters, undertaking research and provided invaluable comments, feedback and moral support. Their assistance was critical in getting this edition finally finished. Similarly, the librarians at the Faculty of Advocates helped with many a reference, especially when the Library was not readily available. The clerking team at Ampersand Stable again showed a seemingly endless patience as they sought to juggle the demands of practice with my desire to find the time to work on this text. A debt of gratitude is always owed to the editors, but special thanks has to be given the editorial team at W. Greens, in particular Kirsty Swain who has been understanding of my very flexible approach to what she called a "deadline" and who has indulged numerous "Brexit" extensions.

But above all, I am grateful to my family who have always supported me in all that I have done. None more so than my wife Kimberley, who has put up with my fretting over completing this book alongside the usual stresses and strains that come with being married to an Advocate. On top of that, our family has arrived since the last edition. Much more of this edition was finished whilst working at home than would otherwise have been expected. As a result, both Archie and Lily contributed greatly by providing regular and welcome distractions (not to mention a constant reminder of what is actually important). And once they were tucked up in bed, Henry provided me with some much appreciated company as I often found myself working into the small hours.

Like the last edition, this text is dedicated to my grandfathers, Tom and George, but now also my grandmother, Isobel, who has joined them since the last edition. Each of them, in their own different but very special way, remain a constant source of inspiration and encouragement in this and every other endeavour.

Paul Reid
at home in Edinburgh
8 June 2020

Preface from the Third Edition

The first edition of *Public Law* in Greens' Concise Scots Law series was published in 2003, about 10 years after I properly acquainted myself with constitutional and administrative law for the first time. During those 10 years, the subject had changed very much. My early education was mostly a matter of legal and constitutional history. The great post-war decisions in administrative law were hardly new; and many lawyers and legal scholars of that vintage regarded the 1980s, in particular, as a retrograde period in the development of the law on civil liberties and human rights. This was the perspective that informed the commitment of the Labour government elected in 1997 to devolution, freedom of information and the enactment of the Human Rights Act. It is fair to say that, at the time, I thoroughly applauded these developments.

They meant, however, that constitutional law and administrative law were no longer only of historic interest. That being so, the writing of the first edition of *Public Law* was a considerable undertaking, one I was only able to assume because I had time to devote to it after completing the Diploma in Legal Practice at Edinburgh University in 2003 with a view to being called to the Scots Bar (as I was in July 2005). The second edition of *Public Law* was published in the autumn of 2007. Even by that time, it was felt that enough had happened to warrant an updating of the first edition. I realised in the course of preparing the second edition, during the summer vacation of 2007, that I would not care to prepare the third. In the event, eight years have passed since the publication of the second edition and the developments in that time have called less for an updating of the book than its rewriting. Paul Reid, Advocate, has undertaken that task and the purpose of this preface is to express my gratitude to him, and my profound admiration. He modestly claims to have built on my original text, but this book is Paul's. I have learned a great deal from it. To my mind, it achieves what a textbook in this series ought to achieve: the right combination of thoroughness and rigour, conveyed in an accessible and intelligible way. I wish the book, and its author, every success.

Jane Smith
June 2015

TABLE OF CONTENTS

TABLE OF CASES

TABLE OF CASES

TABLE OF CASES

TABLE OF CASES

TABLE OF CASES

TABLE OF STATUTES

United Kingdom

Acts of the Parliament of Scotland

TABLE OF STATUTORY INSTRUMENTS

United Kingdom

Scotland

CHAPTER 1

Introduction: A Tale of Two Referendums

INTRODUCTION

There is something about the second decade of a new century that seems to prompt constitutional reform. In the twentieth century, leaving aside the terrors of the First World War, significant constitutional change arrived in the form of the Parliament Act 1911 (curtailing the powers of the House of Lords),[1] Irish home rule[2] and allowing women to enter the House of Commons for the first time.[3] In the twenty-first century, constitutional reform has been the tale of two referendums. First, in September 2014, Scotland voted on the "forever" Union and by a margin of 55.3 per cent to 44.7 per cent for Scotland to remain part of the United Kingdom. Next, in June 2016, the United Kingdom voted on the fate of another union that was, initially at least, meant to be one of "unlimited duration".[4] This time, the decision, by a margin of 51.9 per cent to 48.1 per cent, was to end the United Kingdom's 40-year plus membership of the European Union. That decision ultimately resulted in the United Kingdom, at 23:00 on 31 January 2020, becoming the first country to leave the European Union. Those votes have seen the constitutional arrangements of the United Kingdom tested to the extreme. That current constitutional discourse can be defined by two referendums would have been surprising at the turn of the century, given, as we shall see in Ch.5, the very limited experience that the United Kingdom had of using a referendum. Public law, especially that which would traditionally be regarded as "constitutional" law, often finds itself operating on the border where law meets politics. Never has that been truer than over the second half of the last decade. So as to set what follows in the rest of this book in its contemporary context, it is with the legal issues arising from those two referendums that we shall start. 1–01

[1] On the Parliament Act 1911, see para.6–12, below.
[2] Government of Ireland Act 1914.
[3] Parliament (Qualification of Women) Act 1918.
[4] That was how it was described by the European Court of Justice (as it was then styled) in C-6/64 *Costa v ENEL* [1964] E.C.R. 585 but in the Lisbon Treaty, an exit mechanism was introduced—the now familiar art.50 of the TEU.

2014 INDEPENDENCE REFERENDUM

Calling the referendum: the political basis

1–02 To understand the lead up to the September 2014 vote, we need to start with politics because the Scotland Act 1998 was clear: the Union of the Kingdoms of Scotland and England was a matter that was expressly reserved to the UK Parliament.[5] So how was it that the Scottish Parliament came to legislate for a referendum on Scottish independence and why did it become accepted that the Scottish Parliament was entitled so to legislate (at least on that occasion)? Irrespective of the terms of the Scotland Act 1998, for reasons of practical politics the Scottish Parliament would never legislate for a referendum on independence unless it had a majority of nationalist MSPs.[6] So it was a political prerequisite that the SNP hold an overall majority in the Scottish Parliament. As we will see in Ch.4, below the electoral system used for the Parliament was one that should ordinarily produce coalition or minority government.[7] Given the absence of a second chamber that was not a surprising choice. But the practical consequence was that the SNP required to have an exceptional degree of electoral success before the possibility of calling a referendum on independence could even begin to be envisaged and the question of the Scotland Act 1998 discussed. In 2007, the SNP were returned as the largest party with 47 MSPs (one more than the Scottish Labour Party). That was significantly short of the 65 required to have a majority in the Parliament. In 2010, the SNP Government consulted on a draft Referendum (Scotland) Bill.[8] Without a parliamentary majority[9] the Bill was withdrawn before it was put to a vote. The political landscape changed significantly as a result of the 2011 Scottish general election, which saw the SNP again returned as the largest party in the Parliament. But this time they had 69 MSPs and thus an overall majority. If a similar Bill were to be introduced in that parliamentary session, the Scottish Government could expect to have the votes to secure its passage. And with a clear manifesto commitment to hold such a referendum, the newly returned SNP Government claimed the democratic mandate and legitimacy to hold a referendum. The politics now being in place, the introduction of the necessary enabling legislation appeared inevitable. That required the legal basis on which such a referendum could be held to be addressed.

Calling the referendum: the legal basis

1–03 As we have already noted, the terms of the Scotland Act appeared to be clear and appeared to prohibit the Scottish Parliament legislating to hold an independence referendum. In the 2010 consultation the Scottish Government had maintained

[5] Scotland Act 1998 Sch.6 para.1(b).

[6] The majority of nationalist MSP belong to the Scottish National Party (SNP) but the Scottish Green Party also supported independence. For ease of reference, the discussion that follows talks of the SNP holding a majority but that is shorthand for a nationalist majority in the Scottish Parliament.

[7] See para.4–08, below.

[8] Scottish Government, *Scotland's Future: Draft Referendum (Scotland) Bill Consultation Paper* (Scottish Government, 2010).

[9] Support from the Scottish Green Party (two votes) and an independent MSP (Margo McDonald) gave the SNP Government only 50 votes.

that if the question was worded appropriately, the Scottish Parliament would have the power to legislate for a referendum.[10] That view was disputed by the UK Government. They insisted that any Bill that sought to authorise the holding of an independence referendum, whatever the precise wording of the question might be, would "relate to" the Union and thus fall outside the competence of the Scottish Parliament.[11] The Scottish and the UK Governments did agree that the SNP Government had won a mandate to hold an independence referendum and that it was better for the legal basis to be put beyond doubt rather than be subject to challenge in the courts. That common accord gave rise to what became known as the Edinburgh Agreement.[12] On 15 October 2012, the Scottish and UK Governments signed an agreement that was to allow the Scottish Parliament to legislate for an independence referendum. The Scottish Parliament was to be given the competence to legislate for the referendum by means of a "section 30 Order": that is an Order in Council made in terms of s.30(2) of the Scotland Act 1998 to modify the list of reserved matters. It was a condition of that transfer of power that the referendum be held by the end of 2014 and that a single question be put to the voters with only two possible answers.[13] The date of the referendum, the precise wording of the question and the franchise for the vote were all matters to be determined by the Scottish Parliament. On 12 February 2013 the Privy Council made the Scotland Act 1998 (Modification of Schedule 5) Order 2013[14] giving effect to the terms of the Edinburgh Agreement. The Scottish Parliament now had the legislative competence to pass a Bill authorising the holding of an independence referendum.

Legislating for the referendum

The first step taken by the Scottish Parliament on the road to authorising the referendum was to determine the franchise. This was fixed by the Scottish Independence Referendum (Franchise) Act 2013 ("the Franchise Act"). Here the most noticeable provision was the extension of the franchise to 16 and 17-year-olds, which reflected the Scottish Government's policy that the franchise be extended to that group for all elections. The Franchise Act therefore had to make provision for the registration of those individuals for the purposes of the referendum.[15] Other than that (significant) change, the franchise reflected those for Scottish parliamentary and local government elections. That was consistent 1–04

[10] Scottish Executive, *Choosing Scotland's Future: A National Conversation* (The Stationery Office, 2007), p.35.

[11] Scotland Office, *Scotland's Constitutional Future: A consultation on facilitating a legal, fair and decisive referendum on whether Scotland should leave the United Kingdom* (The Stationery Office, 2012), Cm.8203, p.11. That view was based on the wording, and interpretation, of s.29(3) of the Scotland Act 1998.

[12] The Edinburgh Agreement is available at *http://www2.gov.scot/Resource/0040/00404789.pdf* [Accessed 22 July 2020].

[13] The 2010 consultation by the Scottish Government had proposed that there be two questions: one about independence and one about so-called "devo-max" (a substantial further transfer of powers to the Scottish Parliament). In 2012, the UK Government was opposed to a second question, insisting that a single, clear, question be put so as to ensure a clear and decisive result.

[14] Scotland Act 1998 (Modification of Schedule 5) Order 2013 (SSI 2013/242).

[15] That provision is made in the Scottish Independence Referendum (Franchise) Act 2013 ss.4–9, which required the creation of a "register of young voters" for each electoral area.

with the approach taken for the devolution referendum in 1997.[16] The consequence was eligibility to vote in the referendum was basically tied to residency in Scotland on the date of the referendum: Scots who worked and lived outside Scotland were generally not entitled to vote. The other provision of significance was the blanket disenfranchisement of serving prisoners. That ban, which was found in s.3 of the Franchise Act, was to be subject to judicial challenge.

1–05 As we shall see in Ch.4, the blanket disenfranchisement of serving prisoners by s.3 of the Representation of the People Act 1983 had long been held to be incompatible with art.3 of Protocol 1 to the European Convention on Human Rights.[17] The Franchise Act repeated the prohibition contained in s.3 of the 1983 Act.[18] A number of serving prisoners judicially reviewed the competence of that provision: *Moohan, Petitioner*.[19] There was a superficial attraction to the petitioners' argument: if participating in a parliamentary election every four or five years was a fundamental human right surely participating in a referendum of such constitutional significance as the independence referendum was also protected? That argument, however, ran into difficulties when it confronted the wording of art.3 of Protocol 1. Article 3 of Protocol 1 ("A3P1") requires the UK to "hold free elections at reasonable intervals" to ensure the free expression of the electorate "in the choice of the legislature". The Strasbourg court had held that A3P1 did not cover referendums.[20] The "reasonable intervals" requirement caused an obvious tension: the independence referendum was said to be a "once in a generation" event. If A3P1 applied so as to afford serving prisoners a vote, it raised at least the possibility of a challenge in the years to come that the "reasonable intervals" requirement had been infringed. It was an issue that divided the Supreme Court: the ban survived by five votes to two.

Influential to the minority (Lord Kerr and Lord Wilson) was the fact that the Convention is a "living instrument" whose interpretation evolves with the times. Accordingly, the fact that referendums were not in the contemplation of the framers of the Convention was not fatal to the prisoners' argument.[21] A3P1, said Lord Kerr, had to be interpreted in light of its object and purpose.[22] When that was borne in mind:

> "it is difficult to see how that purpose would be other than frustrated by preventing the safeguard applicable to ordinary legislative elections from applying to the most fundamental of votes."[23]

---

[16] Referendums (Scotland and Wales) Act 1997.

[17] *Smith v Scott* [2007] CSIH 9; 2007 S.C. 345; see para.4–13, below and the cases cited therein.

[18] Franchise Act s.3; see para.10 of the explanatory notes that accompanied the Bill that made the intention to repeat the ban contained in the 1983 Act clear.

[19] *Moohan, Petitioner* [2014] UKSC 67; 2015 S.C. (U.K.S.C.) 1. As explained in Ch.6 below, any provision of an Act of the Scottish Parliament that is incompatible with a Convention right is outwith the legislative competence of the Scottish Parliament with the effect that it is "not law" (Scotland Act 1998 s.29).

[20] *X v United Kingdom* (Application No.7096/75) Unreported 3 October 1975 European Court of Human Rights (concerning the UK referendum on continued membership of the then EEC) and *Bader v Austria* (1996) 22 E.H.R.R. CD213 (concerning the Austrian referendum on accession to the then EC).

[21] *Moohan, Petitioner* [2014] UKSC 67; 2015 S.C. (U.K.S.C.) 1 per Lord Kerr at [67].

[22] *Moohan, Petitioner* [2014] UKSC 67; 2015 S.C. (U.K.S.C.) 1 per Lord Kerr at [67].

[23] *Moohan, Petitioner* [2014] UKSC 67; 2015 S.C. (U.K.S.C.) 1 per Lord Kerr at [68].

The "regular intervals" requirement was, in the minority's view, secondary to the primary aim of A3P1 that citizens should have a full role in the selection of who shall govern them.[24] So far as the Strasbourg case law was concerned, according to Lord Wilson, it was not, as the majority described it, "unequivocal" on the point and the Supreme Court could, and should, go further and extend the application of A3P1 to the independence referendum.[25] The majority took a much narrower view. Lord Hodge, who gave the leading judgment for the majority, found that there was a clear and constant line of decisions from the Strasbourg court that excluded referendums from the scope of A3P1 and that line ought to be followed by the Supreme Court.[26] The "regular intervals" requirement was also influential to the majority: that requirement suggests the framers of the Convention did not have referendums in mind.[27] Furthermore, Lady Hale held that A3P1 does not, and cannot, require a referendum on Scottish independence to be held, thus it follows that the protections that have been implied into A3P1 cannot be applicable to such a vote.[28]

Perhaps the most surprising reason cited by the majority (and expressed in the judgment of Lord Neuberger, with whom the rest of the majority agreed) was what was said to be the consequence of the referendum:

> "... while the main political parties had committed themselves to accept the result of the Referendum, a 'yes' vote would not of itself have triggered independence for Scotland. If there had been a 'yes' vote,[29] Scotland would not have achieved independence unless and until the UK Parliament had voted in favour, and, whatever the main parties had promised, Members of Parliament would have been free, indeed constitutionally bound, to vote as they saw fit."[30]

Assuming that to be correct as a strict proposition of law, it serves to highlight how many of the issues surrounding the referendum operated at the very boundary of the law and politics. Had there been a "yes" vote, as there was to be in the 2016 referendum, the idea that the UK Parliament would then refuse to pass legislation giving effect to that vote is not readily conceivable.

That, unlike what was to happen in relation to the 2016 referendum, was to prove the only time any aspect of the independence referendum was tested in the courts. But it demonstrated that the issues were both legally complex and impossible to divorce entirely from the prevailing political climate. However, the short point to note is the disenfranchisement of serving prisoners stood and the vires of the Franchise Act was vindicated.

---

[24] *Moohan, Petitioner* [2014] UKSC 67; 2015 S.C. (U.K.S.C.) 1, per Lord Kerr at [69], per Lord Wilson at [93]–[96].

[25] *Moohan, Petitioner* [2014] UKSC 67; 2015 S.C. (U.K.S.C.) 1 at [103]–[105]. For discussion of the regard that should be had to Strasbourg authorities, see paras 11–05—11–06.

[26] *Moohan, Petitioner* [2014] UKSC 67; 2015 S.C. (U.K.S.C.) 1 at [9]–[13].

[27] *Moohan, Petitioner* [2014] UKSC 67; 2015 S.C. (U.K.S.C.) 1, per Lord Hodge at [8].

[28] *Moohan, Petitioner* [2014] UKSC 67; 2015 S.C. (U.K.S.C.) 1 at [54]–[55].

[29] Although the outcome of the appeal was advised later the same afternoon (24 July 2014) after the oral arguments had concluded, it was not until 17 December 2014 that the written reasons were provided which allowed Lord Neuberger to reflect the outcome in his judgment.

[30] *Moohan, Petitioner* [2014] UKSC 67; 2015 S.C. (U.K.S.C.) 1 at [47]. See also the decision of the Supreme Court of Canada in *Reference re Secession of Quebec* [1998] 2 S.C.R. 217 where the limits of the law were expressly recognised by that court.

1–06 The substantive legislation that regulated the referendum was the Scottish Independence Referendum Act 2013 ("the Referendum Act"). Section 1 provided for a referendum to be held on 18 September 2014[31] on the question: "Should Scotland be an independent country?"[32] The original wording proposed by the Scottish Government was: "Do you agree that Scotland should be an independent country?" The Electoral Commission was asked for their advice on the wording and intelligibility of that question. "Do you agree . . . " was found by the Electoral Commission's research to have the possibility of leading people towards voting yes hence they recommended the wording that actually appeared in the Referendum Act.[33] It was necessary for the Referendum Act to make provision for the conduct of the campaign. Detailed provision on the conduct of a referendum campaign had been made in the Political Parties, Elections and Referendums Act 2000.[34] The independence referendum, however, having been legislated for by the Scottish Parliament and not Westminster, was not a referendum for the purposes of the 2000 Act.[35] Detailed provision therefore had to be made by the Referendum Act. The principal provisions of note were: the Electoral Commission were to be responsible for monitoring and securing compliance with the campaign rules (s.12); the Electoral Commission were required to take steps to promote public awareness and understanding of the referendum, the question and how to vote (s.23)[36]; and no challenge to the result was permitted other than by judicial review and any such petition had to be lodged within six weeks of the declaration of the result (s.34). The "referendum period" (the time during which the campaigning and funding rules applied) was fixed at 16 weeks (Sch.8) and thus began on 30 May 2014. Schedule 4 to the Referendum Act made provision for detailed "campaign rules".[37] These cover the registration of "permitted participants" (Sch.4 para.3), the selection of "designated organisation" (in other words, the official "yes" and "no" campaigns) (Sch.4 para.6), the regulation of expenses (Sch.4 paras 10–25) and the control of donations to the permitted participants (Sch.4 paras 29–44). These rules largely mirror the provision made in the Political Parties, Elections and Referendums Act 2000 for a referendum that falls within its scope and which are discussed in Ch.5, below.

---

[31] Scottish Independence Referendum Act 2013 s.1(4). The Scottish Ministers had the power to vary this date if it became "impossible or impracticable" to hold the referendum on that date (s.1(5)) so long as the alternative date was no later than 31 December 2014 (s.1(6)).

[32] The question was prescribed by s.1(2).

[33] Electoral Commission, *Referendum on independence for Scotland: advice of the Electoral Commission on the proposed referendum question* (Electoral Commission, 2013), *http://www.electoralcommission.org.uk/__data/assets/pdf_file/0007/153691/Referendum-on-independence-for-Scotland-our-advice-on-referendum-question.pdf* [Accessed 10 June 2020].

[34] Political Parties, Elections and Referendums Act 2000 Pt VII. See para.5–10 et seq.

[35] Political Parties, Elections and Referendums Act 2000 s.101. The Scottish Parliament has now passed its own legislation regulating the conduct of any future referendum called by the Parliament: Referendums (Scotland) Act 2020.

[36] Given the remarkable turnout (just under 85%) there was clearly no issue as to a lack of awareness or understanding!

[37] Schedule 5 made provision for the Electoral Commission to investigate alleged breaches of the campaign rules; Sch.6 made provision for civil sanctions that attached to certain breaches; and Sch.7 made provision for various offences that were created by the Scottish Independence Referendum Act 2013.

The campaign

The "referendum period" may have only begun on 30 May 2014 but the campaign was long underway by that stage. In May and June 2013 the "Yes" and "Better Together" campaigns were launched, and in November 2013 the (SNP) Scottish Government launched its White Paper, *Scotland's Future: Your Guide to an Independent Scotland*.[38] It might have been called a White Paper, but in substance it was a campaigning document and one that the Scottish Government would deliver for free (on request) to any house in the UK. In this document 26 March 2016 was identified as "independence day". From the UK Government came a series of documents (19 in all) called *Scotland Analysis*.[39] These covered a range of topics such as banking, currency, energy, the EU and defence. On 19 June 2014 a concluding document (*United Kingdom, united future: Conclusions of the Scotland analysis programme*)[40] was published setting out the benefits Scotland had gained, and would continue to gain, from the Union. Just like the Scottish Government's White Paper, these documents are best viewed as campaign documents. The Scottish and UK Governments were not the only contributors to the debate. People and organisations from almost all sections of society participated and nothing close to a comprehensive review of the campaign can be attempted in this work.[41] Almost every major campaign issue had constitutional law implications: currency choice (and possible currency "union"); continued membership of the EU (which was an important political issue not just in Scotland but in Spain and other EU countries with separatist parties operating in various regions); and the relative merits of "devo-plus" as opposed to "devo-max" as opposed to independence. By the time polling day arrived, normal politics had been suspended for quite some time and Scotland had a very well-informed electorate, who were daily debating and wrestling with fundamental constitutional problems. Most of these issues were rendered especially difficult because they were "what if . . . " issues. Perhaps the most interesting, for constitutional lawyers if not the rest of the electorate, was what would the constitution of an independent Scotland look like? To that end, a draft Scottish Independence Bill was published in June 2014 and was put out to consultation. That draft Bill had three main purposes: to make provision for Scotland to become independent; to provide an interim constitution; and to make provision for holding a Constitutional Convention to draft a permanent constitution. The consultation period was due to end on 20 October 2014, by which time the referendum had taken place and the result was known.[42] **1–07**

[38] Scottish Government, *Scotland's Future: Your Guide to an Independent Scotland* (Scottish Government, 2013) *http://www.scotland.gov.uk/Publications/2013/11/9348/downloads* [Accessed 31 January 2020].

[39] See *https://www.gov.uk/government/collections/scotland-analysis* [Accessed 31 January 2020].

[40] HM Government, *United Kingdom, united future: Conclusions of the Scotland analysis programme* (The Stationery Office, 2014), Cm.8869, *https://www.gov.uk/government/uploads/system/uploads/attachment_data/file/321369/2902216_ScotlandAnalysis_Conclusion_acc2.pdf* [Accessed 10 May 2020].

[41] For another account of the Independence Referendum, see C.M.G. Himsworth and C.M. O'Neill, *Scotland's Constitution: Law and Practice*, 3rd edn (Haywards Heath: Bloomsbury Professional, 2015), Ch.4.

[42] For a fuller consideration of some of the more interesting aspects of the draft constitution, see paras 1–08—1–10 of the 3rd edition of this work.

The result and its aftermath

1–08 On 18 September 2014, Scotland went to the ballot box. With the eyes of the world focused upon her, Scotland determined the future of the 307-year-old Union. The vote, in terms of its organisation and the logistics, passed off without incident and coped with an unprecedented turnout (turnout was no lower than 75 per cent, with an average turnout of just under 85 per cent). Then, shortly after 6am on the morning of 19 September the result from Fife was declared and a "no" vote became inevitable. The official declaration of the result would not come for a number of hours yet (bad weather delayed some of the ballot papers for the Western Isles getting to the counting centre), but the Union would continue. Shortly after that declaration, the Prime Minister announced a number of measures, accompanied by a seemingly demanding timetable. Those measures included promises for "English votes on English law" (delivered in the form of revisions to the Standing Orders of the House of Commons[43]) and further devolved powers for Scotland. To consider the latter, the Prime Minister also announced the establishment of a commission to report on what further powers should be devolved to Scotland. This fulfilled "the vow" made by the leaders of the three main Westminster parties in the final days of the referendum campaign.[44] A commission, chaired by Lord Smith of Kelvin, recommended a range of further powers for the Scottish Parliament, including control over the voting system and franchise for the Scottish Parliament and establishing the Scottish Parliament and the Scottish Government as permanent institutions. The UK Government undertook to implement the recommendations of the Smith Commission and that resulted in the Scotland Act 2016.

1–09 Various provisions of the 2016 iteration of the Scotland Act are considered at different points in the following chapters, but there are a few points that are worthy of note at this stage. The Smith Commission had been formed, met, consulted, deliberated and reported by the end of November 2014, barely two months after the referendum. By January 2015 the draft clauses had been produced to "make it possible to quickly translate the [Smith Commission Agreement] into law at the beginning of the next Parliament and transfer power to Scotland".[45] The House of Lords Constitution Committee in particular was critical of this approach to such significant and potentially wide-reaching constitutional reform:

> "We do not believe that the referendum and subsequent events constitute a 'clearly justifiable' reason for adopting such an unusual process for initiating significant constitutional change. The undue haste with which the process was conducted... undermines confidence in the outcome."[46]

---

[43] Discussed at para.6–13, below.

[44] "The Vow" was a signed pledge by David Cameron, Ed Miliband and Nick Clegg that was published on the front page of the *Daily Record* on 16 September 2014 that promised "extensive new powers" for the Scottish Parliament.

[45] HM Government, *Scotland in the United Kingdom: An enduring settlement*, p.7.

[46] House of Lords Select Committee on the Constitution, *Proposals for the devolution of further powers to Scotland, 10th Report of Session 2014–15* (The Stationery Office, 2015) HL Paper 145, para.47.

The point is well made: by the time voters in Scotland went to the polls, the options on the ballot paper were independence and further significant devolution. A few of the changes introduced by the 2016 Act serve to illustrate the point.

First, s.1 of the 2016 Act added a new s.63A to the Scotland Act 1998. It provides:

> **"Permanence of the Scottish Parliament and Scottish Government**
> **63A.**—(1) The Scottish Parliament and the Scottish Government are a permanent part of the United Kingdom's constitutional arrangements.
> (2) The purpose of this section is, with due regard to the other provisions of this Act, to signify the commitment of the Parliament and Government of the United Kingdom to the Scottish Parliament and the Scottish Government.
> (3) In view of that commitment it is declared that the Scottish Parliament and the Scottish Government are not to be abolished except on the basis of a decision of the people of Scotland voting in a referendum."

These statements can only be declaratory of an aspiration rather than declaratory of the law. That is because, as explained in Ch.3, below on a traditional understanding of the UK constitution, the Westminster Parliament has the power to make or unmake any law and the only limit on its competence is that it cannot bind its successors.[47] So, the language of permanence can be no more than a statement of desire rather than a legally binding commitment.[48] Similarly, what purports to be an obligation to hold a referendum is also just a statement of desire. Parliament is not bound by its predecessors in substance or in the manner and form of subsequent legislation, thus it would be open to a future Parliament to legislate for the abolition of either devolved institution "notwithstanding s.63A(3) of the Scotland Act 1998".[49] Because, despite all the authority that the Scottish Parliament derives from its democratically elected membership,[50] it is fundamentally a body that has been created by statute.[51] As such, it is, in law at least, just as susceptible to abolition by a future UK Parliament as any other statutory body. That, like so many aspects of the UK constitution, is the strict legal orthodoxy. It does not mean that any future Parliament would be able, as a matter of political reality, to pass such legislation. In a similar vein, by s.2 of the 2016 Act, s.28 of the Scotland Act 1998 (which confers legislative power upon the Scottish Parliament) was amended with a view to asserting the importance of another feature of the devolution settlement:

> "(8) But it is recognised that the Parliament of the United Kingdom will not normally legislate with regard to devolved matters without the consent of the Scottish Parliament."

---

[47] See paras 3–02—3–08, below for a discussion of this orthodox statement of constitutional principle and some of the current challenges to it.

[48] Not all agree. For example, see: K. Campbell, *The "Scotland clauses" and parliamentary supremacy* [2015] Jur. Rev. 259.

[49] On the "manner and form" argument, see para.3–05, below.

[50] As explained, for example, by Lord Hope in *Axa v Lord Advocate* [2011] UKSC 46; 2012 S.C. (U.K.S.C.) 122 at [49].

[51] *Whaley v Lord Watson*, 2000 S.C. 340 at p.349 (Lord President (Rodger)).

That provision reflects what was known as the "Sewel convention".[52] Following, as it does, immediately after a statutory assertion of the UK Parliament's continuing authority to legislate for Scotland on any matter,[53] this too is no more than a statement of legislative desire that could not bind future Parliaments. Nor could it be capable of judicial enforcement. How, for example, could the court give legal effect to the "will not normally" provision? Any doubt that this provision did not provide a judicially enforceable limit on the UK Parliament's legislative competence was, as we shall see shortly, dispelled by the Supreme Court in the first of the major Brexit litigations.[54]

Second, however, there are a group of amendments made by the 2016 Act that appear to have more substance to them. The concept of a "protected subject-matter", which brings with it the need for the Scottish Parliament to have a two-thirds "super majority" to pass legislation on those issues, is introduced by s.11 of the 2016 Act.[55] It does so by amending s.31 of the Scotland Act 1998 and introducing a new s.31A. The latter imposes the two-third majority requirement to pass a provision that relates to a protected subject-matter. The former sets out the list of protected subject-matters: (a) persons entitled to vote at Scottish parliamentary elections; (b) the electoral system employed at such elections; (c) the number of constituencies and regions; and (d) the number of members to be returned for each region. A qualified majority is a sensible provision to guard against the risk of these new competences being exercised for party political advantage by any party that obtained a simple majority in the Parliament. But two questions arise. First, are there any other issues that should fall within the "protected subject-matter"? For example, the rules on the appointment and removal of the judiciary. These are issues that are fundamental to securing the rule of law. Do they deserve the protection that a qualified majority brings? If not, why not? A by-product of the manner in which the 2016 Act was produced is that there was little opportunity to consider how provisions such as these sit in the wider constitutional framework. That brings us to the second point. Is it appropriate to have devolved these powers to the Scottish Parliament? Voting systems and the number of members are not too controversial but the ability to modify the voting age is. That the voting age has now been lowered to 16 for Scottish parliamentary elections[56] throws up yet another anomaly in the UK constitutional arrangements. Why do 16 and 17-year-olds in Scotland not get to vote in a UK parliamentary election but a matter of months later could be permitted vote in the election for their devolved legislature (bearing in mind that 16 and 17-year-olds in Northern Ireland are not be permitted to vote in elections for their devolved legislature)?[57] The speed with which the draft clauses, which formed the basis for the 2016 Act, arrived has allowed no proper debate on

[52] See para.2–10, below.

[53] Scotland Act 1998 s.28(7).

[54] *R (on the application of Miller) v Secretary of State for Exiting the European Union* [2017] UKSC 5; [2018] A.C. 61 at [149]. Not only is it not judicial enforceable, the Supreme Court also made clear that s.28(8) does not convert the Sewel convention into something that the court can interpret the limits of (para.148).

[55] See para.6–20, below.

[56] Scottish Elections (Reduction of Voting Age) Act 2015.

[57] By the time of the next Welsh parliamentary elections, 16 and 17-year-olds in Wales will be entitled to vote in that election: Senedd and Election (Wales) Act 2020.

whether lowering the voting age is appropriate, let alone whether setting different voting ages in different parts of the country is desirable. Of course, all of this is said without discussion of the further competences that it is proposed be devolved to Scotland. But three years after the Scotland Act 2012, which followed the Calman Commission and lengthy consultation, was enacted, it ought to have been surprising that extensive further powers were transferred without, at the very least, a similar sort of consultation process. The process of constitutional change is something we will touch on at the end of this chapter.

There then followed the 2015 General Election, which, until well into the **1–10** count after the polls had closed, appeared set to produce no majority government. In the event, the Conservative party passed the 326 seats needed to form a majority government. So far as Scotland was concerned, however, the result was a resounding success for the SNP: they increased their representation from six seats in 2010 to 56 seats in 2015 (there are only 59 Scottish constituencies). What that says about the functioning of the electoral system is considered in Ch.4, but for present purposes, the result meant that the new UK Government was in a position to not only deliver the proposals of the Smith Commission but also its manifesto commitment to hold an "in/out" referendum on the United Kingdom's membership of the European Union.

2016 EU REFERENDUM

Introduction

This was not the first time the UK electorate had been asked to express their view **1–11** on continued membership of what was now called the European Union. In 1975, little over two years after the UK had joined what was then generally known as the Common Market, the same question was put to the people. On a 65 per cent turnout, 67 per cent voted to continue the United Kingdom's membership. In 1975, calling a referendum on anything was controversial.[58] By 2015, the referendum appeared to have become an accepted, if rarely used, part of the constitution. As result of the European Union Act 2011, referendums were required on a whole host of EU-related decision-making.[59] It appeared inevitable that a referendum on continued membership would arrive, either in terms or by proxy under the 2011 Act. On 17 December 2015, the European Union Referendum Bill received Royal Assent and thereby required that the question "Should the United Kingdom remain a member of the European Union or leave the European Union?" be put to the electorate no later than 31 December 2017.[60] By a Statutory Instrument made on 3 March 2016, 23 June 2016 was fixed as the date for the poll.[61] Controversy has raged over the conduct of the campaign, how it was funded and the reliability of some of the promises that were made. For present purposes, those issues can be put to one side. Like the legislation that enabled the 2014 Scottish independence referendum, there was a general

[58] See para.5–03, below.
[59] As explained at para.10–36, below.
[60] European Union Referendum Act 2015 s.1.
[61] European Union Referendum (Date of Referendum etc.) Regulations 2016, reg.3.

disenfranchisement of convicted prisoners. But this time litigation was prompted by another issue: the franchise was the same as that for UK parliamentary elections with the result that British nationals who had last been registered to vote more than 15 years previously were not entitled to vote in the referendum. That led a group of British nationals who had, exercising their EU-derived right of free movement, moved to live in Europe more than 15 years before to challenge the lawfulness of the restriction.[62] They were, however unsuccessful. The Court of Appeal held that the European Union Referendum Act 2015 did not fall within the scope of EU law and so any claim based on EU law necessarily failed. In any event, the requirement to have been registered to vote in the UK in the last 15 years would not interfere with the right to free movement and, at common law, there was no fundamental right that could take precedence over an Act of Parliament.[63] So, the franchise stood, but it was not the last time the courts would be called upon to adjudicate on issues connected with the referendum.

The result and the immediate aftermath

1–12 On a turnout of 72.2 per cent, and by a majority of just under 1.27 million votes, the United Kingdom voted to leave the EU. It would be a source of controversy further down the line that Scotland (62 per cent to 38 per cent) and Northern Ireland (55.8 per cent to 44.2 per cent) both voted to remain within the EU. Shortly after the result was confirmed, the Prime Minister (David Cameron) indicated he would resign once a successor was chosen. In the event, his successor, Theresa May, was ultimately elected (by members of the Conservative Party) unopposed and assumed office a little more than a month after the referendum. It served as a reminder of the relatively limited role that the general electorate play in the selection of Prime Minister and, having assumed office, not only was there no requirement for a her to call a general election, the Fixed-Term Parliaments Act 2011 prevented her from doing so.[64] The 2015 Act that authorised the referendum was conspicuously silent on what was to happen in the event of a leave vote. That left the new Prime Minister with a number of immediate issues: when should formal notification be given to the EU of the United Kingdom's intention to leave and what did it mean to leave? That latter issue was to prove especially difficult as there appeared to be little consensus between those that had campaigned to leave as to what that would actually look like. In the event, as we shall see, that was to prompt a further change of Prime Minister prior to the UK leaving the EU.

---

62 *Shindler v Chancellor of the Duchy of Lancaster and another* [2016] EWCA Civ 469; [2017] QB 226.

63 On the idea of common law constitutional rights, see para.3–14, below.

64 Fixed Term Parliaments Act 2011, discussed at para.6–02, below.

Notification of intention to leave the EU

On its own, the referendum result was not sufficient to start the process of the UK's departure from the EU. Article 50 of the Treaty on European Union (TEU) provided the framework[65]: 1–13

> "(1) Any member state may decide to withdraw from the Union in accordance with its own constitutional requirements.
> (2) A member state which decides to withdraw shall notify the European Council of its intention. In the light of the guidelines provided by the European Council, the Union shall negotiate and conclude an agreement with that state, setting out the arrangements for its withdrawal, taking account of the framework for its future relationship with the Union. …
> (3) The Treaties shall cease to apply to the state in question from the date of entry into force of the withdrawal agreement or, failing that, two years after the notification referred to in paragraph 2, unless the European Council, in agreement with the member state concerned, unanimously decides to extent this period. …"

It was therefore incumbent upon the UK to give notice of its intention to leave the EU before the formal process for withdrawal would begin. So, whilst the referendum result was not sufficient in itself to start the process, was it a sufficient authority (in other words, consistent with the "constitutional requirements" of the UK) for the Prime Minister to serve the necessary notice on the EU? "Yes," said the Prime Minister, but "no" said the domestic courts. On 3 November 2016, the Divisional Court of the High Court (comprising of the Lord Chief Justice, the Master of the Rolls and one other senior Court of Appeal Judge[66]) held that, before formal notice of withdrawal could be served, serving of the notice required to be authorised by primary legislation.[67] The reaction to the decision was ferocious, with the three members of the court branded by one newspaper as "Enemies of the People".[68] Permission to appeal directly to the Supreme Court was granted, but on 24 January 2017, to a more measured reaction, that appeal was refused.[69] That decision will feature at various points in the chapters that follow, covering, as it does, sovereignty, separation of powers, prerogative powers and the conventions applicable to the devolution arrangements.[70] For now, a relatively brief comment on some of the more important aspects of the judgment should suffice.[71] But before that, there are two curious

[65] Before art.50 TEU was adopted as part of the Lisbon Treaty, there was no exit mechanism from the EU and it had been described (long before the UK signed up to membership) as "*a permanent limitation*" of the sovereign rights of member states: *Costa v Ente Nazionale per l'Energia Elettrica (ENEL)* (C–6/64) [1964] E.C.R. 585 at p.593.

[66] Ordinarily, the Divisional Court consists of two judges, one of whom is a Court of Appeal judge. Accordingly, this composition of the court was about as strong as it can be.

[67] *R (on the application of Miller) v Secretary of State for Exiting the European Union* [2016] EWHC 2768 (Admin); [2018] A.C. 61.

[68] *The Daily Mail*, 4 November 2016.

[69] *R (on the application of Miller) v Secretary of State for Exiting the European Union* [2017] UKSC 5; [2018] A.C. 61.

[70] Indeed, entire books have been devoted to the judgment. For example, Elliot, Williams and Young (eds), *The UK Constitution after Miller: Brexit and beyond* (Hart Publishing; 2018).

[71] For a fuller analysis of various aspects of the judgment, see, for example: A. Hameed, *The rule of recognition and sources of law in Miller* [2019] PL 61; K. Ewing, *Brexit and parliamentary*

features of the whole litigation, as fiercely contested and controversial as it was, that are worth noting. First, with some hindsight (but nothing more than a reasonable amount of foresight could have predicted), the whole litigation was could have been easily avoided. Having been required to seek authority in the form of primary legislation, it was duly delivered by Parliament in the form of the European Union (Notification of Withdrawal) Act 2017. Passed with little meaningful resistance (in sharp contrast to the House of Commons' attitude a few years later), this very short and simple Act could have been passed as soon as it became apparent the government's position was going to be subject to legal challenge. For reasons that have never been explained, the government chose to fight (and lose) through the courts. But it was a defeat that did nothing to prevent notice being served on the EU. Second, the whole case proceeded on the assumption (common amongst all the parties and accepted by the court[72]) that the notice, once given, could not be withdrawn. That assumption was subsequently held to be wrong.[73] As a result, a central plank of the argument in favour of requiring primary legislation has thus fallen away.

1–14 For the majority (the Supreme Court was split 8:3, having sat *en bloc* for the first time[74]), the question turned on the application of orthodox and, it was said, well established principles of the constitution. It is, the majority said, a "fundamental principle of the UK constitution" that, unless permitted by primary legislation, the Royal Prerogative does not permit the executive to change the law.[75] But giving notice under art.50 would inevitably[76] lead to the UK's departure from the EU, irrespective of Parliament's view on the matter, and thus effect significant constitutional change.[77] Accordingly, in the absence of any express Parliamentary approval, that was a result that the executive itself had no power to bring about. The majority went on to point out that their conclusion was consistent with parliamentary sovereignty[78] and if it were otherwise, on the government's argument, the executive could at any point have served notice under art.50 without any authorisation by Parliament and, in theory at least, without, or even in the face of a contrary result in, a referendum.[79] That would be an extremely surprising state of affairs.

---

sovereignty (2017) 80 M.L.R. 711; N. Aroney, *R (Miller) v Secretary of State for Exiting the European Union: three competing syllogisms* (2017) 80 M.L.R. 726; C. Mac Amhlaigh, *Miller: the prerogative and constitutional change* (2017) 21 Edin L.R. 448; and the November 2017 "Brexit Special Extra Issue" of Public Law and the various contributions to that volume.

72 [2017] UKSC 5; [2018] A.C. 61 at [26].

73 C-621/18 *Wightman v Secretary of State for Exiting the European Union* [2019] QB 199, on a reference from the Inner House of the Court of Session (*Wightman v Secretary of State for Exiting the European Union*, 2019 S.C. 111). Of course, had the concession not been made in the *Miller* case, and the correct interpretation of art.50 being a question of EU law, the Supreme Court would have been required to refer the case to the CJEU. In the then prevailing climate, it is inconceivable that would have been done.

74 There were only 11 Justices (the court's full complement being 12) at the time the appeal was heard, hence sitting *en bloc*. To be properly constituted, the Supreme Court must consist of an uneven number of judges (s.42(1)(1) of the Constitutional Reform Act 2005). Accordingly, when it heard the Prorogation case in 2019, it again sat with 11 Justices but that meant Lord Briggs did not sit.

75 [2017] UKSC 5; [2018] A.C. 61 at [50].

76 Because of the assumption mentioned above.

77 [2017] UKSC 5; [2018] A.C. 61 at [81].

78 [2017] UKSC 5; [2018] A.C. 61 at [90].

79 [2017] UKSC 5; [2018] A.C. 61 at [91].

Two further points arising from the judgment should be noticed. First, despite the outrage at the initial decision by the Divisional Court, nobody disputed that the case raised a question of law that the court should determine. As the majority explained:

> "It is worth emphasising that nobody has suggested that this is an inappropriate issue for the courts to determine. It is also worth emphasising that this case has nothing to do with issues such as the wisdom of the decision to withdraw from the European Union, the terms of withdrawal, the timetable or arrangements for withdrawal, or the details of any future relationship with the European Union. Those are all political issues which are matters for ministers and Parliament to resolve. They are not issues which are appropriate for resolution by judges, whose duty is to decide issues of law which are brought before them by individuals and entities exercising their rights of access to the courts in a democratic society."[80]

In short, the case was to present the first in a number of disputes about where the boundary lines rest in respect of the separation of powers. In this case, the question for resolution fell squarely within the judicial sphere. Second, as the minority were at pains to point out, controls over executive power are not exclusively (or even primarily) of a legal character: "[c]ourts should not overlook the constitutional importance of ministerial accountability to Parliament".[81] Applied to the process of leaving the EU, Lord Carnwath explained:

> "Service of an article 50(2) notice will not, and does not purport to, change any laws or affect any rights. It is merely the start of an essentially political process of negotiation and decision-making within the framework of that article. True it is that it is intended to lead in due course to the removal of EU law as a source of rights and obligations in domestic law. That process will be conducted by the executive, but it will be accountable to Parliament for the course of those negotiations and the contents of any resulting agreement."[82]

And arguably that was the most prescient observation in the whole judgment. For, as the withdrawal process worked towards a conclusion, the House of Commons would assert itself in a way that was unprecedented (in modern times, at least) as it sought to hold the government accountable for what was, or was not, happening in the negotiations between the UK Government and the EU. Before that point was reached, however, Parliament went about legislating to ensure sufficient continuity of the law for when the UK left the EU.

Legislative framework for leaving the EU

The European Union (Withdrawal) Act 2018 is the vehicle by which the substance of EU law shall be retained in domestic law following the end of the "implementation period".[83] Once heralded as "the Great Repeal Bill",[84] in fact it serves to retain the vast corpus of EU law as a part of domestic law following the **1–15**

[80] [2017] UKSC 5; [2018] A.C. 61 at [3].

[81] [2017] UKSC 5; [2018] A.C. 61 at [240] (Lord Reed).

[82] [2017] UKSC 5; [2018] A.C. 61 at [259].

[83] On departure from the EU, the UK entered into an "implementation period" where in practice EU law continued to apply. At the time of writing, the implementation period is due to conclude at 23:00 on 31 December 2020 (that being "IP completion day": European Union (Withdrawal Agreement) Act

United Kingdom's departure from the EU (and the end of the implementation period).[85] It will be known as "retained EU law".[86] In Ch.10, we take a closer look at the provisions of the 2018 Act. For present purposes, it is worth mentioning one particular controversy in the passage of the 2018 Act. Importing such a vast body of law into domestic law is bound to throw up what might be described as wrinkles, not least because much of the EU law that is retained is predicated on the UK being a member of the EU and participating in the EU's institutions. Such provisions will make no sense once the implementation period is over. In the language of the 2018 Act, these issues are known as "deficiencies". To deal with such deficiencies, s.8 of the 2018 Act confers upon the government significant legislative authority:

> "**Dealing with deficiencies arising from withdrawal**
> **8.**—(1) A Minister of the Crown may by regulations make such provision as the Minister considers appropriate to prevent, remedy or mitigate—
> (a) any failure of retained EU law to operate effectively, or
> (b) any other deficiency in retained EU law,
> Arising from the withdrawal of the United Kingdom from the EU.
> …
> (5) Regulations under subsection (1) may make any provision that could be made by an Act of Parliament."

As matters currently stand, the power conferred by s.8(1) expires two years after the Implementation Period completion day (currently 31 December 2020 at 23:00). As Professor Elliot put it, if the creation of "retained EU law" was the copy and paste function of the 2018 Act, then s.8 represents the "edit" function.[87] It is an extensive law making power to confer upon the executive and one that caused some concern during the Act's passage. For example, the House of Lords Constitution Committee noted, among a number of concerns with the Bill as it then stood, that:

> "We are concerned that applying a subjective test of 'appropriateness' to a broad term like 'deficiency' makes the regulation-making power in [the clause] potentially open-ended. However, requiring that ministers set out the 'good reasons' to use the power and that it is a 'reasonable course of action', as we recommend … would ameliorate the subjective nature of 'deficiencies'."[88]

Whilst the government resisted an attempt to amend the Bill to impose a necessity requirement before engaging the delegated authority, other concessions

---

2020, s.39), but there is power to amend this date by Regulations. Whether it is amended is likely to depend on what progress is made negotiating the future relationship.

[84] See, for example, *R (on the application of Miller) v Secretary of State for Exiting the European Union* [2017] UKSC 5; [2018] A.C. 61 at [34].

[85] European Union (Withdrawal) Act 2018 s.1A.

[86] That term is defined by s.6(7) of the European Union (Withdrawal) Act 2018.

[87] 1,000 words/The European Union (Withdrawal) Act 2018, 28 June 2018, available at: *https://publiclawforeveryone.com/2018/06/28/1000-words-the-european-union-withdrawal-act-2018/* [Accessed 10 June 2020].

[88] Select Committee on the Constitution, European Union (Withdrawal) Bill, 9th Report of Session 2017–19, HL Paper 69, para.176.

were obtained. For example, the powers cannot be used to amend the 2018 Act,[89] nor can the powers be used to create a new public authority.[90] Schedule 7 to the 2018 Act makes provision for parliamentary scrutiny of the power conferred by s.8.[91] In particular, some regulations must be made using the affirmative procedure (for example, those that transfer an EU legislative power to a UK body or which create or widen the scope of a criminal offence).[92] Where the government proposes to make regulations using the negative resolution procedure,[93] unless a declaration of urgency is made by the minister, the instrument must be laid before the House of Commons for "sifting".[94] This requires the minister to lay a statement before Parliament explaining why the negative procedure is appropriate and why it was chosen. Each House then has 10 sitting days within which to make recommendation as to the procedure to be used. If no recommendation is made, the minister may proceed to make the regulations. If either House makes a recommendation that the minister proceed by affirmative resolution, the minister may accept that recommendation. If it is not accepted, however, a statement must be laid before the House explaining why they do not agree with the recommendation. So, whilst the delegated powers conferred upon the executive remain significant, at least some measure of parliamentary supervision has been built in. How effective it will be, and whether the two-year time-limit on these powers will be extended, remains to be seen.

While the 2018 Act was making its way through Westminster, the Scottish **1–16** Parliament was making its own arrangements to ensure legal continuity following departure from the EU. Those came in the form of the UK Withdrawal from the European Union (Legal Continuity) (Scotland) Bill and took a broadly similar approach to what was to become the 2018 Act (the political disagreements that led to separate Scottish legislation are irrelevant for our purposes). The Bill, however, could not be presented for Royal Assent because it was the subject of the first pre-Assent reference by a Law Officer to the Supreme Court under s.33 of the Scotland Act 1998.[95] Objection was taken to the Bill for a range of reasons. It was argued that the entire Bill was outside competence because it related to the reserved matter of relations with the European Union. A range of other provisions were said to be outside competence because they impermissibly encroached onto reserved matters, were incompatible with EU law or were contrary to the rule of

[89] Nor can they be used to amend or repeal the Human Rights Act 1998 and, subject to very limited qualifications, the Scotland Act 1998 , the Government of Wales Act 2006 and the Northern Ireland Act 1998: s.8(7)(f) and (g) of the European Union (Withdrawal) Act 2018.

[90] European Union (Withdrawal) Act 2018 s.8(7)(d).

[91] For more detail, see Erskine May, *Parliamentary Practice*, 25th edn, at para.32.3 (*https://erskinemay.parliament.uk/section/5666/scrutiny-of-delegated-legislation-made-under-the-european-union-withdrawal-act-2018/* [Accessed 10 June 2020]).

[92] For details of the the affirmative procedure (which requires positive approval by Parliament before the regulation is made), see Erksine May, *Parliamentary Practice*, 25th edn, at para.31.13 (*https://erskinemay.parliament.uk/section/5625/the-affirmative-procedure/* [Accessed 10 June 2020]).

[93] For details of that procedure (where a regulation is subject to annulment by resolution of either House of Parliament) see: Erksine May, *Parliamentary Practice*, 25th edn, para.31.15 (available at: *https://erskinemay.parliament.uk/section/5627/the-negative-procedure/* [Accessed 10 June 2020].

[94] European Union (Withdrawal) Act 2018, Sch.7, para.3.

[95] *UK Withdrawal from the European Union (Legal Continuity) (Scotland) Bill* [2018] UKSC 64; 2019 S.C. (U.K.S.C.) 13. See also: para.6–38, below. See generally: A. McHarg and C. McCorkindale, "The Supreme Court and devolution: the Scottish Continuity Bill Reference" [2019] Jur. Rev. 190.

law. Whilst this wide-ranging attack on the Bill largely failed, a significant number of provisions of the Bill were held to be outside competence and no attempt was made to amend the Bill so as to address that finding.[96] That was largely due to the passage of the 2018 Act, which amended the Scotland Act 1998 so as to include the 2018 Act as an enactment protected from modification by the Scottish Parliament, in the period between the Scottish Parliament passing the Bill and the Supreme Court determining the reference. That produced the first of the two points of general, and lasting, significance determined by the court. At what point did the Supreme Court have to determine the competence of the Bill? Was it the date on which the Scottish Parliament passed the Bill (in this case, 21 March 2018)? Or was it the date on which the court determined the reference (judgment was given on 13 December 2018)? It was, the Supreme Court held, the date on which the reference was determined:

> "We are satisfied that, when addressing the questions in the reference as to whether the Scottish Bill would be within legislative competence, this court must have regard to how things stand at the date when we decide those questions."[97]

While the point had never arisen before (not least because there had never been a pre-Assent reference), that is an unsurprising answer. It would have been a curious outcome if the court had to shut its eyes to a subsequent development that would render a provision of the Bill outside competence in any post-Assent judicial review.[98]

The second point of general, and lasting, significance was the scope of a reference under s.33 of the Scotland Act 1998. In *AXA v Lord Advocate*, the Supreme Court had observed that, in addition to the limitations imposed on devolved competence by the Scotland Act 1998, the common law also set limits on the powers of the Parliament.[99] And in *UK Withdrawal from the European Union (Legal Continuity)(Scotland) Bill*,[100] the UK Law Officers sought to argue that the Bill was contrary to the constitutional framework underpinning the devolution settlement.[101] However, the Court did not accept that such common law grounds of challenge could be presented in a reference under s.33 of the Scotland Act 1998. As it explained:

---

[96] The Scotland Act 1998 s.36(4) requires that the Standing Orders of the Scottish Parliament make provision for the reconsideration of a Bill where the Supreme Court has held that any provision of a Bill would not be within the legislation competence of the Parliament. Such provision is made in r.9.9 of the Standing Orders.

[97] [2018] UKSC 64; 2019 S.C. (U.K.S.C.) 13 at [92].

[98] The reasoning by which the Supreme Court reached that conclusion is set out at paras [93]–[97]. See also: para.6–23, below.

[99] *AXA General Insurance Ltd v Lord Advocate* [2011] UKSC 46; 2012 S.C. (U.K.S.C.) 122 at [47] (Lord Hope) and [149]–[153] (Lord Reed).

[100] [2018] UKSC 64; 2019 S.C. (U.K.S.C.) 13.

[101] More particularly, the argument, as recorded by the court, was the Bill was inconsistent with the constitutional framework underpinning the devolution settlement and with the rule of law principles of legality and legal certainty. The Bill, it was argued, "cuts across the attempts of the UK Parliament and government to deal in a way that applies coherently and consistently across the whole of the UK with a matter within their reserved competence, namely the legal consequences of withdrawal from the EU. It is also said that the existence of parallel legislation on the same subject-matter in Scotland and in the UK as a whole, undermines legal certainty" (at para.25). On the point about the legal consequences of withdrawal from the EU being reserved, the Court disagreed: para.99.

> "There is a difference between a want of legislative competence and more general grounds for judicial review on public law grounds. The result of a want of legislative competence is that a Scottish enactment is a nullity ('not law') (see Scotland Act, s.29(1)). A Scottish enactment which is held by a court to be unlawful on more general public law grounds is not necessarily a nullity. … A reference to this court under s.33 of the Act is concerned only with the extent of the Scottish Parliament's 'legislative competence' (see s.33(1)). This is a term of art in the Scotland Act. It refers back to s.29, which provides that a provision is outside the legislative competence of the Scottish Parliament in the five cases specified in subsec (2). For the purposes of a reference under sec 33, they are exhaustive."[102]

As a result, it is now clear that the pre-Assent reference procedure can only be used to review a Bill under reference to the statutory limitations on the Scottish Parliament's competence set out in s.29 of the Scotland Act 1998.

Securing passage of the Withdrawal Agreement

In November 2018, the UK Government concluded a draft Withdrawal Agreement with the European Union[103] but the United Kingdom was never to ratify the agreement. For those committed to leaving the EU, the Withdrawal Agreement was unacceptable because for a transitional period at least, the UK would remain subject to almost all EU rules. And for those that wished to remain, it still saw the UK leave the EU and, as a result, give up any say in how EU rules were made while, for a period at least, being required to adhere to them. Thus, having managed to prompt opposition from significant sections of two groups that rarely agreed on anything, it proved impossible for the government to secure the agreement of the House of Commons. Three times the House of Commons voted on the agreement; three times it was rejected. On 15 January 2019, the House of Commons voted against the Withdrawal Agreement by 230 votes (the largest vote against the government in parliamentary history), but the government survived a confidence vote the following day. On 12 March 2019, the House of Commons again voted against the agreement, this time by 149 votes (the fourth largest government defeat). With the 29 March 2019 exit day fast approaching, the government proposed to put the Withdrawal Agreement to the House of Commons for a third time on 19 March 2019. But, controversially, the Speaker ruled that motion out of order. Citing a convention that dates back to 1604, but which last appeared to have been relied upon in 1920, the Speaker ruled that the same question, in substance, could not be put to the House twice in the same session.[104] For that reason, the Speaker indicated that it would not be in order (and thus not permissible) for the government to put the Withdrawal Agreement to a vote the following day.[105] Despite (or perhaps because of) the vintage of the convention relied upon by the Speaker, his ruling was (politically, at least) controversial. It meant the government could not seek approval of the Withdrawal Agreement for a third time without making some changes to the wording of any motion. And it all added to what was a very febrile atmosphere as the first exit 1–17

---

[102] [2018] UKSC 64; 2019 S.C. (U.K.S.C.) 13 at [26].

[103] Available at: *https://ec.europa.eu/commission/sites/beta-political/files/draft_withdrawal_agreement_0.pdf* [Accessed 10 June 2020].

[104] Hansard, 18 March 2019, col.775.

[105] Hansard, 19 March 2019, col.776.

date approached over the horizon. But for our purposes, it highlights the important role of the Speaker of the House of Commons.[106] In more sedate times, the Speaker can pass largely unnoticed. But during 2019, the Speaker played a prominent and, at times, critical role in the parliamentary process that accompanied the Brexit process. On 29 March 2019, the Withdrawal Agreement (without the attached political declaration—that satisfied the Speaker that the vote was in order) was put to the House of Commons. It again failed to pass, this time by (a relatively modest) 58 votes.

Getting the Withdrawal Agreement passed by the House of Commons was not the only problem the government was having. Collective Cabinet responsibility, which, as we shall see in Ch.7, is the normal convention under which government operates,[107] appeared to have all but collapsed. It is worth noticing what the Cabinet Manual has to say about collective Cabinet responsibility:

> "The Cabinet system of government is based on the principle of collective responsibility. All government ministers are bound by the collective decisions of the Cabinet, save where it is explicitly set side … In practice, this means that a decision of Cabinet or one of its committees is binding on all members of the Government, regardless of whether they were present when the decision was taken or their personal views."[108]

Despite that, in March 2019, members of the government, including Cabinet ministers repeatedly voted against the government position on Brexit-related votes. The most startling example was the Brexit Secretary (Steve Barclay, MP) who, despite moving a motion on behalf of the government, proceeded to vote against it.[109] He, like the other members of the government that voted against the Prime Minister, retained their ministerial positions. That they felt at liberty to vote against the government, and without consequence, may have fulfilled a short-term political purpose. What longer term damage it has done to what was believed to be an important constitutional convention of collective Cabinet responsibility cannot yet be known. Before turning to events following 29 March 2019, there is another Brexit-related piece of litigation that we need to consider.

The revocability of notice under art.50

1–18 One particular issue that was exercising parliamentarians was what happened if a deal could not be agreed and, in particular, could Brexit be stopped? As we have seen, in *Miller (No.1)*, the court proceeded on the basis of an agreed position amongst the parties that notification under art.50 was not unilaterally revocable. In other words, it had the inevitable consequence that the United Kingdom would leave the European Union. However, a group of politicians sought an answer to that question from the court. And, in the event, the Court of Justice of the

---

[106] On the role of the Speaker generally, see Erskine May, *Parliamentary Practice*, 25th edn, at para.4.23 (available at: *https://erskinemay.parliament.uk/section/6005/the-speaker-as-presiding-officer-of-the-house-of-commons/?highlight=speaker* [Accessed 10 June 2020].

[107] See para.7–28, below.

[108] The Cabinet Manual, 1st edn, October 2011, paras 4.2–4.3 (references omitted). Available at: *https://assets.publishing.service.gov.uk/government/uploads/system/uploads/attachment_data/file/60641/cabinet-manual.pdf* [Accessed 10 June 2020].

[109] *Hansard*, 14 March 2019, col.628 and cols 647–651.

European Union was to disagree with the consensus presented to the Supreme Court: art.50 was, in principle, unilaterally revocable. It is worth briefly tracing the process by which that decision arrived. Proceeding got off to an inauspicious start in the Outer House, where permission to proceed was refused.[110] It was held by the Lord Ordinary that the circumstances in which the art.50 notice could be withdrawn were hypothetical and academic given neither the UK Government nor Parliament had indicated any wish to withdraw the notice.[111] Accordingly, the petition had no real prospect of success. But the Inner House were to disagree.[112] Despite many problems with how the petition had been framed, it was held that when it was distilled to its essence, a case of substance emerged. The court explained:

> "The issue of whether it is legally possible to revoke the notice of withdrawal is, as already stated, one of great importance. On one view, authoritative guidance on whether it is legally possible to do so may have the capacity to influence Members of Parliament in deciding what steps to take in advance of, and at the time of, a debate and vote on the European Union (Withdrawal) Bill. After all, if Parliament is to be regarded as sovereign, the Government's position on the legality of revoking the notice may not be decisive."[113]

In Ch.3, we will consider the separation of powers more closely. For now, it is worth noting that the proper interpretation of art.50, and whether notice of withdrawal was revocable, was not really an issue that touched on parliamentary sovereignty. That, as we shall see,[114] simply provides that the UK Parliament has the power to make or unmake any law. And it is trite that the government's view on the proper interpretation of the law is not determinative. Instead, art.50 being a legal rule, the separation of powers would require that its proper meaning be determined by an independent court. In any event, the Inner House went on to recognise that the petition may be pushing at the boundaries of what properly falls within the scope of judicial review,[115] but permission to proceed was allowed.[116] Accordingly, the case returned to the Outer House for full argument to be heard. Again, however, the petitioners were unsuccessful in the Outer House.[117] The Lord Ordinary held that the question of revocability was hypothetical and academic in that the petitioners (who were all parliamentarians) did not require an answer to the question in order to be able to fulfil their parliamentary roles.[118] Separately, the Lord Ordinary held that the request to "settle a legal question" that had been raised by a number of MPs during the legislative approach was a "clear and dangerous encroachment on the sovereignty

[110] *Wightman v Secretary of State for Exiting the European Union* [2018] CSOH 8.
[111] *Wightman v Secretary of State for Exiting the European Union* [2018] CSOH 8 at [10]–[14].
[112] *Wightman v Advocate General for Scotland* [2018] CSIH 18; 2018 S.C. 388.
[113] *Wightman v Advocate General for Scotland* [2018] CSIH 18; 2018 S.C. 388 at [30].
[114] para.3–02, below
[115] *Wightman v Advocate General for Scotland* [2018] CSIH 18; 2018 S.C. 388 at [30].
[116] This case also clarified the approach to be taken to the test ("a real prospect of success") for granting permission for judicial reviewing proceedings. That is more fully explained at para.14–22.
[117] *Wightman v Secretary of State for Exiting the European Union* [2018] CSOH 61; 2018 S.L.T. 657.
[118] *Wightman v Secretary of State for Exiting the European Union* [2018] CSOH 61; 2018 S.L.T. 657 at [51].

of Parliament".[119] Like the reference to parliamentary sovereignty in the Inner House at the stage of permission, this appears to confuse parliamentary sovereignty and the separation of powers. As traditionally understood, it is the courts (and only the courts) that can settle a dispute over a legal question.[120] Asking them to do so causes no affront to the power of Parliament to make or unmake any law (in other words, if Parliament does not like the legal answer given by the courts, it is at liberty to change the law). Finally, the Lord Ordinary held that if a reference was made to the Court of Justice, that court would decline it on the grounds that the questions posed were hypothetical.[121] Accordingly, he refused to make a reference and dismissed the petition.

Again, the Inner House took a different view.[122] There, it was held that as MPs would require to vote on ratification of any withdrawal agreement, and rejecting that agreement would otherwise result in the United Kingdom leaving the EU without agreement, it was neither academic nor premature to ask whether it was legally competent to revoke the notification that had been given under art.50.[123] And determining the answer to the question was a task that Parliament was quite unsuited to and the government unable to undertake.[124] It was again argued on behalf of the UK Government that answering the questions raised by the petition, which would in turn guide parliamentary debates, would infringe parliamentary privilege. That proposition was rejected this time:

> "To state what the existing law is, or how it applies, does not involve any interference with free speech in Parliament … Nor does the court's opinion compel MPs to vote in any particular way … Nor does the court's opinion involve interference with or criticism of the legislature. It is simply a statement of the existing law, which is precisely the constitutional function of the courts."[125]

Accordingly, the Inner House was persuaded to make a reference to the Court of Justice seeking guidance on the proper interpretation of art.50 and the extent to which it permitted a notice of withdrawal to be revoked.[126] Before turning to events at the Court of Justice in Luxembourg, there is one other point arising out of the Inner House's judgment that should be noticed. What was said about the scope of judicial review may have wider, and lasting, consequences. As the court explained, the starting point is that the principle of access to justice dictates that, in general, anyone who wishes to can come to the court seeking a determination of what the law is in a given circumstance.[127] That general rule is subject to

---

[119] *Wightman v Secretary of State for Exiting the European Union* [2018] CSOH 61; 2018 S.L.T. 657 at [58].

[120] e.g. Dicey, *The Law of the Constitution* (1959), p.413; para.3–02, below.

[121] *Wightman v Secretary of State for Exiting the European Union* [2018] CSOH 61; 2018 S.L.T. 657 at [73].

[122] *Wightman v Secretary of State for Exiting the European Union* [2018] CSIH 62; 2019 S.C. 111.

[123] *Wightman v Secretary of State for Exiting the European Union* [2018] CSIH 62; 2019 S.C. 111 at [27] (Lord President (Carloway)); [37]–[39] (Lord Menzies); [58] (Lord Drummond Young).

[124] *Wightman v Secretary of State for Exiting the European Union* [2018] CSIH 62; 2019 S.C. 111 at [49]–[50] (Lord Drummond Young).

[125] *Wightman v Secretary of State for Exiting the European Union* [2018] CSIH 62; 2019 S.C. 111 at [65] (Lord Drummond Young). See also [28] (Lord President (Carloway)).

[126] The terms of the reference are set out by the Lord President as an appendix to his judgment.

[127] *Wightman v Secretary of State for Exiting the European Union* [2018] CSIH 62; 2019 S.C. 111 at [21] (Lord President (Carloway)).

restrictions, "which are principally resource driven", to ensure that the court does not spend its time answering hypothetical issues or giving judgments that are not aimed at achieving some practical result.[128] Lord Drummond Young recognised that the circumstances before the court were unusual:

> "The present case is a somewhat unusual example of the supervisory jurisdiction, in that the court is ultimately asked to request the CJEU to answer a question on the scope of Art.50 of the TEU. That is not a form of procedure found in traditional administrative law within the United Kingdom. Moreover, the function of the question is to enable certain persons, notably MPs, to be properly informed about the present state of the law in relation to Art 50. Nevertheless, while the form of the proceedings and their effect is different from the traditional application of the supervisory jurisdiction, the underlying purpose is to ensure that those charged with voting on issues of vital importance to the United Kingdom are properly advised on the existing state of the law. That in my opinion falls squarely within the fundamental purpose of the supervisory jurisdiction."[129]

That does, on its face, seem to have the potential to significantly expand the scope of judicial review in practical terms. If ensuring parliamentarians are "properly advised on the existing state of the law" falls squarely within the supervisory jurisdiction, does that allow an MSP to come to the Court of Session and say "the government says this Bill [or clause within the Bill] is necessary to close a loophole in the existing law—can you confirm the loophole exists?" Now, there may well be practical limitations to the circumstances in which a parliamentarian might do so (not least the cost of any form of litigation), but, applying Lord Drummond Young's approach, it would, in principle, have been open to MPs to seek a declarator over the legality of the Iraq war (that being an issue "of vital importance to the United Kingdom" upon which MPs were asked to vote). If that is the true scope of the Court of Session's supervisory jurisdiction, it may, as Lord Reed warned in *Miller (No.1)*, be fraught with risk, not least for the judiciary.[130]

Returning to art.50, after a failed attempt by the UK Government to obtain leave to appeal to the Supreme Court against the making of the reference, the case headed to Luxembourg. The Court of Justice accepted the reference made by the Inner House and appointed it to the expedited procedure. On 27 November 2018, the case was heard by the full court[131] with the Advocate General delivering his opinion the following week[132] and the court issuing its judgment on 10 December 2018.[133] It was held, contrary to the consensus presented to the Supreme Court in *Miller (No.1)*, that a notification under art.50 of an intention to withdraw from the EU was unilaterally revocable by the member state. A further attempt by the UK Government to argue that the question referred by the Court of **1–19**

---

[128] *Wightman v Secretary of State for Exiting the European Union* [2018] CSIH 62; 2019 S.C. 111 at [22] (Lord President (Carloway)).

[129] *Wightman v Secretary of State for Exiting the European Union* [2018] CSIH 62; 2019 S.C. 111 at [68].

[130] *R (on the application of Miller) v Secretary of State for Exiting the European Union* [2017] UKSC 5; [2018] A.C. 61 at [240] (Lord Reed).

[131] See para.10–17, below on the different formations of the CJEU. Sitting as the full court (which requires no less than 17 judges to be present) is an exceptional course.

[132] On the role of the Advocates General at the CJEU, see para.10–17, below.

[133] C-621/18 *Wightman v Secretary of State for Exiting the European Union* [2019] QB 199.

Session was inadmissible because it was hypothetical was rejected by the court.[134] On the substantive issue as to the interpretation of art.50, the UK Government took no position.[135] But both the Council and the Commission of the EU[136] argued that any right to revoke should not be unilateral. If it were, they argued, a member state could revoke its notification shortly before the end of the two-year withdrawal period and then immediately re-notify an intention to withdraw, thus triggering a fresh two-year period. By that means, a member state could negotiate effectively without any time limit. Accordingly, as with any extension of time, it was argued revocation should require the unanimous consent of the European Council.[137] The CJEU did not agree:

> "[T]he notification by a member state of its intention to withdraw does not lead inevitably to the withdrawal of that member state from the European Union. On the contrary, a member state that has reversed its decision to withdraw from the European Union is entitled to revoke that notification for as long as a withdrawal agreement concluded between that member state and the European Union has not entered into force or, if no such agreement has been concluded, for as long as the two-year period laid down in article 50(3) EU, possibly extended in accordance with that provision, has not expired."[138]

The proposal by the Council and Commission that any revocation should require the unanimous approval of the European Council was rejected on the grounds it could result in a member state being forced to leave the EU against its will and such an outcome was incompatible with the principles underlying the Treaties.[139] Accordingly, the debate returned to Westminster, but it had now been established that the United Kingdom could, if it chose to do so, remain a member of the EU on its current terms by unilaterally withdrawing the notice it had given under art.50 of the TEU.

29 MARCH 2019 AND ITS AFTERMATH

1–20 As we have seen, it became obvious that Parliament was not going to pass the Withdrawal Agreement in time for the United Kingdom to leave the EU at 23:00 on 29 March 2019 with transitional arrangements in place. An extension was granted by the European Union, initially until 22 May (if Parliament agreed the Withdrawal Agreement) or 12 April (if it did not). Rather than approve the Withdrawal Agreement, Parliament passed the European Union (Withdrawal) Act 2019.[140] That Act required the Prime Minister to seek a further extension of the

---

[134] C-621/18 *Wightman v Secretary of State for Exiting the European Union* [2019] QB 199 at [20]–[34].

[135] C-621/18 *Wightman v Secretary of State for Exiting the European Union* [2019] QB 199 at [43].

[136] The role and functions of those institutions are explained at paras 10–11—10–15, below.

[137] C-621/18 *Wightman v Secretary of State for Exiting the European Union* [2019] QB 199 at [38]–[42].

[138] C-621/18 *Wightman v Secretary of State for Exiting the European Union* [2019] QB 199 at [69].

[139] C-621/18 *Wightman v Secretary of State for Exiting the European Union* [2019] QB 199 at [72].

[140] This is not to be confused with the 2018 Act bearing the same name. It is an unusual (it was not a Government Bill) and controversial Act (support for it split along Brexiteer/Remainer lines and it was argued by some that it was an example of Parliament stepping outside its proper role of scrutinising the government and holding them to account).

two-year withdrawal period under art.50 TEU. An extension until 30 June was initially sought but ultimately agreement was reached on an extension until 31 October 2019. The 2019 Act was part of a pattern of Parliament, and in particular the House of Commons, asserting itself as against the government. As we shall see later, the government usually has a majority in the House of Commons and it usually has control of the timetable of the House of Commons (thus determining what business it does). Throughout the later stages of the withdrawal process, however, the government lost control of the House of Commons on a number of occasions. Given a government is expected to retain the confidence of the House of Commons, and the House quite clearly did not support the government on its flagship policy, a motion of no confidence in the government might have been expected.[141] But it never came and instead this pattern of Parliament issuing quite specific directions to the government continued. The constitutional propriety of the legislature acting in that way, and in substance micro-managing the executive on the key issue of the day, is not readily reconcilable with a normal understanding of the separation of powers. Holding the government to account is a core function of the legislature; directing its actions in very specific regards is not. The more conventional path would have been for the House of Commons to express its lack of confidence in the government that, depending on how the politics played out, would have resulted in a general election, a change of government or a subsequent expression of confidence. However diffident the House of Commons may have been about expressing its lack of confidence in the Prime Minister and her government, the Prime Minister's own MPs were happy to do so (despite her having seen off a leadership challenge only a few months earlier). On 24 May 2019, the Prime Minister confirmed she would resign as leader of the Conservative Party on 7 June and, when a successor had been chosen, would resign as Prime Minister. For the second time in as many years, a very British transfer of power took place, as the Conservative Party went about selecting a new leader and, by default, a new Prime Minister. It served as another reminder that despite how leader-dominated parliamentary election campaigns have become, voters only ever have an indirect say at the ballot box over who the Prime Minister will be. Boris Johnston was elected leader of the Conservative Party and on 24 July 2019, Theresa May resigned as Prime Minister and was succeed by Mr Johnston. He committed to the United Kingdom leaving the EU on 31 October 2019. Like his predecessor, he did not seek to call an early general election but sought to work with the Parliament he inherited. But again, like his predecessor, he found that the parliamentary arithmetic did not add up and he was unable to muster the necessary support to then call an election.[142] But before that,

[141] As the Supreme Court would explain in the Prorogation case, *R (on the application of Miller) v The Prime Minister* [2019] UKSC 41; [2020] A.C. 373; 2019 S.L.T. 1143: "The Government exists because it has the confidence of the House of Commons. It has no other democratic legitimacy other than that" (at [55]). A motion of no confidence had been tabled by the Leader of the Opposition on 17 December 2018 but it did not come to a vote as the government did not allow any time for the motion to be debated (the Speaker having confirmed they were under no obligation to do so). On 15 January 2019, the Leader of the Opposition again tabled a vote of no confidence. This time there was a vote, and the government won the motion by 326 votes to 306.

[142] Under the Fixed Term Parliaments Act 2011, an early general election (absent a vote of no confidence in the government) requires two-thirds of MPs to support a motion calling for an election.

at the end of August, the new Prime Minister took a decision that would see the United Kingdom's exit from the EU again return to the Supreme Court.

Prorogation of Parliament

1–21 On 28 August 2019, at a meeting of the Privy Council held at Balmoral Castle, an Order in Council was made requiring the prorogation of Parliament at some point between 9 and 12 September 2019 until 14 October 2019. In approving the prorogation, the Queen, as is convention, was acting upon the advice of her Prime Minister. Effect, it was believed at the time, was given to that Order on 10 September 2019 and Parliament was understood to stand prorogued. At the time the Order in Council was made, proceedings were pending before the Court of Session in Edinburgh in which orders were sought preventing the prorogation of Parliament (there having been, since a month or so earlier, speculation that Parliament might be prorogued in the run up to the then "exit day" of 31 October 2019). As soon as the prorogation was announced, similar proceedings were issued in the High Court in London. In Scotland, at first instance, the Lord Ordinary refused the petition on the grounds it raised an issue that was non-justiciable (that is, its subject matter was such that the court could not adjudicate upon it).[143] In England and Wales, a similar conclusion was reached by the Divisional Court (and like *Miller (No.1)*, comprising of the Lord Chief Justice, the Master of the Rolls and another senior Court of Appeal judge).[144] Again, the Divisional Court granted leave to appeal direct to the Supreme Court. There is no equivalent provision for a direct appeal to the Supreme Court from a first instance decision in Scotland,[145] so before the Supreme Court heard the case, the Inner House of the Court of Session gave its judgment. On 11 September 2019, they allowed the appeal, holding that the matter was justiciable and, having regard to the exceptional length of the prorogation (in modern times), the inevitable effect it would have on the ability of Parliament to scrutinise government action and the reasons proffered by the government to justify its course of action, issued a declarator that the advice given to the Queen to prorogue was unlawful and that the purported prorogation that had since happened was unlawful, null and of no effect.[146] That very much put the constitutional cat amongst the proverbial pigeons. It presented the Supreme Court with a case on which the most senior judges in England and Wales disagreed with the most senior judges in Scotland on whether or not the United Kingdom Parliament stood prorogued. Once again, the Supreme Court convened with 11 members.[147]

1–22 For the government, their argument really went back to something Lord Reed (by now, President of the Supreme Court designate) had said in *Miller* in 2017, "[i]t is important for courts to understand that the legalisation of political issues is

[143] [2019] CSOH 70; 2019 S.L.T. 1071.

[144] [2019] EWHC 2381.

[145] There is a provision which allows the Lord Ordinary to "report" a case to the Inner House, which dispenses with a decision in the Outer House (RCS 34). An application to report this case to the Inner House was refused (no reasons for that decision have been published).

[146] *Cherry v Advocate General* [2019] CSIH 49; 2019 S.L.T. 1097.

[147] See fn.74, above for the explanation as to why this is as close to an *en bloc* sitting as the Supreme Court can get.

not always constitutionally appropriate, and may be fraught with risk, not least for the judiciary".[148] In short, when to prorogue Parliament was quintessentially a politically judgment, for the Prime Minister of the day, and not one that he should be called upon to explain in court. For the petitioners, however, it was argued that the power to (advise the Queen to) prorogue Parliament could not be unqualified. What if, they asked, Parliament was prorogued for a year? Or longer? Is it really the case that the court could not intervene? No, said the court.[149] The flaw in the government's case was it left an unreviewable discretionary power in the hands of a public official. In other words, the Prime Minister was, according to the argument, not accountable to the courts for his decision. Nor, having prorogued it, was he accountable to Parliament. And given the Sovereign is, by convention, required to accept the advice tendered to her, there is no accountability there either. The common law has long objected to an unreviewable discretion being placed in the hands of a public official. Accepting that the prorogation decision was reviewable by the courts is consistent with that tradition. Having held that the issue it was being asked to decide was justiciable (i.e. it was not simply a question of political judgment), the court concluded that there was no evidence before it that allowed it to conclude that the Prime Minister had any reason, let alone a good reason, for advising the Sovereign to prorogue Parliament for five weeks. Accordingly, his advice, and the subsequent prorogation, was held to be unlawful with the consequence that the purported prorogation was a legal nullity. It was a decision that, unsurprisingly, divided opinion (but not amongst the Justices, who were unanimous). Leaving the controversy that surrounded the decision to one side, there are aspects of the court's reasoning that are worth dwelling on. We will look at three in particular: what is said of the sovereignty of Parliament; the role and responsibilities of the Prime Minister; and the general approach to reviewing acts of the prerogative. In each respect, the court's approach appears controversial.

As we shall discuss more fully in Ch.3, the sovereignty of Parliament is one of **1–23**
the key principles of the constitution. The classic formulation remains that given by Dicey:

> "[T]he right to make or unmake any law whatever; and, further, that no person or body is recognised by the law of England as having a right to override or set aside the legislation of Parliament."[150]

That formulation was endorsed by the Supreme Court as recently, and as authoritatively, as *Miller (No.1)*.[151] Whatever debate there is about the extent of any qualifications to its absolute terms, the sovereignty of Parliament has long been taken to mean the absolute *legislative* authority of Parliament.[152] And by Parliament, it is meant the House of Commons, the House of Lords and the

---

148 [2017] UKSC 5; [2018] A.C. 61 at [240] (Lord Reed).

149 *R (on the application of Miller) v Prime Minister* [2019] UKSC 41; [2020] A.C. 373; 2019 S.L.T. 1143.

150 Dicey, *The Law of the Constitution* (1959), pp.39–40.

151 [2017] UKSC 5; [2018] A.C. 61 at [43].

152 To take a few examples: Jennings, *Law and the Constitution*, 5th edn, p.152 (where the use of the phrase "legislative omnipotence" is discussed); J.D.B. Mitchell, *Constitutional Law*, 2nd edn, p.64 ("By the sovereignty of Parliament is generally meant the absence of any legal restraint upon the legislative power of the United Kingdom Parliament."); A.W. Bradley and K.D. Ewing, *Constitutional*

Sovereign, coming together to enact legislation ("the Queen in Parliament"). As Goldsworthy explained, there had been a tendency on the part of some to conflate that Diceyian view of the legislative sovereignty of Parliament with what has been described as "political sovereignty":

> "Some historians who refer to parliamentary sovereignty mean the power of the two Houses to control the exercise by the Crown of its prerogatives. But that pertains to what is now called 'responsible government', which is conceptually and practically different from parliamentary sovereignty."[153]

Despite that general consensus about the legislative nature of parliamentary sovereignty, the Supreme Court appeared to give it a wider meaning (or, at least, effect):

> "The first [principle engaged by the case] is the principle of Parliamentary sovereignty: that laws enacted by the Crown in Parliament are the supreme form of law in our legal system, with which everyone, including the Government, must comply. *However, the effect which the courts have given the Parliamentary sovereignty is not confined to recognising the status of legislation enacted by the Crown in Parliament as our highest form of law. Time and again, in a series of cases since the 17th century, the courts have protected Parliamentary sovereignty from threats posed to it by the use of prerogative powers, and in doing so have demonstrated that prerogative powers are limited by the principle of Parliamentary sovereignty.*"[154]

The passage italicised appears to be an innovation on the established understanding of parliamentary sovereignty. The court goes on to cite the *Case of Proclamations*,[155] *Attorney General v De Keyser's Royal Hotel Ltd*[156] and the *Fire Brigades Union*[157] as examples of the court protecting parliamentary sovereignty in the face of an exercise of the prerogative. But arguably those cases are each illustrations of the conventional understanding of the legislative supremacy Parliament prevailing. In each, a purported exercise of the prerogative was inconsistent with the will of Parliament as expressed in primary legislation.[158] In other words, all the court did in those cases was to recognise (and give effect to) the legislation enacted by Parliament as the highest form of law.[159] To the extent that they illustrate the courts "protecting" parliamentary sovereignty from "threats" posed by the prerogative, that is true only in the sense that any time someone purports to override or set aside a provision of an Act of Parliament they threaten Parliament's sovereignty. On that approach to parliamentary sovereignty, the Supreme Court's conclusion that it "must therefore

---

and Administrative Law, 14th edn, pp.54–56 (where what Dicey called the sovereignty of Parliament is described as the "legislative supremacy" of Parliament).

153 J. Goldsworthy, *The Sovereignty of Parliament: History and Philosophy*, p.9.

154 [2019] UKSC 41; [2020] A.C. 373; 2019 S.L.T. 1143 at [41] (emphasis added).

155 (1611) 12 Co Rep 74.

156 [1920] A.C. 508.

157 *R v Secretary of State for the Home Department, Ex p. Fire Brigades Union* [1995] 2 A.C. 513.

158 See para.7–03, below for further discussion of these cases.

159 Ekins, *Parliamentary Sovereignty and the Politics of Prorogation* (2019, Policy Exchange) at p.14. Available online at: *https://policyexchange.org.uk/wp-content/uploads/2019/09/Parliamentary-Sovereignty-and-the-Politics-of-Prorogation3.pdf* [Accessed 10 June 2020].

follow, as a concomitant of parliamentary sovereignty, that the power to prorogue cannot be unlimited" is, at least, an innovation on where the constitution was considered to stand before this litigation.[160]

Next, the court made some interesting comments on the role of the Prime Minister in advising the Sovereign in respect of prorogation. First, the court made clear that it was not interested in the Prime Ministers *motive* for the advice he had given, but it was interested in whether there was a *reason* for the advice and that was a point on which he would be accorded a great deal of latitude.[161] But the court had earlier explained that the Prime Minister had certain constitutional duties when deciding whether to advise a prorogation. As the Sovereign must, by convention, follow the advice she receives in relation to prorogation, and because the Prime Minister is the only person with the power to offer that advice, that "situation does … place on the Prime Minister a constitutional responsibility … to have regard to all relevant interests, including those of Parliament".[162] In other words, the Prime Minister has a "constitutional responsibility" to look beyond his own political interests. That might be thought to be surprising. It was long recognised that in relation to dissolution of Parliament (also a personal prerogative exercised on the advice of the Prime Minister) that the Prime Minister could decide to seek a dissolution at a time of maximum political advantage.[163] Why the Prime Minister owed this constitutional responsibility in respect of prorogation is not explained by the court. In the particular circumstances before the court, and having regard to the relatively limited information that had been made available to it, the court concluded:

> "Nowhere is there a hint that the Prime Minister, in giving advice to Her Majesty, is more than simply the leader of the Government seeking to promote its own policies; he has a constitutional responsibility, as we have explained …
>
> It is impossible for us to conclude, on the evidence which has been put before us, that there was any reason—let alone a good reason—to advise Her Majesty to prorogue Parliament for five weeks …"[164]

On a view, that illustrates the narrowness of the court's decision: it was a case of the Prime Minister having failed to provide the court with sufficient information to reveal his reasons for tendering the advice he did (that being a point on which he benefited from a considerable latitude). But from the Prime Minister's perspective, he could have been forgiven for not appreciating he owed this wider constitutional responsibility, requiring him to put party political issues to one side, when formulating his advice.[165] As was pointed out on his behalf in argument, there are a number of examples of prorogation appearing to have been

[160] [2019] UKSC 41; [2020] A.C. 373; 2019 S.L.T. 1143 at [44]. Craig would (strongly) disagree with that characterisation of this aspect of the court's reasoning. See: P. Craig, "The Supreme Court prorogation and constitutional principle" [2020] P.L. 248 at pp.252–259.

[161] [2019] UKSC 41; [2020] A.C. 373; 2019 S.L.T. 1143 at [57].

[162] [2019] UKSC 41; [2020] A.C. 373; 2019 S.L.T. 1143 at [30].

[163] That being one of the justifications for introducing the Fixed-Term Parliaments Act 2011 which removed that particular prerogative from the hands of the Prime Minister. On the 2011 Act, see para.6–02, below.

[164] [2019] UKSC 41; [2020] A.C. 373; 2019 S.L.T. 1143 at [60]–[61].

[165] Although the court was not necessarily clear on that point. While the Prime Minister had to have regard to all relevant interests (so not just his own political interests), the court also recognised that the decision to advise prorogation "may in some circumstances involve a range of considerations,

used to political advantage of the then governing party without anyone having ever suggested that advice was unlawful.

Finally, the approach taken by the court to the classically recognised distinction between recognising the existence of a prerogative power and controlling the exercise of a recognised power has been almost collapsed. As we shall see in Ch.7, it has long been accepted that it is for the courts to determine whether a prerogative power exists. But stepping in to regulate the exercise of a recognised power is a relatively new development and one which was understood to be subject to limits of justiciability.[166] As we have just seen, the court's conclusion about the Prime Minister's reasons very much gave the impression of having reviewed the exercise of the prerogative power (i.e. did he have a good enough reason for the advice he gave). The court, however, explained the issue was justiciable because what it was being asked to do was define the limits of the prerogative power.[167] As more fully explained in Ch.7, that aspect of the court's reasoning does start to look a little artificial when set against what is said about the Prime Minister's reasons (or, rather, lack of reasons) for the advice he gave.

What effect these broader points have on the future development of the law remains to be seen. This was an exceptional case, arising in exceptional circumstances, and one that was argued and decided at exceptional speed. With those factors in mind, whatever view is taken of the result, its wider implications and future application may have to take into account the circumstances in which it was decided.

2019 GENERAL ELECTION

1–24 Parliament, following the Supreme Court's decision, reconvened (having never actually been prorogued) and the planned exit date of 31 October 2019 was delayed. Once that had happened, the Prime Minister again returned to the House of Commons with a motion for an early general election under the Fixed-term Parliaments Act 2011. On 28 October 2019, that motion failed to achieve the necessary two-third majority meaning the government was denied for a third time the election it now sought. On the following day, however, the House of Commons passed the Early Parliamentary General Election Bill. By 31 October 2019, that Bill had passed the House of Lords and received Royal Assent, becoming the Early Parliamentary General Election Act 2019. It is a very short Act, which quickly gets to the point:

> "**Early parliamentary general election**
> **1.**—(1) An early parliamentary general election is to take place on 12 December 2019 in consequence of the passing of this Act.
> (2) That day is to be treated as a polling day appointed under section 2(7) of the Fixed-term Parliaments Act 2011."

---

including matters of political judgment" ([2019] UKSC 41; [2020] A.C. 373; 2019 S.L.T. 1143 at [51]). So the politics of the matter are not irrelevant, but the Prime Minister must look beyond them to the wider constitutional picture.

166 This issue is discussed more fully at paras 7–02—7–08, below.

167 [2019] UKSC 41; [2020] A.C. 373; 2019 S.L.T. 1143 at [52].

That avoided the two-thirds majority required by the 2011 Act (although, in the event, the Bill received 438 votes on its third reading and thus more than the two-third threshold).[168] But it serves as a reminder that Parliament cannot bind its successors even as to form and that, by a simple majority, Parliament can side step even the requirements of its own legislation.[169] And it begs the question what the point of the 2011 Act is if it can be so readily side-stepped.[170] Parliament was then formally dissolved on 6 November 2019 and the election campaign began.

For the first time in almost a century, the country went to the polls in December. A Conservative Government, with a majority of 80 seats, was returned. Like in 2015, Scotland posed a sharp contrast, where the Conservative party lost seven of its 13 seats and the SNP took 48 of the 56 constituencies (that is, 85 per cent of the seats on just 45 per cent of the votes). The distortive effect of the first-past-the-post system was again on prominent display.[171] On 17 December, the new Parliament met for the first time and the Queen's Speech was delivered on 19 December.

European Union (Withdrawal Agreement) Act 2020

And, after all of that, the European Union (Withdrawal Agreement) Act 2020 passed almost unnoticed. By now, the government had a sufficient majority to ensure a smooth parliamentary passage for its legislation. As a result, on departure from the EU, the UK entered into an "implementation period", which shall expire (unless changed by Regulations) at 23:00 on 31 December 2020.[172] Despite the repeal of the European Communities Act 1972, it shall be treated as remaining in force for the duration of the implementation period.[173] But, in case there was any doubt, the 2020 Act includes its own "sovereignty clause" that appears to have much the same desire, but precisely the same effect, as the previous iteration in the European Union Act 2011.[174] 1–25

Brexit

Then, at 23:00 on 31 January 2020, the United Kingdom left the European Union. In Ch.10, we consider the effect of the continuity legislation and how it has, so far at least, secured a fairly seamless departure. The implementation period is due to end on 31 December 2020. The government has repeatedly stated that there will be no slippage in respect of that date. Whether that is tenable as the coronavirus crisis continues is unclear at the time of writing. 1–26

---

[168] Although an earlier programme motion, which allowed the Bill to pass as fast as it did, did not pass with such support (312:295) so there may have been something of a resignation to the inevitable by the time the third reading vote came.

[169] On the manner and form doctrine, see para.3–05, below.

[170] On the 2011 Act more generally, see para.6–02, below.

[171] But the votes-to-seats ratio was not distorted across the board. For example, in England, Labour won 34% of the seats on 34% of the vote (and their overall share was 31% of the seats on 32% of the vote).

[172] European Union (Withdrawal Agreement) Act 2020 ss.1 and 39.

[173] European Union (Withdrawal Agreement) Act 2020 s.1.

[174] On the "sovereignty clause" in the 2011 Act, see paras.10–37, below.

THE PROCESS OF CONSTITUTIONAL CHANGE

1–27 Finally, there are two points worth noting before we embark on the substance of this book. We have begun by talking about events that have prompted considerable constitutional change and that, in large part, can be attributed to the outcome of two referendums. But throughout the remainder of this book, examples of constitutional change are noted: the introduction of fixed terms for Parliament[175]; the growth of the referendum, in particular as a result of the European Union Act 2011[176]; and the unsuccessful attempt to change the voting system for elections to the House of Commons.[177] The structure of this book means that these changes are discussed at various different points. As a consequence, it is easy to lose sight of an important point that arises: the process by which these changes have been made. As we will see in Ch.3 below, it remains trite to say that the UK Parliament can effect wide ranging constitutional reform in an ordinary Act of Parliament, but the process that gives rise to such an Act merits consideration. And when that is done, the patchwork and disjointed approach to constitutional reform in the UK becomes clear. The House of Lords Constitution Committee has expressed its concern about the ad hoc approach to constitutional reform that is regularly adopted and has called for a clear and consistent approach to be adopted for all significant constitutional changes.[178] That of course raised the question of what is "constitutional" in a country without a single written document that it calls "the constitution". The working definition adopted by the committee was:

> "the set of laws, rules and practices that create the basic institutions of the state, and its component and related parts, and stipulate the powers of those institutions and the relationship between the different institutions and between those institutions and the individual."[179]

Recognising that the current system for constitutional change was flexible, and this was regarded by some as a virtue, the committee explained that flexibility did not overcome the weaknesses inherent in the ad hoc approach to constitutional reform adopted in the UK.[180] Those criticisms included: lack of constrains on government; failure to have regard to wider constitutional arrangements; lack of coherence within government; lack of consistency in the use of particular processes; possibility of changes being rushed; and lack of consultation.[181] What the committee proposed was the introduction of a requirement that a written

---

175 See para.6–02.

176 See paras 10–34—10–37.

177 See para.4–05.

178 House of Lords Select Committee on the Constitution, *The Process of Constitutional Change, 15th report of Session 2010–12* (The Stationery Office, 2011) HL Paper 177, para.15.

179 House of Lords Select Committee on the Constitution, *The Process of Constitutional Change, 15th report of Session 2010–12*, para.10. That definition was first proposed by the same committee in its very first report: House of Lords Select Committee on the Constitution, *Reviewing the Constitution: Terms of Reference and Method of Working, 1st report of Session 2001–2002* (The Stationery Office, 2001) HL Paper 11, para.20.

180 House of Lords Select Committee on the Constitution, *The Process of Constitutional Change, 15th report of Session 2010–12*, paras 20–22.

181 The concerns are discussed in turn in House of Lords Select Committee on the Constitution, *The Process of Constitutional Change, 15th report of Session 2010–12*, paras 20–46.

statement be made to each House of Parliament, by the minister responsible for the Bill in that House, setting out the minister's view on whether the Bill provides for significant constitutional change.[182] Where the minister is of the view that it does provide for such change, they should then be required to explain the processes that the Bill has been subject to and their outcomes.[183]

The report was published over three years before the Scottish independence referendum. In response to that vote, significant constitutional change was promised, change that had not been included in the most recent manifesto of any of the leading parties, and on which no prior consultation had taken place. Proposals were formulated in an exceptionally short period of time and there was no meaningful debate on whether the status quo was (or should be) an option. In short, the process adopted presents the most compelling case yet for the adoption of a fixed and defined process for constitutional reform in the UK. As the Constitution Committee had warned when reporting on the Fixed Term Parliaments Bill (itself a constitutional measure enacted swiftly after the 2010 General Election without proper consultation or regard for its impact on other parts of the constitution),[184] process matters:

> "Process is critical in terms of upholding, and being seen to uphold, constitutional values: particularly those of democratic involvement and transparency in the policy-making process. Moreover, we believe that a proper process is the foundation upon which successful policy is built: the lack of a proper process makes an ineffective outcome more likely."[185]

As we face what is likely to be a further period of significant constitutional change, the process by which that change is made will be all the more important.

Second, it is trite that the United Kingdom has no formal written document **1–28**
that it calls its constitution. As we have seen in the litigation prompted by Brexit, what exactly the constitution requires at particular points is not always obvious. In that context, it is helpful to recall what JDB Mitchell said over half a century ago. Introducing his chapter on the sovereignty or supremacy of Parliament, he explained:

> "Constitutions and constitutional doctrines are the result of history. As has already been emphasised, our overt revolutions occurred relatively early in the history of the modern state, and at times when the writing of a full constitution to crown the revolution had not become customary. These factors affect as strongly the doctrines relating to Parliament as they do doctrines such as those related to conventions. … This background must be borne in mind when considering the doctrine of the sovereignty of Parliament, for some precedents, some of the authoritative writings, must be considered (to an extent at least) in the light of the Parliament which

[182] House of Lords Select Committee on the Constitution, *The Process of Constitutional Change, 15th report of Session 2010–12*, para.71.

[183] House of Lords Select Committee on the Constitution, *The Process of Constitutional Change, 15th report of Session 2010–12*, para.72.

[184] See further, para.6–02. At the time of writing, the House of Lords Constitution Committee is undertaking an inquiry into the operation and implications of the 2011 Act. It ought to report at some point in 2020.

[185] House of Lords Select Committee on the Constitution, *Fixed-term Parliaments Bill, 8th Report of Session 2010–2011* (The Stationery Office, 2010) HL Paper 69, para.160.

> existed contemporaneously with them, and which may be materially different from that which now exists, either in itself or in general acceptance."[186]

Mitchell's warning is about history and its value as precedent applies generally and is not restricted to the principle of sovereignty. It is too early to tell what history will make of the constitutional turmoil through which we have recently passed, but, in considering what the constitution is understood to be, it is important to bear in mind that nothing is immune to the "whirligig of time".[187] Context, as in so many areas of the law, is everything. And that context includes the circumstances in which it is now claimed principles were forged to ensure that they remain relevant to modern society. So, whilst it is generally to history that we must turn to understand what our constitution is today, that history should not be accepted unquestioningly (and certainly not simply because that was how those before us chose to interpret that same history).

---

[186] J.D.B. Mitchell, *Constitutional Law*, 2nd edn (1968), p.63.

[187] That turn of phrase is borrowed from Sir Stephen Sedley and his lecture at Edinburgh University on 20 May 2015 (where the same point was made in relation to human rights and attitudes towards them), which is now reproduced in S. Sedley, *Law and the Whirligig of Time* (Hart Publishing, 2018), Ch.3.

CHAPTER 2

Sources

INTRODUCTION

"A constitution is a thing antecedent to government, and a government is only the creature of a constitution."[1] Clearly, this will not do to describe the British constitution.[2] We do not have a single authoritative document identifying the principal institutions of the state and the powers held by each[3]; and even where a system has a constitution in this sense, it never offers a complete description of that system's constitutional law. The House of Lords Constitution Committee proposed the following definition of the constitution: **2–01**

> "... the set of laws, rules and practices that create the basic institutions of the state, and its component and related parts, and stipulate the powers of those institutions and the relationship between the different institutions and between those institutions and the individual."[4]

The committee also recognised five basic tenants of the UK constitution: sovereignty of the Crown in Parliament; the rule of law; the union state; representative democracy; and membership of the Commonwealth, the European

---

[1] T. Paine, *The Rights of Man*.

[2] There is, however, something of Paine's idea in the arguments of those who suggest that the UK does possess an "antecedent" constitution in the form of the Acts and Treaty of Union of 1707: see, e.g. T.B. Smith, "The union of 1707 as fundamental law" [1957] P.L. 99; D.N. MacCormick, "Does the United Kingdom have a constitution?" (1978) 29 N.I.L.Q. 1; M. Upton, "Marriage vows of the elephant" (1989) 105 L.Q.R. 79.

[3] Although, up to a point, the Scotland Act 1998 may be said to serve as such for Scotland.

[4] House of Lords Select Committee on the Constitution, *The Process of Constitutional Change, 15th report of Session 2010–12* (The Stationery Office, 2011) HL Paper 177, para.10. That definition was first proposed by the same committee in its very first report: House of Lords Select Committee on the Constitution, *Reviewing the Constitution: Terms of Reference and Method of Working, 1st report of Session 2001–2002* (The Stationery Office, 2001) HL Paper 11, para.20. It is broadly consistent with the explanation of the UK constitution offered by the Supreme Court in *R (on the application of Miller and another) v Secretary of State for Exiting the European Union* [2017] UKSC 5; [2018] A.C. 61 at [18]. The description given by the Supreme Court is notable in two respects. First, it is framed by reference to *legal* rules; there is no mention of conventions. Second, it speaks of a UK constitution (and that reflected the general consensus about the relevant principals from all of the parties, from all three jurisdictions, that appeared: [19]) but is properly a short-hand as, for example, the Scottish courts have recognised the existence of established principles of the *Scottish* constitution: *Taylor Clark Leisure Plc v Commissioners for Her Majesty's Revenue and Customs* [2015] CSIH 32; 2015 S.L.T. 281 (see further at para.3–13).

Union and other international organisations.[5] Whilst admittedly not definitive, it has proved to be a helpful working definition.

It is not correct to say that the British constitution is "unwritten".[6] Our constitution is the aggregate of several sources, some written, some not; some legal in character, others non-legal in the sense of not being judicially enforceable or of deriving rather from the realms of legal and political theory. The process of constitutional reform that began in the late 1990s with devolution, in, as we shall see, different forms, to Scotland, Wales and Northern Ireland, and the enactment of the Human Rights Act 1998 saw the constitution become increasingly "written". That process has continued: the Constitutional Reform Act 2005 (which created the UK Supreme Court), the Government of Wales Act 2006 (which has ultimately led to the transfer of limited legislative competence to the Welsh Assembly[7]), the European Union Act 2011 and the Scotland Acts 2012 and 2016 have all resulted in an expansion of the written aspects of the constitution. But the unwritten (or at least, non-statutory) remains as significant as the written: both the Scotland Act and the Human Rights Act are, on the face of it, ordinary statutes enacted in the ordinary way and bearing no imprint of "constitutional" status, but, as we shall see, the courts ascribe to these and other statutes a superior status by virtue of their subject matter, and as a matter of the common law.

Already, then, we have identified two sources of those norms that go to make up our constitutional law: the law of Parliament as enacted in legislation, and the common law as expounded and applied by the courts. These take up much of, but do not exhaust, the field. Inter- and intra-institutional relations are very much the province of any system of constitutional law, and here we must look less at legal rules and more to what are known as constitutional conventions, to the law and custom of Parliament and indeed to broader concepts of legal and political theory, such as the separation of powers and the rule of law, from which certain conclusions about the appropriate balance of power between the institutions of the state may be drawn. Increasingly, the courts talk of "principles" of the constitution that appear to be derived from these broader theories of democracy. It would also be inappropriate to ignore claims to "popular sovereignty" or "the will of the people" that, if they have not made much impact on constitutional law and practice hitherto, have in recent years been asserted with greater vigour and may in the future illuminate not only political choices (e.g. as to the appropriateness of this or that piece of legislation) but also judicial decisions (e.g. as to the legality of Westminster legislation trenching upon the legislative competence devolved to the Scottish Parliament). Finally, one should never be insular in looking for the sources of constitutional law. True, it is that the term "the United Kingdom constitution" implies a strong connection between a constitution, or constitutional law, and the state. But just as the monolithic conception of the state has been weakened from within, by the asymmetric devolution of power from the central legislative and/or executive authorities of the UK to Scotland, Wales and Northern Ireland, so too has it been weakened

---

[5] House of Lords Select Committee on the Constitution, *The Process of Constitutional Change, 15th report of Session 2010–12*, para.10.

[6] The distinction between "written" and "unwritten" constitutions, and the consequences thought to flow from that distinction, has rightly been described as misleading and inexact: C.R. Munro, "What is a constitution?" [1983] P.L. 563.

[7] Which will, by the time of publication, be known as the Welsh Parliament: Wales Act 2017 s.9.

from without. Most obviously, this was a consequence of the UK's membership of the European Union. That may now be over, but it has, as we will see in subsequent chapters, left an indelible mark on the constitution. However, it has also been the consequence of the UK's wider engagement in the global community, wherein the state is increasingly in competition with other authoritative sites of power.[8] These developments have posed significant challenges to British constitutional traditions, and the process of accommodating those challenges within our constitutional law is continuing.

LEGISLATION

Let us begin, at any rate, with legislation—Acts of Parliament—as a source of constitutional law, and let us begin, as it were, at the beginning.[9] Parliament, meaning the UK Parliament at Westminster, is, in its present form, the creation of legislation, which legislation might in that sense be described as "constitutive". Before 1707 there were separate Scottish and English Parliaments. After 1707 there was a Parliament of Great Britain: by the Acts and Treaty of Union, the separate legislatures provided for their own extinction and the creation of a new entity.[10] That entity was enlarged again by the Union with Ireland Act 1800, the effects of which were reversed in large part by the legislation providing for the establishment of the Irish Free State.[11] Over the years, the Parliament thus established progressively redefined its internal composition by means of the Reform Acts,[12] the legislation to modify the power of the House of Lords to block legislation approved by the Commons[13] and, latterly, the legislation to remove **2–02**

[8] N. Walker, "Beyond the unitary conception of the United Kingdom constitution" [2000] P.L. 384; N. MacCormick, *Questioning Sovereignty: Law, State and Nation in the European Commonwealth* (Oxford: Oxford University Press, 1999).

[9] Even this is not going back far enough. Pre-Union enactments of the English and Scottish Parliaments which remain in force include, most importantly, the Bill of Rights 1689 and Claim of Right 1688, whereby the Parliaments finally refuted the claims of the Stuart monarchs to govern by prerogative right; and the Act of Settlement 1700 (extended to Scotland by the Treaty of Union in 1707), which regulated succession to the Crown. As to the status of pre-Union legislation, while many Acts of the Scottish Parliament were repealed pursuant to the Treaty of Union, many were not, and unless subsequently repealed (see, e.g. the Statute Law Revision (Scotland) Acts of 1906 and 1964) or in desuetude, continue in force.

[10] Upton, "Marriage vows of the elephant" (1989) 105 L.Q.R. 79, suggests that the Union involved a delegation of authority by the Scottish and English Parliaments, and that even if, after the Union, there was no need for the old Parliaments, this did not mean that they were "abolished" or that it would be legally impossible to recall them. Suffice to say that, despite the rhetoric attending the first meeting of the new Scottish Parliament on 12 May 1999, that body was indeed new, the creation of an Act of the Westminster Parliament on the terms therein contained, and not the revival of the body dormant since 1707.

[11] Government of Ireland Act 1920, Irish Free State (Constitution) Act 1922 and Irish Free State (Agreement) Act 1922. These provided for the establishment of the Irish Free State as a dominion within the Commonwealth subject to a mechanism—promptly utilised—allowing the six counties of Ulster to opt out. The Irish Free State (or Eire) declared itself a sovereign independent state in the Irish Constitution of 1937; the UK recognised this independence in the Ireland Act 1949.

[12] Notably the Representation of the People Acts 1832, 1867 and 1918. The law relating to the franchise is now contained in the Representation of the People Act 1983, as amended.

[13] Parliament Acts 1911 and 1949.

altogether the right of hereditary peers to sit and vote in the Lords.[14] By the European Communities Act 1972, Parliament incorporated into national law the whole body of what is now called EU law, including future accretions thereto, and, whether intentionally or not, made possible recognition by the courts of the primacy of EU law over inconsistent national law.[15] In the Human Rights Act 1998, Parliament ordained all courts to read and give effect to its enactments, existing and future, in a manner compatible with the "Convention rights",[16] so far as possible; and, where such interpretation was not possible, conferred on the higher courts jurisdiction to make "declarations of incompatibility" in respect of the offending statutory provision(s).[17] In the same session, Parliament made provision for the devolution of legislative competence in relation to Scotland to the Scottish Parliament, subject to various reservations and conditions, and for different forms of devolution to the National Assembly for Wales and Northern Ireland Assembly.

In their different ways—because they are constitutive or definitional, or concern the fundamental rights and freedoms of the individual, or confer authority on new constitutional actors—all of these statutes may be described as "constitutional" in a general sense. The question is whether this carries with it any higher legal status. Traditional constitutional doctrine has it that it does not:

> "[No] Act of the sovereign legislature (composed of the Queen, Lords and Commons) [can] be invalid in the eyes of the courts … it [is] always open to the legislature, so constituted, to repeal any legislation whatever;… therefore no Parliament [can] bind its successors; and … the legislature [has] only one process for enacting legislation, whereby it is declared to be the joint Act of the Crown, Lords and Commons in Parliament assembled… [It] is an invariable rule that in case of conflict between two Acts of Parliament, the latter repeals the earlier."[18]

---

[14] House of Lords Act 1999. Section 1 of the Act is qualified, however, by s.2, which "saves" the right of the Earl Marshal, Lord Great Chamberlain and 90 other hereditary peers elected by their fellows to sit and vote pending further reform of the House of Lords. The exact nature of that reform remains unresolved. As we shall see below, completing the process of reform that began in 1911 has not proved easy.

[15] As the majority put it in *R (on the application of Miller and other) Secretary of State for Exiting the European Union* [2017] UKSC 5; [2018] A.C. 61 at [60]: "It authorises a dynamic process by which, without further primary legislation (and, in some cases, even without any domestic legislation), EU law not only becomes a source of UK law, but actually takes precedence over all domestic sources of UK law, including statutes. This may sound rather dry or technical to many people, but in constitutional terms the effect of the 1972 Act was unprecedented." For a critique of the Supreme Court's reasoning on this point, see M. Elliott, "The Miller Case and Constitutional Statutes", published in M. Elliot, J. Williams and A.L. Young, *The UK Constitution after Miller: Brexit and Beyond*, pp.230–233; see also: D. Feldman, *The Nature and Significance of "Constitutional" Legislation* (2013) 129 L.Q.R. 343. For discussion of the meaning of the "primacy" of EU law, see further below at para.3–09—3–12, and the discussion of the European Union Act 2011 at para.12–45, below. As to whether Parliament knew what it was about in 1972, see D. Nicol, *EC Membership and the Judicialisation of British Politics* (Oxford: Oxford University Press, 2001). The author contends that, despite the explicit assertions by the European Court of Justice of the autonomy and primacy of EU law, MPs did not appreciate the legal and constitutional consequences of accession.

[16] "Convention rights" are those articles of the European Convention on Human Rights listed in Sch.1 to the Human Rights Act 1998.

[17] The operation of the Human Rights Act 1998 is discussed in Ch.11, below.

[18] H.W.R. Wade, "The basis of legal sovereignty" [1955] C.L.J. 172.

In other words, there is no difference in status between, for instance, the Acts of Union on the one hand and the Dentists Act on the other. This is because, on the above reasoning, the only thing that the Westminster Parliament cannot do is detract from its own continuing sovereignty—its ability to make or unmake any law whatever. That being so, any attempt to "entrench" legislation regarded as "constitutional" or otherwise significant would be an exercise in futility: the statute would remain as vulnerable as any other to repeal (express or implied) by a subsequent statute passed in the ordinary way.

We consider that theory in more detail in the next chapter. For now, it suffices to note that it no longer occupies the position of impregnability it once enjoyed. In particular, there has been judicial recognition that the status of Acts of Parliament does differ and that some Acts ought to be regarded as "constitutional". In *Thoburn v Sunderland City Council*, it was argued that provisions of the European Communities Act 1972 had been impliedly repealed by a subsequent, inconsistent Act of Parliament. Laws LJ held that this was not possible: **2–03**

> "Ordinary statutes may be impliedly repealed. Constitutional statutes may not. For the repeal of a constitutional Act or the abrogation of a fundamental right to be effected by statute, the court would apply this test: is it shown that the legislature's *actual*—not imputed, constructive or presumed—intention was to effect the repeal or abrogation? I think the test could only be met by express words in the later statute, or by words so specific that the inference of an actual determination to effect the result contended for was irresistible. The ordinary rule of implied repeal does not satisfy this test. Accordingly, it has no application to constitutional statutes."[19]

If this is so—if "constitutional" statutes are entrenched against implied override—the question is, what qualifies as a constitutional statute? Laws LJ gave some examples: Magna Carta, the Bill of Rights 1689, the Act of Union, the Reform Acts, the European Communities Act 1972 (which illustrates that even a constitutional statute can be repelled), the Human Rights Act 1998 and the devolution statutes. The Supreme Court has more recently included the Claim of Right 1689 and the Constitutional Reform Act 2005 on a similar list.[20] More broadly, Laws LJ described a constitutional statute as:

[19] *Thoburn v Sunderland City Council* [2002] EWHC 195 (Admin); [2003] Q.B. 151 at [63] (emphasis in original). This deals with the situation where a "constitutional" statute clashes with an "ordinary" statute. How the courts would deal with a clash between competing "constitutional" statutes is not clear: see the discussion by Lord Neurberger PSC and Lord Mance JSC in *R. (on the application of Buckingham CC) v Secretary of State for Transport* [2014] UKSC 3; [2014] 1 W.L.R. 324 at [207]–[208].

[20] "The United Kingdom has no written constitution, but we have a number of constitutional instruments. They include Magna Carta, the Petition of Right 1628, the Bill of Rights and (in Scotland) the Claim of Rights 1689, the Act of Settlement 1701 and the Act of Union 1707. The European Communities Act 1972, the Human Rights Act 1998 and the Constitutional Reform Act 2005 may now be added to that list": *R. (on the application of Buckingham CC) v Secretary of State for Transport* [2014] UKSC 3; [2014] 1 W.L.R. 324, per Lord Neuberger PSC and Lord Mance JSC at [207].

> "one which (a) conditions the legal relationship between citizen and state in some general, overarching manner, or (b) enlarges or diminishes the scope of what we would now regard as fundamental constitutional rights."[21]

This definition is not without difficulties.[22] Those difficulties have not prevented the Supreme Court endorsing the assertions of Laws LJ.[23] We may, therefore, safely speak of a category of constitutional statutes (albeit a somewhat open-ended one), which are, at least, resistant to repeal by anything other than express terms or the necessary intendment of a later Act of Parliament.

COMMON LAW

2–04 Professor Mitchell noted the importance of judicial decisions "either as an original source of principle or as a secondary source, when the courts are interpreting a statute".[24] To these categories (which overlap) might be added a third: determining the scope of prerogative power, which is recognised by, but not founded as such on, the common law, and supervising the manner of its exercise. Dicey was referring to the courts as the source of original principles when, in his account of the rule of law, he wrote that, "the general principles of the constitution (as, for example, the right to public liberty, or the right of public meeting) are with us the result of judicial decisions".[25]

In fact, this was a highly questionable proposition. The courts would intervene to protect invasions of individual rights for which there was no lawful authority.[26] But the common law was subordinate to the law enacted by Parliament, at least after 1688–89,[27] and it was less accurate to speak of "rights" of speech, property, assembly and so on than of such residue of liberty as remained after subtracting all the statutory (and common law) restrictions placed upon it. To be sure, the courts had the task of interpreting statutes, and might be more or less protective of the liberty of the subject in doing so.[28] But it is only relatively recently that the courts have begun to speak in terms of "common law constitutional rights".[29] Even there, they draw as much, if not more, inspiration from the post-war human

[21] *Thoburn v Sunderland City Council* [2002] EWHC 195 (Admin); [2003] Q.B. 151 at [62].

[22] See the discussion by Lord Rodger of Earlsferry in *Watkins v Secretary of State for the Home Department* [2006] UKHL 17; [2006] 2 A.C. 395, especially at [62]; G. Marshall, "Metric measures and martyrdom by Henry VIII clause" (2002) 118 L.Q.R. 493.

[23] *R. (on the application of Buckingham CC) v Secretary of State for Transport* [2014] UKSC 3; [2014] 1 W.L.R. 324 at [207]–[208].

[24] J.D.B. Mitchell, *Constitutional Law*, 2nd edn (Edinburgh: SULI; W. Green, 1968), p.23.

[25] A.V. Dicey, *Introduction to the Law of the Constitution*, 10th edn (London: Macmillan, 1959) p.195.

[26] The classic exemplar being *Entick v Carrington* (1765) 19 State Trials 1029.

[27] cf. *Dr Bonhams Case* (1610) 8 Co. Rep. 121, where Coke CJ asserted that "when an Act of Parliament is against common right and reason, or repugnant, or impossible to be performed, the common law will control it, and adjudge such Act to be void".

[28] Probably the least tolerance was shown to statutory provisions purporting to authorise invasions of rights of property: see, e.g. *Cooper v Wandsworth Board of Works* (1863) 14 C.B. N.S. 180. It has been suggested that *Entick v Carrington* is less a ringing assertion of the subjection of government to law than part of this property-fixated tradition: see K.D. Ewing, "The politics of the British constitution" [2000] P.L. 405.

[29] For example, the comments by Lord Hope (at [48]–[52]) and Lord Reed (at [149]–[153]) of *AXA General Insurance Co Ltd v Lord Advocate* [2011] UKSC 46; 2012 S.C. (U.K.S.C.) 122.

rights movement, in particular the European Convention on Human Rights, as from the ancient traditions of the common law itself.[30]

The subjection of the common law to the law of Parliament was a corollary of the asserted supremacy of Parliament, as explained (in differing terms) by writers such as Blackstone and Dicey.[31] It is important to note that at the time Blackstone and (to a lesser extent) Dicey were writing, the law of Parliament encroached upon fewer areas of life than it does today.[32] In that sense, the role of the courts was as much a creative as an interpretive one, for in all the areas untouched by legislation, the common law was the law of the land.[33] This state of affairs did not last. The powers of the state and its organs increased exponentially in the nineteenth and, particularly, twentieth centuries. This was not necessarily for sinister reasons: the establishment and development of the welfare state, for one thing, and the prosecution of two world wars for another, required it, and it came about at the behest of a legislature that was (at least after 1928) elected on the basis of universal adult suffrage. Its consequence, however, was that the role of the courts in developing the common law became less important than their role in interpreting and applying statutes and instruments made under them.

The interpretive role is not value neutral and we may identify two strands of criticism (not necessarily mutually exclusive) levelled at the courts for the way in which they have performed this task. One school depicts the courts as ever apt to thwart the intentions of the legislature when its enactments conflict with the values—or class prejudices—of the judiciary.[34] Others are more concerned with the apparent readiness of the courts (at least in the past) to allow the claims of administrative efficiency and convenience to prevail over the protection of individual freedoms.[35] Associated with the latter if not the former has been a growing perception that the protection of what might be termed "constitutional values" should no longer be left to Parliament alone, or even primarily, given the subordination of Parliament to the executive where the latter commands a majority in the House of Commons. As Lord Hope explained in *AXA General Insurance Co Ltd v Lord Advocate*:

---

[30] For an instructive blending of the two traditions, see Lord Browne-Wilkinson, "The infiltration of a Bill of Rights" [1992] P.L. 397, in which his Lordship suggested that the restrictive approach taken by the courts to the construction of penal and taxing statutes—which threaten, respectively, the liberty and property of the individual—be applied equally to statutes impinging upon other rights as enshrined in the European Convention on Human Rights.

[31] See P.P. Craig, "The sovereignty of the United Kingdom Parliament after *Factortame*" (1991) 11 Y.B.E.L. 221.

[32] Dicey's *Law of the Constitution* was first published in 1885. The same year, Sir Henry J.S. Maine published *Popular Government* (London: 1885), which deplored both the increasing reach of statute law and the increasing domination of Parliament by the executive.

[33] The reference to the common law must include, in Scotland, reference to the civil law, which was a major influence on the development of Scots private law, if not of its public law. Likewise, the institutional writers are regarded as a source of law in Scotland, in the absence of subsequent judicial decisions to the contrary, but as Mitchell noted, the great institutional writers tended not to discuss public law so fully as private law or criminal law. Most constitutional "books of authority" are the works of English writers, and may carry less authority north of the border in consequence: see, generally, Mitchell, *Constitutional Law* (1968), pp.19–26.

[34] See, in particular, J.A.G. Griffith, *The Politics of the Judiciary*, 5th edn (London: Fontana, 1997); also, Ewing, "The politics of the British constitution" [2000] P.L. 405.

[35] See, in particular, the surveys by Sir Stephen Sedley, "The sound of silence: constitutional law without a constitution" (1994) 110 L.Q.R. 270 and "Human rights: a twenty-first century agenda" [1995] P.L. 386.

> "While the judges, who are not elected, are best placed to protect the rights of the individual, including those who are ignored or despised by the majority, the elected members of a legislature of this land are best placed to judge what is in the country's best interests as a whole."[36]

The judicial response to this tension has fused, in a sense, the function of expounding original principle and the function of statutory interpretation. It has been repeatedly held that, in construing legislation, it is to be presumed, absent express words or necessary implication to the contrary, that Parliament intended no infringement of certain "fundamental" rights.[37] In this way, the courts reasserted the authority of the common law as a source of constitutional norms, to such an extent that one commentator discerned a "new and still emerging constitutional paradigm, no longer of Dicey's supreme Parliament to whose will the rule of law must finally bend, but of a bi-polar sovereignty of the Crown in Parliament and the Crown in its courts".[38]

2–05 There is another, discrete sense in which the common law is important as a source of constitutional doctrine, and that is in its treatment of the Crown and prerogative powers. The nature of the Crown and of the prerogative is considered in greater detail in Ch.7; suffice to say for now that the courts have successively denied the Crown any autonomous legislative authority,[39] affirmed the pre-eminence of statute over the prerogative,[40] and asserted the subjection of the prerogative to the supervisory jurisdiction of the courts provided its exercise raises justiciable questions.[41] As we shall see, despite all this, the subjection of the prerogative to law is often more a matter of principle than reality. That is not always, or necessarily, a matter of concern, for in certain circumstances political rather than legal control is apposite. But where called upon to do so, as we saw in *Miller*, the court will step in if required.

Like the prerogative, the privileges of Parliament are rooted in custom,[42] but may be said to exist within the common law in the sense that they are recognised by the courts and (so far as the courts are concerned) are subject to the common law, for while the courts concede Parliament's exclusive jurisdiction in matters of privilege where properly claimed, they assert for themselves the last word on where the outer limits of privilege lie.[43]

---

[36] *AXA General Insurance Co Ltd v Lord Advocate* [2011] UKSC 46; 2012 S.C. (U.K.S.C.) 122 at [49].

[37] See, for example, *R. v Lord Chancellor, Ex p. Witham* [1998] Q.B. 575 QBD; *R. v Secretary of State for the Home Department, Ex p. Pierson* [1998] A.C. 539 HL; *R. v Secretary of State for the Home Department, Ex p. Simms* [2000] 2 A.C. 115 HL; *R. (on the application of Morgan Grenfell & Co Ltd) v Special Commissioners of Income Tax* [2002] UKHL 21; [2003] 1 A.C. 563, per Lord Hoffmann at [8]; and *R (on the application of Privacy International) v Investigatory Powers Tribunal* [2019] UKSC 22; [2019] 2 W.L.R. 1219 at [111].

[38] Sedley, "Human rights: a twenty-first century agenda" [1995] P.L. 386, p.389.

[39] *Case of Proclamations* (1611) 12 Co. Rep. 74 and, in Scotland, *Grieve v Edinburgh and District Water Trustees*, 1918 S.C. 700.

[40] *Attorney General v De Keysers Royal Hotel Ltd* [1920] A.C. 508.

[41] *Council of Civil Service Unions v Minister for the Civil Service* [1985] A.C. 374.

[42] Although the privilege of freedom of speech was given statutory force by the Bill of Rights 1689 art.9. That provision *recognised* the existing principle rather than *creating* it.

[43] *R. v Chaytor (David)* [2010] UKSC 52; [2011] 1 A.C. 684, per Lord Phillips of Worth Matraves PSC at [15]–[16].

CONSTITUTIONAL CONVENTION

In his account of our constitutional rules, Dicey distinguished the legal rules—statutory and common law—from another set of rules consisting of: 2–06

> "[the] conventions, understandings, habits or practices which, though they may regulate the conduct of the several members of the sovereign power, of the ministry, or of their officials, are not in reality laws at all since they are not enforced by the courts. This portion of constitutional law may, for the sake of distinction, be termed the 'conventions of the constitution' or 'constitutional morality'."[44]

For Dicey, the central significance of constitutional conventions was that they prescribed the manner in which the prerogatives of the Crown (or of ministers or servants of the Crown) fell to be exercised. This far from exhausts the field, but it is certainly true that these are the most important, or most clearly established, conventions, and chief amongst them is the convention that requires that the Queen act only on the advice of her ministers.[45] As we shall see, even this rule may admit of exceptions in certain circumstances. One might therefore wonder, how is it possible to speak of conventions as "rules" of the constitution at all, if it is neither necessary that they be always obeyed nor possible (through recourse to the courts) to enforce their observance? As the Supreme Court explained:

> "Judges therefore are neither the parents nor the guardians of political conventions; they are merely observers. As such, they can recognise the operation of a political convention in the context of deciding a legal question ... but they cannot give legal rulings on its operation or scope, because those matters are determined within the political world."[46]

Accordingly, to equate conventions with legal rules is to fall into error. Conventions are not legal rules, by definition. Legal rules are the product of sources we recognise as law constitutive: the Queen in Parliament, the Scottish Parliament acting within the sphere of its competence, and the courts. Conventions, by contrast, are founded on practice and precedent. Breach of a legal rule—stealing, speeding, committing murder—does not invalidate the rule. Breach of a convention, on the other hand, may have a destructive effect, depending on the "degree of stringency and definiteness" the convention possesses.[47] Short of that, the breach may restrict the range of circumstances over which the convention is felt to hold sway, or diminish its binding force within its

---

[44] Dicey, *An Introduction to the Law of the Constitution* (1959), p.24. His insight was not a new one. Mitchell, *Constitutional Law* (1968) cites Gilbert Stuart, who wrote in his *Observations concerning the public law, and the constitutional history of Scotland: with occasional remarks concerning English antiquity* (Edinburgh: William Creech, 1779) that "habits tend to establish a rule, and custom is often as effectual as law".

[45] R. Brazier, "Royal Assent to legislation" (2013) 129 L.Q.R. 184.

[46] *R (on the application of Miller and another) v Secretary of State for Exiting the European Union* [2017] UKSC 5; [2018] A.C. 61 at [146]. See also: *Attorney General v Jonathan Cape Ltd* [1976] Q.B. 752 QBD and C.R. Munro, "Laws and Conventions Distinguished" (1975) 91 L.Q.R. 218.

[47] See F.W. Maitland, *The Constitutional History of England* (Cambridge: The University Press, 1911), p.398.

allotted sphere.[48] What is critical to the crystallisation and survival of a convention, however, is that it has this binding quality: "feeling obliged" is a necessary condition for the existence of a convention, but neither a necessary nor a sufficient condition for the existence of a legal rule.[49]

2–07 The necessity that the key constitutional actors are left "feeling obliged" to adhere to a convention can create some uncertainty as to whether a convention has in fact been established. What then is required to create a constitutional convention? According to Jennings:

> "We have to ask ourselves three questions: first, what are the precedents, secondly, did the actors in the precedents believe that they were bound by a rule; and thirdly, is there a reason for the rule? A single precedent with a good reason may be enough to establish the rule. A whole string of precedents without such a reason will be of no avail, unless it is perfectly certain that the persons concerned regarded them as bound by it."[50]

Constitutional conventions are normally "the product of a slow process of evolution".[51] That is not always so. The more rapid creation of a convention can be illustrated by asking: does the government require the approval of the House of Commons before engaging the military in armed conflict overseas? As we will see in Ch.7, the deployment of the armed forces and the declaration of war are prerogative powers, exercisable by the executive without prior approval by the legislature. However, before deploying armed forces in Iraq in 2003 the then Prime Minister, Tony Blair, asked the House of Commons to vote on his motion requesting approval for the use of military force "to ensure the disarmament of Iraq's weapons of mass destruction".[52] That motion was carried. It was subsequently suggested that events of 2003 meant that similar approval would "almost certainly" have to be obtained in similar circumstances in the future.[53] The next Prime Minister, Gordon Brown, proposed in a Green Paper that a convention to the effect that the consent of the House of Commons should be required before sending the military into armed conflict. That proposal was never taken forward. When the prospect of military intervention in Syria arose, however, the Prime Minister of the day, by then David Cameron, felt obliged to seek approval of UK involvement in any such military intervention. When the House of Commons did not grant that approval, the Prime Minister undertook not to exercise the government's prerogative power to nevertheless deploy the military in Syria and the UK did not participate in the subsequent military

[48] See J. Jaconelli, "The Nature of Constitutional Convention" (1999) 19 L.S. 24 at p.33; J. Jaconelli, "Do Constitutional Conventions Bind?" [2005] C.L.J. 149.

[49] C.R. Munro, *Studies in Constitutional Law*, 2nd edn (London: Butterworths, 1999), pp.78–87.

[50] Sir Ivor Jennings, *The Law and the Constitution*, 5th edn (London: University of London Press, 1959) p.136. That approach to recognising the existence of a constitutional convention was adopted by the Supreme Court of Canada in *Re Resolution to amend the Constitution* [1981] 1 S.C.R. 753.

[51] A. McHarg, "Reforming the United Kingdom constitution: law, convention and soft law" (2008) 71 M.L.R. 853.

[52] *Hansard*, HC Vol.401, col.760 (18 March 2003).

[53] Lord Wilson of Dinton, "The robustness of conventions in a time of modernisation and change" [2004] P.L. 407.

campaign.[54] Events of 2003 proved to have been a sufficient single event to produce the rule: it was, to use Jenning's language, a single precedent underpinned by a very good reason.[55]

The requirement of "feeling obliged" may also help us to clarify what we mean when we speak of "breaches" of convention. The very language betrays a sense of being obliged to act in a particular way, and an expectation of criticism if one acts otherwise. It also suggests that a constitutional actor who acts in a manner other than that ordained by convention will have thought long and hard before doing so, and will probably feel (rightly or wrongly) that they have a good reason for acting in the way they have chosen.[56] For these reasons, the term "breach" may not always, or necessarily, be apposite. But while conventions are not "rules of law" they can be regarded as "rules of the constitution". The difference between a legal rule and a convention being simply the method of enforcement: the former is enforced by the courts and the latter by the political process.[57]

The key characteristics of the operation of constitutional conventions can be illustrated by considering the cardinal convention that governs the exercise of so called "personal prerogatives" of the Queen (assenting to legislation, appointment of the Prime Minister and so on). This list previously included the dissolution of Parliament and the calling of a general election. That personal prerogative has, for now at least, been removed by legislation.[58] By convention, the Queen is required to exercise these only in accordance with the advice of her ministers.[59] Constitutional practice is consistent (if not altogether without ambiguity) and the reasons for it can be located in the importance we attach to such values as responsible government and democratic accountability. Thus, in normal circumstances, the Queen will appoint as Prime Minister the person best able to command the confidence of the House of Commons. In other words, the Queen **2–08**

---

[54] *Hansard*, HC Vol.566, cols 1555–1556 (29 August 2013).

[55] See McHarg, "Reforming the United Kingdom constitution: law, convention and soft law" (2008) 71 M.L.R. 853, who discusses why the Green Paper should not be considered the source of the convention.

[56] Jaconelli, "The Nature of Constitutional Convention" (1999) 19(1) L.S. 24 discusses this point under reference to Ronald Dworkin's account of the nature of practices in *Law's Empire* (London: Fontana, 1986). Dworkin agrees that practices have an element of uncertainty which is open to interpretative dispute. On this view, it is not enough to act solely on the basis of the "raw empirical data" consisting in past precedents; rather, one must supplement the data with questions of the rationale for applying the convention in the present circumstances.

[57] C. Turpin and A. Tomkins, *British Government and the Constitution: text and materials*, 7th edn (Cambridge: Cambridge University Press, 2011), pp.182–183.

[58] Fixed-Term Parliaments Act 2011 s.3; s.6(1) of the 2011 Act preserves Her Majesty's power to prorogue Parliament. The 2011 Act, however, otherwise prescribes when, and in what circumstances, an election can now be called. Parliament is then dissolved on the seventeenth working day before the election (s.3(1)). For a critical analysis of the 2011 Act see M. Ryan, "The Fixed-Term Parliaments Act 2011" [2012] P.L. 213. Various noises have been made about the repeal of the Act but no proposals have yet been forthcoming.

[59] R. Blackburn, "Monarchy and the personal prerogatives" [2007] P.L. 546 (who argues that the approach of "personal prerogatives" is "wrong, misconceived, and belongs to an earlier era"; despite the cogency of his argument, the phrase remains in common currency and is used here, subject to Professor Blackburn's warnings); see also R. Blackburn, "The prerogative power of dissolution of Parliament: law, practice and reform" [2009] P.L. 766.

will appoint either the leader of the largest party (especially where that party has an overall majority) or, where a coalition has been formed, the leader of the largest party within that coalition.

As we saw in 2010, the Queen exercised no personal choice in the aftermath of a general election that produced no clear winner. In 2010, there were three possibilities: a Conservative-Liberal Democrat coalition, a Labour-Liberal Democrat coalition or a minority Conservative government.[60] Coalition talks between the Conservatives and the Liberal Democrats took a number of days. During that period, the incumbent Prime Minister, Gordon Brown, remained in office. By failing to tender his resignation immediately after the election (as would ordinarily be expected of a defeated incumbent) he afforded space to the parties to negotiate a coalition agreement. As a result, the Queen was not placed in a position where she may have required to intervene in those discussions. For much of 2019, the Prime Minister (first Teresa May and then Boris Johnson) could not be said to command the confidence of the House of Commons on their central policy: Brexit. The government had no majority on that issue and was subject to a series of defeats. Absent the fixed-term Parliaments Act, an election would have been inevitable. One eventually came but throughout, despite the difficulties the Prime Minister faced in the House of Commons, it was never a matter for the Palace.[61] Those events underscore the flexibility of the constitution, and, in particular, the conventions surrounding the appointment of the Prime Minister. Just as King George V was not required to exercise any personal choice in the 1920s when twice a general election failed to produce a clear winner, nor was his granddaughter nearly a century later: political circumstances dictated the outcome. Any alternative, which saw an unelected and hereditary Head of State exercise a personal choice in the appointment of Prime Minister, in a representative democracy, could be described as, at best, unfortunate.[62]

What does this tell us about the conventions surrounding the choice of Prime Minister? It suggests that despite being labelled a "personal prerogative" of the Sovereign, the prevailing political atmosphere should ensure that no personal choice is required on the Sovereign's part. Any other situation would be dangerous for the monarchy as an institution. The 2011 Act removes the need to theorise about when, if at all, the Queen could act contrary to the advice of her Prime Minister in relation to the dissolution of Parliament. History, however, teaches us that it would only have been in the rarest of circumstances that such a course would have been appropriate. In 1926, the minority Liberal Prime Minister in Canada requested a dissolution from the Sovereign's representative, the Governor General. The Governor General believed that the Conservative leader could form a government having majority support in the existing Parliament, and refused. The Prime Minister resigned and the Governor General appointed the Conservative leader in his place. Days later, the new government

[60] For a general and insightful discussion of the issues arising from the 2010 election result, see V. Bogdanor, *The Coalition and the Constitution* (Oxford: Hart, 2011).

[61] Of course, whilst it is right to say that the Prime Minister (both May and, before the 2019 election, Johnston) could not be said to command the confidence of the House of Commons on their flagship policy (namely, Brexit), nobody else appeared better placed to command the confidence of the House on that issue.

[62] Blackburn, "Monarchy and the personal prerogatives" [2004] P.L. 546.

was defeated on a motion of confidence, leading to the dissolution that had been denied to its Liberal predecessor. In the general election that followed, the Liberals were returned with a convincing majority. Again, in 1975, the Governor General of Australia was moved to exercise the prerogative of dismissing a Prime Minister and his government.[63] The Australian Senate (in which the opposition had a majority) had refused to pass money bills authorising government expenditure. This had led to a rapid depletion in the funds available to maintain public services. Prime Minister Whitlam requested the Governor General to dissolve the Senate. The Governor General insisted on a full dissolution so that a general election could be held. When Whitlam refused to change his advice, the Governor General dismissed him and his government and appointed the Leader of the Opposition in his place on condition that he would guarantee supply and advise a dissolution and general election.

It is not obvious that the circumstances of either case were so extreme as to justify departure from the normal convention. In the Australian case, for instance, the more astute course would have been to follow the advice given and let the electorate decide, in the fullness of time, whether Whitlam's advice had been sound. Resolution of the crisis would then have rested where it properly belonged, firmly in the arena of democratic politics. On this view, the Sovereign should only exercise her prerogatives personally and without advice where the advice tendered is clearly an abuse of the system or where necessary to safeguard the parliamentary and democratic bases of the constitution.[64] The point remains that even this convention is less than absolute in its terms, and does not altogether exclude the possibility of the Sovereign exercising effective political power. This may not commend itself to those of a republican bent. On the other hand, it generally works, and it is not as though the alternative solutions to such occasional crises are themselves free of problems.[65]

Other conventions are less prescriptive still, perhaps not least the convention 2–09
of ministerial responsibility. This has a collective and an individual dimension. Collective ministerial responsibility:

> "requires that Ministers should be able to express their views frankly in the expectation that they can argue freely in private while maintaining a united front

[63] This despite the fact that the exercise of the prerogative of dismissal had been described not so very long before as "not being within the scope of practical politics": *Adegbenro v Akintola* [1963] A.C. 614 PC (Nigeria), per Lord Radcliffe at p.631.

[64] The advice would have to be extreme and patently an abuse of power. As we saw in Ch.1, in the *Prorogation case*, the advice given to the Queen was found by the Supreme Court to have been unlawful. That was after the Court of Session and the High Court had reached differing conclusions on the issue. There was no serious suggestion that the Queen ought to have refused to follow the advice when it was tendered and rightly so given it was a point that divided legal opinion (albeit not the Justices of the Supreme Court).

[65] See A. Tomkins, "In Defence of the Political Constitution" (2002) 22 O.J.L.S. 157. The author contrasts the British constitutional handling of a hung Parliament with the debacle that followed the American Presidential election in 2000, suggesting that the latter demonstrates the futility and undesirability of seeking to find the answer to all political disputes in law (see *Bush v Gore* (2000) S31 US 98).

> when decisions have been reached. This in turn requires that the privacy of opinions expressed in Cabinet and Ministerial Committees, including in correspondence, should be maintained."[66]

A minister that cannot adhere to this principle ought to resign from the government.[67] Individual ministerial responsibility in its classic form involves the minister in charge of a government department assuming responsibility for all that is done by his officials in his name, such that an official's mistake is deemed to be the minister's mistake and, if sufficiently serious, warrant for his resignation. The sanction attaching to a lapse from collective ministerial responsibility is clear enough: if the minister neglects to resign, they may simply be sacked. The sanction attaching to a departure from the strictures of individual ministerial responsibility, however, is less clear. In the days when Parliament was less apt to operate on rigid party lines, MPs might have forced an incompetent minister's resignation by withdrawing their confidence from him or her. Now, this is virtually inconceivable provided the government has majority support: government backbenchers are unlikely, to put it mildly, to force the resignation of one of their own. Is there, then, evidence that ministers resign in circumstances of departmental failure through a sense of obligation to do so? Professor Finer doubted it.[68] Having studied the instances of ministerial resignation over the course of the preceding century, he concluded that:

> "All [the convention] says (on examination) is that if the minister is yielding, his Prime Minister unbending and his party out for his blood—no matter how serious or trivial the reason—the minister will find himself without parliamentary support. [But] that is a statement of fact, not a code."

It is of note that the Ministerial Code now talks about a minister's duty to account as opposed to their responsibility.[69] As we will see in Ch.7, the distinction between "accountability" and "responsibility" has become of increasing importance in recent years. It is true that ministers do not routinely fall on their swords in the manner the convention seems to prescribe. Famous examples do not denote consistent compliance.[70] But some ministers at least have felt an obligation to resign, and "in everyday political discourse, too, the rule continues to be treated as if it had practical content".[71] Thus we need not accept Finer's

---

66 Cabinet Office, *Ministerial Code* (The Stationery Office, 2010, revised August 2019) para.2.1, *https://assets.publishing.service.gov.uk/government/uploads/system/uploads/attachment_data/file/826920/August-2019-MINISTERIAL-CODE-FINAL-FORMATTED-2.pdf* [Accessed 15 April 2020].

67 In this context, "Minister" includes all members of the government, including parliamentary private secretaries (para.3.9 of the Ministerial Code).

68 S.E. Finer, "The Individual Responsibility of Ministers" (1956) 34(4) *Public Administration* 377.

69 For example, para.4.6 of the Ministerial Code: "The Minister in charge of a department is solely accountable to Parliament for the exercise of the powers on which the administration of that department depends."

70 Among the classic cases are those of Sir Thomas Dugdale, who resigned as Minister of Agriculture in 1954 after an inquiry found maladministration by officials in his department; the Foreign Secretary, Lord Carrington, and two Foreign Office ministers, who resigned in 1982 amidst claims that the Foreign Office had culpably misinterpreted signals of Argentinian intention in the period preceding the Falklands conflict; and the Home Secretary, Leon Brittan MP, who resigned in 1986 after one of his officials leaked confidential legal advice to the press.

71 Munro, *Studies in Constitutional Law* (1999), p.86.

conclusion that there is no convention of resignation at all, even if we concede that it is not a convention of great "stringency and definiteness". Further, as we shall see in Ch.7, it does not necessarily do to focus exclusively on the "blame and sanction" aspect of the convention of ministerial responsibility. It has been forcefully argued that the convention has had a strong influence on the internal structuring of government.[72] Moreover, in point of fact, ministers do answer to Parliament for the actions and decisions of their departments, and do not routinely or systematically mislead Parliament in doing so. Viewed thus, whether or not a minister resigns may be less important than the adequacy (or otherwise) of the convention as a vehicle for securing the accountability of the executive to Parliament.

So far we have been talking about the operation of constitutional conventions at the UK level. To what extent may it be said that conventions have developed in the context of the devolved Scottish institutions? It may still be too soon to speak of "indigenous" conventions, the products of consistent and uniform practice. In the last decade, we have seen coalition government, minority government and the supposedly impossible majority government. What should be considered "the norm" is yet to be established. But two aspects of the devolution settlement are interesting in this regard. First, the Scotland Act 1998 clothes in the language of legislation the conventions that, at Westminster, govern the choice of Prime Minister.[73] The appointment of the First Minster is made by the Queen from among the members of the Scottish Parliament. Section 46(4) of the Scotland Act 1998 provides that the Presiding Officer shall recommend to the Queen the appointment of that MSP who is nominated by the Parliament in accordance with the section. Nowhere does the Act state in terms that the nomination must be accepted, but the intention of the section is clear; whatever arguments might be made about the strict legal position, here at least we can probably speak of a convention that the Queen will act in this matter on the advice of the Presiding Officer alone. **2–10**

Second, there is a convention, originally called the "Sewel Convention", whereby Westminster is obliged to seek the consent of the Scottish Parliament before proceeding to enact legislation touching on devolved matters.[74] The Sewel Convention is named for the Scottish Office Minister who, during the parliamentary debates on the Scotland Bill, sought to assuage concern that, after devolution, Westminster would exploit its unimpaired legislative competence to frustrate the work of the Scottish Parliament:

---

[72] T. Daintith and A. Page, *The Executive in the Constitution: Structure, Autonomy and Internal Control* (Oxford: Oxford University Press, 1999).

[73] The Scottish Parliament has always been a fixed term parliament. The Scotland Act 1998 was effectively a codification of the conventions that, at that time, regulated Westminster. Those conventions have now been codified for Westminster as well in the form of the Fixed-Term Parliaments Act 2011.

[74] See B.K. Winetrobe, "Counter-devolution? The Sewel convention on devolved legislation at Westminster" (2001) 6(4) S.L.P.Q. 286; N. Burrows, "It's Scotland's Parliament: Let Scotland's Parliament Legislate", 2002 Jur. Rev. 213; A. Page and A. Batey, "Scotland's Other Parliament: Westminster Legislation about Devolved Matters in Scotland since Devolution" [2002] P.L. 501; J. Munro, "Thoughts on the 'Sewel Convention'", 2003 S.L.T. (News) 194.

> "The government would expect a convention to be established that Westminster would not normally legislate with regard to devolved matters in Scotland without the consent of the Scottish Parliament."[75]

This principle was endorsed by the House of Commons Select Committee on Procedure in 1999, and further reinforced by guidance concerning its operation in the Memorandum of Understanding between the UK Government and Scottish Executive and documents issued by the Privy Council Office in 1999 and by the Constitution and Parliamentary Secretariat in 2001. Where consent is required, it is sought by way of a "legislative consent motion" (formerly known as "Sewel motion") laid before the Scottish Parliament[76] by the appropriate Scottish Minister following consultation between the UK Government and the Scottish Government. So firmly established is the Sewel Convention that it has now received statutory recognition. The Scotland Act 2016 amended the 1998 Act so as to insert s.28(8):

> "(8) But it is recognised that the Parliament of the United Kingdom will not normally legislate with regard to devolved matters without the consent of the Scottish Parliament."[77]

Immediately preceding that provision is s.28(7), which is an unequivocal assertion of the continuing legislative supremacy of the UK Parliament, "This section does not affect the power of the Parliament of the United Kingdom to make laws for Scotland". That, like s.28(8), is simply declaratory of the existing position: without s.28(7) the UK Parliament still has power to legislate on devolved matters and without s.28(8) the Sewel Convention existed. Whilst there may be some benefit in formally recognising a convention such as the Sewel Convention,[78] s.28(7) is otiose.

2–11 It was not anticipated that legislative consent motions would be used routinely. In fact, they are commonplace.[79] Legislative consent has routinely been sought where the convention dictated it was required. And it has invariably been granted.[80] Each time consent has been withheld, the UK Parliament has proceeded to legislate in any event. That points to a consistent practice and one that accords with what is now said in s.28(8) of the Scotland Act 1998: the UK

[75] *Hansard*, HL Vol.592, col.791 (21 July 1998). Whether such a statement can create a convention ahead of time (i.e. before the Scottish Parliament had been created) raises an interesting doctrinal point. Jaconelli suggests that, even if ultimately we can trace the emergence of a convention back to a particular event, such as a statement made in the legislature, the statement "attains that status [as a convention] in truth only when [it has] set in motion a chain of actions and expectations based on [its] observance" (Jaconelli, "The Nature of Constitutional Convention" (1999) 19(1) L.S. 24 at 33).

[76] Standing Orders of the Scottish Parliament, Pt 9B.

[77] Similar provision has also been made in relation to Wales: Government of Wales Act 2006, s.107(6).

[78] The Supreme Court's view was that "the purpose of the legislative recognition of the convention was to entrench it as a convention.": *R (on the application of Miller and another) v Secretary of State for Exiting the European Union* [2017] UKSC 5; [2018] A.C. 61 at [149].

[79] As at April 2020 207 legislative consent motions had been presented to the Scottish Parliament, *https://www.parliament.scot/parliamentarybusiness/Bills/31313.aspx* [Accessed 16 April 2020].

[80] Only three such motions have not been agreed: Welfare Reform Bill (December 2011; this Bill introduced the universal credit benefit scheme; consent was only partially withheld); the European Union (Withdrawal) Bill (May 2018; consent was withheld in full); and the European Union (Withdrawal Agreement) Bill (January 2020; consent was withheld in full).

Parliament "will not normally legislate" on devolved matters without consent. The convention does not confer upon the Scottish Parliament a veto over UK legislation that has a devolution element. It remains a convention and if consent is not sought, or it is sought and refused, there is no bar on the UK Parliament proceeding to legislate.[81] As the Supreme Court explained:

> "The Sewel convention has an important role in facilitating harmonious relationships between the UK Parliament and the devolved legislatures. But the policing of its scope and the manner of its operation does not lie within the constitutional remit of the judiciary, which is to protect the rule of law."[82]

And so it was with the Brexit-enabling legislation. Consent was not forthcoming from the Scottish Parliament (reflective, it was argued, of how the Scottish electorate had voted in the 2016 referendum), but any consequence from proceeding with the UK Bills was political only. That was much lamented by some and was said to undermine devolution. But, on the contrary, it illustrates a convention working in practice (and it is how conventions have always been understood to work).[83] But given what has been said about the importance of the Sewel Convention to facilitating the smooth running of devolution, there is a good argument for giving the convention some (political) teeth.[84]

Leaving Brexit-related troubles, there are good reasons for consent not being an absolute requirement. What if the Scottish Parliament, under the control of a majority government, were to refuse all legislative consent motions on principle, even where the arguments for UK-wide legislation were compelling? It is hard to conceive of a good reason why the UK Government and Parliament should refuse to legislate in the face of such an arbitrary policy (especially if there was an obvious benefit from a UK-wide approach). In the previous edition of this work, it was asked whether the extent of popular support for any refusal of consent by the Scottish Parliament would be determinative of the UK Government and Parliament's response. The lesson of the Brexit-enabling legislation suggests it is not (at least where the legislation in issue pursues a genuinely UK-wide policy in relation to which a tailored sub-national solution is not practicable). So, the Sewel Convention, like any convention, is binding only to the extent the relevant actors feel bound. But that does not undermine its importance, it just recognises it for what it is: a convention, not a law.

---

[81] That point should never have been in doubt, but it was made clear by the Supreme Court in *UK Withdrawal from the European Union (Legal Continuity) (Scotland) Bill* [2018] UKSC 64; 2019 S.C. (U.K.S.C.) 13 at [20].

[82] *R (on the application of Miller and another) v Secretary of State for Exiting the European Union* [2017] UKSC 5; [2018] A.C. 61 at para.151. To similar effect, see: *UK Withdrawal from the European Union (Legal Continuity) (Scotland) Bill* [2018] UKSC 64; 2019 S.C. (U.K.S.C.) 13 at [20].

[83] Arguably the court has, on occasion, taken a more generous view of conventions and its role in relation to them. See T. Mullen, *The Brexit case and constitutional conventions* (2017) 21 Edin L.R. 442. For example, in *R (on the application of Evans) v Attorney General* [2015] UKSC 21; [2015] A.C. 1787 it might be thought that constitutional conventions played a surprisingly prominent role (at least before the Tribunal).

[84] See: P. Reid, "Time to Give the Sewel Convention Some (Political) Bite?", U.K. Const. L. Blog, 26 January 2017 (at: *https://ukconstitutionallaw.org/2017/01/26/paul-reid-time-to-give-the-sewel-convention-some-political-bite/* [Accessed 4 May 2020]).

INTERNATIONAL LAW

2–12 As a Member State of the European Union, the UK was obliged to give effect to and apply directly effective norms of EU law, and that obligation was discharged through the medium of the European Communities Act 1972. The incorporation of EU law had momentous consequences for our constitutional law, as we shall see the next chapter. And those ripples continue, and will continue for some time to come, given the general transposition of EU law into domestic law on Exit Day.[85] That, however, is a consequence of what was EU law being brought into, and becoming a true part of, domestic law. But to what extent might other international legal norms serve as a source of domestic constitutional law? Rules of customary international law, the product of consistent and uniform state practice that comes to reflect an *opinio juris* that particular conduct is proscribed or, as the case may be, required by international law, constitute rules of Scots law, whether or not codified in international treaties.[86] Thus, established principles of international humanitarian law on the prohibition of torture and other crimes against humanity would form part of Scots law independently of their incorporation (or otherwise) into national law by statutes. Rules of international law derived from treaties (unless they have customary law status) differ. Some constitutional systems, which are described as "monist", hold that when a state signs and ratifies an international treaty, the contents of that treaty automatically become part of its domestic law, directly enforceable as such before its courts. The UK, however, subscribes to the "dualist" position, which holds that a treaty does not form part of national law unless and until incorporated into the law by legislation. The process for ratification of treaties by the UK has now been put on a statutory footing.[87] Unless incorporated, however, the treaty cannot create rights or duties enforceable before the national courts. The rationale for this is that the signing of a treaty is an executive, not a legislative, act, and the government should not be permitted to burden citizens with obligations unsanctioned by Parliament.[88] Lord Steyn has noted that this reasoning is quite beside the point in relation to human rights treaties, which by definition do not impose burdens on individuals.[89] Lord Kerr (in the course of dissenting) has adopted this argument and strongly advocated that human rights enshrined in international treaties to

---

85 The mechanism by which that was done is more fully explained in Ch.10, below.

86 See *R. (on the application of European Roma Rights Centre) v Prague Immigration Officer* [2004] UKHL 55; [2005] 2 A.C. 1; *Lord Advocates Reference (No.1 of 2000)*, 2001 J.C. 143. It follows that, whereas questions of foreign law (including English law) constitute questions of fact on which evidence may be led, questions of customary international law constitute questions of law for the judge to determine.

87 Constitutional Reform and Governance Act 2010 Pt 2.

88 See *JH Rayner (Mincing Lane) Ltd v Department of Trade and Industry* [1990] 2 A.C. 418 HL, per Lord Oliver at [500], approved in *Moohan v Lord Advocate* [2014] UKSC 67; 2015 S.C. (U.K.S.C.) 1 at [29].

89 *Re McKerr* [2004] UKHL 12; [2004] 1 W.L.R. 807, per Lord Steyn at [49]–[50]. These comments built on his extrajudicial comments: Lord Steyn, "Democracy Through Law" [2002] E.H.R.L.R. 723. Under reference to *Thomas v Baptiste* [2000] 2 A.C. 1 PC (Trinidad and Tobago) and *Lewis v Attorney General of Jamaica* [2001] 2 A.C. 50 PC (Jamaica), in which the Judicial Committee of the Privy Council held that condemned men in Caribbean countries could not be executed until the determination of their appeals to the Inter-American Human Rights Committee, a body whose jurisdiction depends upon an unincorporated treaty, Lord Steyn suggests that there is "scope for the evolution of a more realistic notion", which would place human rights treaties in a special category.

which the UK is party should be directly enforceable in domestic law.[90] Nonetheless, the weight of authority remains firmly in favour of dualist orthodoxy.[91]

This is not to say that unincorporated international treaties have no domestic legal effect. As Diplock LJ held in *Salomon v Commissioners of Customs and Excise*:

> "There is a prima facie presumption that Parliament does not intend to act in breach of international law, including therein specified treaty obligations; and if one of the meanings that can reasonably be attributed to the legislation is consonant with the treaty obligations and another or others are not, the meaning which is so consonant is to be preferred." [92]

Thus, where a statutory provision was ambiguous, international treaties to which the UK was party could be relied on as an aid to construction and there is a strong presumption in favour of interpreting a statute so as to avoid placing the UK in breach of its international law obligations.[93] An equivalent presumption applies when developing the common law[94] and unincorporated treaties can be used to resolve ambiguities in the common law.[95] As we shall see, prior to the incorporation of the "Convention rights" by the Human Rights Act 1998, the European Convention on Human Rights was particularly influential in this respect.[96] But there is no reason in principle why exactly the same approach should not apply in relation to other, as yet unincorporated, treaty provisions,[97] in

See also Lord Collins, "Foreign Relations and the Judiciary" (2002) 51(3) I.C.L.Q. 485. For a robust response to this argument see, P. Sales and J. Clement, "International Law in Domestic Courts: The Developing Framework" (2008) 124 L.Q.R. 388.

[90] *R. (on the application of JS) v Secretary of State for Work and Pensions* [2015] UKSC 16; [2015] 1 W.L.R. 1449 at [254]–[256].

[91] See, in addition to *JH Rayner (Mincing Lane) Ltd v Department of Trade and Industry* [1990] 2 A.C. 418, *R. v Lyons (Isidore Jack)* [2002] UKHL 44; [2002] 3 W.L.R. 1562, per Lord Hoffmann at [27], [28]; and *Whaley v Lord Advocate*, 2004 S.C. 78, per Lord Brodie at [41]–[44].

[92] *Salomon v Commissioners of Customs and Excise* [1967] 2 Q.B. 116 CA at p.143. See also Lord Hughes' summary of the circumstances where an unincorporated international treaty may be relevant in domestic law in *R (on the application of JS) v Secretary of State for Work and Pensions* [2015] UKSC 16; [2015] 1 W.L.R. 1449 at [137] and Lord Kerr's fuller discussion on the status of international law in the same case at [234]–[257].

[93] *Assange v Swedish Prosecution Authority* [2012] UKSC 22; [2012] 2 A.C. 471, per Lord Dyson at [122].

[94] *A v Secretary of State for the Home Department (No.2)* [2005] UKHL 71; [2006] 2 A.C. 221, per Lord Bingham of Cornhill at [27].

[95] *Derbyshire CC v Times Newspapers Ltd* [1993] A.C. 534 HL.

[96] If only latterly in Scotland. It was held in *Kaur v Lord Advocate*, 1980 S.C. 319 that, "as the Convention was not part of the municipal law of the United Kingdom, the court was not, so far as Scotland was concerned, entitled to have regard to the Convention either as an aid to construction or otherwise" (per Lord Ross at p.330). This remained the position in Scots law until the First Division held in *T, Petitioner*, 1997 S.L.T. 724, that it could no longer be justified and should be departed from. Section 3 of the Human Rights Act 1998 now requires the courts to read and give effect to all legislation, whenever enacted, consistently with the Convention rights so far as possible to do so; s.4 authorises certain higher courts to make declarations of incompatibility in respect of provisions of primary legislation which cannot be so construed (and it should be noted that provisions of Acts of the Scottish Parliament which are incompatible with the Convention rights are invalid and may be struck down accordingly).

[97] Indeed reference is regularly made to such treaties as the Universal Declaration of Human Rights, the International Covenant on Civil and Political Rights and the UN Convention on the Rights of the

particular in the field of human rights. The European Court of Human Rights is already prepared to have regard to unincorporated international treaties to which the UK is a party when determining whether there has been an infringement of the Convention rights.[98]

Child: see R. Clayton and H. Tomlinson, *The Law of Human Rights* (Oxford: Oxford University Press, 2000), paras 2.09–2.60. So far as the latter Convention is concerned, it was precisely what status it had in domestic law that divided the Supreme Court on the question of whether the "benefits cap" was lawful: *R. (on the application of JS) v Secretary of State for Work and Pensions* [2015] UKSC 16; [2015] 1 W.L.R. 1449.

[98] See, for example *Wilson v United Kingdom* (2002) 35 E.H.R.R. 20, where regard was had to the European Social Charter 1961 and International Labour Organisation Conventions Nos 87 and 98.

CHAPTER 3

Foundations

INTRODUCTION

Less than half a century ago, the central tenet of the law of the constitution, that of the supremacy of Parliament, was so firmly established that the Senior Law Lord felt able to say: 3–01

> "The idea that a court is entitled to disregard a provision in an Act of Parliament on any ground must seem strange and startling to anyone with any knowledge of the history and law of our constitution."[1]

It may, therefore, be thought surprising that the First Division of the Court of Session, in 2011, felt able to say:

> "There can accordingly be seen to be an as yet unresolved issue at the highest judicial level as to whether an Act of the United Kingdom Parliament could, in any circumstances, be open to challenge in the courts."[2]

Those comments were echoed in the Supreme Court.[3] Immediately, Allan's warning rings true:

> "A student of British constitutional law is confronted by an intimidating series of antinomies; and it is quickly apparent that there is great scope for argument about fundamental ideas and doctrines."[4]

In this chapter, we begin by considering the supremacy of Parliament and we will look at the recent developments that led the highest courts in the land to openly speculate about its future. Any fall in support for the supremacy of Parliament appears to have been offset by a rise in support for the rule of law, "[t]he rule of

---

[1] *British Railways Board v Pickin* [1974] A.C. 765 HL, per Lord Reid at p.782; he went on to say, "[i]n earlier times many learned lawyers seem to have believed that an Act of Parliament could be disregarded in so far as it was contrary to the law of God or the law of nature or natural justice, but since the supremacy of Parliament was finally demonstrated by the Revolution of 1688 any such idea has become obsolete." That comment is worth bearing in mind as we discuss the contemporary debate around parliamentary supremacy.

[2] *AXA General Insurance Co Ltd v Lord Advocate* [2011] CSIH 31; 2011 S.C. 662 at [67].

[3] *AXA General Insurance Co Ltd v Lord Advocate* [2011] UKSC 46; 2012 S.C. (U.K.S.C.) 122, per Lord Hope of Craighead DPSC at [50], "The question whether the principle of the sovereignty of the UK Parliament is absolute or may be subject to limitation in exceptional circumstances is still under discussion".

[4] T.R.S. Allan, *The Sovereignty of Law* (Oxford: OUP, 2013), p.1.

law enforced by the courts is the ultimate controlling factor on which our constitution is based".[5] It has also been declared by Parliament to be "an existing constitutional principle".[6] The rule of law is an idea that can be traced back as far as Aristotle[7] and it was a concept that Dicey too wrote about.[8] Despite that pedigree, it has proved a notoriously difficult concept to define. In the second part of this chapter we will look at the various tenets of the rule of law and consider how they relate to the continuing supremacy of Parliament. Finally, we look at the separation of powers, a concept that for many years the United Kingdom did not appear, formally at least, to adhere to. In recent years, however, steps have been taken to ensure an institutional separation of powers that compliments the pre-existing functional separation. But it is with what was traditionally seen as the "bedrock"[9] of the constitution that we begin: the supremacy of Parliament.

PARLIAMENTARY SUPREMACY

The traditional approach

3–02 "The principle of parliamentary sovereignty means neither more nor less than this, namely, that Parliament . . . has, under the English constitution, the right to make or unmake any law whatever; and further, that no person or body is recognised by the law as having a right to override or set aside the legislation of Parliament."[10]

That statement of principle has the support of a long and impressive line of authority. We have already seen what Lord Reid had to say about the matter in *British Railways Board v Pickin*. He was not the first senior judge to make such remarks nor was he the last. As to the first proposition (that Parliament can "make or unmake any law whatever"), it is of course true that "one does not establish that Parliament can do anything merely by pointing to a number of things that it has done, however impressive".[11] But some support for Dicey's thesis can be drawn from the many statutes that Parliament has passed, both before and after Dicey's time, whereby important constitutional change, or retrospective or extraterritorial legislation, has been enacted.[12] The second proposition (that no person or body can set aside the legislation of Parliament) has, as we shall see, an even stronger pedigree.

---

[5] *R. (on the application of Jackson) v Attorney General* [2005] UKHL 56; [2006] 1 A.C. 262, per Lord Hope of Craighead at [107].

[6] Constitutional Reform Act 2005 s.1(a).

[7] B.Z. Tamanaha, *On the Rule of Law: History, Politics, Theory* (Cambridge: Cambridge University Press, 2004), pp.8–9; *Aristotle's Politics and Athenian Constitution*, edited and translated by J. Warrington (London: J.M. Dent, 1959) book III, s.1287, p.97.

[8] A.V. Dicey, *The Law of Constitution*, 10th edn (London: Macmillan, 1959), pp.99–119.

[9] *R. (on the application of Jackson) v Attorney General* [2005] UKHL 56; [2006] 1 A.C. 262, per Lord Bingham of Cornhill at [9].

[10] Dicey, *The Law of the Constitution* (1959), pp.39–40.

[11] C.R. Munro, *Studies in Constitutional Law*, 2nd edn (London: Butterworths, 1999), p.13.

[12] That is not to say that important constitutional change does not require special consideration. See the consideration of the process of constitutional change by the House of Lords Select Committee on the Constitution, *The Process of Constitutional Change, 15th report of Session 2010–12* (The

The Diceyian doctrine of parliamentary supremacy has three consequences. First, it has a positive effect and ensures that the courts obey any new Act of Parliament. As Lord Morris explained in *Pickin*, "[i]n the courts there may be argument as to the correct interpretation of the enactment: there must be none as to whether it should be on the statute book at all".[13] That bars any argument that Parliament lacked the legal power to enact any particular law. It is important to distinguish between *political* limitations on Parliament's ability to legislate and *legal* limitations. Dicey himself recognised the former: Parliament may have the legal power to pass any legislation it wished but that was not the same as saying there were no limits whatsoever on the legislative competence of Parliament.[14] Moral or political considerations may prevent Parliament legislating as it wishes. But once it has legislated, the court cannot entertain an argument that an Act of Parliament is beyond its competence or somehow "unconstitutional". As Lord Reid explained in *Madzimbamuto v Lardner-Burke*:

> "It is often said that it would be unconstitutional for the United Kingdom Parliament to do certain things, meaning that the moral, political and other reasons against doing them are so strong that most people would regard it as highly improper if Parliament did these things. But that does not mean that it is beyond the power of Parliament to do such things. If Parliament chose to do any of them, the courts could not hold the Act of Parliament invalid."[15]

The question that flows from this is: what is an Act of Parliament? Dicey described the Queen in Parliament as the sovereign power. It is not the House of Commons alone that is supreme, but it is the will of the House of Commons, the House of Lords (subject to the provisions of the Parliament Acts 1911–1949) and the Queen that is accorded this special status. This reflected a number of decisions at the time Dicey was writing (and which have gone unquestioned since).[16] Once an Act of Parliament reaches the statute book, there can be no inquiry by the court as to how it got there. To do otherwise would be to review the internal proceedings of Parliament. Such a review is precluded by the terms of

---

Stationery Office, 2011) HL Paper 177, para.1: "The constitution is the foundation upon which law and government are built. The fundamental nature of the constitution means that it should be changed only with due care and consideration."

[13] *British Railways Board v Pickin* [1974] A.C. 765 at p.789. Ungoed-Thomas J made the same point in *Cheney v Conn* [1968] 1 W.L.R. 242 (ChD) at p.247: ". . . what the statute itself enacts cannot be unlawful . . . and it is not for the court to say that a parliamentary enactment, the highest law in the country, is illegal." As we will see below, these comments must now be read as subject to what happened in *R. (on the application of Jackson) v Attorney General* where a challenge to the validity of the Hunting Act 2004 was heard by the court, a situation that the Court of Appeal recognised as novel ([2005] EWCA Civ 126; [2005] Q.B. 579 at [11]–[13]) as did the House of Lords ([2005] UKHL 56; [2006] 1 A.C. 262, per Lord Bingham of Cornhill at [8] and Lord Nicholls of Birkenhead at [49]). Of particular note is the concession by the Attorney General that "there was no absolute rule that the courts could not consider the validity of a statute".

[14] Dicey, *The Law of the Constitution* (1959), pp.76–84.

[15] *Madzimbamuto v Lardner-Burke* [1969] 1 A.C. 645 PC (Rhodesia) at p.723.

[16] "If an Act be penned that the King with the assent of the Lords, or with the assent of the Commons, it is no Act of Parliament, for three ought to assent to it scilicet the King, the Lords and the Commons, or otherwise it is not an Act of Parliament": *The Prince's Case* (1606) 8 Co. Rep. 481; *Stockdale v Hansard* (1839) 9 Ad. & El. 1, per Lord Denman at [108]. *The Prince's Case* ought to be treated with caution, referring as it does to the pre-Union Parliament of England and not the post-Union Parliament.

art.9 of the Claim (and in England and Wales, the Bill) of Rights. This gives rise to what is known and the "enrolled bill rule". Lord Campbell LC explained the rule in (the Scottish case) *Edinburgh & Dalkeith Railway v Wauchope*:

> "All that a Court of Justice can do is look to the Parliamentary Roll; if from that it should appear that a Bill has passed both Houses and received Royal Assent, no Court of Justice can inquire into the mode in which it was introduced into Parliament, nor into what was done previous to its introduction, or what passed in Parliament during its progress through Parliament."[17]

If there is a suggestion that an Act, whether private or public, has been obtained improperly or through fraud, that is a matter for Parliament to investigate and, if necessary, repeal the offending Act. Whilst it remains on the statute book, however, the courts must give effect to it.[18]

What, however, of an Act of Parliament that is passed in accordance with the provisions of the Parliament Acts 1911–1949: do such Acts benefit from the enrolled Bill rule as explained by Lord Campbell LC? That question arose in *R (on the application of Jackson) v Attorney General*.[19] The Parliament Acts allow for a Bill to pass without the consent of the House of Lords. Where a Bill is passed using that procedure, it becomes an Act of Parliament and primary legislation. It is not of an inferior quality because the House of Lords did not assent it to.[20] But it is not an Act of a sovereign parliament, one with the power to make or unmake any law, because the Parliament Acts prohibit the passing of certain legislation (for example, extending the life of Parliament) without the assent of the House of Lords.[21] The workings of the Parliaments Acts are considered in more detail in Ch.6. For present purposes, however, it is important to note the challenge that was mounted to the Hunting Act 2004. This controversial piece of legislation, which sought to make it an offence to hunt wild animals with a dog, was passed under the Parliament Acts after the House of Lords refused to pass it. After Royal Assent was given, a number of individuals with an interest in fox-hunting challenged the Act arguing that it was not a valid Act of Parliament. On a simple application of the dicta from *Edinburgh & Dalkeith Railways* and *Pickin* the challenge ought to have fallen to be rejected. But the claim was entertained by the courts, and was ultimately determined by a then unprecedented panel of nine Law Lords. Why? Lord Bingham explained that he was persuaded that the case should be heard for two reasons. First, unlike *Pickin*, the court was not being asked to enquire into the internal workings of Parliament to ascertain whether it had been misled when enacting the legislation

[17] *Edinburgh & Dalkeith Railway v Wauchope* (1842) 8 Cl. & F. 710.

[18] *Lee v Bude and Torrington Junction Railway* (1871) L.R. 6 C.P. 576; *British Railways Board v Pickin* [1974] A.C. 765.

[19] *R. (on the application of Jackson) v Attorney General* [2005] UKHL 56; [2006] 1 A.C. 262. For a general discussion of this important case, see Lord Cooke of Thorndon, "A Constitutional Retreat" (2006) 122 L.Q.R. 224; M. Plaxton, "The Concept of Legislation: *Jackson v Her Majesty's Attorney General*" (2006) 69 M.L.R. 249.

[20] *R. (on the application of Jackson) v Attorney General* [2005] UKHL 56; [2006] 1 A.C. 262, per Lord Bingham of Cornhill at [24]–[25].

[21] Although commenting obiter, the majority of the House of Lords held that such limitations could not be removed by a two-step process: amending the Parliament Acts, using their own procedure, to remove the limit and then passing legislation to extend the life of Parliament. It is noteworthy that this was not a view shared by Lord Bingham.

and, unlike *Edinburgh & Dalkeith Railways*, the court looks to the parliamentary roll and does not see a Bill that has passed both Houses of Parliament. That gave rise not to a question of parliamentary procedure but to a question of law. Lord Bingham's second reason was "more practical":

> "The appellants have raised a question of law which cannot, as such, be resolved by Parliament. *But it would not be satisfactory, or consistent with the rule of law, if it could not be resolved at all.* So it seems to me necessary that the courts should resolve it, and that to do so involves no breach of constitutional propriety."[22]

From *Jackson* we learn that the rule that appears from *Pickin* and *Edinburgh & Dalkeith Railways* is not absolute: it does not apply to Acts passed under the Parliament Acts. Furthermore, we learn that the court has jurisdiction to entertain a challenge to the validity of an Act of Parliament where the rule of law demands it. That is an idea we shall return to shortly.

The second consequence of the Diceyian doctrine of parliamentary supremacy is a negative effect. Nobody else can override the wishes of Parliament, be it the courts or another, competing, legislature. For example, in relation to matters where legislative competence has been devolved to the Scottish Parliament, the UK Parliament retains the power to legislate (with or without the blessing of the Scottish Parliament).[23] In relation to the courts, Dicey recognised that:

> "Parliament is the supreme legislator, but from the moment Parliament has uttered its will as law giver, that will becomes subject to the interpretation put upon it by the judges."[24]

But to ensure that the courts do not override the wishes of Parliament, the process of statutory interpretation is an attempt to discover the intention of Parliament in using the words it has chosen, thereby giving effect to that intention.[25] As we shall see below, the Human Rights Act 1998, and the interpretative obligation imposed on the courts by virtue of s.3 of that Act, have required the courts to be careful not to overstep the bounds of their legitimate constitutional role.

---

22 *R. (on the application of Jackson) v Attorney General* [2005] UKHL 56; [2006] 1 A.C. 262 at [27] (emphasis added); Lord Nicholls (at [51]) reached the same conclusion for similar reasons: "This question of statutory interpretation is properly cognisable by a court of law even though it relates to the legislative process. Statutes create law. The proper interpretation of a statute is a matter for the courts, not Parliament. This principle is as fundamental in this country's constitution as the principle that Parliament has exclusive cognizance (jurisdiction) over its own affairs"; and Lord Hope of Craighead at [107] and [110]–[116].

23 Scotland Act 1998 s.28(7) makes the point specifically but it was unnecessary to secure the result. See also: *R (on the application of Miller) v Secretary of State for Exiting the European Union* [2017] UKSC 3; [2018] A.C. 61 at [147]–[151]. With regard to how the UK Parliament exercises its legislative powers in devolved areas, see the discussion in relation to legislative consent motions at para.2–10.

24 Dicey, *The Law of the Constitution* (1959) p.413.

25 On interpretation of legislation, see *Craies on Legislation: A Practitioners' Guide to the Nature, Process, Effect and Interpretation of Legislation*, edited by D. Greenberg, 10th edn (London: Sweet and Maxwell, 2012) Ch.16; D. Bailey and L. Norburry, *Bennion Statutory Interpretation*, 7th edn (London: LexiNexis, 2019); *Edwards v Chesterfield Royal Hospital NHS Foundation Trust* [2011] UKSC 58; [2012] 2 A.C. 22, per Lord Phillips of Worth Matravers PSC at [79].

3–03 Finally, the supremacy of Parliament has the effect that Parliament cannot bind her successors.[26] This, for Dicey, was the only limit on the powers of a sovereign legislature. Sovereignty was continuing and, on Dicey's logic, inescapable short of revolution. It followed that there could be no difference in the "ranking" of Acts of Parliament: all Acts were of equal standing and authority. That produced what is known as the doctrine of implied repeal:

> "The Legislature cannot, according to our constitution, bind itself as to the form of subsequent legislation, and it is impossible for Parliament to enact that in a subsequent statute dealing with the same subject matter there can be no implied repeal. If a subsequent Act of Parliament chooses to make it plain that the earlier statute is being to some extent repealed, effect must be given to that intention just because it is the will of the Legislature."[27]

The result of the doctrine of implied repeal is that the court gives effect to the most recent expression of Parliament's intention: if the terms of an Act from 2005 and 2015 are irreconcilable, the court will give effect to the terms of the 2015 Act on the basis it has impliedly repealed the 2005 Act. The doctrine of implied repeal has, however, undergone modification in recent years.[28] In *Thoburn v Sunderland City Council*, Laws LJ recognised that not all Acts of Parliament are equal: there are some statutes that should be regarded as "constitutional" and thus protected from implied repeal as it is traditionally understood.[29] This distinction between "ordinary" Acts and "constitutional" Acts, although difficult to draw,[30] has subsequently been endorsed by the Supreme Court.[31] And although Laws LJ made reference to "Acts" and "statutes", it is probably better to think of constitutional "provisions", recognising the fact that one section of an Act may be "constitutional" whereas the rest of its provisions may be very "ordinary".[32] The distinction that Laws LJ drew is traced back to the court's core function when interpreting an Act of Parliament, namely to ascertain the intention of Parliament when passing the legislation.[33] As Laws LJ explained:

---

[26] See Lord Hope's comments in *R. (on the application of Jackson) v Attorney General* [2005] UKHL 56; [2006] 1 A.C. 262 at [113].

[27] *Ellen Street Estates Ltd v Minister of Health* [1934] 1 K.B. 590 CA, per Maugham LJ at p.597. See also: *Vauxhall Estates Ltd v Liverpool Corp* [1932] 1 K.B. 733 (KBD) and, for a more modern statement of the same rule, *Thoburn v Sunderland City Council* [2002] EWHC 195 (Admin); [2003] Q.B. 151 at [37]: "The rule is that if Parliament has enacted successive statutes which on the true construction of each of them makes irreducibly inconsistent provisions, the earlier statute is impliedly repealed by the latter."

[28] For a discussion of the uncertainty surrounding the scope of implied repeal, see A.L. Young, *Parliamentary Sovereignty and the Human Rights Act* (Oxford: Hart, 2009), Ch.2.

[29] *Thoburn v Sunderland City Council* [2002] EWHC 195 (Admin); [2003] Q.B. 151 at [59]–[64].

[30] D. Feldman, "The nature and significance of 'constitutional' legislation" (2013) 129 L.Q.R. 343.

[31] *R. (on the application of Buckingham CC) v Secretary of State for Transport* [2014] UKSC 3; [2014] 1 W.L.R. 324, per Lord Neuberger PSC and Lord Mance at [207]–[208].

[32] Feldman, "The nature and significance of 'constitutional' legislation" (2013) 129 L.Q.R. 343, [352]–[353].

[33] For the moment, we are considering how the idea of constitutional statues impacts on the doctrine of implied repeal. It is worth noting at this stage, however, that the courts have held that the same approach should be taken to the interpretation of "constitutional" legislation as any other legislation (*Imperial Tobacco Ltd v Lord Advocate* [2012] UKSC 61; 2013 S.C. (U.K.S.C.) 153; *Attorney General v National Assembly for Wales Commission* [2012] UKSC 53; [2013] 1 A.C. 792; D.

> "Ordinary statutes may be impliedly repealed. Constitutional statutes may not. For the repeal of a constitutional Act or the abrogation of a fundamental right to be effected by statute, the court would apply this test: is it shown that the legislature's actual—not imputed, constructive or presumed—intention was to effect the repeal or abrogation? I think the test could only be met by express words in the latter statute, or by words so specific that the inference of an actual determination to effect the result contended for was irresistible. The ordinary rule of implied repeal does not satisfy this test. Accordingly, it has no application to constitutional statues."[34]

This idea that Parliament requires to use clear language to obtain particular results was not new nor does it necessarily undermine parliamentary supremacy. Lord Hoffmann had explained a few years earlier that, in relation to fundamental principles of human rights, Parliament, because it was supreme, had the power to legislate contrary to those rights but the courts would only accept Parliament intended to do so where express and clear words had been used.[35] Laws LJ did little more than apply the same rule of statutory interpretation to "constitutional" statutes more generally. So far as parliamentary supremacy is concerned, the modification to the doctrine of implied repeal set out by Laws LJ preserves Parliament's right to "make or unmake any law". All it does is require Parliament to do so using words that make that intention clear (expressly or giving rise to an "irresistible" inference) when it comes to statutes which condition the relationship between the citizen and the state or alter the scope of fundamental constitutional rights.[36] In *H v Lord Advocate*[37] the Supreme Court, in the context of explaining how the Scotland Act could be repealed or modified, said this:

> "But in my opinion only an express provision [*modifying s.57(2) of the Scotland Act*] could be held to lead to such a result. This is because of the fundamental constitutional nature of the settlement that was achieved by the Scotland Act. This in itself must be held to *render it incapable of being altered otherwise than by an express enactment*. Its provisions cannot be regarded as vulnerable to alteration by implication from some other enactment in which an intention to alter the Scotland Act *is not set forth expressly on the face of the statute*."[38]

It has been suggested that these remarks qualified what Laws LJ had said in *Thoburn* with the result that an "irresistible" inference was no longer sufficient to amend the Scotland Act (and, by implication, any other "constitutional"

Feldman, "Statutory interpretation and constitutional legislation" (2014) 130 L.Q.R. 473). This point is developed further in Ch.6, when considering the operation of the Scotland Act.

[34] *Thoburn v Sunderland City Council* [2002] EWHC 195 (Admin); [2003] Q.B. 151 at [63]. This passage was approved by the Supreme Court in *R (Miller) v Secretary of State for Exiting the European Union* [2018] A.C. 61 at [66].

[35] *R. v Secretary of State for the Home Department, Ex p. Simms* [2000] 2 A.C. 115 HL, per Lord Hoffmann at [131]. In *R. (on the application of Jackson) v Attorney General* [2005] UKHL 56; [2006] 1 A.C. 262 at [159] Baroness Hale made the same point: "... courts will, of course, decline to hold that Parliament has interfered with fundamental rights unless it has made its intentions crystal clear". See also fn.230, below

[36] *Thoburn v Sunderland City Council* [2002] EWHC 195 (Admin); [2003] Q.B. 151 at [60] and [64]

[37] *H v Lord Advocate* [2012] UKSC 24; 2012 S.C. (U.K.S.C.) 308; [2013] 1 A.C. 413.

[38] *H v Lord Advocate* [2012] UKSC 24; 2012 S.C. (U.K.S.C.) 308; [2013] 1 A.C. 413, per Lord Hope of Craighead DPSC at [30] (emphasis added).

statute).[39] That argument, however, appears to overstate what the Supreme Court said in *H v Lord Advocate*. The Supreme Court heard limited oral argument on the point (it arose in the context of whether the Supreme Court had jurisdiction to hear an extradition appeal from the High Court of Justiciary which in turn required that apparently conflicting provisions of the Extradition Act 2003 and the Scotland Act 1998 be reconciled). Had there been an intention to review, with a view to modifying, what Laws LJ had said in *Thoburn* the court can be expected to have insisted upon the point being fully argued.[40] Furthermore, when Law LJ's decision in *Thoburn* was discussed a little over a year later in *R. (on the application of Buckingham CC) v Secretary of State for Transport* there was no suggestion that his remarks had been qualified by what Lord Hope said in *H v Lord Advocate*. For the moment, the better view is that for Parliament to amend or repeal the provisions of a "constitutional" statute, it must use words that make that intention clear, whether expressly or by way of an irresistible inference.

3–04 Challenges to the doctrine of parliamentary supremacy are not new. We consider three contemporary challenges below: the European Union, common law constitutionalism and the Human Rights Act 1998. But first it is necessary to examine some older arguments against the idea of parliamentary supremacy. The first challenge we need to consider relates to the Acts of Union and the argument that the UK Parliament was "born unfree".[41] Is Parliament limited by the terms of the Acts of Union, for example that the Court of Session continues for all time coming?[42] Dicey's view was clear, "... neither the Act of Union with Scotland nor the Dentists Act 1878 has more claim than the other to be considered a supreme law".[43]

There is an obvious difference between the Act of Union and the Dentists Act 1878 (and, indeed, any other Act passed by Parliament): the Dentists Act was passed by Parliament whereas the Act of Union *founded* Parliament. Dicey did recognise that the drafters of the Union legislation intended it to be binding on the legislature it created.[44] The argument that the Acts of Union represent "fundamental law" and thus impose some limits on the legislative competence of the UK Parliament has found some judicial support. In *MacCormick v Lord Advocate* Lord President Cooper famously observed:

> "The principle of the unlimited sovereignty of Parliament is a distinctively English principle which has no counterpart in Scottish constitutional law... I have difficulty in seeing why it should have been supposed that the new Parliament of Great Britain must inherit all of the peculiar characteristics of the English

---

[39] A. Perry and F. Ahmed, "The Quasi-Entrenchment of Constitutional Statues" (2014) 73 C.L.J. 514.

[40] *H v Lord Advocate* [2012] UKSC 24; 2012 S.C. (U.K.S.C.) 308; [2013] 1 A.C. 413, per Lord Mance at [73].

[41] T.B. Smith, "The Union of 1707 as fundamental law" [1957] P.L. 99. See also J.D.B. Mitchell, *Constitutional Law*, 2nd edn, (Edinburgh: SULI; W. Green, 1968), pp.93–98; N. MacCormick, "Does the United Kingdom have a constitution?" (1978) 29 N.I.L.Q. 1; M. Upton, "Marriage vows of the elephant: the Constitution of 1707" (1989) 105 L.Q.R. 79; J.D. Goldsworthy, *The Sovereignty of Parliament: History and Philosophy* (Oxford: Clarendon Press, 1999), pp.165–173; Munro, *Studies in Constitutional Law* (1999), pp.137–142; E. Wicks, "A new constitution for a new state? The 1707 Union of England and Scotland" (2001) 117 L.Q.R. 109; *R. (on the application of Jackson) v Attorney General* [2005] UKHL 56; [2006] 1 A.C. 262, per Lord Hope of Craighead at [106].

[42] Act of Union 1707 art.XIX.

[43] Dicey, *The Law of the Constitution* (1959), p.145.

[44] Dicey, *The Law of the Constitution* (1959), p.69.

> Parliament but none of the Scottish Parliament, as if all that happened in 1707 was that Scottish representatives were admitted to the Parliament of England. That is not what was done."[45]

In that case, the Lord Advocate conceded that certain articles of the Union were unalterable, for example those protecting the Church and the independent legal system. The Lord President, however, went on to doubt whether a breach of the Acts of Union would be a justiciable issue in the courts of either Scotland or England and Wales. It is also worth noting that, although the Lord President questions whether Scots and English law took the same view of parliamentary supremacy before the Union, Scottish courts have supported the Diceyian orthodox since.[46] In *Gibson v Lord Advocate*, Lord Keith reserved his opinion as to the effect of a hypothetical Act of Parliament purporting to abolish the Church of Scotland or the Court of Session but held that arguments about whether changes to Scots private law were "for the evident utility" of the subjects of Scotland (as required by art.XVIII of the Union legislation) would not be justiciable. There is a logical attraction to the fundamental law argument but sustaining it faces significant difficulties.[47] As Munro explains, nearly every article of the legislation has been altered or repealed to a greater or lesser extent.[48] Even T.B. Smith, a great proponent of the fundamental law theory, accepted that "many changes have been made, even of the most fundamental clauses".[49] That leaves one asking what exactly is beyond the reach of Parliament? The requirement (in art.XXII) that a prescribed number of Scots sit in the House of Lords was competently altered by the House of Lords Act 1999,[50] the Acts of Union now take effect subject to the provisions of the Scotland Act 1998[51] and the appellate jurisdiction of the House of Lords has been abolished and transferred to the new Supreme Court,[52] a matter that was previously thought to have been inhibited by the terms of the Acts of Union.[53]

In reality, we will only learn if certain provisions of the Union legislation are beyond the reach of Parliament if an attempt is made to legislate contrary to them. That the Acts of Union confer no power on the courts to review Acts of Parliament on the grounds of non-conformity with the terms of the Union cannot be decisive: the constitution of the United States did not confer such a power on

---

45 *MacCormick v Lord Advocate*, 1953 S.C. 396 at p.411. There is some suggestion in the institutional writers that the pre-Union Parliament of Scotland was in fact sovereign. See, for example, Stair, IV, 1, 61.

46 *Mortensen v Peters* (1906) 8 F. (J.) 93, per Lord Justice General Dunedin at p.100 (sitting with a full bench), the continuing force of which was affirmed by the Lord Ordinary (Brodie) in *Whaley v Lord Advocate*, 2004 S.C. 78.

47 As Lord Hope of Craighead put it in *Lord Gray's Motion*, 2000 S.C. (H.L.) 46 at [59D]–[E], "... the argument that the legislative powers of the new Parliament of Great Britain were subject to the restrictions expressed in the Union Agreement by which it was constituted cannot be dismissed as entirely fanciful". Lord Slynn of Hadley, in the same case, doubted whether even a provision regarded as fundamental to the constitution could not be altered by Parliament (at p.49I).

48 Munro, *Studies in Constitutional Law* (1999), p.138–139.

49 T.B. Smith, "Two Scots Cases" (1953) 69 L.Q.R. 512, 515.

50 *Lord Gray's Motion*, 2000 S.C. (H.L.) 46.

51 Scotland Act 1998 s.37.

52 Constitutional Reform Act 2005 Pt 3.

53 Mitchell, *Constitutional Law* (1968), p.11; Wicks, "A new constitution for a new state? The 1707 Union of England and Scotland" (2001) 117 L.Q.R. 109, [118]–[119].

the Supreme Court but it was claimed as necessary to uphold the constitution.[54] Whether the Scottish (or England and Welsh) court would claim a similar power if faced with an Act of Parliament that, say, purported to abolish the Court of Session is unknown. They have, however, never thought it necessary to qualify their clear statement on the supremacy of Parliament that we considered above to guard against the possibility.

3–05 The next challenge we need to consider is the "manner and form" argument: if Parliament cannot bind its successors as to the content of future legislation can it bind them as to the process by which they legislate?[55] On this argument, should Parliament wish to entrench a particular statute, it could provide that none of the provisions of the Act might be repealed or amended without, for example, a two-thirds majority in both Houses of Parliament.[56] The evidence to support this view is derived primarily from Commonwealth cases, notably *Attorney General of New South Wales v Trethowan*[57] and *Bribery Commissioner v Ranasinghe*,[58] both decisions of the Privy Council, as well as the South African case of *Harris v Minister of the Interior*.[59] In *Trethowan*, the legislature of New South Wales passed an Act, in 1929, providing that no Bill that would abolish the upper house of the legislature be presented for Royal Assent unless it had been approved by the electorate in a referendum. The opposition Labour party in 1929 were committed to the abolition of the upper house. When they won the general election of 1930 two Bills were passed by both houses: the first repealing the referendum requirement and the second abolishing the upper house. Neither were approved by a referendum. An injunction was granted by the Supreme Court of New South Wales and an appeal to the Privy Council was unsuccessful. On one level, that decision supports the "manner and form" argument. But it is not very helpful in understanding the extent to which the Westminster Parliament is subject to such an argument. Dicey had little difficulty classifying the New South Wales legislature as a non-sovereign body.[60] It was subordinate to the Colonial Laws Validity Act 1865 and in particular s.5.[61] The decision therefore turned on the correct interpretation of s.5 of the 1865 Act, which was held to require the offending legislation to be approved in a referendum. So to compare the legislature of New South Wales with the Westminster Parliament is to compare apples and oranges.

Harris perhaps presents a closer analogy. *Harris* concerned the Separate Representation of Voters Act 1951, passed pursuant to the new apartheid policy of

---

54 *Marbury v Madison* (1803) 1 Cranch 137.

55 On this, see generally J.D. Goldsworthy, *Parliamentary Sovereignty: Contemporary Debates* (Cambridge: Cambridge University Press, 2010) Ch.7.

56 See, for example, Sir Ivor Jennings, *The Law and the Constitution*, 5th edn (London: University of London Press, 1959), pp.152–159; R.F.V. Heuston, *Essays in Constitutional Law*, 2nd edn (London: Stevens, 1964), Ch.1.

57 *Attorney General of New South Wales v Trethowan* [1932] A.C. 526 PC (Australia).

58 *Bribery Commissioner v Ranasinghe* [1965] A.C. 172 PC (Ceylon).

59 *Harris v Minister of the Interior* [1952] 1 T.L.R. 1245.

60 Dicey, *The Law of the Constitution* (1959) Ch.2.

61 Section 5 of the 1865 Act provided: ". . . every Representative Legislature shall, in respect to the Colony under its jurisdiction, have, and be deemed at all times to have had, full power to make laws respecting the Constitution, Power and Procedure of such legislature; provided that such laws shall have been passed in such manner and form as may from time to time be required by any Act of Parliament, Letters Patent, Order in Council, or Colonial law for the time being in force in the said colony."

the Union Parliament of South Africa, acting by simple majority, both Houses sitting separately. Voters who were deprived of their rights by the 1951 Act argued that it was invalid because it was contrary to s.35 of the South Africa Act 1909 (an Act of the UK Parliament). Section 35 required certain legislation of the South African Parliament, including the 1951 Act, to be passed by both Houses sitting together and agreed to by not less than two-thirds of the total number of members of both Houses. The South African Government argued that the Union Parliament had, since 1909, full legislative sovereignty and so was free to disregard the provisions of s.35 of the 1909 Act. The court disagreed, with Centlivres CJ holding:

> "A State can unquestionably be sovereign although it has no legislature which is completely sovereign... In the case of the Union, legal sovereignty is or may be divided between Parliament as ordinarily constituted and Parliament as constituted under [s.35]. Such a division of legislative power is no derogation from the sovereignty of the Union and the mere fact that that division was enacted in a British statute which is still in force in the Union cannot affect the question in issue... The South Africa Act created the Parliament of the Union. It is that Act... which prescribes the manner in which the constituent elements of Parliament must function for the purpose of passing legislation... [I]t follows that... courts of law have the power to declare the Act of 1951 invalid on the ground that it was not passed in conformity with the provisions of section 35."[62]

While this passage crisply articulates the nub of the manner and form argument, it again does not tell us much about the UK Parliament. The decision in *Harris* turned on the application of s.35 of the 1909 Act. But as Lord Pearce explained in *Ranasinghe*, "in the United Kingdom there is no governing instrument which prescribes the law-making powers and the forms which are essential to those powers".[63] There being no such instrument in the United Kingdom, it is hard to see how the "manner and form" argument could gain much traction as against our Parliament. Whilst the Fixed-term Parliaments Act 2011 did not seek to condition the future ability to legislate, it did seek to limit the circumstances in which an early general election could be called (by requiring, inter alia, a two-thirds majority in support of such an election in the House of Commons).[64] As we saw in Ch.1, the Early Parliamentary General Election Act 2019 easily side-stepped that requirement and serves to illustrate how difficult, if not impossible, it is for one Parliament to bind the hands of its successor as to the form any that any decision must take.[65]

We have seen that the courts accept whatever the Queen in Parliament enacts (both Houses acting by simple majority) as law. That being a rule of the common law, on one view it should be open to modification by Parliament. Does this allow a change to the "manner and form" of legislation? No. For Parliament to modify the rule would be to limit (or potentially abandon) its sovereignty and that, as we have seen, is the one thing Parliament cannot do. The point was explained by Professor Wade in his seminal article in 1955: 3–06

[62] *Harris v Minister of the Interior* [1952] 1 T.L.R. 1245.

[63] *Bribery Commissioner v Ranasinghe* [1965] A.C. 172 at p.195.

[64] For a further discussion of the 2011 Act, see para.6–02, below.

[65] See para.1–24, above.

> "[T]he rule that the courts obey Acts of Parliament is above and beyond the reach of statute... because it is itself the source of authority of statute. This puts it into a class by itself among rules of the common law... The rule of judicial obedience is in one sense a rule of common law, but in another sense—which applies to no other rule of common law—it is the ultimate political fact upon which the whole system of legislation hangs. Legislation owes its authority to the rule: the rule does not owe its authority to legislation. To say that Parliament can change the rule... is to put the cart before the horse. The rule is unique in being unchangeable by Parliament—it is changed by revolution, not by legislation; it lies in the keeping of the courts and no Act of Parliament can take it from them."[66]

Such a revolution occurred in Rhodesia when the Rhodesian courts ceased to recognise UK statutes as supreme and instead relocated their rules of recognition to the revolutionary constitution of 1965.[67] But there has been no such change in the United Kingdom and what the courts recognise as law remains the will of the Queen in Parliament.

3–07 Finally, did Parliament bind its successors when legislating for the independence of former British colonies? Take, for example, s.4 of the Statute of Westminster 1931 that provided that no subsequent Act of Parliament would extend, or be deemed to extend, to a dominion unless it was expressly declared in the Act that the dominion had requested and consented to its enactment. Did Parliament thereby deprive itself of the competence to legislate for a dominion without the request and consent of the dominion? Lord Sankey LC described the notion that Parliament could repeal or disregard s.4 as "theory [having] no relation to realities"[68] and in *Ndlwana v Hofmeyr*, Stratford ACJ insisted that "freedom once conferred cannot be revoked".[69] But here we see again the difference between the legal limits on the legislative competence of Parliament and the political or other limits. As a matter of legal theory, Parliament could have repealed or disregarded the terms of s.4 of the 1931 Act. That is not the same thing as the courts of the dominion paying heed to it. As Sir Robert Megarry VC explained in *Manuel v Attorney General*:

> "I have grave doubts about the theory of the transfer of sovereignty as affecting the competence of Parliament.... As a matter of law the courts recognise Parliament as being omnipotent in all save the power to destroy its own omnipotence. Under the authority of Parliament the courts of a territory may be released from their legal duty to obey Parliament, but that does not trench on the acceptance by the... courts of all that Parliament does. Nor must validity in law be confused with practical enforceability."[70]

---

[66] H.W.R. Wade, "The basis of legal sovereignty" [1955] C.L.J. 172, 187; this analysis that was approved by Lord Denning MR in *Blackburn v Attorney General* [1971] 2 All E.R. 1380 at p.1387; it is not an approach that found favour with Lord Bingham: "To my mind, it has been convincingly shown that the principle of parliamentary sovereignty has been recognized as fundamental in this country not because the judges invented it but because it has for centuries been accepted as such by judges and others officially concerned in the operation of our constitutional system. The judges did not by themselves establish the principle and they cannot, by themselves, change it" (T.H. Bingham, *The Rule of Law* (London: Allen Lane, 2010), p.167).

[67] *R. v Ndhlovu* (1968) 4 S.A. 515; see also *Madzimbamuto v Lardner-Burke* [1969] 1 A.C. 645 that held that the regulations made by the rebel regime were void.

[68] *British Coal Corp v The King* [1935] A.C. 500 PC (Canada).

[69] *Ndlwana v Hofmeyr* [1937] A.D. 229.

[70] *Manuel v Attorney General* [1983] Ch. 77 CA (Civ Div) at p.89.

So independence to the colonies did not undermine the legislative supremacy of Parliament; it simply released certain courts from the obligation to give effect to the will of Parliament.

Having examined some of the traditional challenges to the supremacy of Parliament, it is time to turn and consider three more contemporary challenges. The first comes in the form of the European Union and the consequences of UK membership. Then we will consider the rise of what is known as common law constitutionalism before finally assessing the impact of the Human Rights Act. Vernon Bogdanor has said, "[i]n practice... if not in law, Parliamentary sovereignty is no longer the governing principle of the British constitution".[71] Have these three contemporary challenges to the supremacy of Parliament really taken us to that stage? 3–08

Parliamentary supremacy and the European Union[72]

To understand the significance of UK membership of the European Union, it is necessary to first understand a bit about the state of EU law when the UK joined in 1973.[73] In 1963, in the case of *Van Gend en Loos v Nederlandse Administratie der Belastingen*, the European Court of Justice explained, "... the Community constitutes a new legal order of international law for the benefit of which states have limited their sovereign rights".[74] The court returned to this theme a year later, in the Italian case of *Costa v ENEL*. The language could hardly have been clearer: 3–09

> "By creating [the] Community... the Member States have limited their sovereign rights, albeit within limited fields, and have thus created a body of law which binds both their nationals and themselves ... The transfer by the states from their domestic legal systems to the Community legal system of the rights and obligations arising under the Treaty carries with it a permanent limitation of their sovereign rights, against which a subsequent unilateral act incompatible with the concept of the Community cannot prevail."[75]

The primacy of EU law over conflicting national law was not explicit in the founding treaties. However, within little more than a decade, the Court of Justice

---

[71] V. Bogdanor, *The New British Constitution* (Oxford: Hart, 2009), pp.13–14; for a discussion of Bogdanor's views on sovereignty, see R. Gordon QC, "Constitutional Change and Parliamentary Sovereignty—the Impossible Dialetic" in M. Qvortrup (ed.), *The British Constitution: Continuity and Change, A Festschrift for Vernon Bogdanor* (Oxford: Hart, 2013), Ch.9. See also M. Elliott, "Parliamentary sovereignty in a changing constitutional landscape" in J. Jowell and C. O'Cinneide (eds), *The Changing Constitution*, 9th edn (Oxford: Oxford University Press, 2019), Ch.2.

[72] For a fuller discussion of the consequences of membership of the EU, see: M Gordon, *Parliamentary Sovereignty in the UK Constitution*, (Oxford: Bloomsbury, 2017), c.4.

[73] Throughout this section reference is made to the "European Union" and the "EU". This is done for simplicity. As is explained in Ch.10 below, the EU as we know it today has gone through various iterations and it was, in fact, the EEC that the UK joined in 1973. At the time of writing, the UK has left the EU but remains in the implementation/transition period, during which it is treated as effectively being a Member State. See further para.10–39, below. For a review of the UK's relationship with the EU prior to, and during, its membership, see *R (on the application of Miller and another) v Secretary of State for Exiting the European Union* [2017] UKSC 3; [2018] A.C. 61 at [13]–[33].

[74] *Van Gend en Loos v Nederlandse Administratie der Belastingen* (C–26/62) [1963] E.C.R. 1 at p.12.

[75] *Costa v Ente Nazionale per l'Energia Elettrica (ENEL)* (C–6/64) [1964] E.C.R. 585 at p.593.

had made it clear that national law must come second where there was a conflict. In *International Handelsgesellschaft* the European Court of Justice confirmed that EU law in all its forms prevails over national law, including the provisions of national constitutions, where there is a conflict.[76] All of this was clear, or at least ought to have been, when the UK sought membership in the early 1970s. For completeness, it is worth noting that the European Court of Justice took these various statements to their logical conclusion in their judgment in *Simmenthal* where they said that a national court must "apply Community law in its entirety and protect rights which the latter confers on individuals, and must accordingly set aside any provision of national law which may conflict with it, whether prior or subsequent to the Community rule".[77] Those statements from the Court of Justice are obviously irreconcilable with a conventional understanding of the Diceyian doctrine of parliamentary supremacy.

In passing the European Communities Act 1972 Parliament had to, as best it could, allow the UK to fulfil its obligations under the treaties and join what is now the EU. The key provision is s.2 of the 1972 Act. Subsection (1) provides:

> "All such rights, powers, liabilities, obligations and restrictions from time to time created or arising by or under the Treaties, and all such remedies and procedures from time to time provided for by or under the Treaties, as in accordance with the Treaties are without further enactment to be given legal effect or used in the United Kingdom shall be recognised and available in law, and be enforced, allowed and followed accordingly."

At a stroke, Parliament had commanded that directly effective provisions of EU law should prevail over inconsistent national law and, as we have seen, EU law would require that rule to apply to Acts of Parliament as well.[78] We have already seen that the 1972 Act is now regarded as part of the group of "constitutional statutes" identified by Laws LJ in *Thoburn* and so is immune from implied repeal. But could Parliament do what it sought to achieve in s.2? Is s.2 not a clear attempt to bind its successors? And despite what the Court of Justice may have said, would the domestic courts really set aside an Act of Parliament if it conflicted with the terms of EU law? An early indication of the attitude of the courts was given by Lord Denning MR in *Macarthys Ltd v Smith*, where he held:

> "Under section 2(1) and (4) of the European Communities Act 1972, the principles laid down in the Treaty are 'without further enactment' to be given legal effect in the United Kingdom; and have priority over any enactment 'passed or to be passed' by our Parliament . . . In construing our statute, we are entitled to look to the Treaty as an aid to its construction; but not only as an aid but as an overriding force. If . . . it should appear that our legislation is deficient or is inconsistent with Community

---

[76] *International Handelsgesellschaft MbH v Einfuhr und Vorratsstelle fur Getreide und Futtermittel* (C–11/70) [1970] E.C.R. 1125.

[77] *Amministrazione delle Finanze dello Stato v Simmenthal SpA* (C–106/77) [1978] E.C.R. 629.

[78] For a contemporary discussion of the issues, see S.A. de Smith, "The Constitution and the Common Market: A Tentative Appraisal" (1971) 34 M.L.R. 597; H.W.R. Wade, "Sovereignty and the European Communities" (1972) 88 L.Q.R. 1. See also: *R (on the application of Miller and another) v Secretary of State for Exiting the European Union* [2017] UKSC 3; [2018] A.C. 61 at [63].

> law by some oversight of our draftsmen then it is our bounden duty to give priority to Community law. Such is the result of section 2(1) and (4) of the European Communities Act 1972."[79]

This answer avoids the main issue, however. The Act in question in *Macarthys* was the Equal Pay Act 1970, in other words an Act that pre-dates the 1972 Act. Any conflict could be resolved by an application of the doctrine of implied repeal in its classic sense. The more important question was how would the court treat an Act that post-dates the 1972 Act and that conflicts with EU law? That was the issue that arose in the *Factortame* litigation.

In *Factortame* a number of English-registered companies whose managers and shareholders were primarily Spanish nationals lost their right to exploit the UK's fishing quota when the Merchant Shipping Act 1988 made the right conditional on nationality requirements they were unable to meet. The companies argued that the 1988 Act was unlawful as being in breach of the EU treaties. The House of Lords referred the case to the Court of Justice for a preliminary ruling; that court duly held that the 1988 Act was incompatible with EU law. The case then returned to the House of Lords where the question of remedy arose. What was the House of Lords to do with an Act that post-dated the 1972 Act but was inconsistent with EU law? The Court of Justice authorities were, as we have seen, clear on the point: the Act must be disapplied. In the House of Lords, Lord Bridge held: 3–10

> "Some public comments on the decision of the Court of Justice . . . have suggested that this was a novel and dangerous invasion by a Community institution of the sovereignty of the United Kingdom Parliament. But such comments are based on a misconception. If the supremacy within the European Community of Community law over the national law of Member States was not always inherent in the EEC Treaty it was certainly well established in the jurisprudence of the Court of Justice long before the United Kingdom joined the Community. Thus whatever limitation of its sovereignty Parliament accepted when it enacted the European Communities Act 1972 was entirely voluntary. Under the terms of the 1972 Act it has always been clear that it was the duty of a United Kingdom court, when delivering final judgment, to override any rule of national law found to be in conflict with any directly enforceable rule of Community law."[80]

Two points of significance arise from this passage. First, Lord Bridge speaks of a "limitation of sovereignty". This is something that is inconsistent with the very essence of the Diceyian theory of parliamentary supremacy.[81] The House of Lords had, argued Wade, effected a revolution.[82] Second, Lord Bridge is at pains to emphasise that any limitation of Parliament's sovereignty was its own choice.[83] This again conflicts with the Diceyian view of parliamentary supremacy: being

---

[79] *Macarthys Ltd v Smith* [1979] 3 All E.R. 325 at p.329.

[80] *R. v Secretary of State for Transport, Ex p. Factortame Ltd* [1991] 1 A.C. 603 HL at pp.658–659.

[81] A.V. Dicey, *The Law of the Constitution* (1959), p.91: "There does not exist in any part of the British Empire any person or body of persons, executive, legislative or judicial, which can pronounce void any enactment passed by the British Parliament on the ground such enactment being opposed to the constitution, or on any ground whatever, except of course its being repealed by Parliament."

[82] H.W.R. Wade, "Sovereignty—Revolution or Evolution?" (1996) 112 L.Q.R. 568.

[83] Which is contrary to Wade's view that parliamentary sovereignty lies in the keeping of the courts: Wade, "The basis of legal sovereignty" (1955) 13 C.L.J. 172, 187, discussed at para.3–03, above.

sovereign it was said Parliament could not abandon its own sovereignty. A similar approach was taken by the House of Lords a few years later in *R. v Secretary of State for Employment, Ex p. Equal Opportunities Commission*, which confirmed that the UK courts had jurisdiction to review primary legislation said to be in breach of EU law.[84]

3–11 It has been argued that the decision in *Factortame* does not necessarily undermine the doctrine of parliamentary supremacy. As Goldsworthy has explained, the conflict between the Merchant Shipping Act 1988 and the 1972 Act was inadvertent and Parliament had been assured during the passage of the 1988 Act that it was compatible with EU law. What the court did in *Factortame* was to correct an oversight by Parliament and give effect to its intention: that the 1988 Act should not breach EU law.[85] But that is to overlook what the House of Lords in fact did: it questioned and then set aside an Act of Parliament on the grounds it was not consistent with EU law. That cannot be reconciled with Dicey's statement that "that no person or body is recognised by the law as having a right to override or set aside the legislation of Parliament".[86] The Diceyian doctrine of parliamentary supremacy now had to be read as subject to the requirements of EU law. It was that factor that led Wade to describe the decision as a "revolution".

3–12 *Factortame* did leave one question open: what if Parliament expressly stated its intention to derogate from EU law but without withdrawing from the EU? This would produce an acute tension: on the one hand, there is the power to make or unmake any law, while on the other hand a clear rule of EU law that conflicting national rules, whatever their domestic standing, must be set aside if in conflict with EU law. Could the UK pick and choose the EU law obligations it complied with?

Lord Denning MR had addressed this issue in *Macarthys*:

> "If the time should come when our Parliament deliberately passes an Act with the intention of repudiating the Treaty or any provision of it or intentionally of acting inconsistently with it and says so in express terms then I should have thought that it would be the duty of our courts to follow the statute of our Parliament."[87]

That view is supported by Goldsworthy, who said "[i]t is the business of the government and Parliament, not the courts, to decide whether or not Britain should abide by its treaty commitments".[88] But that is to ignore the content of EU law. As the Court of Justice emphasised in *Costa*:

---

[84] *R. v Secretary of State for Employment, Ex p. Equal Opportunities Commission* [1995] 1 A.C. 1 HL.

[85] Goldsworthy, *Parliamentary Sovereignty: Contemporary Debates* (2010), pp.288–290.

[86] Dicey, *The Law of the Constitution* (1959), pp.39–40.

[87] *Macarthys Ltd v Smith* [1979] 3 All E.R. 325 at p.329. That is consistent with what Lord Diplock had said in *Gartland v British Rail Engineering Ltd* [1983] 2 A.C. 751 HL at p.771 where he said that legislation passed after a treaty was entered into "are to be construed, if they are reasonably capable of bearing such a meaning, as intended to carry out the obligation".

[88] Goldsworthy, *Parliamentary Sovereignty: Contemporary Debates* (2010), p.287.

> "The executive force of Community law cannot vary from one State to another in deference to subsequent domestic laws, without jeopardising the attainment of the objectives of the Treaty."[89]

As long as s.2 of the 1972 Act remained in force effect had to be given to the treaties and, in particular, the rule that EU law takes precedence.[90] By virtue of s.2, the entire corpus of EU law was a part of domestic law. That led other commentators to suggest that it would not be open to Parliament to pick and choose the EU obligations it complied with: it is all or nothing.[91] That would appear to have been the preferable view. The functioning of the EU is contingent upon Member States not selecting the obligations they are willing to comply with while seeking to draw all the benefits of membership. As we saw, this aspect of EU law was clear when the UK joined and it is one they ought to be held to whilst remaining a member. Not dissimilar arguments were advanced in *Thoburn*. As we have seen, Laws LJ held that the 1972 Act was exempt from the doctrine of implied repeal. But he rejected the argument that was because of requirements of EU law. Rather, it was the result of national law:

> "The British Parliament has not the authority to authorise [a limit on its sovereignty]. Being sovereign, it cannot abandon its sovereignty. Accordingly there are no circumstances in which the jurisprudence of the Court of Justice can elevate Community law to a status within the corpus of English domestic law to which it could not aspire by any route of English law itself. This is, of course, the traditional doctrine of sovereignty. If is to be modified, it certainly cannot be done by the incorporation of external texts. The conditions of Parliament's legislative supremacy in the United Kingdom necessarily remain in the United Kingdom's hands."[92]

While this does not answer directly the question of whether Parliament can pick and choose its EU law obligations, it makes one thing clear: had the need arisen, the answer would have been found in domestic, and not EU, law.[93] Parliament has also made a similar statement, in the form of s.18 of the European Union Act 2011.[94]

Thoburn also belongs to a group of cases that form the second contemporary attack on the classic Diceyian view of parliamentary sovereignty and that found

---

[89] *Costa v ENEL* (C–6/64) [1964] E.C.R. 585 at p.594.

[90] To the extent that the corpus of EU law shall be retained in domestic law at the end of the transition/implementation period, the principle of EU supremacy is retained for pre-exit legislation. That is more fully explained at para.10–41, below.

[91] P. Craig, "Report on the United Kingdom" in A.M. Slaughter, A.S. Sweet and J.H.H. Weiler (eds), *The European Court and National Courts: Doctrine and Jurisprudence* (Oxford: Hart, 1998).

[92] *Thoburn v Sunderland City Council* [2002] EWHC 195 (Admin); [2003] Q.B. 151 at [59]. The approach was approved by Lord Reed in *R. (on the application of Buckingham CC) v Secretary of State for Transport* [2014] UKSC 3; [2014] 1 W.L.R. 324 at [79]. On that case the various constitutional issues that were discussed see P. Craig, "Constitutionalising constitutional law: HS2" [2014] P.L. 373.

[93] The same approach has been taken by the constitutional courts of a number of other Member States, for example Germany, Czech Republic and Poland. See D.A.O. Edward and R.C. Lane, *Edward and Lane on European Union Law* (Cheltenham: Edward Elgar, 2013), para.6.19 and cases cited therein.

[94] See the discussion at para.10–37, below on the need for, and effect of, this particular statutory provision.

the basis for our discussion of common law constitutionalism. We turn to that next. But, for now, although the UKs membership of the EU has been brought to an end, it has probably left an indelible mark on the UK constitution. It was as a consequence of EU membership that the courts developed the concept of a "constitutional statute" (and, through it, qualified the doctrine of implied repeal). That concept is now a recognised feature of the constitution and will survive the UK's exit from the EU. And in *Factortame*, in practical terms at least, the courts recognised the right to disapply an Act of Parliament. EU law may have been the context in which it was done, but that it could be done at all simply begs the question whether it could be done again. That takes us onto the idea of common law constitutionalism.

Parliamentary supremacy and common law constitutionalism

3–13 From the discussion above the common law's view of parliamentary supremacy ought to have appeared fairly clear: the idea that the provisions of an Act of Parliament could be set aside should appear "strange and startling". Starting with a number of extrajudicial writings in the 1990s,[95] however, the suggestion that there were some, albeit extreme, circumstances where the common law would reject legislation passed by Parliament began to take hold. As we have just seen, reflecting his extrajudicial writings, the idea of common law constitutionalism is woven through Law LJ's judgment in *Thoburn*. The debate reached a new level, however, following some obiter dicta comments by Lord Steyn, Lord Hope of Craighead and Barnoess Hale of Richmond in their speeches in the case of *R. (on the application of Jackson) v Attorney General*.[96] The relevant passages merit repetition. First, Lord Steyn:

> "The classic account given by Dicey of the doctrine of the supremacy of Parliament, pure and absolute as it was, can now be seen to be out of place in the modern United Kingdom. Nevertheless, the supremacy of Parliament is still the *general* principle of our constitution. It is a construct of the common law. The judges created this principle. If that is so, it is not unthinkable that circumstances could arise where the courts may have to qualify a principle established on a different hypothesis of constitutionalism."[97]

Lord Hope went on to say:

> "Our constitution is dominated by the sovereignty of Parliament. But parliamentary sovereignty is not longer, if it ever was, absolute . . . It is no longer right to say that its freedom to legislate admits of no qualification whatever. Step by step, gradually

[95] Lord Woolf, "Droit public—English style" [1995] P.L. 57; Sir John Laws, "Law and democracy" [1995] P.L. 72; Sir Stephen Sedley, "Human rights: a twenty-first century agenda" [1995] P.L. 386. For a response, see J.A.G. Griffith, "The brave new world of Sir John Laws" (2000) 63 M.L.R. 159. A similar argument had opened up in New Zealand, in the 1980s, a country also thought to possess a legislature with unlimited sovereign power (and, of course, a country with an uncodified constitution): *Taylor v New Zealand Poultry Board* [1984] 1 N.Z.L.R. 394, per Cooke J at p.398: "Some common law rights presumably lie so deep that even Parliament could not override them."

[96] *R. (on the application of Jackson) v Attorney General* [2005] UKHL 56; [2006] 1 A.C. 262.

[97] *R. (on the application of Jackson) v Attorney General* [2005] UKHL 56; [2006] 1 A.C. 262 at [102] (emphasis in original).

> but surely, the English principle of the absolute legislative sovereignty of Parliament which Dicey derived from Coke and Blackstone is being qualified."[98]

Lord Hope continued:

> "The rule of law enforced by the courts is the ultimate controlling factor on which our constitution is based. The fact that your Lordships have been willing to hear this appeal and to give judgment upon it is another indication that the courts have a part to play in defining the limits of Parliament's legislative sovereignty."[99]

Finally, Baroness Hale:

> "The courts will treat with particular suspicion (and may even reject) any attempt to subvert the rule of law by removing governmental action affecting the rights of the individual from all judicial scrutiny."[100]

In the same passage, Lady Hale went on to say, "[i]n general, however, the constraints upon what Parliament can do are political and diplomatic rather than constitutional".

These passages are remarkable for the fact they contain dicta openly questioning the continuing validity of the central tenet of the constitution that is, as we have seen, supported by an almost unwavering line of judicial authority. It was in large part these remarks that led the First Division in *AXA General Insurance Co Ltd v Lord Advocate* to describe the question of parliamentary supremacy as an "as yet unresolved issue".[101]

Are there other principles of the constitution that could trump that of parliamentary supremacy? Lord Hoffmann spoke of "principles of fundamental human rights which exist at common law" in *R. v Secretary of State for the Home Department, Ex p. Simms*[102] and Lord Reed, in *AXA*, spoke of Parliament, when enacting the Scotland Act 1998, not having legislated in a vacuum but having legislated for "a liberal democracy founded on particular constitutional principles and traditions".[103] The court now regularly talks of fundamental principles of the constitution. No definitive list exists. Such a list would certainly include parliamentary sovereignty. That was one of the two fundamental principles engaged in the Prorogation case (the other being parliamentary accountability).[104] That case also made express reference to, and relied upon, the separation of 3–14

---

[98] *R. (on the application of Jackson) v Attorney General* [2005] UKHL 56; [2006] 1 A.C. 262 at [104]; Lord Hope has also discussed his comments in *Jackson* extrajudicially: Lord Hope, "Sovereignty in Question" (W.G. Hart Legal Workshop, 28 June 2011) *http://www.supremecourt.uk/docs/speech_110628.pdf* [Accessed 12 June 2020].

[99] *R. (on the application of Jackson) v Attorney General* [2005] UKHL 56; [2006] 1 A.C. 262 at [107].

[100] *R. (on the application of Jackson) v Attorney General* [2005] UKHL 56; [2006] 1 A.C. 262 at [159].

[101] *AXA General Insurance Co Ltd v Lord Advocate* [2011] CSIH 31; 2011 S.C. 662 at [67].

[102] *R. v Secretary of State for the Home Department, Ex p. Simms* [2000] 2 A.C. 115 at [131G].

[103] *AXA General Insurance Co Ltd v Lord Advocate* [2011] UKSC 46; 2012 S.C. (U.K.S.C.) 122 at [153].

[104] *R (on the application of Miller) v The Prime Minister* [2019] UKSC 41; [2020] A.C. 373; 2019 S.L.T. 1143, [41] and [46].

powers.[105] The rule of law is regularly cited as a fundamental principle of the constitution. For example, "[a]uthority is not needed (although much exists) to show that there is no principle more basic to our system of law than the maintenance of [the] rule of law itself and the constitutional protection afforded by judicial review".[106] It also has statutory recognition.[107] And in *UNISON*, a constitutional right of access to a court or similar judicial body was relied upon when determining a challenge to an increase in fees for using the Employment Tribunal.[108] It has even been suggested that there may be common law principles of a distinctive Scottish constitution.[109] It is neither necessary, nor desirable, to attempt to catalogue such rights as have been recognised for our purposes. What is important is the recognition by the courts (and therefore the common law) that there is a number of fundamental principles of the constitution, of which parliamentary sovereignty is one. It may be a prominent principle, but it is unclear whether it is *primus inter pares*.[110] As the Supreme Court observed in *HS2*, it is not clear how a clash between competing constitutional principles would be resolved.[111] If parliamentary sovereignty and the rule of law were to clash head-on, it cannot now be said with any confidence that parliamentary sovereignty would necessarily prevail.[112] In *Walton*, Lord Reed also explained that the "constitutional function" of the court when exercising its supervisory jurisdiction was "maintaining the rule of law".[113] That statement was unqualified.

---

[105] *R (on the application of Miller) v Prime Minister* [2019] UKSC 41; [2020] A.C. 373; 2019 S.L.T. 1143 at [34] and [40].

[106] *R (on the application of Cart) v Upper Tribunal* [2011] UKSC 28; [2012] 1 A.C. 663 at [122] (Lord Dyson). Approved by Lord Carnwath in *R (on the application of Privacy International) v Investigatory Powers Tribunal* [2019] UKSC 22; [2019] 2 W.L.R. 1219 at [119].

[107] Constitutional Reform Act 2005 s.1.

[108] *R (on the application of UNISON) v Lord Chancellor* [2017] UKSC 51; [2017] 3 W.L.R. 409 at [65] (Lord Reed). Lord Sumption made the same point in *R (on the application of Privacy International) v Investigatory Powers Tribunal* [2019] UKSC 22; [2019] 2 W.L.R. 1219 at [182].

[109] *Taylor Clark Leisure Plc v Commissioners for Her Majesty's Revenue and Customs* [2015] CSIH 32; 2015 S.C. 595, per Lord President (Gill) at [16]. The "established principle of the Scottish constitution" discussed in that case concerned rights of audience before the Court of Session. But the Lord President's remarks do raise the intriguing question of what other principles of the Scottish constitution exist and to what extent, if any, they may differ from the "English" or the "UK" constitution. That suggestion should be treated with a degree of caution. For a long time, the Scottish courts, and the leading textbooks, accepted that on matters of constitutional law affecting the UK, the law in Scotland was the same as that in England and Wales. So, the extent to which a distinctively Scottish constitution, capable of generating its own common law principles, exists must be doubtful. See the discussion by Prof. Page in: A. Page, *Constitutional Law of Scotland*, paras 1–39—1–44.

[110] In *R (on the application of Miller and other) v Secretary of State for Exiting the European Union* [2017] UKSC 3; [2018] A.C. 61 at [43], the majority of the Supreme Court (sitting *en bloc* for the first and only time) held that "Parliamentary sovereignty is *a* fundamental principle of the UK constitution". It did not describe it as "the" fundamental principle of the constitution.

[111] *R. (on the application of Buckingham CC) v Secretary of State for Transport* [2014] UKSC 3; [2014] 1 W.L.R. 324 at [207]. In that case, the context was a clash between the supremacy of EU law (which had been recognised, as we saw above, as in practical terms qualifying the legislative supremacy of Parliament) and Art.9 of the Bill of Rights (which protects from review proceedings in Parliament).

[112] Although, as Lord Reed pointed out in *AXA General Insurance Co Ltd v Lord Advocate* [2011] UKSC 46; 2012 S.C. (U.K.S.C.) 122 at [141], it has never been said that parliamentary sovereignty is the *only* reason Acts of Parliament are immune from judicial review. There may be other reasons for reaching that same conclusion. Some of those reasons are explored by Goldsworthy in J. Goldsworthy, *The Sovereignty of Parliament* (Oxford; OUP, 1999), pp.254–255.

[113] *Walton v Scottish Ministers* [2012] UKSC 44; 2013 S.C. (U.K.S.C.) 67 at [90].

Could it include maintaining the rule of law in the face of an Act of Parliament that would otherwise undermine it? There is no reason, in principle, why that should not be so.[114] As we have seen, the constitution of the United States does not expressly authorise the court to strike down legislation that conflicts with the constitution. It was a power claimed by the US Supreme Court as necessary to protect the constitution.[115] In Canada, the Supreme Court has read in principles that underlie the constitution and that will be protected by the courts.[116] And in India, the Supreme Court has gone as far as to strike down a constitutional amendment (which was otherwise passed in accordance with the written constitution) because it offended principles that underpin the constitution.[117] The more difficult question, perhaps, is whether such a change should be made by the courts acting on their own initiative.[118] As Professor Wade explained:

> "Even without a [break in legal continuity] there might be a shift in judicial loyalty if we take into account the dimension of time ... [N]ew generations of judges might come to accept that there had been a new constitutional settlement based on common consent and long usage, and that the old doctrine of sovereignty was ancient history... The judges would then be adjusting their doctrine to the facts of constitutional life, as they have done throughout history."[119]

A change to such a fundamental rule of the constitution ought to be made, if possible, with the consent of the various constitutional actors. If the courts cease to recognise Acts of Parliament as beyond challenge it would be preferable if this was the result of a consensus having emerged as to what the new fundamental rule of the constitution ought to be, as opposed to one branch of the state unilaterally declaring it.[120] That is not least because it is by no means certain that such a step by the court would be accepted by the other limbs of the state or by the public. And if that were to be the case, untold damage could be done to the standing of the judiciary.[121]

---

[114] Most recently, see Lord Carnwath's (obiter) comments in *R (on the application of Privacy International) v Investigatory Powers Tribunal* [2019] UKSC 22; [2019] 2 W.L.R. 1219 at [144].

[115] *Marbury v Madison* (1803) 1 Cranch 137.

[116] *Reference re the Secession of Quebec* [1998] 2 S.C.R. 217.

[117] *Golaknath v Punjab*, 1967 A.I.R. 1643; see the discussion of the "Basic Structure Doctrine" in S.P. Sathe, "India: From Positivism to Structuralism" in J.D. Goldsworthy (ed), *Interpreting Constitutions: A Comparative Study* (Oxford: Oxford University Press, 2006), pp.242–248. The idea of a constitution that has a basic structure, or architecture, has also been discussed in Canada: *Reference re Senate Reform*, 2014 S.C.C. 32 at [25]–[27].

[118] On the process of constitutional change, see House of Lords Select Committee on the Constitution, *The Process of Constitutional Change, 15th report of Session 2010–12*. The sovereignty of Parliament had earlier been recognised by the same committee as one of the central tenets of the constitution: House of Lords Select Committee on the Constitution, *Reviewing the Constitution: Terms of Reference and Method of Working, 1st report of Session 2001–2002* (The Stationery Office, 2001) HL Paper 11, para.20.

[119] H.W.R. Wade, *Constitutional Fundamentals* (London: Stevens, 1989).

[120] Bogdanor, *The New British Constitution* (2009), pp.280–282; Bingham, *The Rule of Law* (2010) p.170. See generally C. Turpin and A. Tomkins, *British Government and the Constitution: Text and Materials*, 7th edn (Cambridge: Cambridge University Press, 2011), pp.71–75; Young, *Parliamentary Sovereignty and the Human Rights Act* (2009), pp.82–93.

[121] D. Oliver, *Parliament and the Courts: A Pragmatic (or Principled) Defence of the Sovereignty of Parliament*, in A. Horne and G. Drewry (eds.), *Parliament and the Law*, (Oxford: Bloomsbury, 2018) at pp.304–307.

3–15 But the United Kingdom is not there yet. Common law constitutionalism is only to be found in academic journals and obiter dicta comments. There is no "common consent" that there has been a shift away from parliamentary supremacy. Quite the reverse. A staunch defence of the Diceyian view of parliamentary supremacy was given by Lord Bingham, writing after his retirement. He argued:

> "We live in a society dedicated to the rule of law; in which Parliament has power, subject to limited, self-imposed restraints, to legislate as it wishes; in which Parliament may therefore legislate in a way which infringes the rule of law; and in which the judges, consistently with their constitutional duty to administer justice according to the laws and usages of the realm, cannot fail to give effect to such legislation if it is clearly and unambiguously expressed."[122]

The same argument was advanced by Goldsworthy[123] along with several eminent judges.[124] If, however, it is accepted that there are some limits to the legislative competence of Parliament (for example, as a result of EU law) then it is hard to understand why, as a matter of principle, there should be no other limits.[125] Why should an Act of Parliament have had to yield to the requirements of the free movement of goods within the EU but not to fundamental principles of human rights? It may be dangerous for Parliament to assume it could, in a modern democracy, legislate in flagrant breach of the rule of law or fundamental human rights.[126] If it did, it may find it had not the power to do so. In the Human Rights Act 1998 the UK now has a stronger protection of such rights. And that Act represents the third contemporary challenge to the Diceyian orthodox.

Parliamentary supremacy and the Human Rights Act[127]

3–16 The working of the Human Rights Act 1998 is considered in more detail in Ch.11. For present purposes, we are interested in how the Act impacts on parliamentary supremacy. The Human Rights Act has been said to have been carefully crafted to ensure that parliamentary supremacy was preserved whilst allowing certain rights within the European Convention on Human Rights to be available in domestic courts.[128] Similar statements were made repeatedly in the Bill's passage through both Houses of Parliament. The key provisions for this present discussion are ss.3 and 4 of the Act. Section 3 provides:

---

[122] Bingham, *The Rule of Law* (2010), p.168.

[123] Goldsworthy, *Parliamentary Sovereignty: Contemporary Debates* (2010), pp.304–318. But compare what he said about a judge's moral duty in respect of "evil" legislation in J. Goldsworthy, *The Sovereignty of Parliament* (Oxford: OUP, 1999) at p.254. See also his general response to common law constitutionalism in *The Sovereignty of Parliament* at pp.277–279.

[124] Lord Neuberger MR (as he then was), "Who are the Masters Now?" (Lord Alexander of Weedon Lecture, 7 April 2011); and Jonathan Sumption, QC (as he then was), "Judicial and Political Decision-Making: the uncertain boundary" (F.A. Mann Lecture, 8 November 2011).

[125] A. Kavanagh, *Constitutional Review under the Human Rights Act* (Cambridge: Cambridge University Press, 2009), pp.413–415

[126] J. Jowell, "The Rule of Law and its Underlying Values" in *The Changing Constitution* (2011), p.32.

[127] See generally, Young, *Parliamentary Sovereignty and the Human Rights Act* (2009) and Kavanagh, *Constitutional Review under the Human Rights Act* (2009), Chs 10 and 11.

[128] See, for example, Lord Steyn's comments in *R v DPP, Ex p. Kebeline* [2000] 2 A.C. 326 at [367].

> "So far as it is possible to do so, primary legislation and subordinate legislation must be read and given effect in a way which is compatible with the Convention rights."

Section 4 provides that where the courts are satisfied that a legislative provision is incompatible with Convention rights, and that incompatibility cannot be cured by using s.3, then a "declaration of incompatibility" shall be made. Such a declaration does not affect the continuing validity, operation or enforcement of the offending provision.[129] The courts, therefore, are given no power to strike down or disapply an Act of Parliament. Where a declaration of incompatibility is made, the offending legislation can be cured by means of subordinate legislation.[130] So far, so good for the traditional view of parliamentary supremacy.

However, the key question is when should the courts interpret a provision using their power under s.3 and when should they make a declaration under s.4? The more readily the courts are prepared to resort to s.4, the greater the control that Parliament retains over the content and meaning of its legislation. However, if greater use is made of s.3 to interpret, gloss, stretch or potentially change the meaning of the words used by Parliament, the less control Parliament retains over the effect of its legislation. In other words, over use of s.3 threatens to restrict or impinge upon parliamentary supremacy by giving the words used by Parliament a meaning or effect that was never intended by it.[131] There were early tensions within the House of Lords over to what extent s.3 should be used to interpret legislation in a manner consistent with Convention rights.[132] In *Ghaidan v Godin-Mendoza* Lord Rodger of Earlsferry explained the correct approach to s.3 of the Act: 3–17

> "[The] key to what it is possible for the courts to imply into legislation without crossing the border from interpretation to amendment does not lie in the number of words that have to be read in. The key lies in a careful consideration of the essential principles and scope of the legislation being interpreted. If the insertion of one word contradicts those principles or goes beyond the scope of the legislation, it amounts to impermissible amendment. On the other hand, if the implication of a dozen words leaves the essential principles and scope of the legislation intact but allows it to be read in a way which is compatible with Convention rights, the implication is a legitimate exercise of the powers conferred by section 3(1)."[133]

Where s.3 cannot be used in that manner, it falls to the court to make a declaration of incompatibility under s.4. This approach to ss.3 and 4 proceeds on the understanding that Parliament had not intended to legislate in breach of Convention rights and thus the court corrects, where it can, any inadvertent or unintended incompatibility with Convention rights. In that respect, the minister responsible for the Bill must state to Parliament whether, in their view, the Bill is compatible with Convention rights or, alternatively, that they are unable to make

---

[129] Human Rights Act 1998 s.4(6)(a).

[130] Human Rights Act 1998 s.10.

[131] These issues are more fully discussed at paras 11–07—11–13, below.

[132] Compare Lord Steyn's approach in *R. v A* [2001] UKHL 25; [2002] 1 A.C. 45, which advocated an extensive use of s.3 and Lord Nicholls more moderate approach in *Re S (Children) (Care Order: Implementation of Care Plan)* [2002] UKHL 10; [2002] 2 A.C. 291.

[133] *Ghaidan v Godin-Mendoza* [2004] UKHL 30; [2004] 2 A.C. 557 at [122].

such a statement but the government nevertheless wish the House to proceed with the Bill.[134] Thus if Parliament intends to legislate contrary to Convention rights, it ought to be clear that that was the intention. Furthermore, where the courts issue a declaration of incompatibility, it is open to Parliament to take no remedial action, as has happened in respect of the blanket ban on prisoners voting.[135] Seven years after the declaration of incompatibility was originally made, the Supreme Court refused to make a further declaration: the matter was one for Parliament.[136]

3–18 It can be seen, therefore, that the Human Rights Act ultimately leaves the last word with Parliament. A consequence of that approach is that the protection of some Convention rights is incomplete (for example, those of disenfranchised prisoners) but parliamentary supremacy remains intact. But the Human Rights Act does not compromise Parliament's ability to legislate contrary to Convention rights if it so desires, but to do so effectively it will need to use clear and express language. As Lord Bingham explained (when speaking about the presumption expressed by Lord Hoffmann in *Simms* and which has parallels to s.3) this is no bad thing:

> "... if, as sometimes happens, the executive as the proponent of legislation wants to introduce a provision that would strike ordinary people as unfair or disproportionate or immoral, the need to spell out that intention explicitly on the face of the bill must operate as a discouragement, not least because of the increased risk of media criticism and parliamentary and popular resistance."[137]

If that is the combined effect of ss.3, 4 and 19 of the Human Rights Act then far from undermining Parliament, it ought to strengthen it.

Conclusions on parliamentary supremacy

3–19 Despite the contemporary debate about whether the Diceyian model of parliamentary supremacy *ought* to endure, there can be little doubt that it does in fact endure. It is vouched by authority of the highest order that has been recently re-affirmed. It is also attested to by the fact that there is no record of the courts having ever invalidated or disapplying the provisions of an Act of Parliament without some parliamentary authority for doing so.[138] But there is undoubtedly a shift in attitudes. Openly speculating on the continence of the doctrine in the highest courts would have been unthinkable two or three decades ago yet, as we have seen, judges in both the Inner House of the Court of Session and the Supreme Court/House of Lords have engaged in just such speculation. Perhaps

---

[134] Human Rights Act 1998 s.19.

[135] See the discussion below at para.4–14; the relevant provision of the Representation of the People Act 1983 was declared to be incompatible by the Registration Appeal Court (Scotland) in *Smith v Scott* [2007] CSIH 9; 2007 S.C. 345.

[136] *McGeoch v Lord President of the Council* [2013] UKSC 63; 2014 S.C. (U.K.S.C.) 25. So far as Scotland is concern, and with competence over the franchise for Scottish elections having been devolved, those prisoners serving a sentence of less than one year: Scottish Elections (Franchise and Representation) Act 2020.

[137] Lord Bingham, "Dicey Revisited" [2002] P.L. 39, 48.

[138] T. Bingham, *The Rule of Law* (London: Allan Lane, 2010), p.163 citing J Goldsworthy, *The Sovereignty of Parliament* (Oxford: OUP, 1999).

the more important question is if there is to be a shift away from parliamentary supremacy as the touchstone of our constitution, who should initiate the move? Lord Millett, in *Ghaidan v Godin-Mendoza*, accepted that the doctrine of parliamentary supremacy was not "sacrosanct" but if it were to be changed, it should be done by the legislature and not "judicial activism".[139] That view is supported by a number of other judges.[140] However, Laws LJ, Lord Steyn and Lord Hope would say that parliamentary supremacy is a creature of the common law and what the common law giveth, the common can taketh away. Professor Wade would support this stance. Goldsworthy would strongly disagree.[141] At present, the rule of parliamentary supremacy represents the "rule of recognition"[142] or "*grundnorm*"[143] in our legal system. It has attained that status, and derived its authority, from its acceptance by the judges and other constitutional actors. Any change in that rule of recognition ought not to lie exclusively in the hands of the courts or the legislature but in both, acting together, to form a new consensus, a consensus shared by the people.

A point that has not arisen in our discussion so far is the increasing use of referendums in the United Kingdom.[144] What, if any, impact does that have for parliamentary supremacy? Dicey himself came to advocate the introduction of the referendum in the UK.[145] He proposed a Referendum Act that would require popular approval of any legislative measure that alters provisions of the highest constitutional importance. Any measure not so approved should be "held invalid by every court of law".[146] Such a proposal would flatly contradict the classic, Diceyian, view of parliamentary supremacy. We discuss the rise of the referendum in Ch.5. If the referendum does become a common feature of our constitution, a fourth flank is likely to be opened in the battle over continuing parliamentary supremacy. And this line of attack appears to have been endorsed by Dicey himself.

At present, however, the law remains clear: assuming Parliament uses sufficient clear language, it retains the power to make or unmake any law, subject to the courts ability to disapply, for what remains of the transition/implementation period, any provision that conflicts with EU law. If that is to change, it is likely to be justified, at least in part, by a need to secure the rule of law. And it is to the rule of law that we now turn.

---

139 *Ghaidan v Godin-Mendoza* [2004] UKHL 30; [2004] 2 A.C. 557 at [57].

140 Bingham, *The Rule of Law* (2010), Ch.12; Lord Neuberger MR, "Who are the Masters Now?" (Lord Alexander of Weedon Lecture, 7 April 2011); and J. Sumption QC, "Judicial and Political Decision-Making: the uncertain boundary" (F.A. Mann Lecture, 8 November 2011).

141 J. Goldsworthy, *The Sovereignty of Parliament* (Oxford: OUP, 1999), pp.6–7, where he introduces his argument that parliamentary sovereignty is actually constituted as a fundamental rule as a result of a common consensus between senior officials in all three branches of the State.

142 H.L.A. Hart, *The Concept of Law*, 2nd edn (Oxford: Clarendon Press, 1994), pp.149–150.

143 H. Kelsen, *Pure Theory of Law* (translation from the revised 2nd edn, German edn by M. Knight); H. Kelsen, *General Theory of Law and State* (translated by A. Wedbery) (Cambridge Mass.: Harvard University Press, 1949).

144 On which see Bogdanor, *The New British Constitution* (2009), Ch.7.

145 A.V. Dicey, "The Referendum and its Critics" (1910) 212 *Quarterly Review* 538; see also: R. Weill, "Dicey was not Diceyan" (2003) 62 C.L.J. 474; Young, *Parliamentary Sovereignty and the Human Rights Act* (2009), pp.98–101.

146 Dicey, "The Referendum and its Critics" (1910) 212 *Quarterly Review* 538, 554.

THE RULE OF LAW

Introduction

3–20 The idea of the rule of law began to develop as a principle of the British constitution in the nineteenth century, but it has more ancient roots.[147] Its importance as a constitutional principle is now taken as read and has found itself embodied in statute.[148] Section 1 of the Constitutional Reform Act 2005 provides:

> "This Act does not adversely affect—(a) the existing constitutional principle of the rule of law; or (b) the Lord Chancellor's existing constitutional role in relation to that principle."

Section 17 of the Act goes on to amend the terms of the Promissory Oaths Act 1868 so as to require the Lord Chancellor to take an oath that he will "respect the rule of law, defend the independence of the judiciary and discharge my duty to ensure the provision of resources for the efficient and effective support of the courts for which I am responsible".

No attempt is made to define "the rule of law" in the 2005 Act. That reflects the fact that there is no general consensus about what it includes.[149] Some argue that the rule of law should be content free.[150] In other words, the rule of law should be about the form that law takes and the procedures for making law. It should not, the argument goes, trouble itself with the content of the law. The rule of law, on this understanding, should not be confused with, or be seen to require, other attributes (such as democracy, social justice, equality or the protection of human rights) to which a "good" constitution ought to aspire. The attributes that this narrow view of the rule of law would require include a requirement that laws be prospective in operation, open and clear. The law should be relatively stable. The making of particular laws or rules, whether legislative or administrative in nature, should be guided by open, stable, clear and general norms. This all requires that the courts play a role in securing even this narrow vision of the rule of law. An independent judiciary, who observe the principles of natural justice, and ready access to open courts are important features of this construction of the rule of law.[151] Rather than trying to capture all of the virtues of the state under the banner "the rule of law", this vision of the rule of law makes the more modest

---

[147] Tamanaha, *On the Rule of Law: History, Politics, Theory* (2004), pp.8–9; *Aristotle's Politics and Athenian Constitution* (1959) book III, s.1287, p.97.

[148] As Lord Steyn put it, an "overarching principle of constitutional law": Lord Steyn, "Democracy through law" [2002] E.H.R.L.R. 723. But the usefulness of the doctrine was not always so readily accepted: "The ground is then shifted slightly and what becomes sacred and untouchable is something called the Rule of Law. The Rule of Law is an invaluable concept for those who wish not to change the present set-up" (J.A.G. Griffith, "The Political Constitution" (1979) 42 M.L.R. 1, 15).

[149] That might be because an agreed definition is difficult to identify. As Lord Bingham put it: "If any of us were buttonholed in the street by an intellectually curious Martian who asked what was meant by the 'rule of law'—an expression he had observed much used in some of the more pretentious journals—our definition might be more or less incoherent." (Bingham, *Should public law remedies be discretionary?* [1991] PL 64).

[150] Perhaps the strongest advocate of this vision of the rule of law was Joseph Raz, see, in particular: J. Raz, "The Rule of Law and its Virtue" (1977) 93 L.Q.R. 195.

[151] See, for example, *Guardian News and Media Ltd v AB and CD* [2014] EWCA Crim B1, per Gross LJ at [2].

claim that respect for the rule of law is a necessary, if not a sufficient, condition for respecting individual freedom and human dignity.

The narrow view of the rule of law has the problem that it could maintain a state that supported arbitrary discrimination or other human rights abuses so long as the law was made in the appropriate manner and administered by independent courts. That has led others to argue for a fuller vision of the rule of law, one which includes specific rights for individuals.[152] Such a model is not without its difficulties. Which rights are protected by the rule of law? Are they unalienable and thus beyond the reach of future generations who may wish to order society differently? A further problem arises in the British constitutional context. The logical conclusion of any substantive vision of the rule of law requires the imposition of legal limitations on the legislature.[153] On this view, the rule of law sets its face against arbitrary power; arbitrary power is power unconstrained by law; the legislative supremacy of Parliament is unconstrained by law and therefore arbitrary; being arbitrary, it must be subject to judicial control (even if only on limited grounds). But since there "cannot be an infinite regress of lawmakers able to impose limits on the authority of each one in turn",[154] this argument necessarily involves the substitution of judicial for legislative supremacy. Only one institution can have the last word on whether or not law is valid.

The suggestion that, as a matter of the rule of law, that institution must be the courts can be resisted on a number of grounds. The first argument deployed is usually that such "judicial supremacy" is undemocratic.[155] The substantive rights said to be captured by the rule of law are rarely absolute. Once it is accepted these rights require to be qualified or balanced against each other, difficult choices are not made any easier by leaving the decision to the judiciary as opposed to the elected legislature.[156] The argument runs deeper than the democratic accountability of judges. Judicial decisions arise out of adversarial litigation. That process is ill-suited to the balancing of various competing interests and rights: that is a quintessentially legislative function.[157] Finally, given judicial decision-making is inherently retrospective, there is a necessary tension with the rule of law's emphasis on the prospectivity of the law.[158]

In *A v Secretary of State for the Home Department*, however, Lord Bingham defended judicial decision making and its democratic values:

---

[152] See, for example, Woolf et al, *De Smith's Judicial Review*, 8th edn (London: Sweet & Maxwell, 2018), para.1–023. J. Jowell, *The Rule of Law* in J. Jowell and C. O'Cinneide (eds), *The Changing Constitution*, 9th edn (Oxford: Oxford University Press, 2019), Ch.1. For a comparison between the two models, see R. Dworkin, "Political Judges and the Rule of Law" in R. Dworkin, *A Matter of Principle* (Oxford: Oxford University Press, 1985), Ch.1.

[153] We have seen the seeds of this argument above, at para.3–13, where the idea of common law constitutionalism was discussed.

[154] J.D. Goldsworthy, "Legislative sovereignty and the rule of law" in T. Campbell, K.D. Ewing and A. Tomkins (eds), *Sceptical Essays on Human Rights* (Oxford: Oxford University Press, 2001), Ch.4.

[155] See, for example, Griffith, "The brave new world of Sir John Laws" (2000) 63 M.L.R. 159; K.D. Ewing, "The Human Rights Act and Parliamentary Democracy" (1999) 62 M.L.R. 79.

[156] Griffith, "The political constitution" (1979) 42 M.L.R. 1. On that general theme, see: J Sumption, *Trials of the State* (London: Profile Books, 2019), in particular Ch.2 (*In Praise of Politics*).

[157] L.L. Fuller, "The Forms and Limits of Adjudication" (1978) 92 Harvard L.R. 353.

[158] R. Ekins, "Judicial Supremacy and the Rule of Law" (2003) 119 L.Q.R. 127.

> "I do not in particular accept the distinction which [the Attorney General] drew between democratic institutions and the courts. It is of course true that the judges in this country are not elected and are not answerable to Parliament. It is also of course true . . . that Parliament, the executive and the courts have different functions. But the function of independent judges charged to interpret and apply the law is universally recognised as a cardinal feature of the modern democratic state, a cornerstone of the rule of law itself. The Attorney General is fully entitled to insist on the proper limits of judicial authority, but he is wrong to stigmatise judicial decision-making as in some way undemocratic."[159]

That does not allow the courts to second guess the judgment of the executive or the legislature without restraint. As Lord Bingham also explained, it is necessary to have regard to the concept of "relative institutional competence":

> "The more purely political . . . a question is, the more appropriate it will be for political resolution and the less likely it is to be an appropriate matter for judicial decision. The smaller, therefore, will be the potential role for the court. It is the function of political and not judicial bodies to resolve political questions. Conversely, the greater the legal content of any issue, the greater the potential role of the courts, because under our constitution and subject to the sovereign power of Parliament it is the function of courts and not of political bodies to resolve legal questions."[160]

That suggests that a middle way can be found. Lord Bingham acknowledges the role of the court, even where the legal content is high, is subject to the supremacy of Parliament. That is a clear rejection of the logical end point of a fuller ideal of the rule of law. But it is also a rejection of the narrow formulation favoured by Raz and others. To understand how such a middle way can be navigated, it is necessary now to turn and consider what the rule of law actually means. Can we find an acceptable definition of this important term (one which has been described as the "ultimate controlling factor" upon which our constitution is based)?[161] To do that, we will consider two theories. First, Dicey and his views on the rule of law, which, despite coming under heavy criticism, remain influential. The second is the vision of the rule of law set out by Lord Bingham after his retirement as the Senior Law Lord. Once we have done that, we then turn to consider the different means by which the rule of law is protected in the United Kingdom.

---

159 *A v Secretary of State for the Home Department* [2004] UKHL 56; [2005] 2 A.C. 68 at [42]; see also Lord Hope at [108]. For support for Lord Bingham's stance, see J. Jowell, "Judicial Deference: Servility, Civility or Institutional Capacity?" [2003] P.L. 592 and R. Clayton, "Judicial deference and 'democratic dialogue': the legitimacy of judicial intervention under the Human Rights Act 1998" [2004] P.L. 33.

160 *A v Secretary of State for the Home Department* [2004] UKHL 56; [2005] 2 A.C. 68 at [29].

161 *R. (on the application of Jackson) v Attorney General* [2005] UKHL 56; [2006] 1 A.C. 262, per Lord Hope of Craighead at [107].

Dicey on the rule of law

Dicey's approach to the rule of law perhaps exemplifies the debate that has been outlined above and the difficulty in drawing any hard and fast lines. Dicey has been described as offering both a formal[162] and a substantive[163] concept of the rule of law. Dicey's views on the rule of law have been the subject of substantial, and sustained, criticism but they were the first clear articulation of the concept in terms of British constitutional law. For Dicey the rule of law sat with parliamentary sovereignty as the two fundamental doctrines of the constitution.[164] While parliamentary supremacy concerned itself with Parliament's relationship with the law, the rule of law concerned the executive's relationship with the law. 3–21

Dicey understood the rule of law to have three facets.[165] First, he took the rule of law to mean "the absolute supremacy or predominance of regular law as opposed to the influence of arbitrary power".[166] Arbitrariness, prerogative, even "wide discretionary authority on the part of government" were, for Dicey, incompatible with the rule of law. But this equation of discretion and arbitrariness is misconceived. No workable scheme of social welfare or regulation can be cast in terms of rules alone. Those charged with implementing and administering the scheme must be entrusted with a discretion in order to adapt and apply its general principles to the circumstances of specific cases. Consequently, Parliament regularly confers wide discretionary powers on public authorities and officials. That is plainly compatible with a narrow view of the rule of law: having the imprimatur of the legislature, its legal pedigree is beyond question. However, discretionary power and the rule of law can coexist. This does not dismiss Dicey's first branch of the rule of law entirely. Dicey's attack was on arbitrary power, which is not readily reconcilable with the idea of government under law. The issue thus becomes whether we have appropriate legal (and political) controls with which to regulate the exercise of discretionary power so as to ensure that it is not exercised in an arbitrary manner. Those controls are considered below.

Second, Dicey saw the rule of law as requiring "the equal subjection of all classes to the ordinary law of the land administered by the ordinary Law courts".[167] Dicey drew a distinction between the arrangements in Britain and those in continental systems, such as France, which had a distinct system of public law administered by separate courts. "With us", Dicey explained, "every official, from the Prime Minister down to a constable or collector of taxes, is under the same responsibility for every act done without legal justification as any other citizen." This proposition too is hard to sustain. It is simply wrong to say that there is equality before the law in the United Kingdom today. Leaving aside issues of access to the courts (which are touched on below) the state has a whole

---

[162] For example, P. Craig, "Formal and substantive conceptions of the rule of law: an analytical framework" [1997] P.L. 467.

[163] Perhaps most trenchantly by Jennings, *The Law and the Constitution* (1959).

[164] Dicey, *The Law of the Constitution* (1959), pp.183–184.

[165] Dicey, *The Law of the Constitution* (1959), pp.188–203.

[166] Dicey, *The Law of the Constitution* (1959), p.202.

[167] Dicey, *The Law of the Constitution* (1959), p.202.

host of special rights, privileges and immunities before the law.[168] Furthermore, the distinction between ordinary courts in Britain and the administrative courts in France has become less marked during the twentieth century as Parliament moved an increasing number of disputes away from the courts and into specialist tribunals.[169]

Finally, the rule of law, according to Dicey, means that:

> "with us the law of the constitution, the rules which in foreign countries naturally form part of a constitutional code, are not the source but the consequence of the rights of individuals, as defined and enforced by the Courts."[170]

The British constitution, on this account, was the product of the ordinary law, developed by the courts on a case by case basis, as distinct from (and, implicitly, superior to) a constitutional order superimposed in the manner of a written constitution. This third meaning of the rule of law is perhaps the most curious. Dicey clearly regarded individual rights and liberties as secured by the rule of law: the right to personal freedom, right to freedom of discussion and the right of public meeting were all discussed by Dicey in the section concerned with the rule of law.[171] In that sense Dicey gave a fuller, or substantive, account of the rule of law. But he did not (obviously) take that to the logical conclusion discussed above. Parliament retained the right to make or unmake any law. That being so, if the government of the day, commanding a majority in the House of Commons, forces through illiberal legislation (perhaps using the Parliament Acts) there is nothing the courts can do about it. For Dicey, however, parliamentary supremacy and the rule of law were not to be viewed as counterbalancing forces but in fact being mandated by each other. They are complementary.[172] This appears to be based on Dicey's belief that Parliament would not enact laws harmful to the interests of its electors: Dicey only ever advocated the absence of *legal* limits on the competence of Parliament. As he explained:

> "Parliament, though sovereign, unlike a sovereign monarch who is not only a legislator but a ruler, that is head of the executive government, has never been able to use the powers of the government as a means of interfering with the regular course of law; and what is even more important, Parliament has looked with

[168] To take but a few examples: in the absence of express terms (or necessary implication) to the contrary, the Crown is not bound by the burden of a statute (*Lord Advocate v Dumbarton DC*, 1990 S.C. (H.L.) 1; recently re-affirmed by the Supreme Court in *R (Black) v Secretary of State for Justice* [2017] UKSC 81; [2018] A.C. 215, although it was noted that the rule was so well established that that abolition or modification of it should not be done by the court but the Law Commission and Parliament were encouraged to look at the matter: para.35); the Crown has immunity from coercive remedies (interdict and implement in Scotland; injunction and specific performance in England and Wales) in civil proceedings (Crown Proceedings Act 1947), although "civil proceedings" have now been held not to include proceedings for judicial review (*M v Home Office* [1994] 1 A.C. 377 HL; *Davidson v Scottish Ministers* [2005] UKHL 74; 2006 S.C. (H.L.) 41).

[169] These have now been brought together under the unified tribunal structure: Tribunals, Courts and Enforcement Act 2007 and Tribunals (Scotland) Act 2014. See paras 8–06—8–11, below.

[170] Dicey, *The Law of the Constitution* (1959), p.203.

[171] Dicey, *The Law of the Constitution* (1959), pp.206–283.

[172] Dicey, *The Law of the Constitution* (1959), p.406. See also T.R.S. Allan, *Law, Liberty and Justice: the Legal Foundations of British Constitutionalism* (Oxford: Clarendon Press, 1994), p.282; Laws, "Law and Democracy" [1995] P.L. 72; T.R.S. Allan, *The Sovereignty of Law* (Oxford: OUP, 2013), Ch.5 (*Legislative Supremacy and the Rule of Law*).

> disfavour and jealously on all exemptions of officials from the ordinary liabilities of citizens or from the jurisdiction of the ordinary Courts; Parliamentary sovereignty has been fatal to the growth of 'administrative law'."[173]

The last sentence, at least, is clearly out of place in the modern United Kingdom. But the rest of this passage also highlights how times have changed since Dicey was writing. Parliament has been, in modern times, dominated by the executive. It is a necessary condition (by convention at least) that the executive commands the support of the majority of the House of Commons.[174] That fact, coupled with the provisions of the Parliament Acts, do allow a confusion between executive and legislative functions.[175] Thus a tension can be seen between the Diceyian model of parliamentary supremacy and the rule of law. Maintaining the former necessarily leads to, at least, the risk of an incomplete protection of the latter.

Bingham on the rule of law[176]

A more contemporary definition of the rule of law was given by Lord Bingham: 3–22

> "The core of the existing principle is, I suggest, that all persons and authorities within the state, whether public or private, should be bound by and entitled to the benefit of laws publically made, taking effect (generally) in the future and publically administered in the courts."[177]

Lord Bingham acknowledged that this formulation of the rule of law has been heavily influenced by Dicey. Lord Bingham went on to explain that his formulation of the rule of law brings with it eight sub-rules[178]:

(i) "the law must be accessible and so far as possible intelligible, clear and predictable";
(ii) "questions of legal right and liability should ordinarily be resolved by application of the law and not the exercise of discretion";
(iii) "the laws of the land should apply equally to all, save to the extent that objective differences justify differentiation";

---

[173] Dicey, *The Law of the Constitution* (1959), p.409. One of Dicey's staunchest supporters, Goldworthy, has also suggested that the doctrine of parliamentary sovereignty does not actually entail that judges should actually enforce statues: "Parliament has legal authority to enact [statutes which violate deeper principles of political morality], and that judges have a legal duty to enforce them, but not that judges would be morally justified in enforcing them. Legal validity and authority are not the same as moral validity and authority. Judges may have a legal but not a moral duty to enforce an evil statute." (J. Goldsworthy, *The Sovereignty of Parliament* (Oxford: OUP, 1999), p.254.

[174] Or, as the Supreme Court put it in *R (on the application of Miller) v Prime Minister* [2019] UKSC 41; [2020] A.C. 373; 2019 S.L.T. 1143 at [55]: "The Government exists because it has the confidence of the House of Commons. It has no democratic legitimacy other than that."

[175] This increasingly troubled Dicey and was at the root of his proposed Referendums Act, discussed in Ch.5, below.

[176] What follows is a necessarily brief synopsis of Lord Bingham's discussion of the rule of law that is set out in his lecture on the topic, "The Rule of Law", which is published at [2007] C.L.J. 67 the themes of which are more fully discussed in his book, Bingham, *The Rule of Law* (2010). The book in its entirety is commended to anyone who has an interest in the issue of the rule of law.

[177] Bingham, *The Rule of Law* (2010), p.8.

[178] Bingham, *The Rule of Law* (2010), Chs 3–10 (respectively).

(iv) "ministers and public officers at all levels must exercise the powers conferred on them in good faith, fairly for the purpose for which the powers were conferred, without exceeding the limits of such powers and not unreasonably";
(v) "the law must afford adequate protection of fundamental human rights";
(vi) "means must be provided for resolving, without prohibitive cost or inordinate delay, bona fide civil disputes which the parties themselves are unable to resolve";
(vii) "adjudicative procedures provided by the state should be fair"; and
(viii) "the rule of law requires compliance by the state with its obligations in international law as in national law".

Lord Bingham's formulation and his sub-rules can be seen to share characteristics of both the narrow view of the rule of law (for example, sub-rules (i)–(iv)) but also a more substantive vision of the rule of law (for example, sub-rules (v) and (vi)). Access to justice is a topical example to choose.[179] As Lord Bingham explained an "unenforceable right or claim is a thing of little value to anyone" and it is important the courts are not open to everyone in the same way that anyone (who has the money) can stay at the Ritz Hotel.[180] The jurisdictions of the United Kingdom have long subsidised access to the courts for those who did not have the means to pay for professional representation. But legal aid, especially for civil litigation, is a contentious issue. As successive cuts have been made to legal aid budgets, and access to the courts has become more difficult for more and more families, strain is placed on the rule of law.[181] But would there come a point when legal aid was cut so far that it would infringe the rule of law? And if so, could such legislation (assuming the cut to have been made by Act of Parliament) be reviewable on the grounds it does not comply with the rule of law?[182]

3–23 Despite supporting a more substantive content to the rule of law, Lord Bingham denies that his formulation necessarily leads to the rule of law supplanting parliamentary supremacy as the ultimate rule of our constitution. As we have already seen, Lord Bingham argues that Parliament retains the right to legislate contrary to the rule of law if sufficiently clear words are used.[183] That potentially gives rise to an incomplete protection of the rule of law. As Lord Bingham noted earlier in his work:

> "It is a good start for public authorities to observe the letter of the law, but not enough if the law in a particular country does not protect what are regarded as the basic entitlements of a human being."[184]

---

[179] See, generally, Lord Neuberger, "Justice in the Age of Austerity" (Tom Sargant Memorial Lecture, 15 October 2013) *http://www.supremecourt.uk/docs/speech-131015.pdf* [Accessed 15 June 2020].

[180] Bingham, *The Rule of Law* (2010), pp.85–86.

[181] See, for example, the controversy surrounding whether a complex fraud trial could continue where barristers involved refused to appear at the reduced legal aid rates that had been imposed: *R. v Crawley (Scott)* [2014] EWCA Crim 1028; [2014] 2 Cr. App. R. 16.

[182] In *R (on the application of UNISON) v Lord Chancellor* [2017] UKSC 51; [2017] 3 W.L.R. 409 an order (therefore, secondary legislation) that had significantly increased fees for the Employment Tribunal was quashed because of, inter alia, its consequences for access to justice. Of particular note, see the comments by Lord Reed at [66]–[73], which deserve to be read in full.

[183] Bingham, *The Rule of Law* (2010), p.168; see para.3–14, above.

[184] Bingham, *The Rule of Law* (2010), p.84.

The protection of the rule of law, as Lord Bingham recognised, rests on trusting Parliament not to abuse its legislative supremacy. An obvious assault on the rule of law (for example, the fabled legislation requiring the slaughter of all blue-eyed babies) can safely be ruled out. But as we saw with legal aid, more subtle infringements of the rule of law cannot be excluded. Lord Bingham recognises that the constitution has become "unbalanced" in this regard and may, in time, require reconsideration.[185]

As we have seen, both Dicey and Bingham's visions of the rule of law result in incomplete protection so long as parliamentary supremacy remains. But to what extent is that only an academic concern? To answer that, we need to consider how the rule of law is currently safeguarded in the United Kingdom.

Protecting the rule of law

All three branches of the state (judiciary, legislature and executive) have an important role to play in protecting the rule of law. We have already seen the statutory obligation placed on the Lord Chancellor in that regard. They, with the other Law Officers, play an important role in ensuring the executive respect the rule of law. The legislature (be it Westminster or Holyrood) have a role to play as well. For example, s.1 of the Judiciary and Courts (Scotland) Act 2008 places an obligation on the First Minister, the Lord Advocate, the Scottish Ministers and MSPs to "uphold the continued independence of the judiciary"—as we have seen, an essential component of the rule of law. But it is the judiciary that play the most important role in securing the rule of law, through applying the common law and interpreting the legislation passed by Parliament. **3–24**

Dicey (through his second characteristic of the rule of law) and Bingham (through his third sub-rule) saw the courts playing an important role in the protection of the rule of law. This is most obviously done through their development of the common law. In our discussion of common law constitutionalism we have seen the courts asserting the common law's role in giving content to, and protection for, the rule of law. The common law has long protected some basic rights, which have been said to include: access to a judicial remedy; right to life; liberty of the person; right to a fair hearing; prohibition on the retrospective imposition of criminal penalty; freedom of expression; and many others.[186] At its core is the principle of legality. This requires the courts to apply the rule of law and other constitutional principles unless Parliament has clearly and expressly excluded them.[187] It also requires the executive to act in accordance with the law, including the law of delict. Thus, in *Entrick v Carrington*, the court rejected the assertion that "state necessity" was sufficient warrant for authorising the King's Messengers to break in to Entrick's house and seize his books and papers: **3–25**

---

185 Bingham, *The Rule of Law* (2010), p.169.

186 Woolf et al., *De Smith's Judicial Review* (2013), para.5–042. See also the more general discussion of at paras 5–047—5–048 of the 8th edn (2018).

187 *R. v Secretary of State for the Home Department, Ex p. Simms* [2000] 2 A.C. 115, per Lord Hoffmann at [131]; subject to the caveat that the courts *may* reject a blatant attempt to subvert the rule of law: *R. (on the application of Jackson) v Attorney General* [2005] UKHL 56; [2006] 1 A.C. 262, per Baroness Hale of Richmond at [159].

> "Every invasion of private property is a trespass. No man can set his foot upon my ground without my licence, but he is liable to an action . . . If he admits the fact, he is bound to show by way of justification that some positive law has empowered or excused him. The justification is submitted to the judges, who are to look into the books, and see if such a justification can be maintained by the text of the statute law, or principles of the common law . . . It is said that it is necessary for the ends of government to lodge such a power [*of search and seizure*] with a state officer . . . but with respect to the argument of state necessity, or to a distinction that has been aimed at between state offences and others, the common law does not understand that kind of reasoning, nor do our books take notice of any such distinction."[188]

A more recent example is *R. v Davis*, where the House of Lords held that the common law conferred a right on an accused to confront his accusers.[189] An order by a trial judge that allowed witnesses to use pseudonyms, to be hidden behind a screen, have their voice mechanically distorted and prohibited the accused's counsel from asking any questions that may have allowed the witnesses to be identified was unlawful.[190]

But the protection offered by the principle of legality is limited. It does not require the state to found on a positive legal authority for all that it does. Rather, such authority is only required where necessary to validate what would otherwise constitute a legal wrong. *Malone v Metropolitan Police Commissioner* illustrates the significance of that distinction.[191] Mr Malone was prosecuted for handling stolen goods. It came to light during his trial that evidence had been recovered in the form covert recordings of his telephone conversations (in other words, a phone tap). The Secretary of State, on the request of the police, had authorised the Post Office (who then ran the telephone network) to record Mr Malone's telephone calls. Mr Malone sought a declaration that such phone tapping was unlawful. He was unsuccessful. There had been no trespass on to his property and the common law, at that point, did not protect a person's privacy. Accordingly, Mr Malone could point to no unlawful act by those that had recorded his telephone conversations. That was fatal to his claim:

> "If the tapping of telephones by the Post Office at the request of the police can be carried out without any breach of the law, it does not require any statutory or common law power to justify it: it can lawfully be done simply because there is nothing to make it unlawful."[192]

When Mr Malone's case reached the European Court of Human Rights in Strasbourg, however, the absence of a legal basis for the actions of the police was fatal to its compatibility with art.8 of the European Convention on Human Rights.[193] *Malone* is simply one example of the haphazard protection of the rule of law by the common law. An equally stark example is that of *Liversidge v*

---

188 *Entrick v Carrington* (1765) State Trials 1030.

189 *R. v Davis (Iain)* [2008] UKHL 36; [2008] 1 A.C. 1128.

190 That result was swiftly reversed by legislation in the form of the Criminal Evidence (Witness Anonymity) Act 2008, although the effect was ameliorated by requiring the trial judge to ensure that the requirements of art.6 of the European Convention on Human Rights were still fulfilled.

191 *Malone v Metropolitan Police Commissioner* [1979] Ch. 344 (ChD).

192 *Malone v Metropolitan Police Commissioner* [1979] Ch. 344, per Sir Robert Megarry VC at p.367A.

193 *Malone v United Kingdom* (1984) 7 E.H.R.R. 14.

Anderson that saw the House of Lords uphold the detention of Mr Liversidge without charge, without trial and without limit of time.[194] The case is most memorable for Lord Atkin's stinging dissent:

> "In this country, amid the clash of arms, the laws are not silent. They may be changed, but they speak the same language in war as in peace."[195]

But his comments were just that, a dissent. The laws must have sounded very quiet indeed to Mr Liversidge as he languished in his cell within Brixton prison at the behest of the Secretary of State. It took the best part of four decades before the common law recognised that Lord Atkin had been correct all along.[196] Whatever the reasons for decisions such as *Malone* or *Liversidge*, they serve to underscore the uncertain protection that the common law can afford to the rule of law.

It is not just through the common law that the judiciary seek to protect the rule of law. The approach of the courts to statutory interpretation also plays an important role. Once Parliament has spoken (in the form of legislation) the meaning to be given to those words is a matter for the courts. As we have seen, the court will not uphold a construction of an Act that infringes fundamental rights unless Parliament has clearly and expressly authorised such an infringement. What amounts to an express authorisation can be controversial. The decision in *R (on the application of Evans) v Attorney General* is illustrative.[197] Here, various letters written by the Prince of Wales to various government departments were sought under freedom of information legislation. That request had been upheld by the Upper Tribunal (a decision against which the government could have but did not appeal). Rather than release the letters, however, the Attorney General issued a certificate under s.53(2) of the Freedom of Information Act 2000 effectively overriding the decision of the Upper Tribunal. It is instructive to consider how the court approached of s.53(2) of the 2000 Act. Read short, that section allowed the Attorney General to override a decision notice or an enforcement notice under the 2000 Act requiring the production of a document where the Attorney "has on reasonable grounds formed the opinion that ... there has been no failure" to comply with the general obligation to disclose information imposed by s.1 of the 2000 Act. For Lord Neuberger, writing the leading judgment, Parliament would have had to use "crystal clear" language to allow the executive to override a judicial decision (such as that of the Upper Tribunal in this case). And the language of s.53(2) was not "crystal clear".[198] But while Lord Neuberger invoked the rule of law in support of (indeed, requiring) his decision, Lord Wilson (dissenting) complained that the result did not interpret but rather re-wrote s.53(2) of the 2000 Act. Furthermore, for all the reliance placed upon the rule of law, he pointed out that "the most precious" of constitutional principles

---

[194] *Liversidge v Anderson* [1942] A.C. 206 HL; see also Lord Bingham, "Mr Perlzweig, Mr Liversidge, and Lord Atkin", 16 October 1997, republished in Lord Bingham, *The Business of Judging* (Oxford: Oxford University Press, 2000), pp.211–221. Further discussion at para.13–02.

[195] *Liversidge v Anderson* [1942] A.C. 206 at p.244.

[196] *Inland Revenue Commissioners v Rossminster Ltd* [1980] A.C. 952 HL, per Lord Diplock at [1011].

[197] [2015] UKSC 21; [2015] A.C. 1787.

[198] [2015] UKSC 21; [2015] A.C. 1787 at [58].

(parliamentary sovereignty) was conspicuous by its absence.[199] That the most senior judges can so sharply disagree simply serves to illustrate how fine a line it is that the court must tread in upholding the rule of law whilst at the same time retaining the overall constitutional balance.

Conclusions on the rule of law

3–26 Despite its increasingly important place in our constitution, a definition of the rule of law that is acceptable to all remains elusive. The truth appears to lie somewhere between the narrow and the substantive visions of the rule of law that have been advocated. What we have seen, however, is that while parliamentary supremacy remains in its orthodox form, the protection of the rule of law can never be complete.

SEPARATION OF POWERS

Introduction

3–27 "Everybody knows that the separation of powers is a good thing. It is less easy to say how it came to be this way."[200] For supposedly fundamental doctrines of the constitution, the meaning and force of both parliamentary supremacy and the rule of law turn out to be surprisingly contested questions. So too the doctrine of the separation of powers, which Britain was once taken to exemplify, which was subsequently written off as irrelevant, but which has had the withal to cling on to its claim to be a central feature of the constitution.[201] Indeed, in recent years, it has had somewhat of a revival.

The classic statements of the separation of powers doctrine were made in the period prior to the Glorious Revolution, although the idea underpinning the doctrine can be found in the experiments with mixed government in Ancient Greece and Rome. The classic formulation of the doctrine was given by Montesquieu in *The Spirit of the Laws*:

> "In every government there are three sorts of power . . . that of making laws, that of executing public affairs and that of adjudicating on crimes and individual cases . . . When the legislative and executive powers are united in the same person or in the same body of magistrates, there can be no liberty . . . Again, there is no liberty if the

[199] [2015] UKSC 21; [2015] A.C. 1787 at [168].

[200] S. Sedley, *Lions Under the Throne: Essays on the history of English Public Law* (Cambridge: CUP, 2015), p.172. The entire of Ch.9 (*The Separation of Powers*) is commended.

[201] In defence of the separation of powers, see M.J.C. Vile, *Constitutionalism and the Separation of Powers* (1967); Munro, *Studies in Constitutional Law* (1999), Ch.8; E. Barendt, "Separation of powers and constitutional government" [1999] P.L. 599; N.W. Barber, "Prelude to the separation of powers" [2001] C.L.J. 59.

> power of judging is not separated from the legislature and executive. There would be an end to everything if the same man or the same body . . . were to exercise those powers."[202]

Thus, the crucial evil that the separation of powers seeks to avoid is the concentration of too much power in too few hands, with all that that implies in terms of loss of liberty. This may be achieved by a rigid separation of the legislative, executive and judicial functions, and their allocation to three distinct agencies; more probably, it will be achieved by structuring the institutions of the state in such a way that no one institution has complete autonomy in the exercise of its functions, but is subject to a degree of control by one or both of the others.[203] On this account, it is less important to correctly identify and distribute particular functions of the state than to ensure that at no one time does one branch of the state have too much power by comparison with the others: the "health" of a constitution is a function of the efficacy of the "checks and balances" whereby the different institutions may encroach upon one another's territory. That, as we saw in Ch.1 and to which we will return in a moment, was at the heart of the Prorogation case.

On the face of it, our constitutional arrangements appear to conform to this doctrine: we have legislatures, executive authorities and judicial organs, each performing its respective role.[204] Why then did it become so fashionable to dismiss the separation of powers as a "tiresome talking point"?[205] There are obvious institutional overlaps.[206] When not simply ignoring it, critics of the separation of powers would enumerate in exhaustive detail the instances of Parliament performing non-legislative functions, of the government making laws and adjudicating upon them,[207] of the judiciary acting non-judicially. There is some truth in these observations, but they tend to give an incomplete and distorted impression. It is true that Parliament has a penal jurisdiction in the protection and enforcement of its privileges, but it has not been used for more

---

[202] Montesquieu, *The Spirit of the Laws* (1749). Although influenced by British constitutional arrangements, the theories of Montesquieu were to have their greatest impact in the exercise in constitutional design which took place in the United States of America following the Declaration of Independence.

[203] Montesquieu insisted, however, that the judicial power be wholly independent of the other two branches of government.

[204] Sir Stephen Sedley has argued that the separation of powers in the United Kingdom is bipolar: the power of Parliament to make the law and the power of the courts to decide, case by case, what the law is. In that model, the executive is subordinate to both. See: S. Sedley, *Lions Under the Throne: Essays on the history of English Public Law* (Cambridge: CUP, 2015), p.173.

[205] S.A. de Smith, "The Separation of Powers in New Dress" (1966) 12 McGill L.J. 491.

[206] The Sovereign, for example, is part of the legislature, the executive and the judiciary, if only in a formal sense; the government is drawn from Parliament; and, until October 2009, the most senior judges sat in the House of Lords.

[207] Something which the recent Governments got a taste for: consider, for example, the general anti-avoidance rule contained in s.207 of the Finance Act 2013 which make financial arrangements "abusive" if they "exploit" "shortcomings" in the Act. So the Finance Act 2013 means not only what Parliament said, but what the Government would wish it had said when and if a loophole is found. As Greenberg explains, this is a very serious blurring of the separation of powers as between the three institutions of the state and one which was introduced without any constitutional complaints: D. Greenberg, "Dangerous Trends in Modern Legislation" [2015] P.L. 96, [100]–[103] (the article rewards consideration in full).

than a century.[208] A great deal of legislative power is delegated by Parliament to ministers, local authorities and others, but primary legislation prescribes the scope and limits of these powers, subordinate legislation is subject to parliamentary approval, and the courts can invalidate subordinate legislation that is found to be ultra vires. Certain judicial functions are performed by administrative tribunals or officials, but since the Franks Report on administrative tribunals and inquiries, and the legislation to which it led, such tribunals have been absorbed into the machinery of justice, and their determinations are subject either to appeal or review by the ordinary courts.[209] So the various functions of the state do stray across institutional boundaries to some extent. But Montesquieu himself did not insist on an absolute division of the functions of the state between separate institutions. It may be that the critics of the doctrine have perpetuated the pure theory that, in its lack of correspondence to actual constitutional arrangements, is easier to knock down.

Judicial recognition of the separation of powers

3–28 There are numerous references in the case law to the separation of powers. For example, in *Duport Steels Ltd v Sirs*, Lord Diplock remarked:

> "At a time when more and more cases involve the application of legislation which gives effect to policies that are the subject of bitter public and parliamentary controversy, it cannot be too strongly emphasised that the British constitution, though largely unwritten, is firmly based on the separation of powers: Parliament makes the laws, the judiciary interprets them."[210]

Again, in *Secretary of State for the Home Department v Rehman*, where the question was whether and to what extent the Special Immigration Appeals Committee could question the Home Secretary's decision that a person's deportation was "in the interests of national security", Lord Hoffmann held:

> "However broad the jurisdiction of a court or tribunal, whether at first instance or on appeal, it is exercising a judicial function and the exercise of that function must recognise the constitutional boundaries between judicial, executive and legislative power."[211]

Similarly, in *Belmarsh*, on the question whether there existed "a public emergency threatening the life of the nation" so as to entitle the government to derogate from the United Kingdom's obligations under the European Convention

---

[208] It is almost inconceivable that it will ever be used again, certainly since the decision of the European Court of Human Rights in *Demicoli v Malta* (1991) 14 E.H.R.R. 47. There, a journalist had been convicted of a breach of parliamentary privilege for criticising MPs by a tribunal numbering amongst its membership two of the MPs named in his article. The court held that his rights to a fair trial under art.6 had been violated. See also *R. v Chaytor (David)* [2010] UKSC 52; [2011] 1 A.C. 684 for a discussion of the House of Commons penal jurisdiction.

[209] Although review by the courts of tribunal decisions is increasingly restricted: *Eba v Advocate General for Scotland* [2011] UKSC 29; 2012 S.C. (U.K.S.C.) 1; *R. (on the application of Cart) v Upper Tribunal* [2011] UKSC 28; [2012] 1 A.C. 663.

[210] *Duport Steels Ltd v Sirs* [1980] 1 W.L.R. 142 at p.157.

[211] *Secretary of State for the Home Department v Rehman* [2001] UKHL 47; [2003] 1 A.C. 153 at [49].

on Human Rights, the majority of the House of Lords accepted that this was an issue calling for the exercise of "pre-eminently political judgment", in consequence of which great (if not overriding) weight was to be attached to the views of executive and legislature.[212] In *M v Home Office*, the relationship between the courts and the executive was at stake. M had arrived from Zaire and sought asylum in the UK. His claim was rejected and in March 1991 his application for leave to judicially review that decision was refused. He was to be removed to Zaire on the evening of 1 May 1991. Earlier in the day of 1 May, a fresh application for judicial review was presented (by newly instructed solicitors and counsel). The High Court judge before whom the case called understood counsel for the Home Office to have given an undertaking that M would not be removed pending determination of his application. It had not been understood by the Home Office that such an undertaking had been tendered (and it was said on appeal, by fresh counsel for the Home Office, that original counsel had no instructions to offer such an undertaking) and M was removed as planned. Having been advised of this, the judge required the Secretary of State to procure M's return forthwith. Arrangements were made to return M to the UK on 2 May. That afternoon, the Home Secretary learned of what had happened. Satisfied that the original asylum decision was correct, and having been advised that the order to return M had been made without jurisdiction, the Home Secretary cancelled the return arrangements. Proceedings were then instituted against the Home Secretary for contempt. In short, the question for the court was whether the Crown obeyed orders of the court by grace or under obligation? Relying on s.21 of the Crown Proceedings Act 1947,[213] Simon Brown J held that neither the Crown nor its departments, ministers or officials could be found in contempt. That conclusion was reversed by a divided Court of Appeal, during which Nolan LJ memorably remarked:

> "The proper constitutional relationship of the executive with the courts is that the courts will respect all acts of the executive within its lawful province, and that the executive will respect all decisions of the courts as to what its lawful province is."[214]

The Court of Appeal went on to hold that, whilst the Crown and the Home Office lacked sufficient legal personality to be subject to contempt proceedings, the Secretary of State had personally decided not to comply with the order of the judge and was therefore in contempt. That conclusion was upheld by an unanimous House of Lords, although it was clarified that the finding of contempt should be against the minister in his official capacity so that the court was clear that it was the department for which the minister was responsible that was guilty of the contempt and not the minister personally.[215]

---

[212] *A v Secretary of State for the Home Department* [2004] UKHL 56; [2005] 2 A.C. 68, per Lord Bingham of Cornhill at [29]; Lord Hoffmann dissented on that point at [95]–[97].

[213] See paras 7–09—7–11, below.

[214] *M v Home Office* [1992] QB 270 at p.314.

[215] *M v Home Office* [1994] 1 A.C. 377 at p.426 (Lord Woolf). That means there is no prospect of the minister being fined or imprisoned for contempt, which has been said to leave a gap in that there is no coercive means by which the court's orders can be enforced against the Crown (see, for example, S. Sedley (who argued the case for M in the Court of Appeal; he had been appointed to the bench before the House of Lords heard the case), "The Crown in its own courts", in S. Sedley, *Ashes and Sparks:*

3–29 The Privy Council has on a number of occasions struck down retrospective criminal legislation or legislation transferring sentencing powers to the executive as unconstitutional usurpations of the judicial function,[216] and separation of powers thinking may be said to inform decisions such as *Commissioners of Customs and Excise v Cure & Deeley Ltd*,[217] where the Court of Appeal declined to interpret a statute so as to permit an administrative authority to make the final decision on a person's liability to tax. More broadly, it is notable how often the separation of powers crops up as a tool of criticism of aspects of constitutional practice. The Franks Report in 1957, and the concerns that prompted the establishment of the Committee on Administrative Tribunals and Inquiries and which has more recently seen the establishment of the unified tribunal structure,[218] may be seen as a powerful vindication of the continuing relevance of the reasoning underpinning the separation of powers doctrine.[219] The idea of the separation of powers is interconnected with the rule of law in our modern constitution. As Lord Phillips explained *R. (on the application of Cart) v Upper Tribunal*:

> "The administration of justice and upholding of the rule of law involves a partnership between Parliament and the judges. Parliament has to provide the resources needed for the administration of justice.... Parliament has not sought to oust or fetter the common law powers of judicial review of the judges of the High Court and I hope that Parliament will never do so. It should be for the judges to decide whether the statutory provisions for the administration of justice adequately protect the rule of law and, by judicial review, to supplement these should it be necessary. But, in exercising the power of judicial review, the judges must pay due regard to the fact that, even where the due administration of justice is at stake, resources are limited."[220]

In that passage, Lord Phillips captures the need for institutional respect between the organs of the state and a need that each respects the competences of the other. Whilst the United Kingdom may not have the formal, and strict, separation of powers that can be found in countries such as the United States, the idea remains an important element of our constitution.

Essays on Law and Justice (Cambridge: CUP, 2011), Ch.28). The Scottish Ministers can be found in contempt for breach of an undertaking. The relevant principles are summarised by the Lord Ordinary (Pentland) in *Smith v Scottish Ministers*, 2015 S.L.T. 131 at [13]. See also: *Beggs v Scottish Ministers*, 2005 1 S.C. 342.

216 See, e.g. *Liyanage v The Queen* [1967] 1 A.C. 259 PC (Ceylon) and *Hinds v The Queen* [1977] A.C. 195 PC (Jamaica).

217 *Commissioners of Customs and Excise v Cure & Deeley Ltd* [1962] 1 Q.B. 340.

218 On the tribunal structure generally, see paras 8–06—8–11, below.

219 As may the earlier report of the Donoughmore Committee on Ministers' powers, which reported in 1929 and which was set up to consider whether the increasing use of delegated legislative power required to be checked. The committee concluded that it did not, subject to appropriate safeguards to prevent abuse.

220 *R. (on the application of Cart) v Upper Tribunal* [2011] UKSC 28; [2012] 1 A.C. 663 at [89].

Recent experience of the separation of powers

As ever, the tide ebbs and flows. Recently, the courts have been more willing to review areas that may previously have been thought to be "off limits". For example, in *Belhaj v Straw* the claimants sought to challenge their alleged "rendition" and subsequent mistreatment in which the UK Government was said to have been complicit.[221] Pleas that the action be dismissed on account of state immunity and the "act of state" doctrine were rejected by the Court of Appeal: **3–30**

> "... the stark reality is that unless the English courts are able to exercise jurisdiction in this case, these very grave allegations against the executive will never be subjected to judicial investigations ... there is ... no alternative international forum with jurisdiction over these issues. As a result, these very grave allegations would go uninvestigated and the appellants would be left without any legal recourse or remedy."[222]

Here we see the Court of Appeal, although not expressly, balancing the rule of law (the need for the actions of the executive to be subject to review) and the separation of powers (the court respecting its proper constitutional function).[223] A similar concern underlay much of the debate in the Prorogation case.[224] There it was argued on behalf of the Prime Minister that he was accountably only to Parliament for the advice tendered to the Queen in respect of prorogation. Given the prorogation did not happen immediately, and Parliament had sufficient time to pass Brexit-related legislation but did not legislate to reverse the prorogation, the court should not, it was said, enter the political arena. Not so, said the Supreme Court:

> "[I]f the issue before the court is justiciable, deciding it will not offend against the separation of powers. As we have just indicated, the court will be performing its proper function under our constitution. Indeed, by ensuring that the Government does not use the power of prorogation unlawfully with the effect of preventing Parliament from carrying out its proper functions, the court will be giving effect to the separation of powers."[225]

Of course, the problem with the Prime Minister's argument was that it relied upon the court accepting that a discretionary power rested in the Prime Minister's hands that was subject to no right of review in the court (and parliamentary accountability is a poor substitute given the majority a Prime Minister can normally be expected to have). The court was always likely to be sceptical of the idea of an unreviewable discretionary power and so it proved.

Two cases serve to illustrate the sort of tension that the separation of powers can produce for the judiciary, who must be careful about defining the limits of

[221] *Belhaj v Straw* [2014] EWCA Civ 1394; [2015] 2 W.L.R. 1105. The decision was upheld by the Supreme Court: [2017] UKSC 3; [2017] A.C. 964.

[222] *Belhaj v Straw* [2014] EWCA Civ 1394; [2015] 2 W.L.R. 1105 at [119].

[223] For a general discussion of the issues surrounding the courts approach to respecting its proper constitutional function, see A. Paterson, *Final Judgment* (Oxford: Hart, 2013), Ch.7.

[224] *R (on the application of Miller) v Prime Minister* [2019] UKSC 41; [2020] A.C. 373; 2019 S.L.T. 1143.

[225] *R (on the application of Miller) v Prime Minister* [2019] UKSC 41; [2020] A.C. 373; 2019 S.L.T. 1143 at [34].

their own constitutional function. They are *R (on the application of Evans) v Attorney General*[226] and *R (on the application of Nicklinson) v Ministry of Justice*.[227] *Evans*, as we saw above, concerned a freedom of information request to disclose letters sent by the Prince of Wales to various members of the government. Under s.53(2) of the Freedom of Information Act 2000, a minister (in this case, the Attorney General) had the power to prevent the release of documents that were otherwise disclosable. The (constitutional) problem was explained by Lord Neuberger:

> "A statutory provision which entitles a member of the executive (whether a Government Minister or the Attorney General) to overrule a decision of the judiciary merely because he does not agree with it would not merely be unique in the laws of the United Kingdom. It would cut across two constitutional principles which are also fundamental components of the rule of law.
>
> First, subject to being overruled by a higher court or (given Parliamentary supremacy) a statute, it is a basic principle that a decision of a court is binding as between the parties, and cannot be ignored or set aside by anyone, including (indeed it may fairly be said, least of all) the executive. Secondly, it is also fundamental to the rule of law that decisions and actions of the executive are [subject to limited exceptions] reviewable by the court at the suit of an interested citizen. Section 53, as interpreted by the Attorney General's argument in this case, flouts the first principle and stands the second principle on its head."[228]

In short, s.53(2) of the 2000 Act had been used in a way that ran contrary to the separation of powers. The release of the letters having been the subject of judicial decision, the executive could not set that decision to one side simply because it disagreed with the outcome. Parliament could, Lord Neuberger accepted, authorise such a course but only where the intention had been made "crystal clear".[229] That is because so long as Parliament is accepted as having the authority to legislate contrary to the rule of law or cardinal features of the constitution (and we shall not revisit our earlier discussion on whether that holds true), the courts will not accept that Parliament intended such a result where it has used general or ambiguous words.[230] *Evans* represents an example of the courts defining and policing the boundary between the respective organs of the state and doing so with the avowed aim of protecting the separation of powers.

Nicklinson is illustrative of the restraint that the judiciary often have to show so as to respect those same boundaries. Not all questions that come before the courts can properly be answered by the courts. *Nicklinson* was such a case. Here, the claimants were suffering from irreversible physical disabilities but were of sound mind and were aware of their predicament. In short, they wanted to be able to end their lives at a time, and in a manner, of their own choosing. But to do so would require assistance due to their physical condition. They sought to challenge s.2 of the Suicide Act 1961, which would render anyone who assisted them to end

---

[226] [2015] UKSC 21; [2015] A.C. 1787.
[227] [2014] UKSC 38; [2015] A.C. 657.
[228] [2015] UKSC 21; [2015] A.C. 1787 at [51]–[52].
[229] [2015] UKSC 21; [2015] A.C. 1787 at [58].
[230] [2015] UKSC 21; [2015] A.C. 1787 at [57], citing *AXA General Insurance Co Ltd v Lord Advocate* [2011] UKSC 46; 2012 S.C. (U.K.S.C.) 122 at [152] (Lord Reed) and *R v Secretary of State for the Home Department, Ex p. Pierson* [1998] A.C. 539 at p.575 (Lord Browne Wilkinson) in support.

their lives liable to criminal prosecution (indeed, a prosecution for murder, depending on the circumstances, was not impossible). One claimant sought a declarator that the common law defence of necessity was available to such a charge (failing which a declaration that the law of murder and assisted suicide was incompatible with art.8 of the Convention). The other claimant sought an order requiring the Director of Public Prosecutions to clarify his policy on when he would consent to a prosecution under s.2 of the 1961 Act in these circumstances.[231] The Supreme Court was sharply divided on whether it was institutionally appropriate for the court to determine whether s.2 of the 1961 Act was compatible with art.8 of the Convention. Lord Neuberger, for the majority that held it was institutionally appropriate, recognised the issue was challenging for the court to grapple with but he was not prepared to hold that, in principle, it could not determine it.[232] But he would not have been prepared to grant a declaration of incompatibility.[233] For a minority, however, it was simply not appropriate for the court to determine the issue:

> "the social and moral dimension of the issue, its inherent difficulty, and the fact that there is much to be said on both sides makes Parliament the proper organ for deciding it.
>
> ...
>
> the issue is an inherently legislative issue for Parliament, as the representative body in our constitution, to decide. The question what procedures might be available for mitigating the indirect consequences of legalising assisted suicide, what risks such procedures would entail, and whether those risks are acceptable, are not matter which under our constitution a court should decide."[234]

This represents the second aspect the courts have to be careful about. Adversarial litigation is not always the best (indeed, some would suggest rarely the best) forum in which to determine controversial issues of policy. Each party appearing before the court represents a particular interest and is seeking a particular outcome. And not all interests are represented. Despite the cast of parties that were involved before the Supreme Court in *Nicklinson*, it is but a fraction of those that could be expected to engage with a consultation, whether by government or the Law Commission, on the same point. *Nicklinson* represents an extreme example. But the point arises day in, day out in public law cases where the court has to determine whether it has sufficient expertise (for example, in relation to matters of national security) or where discretion vested in the decision-maker is sufficiently broad that any review beyond procedural impropriety is inappropriate (for example, decisions on the allocation of finite resources).[235]

The risk for the court is well captured by Lord Bingham: **3–31**

---

[231] That policy had been issued following another set of proceedings which raised very similar issues: *R (Purdy) v Director of Public Prosecutions* [2009] UKHL 45; [2010] 1 A.C. 345.

[232] [2014] UKSC 38; [2015] A.C. 657 at [112].

[233] [2014] UKSC 38; [2015] A.C. 657 at [125]–[129]. Interestingly, at [127] Lord Neuberger suggests that "the court would owe a duty, not least to Parliament, not to grant a declaration without having reached and expressed some idea of how the incompatibility identified by the court could be remedied". cf. para.11–12, below.

[234] [2014] UKSC 38; [2015] A.C. 657 at [223]–[234] (Lord Sumption).

[235] See generally, *De Smith's Judicial Review* (2018), paras 1–040—1–049.

> "The democratic process is likely to be subverted if, on a question of moral or political judgment, opponents of the Act achieve through the courts what they could not achieve in Parliament."[236]

But, for some, the courts have in recent years gone too far.[237] Most recently it was expressed by Lord Sumption (after he had retired from the Supreme Court) thus:

> "Judges have always made law. To decide disputes between litigants, they have to fill the gaps, supplying answers that cannot be found in existing legal sources. They have to be prepared to change existing judge-made rules if they are mistaken, redundant or outdated. The common law, which has grown up organically through the decisions of generations of judges, remains a major source of our law. Judges have traditionally done this within an existing framework of legal principle, and without trespassing on the functions of Parliament and the executive. In the last three decades, however, there has been a change of judicial mood. The courts have come to share the general suspicion of the political process and of political reasoning as an element in public decision-making. They have developed a broader concept of the rule of law which greatly enlarges their constitutional role. They have claimed wider supervisory authority over the other organs of the state. They have inched their way towards a notion of fundamental law overriding ordinary processes of political decision-making. If you were to sit in on an appeal in the Supreme Court on a question of public law, you would notice that in addition to the advocates of the parties, there are various lawyers representing 'interveners'. These are single-issue pressure groups with highly specific political agendas. Often, they are agendas which they have failed to persuade Parliament to adopt but hope to impose through the courts. Their presence is symptomatic of a profound change in the constitutional role of the courts. To adapt the famous dictum of the German military theorist Clausewitz about war, law is not the continuation of politics by other means."[238]

While matters may not be quite as stark as Sumption suggests, it emphasises the importance of the court taking care over where it draws the boundary of its own authority.

3–32 So far, we have focused on the relationship between the courts and the executive and legislature. But the separation of powers also requires a boundary between the executive and the legislature. In a sense, this is the most blurred aspect of the separation of powers in the UK because the executive necessarily sit and constitute a majority (or, at least, have the support of a majority) of the legislature. Ordinarily, when the executive has a stable majority in the House of Commons, Parliament will pass the legislation that the executive introduces. This should not mask the fact that the enactment of legislation is not an entitlement of the executive. During the Brexit process, the House of Commons became uncharacteristically assertive and not only did the government find itself unable to pass the legislation it wished (at least in relation to leaving the EU), but it found Parliament passing legislation that the government was positively opposed

---

[236] *R. (on the application of Countryside Alliance) v Attorney General* [2007] UKHL52; [2008] 1 A.C. 719 at [45]. See also, *AXA General Insurance Co Ltd v Lord Advocate* [2011] UKSC 46; 2012 S.C. (U.K.S.C.) 122, per Lord Hope at [49].

[237] The concern is not especially new and was being expressed by some commentators at the end of the last century: e.g. J. Goldsworthy, *The Sovereignty of Parliament*, p.3.

[238] J. Sumption, *Trials of the State: Law and the Decline of Politics* (London: Profile Books, 2019), pp.34–35.

to.[239] Parliament did at times appear to stray close to, if not beyond, the proper constitutional boundary as it all but micro-managed government policy on negotiations with the EU.[240] On the other hand, as we saw in Ch.1, the European Union (Withdrawal) Act 2018 conferred sweeping powers on the executive to amend the law (so as to address "deficiencies" arising from the importation of retained EU law) with limited parliamentary oversight.[241] Conferring too broad a power on the executive to amend legislation risks just as great an afront to the separation of powers as an overreaching judiciary or a micromanaging Parliament. In short, the separation of powers requires that each branch of the state be careful to respect the boundary of its own competences.

Devolution and the separation of powers

Going forward, it may be argued that the tripartite division of powers, and indeed the whole focus of the doctrine on the state, no longer provides an accurate or adequate picture of a constitution. This is not to abandon the doctrine, but to seek to strengthen it: the separation of powers in the modern age is as much concerned with the proper allocation of competence between national and supranational institutions, or between separate legislatures, as it is with the balance between legislature and executive, or legislature and the courts.[242] On this view, the separation of powers, properly understood, aims not only to safeguard individual liberty, but also to secure efficiency in government, in the sense that a given function should be allocated to the institution best fitted to discharge it.[243] In that regard, the separation of powers doctrine may acquire added significance as the devolution settlement beds down and questions are raised about the balance of competences it presently enshrines. 3–33

[239] For example, the European Union (Withdrawal) (No.2) Act 2019.

[240] Again, the European Union (Withdrawal) (No.2) Act 2019 is illustrative where it went as far as dictating the terms of a letter that the Prime Minister required to send to the President of the European Council if certain conditions were met.

[241] See para.1–15. See also para.10–43.

[242] Barber, "Prelude to the separation of powers" (2001) 60(1) C.L.J. 59.

[243] Barber, "Prelude to the separation of powers" (2001) 60(1) C.L.J. 59, under reference to John Locke, James Madison (The Federalist Papers, No.47) and the decision of the Supreme Court in *Myers v United States* (1926) 272 U.S. 52.

CHAPTER 4

Elections

INTRODUCTION

In a democratic society, a number of basic decisions have to be made about how the holders of elected office are to be chosen: by what system will a candidate be elected; who will be entitled to vote in any election; who will be entitled to stand as a candidate; how frequently shall an election be held; and how is any election campaign to be funded and conducted. The United Kingdom is under an obligation, in terms of art.3 of the First Protocol to the European Convention on Human Rights: **4–01**

> "to hold free elections at reasonable intervals by secret ballot, under conditions which will ensure the free expression of the opinion of the people in the choice of the legislature".

The substantive content of that right is a matter that has proved controversial and we shall return to it later. But there is a universal consensus that elections be by secret ballot and regular meetings of Parliament pre-date (by centuries) the modern concept of democracy but the principle endures.[1] There is a general consensus that all those above a certain age (and who are not subject to a legal disability) be entitled to vote, although there is disagreement around the edges: what should the age at which an individual becomes eligible to vote be (16 or 18?), and should criminals serving a prison sentence be automatically disenfranchised? The former arose from the Scottish independence referendum, where the voting age was 16 and there are now different voting ages for Scottish and UK parliamentary elections.[2] The latter arises from a series of court decisions

---

[1] Meeting of Parliament Act 1694 s.2 required that the pre-Union English Parliament be summoned afresh every three years. The Septennial Act 1715 extended that period (as the name suggests) to seven years only for it to be shorted to five years by the Parliament Act 1911 s.7. These were minimum requirements. The Fixed-term Parliaments Act 2011 specifies the precise date on which the general election will be held and, as a consequence, prescribes the length of Parliament (now fixed at five years). Although in practice, that period has proved a lot less "fixed" that was intended. On the 2011 Act, see para.6–02, below. On some of the technical legalities surrounding summoning a new Parliament, see O. Gay and B.K. Winetrobe, "Putting out the Writs" [1997] P.L. 385.

[2] The Smith Commission proposed that the Scottish Parliament be empowered to determine the franchise, including the voting age, for Scottish Parliamentary elections; HM Government, *Scotland in the United Kingdom: An enduring settlement* (The Stationery Office, 2015) Cm.8990. A s.30 order (Scotland Act 1998 (Modification of Schedules 4 and 5 and Transfer of Functions to the Scottish Ministers etc.) Order 2015 (SI 2015/692)) was then made to transfer competence to determine the

to the effect that art.3 of the First Protocol prohibits the automatic disenfranchisement of serving prisoners.[3] Both are discussed more fully below. The idea of free, fair and regular elections is easy to state but the devil, as all too often is the case, lurks in the detail. Political interest in reforming electoral law is normally inversely proportionate to the ability to do anything about it.[4] That is perhaps unsurprising, given the prevailing system will have produced the election of those holding power. But the result is a rather patchwork electoral law, based largely on Victorian laws, which is often confusing for both the electorate and those seeking election.[5] Until recently, one saving grace was that electoral law was largely reserved and thus, while the electoral systems employed varied, the regulatory framework was broadly consistent throughout the United Kingdom. That can no longer be said with competence over certain aspects of electoral law having been devolved and the Scottish Parliament currently considering two Bills to reform (devolved) electoral law.[6]

In this chapter we will consider the following topics. First, we will look at electoral systems. Voters in Scotland currently use three different systems depending on which representatives they are being asked to elect. Next, we will consider the question of the franchise: who is entitled to vote? Third, we will consider the rules on candidacy and who is entitled to seek election. Finally, we will review the regulations governing the funding and conduct of election campaigns. Each of those topics are concerned with "representative democracy": the selection by the electorate of individuals to take collective decisions on their behalf. Until recently, the United Kingdom could safely be described as a representative democracy. There has, however, been a recent growth in "direct democracy": the use of the referendum to canvass the opinion of the electorate on a particular question. The increasing resort to direct democracy in the United Kingdom, its interrelationship with representative democracy and its consequences for the constitution are considered in the next chapter. But before that, and before considering the detail of the UK's electoral arrangements, it is helpful to briefly consider what we mean by a "representative democracy".

4–02 The House of Commons, the Scottish Parliament and the various other elected assemblies comprise of members who have been elected to represent a certain section of the population. The section they represent is invariably determined on

voting age. The Scottish Elections (Reduction of Voting Age) Act 2015 has now reduced the voting age in Scotland to 16 (s.1 of the 2015 Act, which inserts a new s.1A in the Representation of the People Act 1983).

[3] *Hirst v United Kingdom* (2005) 42 E.H.R.R. 41; *Smith v Scott* [2007] CSIH 9; 2007 S.C. 345; *R. (on the application of Chester) v Secretary of State for Justice* [2013] UKSC 63; 2014 S.C. (U.K.S.C.) 25; [2014] A.C. 271; *McHugh v United Kingdom* (51987/08), *The Times*, 12 February 2015. This line of authority is more fully discussed below at paras 4–11—4–13, above.

[4] Independent Commission on the Voting System, *Report of the Independent Commission on the Voting System* (The Stationery Office, 1998) Cm.4090–I, para.23.

[5] A joint consultation was launched by the Law Commission, the Scottish Law Commission and the Northern Ireland Law Commission in December 2014 having reviewed electoral law with a view to bringing forward proposals for reform to rationalise the law and ensure it was fit for modern times. An interim report was issued in February 2016 (*https://www.scotlawcom.gov.uk/index.php/download_file/view/1354/592/* [Accessed 5 May 2020]) and a final report is expected in the first half of 2020.

[6] Scottish Elections (Franchise and Representation) Bill (which purports to address the prisoner voting issue; the Bill received Royal Assent in April 2020—see para.4–14, below) and the Scottish Elections (Reform) Bill.

a geographical basis.[7] But what is the role of these representatives? There are two competing theories.[8] On the one hand, these representatives can be seen as a delegate sent by their constituents to represent the views of those constituents. This requires the representative to ascertain or understand their constituents' views on a particular matter and to vote in accordance with those views. In short, they should reflect the wishes of their constituents. On the other hand, there is the "trustee" theory. A representative is not elected to simply advocate the local interests of the area they represent and to do as their constituents would wish. Once elected they are to act in the national interest. They cannot be bound by the views of their constituents because they have not participated in the debates and do not have regard to the "bigger picture". What is represented is not the people of the constituency but their interests. Which theory prevails? In the UK, the answer is neither but the ideas proved controversial in the Brexit fallout because, unusually, MPs knew exactly what their constituents thought of the issue. What was a "remain" supporting MP to do if a majority of their constituents voted to leave? The conventional view would have been that Members of Parliament are expected to advocate local causes where appropriate but equally are not expected to be bound by local views when they come to cast their vote. The party system, and the whipping of the vote, does not allow for that. The answer probably depends on the circumstance. Ordinarily, representatives act as "trustee" and their constituents are quite content that they exercise their own judgment and vote as they see fit.[9] But some matters are of greater concern to constituents. Issues that would have a direct (and normally negative) impact on the constituency are issues on which constituents will expect their representative to have regard to their views and, in some circumstances, vote in accordance with their wishes. Bearing in mind that any representative requires their mandate to be renewed by their constituents, ignoring the constituents' wishes on such issues can prove (politically) fatal.

ELECTORAL SYSTEMS

Introduction

Different systems are used to elected representatives for different bodies. In Scotland, three different systems are used: first past the post for elections to the UK Parliament; the additional member system for elections to the Scottish Parliament; and the single transferrable vote for local government elections in Scotland. A fourth system used to be used: the regional list system for elections to the European Parliament. 4–03

[7] It was not always thus. Until 1950, certain universities returned an MP, a practice that dated back to the ancient Scottish universities who had a representative in the pre-Union Parliament. The university constituencies were abolished by the Representation of the People Act 1948.

[8] What follows is a brief overview. This issue is more fully discussed in C. Morris, *Parliamentary Elections, Representation and the Law* (Oxford: Hart, 2012), Ch.2.

[9] Their MP will, after all, have ordinarily been standing under the banner of a political party and that party's election manifesto will have given voters a fair idea as to how their MP would vote on a range of issues.

UK Parliament

4–04 Elections to the UK Parliament are conducted under the first past the post system (which is also referred to as the plurality system). It is a system that is also used in Canada and the United States, but otherwise eschewed by the most of the democratic world. It requires the electoral area (in the case of elections to Westminster, the entire UK) to be divided into a number of constituencies.[10] There are currently 650 constituencies: this figure was due to be reduced to 600 in time for the election, which had been expected in 2020.[11] That timetable has slipped again. Each of these constituencies should be broadly the same size.[12] A single Member of Parliament is then returned by the electorate of each constituency. The greatest virtue of the first past the post system is its simplicity: the winner is the person who gets the most votes. There is no need to receive a majority of the votes cast (never mind a majority of the voters in the constituency) but just one more vote than the nearest rival. In other words, the winner takes it all. Casting a vote under the first past the post system is also simple. All that a voter need do is place a cross against his or her preferred candidate. And counting the votes is also simple for each ballot paper should only have one cross on it, against one candidate. Any ballot paper that has more than a single cross will be discarded as spoilt and not counted. The simplicity of the count also makes the system relatively cheap to operate. Furthermore, the first past the post system is said to provide a strong link between the constituency and the MP: whether they voted for him or her or not, each voter knows who their designated representative in Parliament is. Finally, it is said that the first past the post system should produce a clear result and with it a "strong" government. That argument lost a degree of credibility following the outcome of the 2010 UK general election, which produced the Conservative-Liberal Democrat coalition government with no one party having achieved an overall majority in the House of Commons. The 2010 election was the first time since February 1974 that the result of the general election had not produced a government with an overall

---

[10] Provision for which is made by the Parliamentary Constituencies Act 1986 (which was a consolidation of pre-existing legislation on the matter, namely the House of Commons (Redistribution of Seats) Acts 1949 to 1979).

[11] Parliamentary Constituencies Act 1986 Sch.2 para.1 requires that there be 600 constituencies. The number (600) was fixed by the Parliamentary Voting and Constituencies Act 2011 s.11(1). Prior to that amendment, the 1986 Act required the number of constituencies to "not be substantially greater than" 613, no fewer than 35 of which should be Welsh and between 16 and 18 (and ordinarily 17) of which should be in Northern Ireland. The requirement that there be not fewer than 71 Scottish constituencies was removed by the Scotland Act 1998 (Sch.9 para.1). Prior to the establishment of the Scottish Parliament, Scotland had been proportionately over-represented and the advent of devolution was regarded as the right time to equalise representation throughout Great Britain. The reduction to 600 MPs was due to come into effect in time for the 2015 general election. However, in January 2013 Parliament voted to defer the necessary boundary review until October 2018 with the effect that there will remain 650 MPs until the 2020 general election (Electoral Registration and Administration Act 2013 s.6).

[12] Parliamentary Constituencies Act 1986 Sch.2 para.2 requires that the electorate in any constituency shall be no less than 95%, and no more than 105%, of the United Kingdom electoral quota. The "United Kingdom electoral quota" is the total electorate of the United Kingdom (excluding the Isle of Wright [which shall have two constituencies], Orkney and Shetland [which shall be one constituency] and Comhairle nan Eliean Siar [which shall also be a single constituency] on account of their particular geographical locations: Sch.2 para.6) divided by 596.

majority in the House of Commons. "Normality" (somewhat unexpectedly) resumed in 2015 with a majority government being returned.[13] But as we saw in Ch.1, above the 2015 election result raised other questions about the first past the post system and minority government was to return between 2017 and 2019.

If the first past the post system is so simple and relatively cheap to operate then why do so few countries employ it? Because the first past the post system comes at a price and that price is the translation of the electorates' votes into seats allocated to the various parties in the House of Commons. As Munro put it, "[the first past the post system] provides only a rough and ready translation of electors' wishes".[14] Sometimes, it does barely that. To some, that might seem like a fairly fundamental flaw in the electoral system of a representative democracy. What does Munro mean? That is best explained by considering a number of recent election results and the number of seats won by each of the three main parties.

Table 1: Share of the vote and seats in House of Commons (1983–2019)

	2010		**2015**		**2017**		**2019**	
	% vote	**Seats (%)**	**% vote**	**Seats (%)**	**% vote**	**Seats (%)**	**% vote**	**Seats (%)**
Con	36.1%	306 (47.7%)	36.9%	331 (50.9%)	42.4%	318 (48.9%)	43.6%	365 (56.2%)
Lab	29.0%	258 (40.2%)	30.4%	232 (35.7%)	40.0%	262 (40.3%)	32.2%	203 (31.2%)
Lib Dem	23.0%	57 (8.9%)	7.9%	8 (1.2%)	7.4%	12 (1.8%)	11.5%	11 (1.7%)
Other	5.9%	20 (3.1%)	24.8%	78 (12%)	10.2%	58 (8.9%)	12.7%	71 (10.9%)
	1992		**1997**		**2001**		**2005**	
	% vote	**Seats (%)**	**% vote**	**Seats (%)**	**% vote**	**Seats (%)**	**% vote**	**Seats (%)**
Con	41.9%	336 (51.6%)	30.7%	165 (25.0%)	31.7%	166 (25.2%)	32.3%	197 (30.5%)
Lab	34.4%	271 (41.6%)	43.2%	418 (63.4%)	40.7%	412 (62.5%)	35.2%	356 (55.1%)
Lib Dem	17.8%	20 (3.1%)	16.8%	46 (7.0%)	18.3%	52 (7.9%)	22.1%	62 (9.6%)
Other	5.8%	24 (3.7%)	9.3%	30 (4.6%)	9.3%	29 (4.4%)	10.4%	31 (4.8%)

[13] V. Bogdanor, *The Coalition and the Constitution* (Oxford: Hart, 2011), pp.123–127.

[14] C.R. Munro, *Studies in Constitutional Law*, 2nd edn (London: Butterworths, 1999), p.107.

	1983[15]		1987					
	% vote	Seats (%)	% vote	Seats (%)				
Con	42.4%	397 (61.1%)	42.2%	375 (57.5%)				
Lab	27.6%	209 (32.2%)	30.8%	229 (35.1%)				
Lib Dem	25.4%	23 (3.5%)	22.6%	22 (3.4%)				
Oth-ers	4.6%	21 (3.2%)	4.4%	26 (4.0%)				

The first past the post system favours a two party system. As a consequence, the other, smaller, parties are significantly disadvantaged.[16] To succeed under the first past the post system a political party requires to have concentrated support in a number of constituencies rather than a moderate, across the board, support. For it does not matter that a party comes second, or a close third, by a narrow margin in dozens of seats as that will not translate into seats. To win a seat, a candidate need only poll one more vote than any of the others. With that comes absolutely victory in that constituency. The problems caused by the potentially unrepresentative outcomes produced by the first past the post system were easily overlooked when the two main parties (Conservatives and Labour) dominated: between 1931 and 1970, on average they received over 90 per cent of the vote between them. That is no longer the case. In 2015, more than a third of the votes were for parties other than the two main parties. As can be seen from Table 1, this was not a new issue. The Liberal Democrats (or their previous incarnations) have regularly received a much smaller allocation of the seats in the House of Commons than their share of the vote would suggest was fair. The result of the 1983 election remains, over 30 years on, one of the best examples of the deficiencies in the first past the post system: Labour and the Liberals received 27.6 per cent and 25.4 per cent of the vote respectively but the first past the post system translated that into 209 seats for Labour and 23 seat for the Liberals. The 1983 election is not an isolated example. In 1992, despite polling just under 18 per cent of the vote, the Liberals won only 3 per cent of the seats. Five years later, their share of the vote fell by 1 per cent but their share of the seats in the House of Commons more than doubled. Little had changed by 2010 when the Liberal Democrats received 23 per cent of the vote, only 6 per cent less than Labour but that translated into to 8.9 per cent of the seats for the Liberal Democrats but 40.2 per cent of the seats for Labour (not too dissimilar from 1983!). Lest it be thought that the first past the post system only disadvantages the smaller parties, Labour and the Conservatives

[15] The Liberal Democrats were then in the form of the Liberal/SDP Alliance (as they were again in 1987).

[16] The 2015 result altered that traditional narrative slightly. The SNP are now the "third party" in the House of Commons and far from being disadvantaged by the first past the post system, it benefitted them significantly. But that was a result of the fact the SNP only contested seats in Scotland. Again, see the discussion of the 2015 election in Ch.1, above.

could have cause to grumble. For example, compare the Conservative result in the 2010 election (36.1 per cent of the vote yielding 306 seats) with the Labour result in 2005 (35.2 per cent of the vote yielding 356 seats). It is also a problem in Scotland, as can be seen from Table 2, where the recent electoral dominance of the SNP has produced a Scottish representation at Westminster that is not nearly reflective of the totality of votes actually cast (with 2015 being a particularly egregious example). It is little wonder that the Liberal movement have advocated reform of the electoral system for more than a century.[17]

Table 2: Share of the vote and seats in House of Commons in respect of Scottish constituencies (2010–2019)

	2010		**2015**		**2017**		**2019**	
	% vote	**Seats (%)**	**% vote**	**Seats (%)**	**% vote**	**Seats (%)**	**% vote**	**Seats (%)**
SNP	19.9%	6 (10.2%)	50%	56 (94.9%)	36.9%	35 (59.3%)	45%	48 (81.4%)
Con	16.7%	1 (1.7%)	14.9%	1 (1.7%)	28.6%	13 (20%)	25.1%	6 (10.2%)
Lab	42%	41 (69.5%)	24.3%	1 (1.7%)	27.1%	7 (11.9%)	18.6%	1 (1.7%)
Lib Dem	18.9%	11 (18.6%)	7.5%	1 (1.7%)	6.8%	4 (6.8%)	9.5%	4 (6.8%)
Other	2.5%	0	3.3%	0	0.6%	0	1.8%	0

It is worth dwelling for a few moments longer on the outcome of the 2015 election. Until well into the count after the polls had closed, it appeared that again the electorate would have failed to return a majority government. In the end, the Conservative party passed the 326 seats needed to form a majority government. In Scotland, the SNP increased their representation: from six seats in 2010 to 56 in 2015. That left only three constituencies that did not return an SNP MP. Once those results are broken down a little further, the 2015 result highlights the case for reform. **4–05**

Table 3: 2015 General Election result in UK

Party	**Votes**	**%**	**Seats**	**%**
Conservative	11,334,920	36.9%	331	50.9%
Labour	9,347,326	30.4%	232	35.7%
Liberal Democrat	2,415,888	7.9%	8	1.2%

[17] The first past the post system survived a challenge that is was incompatible with art.3 of the First Protocol to the European Convention on Human Rights (read with art.14): *Liberal Party v United Kingdom* (1980) 4 E.H.R.R. 106.

Party	Votes	%	Seats	%
SNP	1,454,436	4.7%	56	8.6%
UKIP	3,881,129	12.6%	1	0.2%
Greens	1,157,613	3.8%	1	0.2%
Total votes cast: 30,698,210	Turnout: 66.1%		Seats available: 650	

On a purely proportionate allocation of seats (recognising that even systems of proportionate representation rarely produce an exact representation of the votes cast), the allocation of seats in the House of Commons would have been: Conservative 240; Labour 198; Liberal Democrat 51; SNP 31; UKIP 82 and Greens 25. No party would be close to a majority and the third largest party in the House of Commons would be UKIP. The most startling comparison is between the fortunes of UKIP and the Greens (whether individually or taken together) as compared to the SNP. In return for just under 1.5 million votes the SNP secured 56 seats in the House of Commons. For just under 5 million and 1.2 million votes respectively, UKIP and Greens secured a single seat each. On a proportionate allocation of seats, UKIP would have secured almost three times more seats than the SNP. In a representative democracy, an electoral system that can produce such a result ought to be a matter of concern. Of course, the SNP only fielded candidates in 59 of the 650 constituencies so necessarily have a more concentrated vote. It is a known feature of the first-past-the-post system that it rewards parties that have such a support. But the SNP anomaly cannot be justified, or explained, by pointing to the results in Scotland alone. They simply make the problem more acute.

Table 4: 2015 General Election result in Scotland

Party	Votes	%	Seats	%
SNP	1,454,436	50.0%	56	94.9%
Labour	707,147	24.3%	1	1.7%
Conservative	434,097	14.9%	1	1.7%
Liberal Democrat	219,675	7.5%	1	1.7%
Total votes case: 2,910,465	Turnout: 71.1%		Seats available: 59	

The SNP secured 95 per cent of the seats in Scotland on 50 per cent of the votes cast (which in turn represents 35.5 per cent of the registered electorate). They can be seen to be large benefactors from the current system. A purely proportionate result would have given the SNP 30 seats (still five times more than they won at the 2010 election and thus, on any measure, a significant electoral success), Labour 15 seats, the Conservative party eight or nine seats and the Liberal Democrats four or five seats. This result raises a real question about the democratic deficit in Scotland and about an electoral system that allows a landslide in terms of seats in Parliament on only half of the votes cast.

It was a condition of the coalition agreement that was forged by the Conservatives and the Liberal Democrats in May 2010 that a referendum be held on changing the voting system for elections to the House of Commons.[18] Securing electoral change was a long-held ambition of the Liberal Democrats. Alternatives to the first past the post system were studied in exhaustive detail by the independent commission appointed after the 1997 general election under the chairmanship of the late Lord Jenkins. The commission recommended that the first past the post system be replaced by a two vote mixed system, described in the *Jenkins Report* as "limited AMS" or "AV top-up". The acronym "AMS" stands for the additional member system of voting.[19] As the name implies, it is not a system that operates alone; its object, rather, is to mitigate the unfairness involved in a strictly majoritarian system. In effect, at any election involving the additional member system, there are two types of candidate: the constituency candidates, elected by the first past the post system or some similar method, and the additional or top up candidates, elected in accordance with proportional representation. "AV" stands for the alternative vote system. It works on the basis of single member constituencies in the same way as the first past the post system. It differs from the first past the post system in that the voter does not simply cast a vote for his preferred candidate, but ranks the candidates listed on the ballot paper in order of preference. If one candidate wins 50 per cent or more of the first preference votes, that candidate is elected to represent the constituency. Failing that, the candidate receiving the lowest number of first preferences is eliminated and their supporters' second preferences are redistributed. The process of elimination and redistribution continues until one candidate secures an overall majority of votes by comparison to the others.[20] But this is to use the word "majority" in the loosest sense: the alternative vote system may produce results even less representative of voter preferences than the first past the post system. The Jenkins Commission itself recognised that the alternative vote system unmitigated by a second, more proportionate method of voting, would not constitute an acceptable alternative to first past the post. Hence its recommendation for a combination of the alternative vote and additional member systems, whereby some four-fifths of MPs would be elected on the basis of single member constituencies, but using the alternative vote system rather than the first past the post system, with the remaining top up members being elected on a second vote based on regional lists. The alternative vote top up was not, however, the alternative to the first past the post system that the electorate were offered in the 2011 referendum.[21] What was offered was the alternative vote system: the system 4–06

[18] See Bogdanor, *The Coalition and the Constitution* (2011) Ch.5.

[19] As we shall see, this forms part of the system adopted for elections to the Scottish Parliament.

[20] The alternative vote system was recommended for use in county constituencies by an all-party Speaker's Conference in 1917; and in 1931, a Bill providing for the adoption of the system was actually passed by the House of Commons. The Bill was rejected by the House of Lords and nothing more was heard of it after the fall of the second Labour Government later that year.

[21] The referendum was enabled by the Parliamentary Voting System and Constituencies Act 2011. That Act provided that the minister "must" make an order bringing into force the provisions that would have introduced the alternative vote system in the event that more votes were cast for "yes" than "no" in the referendum (s.8(1)). Any by-election during the term of the 2010–2015 would have been conducted under the first past the post system with the alternative vote system being introduced

rejected by the Jenkins Commission and derided by the Liberal Democrats themselves. The alternative vote system did not offer proportionate representation thus it did not address the fundamental concern of many of those that advocated electoral reform. The electorate were presented with a choice between the first past the post system and the alternative vote system. The choice did not engender much enthusiasm amongst voters with a turnout of only 42.2 per cent (dropping as low as 27.2 per cent in one area). Those that did vote were fairly emphatic with 67.9 per cent voting "no". Thus, the first past the post system survived, warts and all, and the prospect of electoral reform in relation to the House of Commons appears to have retreated to the very distant horizon. In the immediate aftermath of the 2015 general election, there was renewed noise about the unfairness of the first-past-the-post system: the United Kingdom Independence Party (UKIP) in particular were unhappy about their return in terms of seats. But given the continuing dominance of Brexit in the political agenda, it is unlikely that anything will be done to address the electoral system. And given any attempt would likely require a further referendum,[22] and a more proportionate system would likely produce more regular coalition or minority governments, it is hard to foresee much enthusiasm for revisiting this issue for the foreseeable future. It is, however, noteworthy that when the House of Commons has had to choose an electoral system for other representative bodies, it has invariably chosen some form of proportionate representation.

Scottish Parliament

4–07 Voters in the Scottish Parliamentary elections require to cast two votes: one for a constituency MSP and one for a "regional" MSP. Constituency MSPs are elected using the first past the post system (styled the "simple majority system" in the Scotland Act 1998) while "regional" MSPs are elected using the additional member system of proportionate representation.[23] There are 73 single member constituencies for the Scottish Parliament.[24] There are eight "regions", each

---

for the 2015 general election (s.8(3)). In the event, there were more "no" votes than "yes" and, accordingly, the relevant provisions of the 2011 Act have now been repealed (s.8(2); Parliamentary Voting System and Constituencies Act 2011 (Repeal of Alternative Vote Provisions) Order 2011 (SI 2011/1702)).

[22] See para.5–06, below.

[23] Scotland Act 1998 s.1(2) and (3).

[24] Scotland Act 1998 Sch.1 para.1. The Scotland Act originally provided that the constituencies for the Scottish Parliament would be the same as those for the UK Parliament (save for Orkney and Shetland being split into separate constituencies for the purposes of the Scottish Parliament). However, when Scottish representation was reduced at Westminster it was not thought appropriate to reduce the number of MSPs. Accordingly, the Scotland Act was amended by the Scottish Parliament (Constituencies) Act 2004 and the number of constituencies became a matter regulated by Order in Council (Sch.1 para.6). The matter is currently regulated by the Scottish Parliament (Constituencies and Regions) Order 2014 (SI 2014/501) Sch.1). The size of each constituency should be as near the "electoral quota" as is "practicable" (Scotland Act 1998 Sch.1 para.12 r.2(1)). The "electoral quota" is the total electorate divided by 71 (Scotland Act 1998 Sch.1 para.12 r.2(3)). Originally, determination of constituencies of the Scottish Parliament was a reserved matter (Scotland Act 1998 Sch.4 para.4) but the Scotland Act 2016 conferred competence upon the Parliament to vary these (subject to the requirement of a 'super-majority', on which, see para.6–20, below).

returning seven MSPs.[25] Accordingly, there are 129 MSPs in total. Candidates may stand as both a constituency candidate and a regional candidate in the same election.[26] But a candidate may only stand for election in one constituency[27] and in one region.[28] So far as the regions are concerned, a registered political party[29] may list up to 12 candidates in each region but the list may include only one person.[30] The purpose of the regional members, and allocating those seats under a system of proportionate representation, is to ameliorate the effects of the first past the post system. The consequence should be a parliament that is more representative of the votes actually cast. As Table 5 shows, the electoral system has been fairly successful in this respect.

Table 5: Results of General Elections to the Scottish Parliament (2003–2016)[31]

Party/ Year	**Constituency**		**Regional**		
2003	**% vote**	**Seats (%)**	**% vote**	**Seats (%)**	**Total Seats (%)**
Lab	34.6%	46 (63.0%)	29.3%	4	50 (38.8%)
SNP	23.8%	9	20.9%	18	27 (20.9%)
Lib Dem	15.4%	13	11.8%	4	17 (13.2%)
Con	16.6%	3	15.5%	15	18 (14.0%)
Other	7.7%	2	16.5%	15	17 (13.2%)

[25] The current regions are: Central Scotland, Glasgow, Highlands and Islands, Lothian, Mid Scotland and Fife, North East Scotland, South Scotland and West Scotland (Scottish Parliament (Constituencies and Regions) Order 2014 (SI 2014/501) Sch.2). Each region consists of specific constituencies, which are listed in the 2014 Order. The electorate in each region should, as far as is "practicable", be the same (Scotland Act 1998 Sch.1 para.13 r.2).

[26] Scotland Act 1998 s.5(1).

[27] Scotland Act 1998 s.5(2).

[28] Scotland Act 1998 s.5(8).

[29] As defined as Pt II of the Political Parties, Elections and Referendums Act 2000 ("PPERA") (Scotland Act 1998 s.5(9)). The (legal) concept of a political party was first introduced by the Registration of Political Parties Act 1998.

[30] Scotland Act 1998 s.5(6).

[31] Source, Scottish Parliament, "Election Results", *http://www.parliament.scot/msps/election-results.aspx* [Accessed 7 May 2020].

2007	% vote	Seats (%)	% vote	Seats (%)	Total Seats (%)
Lab	32.1%	37 (50.1%)	29.1%	9 (16.1%)	46 (35.7%)
SNP	32.9%	21 (28.9%)	31.0%	26 (46.4%)	47 (36.4%)
Lib Dem	16.2%	11 (15.1%)	11.3%	5 (8.9%)	16 (12.4%)
Con	16.6%	4 (5.5%)	13.9%	13 (23.2%)	17 (13.2%)
Other	0.2%	0 (0%)	8.9%	3 (5.4%)	3 (2.4%)
2011	**% vote**	**Seats (%)**	**% vote**	**Seats (%)**	**Total Seats (%)**
Lab	31.7%	15 (20.5%)	26.3%	22 (39.3%)	37 (28.7%)
SNP	45.4%	53 (72.6%)	44.0%	16 (28.6%)	69 (53.5%)
Lib Dem	7.9%	2 (2.7%)	5.2%	3 (5.4%)	5 (3.9%)
Con	13.9%	3 (4.1%)	12.4%	12 (21.4%)	15 (11.6%)
Other	1.1%	0 (0%)	12.1%	3 (5.4%)	3 (2.3%)
2016	**% vote**	**Seats (%)**	**% vote**	**Seats (%)**	**Total Seats (%)**
Lab	22.7%	3 (4.1%)	20.0%	21 (37.5%)	24 (18.6%)
SNP	46.7%	59 (80%)	43.7%	4 (7.1%)	63 (48.8%)
Lib Dem	7.9%	4 (5.5%)	5.5%	1 (1.8%)	5 (3.9%)

Con	22.1%	7 (9.6%)	24.0%	24 (42.9%)	31 (24.0%)
Other[32]	0.6%	0 (0%)	6.9%	6 (10.7%)	6 (4.7%)

In 2007, as a result of the additional member system, the result of the election was altered: on the first past the post votes alone, Labour would have had a majority in the Scottish Parliament of a single seat, having won 37 of the 73 constituencies on offer. However, once the regional members were added, the SNP became the largest party, albeit without an overall majority, and proceeded to govern as a minority administration. The 2011 and 2016 elections also provide good examples of the effects of the additional member system. On both occasions, based on first past the post votes, the SNP won a landslide, securing the vast majority of the seats but on only 45 per cent or so of the vote. The final result, however, still handed the SNP more seats than a strictly proportionate allocation would have afforded them (albeit the gain was marginal in 2016) and allowed them to continue to govern and, in 2011, as a majority government. The 2003 election saw a similar correction of a first past the post landslide: this time reducing Labour's 63 per cent of the constituency seats to only 39 per cent of the total number of seats and thus compelling them to govern in coalition with the Liberal Democrats. So, in securing a more representative result, and in avoiding one party governing with a majority as a result of a grossly exaggerated allocation of seats, the combination of the first past the post system with the additional member system has served the Scottish Parliament reasonably well.

As is common with systems of proportionate representation, coalition or minority government often results. This was true of the Scottish Parliament until the 2011 election in which the SNP achieved the supposedly impossible: an absolute majority. There are good reasons why that was meant to be impossible and we will touch on those in a moment. But before that, it is necessary to explain how the regional seats are allocated under the additional member system.

The method of allocating the seven available seats in each region is complex **4–08**
and will only be outlined here. Once the regional votes have been counted, each party and each individual candidate is allotted a "regional figure" calculated in accordance with a formula prescribed by s.7(2) of the Scotland Act 1998. The first regional seat is awarded to the party or individual candidate having the highest regional figure. Where a seat is awarded to a party in this way, it is then necessary, in order to maintain proportionality in the distribution of seats, to recalculate that party's regional figure. Again, the arithmetic is prescribed by the Act. Each successive seat is awarded to the party or candidate having, on that particular round, the highest regional figure, until all seven seats are filled. If, at any stage of the process, that figure is shared between two parties or between a party and an individual candidate, the Act provides that a regional seat shall be allocated to each. The use of party lists in the election of regional members obviates the need for by-elections should a regional seat fall vacant during the life of the Parliament: the regional returning officer will simply notify the Presiding Officer of the next named nominee in the appropriate party's regional list (no

[32] The only "Other" party that won seats at the 2016 election was the Green Party.

doubt having first ascertained that he or she is willing to serve). On purely practical grounds, the Scotland Act makes no provision for regional by-elections in other situations, as where a party's regional list is exhausted, or where a regional seat held by an individual candidate falls vacant. This has happened only once so far (following the death of Margo MacDonald MSP in April 2014). Having been elected as a regional MSP from a list that contained only her name, the seat remained vacant until the 2016 election. Constituency MSPs, however, are replaced during the life of the Parliament by means of a by-election. Where the seat of a constituency MSP falls vacant by reason of the death, disqualification or resignation of the incumbent, the Presiding Officer will appoint a date for a by-election to fill the vacancy unless such date would fall within three months of the date of the next ordinary general election. In that event, the seat will remain vacant until filled in the usual way.

4–09 It is worth pausing to reflect on why it was thought necessary to devise a system that produced a more proportionate result. Democratic claims cannot be enough. If they were, the continuing use of the first past the post system for the House of Commons would be indefensible. But an electoral system must also serve the institution it selects members for. The obvious difference between Holyrood and Westminster is the absence of a second chamber in Edinburgh. As discussed in more detail in Ch.6, the House of Lords acts as a form of handbrake on the House of Commons (dominated as it usually is by the executive): the executive can almost always prevail (using the Parliament Acts if necessary) but, like driving a car with the handbrake on, forcing legislation through against the wishes of the House of Lords takes longer, makes more noise and risks causing longer term damage. Had the Scottish Parliament been elected using only the first past the post system there would have been no equivalent "handbrake". Instead, the handbrake function is built into the electoral system: by ensuring a more proportionate representation the chances of a single party having an overall majority are significantly reduced. That requires the executive (where it lacks an overall majority) to either compromise when forming a coalition with one or more of the other parties or to govern as a minority administration and thus compromise on its legislative agenda. It was not expected that the electoral system adopted for the Scottish Parliament would produce a single party majority government. That made the 2011 election result all the more remarkable. For when there is a single party majority government at Holyrood, there is no effective "handbrake" function on the executive.[33] That gives rise to obvious concerns (as discussed in Ch.3) in relation to the separation powers.

4–10 In the aftermath of the 2014 referendum, commitments were made to transfer legislative competent to the Scottish Parliament in relation to various aspects of electoral law. That was, in the Scotland Act 2016, duly done. Now the Parliament has legislative competence over various aspects of electoral law, including the franchise, the electoral system, the number of constituencies, the number of regions and the number of members returned from each region. But with the transfer of these powers came the introduction of the concept of a "super-majority" to pass legislation related to "protected subject-matter". In short, any

[33] That a majority government was, against expectations, returned under the electoral system perhaps explains the introduction of "protected subject-matter" and the need for a qualified (two-thirds) majority to pass certain legislation. See para.6–20, below.

legislation that makes changes to the aspects of electoral law that were devolved by the 2016 Act engages the requirement for a two-thirds majority to secure its passage. It is incumbent upon the Presiding Officer, after the last point in the legislative process at which a Bill can be amended but before a vote on whether to pass it, to decide whether any provision in the Bill relates to a protected subject-matter.[34] Where the President Officer decides that a provision of the Bill does relation to a protected subject-matter, the Bill cannot pass unless two-thirds of the MSPs vote in favour of it.[35] Given the obvious scope for abuse by a party with an overall majority, and in the absence of a revising chamber, a "super-majority" seemed an inevitable consequence of devolving these competences to the Parliament.[36]

Local government

Finally, Scottish voters use another form of proportional representation when electing their local government representatives: the single transferrable vote. These were the only Scottish elections that were initially devolved to the Scottish Parliament and it was the Scottish Parliament that adopted the single transferrable vote under the Local Governance (Scotland) Act 2004. The single transferrable vote was first used at the local government elections in 2007. It requires each local government area[37] to be divided into a number of wards. There is a separate election for each ward and each ward returns three or four councillors.[38] With the single transferrable vote the voter does not merely vote for one party or candidate, but expresses their preferences for the candidates in numerical order. The first candidate whose "first preference votes" meet a predetermined quota is awarded the first seat in the constituency.[39] The voter's second (and subsequent) preference votes are then redistributed to the appropriate candidates until someone else achieves the quota figure. If no candidate meets the quota on the first round of counting, the candidate receiving the lowest number of first preferences is eliminated, with second and subsequent preferences being redistributed to other candidates as appropriate. The process continues until enough candidates have met the quota to fill the seats available in the constituency. Complex it may be, but it was adopted in Northern Ireland with the acknowledged aim of reducing the risk of the electorate splitting along sectarian lines and in practice has worked well there. It also appears to have worked well in the two Scottish local government elections that have been held under it.[40] 4–11

[34] Scotland Act 1998 s.31(2A). It is interesting to note that, quite sensibly, the Presiding Officer has to form this view after the last point at which the Bill can be amended. That contrasts with his duties in relation to legislative competence, where that certification is given at the start of a Bill's process and does not need revised once it is in final form.

[35] Scotland Act 1998 s.31A.

[36] It does raise other issues, however, and these are considered at para.6–17, below.

[37] A "local government area" is defined by the Local Government etc. (Scotland) Act 1994, which in its present form provides for Scotland to be subdivided into 32 local government areas.

[38] Local Governance (Scotland) Act 2004 s.1(2).

[39] That quota, and the allocation of seats, is prescribed by the Scottish Local Government Election Rules (Scottish Local Government Elections Order 2011 (SSI 2011/399) Sch.1 rr.47–53).

[40] The single transferable vote was recommended for adoption in the UK's urban constituencies by the 1917 Speaker's Conference, and was actually used in a number of the old multi-member university seats until their abolition in 1948. The principal objection to its adoption for Westminster

European Parliament

4–12 For completeness, it is worth noting the system that previously applied to elections to the European Parliament. Those were conducted under the regional list system.[41] This operated in much the same way as the second vote for the Scottish Parliament. At the time of the United Kingdom's exit from the European Union, 73 MEPs were elected to represent it.[42] The United Kingdom was divided into a number of electoral regions: Scotland, Wales and Northern Ireland each constitute a region and England and Gibraltar were divided into nine regions.[43] The 73 seats in the European Parliament were then divided between the regions. In the year before a European Parliamentary election, the Electoral Commission[44] was required to review the distribution of MEPs between the regions and report to the Secretary of State. In carrying out that review, the Commission had to consider whether the ratio of electors to MEPs is as nearly as possible the same for each region. If it is not, the Commission's report to the Secretary of State had to include a recommendation of a distribution of seats that would achieve that result.[45] At the last UK elections to the European Parliament, Scotland returned six MEPs.[46]

On polling day, voters were presented with a ballot paper that lists each of the political parties that are fielding candidates along with any independent candidates. It was a "closed list" system: the voter did not rank a party's candidates in order of preference, they simply vote for their preferred party (or independent candidate) and any seats were allocated in accordance with the order in which candidates have been ranked by their party.[47] Once the votes had been tallied for the region, seats were allocated using a quota system.[48] A party's "quota" was the number of votes they received divided by the number of seats they have already been allocated plus one. How this system operated is probably best illustrated with an example rather than more words:

---

elections, at least, was identified by the Independent Commission on the Voting System, *Report of the Independent Commission on the Voting System* in the following terms (para.94): "In Britain, with a population of 58.5 million as against Ireland's 3.5 million, the multi-member STV constituencies (unless there were to be a massive increase in the number of MPs, which the Commission regards as unacceptable) would need to be approximately four or five times as large as the Irish constituencies. This would make them geographically far-flung in rural or semi-rural areas, and, even in concentrated urban areas, constituencies of about 350,000 electors would entail a very long ballot paper and a degree of choice which might be deemed oppressive rather than liberating."

[41] European Parliamentary Elections Act 2002 s.2. In Northern Ireland, the single transferrable vote system is employed: s.3 of the 2002 Act. That is the system employed in Scottish local government elections and is explained at para.3–10, below. Obviously, these elections are of historical interest only now.

[42] That number fluctuated as the size of the European Union has changed. When the 2002 Act was first enacted, the number was 87 but was reduced by the European Union Act 2011 s.16(2).

[43] The regions were prescribed in Sch.1 to the 2002 Act and were: East Midlands, Eastern, London, North East, North West, South East, South West (which includes Gibraltar), West Midlands and Yorkshire and the Humber.

[44] On which, see para.4–16.

[45] European Parliamentary Elections Act 2002 Sch.1A.

[46] European Parliamentary Elections Act 2002 s.1(3).

[47] European Parliamentary Elections Act 2002 s.2(8).

[48] European Parliamentary Elections Act 2002 s.2(5)–(7).

Table 6: Allocation of seats under regional list system

	Region x; six seats to be allocated					
Party	**Seat 1**	**Seat 2**	**Seat 3**	**Seat 4**	**Seat 5**	**Seat 6**
A	250,000/1	250,000/1	250,000/2 125,000	250,000/2 125,000	250,000/2 125,000	250,000/2 125,000
B	450,000/1	450,000/2 225,000	450,000/2 225,000	450,000/3 150,000	450,000/3 150,000	450,000/4 112,500
C	100,000/1	100,000/1	100,000/1	100,000/1	100,000/1	100,000/1
D	175,000/1	175,000/1	175,000/1	175,000/1	175,000/2 87,500	175,000/2 87,500
	Party B	**Party A**	**Party B**	**Party D**	**Party B**	**Party A**

In that example, the final seat allocation is three for party B, two for party A and one for party D. In percentage terms, party B won 50 per cent of the seats, party A won 33.3 per cent of the seats and party D won 16.7 per cent of the seats. Their respective share of the vote was: party A 25.6 per cent, party B 46.2 per cent, party C 10.2 per cent and party D 17.9 per cent. So, we can see that the regional list system also produced a broadly proportionate allocation of seats.

THE FRANCHISE

The franchise (that is, who is entitled to vote[49]) is determined by the Representation of the People Act 1983. That Act was itself a consolidation of the pre-existing law that dated back to Victorian times[50] but has been heavily amended, most recently (and most significantly) by the Political Parties, Elections and Referendums Act 2000. Critical to being entitled to vote is being registered to vote.[51] Entitlement to be registered depends (together with criteria relating to age, capacity and citizenship) on being resident in the constituency or electoral area on the "relevant date". Previously, the 1983 Act prescribed a single annual qualifying date[52] on which a person's residence fell to be tested. The 2000 Act amended s.4 of the 1983 Act so as to define the "relevant date" as the date on which an application for registration is made or, in the case of a person applying for registration pursuant to a declaration of local connection or a service 4–13

[49] There are detailed rules on *how* the franchise is to be exercised. For Scottish elections, see; Scottish Parliament (Elections etc.) Order 2015 (SSI 2015/425), Pt 2.

[50] The Representation of the People Act 1983 (1983 Act) is, according to its long title, a consolidation of the Representation of the People Acts of 1949, 1969, 1977, 1978 and 1980. The 1949 Act was again a consolidation of "certain enactments relating to parliamentary . . . elections" (according to its long title), the main such enactment being the Representation of the People Act 1867.

[51] Being registered to vote is also a precondition to being entitled to make a donation to a political party: see para.4–19, below.

[52] 10 October.

declaration, the date on which the declaration was made. This "rolling system" allows a person to be entered on and removed from the electoral register at any time of year.

Sections 5 and 7 of the 1983 Act make provision as to the meaning of "residence" for the purposes of registration.[53] Patients resident in a mental hospital, whether on a voluntary or detained basis, are able either to register in respect of the hospital, if they are likely to be there some time, or to register at some other address (such as the address the patient would regard as their home address were they not in hospital). Alternatively, such patients may make a "declaration of local connection". Remand prisoners[54] may register at the establishment where they are being held, at some other address or by means of a declaration of local connection. Convicted prisoners who are entitled to vote (that being a limited number of Scottish prisoners in relation to Scottish elections only) are invariably registered at where they would have been living but for their incarceration.[55] Homeless persons who would not otherwise be able to satisfy a residence-based test may also make a declaration of local connection. Declarations of local connection must state the declarant's name, an address to which correspondence may be sent (or an undertaking to collect correspondence from the electoral registration office), the date of the declaration and a statement that the declarant falls into one of the categories permitted to make a declaration of local connection. They must also state that the declarant conforms to the nationality requirements and is 18 years of age or over (or, if not, his date of birth). Section 7 of the 2000 Act repeals and replaces s.12 of the 1983 Act, enabling service personnel to vote in the same way as other voters or as overseas electors, as well as by way of a service declaration. Last, s.12 of and Sch.4 to the 2000 Act make significant changes to the rules relating to absent voting (voting by post or by proxy) at parliamentary or local government elections, including local elections in Scotland.

4–14 The scope of the franchise is largely uncontroversial, save for the blanket exclusion of convicted prisoners. That matter has attracted significant judicial attention in recent years. The 1983 Act deprives any person who has been convicted of a criminal offence and who is serving a prison sentence (irrespective of length) of the right to vote.[56] To that extent, the 1983 Act is incompatible with art.3 of the First Protocol to the European Convention on Human Rights and a declaration to that effect was first made by the (Scottish) Electoral Registration Court in 2007.[57] The Grand Chamber of the European Court of Human Rights has declined to change its stance on the correct interpretation of art.3 of the First

---

[53] Without prejudice to the case law that has accumulated on whether a person is resident in a constituency such as to be entitled to be registered to vote there, see, e.g. *Scott v Phillips*, 1974 S.L.T. 32; *Hipperson v Newbury District Electoral Registration Officer* [1985] Q.B. 1060 CA (Civ Div).

[54] For whom provision is made in the new s.7A of the 1983 Act, inserted by the Political Parties, Elections and Referendums Act 2000.

[55] Scottish Elections (Franchise and Representation) Act 2020 ss.5 and 6. Ultimately a prisoner can be registered at the address of the prison but there are a range of other options and that prison address is very much a last resort.

[56] See s.3 of the 1983 Act.

[57] *Smith v Scott* [2007] CSIH 9; 2007 S.C. 345. The matter was most recently considered by the Supreme Court in *R. (on the application of Chester) v Secretary of State for Justice* [2013] UKSC 63; 2014 S.C. (U.K.S.C.) 25; [2014] A.C. 271. Interestingly, as is discussed in the following chapter, art.3 of the First Protocol to the European Convention was not infringed by the blanket disenfranchisement

Protocol.[58] The Supreme Court has now accepted the Grand Chamber's interpretation.[59] That has not been an end of the matter. Parliament, that is the Westminster Parliament, has not remedied the incompatibility in so far as elections for which it has sole legislative responsibility in relation to the franchise are concerned. Indeed, it has specifically refused to do so.[60] In April 2020, the Scottish Parliament, using its new powers in relation to the franchise, passed the Scottish Elections (Franchise and Representation) Act 2020. That Act excludes prisoners serving a period not exceeding 12 months from the general disenfranchisement.[61] Whether that is sufficient to satisfy the Strasbourg Court, in particular having regard to the presumption against sentences of less than 12 months that must seriously reduce the number of prisoners that benefit from the change,[62] remains to be seen. The saga of the right of prisoners to vote is considered in more detail in Ch.11 in the context of the Human Rights Act 1998 and the limits of a declaration of incompatibility.[63] For present purposes, it is sufficient to note that: it is acceptable, in terms of art.3 of the First Protocol, for some convicted prisoners to be disenfranchised as a result of their imprisonment, but such disenfranchisement must be proportionate; a blanket ban on serving prisoners voting in an election is not proportionate and is incompatible with art.3 of the First Protocol; there is a clear and consistent line of authority from the Grand Chamber to that effect; that line of authority has been accepted (although to some extent reluctantly) by the Supreme Court; s.3 of the 1983 Act is therefore incompatible with art.3 of the First Protocol; but it is for (the Westminster) Parliament to address the issue as it is not possible to read the offending section in such a way as to remedy the incompatibility. Despite the UK being required, as a matter of international law, to amend the 1983 Act so as to address the incompatibility, there is (perhaps understandably) little political enthusiasm for enfranchising even a proportion of the prison population. Those prisoners that were disenfranchised at the 2010 UK general election, and who complained to the Strasbourg Court, had their complaint that their right under art.3 of the First Protocol had been infringed upheld but were refused any financial compensation.[64] At the time of writing, 13 years after the declaration of incompatibility in *Smith v Scott*, the blanket disenfranchisement of serving prisoners remains in place for all elections other than those to the Scottish Parliament and Scottish local authorities.

---

of serving prisoners for the Scottish independence referendum: *Moohan, Petitioner* [2014] UKSC 67; 2015 S.L.T. 2 (a point on which the Supreme Court split 5:2).

[58] *Hirst v United Kingdom* (2005) 42 E.H.R.R. 41; *Scoppola v Italy* (2012) 56 E.H.R.R. 19.

[59] *R. (on the application of Chester) v Secretary of State for Justice* [2013] UKSC 63; 2014 S.C. (U.K.S.C.) 25; [2014] A.C. 271, where it was made clear (albeit with some reluctance on the part of several justices) that the European Court's jurisprudence on art.3 of the First Protocol stands.

[60] There are arguments both ways, as Laws LJ explained in *R. (on the application of Chester) v Secretary of State for Justice* [2010] EWCA Civ 1439; [2011] 1 W.L.R. 1436 at [32]–[34].

[61] Scottish Elections (Franchise and Representation) Act 2020 s.5.

[62] cf. the response of the Faculty of Advocates to the consultation on the Bill: *http://www.advocates.org.uk/media/3045/final-faculty-response-6-march-2019-3.pdf* [Accessed 5 May 2020].

[63] See para.11–13.

[64] *McHugh v United Kingdom* (51987/08), *The Times*, 12 February 2015.

CANDIDATES FOR ELECTION

4–15 There are relatively few rules on who may stand as a candidate for election to the House of Commons. Statute does not positively define who may be a candidate.[65] Instead, a person may stand as a candidate for election provided they do not fall within any of the prescribed exclusions. "Aliens" (persons who are neither Commonwealth citizens nor British protected person nor a citizen of the Republic of Ireland)[66] are not eligible to be members of Parliament.[67] A candidate must have attained the age of 18 on the day they are nominated.[68] Mental illness is no longer a bar to membership of the House of Commons.[69] Peers that have a seat in the House of Lords cannot be a member of the House of Commons, but those hereditary peers who are excluded in terms of the House of Lords Act 1999 may now be a member of the House of Commons.[70] The House of Lords Reform Act 2014 makes provision for members of the House of Lords to resign their membership of that House. A peer that resigns in terms of that Act becomes eligible for membership of the House of Commons.[71] Other persons that are excluded from membership of the House of Commons include: clergy that sit in the House of Lords as Lords Spiritual[72]; certain bankrupts[73]; holders of any office prescribed by the House of Commons Disqualification Act 1975[74]; persons convicted of an offence and sentenced to a period of imprisonment of one year or more, while detained (or unlawfully at large) in pursuance of that sentence[75]; a person convicted of being personally guilty of corrupt practices[76]; a person convicted of being personally guilty of illegal practices.[77] Where a person wishes to stand as a candidate on behalf of a party, that party must be a registered party in accordance with the Political Parties, Elections and Referendums Act 2000.[78]

---

[65] "Candidate" is defined by statute (1983 Act s.118A, inserted by s.135(2) of PPERA) but it is restricted to the time after the election has been called.

[66] British Nationality Act 1981 s.50(1); Ireland Act 1949 s.3; Electoral Administration Act 2006 s.18.

[67] Act of Settlement 1700 s.3; *Tipperary* case (1875) 3 O'M. & H. 19.

[68] Electoral Administration Act 2006 s.17.

[69] Mental Health (Discrimination) Act 2013 s.1(2).

[70] House of Lords Act 1999 ss.1–3.

[71] House of Lords Reform Act 2014 s.4(5).

[72] House of Commons (Removal of Clergy Disqualification) Act 2001.

[73] Insolvency Act 1986 ss.426A–427 (as amended by the Enterprise Act 2002 s.266).

[74] The list is constantly changing but includes: most judicial office holders (House of Commons Disqualification Act 1975 Sch.1) members of a wide range of bodies (from the Forestry Commission to the UK Sports Council including civil servants and police officers) (Sch.2) and an even wider range of specific offices (Sch.3).

[75] Representation of the People Act 1981 s.1. That produces the frankly absurd result that a prisoner serving a sentence of less than 12 months can stand for election but is prohibited from voting in that election. The Recall of MPs Act 2015 now provides that an MP that is sentenced to a term of imprisonment or suspended from the House of Commons for at least 21 days may face a "recall petition" that would trigger a by-election in their constituency should a sufficient number of their constituents support such a move. There have so far been three recall petitions, two of which were successful. Details are set out in a recent House of Commons Library Briefing Paper: *https://researchbriefings.parliament.uk/ResearchBriefing/Summary/SN05089* [Accessed 13 May 2020].

[76] 1983 Act s.160. The disqualification lasts for five years from conviction.

[77] 1983 Act s.159. The disqualification lasts for three years from conviction.

[78] PPERA s.22(1). This does not prevent a person standing as an "independent" candidate. On registration of political parties, see para.4–17, below.

A candidate must pay a deposit, which is lost in the event they receive fewer than one-twentieth of the votes cast.[79] Qualification to stand for election to, and to be a member of, the Scottish Parliament is prescribed by s.15 of the Scotland Act 1998 and the Scottish Parliament (Disqualification) Order 2015.[80] Those provisions largely replicate the disqualifications that apply to the House of Commons.

CONDUCT OF ELECTIONS

Introduction

Article 3 of the First Protocol to the European Convention on Human Rights requires that the state provide for "free elections . . . which will ensure the free expression of the opinion of the people". Accordingly, the conduct of election campaigns is a heavily regulated matter. Prior to 2000, the controls on the conduct of elections focused on the constituency level of an election campaign: there were virtually no controls on the conduct of the national campaign or on the expenditure incurred by parties at that level, or indeed on the financing of political parties. The Political Parties, Elections and Referendums Act 2000 (PPERA) changed all of that. The PPERA made fresh provision for the registration and regulation of political parties,[81] for the financing and expenses of registered political parties, for the conduct of election and referendum campaigns and for proceedings in connection with elections.[82] The older controls on the conduct of campaigns at a constituency level, provided for by the Representation of the People Act 1983, continue in force. Before turning to consider the various provisions introduced by PPERA, it is helpful to start with the body that was created to oversee this new system of regulation of elections, the Electoral Commission. 4–16

The Electoral Commission

The Electoral Commission was established by Pt 1 of the PPERA. Its statutory remit is considerable. It is charged, first, with reporting on the administration of, inter alia, parliamentary general elections, European parliamentary general elections,[83] Scottish parliamentary general elections, the election of police and crime commissioners[84] and certain referendums. Its other functions include 4–17

[79] 1983 Act Sch.1 rr.9 and 53(3). The deposit is, and has been since 1985, currently £500.

[80] Scottish Parliament (Disqualification) Order 2015 (SI 2015/350).

[81] Re-enacting, with modifications, the provisions of the Registration of Political Parties Act 1998.

[82] It should, however, be noted that many of the amendments made to earlier legislation by the Political Parties, Elections and Referendums Act 2000 do not apply to Scottish local government elections (which are a devolved matter).

[83] European elections remain part of the statutory remit at the time of writing but is due to be repealed on 31 December 2020 (when the transitional period ends): European Parliamentary Elections Etc. (Repeal, Revocation, Amendment and Saving Provisions) (United Kingdom and Gibraltar) (EU Exit) Regulations 2018.

[84] As added by the Police Reform and Social Responsibility Act 2011 (which applies only to England and Wales).

reviewing, and reporting to the Secretary of State on matters relating to elections and referendums, including the distribution of seats at parliamentary elections, the conduct of local government elections, the registration and regulation of political parties and political party funding.[85] It must be consulted on changes to electoral law.[86] It may express views on party political broadcasting, to which independent broadcasters are required to have regard.[87] It may provide advice and assistance on electoral matters to bodies including registered political parties, the Scottish Parliament, Scottish Government and councils constituted under the Local Government etc. (Scotland) Act 1994.[88] More broadly, it has a general duty to promote public awareness of electoral systems, systems of local and national government in the United Kingdom (including the devolved administrations, but excluding Scottish local government unless the Scottish Ministers by order provide otherwise).[89]

In January 2007, the Committee on Standards in Public Life published *A Review of the Electoral Commission*.[90] It was withering in its assessment of the Commission's performance since its establishment. During that time, as the *Review* points out, there has been a marked fall in confidence in the integrity of the system of electoral administration and in the framework for the regulation of political party funding—both matters falling within the statutory remit of the Commission.[91] The width of that remit, in the view of the Committee on Standards in Public Life, is at the root of the problem.[92] It recommended a comprehensive reconfiguration of the Electoral Commission so as to focus its role as the regulator of party funding and campaign expenditure on the one hand, and electoral administration on the other. The result was the Political Parties and Elections Act 2009, which strengthened the Electoral Commission's investigatory powers[93] and provides the Commission with a range of civil sanctions that it can

---

[85] The Commission does not, however, have power to review or report on (among other things) the funding of political parties under s.97 of the Scotland Act 1998; the conduct of referendums held pursuant to an Act of the Scottish Parliament (although it was given a role in the independence referendum by the Scottish Independence Referendum Act 2013 s.12); or (subject to s.19 of PPERA) on the conduct of local elections in Scotland.

[86] PPERA, s.7. This includes changes to provision made by the Scottish Ministers under s.12 of the Scotland Act 1998 or the Secretary of State (under s.12A) in relation to the conduct of elections in Scotland.

[87] PPERA s.11.

[88] PPERA s.10.

[89] PPERA s.13.

[90] Committee on Standards in Public Life, *A Review of the Electoral Commission, 11th Report* (The Stationery Office, 2007) Cm.7006.

[91] This fall in confidence the Committee attributes, on the one hand, to the perceived increase in voter fraud (driven in part by the introduction of such initiatives as on-demand postal voting); and, on the other, to the controversy surrounding undeclared loans taken out by the major political parties prior to the 2005 general election. The latter prompted the Prime Minister to appoint Sir Hayden Phillips to conduct a review of party funding. Sir Hayden's report, *Strengthening Democracy: Fair and Sustainable Funding of Political Parties* (The Stationery Office, 2007) was published in March 2007. In relation to the proper role of the Electoral Commission, it endorses the views of the Committee on Standards in Public Life in every material respect.

[92] As the *Review* observes, the various functions with which the Commission is charged are not mutually compatible and, in choosing to concentrate on issues such as the promotion of public engagement in the electoral process, the Commission has neglected its more contentious regulatory roles.

[93] See now PPERA s.146 and Sch.19B.

now impose.[94] The introduction of these civil sanctions was important: previously the Commission faced a choice of doing nothing or instigating a criminal prosecution. That had led to the Commission, on occasion, to take no action in response to acknowledged breaches of PPERA.[95] A more proportionate response is now available to the Commission and is to be welcomed.

Registration of political parties

Until the introduction of a voluntary register by the Registration of Political Parties Act 1998, there was no system for the registration of political parties in the UK. The PPERA changed that and the whole regulatory regime contained in that Act now revolves around the registration of political parties. Unless registered, a party cannot field candidates at any election in the UK other than elections to community councils (or their English equivalents, parish councils).[96] This is without prejudice to the right of any person who does not purport to represent any party[97] to stand for election. The register of political parties previously maintained by the Registrar of Companies under the Registration of Political Parties Act 1998 was replaced with two new registers maintained by the Electoral Commission.[98] The Great Britain Register contains details of parties intending to contest elections in one or more of England, Scotland or Wales; the Northern Ireland Register contains details of parties intending to contest elections in Northern Ireland. An entry in the Great Britain Register must be marked to indicate the part or parts of Great Britain in respect of which the party in question is registered. A party can apply to be registered in both registers, but the party as registered in the Great Britain Register and the party as registered in the Northern Ireland Register are required to be constituted as two separate parties with separate financial affairs. **4–18**

Each registered party must register a person as the party's leader, the party's nominating officer and the party's treasurer (although the same person may hold all three offices).[99] The nominating officer has responsibility for the submission by representatives of the party of lists of candidates for elections, the issuing of certificates attesting that a candidate in an election is a representative of the party and the approval of descriptions and emblems used on nomination and ballot papers at elections. The treasurer has responsibility for compliance on the part of the party with the provisions of Pts III and IV of PPERA (concerning accounting

---

[94] See now PPERA s.150 and Sch.19C.

[95] See, for example, the much-criticised decision the Commission took in relation to Wendy Alexander and her failure to timeously return an impermissible donation: Electoral Commission, "Statement by the Electoral Commission" (3 June 2008). The Alexander affair (and its wider implications) are discussed in: N.S. Ghaleigh, B. Kemp and P. Reid, "Politics as a profession: electoral law, Parliamentary standards and regulating politicians" [2012] P.L. 658.

[96] Nor, in terms of PPERA s.37 can broadcasters transmit party political broadcasts on behalf of a party that is not registered.

[97] That is, a person whose nomination paper describes him or her as "independent" or as "the Speaker seeking re-election", or which gives no description at all.

[98] PPERA s.23.

[99] PPERA s.24.

requirements[100] and the control of donations) and, unless a different person is registered as the party's campaigns officer, with the provisions of Pts V–VII (concerning campaign expenditure, third party expenditure and referendums).

A party may not be registered unless it has adopted a scheme that sets out the arrangements for regulating the financial affairs of the party for the purposes of PPERA and which has been approved in writing by the Electoral Commission.[101] In particular, the scheme must specify whether the party is to be regarded as a single organisation with no division of responsibility for the financial affairs and transactions of the party for the purposes of PPERA's accounting requirements, or as consisting of a central organisation and one or more separate accounting units (that is, constituent or affiliated organisations, each of which is responsible for its own financial affairs). In the latter case, the scheme must identify the various accounting units within the party by name, and in every case, must include such other information as may be required by regulations made by the Electoral Commission. The Commission may either approve a scheme as submitted, or give notice to a party requesting it to submit a revised scheme. The same process applies where a registered party wishes to replace an approved scheme with a revised scheme.

4–19 Applications for registration must be in the form prescribed by the PPERA,[102] specifying: a name to be the party's registered name[103]; the address of the party's headquarters, or an address to which communications to the party may be sent; the name and home address of each of the party's registered officers; a copy of the party's constitution and a draft of the accounting scheme submitted to the Electoral Commission; (where the party has accounting units) the name of each accounting unit, its address and the name of its treasurer; and such additional information as the Electoral Commission may prescribe in regulations. A party may also apply to register up to three emblems to be used by the party on ballot papers. The Electoral Commission is obliged to grant applications unless the application falls foul of the conditions prescribed in s.28(4).[104] Applications must be signed by the proposed registered leader or nominations officer, the treasurer and (where a party has one) by the campaigns officer, each of whom must declare that they are authorised to sign the application on the party's behalf. Thereafter, subject to applying to change registered particulars, the registered treasurer of a party must, at the time of sending its annual statement of accounts to the Electoral Commission, also give notification to the commission confirming that its registered particulars remain accurate.

---

[100] Unless the party has accounting units, in which case the treasurer is only responsible for compliance with the accounting requirements by the party's central organisation. Compliance with the requirements of PPERA Pts III and IV by each accounting unit is the responsibility of the person registered as treasurer of the unit.

[101] PPERA s.26.

[102] PPERA s.28 and Sch.4 Pt 1.

[103] As to registered names and descriptions, see now also Pt 7 of the Electoral Administration Act 2006.

[104] For example, the party proposes to register a name that: has already been registered by another party; is likely to result in voters confusing the party with another registered party; comprises more than six words; or is obscene, offensive or includes words the publication of which might amount to the commission of an offence.

Donations to political parties[105]

One of the main objectives in requiring political parties to be registered was to allow greater control of, and transparency in respect of, their funding. Following the PPERA, donations to political parties is now a heavily regulated matter.[106] It was not always so. Funding of political parties has long been a controversial topic.[107] Political parties have access to very limited public funds. Once a party has managed to secure a foothold in Parliament it is eligible for a contribution from public funds towards its parliamentary work (but not its election expenses).[108] At election time, candidates are entitled to such benefits as free postage (for one constituency mail shot) and free use of public buildings for election meetings. If a party is sufficiently sizeable to register on the national scale, it is also entitled to at least one party election broadcast.[109] Beyond that, the amount a party has to spend at election time on advertising and other forms of promotion depends on its membership income (which, for almost all parties, is in radical decline)[110] and, crucially, support from companies, trades unions, private individuals and others. It is the latter, and the terms on which it is provided, that has perennially caused controversy. Having investigated the matter in the context of its Fifth Report, the Committee on Standards in Public Life was unpersuaded of the case for state funding of political parties. Its recommended solution involved limits on campaign expenditure coupled with new requirements of disclosure and registration. Those recommendations provided the foundation for Pt IV of the PPERA concerning donations to political parties. **4–20**

"Donation" is defined by s.50 of PPERA to include: any gift to a party of money or other property[111]; any sponsorship provided in relation to the party[112]; any subscription or other fee paid for affiliation to, or membership of, the party; **4–21**

[105] What follows is necessarily an overview of what is becoming an increasingly complex and technical subject; M. Smyth, P. Barratt and F. Campbell, *The Law of Political Donations* (London: Wildy, Simmonds & Hill, 2012) is commended to anyone in search of further detail.

[106] Donations to members of registered parties, members associations and certain elected offices are also controlled by a near identical scheme: see PPERA s.71 and Sch.7.

[107] See K.D. Ewing, *The Funding of Political Parties* (Cambridge: Cambridge University Press, 1987); more recently, Committee on Standards in Public Life, *The Funding of Political Parties in the United Kingdom, Fifth Report* (The Stationery Office, 2008) Cm.4057–I and, now, the House of Commons Constitutional Affairs Committee, *Party Funding, First Special Report of Session 2006–2007* (The Stationery Office, 2007) HC 222 and Phillips, *Strengthening Democracy: Fair and Sustainable Funding of Political Parties*.

[108] Known as "Short money" in the House of Commons (see, Erskine May, 25th edn, para.4.8) and "Cranborne money" in the House of Lords, this system of funding has a statutory foundation in relation to the Scottish Parliament in the Scotland Act 1998 s.97.

[109] On party election broadcasts, see para.4–26, below.

[110] The SNP buck that trend having seen a huge growth in their membership following the 2014 referendum.

[111] This includes the provision of property, services, facilities or other consideration of monetary value for payment of a sum less than the market value of the property transferred; and also includes bequests.

[112] Defined in s.51 as money or other property transferred to the party or to any person for the benefit of the party for the purpose of helping the party to meet any defined expenses (i.e. expenses in connection with a conference, meeting or other event organised by or on behalf of the party; the preparation, production or dissemination of any publication by or on behalf of the party; or any study or research organised by or on behalf of the party) or to secure that to any extent such expenses are not incurred.

any money spent (otherwise than by or on behalf of the party) in paying any expenses incurred by the party; any money lent to the party otherwise than on commercial terms; and the provision otherwise than on commercial terms of any property, services or facilities for the use or benefit of the party, including the services of any person. Anything given or transferred to any officer, member, trustee or agent of a registered party in that capacity is also to be regarded as a donation to the party. Section 52 then lists items that are not to be regarded as donations, including: grants made to cover security costs at party conferences; payments made by or on behalf of the European Parliament for the purpose of assisting MEPs in the performance of their functions[113]; the transmission by a broadcaster, free of charge, of a party political broadcast or referendum campaign broadcast; any other facilities provided in pursuance of any right conferred on candidates or a party at an election or a referendum by any enactment; the voluntary provision by any individual of their own services, in their own time and free of charge; payments made for the hire of a stand at a party conference (provided the payment does not exceed a maximum deemed by the Electoral Commission to be reasonable). Any donation worth less than £500 also falls outwith the PPERA scheme entirely.[114]

Donations may only be accepted from "permissible donors".[115] The concept of a "permissible donor" was at the heart of the PPERA reforms. In short, the objective was to prevent foreign donations to political parties. The rational is obvious: only those that have a sufficient connection to the UK should be allowed to contribute to funding politics in the UK. Where a political party receives a donation from an impermissible donor (or it is unable to satisfy itself that the donor is permissible), it must return the donation within 30 days.[116] Failure to do so is a criminal offence.[117] Who, then, is a "permissible donor"? A list is set out in s.54(2) and includes: an individual registered in an electoral register[118]; a registered company[119]; a registered party; a registered trade union; a building society; a registered limited liability partnership; a registered friendly society; and an unincorporated association that carries on its activities wholly or mainly in the UK. The objective of the list was to provide a clear and simple way of verifying a donor's entitlement to make a donation. It was with that in mind that a proposal that an individual who was not on the electoral register but was entitled to be on it should be a permissible donor was rejected.[120] Ascertaining the permissibility of a donation from an individual was therefore a clear and simple

113 That provision remains on the statute book at the time of writing but is due to be repealed on 31 December 2020 at the end of the transition period: European Parliamentary Elections Etc. (Repeal, Revocation, Amendment and Saving Provisions) (United Kingdom and Gibraltar) (EU Exit) Regulations 2018.

114 PPERA s.52(2)(b). The limit was originally £200 but it was increased to £500 by the Political Parties and Elections Act 2009 s.20(1).

115 PPERA s.54.

116 PPERA ss.56(1) and 57.

117 PPERA s.56(3).

118 An "electoral register" is defined by PPERA s.54(8).

119 Registered under the Companies Act 2006, incorporated in the UK or another EU Member State and carrying on business in the United Kingdom.

120 The recommendation was made by the Neill Committee in Committee on Standards in Public Life, *The Funding of Political Parties in the United Kingdom, Fifth Report,* para.5.20. The recommendation was specifically rejected in the government's response to the Neill Committee's

process: check the electoral register (itself, a simple task) and if the person does not appear on it the donation must not be accepted. Changes introduced by the Political Parties and Elections Act 2009 will complicate this issue in some circumstances. The 2009 Act (although the relevant provision still has not yet been bought into force) requires any person making a donation in excess of £7,500 (whether in a single donation or a series of donations in the same calendar year) to be domiciled and tax resident in the United Kingdom.[121] Thus, a political party receiving such a donation will need to check not only that the donor is on the electoral register but also their tax status. There is no register that can be checked to ascertain that and determining a person's residence for tax purposes and their domicile is often a complicated business.[122] Whilst the policy behind the amendment (to restrict donations from those that, although on the electoral register, do not pay tax in the United Kingdom) is understandable, it results in an unfortunate dilution of what was otherwise a clear system and renders compliance more difficult that the original scheme anticipated.

Retaining an impermissible donation has two consequences. First, the party and its treasurer commit a criminal offence.[123] It is a defence for a party or its treasurer to show that all reasonable steps were taken to verify (or ascertain) whether the donation was permissible and as a result the treasurer believed the donation to be permissible.[124] As an alternative to criminal prosecution, the Electoral Commission now has a range of civil sanctions that it may impose upon a person that commits an offence under PPERA.[125] Second, the Electoral Commission can seek an order for forfeiture of "an amount equal to the value of the donation".[126] Forfeiture allows the political party to be deprived of the benefit of an impermissible donation. Such an application is made to the sheriff (in Scotland) or to the magistrate (in England and Wales)[127] and can be made irrespective of whether proceedings have been brought for an offence connected with the donation.[128] An appeal lies, at the instance of the political party, to the Court of Session or the Crown Court.[129] The decision of the sheriff (or magistrate) is amenable to judicial review at the instance of the Electoral Commission.[130] Whether to order forfeiture, and how much of the impermissible **4–22**

---

report: HM Government, *The Funding of Political Parties in the United Kingdom: the Government's proposals for legislation in response to the Fifth Report of the Committee on Standards in Public Life* (The Stationery Office, 1999) Cm.4413, para.4.6.

121 Political Parties and Elections Act 2009 s.10, inserting s.54(2ZA) and s.54B into PPERA.

122 Smyth, Barratt and Campbell, *The Law of Political Donations* (2012), pp.43–46.

123 PPERA s.56(3) and (4). Upon conviction on indictment the court may impose a fine or a period of imprisonment of up to one year; upon summary conviction the court may impose a fine up to the statutory maximum or a period of imprisonment of up to six months (PPERA s.150 and Sch.20).

124 PPERA s.56(3A); this provision was inserted by the Political Parties and Elections Act 2009 s.12 and reflects the grounds on which the Electoral Commission did not initiate criminal proceedings against Wendy Alexander in 2008 when she failed to return an impermissible donation within the 30-day period.

125 These were introduced by the Political Parties and Elections Act 2009 and are now to be found in PPERA s.147 and Sch.19C.

126 PPERA s.58(2).

127 PPERA s.58(5).

128 PPERA s.58(4).

129 PPERA s.59.

130 *R. (on the application of Electoral Commission) v Westminster Magistrates' Court* [2009] EWHC 78 (Admin); [2009] A.C.D. 23.

donation should be forfeited, are matters of discretion for the sheriff (or magistrate). That was made clear by the Supreme Court in *R. (on the application of Electoral Commission) v Westminster Magistrates' Court*.[131] That case was the culmination of litigation arising out of UKIP's acceptance of 69 donations totalling over £350,000 from a party member who was not on the electoral register and was thus an impermissible donor. Sixty-two of those donations were made when both UKIP and the donor were ignorant of the fact he was an impermissible donor. The remaining seven (amounting to just under £15,000) were made after UKIP became aware the donor was not a permissible donor. The Electoral Commission made an application for a forfeiture order covering all donations that were in excess of £200 (the then minimum threshold to fall within the 2000 Act scheme). At first instance, the magistrate ordered forfeiture in the sum of £14,481 (representing the seven donations received once the donor's status was known to UKIP). The Electoral Commission sought judicial review of that decision. By the time the case reached the Supreme Court the issue had become focused: was there a presumption in favour of forfeiture where a donation came from an impermissible donor? The Supreme Court split 4:3. The minority (Lords Rodger, Brown and Walker) were of the view that there was a strong presumption in favour of forfeiture, especially in a case such as the present where the donation had been retained by the party.[132] As Lord Brown put it:

> "... in any case where neither the benefit nor its value has ever been returned, it is difficult to see how the discretion could properly be exercised other than by an order for forfeiture. How, in those circumstances, could a court properly allow a party to retain the value of a donation which Parliament has plainly ordained that it should never have accepted?"[133]

That reasoning is fairly compelling and would have resulted in forfeiture of the entire amount that UKIP had received. But the majority (Lords Phillips, Mance, Kerr and Clarke) took a more nuanced view of the forfeiture rules: where a donation has been accepted from an impermissible source, there is an initial presumption in favour of forfeiting the donation; there is an onus on the party to show why such a donation should not be forfeited; a "first step" in discharging that onus will be show that it was not in fact a "foreign donation"; that can be done by showing an individual was entitled to be entered on the electoral register; if it can be shown that the individual was in a position to qualify as a permissible donor, the initial presumption in favour of forfeiture will have been rebutted.[134]

---

[131] *R. (on the application of Electoral Commission) v Westminster Magistrates' Court* [2010] UKSC 40; [2011] 1 A.C. 496.

[132] *R. (on the application of Electoral Commission) v Westminster Magistrates' Court* [2010] UKSC 40; [2011] 1 A.C. 496, per Lord Rodger at [69] and Lord Brown at [95].

[133] *R. (on the application of Electoral Commission) v Westminster Magistrates' Court* [2010] UKSC 40; [2011] 1 A.C. 496 at [95]. Lord Rodger's interpretation of s.54(1) (at [58]) was equally compelling: "Nothing could be clearer than the language used by Parliament and nothing could be clearer than the intention behind the language: political parties were not to accept donations from any individual who was not registered in an electoral register. In particular, parties were not to accept donations from individuals who were entitled to be registered, but who were not on the register. That situation would be adequately catered for by the simple expedient of the individual concerned getting himself registered: the party could then accept a donation from him."

[134] *R. (on the application of Electoral Commission) v Westminster Magistrates' Court* [2010] UKSC 40; [2011] 1 A.C. 496, per Lord Phillips at [47]–[49].

In relation to the sum to be forfeited, the majority went on to hold that the power to order forfeiture of "an amount equal to the value of the donation" was not an all or nothing power: it implicitly contains the power to order forfeiture of a lower sum.[135] That was necessary, said Lord Phillips, to ensure the sum forfeited was proportionate to the culpability of the party.[136] Nothing in this decision changes the fact that a party may not accept a donation from a person that is not on the electoral register and to do so remains a criminal offence. But it does mean that forfeiture of that donation is unlikely if the donor was eligible to be on the electoral register. To that extent, what appears on the face of the PPERA to be a strong incentive to carefully check the electoral register on receipt of a donation has been significantly watered down.

Campaign expenditure

The idea that an election result can be "bought" should be repugnant in a democracy. As we have just seen, regulation of donations to political parties is a relatively new development.[137] Such expenditure is now controlled by a combination of the Representation of the People Act 1983 and Pts V and VI of the PPERA. So far as the 1983 Act is concerned, the relevant provisions are to be found in Pt II of that Act, in particular ss.72–90D. A summary of the key provisions will suffice.[138] The 1983 Act concerns itself with "election expenses". An "election expense" is any expense incurred at any time after the date on which a person becomes a candidate in respect of matters specified in Pt 1 of Sch.4A and which is used for the purpose of the candidate's election.[139] The matters prescribed in Sch.4A include: advertising of any nature; unsolicited material addressed to electors; transport costs; public meetings; costs of engaging an election agent; and accommodation and administrative costs. **4–23**

The Political Parties, Elections and Referendums Act 2000 now adds to those rules. Part V concerns the control of campaign expenditure. "Campaign expenditure" is defined as "expenses incurred by or on behalf of the party which are expenses falling within Part 1 of Schedule 8 and so incurred for election purposes",[140] but it excludes anything that falls to be included in a return as election expenses by a candidate (or the equivalent return in respect of a recall **4–24**

[135] *R. (on the application of Electoral Commission) v Westminster Magistrates' Court* [2010] UKSC 40; [2011] 1 A.C. 496, per Lord Phillips at [50]–[51].

[136] Again, the minority's view on this point is compelling: *R. (on the application of Electoral Commission) v Westminster Magistrates' Court* [2010] UKSC 40; [2011] 1 A.C. 496, per Lord Rodger at [64]–[69] and Lord Brown at [90]–[92]. As Lord Rodger explains in that passage, the consequence of the majority's decision appears to be that large impermissible donations are harder to forfeit than smaller impermissible donations: that would be an odd result.

[137] The rules in the UK can be contrasted to the approach taken in the US, where there are few restrictions on campaign expenditure as the US Supreme Court has consistently taken the view that such regulations infringe the First Amendment of the US Constitution. Most recently, see *Citizens United v Federal Election Commission*, 558 U.S. 310 (2010).

[138] Fuller discussion of these provisions can be found in R. Clayton, *Parker's Law and Conduct of Elections* (Croydon: Charles Knight, 1996), Ch.8.

[139] 1983 Act s.90ZA(1); "for the purpose of the candidate's election" is widely defined as "with a view to, or otherwise in connection with, promoting or procuring the candidate's election at the election" (s.90ZA(3)).

[140] PPERA s.72(1).

petition under the Recall of MPs Act 2015).[141] The matters listed in Pt 1 of Sch.8 include: party political broadcasts; advertising of any nature; unsolicited material addressed to electors; any manifesto or equivalent document; costs associated with polling or market research; the provision of services or facilities in connection with press conferences or other media dealings; transport; and rallies or other party meetings (but excluding party conferences). Campaign expenditure does not include anything that falls to be included in a return as to election expenses in respect of a candidate or candidates at a particular election. Nor does it include such items as: expenses in respect of newsletters issued by or on behalf of the party in order to inform the local electorate about a representative or candidate; the costs of employing party staff; or travelling expenses incurred by an individual from his own resources and not reimbursed.[142] Responsibility in relation to campaign expenditure is vested in the treasurer of a party and such deputy treasurers (not exceeding 12) as they may appoint.[143] No "campaign expenditure" may be incurred without authorisation of the treasurer, a deputy or somebody that is authorised on their behalf.[144] The obligations imposed by the PPERA are onerous and time consuming, especially for smaller parties that have limited resources. Limits are imposed on the amount of "campaign expenditure" that may be incurred during specified periods. Those limits are set out in Sch.9 of the 2000 Act. For a UK general election, Scotland, Wales, Northern Ireland and England are treated separately. The amount of "campaign expenditure" a party may incur is (at least in the first instance) tied to the number of seats they are contesting in each part of the UK. Where a registered party contests one or more seats in a part of the UK the amount of campaign expenditure that may be incurred in that part of the UK is £30,000 per constituency in that part of the country.[145] There is, in relation to Great Britain, a minimum amount a party fielding a candidate may spend: in England that is £810,000, in Scotland £120,000 and in Wales £60,000.[146] For a Scottish general election, campaign expenditure is limited to £12,000 per constituency that is being contested and £80,000 for each region that is contested.[147] There is no minimum amount. Breaching those limits is a criminal offence, which is committed both by the treasurer (or deputy) that authorised the expenditure and by the party.[148]

It may be helpful to put those figures into context:

---

141 PPERA s.72(7).
142 PPERA Sch.8 Pt 1 para.2.
143 PPERA s.74.
144 PPERA s.75.
145 PPERA Sch.9 para.3(2) and (4).
146 PPERA Sch.9 para.3(3).
147 PPERA Sch.9 para.5(2). The power to vary this sum will be devolved if legislation is passed to give effect to the Smith Commission. At the time of writing, the current draft of the relevant clause is cl.7 of the Draft Scotland Clauses 2015 which are annexed to the Command Paper, HM Government, *Scotland in the United Kingdom: An enduring settlement*.
148 PPERA s.79(2).

Table 7: Campaign expenditure during 2010–2017 UK and 2011 and 2015 Scottish general elections[149]

Party	2010 UK	2015 UK	2017 UK	2011 Scottish	2016 Scottish
Con	£16,682,874	£15,587,957	£18,565,102	£273,462	£978,921
Lab	£8,009,483	£12,099,263	£11,003,980	£816,889	£337,814
Lib Dem	£4,787,595	£3,529,106	£6,788,316	£176,300	£186,477
SNP	£315,776	£1,475,478	£1,623,127	£1,141,662	£1,465,542
Cap if contesting all constituencies in Great Britain at UK election: £18,960,000 Cap if contesting all seats and regions at Scottish election: £1,516,000					

From those figures alone, it is clear that there is a wide disparity in the amount the different parties spend during a general election campaign. The amount spent in 2010 and 2011 was substantially less than was spent in 2005 and 2007 respectively. Although no party has yet spent the limit of their entitlement, imposing a limit on expenditure does ensure that there is only so far that the gulf can open.

Part VI of the PPERA is concerned with controls on third party participation in national election campaigns. These provisions are a response to the European Court of Human Rights decision in *Bowman v United Kingdom*.[150] As it then stood, s.75 of the 1983 Act made it an offence for a person other than a candidate or their agent to incur expenditure in excess of £5 during an election period "with a view to promoting or procuring the election of a candidate" at that election, which might be contravened as much by denigrating a candidate (since their opponents stood to benefit) as by actively promoting them. That rule was held to be a disproportionate restriction on freedom of expression, contrary to art.10 of the Convention. Part VI now allows for greater third-party participation in national election campaigns, but still subject to strict limits.[151] For the 2010 general election just under £3,000,000 of "controlled expenditure" was incurred by third parties. That fell to £1,780,000 in 2015 but rose again to just over £2,500,000 in 2017.[152] In the 2011 Scottish general election approximately £100,000 of such expenditure was incurred and much the same figure was again spent in the 2016 Scottish general election. The Pt VI regime was further expanded by the Transparency of Lobbying, Non-Party Campaigning and Trade

[149] Source, the Electoral Commission. At the time of writing figures were not available for the 2019 UK general election.

[150] *Bowman v United Kingdom* (1998) 26 E.H.R.R. 1.

[151] In relation to a Scottish general election, the limit is £75,800 of "controlled expenditure" during the "relevant period": PPERA Sch.10 para.5. The limits for a UK general election vary as between Scotland, England, Wales and Northern Ireland and are determined in accordance with PPERA Sch.10 para.3. In relation to Scotland, the limit is £20,000 plus 2% of the maximum campaign expenditure limit in Scotland.

[152] At the time of writing, figures are not available for the 2019 election.

Union Administration Act 2014 that brought charities, certain Scottish partnerships and certain bodies established by Royal Charter within the scope of Pt VI of the 2000 Act.[153] The 2014 Act also introduces limits to the amount third parties can spend in a single parliamentary constituency.[154]

Television coverage, electoral broadcasts and debates

4–25 Television coverage of election campaigns has long been regulated. The power and reach of television mean it could have a significant impact on the outcome of an election if favourable coverage was to be given to one party or candidate as compared to the rest. There are no equivalent restrictions on the printed media: newspapers and the like are free to be as partisan as they please during an election campaign. Under s.320 of the Communications Act 2003, in relation to matters of political or industrial controversy or current public policy, broadcasters (both television and radio) must avoid all expressions of the views or opinions of the broadcaster, preserve due impartiality and prevent undue prominence being given to the views of any particular person or body. The preservation of impartiality can be satisfied by a series of programmes taken as a whole and the prevention of undue prominence can be secured by viewing the service in question's coverage as a whole. "Political" in this context is not restricted to party political but includes social advocacy bodies.

4–26 Adverts "directed towards a political end" are prohibited in the United Kingdom.[155] That phrase is given a wide meaning and includes, inter alia: a broadcast with the purpose of influencing the outcome of an election or referendum; bringing about a change in the law; influencing the policies or decisions of a government; influencing public opinion on a matter of public controversy; and promoting the interests of any group for political ends.[156] Having such a blanket ban on access to the broadcast media is an obvious restriction of the art.10 right to freedom of expression. It is, however, a proportionate interference with that right.[157] Lord Bingham, in *R. (on the application of Animal Defenders International) v Secretary of State for Culture, Media and Sport*, explained the rationale that underpins the duties imposed on broadcasters and the ban on political adverts:

> "The fundamental rationale of the democratic process is that if competing views, opinions and policies are publicly debated and exposed to public scrutiny the good will over time drive out the bad and the true prevail over the false. It must be

---

[153] Transparency of Lobbying, Non-Party Campaigning and Trade Union Administration Act 2014 s.32 (which amends PPERA s.88).

[154] Transparency of Lobbying, Non-Party Campaigning and Trade Union Administration Act 2014 s.29 (which amends PPERA ss.94, 96 and Sch.10). A mechanism is introduced to calculate the limit, which is currently £9,750.

[155] Communications Act 2003 s.321(2).

[156] Communications Act 2003 s.321(3). These restrictions do not have a territorial limitation: they apply to *any* election, referendum, government, policy or body and not just those in the United Kingdom. See *R. (on the application of London Christian Radio Ltd) v Radio Advertising Clearance Centre* [2013] EWCA Civ 1495; [2014] 1 W.L.R. 307.

[157] *R. (on the application of Animal Defenders International) v Secretary of State for Culture, Media and Sport* [2008] UKHL 15; [2008] 1 A.C. 1312; *Animal Defenders International v United Kingdom* (2013) 57 E.H.R.R. 21.

> assumed that, given time, the public will make a sound choice when, in the course of the democratic process, it has the right to choose. But it is highly desirable that the playing field of debate should be so far as practicable level. This is achieved where, in public discussion, differing views are expressed, contradicted, answered and debated. It is the duty of broadcasters to achieve this object in an impartial way by presenting balanced programmes in which all lawful views may be ventilated. It is not achieved if political parties can, in proportion to their resources, buy unlimited opportunities to advertise in the most effective media, so that elections become little more than an auction. Nor is it achieved if well-endowed interests which are not political parties are able to use the power of the purse to give enhanced prominence to views which may be true or false, attractive to progressive minds or unattractive, beneficial or injurious. The risk is that objects which are essentially political may come to be accepted by the public not because they are shown in public debate to be right but because, by dint of constant repetition, the public has been conditioned to accept them. The rights of others which a restriction on the exercise of the right to free expression may properly be designed to protect must, in my judgment, include a right to be protected against the potential mischief of partial political advertising."[158]

Those comments pre-date the explosion in use of social media, which falls outside the scope of the 2003 Act. But Lord Bingham's remark that the underlying policy objection is not achieved if "political parties can, in proportion to their resources, buy unlimited opportunities to advertise in the most effective media" has an obvious resonance with the increasing influence of social media in shaping public opinion. The regulation of social media has been controversial and, so far as elections are concerned, is being considered by the Law Commissions.[159]

Political parties (or at least some of them) are given some access to the airwaves. Broadcasters and licenced radio stations are required to carry "party political broadcasts".[160] In the run up to an election, these are known as party election broadcasts. It is for the broadcasters, following, in the case of commercial broadcasters, the rules set down by Ofcom, to determine the number of broadcasts each political party should receive, having regard to their duty to ensure a fair overall coverage. Under the current Ofcom rules,[161] the "major parties" (in Great Britain they were the Conservative Party, Labour and the Liberal Democrats)[162] should receive at least two broadcasts. In determining the allocation of broadcasts, regard is had to each party's past electoral support and/or current levels of support. For these purposes, each nation of the UK is considered separately. For the UK general election, at least one broadcast should be allocated to any party that is contesting at least one-sixth of the seats that are up for election. Detailed rules are made by Ofcom about the length of broadcasts and the time of day that broadcasters must carry them. Unsurprisingly, the allocation of broadcasts is controversial. 4–27

---

[158] *R. (on the application of Animal Defenders International) v Secretary of State for Culture, Media and Sport* [2008] UKHL 15; [2008] 1 A.C. 1312 at [28].

[159] *https://www.lawcom.gov.uk/project/electoral-law/* [Accessed 5 May 2020].

[160] Communications Act 2003 s.333(1).

[161] Ofcom, *Ofcom Rules on Party Political and Referendum Broadcasts* (March 2017) *https://www.ofcom.org.uk/__data/assets/pdf_file/0035/99188/pprb-rules-march-2017.pdf* [Accessed 9 April 2020].

[162] The SNP are a "major party" in Scotland.

A more recent development is debates between the party leaders in the run up to an election. Unlike party political broadcasts, there is little regulation about the number and content of any debates (as the run up to the 2015 election showed). They were first used in advance of the 2010 general election in which the leaders of the three main parties (Labour, the Conservatives and the Liberal Democrats) took part. Such debates are an import from the US, where televised debates between the presidential candidates have been a feature of elections since the mid-1970s.[163] Matters are simpler in the US where the two main parties (the Republicans and the Democrats) dominate and where the electorate are voting to choose the President rather than electing a legislature.[164] Presidential debates normally consist of the candidate from each party.[165] It is not as straightforward in the UK. A challenge was mounted to the 2010 debates by the SNP, who claimed their leader was entitled to participate, representing as he did the largest party in Scotland. Accordingly, it was argued that broadcasting the debates in Scotland would breach the broadcasters' obligation of impartiality.[166] Their application for interim interdict to prevent the broadcasting of the debate in Scotland failed.[167] It did so for a number of reasons: placed in the context of the planned coverage of the election campaign, broadcasting the debate did not prevent impartial coverage of the overall campaign; it was too late to prevent broadcast of the third debate (it being likened to denying the audience act three of a three act play); and the terms of the order lacked sufficient precision. Although unsuccessful, the case highlights a problem with presidential-style debates in a parliamentary democracy in the UK: whilst voters in Scotland may have an interest in seeing a representative of the SNP (or Welsh voters seeing Plaid Cymru) the voters in Yorkshire or East Anglia or Devon will have little, if any, interest as they are unlikely to have the option of voting for a candidate from those regional parties. That issue arose in 2015 where the parties again disagreed on who should be entitled to participate in any televised debates. Eventually there was a single debate, with seven party leaders appearing.[168] That still led to complaints from the Democratic Unionist Party in Northern Ireland about their omission. Other debates followed between the opposition leaders, and in Scotland between the Scottish political leaders. But the agreement was forged against the background of broadcasters threatening to leave an empty chair in the place of

---

[163] The first debate was in the 1960 campaign between Kennedy and Nixon. It was not until 1976 that a presidential debate was held again and since then they have been an ever-present feature of the US presidential election campaign. The number, timing and location of the debates is always a controversial matter and one which is determined by the Commission on Presidential Debates, *http://www.debates.org* [Accessed 22 July 2020].

[164] The United States adheres to a strict version of the separation of powers. With the exception of the Vice-President who chairs the Senate (the upper chamber of the US legislature) members of the executive do not sit in the legislature. Voters in the US cast a different ballot to elect their "Senator" (who sits in the upper chamber) and the "Representative" (who sits in the lower chamber).

[165] In 1992 the Republican (President G.H.W. Bush) and Democrat (then Governor Clinton) candidates were joined by independent candidate Ross Perot and in 1976 a third candidate (Congressman Anderson) sought to participate in the debates. Otherwise, the debates have been a two-party affair.

[166] The challenge was made to the broadcast of the third debate, which was due to be screened by the BBC. At the point the case was heard the first two debates had already been screened by other broadcasters.

[167] *Scottish National Party v BBC* [2010] CSOH 56; 2010 S.C. 495.

[168] Conservative, Labour, Liberal Democrat, SNP, Plaid Cymru, UKIP and the Greens.

any leader who did not participate and sharp divisions between the leaders on the appropriate number and form of debate. In both 2017 and 2019, there were two "head-to-head" debates between the leaders of the Conservative and Labour parties (a third one in 2019 was cancelled at short notice) and then a range of other debates, some with party leaders, some with only a selection of the parties invited. But, unlike the strict regulation around party election broadcasts, debates have been a matter of negotiation, and to an extent brinksmanship, between political parties and the broadcasters. This all highlights that televised leadership debates in the run up to a general election do not sit easily with the UK's parliamentary style democracy. But they are likely to be here to stay and thus ought to be properly regulated. Just as it took the US a number of electoral cycles to learn to work with such debates, the same seems likely to be true of the UK.

CHALLENGING AN ELECTION RESULT[169]

It was previously an aspect of parliamentary privilege that it was for the House of Commons, and the House of Commons alone, to determine the outcome of any controverted election. That remained the position until the Parliamentary Elections Act 1868 by which the House delegated its jurisdiction to the civil courts.[170] The Representation of the People Act 1983 now governs challenges to an election result and primarily relies upon private challenge. The 1983 Act applies to elections to the UK Parliament and local government.[171] Those provisions are applied by the Scottish Parliament (Elections etc.) Order 2015 to elections to the Scottish Parliament.[172] Legal proceedings questioning an election must be taken in accordance with Pt III of the Representation of the People Act 1983.[173] The procedure set out below relates to the challenge to an election to the UK Parliament. The same procedures have, however, been largely adopted in relation to the Scottish Parliament.[174] **4–28**

A challenge must come in the form of a parliamentary election petition.[175] These are essentially private proceedings, which is surprising given the obvious public interest in the legitimacy of an election result. Three categories of persons have title to raise such a petition: (a) a person who voted, or who had the right to vote, at the election; (b) a person claiming to have had the right to be elected or

[169] Law Commission, Scottish Law Commission and Northern Ireland Law Commission, *Electoral Law: A Joint Consultation* (The Stationery Office, 2014) L.C.C.P. 218, S.L.C.D.P. 158, N.I.L.C. 20, Ch.13 contains a comprehensive survey of this particularly complex corner of electoral law with a number of proposals for reform. Their final report (SLC No.256) was published shortly before this text was finalised so its recommendations are not reflect here. But the paper is available at: *https://s3-eu-west-2.amazonaws.com/lawcom-prod-storage-11jsxou24uy7q/uploads/2020/03/6.6339_LC_Electoral-Law_Report_FINAL_120320_WEB.pdf* [Accessed 5 May 2020].

[170] For a brief history, see *Erksine May Parliamentary Practice*, edited by M. Jack, 25th edn (available online, for free, at: *https://erskinemay.parliament.uk* [Accessed 13 May 2020]) at para.2.22.

[171] So far as local government elections in Scotland are concerned, that is as a result of the Scottish Local Government Elections Order 2011 (SSI 2011/399).

[172] Scottish Parliament (Elections etc.) Order 2015 (SI 2015/425).

[173] In what follows, we consider the procedure for challenging a parliamentary election result. Broadly similar provision is made by the 1983 Act to challenge a local government election result.

[174] Scottish Parliament (Elections etc.) Order 2015 (SI 2015/425) art.82 and Sch.6.

[175] 1983 Act s.120.

returned at the election; and (c) a person alleging themselves to have been a candidate at the election.[176] The respondent to such a petition is either the person whose election or return is being complained of or, where the petition complains about the conduct of the returning officer, the returning officer.[177] The form of petition and the procedures to be adopted in determining the petition are prescribed by the Rules of Court.[178] The timescales for challenging an election result are, for understandable reasons, short. The default time limit for presenting a parliamentary election petition is within 21 days of the election that is complained about.[179] Where, however, the complaint is of corrupt practices and specifically alleges a payment of money or other reward in furtherance of the alleged corrupt practice, a petition may be presented within 28 days of the date of the payment.[180] Other time limits apply where the allegation is of an illegal practice.[181] The grounds of challenge are not easily distilled from the various statutes that apply. In their consultation paper, the Law Commissions identified three grounds on which an election result can be annulled:

> "(a) a breach of electoral law during the conduct of the election which was either: (i) fundamental; or (ii) materially affected the result;
> (b) corrupt or illegal practices committed either: (i) by the winning candidate personally or through that candidate's agent; or (ii) by anyone else, to the benefit of the winning candidate, where such practices were so widespread that they could reasonably be supposed to have affected the result; or
> (c) the winning candidate was at the time of the election disqualified from office".[182]

A parliamentary election petition is tried by two judges, who constitute "the election court".[183] The election court has the same powers, jurisdiction and authority as a judge of the Court of Session, but importantly it is not the Court of Session.[184] It is a UK statutory body exercising a jurisdiction that was previously the exclusive preserve of Parliament itself.[185] Unlike civil cases, where the Court of Session always sits in Parliament House in Edinburgh, the election court should ordinarily sit within the constituency for which the election was held.[186]

---

176 1983 Act s.121(1).
177 1983 Act s.121(2).
178 In Scotland, Ch.69 of the Rules of the Court of Session 1994, read with ss.136 to 157 of the 1983 Act. The normal rules as to pleading do not apply: *Morrison v Carmichael*, 2016 S.C. 585 at [34].
179 1983 Act s.122(1).
180 1983 Act s.122(2).
181 1983 Act s.122(3) and (4). Generally, 31 days after delivering an election expenses return to the returning officer or, where it is alleged that payment of money or some other act has been done, within 28 days of that payment or act.
182 Law Commission, Scottish Law Commission and Northern Ireland Law Commission, *Electoral Law: A Joint Consultation*, para.13.12.
183 1983 Act s.123(1). A rota is maintained of judges who may be selected to hear election petitions. At the time of writing, the Scottish judges who could hear such petitions were Lord Eassie and Lady Paton (Court of Session Practice Direction No.1 of 2014).
184 1983 Act s.123(2).
185 Until the Parliamentary Elections Act 1868 transferred that jurisdiction to the courts. *Morrison v Carmichael*, 2016 S.C. 585 at [34].
186 1983 Act s.123(3). In *Morrison v Carmichael*, 2016 S.C. 585, which concerned a challenge to the result in the Orkney and Shetland constituency, the court sat in Parliament House in Edinburgh, but its proceedings were live-streamed.

Having heard the necessary evidence, the election court must then determine whether the member whose election is complained of has been duly returned or elected or whether that election was void.[187] That determination must be communicated to the Speaker of the House of Commons forthwith.[188] Where the court is divided on whether the member has been properly elected (being a court of two judges there will be no majority) the election shall stand.[189] Where an allegation of corrupt or illegal practices was made in the petition, the election court shall also report to the Speaker (or Clerk to the Scottish Parliament) whether any such allegation has been proved to have been committed by or with the knowledge and consent of any candidate at the election and the nature of the corrupt or illegal practice.[190] The report must also name all those who have been proved to have been guilty of any corrupt or illegal practice, but where they were not a party to the petition proceedings, the election court must first give that person the opportunity to be heard and, if appropriate, lead evidence to defend why they should not be so reported.[191] A candidate's election is void if they are reported by an election court as personally guilty, or guilty by their agents, of any corrupt or illegal practice.[192] Where the election court finds that corrupt or illegal practices or illegal payments, employments or hirings were made in the context of the election campaign and with the view to procuring the election of any person prevailed so extensively that they may be reasonably supposed to have affected the result, the election result shall be void.[193] The 1983 Act makes no provision for an appeal from the findings of the election court. But being a statutory body, any decision is amenable to judicial review.[194] Having reported to the Speaker, the election court is functus; there is no standing election court.

Such challenges are rare. Most recently, in 2015, the election of Alastair Carmichael (then the MP for Orkney and Shetland) was subject to challenge.[195] **4–29** There, a group of constituents asserted that he had committed an "illegal practice" by denying his involvement in a leak concerning the First Minister's desired outcome for the (UK) election. In short, the Election Court held that Carmichael had made a false statement for the purpose of affecting his return as the MP for the constituency.[196] They were not, however, satisfied that this fell within s.106(1) of the 1983 Act in that it did not relate to his personal character or conduct.[197] That appeared to be because leaking (or, where done by a minister, as Carmichael was at the relevant time, "briefing") is so well-established as part of

---

187 1983 Act s.144(1).

188 1983 Act s.144(2); in the case of the Scottish Parliament, the determination is relayed to the Clerk of the Scottish Parliament.

189 1983 Act s.144(3)(a).

190 1893 Act ss.144(4) and 158.

191 1983 Act s.160.

192 1983 Act s.159(1).

193 1983 Act s.164.

194 *R. (on the application of Woolas) v Parliamentary Election Court* [2010] EWHC 3169 (Admin); [2012] Q.B. 1.

195 *Morrison v Carmichael*, 2016 S.C. 585 (decision in relation to relevancy of the petition) and 2016 S.C. 598 (substantive decision having heard evidence).

196 *Morrison v Carmichael*, 2016 S.C. 598 at [61]–[65].

197 *Morrison v Carmichael*, 2016 S.C. 598 at [58]–[59].

the political culture that there is no adverse inference to be drawn about the character of a person involved in a leak (or "briefing").[198] As the Court observed:

> "Members of the public cannot … assume that a member of Parliament or officer-holder will never be involved in a politically-motivated leaking exercise, all the more so during an election campaign."[199]

So, despite having been found (beyond reasonable doubt) to have made a false statement for the purpose of positively affecting his return as the MP, the election result stood. To some, that was entirely to be expected as people know to take what they are told, in particular around elections, with a pinch of salt. For others, it was no doubt disappointing that the court did not intervene where it had been found that the candidate had made a false statement.[200] Whilst there was concern at the time that this challenge might mark the start of more frequent challenges to election results,[201] and scrutiny of what candidates had said during the campaign, there were no similar challenges to the Westminster or Holyrood elections since *Morrison*.

4–30 Despite the rarity of a challenge, the rules concerning challenges to election results are, in the Law Commissions' words, "complex and inaccessible".[202] At the time of writing, the outcome of the Commissions' project on electoral law is awaited but their provisional proposals for reform included: bringing the law regarding challenging elections together in a single piece of primary legislation[203]; the grounds of challenge should be restated and positively set out; the election court should be abolished with challenges being heard by the ordinary courts; returning officers should be given standing to raise a petition; and the possibility of introducing "public interest" challenges. Whatever the outcome of the consultation, some codification of the rules relating to challenging election results would be welcome.

---

198 *Morrison v Carmichael*, 2016 S.C. 598 at [52].

199 *Morrison v Carmichael*, 2016 S.C. 598 at [53].

200 Which, as the court noted, is just another way of calling something a lie: 2016 S.C. 598 at [44].

201 A concern that was debunked centuries ago: "If wrongs be multiplied, remedies must be multiplied." (*Ashby v White* (1703) 2 Ld. Raym. 938, cited by S. Sedley, *Lions Under the Throne, Essays on the History of English Public Law*, p.151).

202 Law Commission, Scottish Law Commission and Northern Ireland Law Commission, *Electoral Law: A Joint Consultation*, para.13.13.

203 That may be unlikely given the transfer of competence of various aspects of electoral law to the Scottish Parliament by the Scotland Act 2016.

CHAPTER 5

Referendums

INTRODUCTION

In the previous chapter we considered the electoral systems by which democracy in the United Kingdom has been traditionally assured. Referendums are a relative new-comer to our democracy. But they have made their mark. The second decade of this century was defined by two referendums: 2014 on Scottish independence and 2016 on continuing EU membership. The purpose of this chapter is not to get into the merits of those two polls, let alone the aftermath that followed each. Instead, it is to consider referendums, and their use in the United Kingdom, in their proper constitutional context. There is now detailed regulation of how a referendum ought to be conducted but there is little regulation of when a referendum ought to be held. The effect of the referendums on devolution in 1978 and 1997 appears to have established a convention that the people should be asked to approve a scheme of devolution.[1] In 2011 the people of Wales were asked to approve the transfer of limited legislative competence to the Welsh Assembly. They did so, with 63.5 per cent of those voting in favour. The people of Scotland, however, were not asked to approve the changes to their devolution settlement that were introduced by the Scotland Act 2012 (nor those that followed in the Scotland Act 2016[2]). So even in relation to devolution, it is unclear when a referendum ought to be called. It had always been accepted that Scotland could not leave the Union without a positive vote in such a referendum and in September 2014, on an unprecedented turnout of 85 per cent, Scotland voted by a margin of 55:45 to remain a part of the United Kingdom. Similarly, legislation provides that Northern Ireland shall not leave the Union without the people of that province voting to do so in a referendum (or, as it is referred to in the Northern Ireland Act 1998, a border poll). So devolution and independence appear to require (politically at least) a referendum. Even before June 2016, the UK's relationship with the EU was a potentially fertile source of referendums. In 1975, the first ever referendum was held on the UK's continued membership of what was then the EEC. Even without the 2016 referendum, an EU-related 5–01

[1] This applies not only to sub-national devolution but also to regional devolution: a referendum preceded the establishment of the Greater London Assembly and the creation of a directly elected mayor. The people of the north east of England rejected regional devolution in a referendum and as a result none has been forthcoming. Similarly, 9 out of 10 cities that were asked whether they wanted a directly elected mayor in 2012 said no.

[2] Albeit by the end of the 2014 referendum campaign, the choice for the Scottish people appeared to be between independence and further devolution; the status quo was not really on the ballot paper. See para.1–09, above.

referendum was all but inevitable. Until the UK's departure from the EU, the European Union Act 2011 required a referendum before certain amendments to the treaties could be ratified by the United Kingdom as well as a range of other, relatively technical, decisions could be taken by the UK in relation to the EU.[3] As we have seen, a proposal to change the electoral system for the House of Commons was submitted to a referendum, it having long been accepted that direct approval by the people was necessary before any such change could be made. But it is not only national, constitutional, questions that have been submitted to the people in a referendum. Referendums occur at a much more local level too. For example, the people of Aberdeen were asked to approve plans to replace Union Terrace Gardens (in 2012) and the residents of Edinburgh were asked to approve (but rejected) proposals to introduce congestion charging (in 2005). This ad hoc use of the referendum, often for political as opposed to constitutional reasons, has been lamented by the House of Lords Constitution Committee.[4]

The first question we will consider in this chapter is when, in a representative democracy, should resort be had to the people in a referendum? Despite the fact the first nationwide referendum was not held until 1975, use of the referendum has been advocated for over a century. One such advocate was Dicey and we will begin by considering some of his thoughts on the use of referendums. We will then turn to consider the range of circumstances in which a referendum has been held, or where legislation now requires that one be held, in an attempt to understand what the contemporary requirements of the constitution are. The second issue we will consider in this chapter is the regulation of referendums and referendum campaigns. Despite the infrequency with which they have been held, detailed provision was introduced for their regulation in 2000. That regulatory framework will be outlined. Perhaps the most notable omissions from this chapter on referendums are the 2014 Scottish independence referendum and the 2016 EU referendum: we have already considered those in Ch.1.

DICEY ON THE REFERENDUM[5]

5–02 Given what we have seen about Dicey's views on parliamentary sovereignty, it is perhaps surprising to learn that he was a strong advocate for the introduction of the referendum:

> "...the final decision of the nation's destiny must be referred to a more august tribunal than the House of Commons, or even than Parliament."[6]

---

[3] The details of these are now largely of historical interest but they are briefly sketched out at para.10–36, below.

[4] House of Lords Select Committee on the Constitution, *Referendums in the United Kingdom, 12th Report of Session 2009–2010* (The Stationery Office, 2010) HL Paper 99, para.62.

[5] See generally: A.V. Dicey, "The Referendum" (1894) 23 *National Review* 65; A.V. Dicey, "The Referendum and its Critics" (1910) 212 *Quarterly Review* 538; R. Weill, "Dicey was not Diceyan" (2003) 62(2) C.L.J. 474.

[6] Dicey, "The Referendum" (1894) 23 *National Review* 65, 71.

Dicey's comments have to be set in the context of the time he was writing. He was a staunch opponent of Irish Home Rule, a measure that the House of Commons seemed determine to pass but which Dicey thought the majority of the population were opposed to. He was also increasingly concerned by the role played by the party system in the House of Commons, which was, by the end of the nineteenth century, becoming increasingly powerful. The consequence, feared Dicey, was that the House of Commons, freely chosen by the electorate, may nonetheless fail to represent the views of the nation.[7] Dicey proposed a Referendum Act that would require approval by the people of any Act of Parliament effecting constitutional reform. The requirement, Dicey believed, should be judicially enforceable. His proposed Act provided:

> "Any Bill, or so-called Act, passed by both Houses of Parliament and assented to by the Crown, which, whilst affecting any one of the scheduled Acts, had not been sanctioned by and on appeal under the Referendum Act, should be held invalid by every court of law throughout the British Empire."[8]

Such a provision obviously causes a problem for what is regarded as the Diceyian view of parliamentary supremacy: it simultaneously purports to bind Parliament's successors (but perhaps only in terms of the "manner and form" of legislation),[9] it appears to recognise a hierarchy of Acts of Parliament[10] and it authorises the courts to invalidate an Act of Parliament. In other words, it appears to contradict the three cardinal features of Dicey's own vision of parliamentary supremacy. Dicey sought to reconcile his Referendum Act and parliamentary supremacy by explaining no party leader would wish to incur the resentment of the electorate by denying them their say in a referendum but that Parliament could override his proposed Referendum Act if it was necessary to protect the State "against imminent peril, e.g. foreign invasion".[11] Dicey's Referendum Act would ultimately have been binding only in a political sense and the supremacy of Parliament preserved. As we saw in the aftermath of the 2016 referendum, the political force of a referendum result was a strong as Dicey anticipated it would be.

Leaving that to one side for now, for present purposes it is helpful to consider the function that Dicey saw the referendum performing. The referendum, for Dicey, "places the electorate in the position once occupied in England by the Crown; it is the nation's veto . . . It establishes the only conservative check on legalisation which is clearly in harmony with those democratic principles which in the modern world form the moral bases of government."[12]

Dicey recognised that there were forceful arguments against his vision of the referendum: it was conservative in that it can only block change not initiate it; the referendum ought to be useless because a fairly elected House of Commons

[7] Dicey, "The Referendum and its Critics" (1910) 212 *Quarterly Review* 538.

[8] Dicey, "The Referendum and its Critics" (1910) 212 *Quarterly Review* 538, at p.554.

[9] See para.3–05, above.

[10] A consequence Dicey had already recognised: "[The referendum] may undoubtedly be so used as to establish a clear distinction between laws which effect permanent changes to the Constitution and ordinary legislation" (Dicey, "The Referendum" (1894) 23 *National Review* 65, 69).

[11] Dicey, "The Referendum and its Critics" (1910) 212 *Quarterly Review* 538, p.555.

[12] Dicey, "Parliamentarism", lecture of 30 August 1898, reproduced in J.W.F. Allison (ed), *Comparative Constitutionalism: AV Dicey* (Oxford: Oxford University Press, 2013), p.147.

should represent the wishes of the nation; and the referendum threatened to diminish the importance of Parliament.[13] Those concerns were, for Dicey, outweighed by the benefits of the system: it allows the people to pronounce on whether a particular change *should* be made while leaving to Parliament the detail of *how* such a change was implemented, and it "cuts at the root of parliamentary intrigue" allowing the people to override the will of the politicians.[14]

Despite Dicey's best efforts, however, Home Rule for Ireland was passed, the absolute veto of the House of Lords restricted and the referendum never adopted. It would be nearly three-quarters of a century until the United Kingdom used the referendum. Dicey's discussion of the referendum, however, offers a helpful introduction to the more contemporary issues that now arise.

THE REFERENDUM IN THE UK

5–03 It was in 1975 that the United Kingdom had its first nationwide referendum. Two years previously, a border poll had been held in Northern Ireland to determine whether the province should remain within the United Kingdom. On a 58.7 per cent turnout, 98.9 per cent of the votes cast were in favour of remaining in the United Kingdom. The poll was, however, boycotted by the nationalist community. In 1975, however, the people of the United Kingdom were asked: "Do you think the UK should stay in the European Community (Common Market)?"[15] Whether to hold a referendum was a deeply controversial topic, primarily due to concerns about its effect on the doctrine of parliamentary supremacy.[16] Continued membership of the EEC was said to be so significant that it was the sole exception to the principle that decisions be taken by Parliament and not by the people directly in a referendum.[17] Once the referendum genie was out of the bottle, however, others feared that it would not be possible to get it back in. Despite those constitutional arguments on whether the poll should have been held in the first place, when it came to the vote, on a 65 per cent turnout, 67 per cent voted in favour of the UK remaining within the "Common Market".

Despite government assurances in advance of the 1975 referendum that no precedent was being set and the vote was in response to a unique situation, it was not the last referendum of the decade. The devolution legislation of the 1970s, as originally introduced, contained no requirement for approval by the people of Scotland and Wales, respectively, in a referendum. Backbench pressure saw the government amend the Scotland and Wales Bill so as to introduce a referendum requirement. When the Scotland and Wales Bill ran out of parliamentary time, devolution legislation was again introduced in the 1977–78 session of Parliament, this time in the form of separate Bills for Scotland and Wales. This time, however, the Scotland Bill was amended during its passage to introduce what would become s.85(2) of the Scotland Act 1978. Section 85(2) required the

[13] Dicey, "Parliamentarism" in *Comparative Constitutionalism: AV Dicey* (2013), pp.148–149.

[14] Dicey, "Parliamentarism" in *Comparative Constitutionalism: AV Dicey* (2013), p.148.

[15] Referendum Act 1975 Schedule.

[16] For example, see C. Dike, "The case against parliamentary sovereignty" [1976] P.L. 283.

[17] *Hansard*, HC Vol.881, cols 1742–1743 (22 November 1974) quoted by V. Bogdanor, *The New British Constitution* (Oxford: Hart Publishing, 2009), p.182.

Secretary of State to lay before Parliament an Order in Council for the repeal of the Act if it appeared that less than 40 per cent of the persons *entitled to vote* in the referendum had voted "yes".[18] An abstention therefore became a "no" vote and thus the lower the turnout the larger the margin of victory would have to be before a "yes" on the ballots cast became an effective "yes". In the event, on a turnout of 63 per cent, 52 per cent voted "yes", which equated to approximately 33 per cent of the electorate. Devolution for Scotland had, at that stage, been rejected.[19] When Labour returned to power in 1997, however, devolution was resurrected. Again, it was accepted that the people of Scotland and Wales should express a desire for devolution in a referendum before any system was implemented. But this time, the poll was to be held before Parliament passed devolution legislation. The Referendums (Scotland and Wales) Act 1997 was passed requiring polls to be held in September 1997. This time, no turnout threshold was included. On 11 September 1997 Scotland voted in favour of the establishment of a Scottish Parliament (74 per cent "yes", 26 per cent "no", turnout 61 per cent) and to vest it with limited tax varying powers (64 per cent "yes", 36 per cent "no"). Matters were much closer in Wales a week later: on a 50 per cent turnout, 50.3 per cent voted in favour of the establishment of a Welsh Assembly with 49.7 per cent voting against. The following year, the Scotland Act and the Government of Wales Act were passed by Parliament and the inaugural elections for the two new bodies were held in May 1999. We will return to consider what lessons can be learned from the UK's experience of the referendum thus far. But at this point it worth noting that had the 40 per cent threshold applied to the 1997 devolution referendums Scotland would have a Parliament *without* tax varying powers and Wales would have no Assembly.

Two other referendums took place in 1998: in Northern Ireland the Belfast Agreement was approved by the people of that province (71 per cent "yes", 29 per cent "no", turnout 80 per cent)[20] and in London the establishment of the Greater London Authority with a directly elected mayor and council were approved, in a manner of speaking, by Londoners (72 per cent "yes", 28 per cent "no", but a turnout of only 34 per cent). Similar devolution to the north east of England proved significantly less popular with the electorate there in 2004: on a 48 per cent turnout, only 22 per cent voted in favour. There have been no further referendums on devolution to other regions of England and the relevant legislation (the Regional Assemblies (Preparations) Act 2003) has now been repealed in its entirety.[21]

Two further referendums were held in 2011. First, on 3 March 2011, the people of Wales were asked to decide whether limited legislative competence should be granted to the Welsh Assembly. Unlike 1997, when Parliament had not **5–04**

[18] An equivalent amendment was made to the Wales Bill, resulting in what became s.80(2) of the Wales Act 1978. In the event, it was academic. On a 58% turnout, only 20% voted "yes" and thus Welsh devolution was comprehensively rejected.

[19] The appropriate Order in Council was laid before Parliament and approved but not before the government considered asking its MPs to vote against it and thus save the devolution project. See the discussion by Bogdanor, *The New British Constitution* (2009), pp.183–184.

[20] A referendum was simultaneously held in the Republic of Ireland as the Good Friday Agreement required approval in both referendums. For a discussion of some of the particular issues arising from the Good Friday Agreement referendums, see G. Gilbert, "The Northern Ireland Peace Agreement, Minority Rights and Self-Determination" (1998) 47 I.C.L.Q. 943.

[21] Local Democracy, Economic Development and Construction Act 2009 Sch.7(4) para.1.

yet passed legislation on the matter, provision had been made in the Government of Wales Act 2006. Under the 2006 Act, it was for the Welsh Assembly to request that the Secretary of State hold a referendum on the subject.[22] As with 1997, what was required was a majority of *votes cast* in a referendum and not any specific percentage of the electorate. The transfer of limited legislative competence to the Welsh Assembly was approved with 63.5 per cent voting in favour (36.5 per cent voting "no", with a turnout of 35.6 per cent). Then, in May 2011, only the second ever UK wide referendum was held. The electorate were asked to approve a change to the voting system for the House of Commons. This was a central plank of the Liberal Democrats coalition negotiations following the 2010 general election. When it was put to the electorate, however, it was roundly defeated. Turnout was only 42.2 per cent (the highest it reached was 63 per cent in Eastwood but it sank as low as 27.2 per cent in Newham, London)[23] and 67.9 per cent of those voting voted "no".

Finally, of course, the two most recent, and most prominent, referendums. First, the Scottish people went to the polls on 18 September 2014 to answer the question: "Should Scotland be an independent country?" On a turnout of 84.6 per cent, 44.7 per cent answered that question "yes" whereas 55.3 per cent answered the question "no".[24] The obvious consequence of that result is that Scotland shall, for the time being at least, remain a part of the UK. Second, on 23 June 2016, the UK held only its third ever nationwide referendum to answer the question: "Should the United Kingdom remain a member of the European Union or leave the European Union?" On a turnout of 72.2 per cent, 48.1 per cent answered that question "remain" whereas 51.9 per cent answered that question "leave". In response to that result, the United Kingdom ceased to be a member of the European Union at 23:00 on 31 January 2020. Some of the issues arising from those result have already been discussed in Ch.1, above.

Before turning to consider what we can learn from the UK's experience of the referendum, it is worth noting that referendums happen on a local level too. For example, residents of Edinburgh were asked to approve the introduction of a congestion charge in 2005. That was a postal referendum and the proposal was rejected: 74.4 per cent voted "no" on a turnout of 61.8 per cent. In 2012, the people of Aberdeen were asked to choose between two proposals for the redevelopment of Union Terrace Gardens. Again, this was a postal referendum (although online and telephone voting were available). Turnout was 52 per cent with the City Garden Design Project being favoured by 52.3 per cent of the voters. And in 2016, voters in St Ives were asked to support a ban on second

[22] Government of Wales Act 2006 s.104. Similar provision is now made under the Wales Act 2014 (s.12) in relation to the possible transfer of limited powers in relation to income tax. Curiously, it is for the Welsh Assembly, in requesting that the referendum be held, to state the voting age (16 or 18) (s.13(2)). Sixteen was of course the voting age in Scotland for the independence referendum but 18 was be the voting age for the EU referendum. The age of enfranchisement has now been reduced to 16 for all elections over which it has competence: Scottish Elections (Reduction of Voting Age) Act 2015.

[23] C. Rallings and M. Thrasher, *The 2011 Referendum on the Parliamentary Voting System: aspects of participation and administration* (Plymouth: Elections Centre, University of Plymouth, 2011), prepared on behalf of the Electoral Commission.

[24] The turnout was noteworthy: 3.62 million votes were cast out of an electorate of 4.28 million. That level of public participation in democracy was unprecedented in modern times. Turnout peaked in East Dumbartonshire (at 91 per cent) and dropped no lower than 75 per cent (in Glasgow).

homes in the town (which they did, with 83.2 per cent voting for the ban on a turnout of 42.7 per cent). Despite the failure of regional government in England and Wales in 2004, in 2012 referendums were held in 10 different cities across England asking the local population whether they wished to have a directly elected mayor. Only Bristol voted in favour.[25] Various other local referendums have been held across the country. As we will consider below, referendums at this level present some of their own issues.

One final point before moving on: there is no (enforceable) obligation to hold a referendum. In Ch.15 we consider when a substantive legitimate expectation that gives rise to an enforceable right in public law can occur. For present purposes, however, it is sufficient to note that a ministerial (even a Prime-ministerial) promise to hold a referendum on any particular issues cannot give rise to an enforceable obligation on the government to arrange such a referendum.[26]

That brief review of the use of the referendum in the United Kingdom helps us answer the question posed above: when, in a representative democracy, should resort be had to the people in a referendum? But it also shows that the question really has two parts to it: first, on what issues should a referendum be held, and second, should the referendum be held before or after Parliament has legislated on the matter? A further question arises from the UK's experience of the referendum: what provision, if any, should be made in relation to minimum levels of turnout to legitimise a referendum result? We will now turn to consider each of those issues. 5–05

Statute now requires that a referendum be held on a number of issues, including: (a) before Northern Ireland can cease to be part of the UK[27]; (b) before limited tax varying powers are conferred on the Welsh Assembly[28]; (c) the adoption of certain planning decisions in England and Wales[29]; and (d) increasing, in certain circumstances, council tax charges in England and Wales.[30] That apart, the calling of a referendum is a matter for the government of the day, constrained to a certain extent by convention. Generally, referendums have been called where the decision was believed to be of significant constitutional importance (devolution, independence or continued membership of the EU). Referendums on each of these issues can be labelled "constitutional referendums". This is a phrase that Tierney defines as "any direct citizen vote on the

---

[25] The cities that rejected a directly elected mayor were: Birmingham, Bradford, Coventry, Leeds, Manchester, Newcastle-upon-Tyne, Nottingham, Sheffield and Wakefield. Doncaster voted to retain their mayor. The referendums were held in terms of s.9N of the Local Government Act 2000 (that section having been inserted by Sch.2 para.1 of the Localism Act 2011). See Electoral Commission, *Local elections and referendums in England 2012: Report on the administration of the elections and referendums held on 3 May 2012* (Electoral Commission, 2012).

[26] *R. (on the application of Wheeler) v Office of the Prime Minister* [2008] EWHC 1409 (Admin) at [41]; *Wheeler v Office of the Prime Minister* [2014] EWHC 3815 (Admin); [2015] 1 C.M.L.R. 46 at [41]–[48].

[27] Northern Ireland Act 1998 s.1 and Sch.1.

[28] Wales Act 2014 s.12.

[29] Town and Country Planning Act 1990 Sch.4B (as inserted by Sch.10 of the Localism Act 2011).

[30] Local Government Finance Act 1992 Ch.4ZA (as inserted by the Localism Act 2011 s.72 and Sch.5). Prior to the UK's departure from the EU, the European Union Act 2011 required (by s.4) that a referendum be held before any new exclusive competence was conferred upon the EU, or an existing competence extended, along with various other, more technical, decisions could be taken by the UK at EU level. Those provisions were never called into action.

specific issue of constitutional change or constitutional creation".[31] Tierney identifies four types of constitutional process where the referendum is now regularly used: founding of new states (e.g. Montenegro in 2006); amendment or adoption of a constitution; establishing devolution; and transfer of sovereign powers to international institutions.[32] A border poll under the Northern Ireland Act 1998, which is necessary before Northern Ireland could leave the UK, would also fall into this category. Convention must now require a referendum to approve the introduction of devolution to a region: the effect of the 1998 vote in London and, more particularly the 2004 vote in the north east would appear to provide a precedent. The extension of devolution, however, is not as clear cut. The Government of Wales Act 2006 required approval in a referendum before limited legislative competence was conferred on the Welsh Assembly. Similarly, the Wales Act 2014 now requires a referendum before income tax varying powers are conferred on the Assembly. On the other hand, the Scotland Act 2012 was introduced without being approved by the Scottish people in a referendum. Although the 2012 Act made limited changes to the legislative competences of the Scottish Parliament it did significantly alter the devolved competences in relation to taxation. Despite a specific question on that issue being posed in the 1997 referendum, there was no great call for a referendum on the 2012 Act. That may be explained by attention having been focused on the 2014 independence referendum: it would have been odd if the Scottish people were asked to approve a revised devolution scheme at the same time as plans were being laid for a referendum on independence. Following that referendum, the Scotland Act 2016 came into force without any suggestion it required popular approval at the ballot box. In Wales, the result in 1997 can explain the requirement for a referendum before the Welsh Assembly was granted legislative competence. The margin of victory for the "yes" vote was so slight that testing the people of Wales continuing enthusiasm for devolution before extending it further appears eminently reasonable. What the contrast between Scotland and Wales shows is the continuing flexibility of the United Kingdom's constitutional arrangements and its ability to tailor a solution for a particular set of circumstances. Referendums have, however, also been called for apparently political reasons. The 1975 referendum on continued membership of the EEC falls into that category, as would the promised, but never held, referendum on adopting the euro. Both issues were highly controversial and divisive within the government. By submitting (or, in the case of the euro, undertaking to submit) the matter to the people in a referendum the political sting was drawn from it. No comment is made on the motives behind the 2016 EU referendum: the historians can address that in due course. The local referendums in Edinburgh and Aberdeen on congestion charging and redeveloping Union Terrace Gardens perhaps fall into

[31] S. Tierney, *Constitutional Referendums: The Theory and Practice of Republican Deliberation* (Oxford: Oxford University Press, 2012), p.11.

[32] Tierney, *Constitutional Referendums: The Theory and Practice of Republican Deliberation* (2012) p.1. Tierney also explains (pp.11–14) that "constitutional referendums" can be further subdivided into "constitution-changing" and "constitution-framing". The former occur within the existing constitutional structure of the state whereas the latter usually transcend the existing constitutional order. In the United Kingdom, referendums (including the Scottish independence referendum and the provisions of the Northern Ireland Act 1998) are best understood as falling into the former category as they have all been accommodated within the existing constitutional structure of the state.

this category as well. So far as St Ives is concerned, the referendum served to provide added legitimacy to a decision that some will have disagreed with.

The House of Lords Constitution Committee expressed their concern at the ad hoc manner in which referendums have been used and called for cross-party agreement on the circumstances in which they should be used.[33] The Committee recommended that if they are to be used, they should be restricted to "fundamental constitutional issues". Recognising that a comprehensive definition of "fundamental constitutional issues" would be impossible (and unwise) they considered that any of the following issues would fall to be determined by a referendum: a proposal to abolish the Monarchy; a proposal to leave the EU; secession of the nations of the UK from the Union; abolition of either House of Parliament; changes to the electoral system for the House of Commons; adoption of a written constitution; and a proposal to change the currency used in the UK.[34] In relation to local referendums (of the sort that took place in Edinburgh, Aberdeen and St Ives), the Committee was left unconvinced that they were the most effective way to increase citizen engagement with the local democratic process.[35] 5–06

The other issue to consider in relation to the calling of a referendum is the question of timing. As we saw, the 1978 devolution referendums were called after Parliament had legislated on the matter. The people were being asked to approve the legislation enacted by Parliament. This was the Diceyian vision of the referendum: "the nation's veto". But by asking the people to vote after Parliament has legislated, a number of problems arise. First, Parliament may find itself enacting legislation that its members are not actually in favour of, but they would prefer to take the chance of trying to persuade the people to reject it.[36] This leads to a second problem. In that scenario, it is not in the interests of those opposed to the substance of the measure to seek to improve the legislation as it makes its way through Parliament. The more problems they can point to in the legislation, the greater the chance they can persuade the people to reject the measure. Third, it is a considerable waste of parliamentary time for potentially complex and controversial issues to be debated by both Houses and then passed only for it to be vetoed by the electorate. Finally, having the approval of the people before the legislative process begins helps secure the passage of the legislation when it comes before Parliament. That is certainly true of leaving the EU: pre-referendum there was nothing like a majority in the House of Commons for leaving the EU, but after the people had expressed their view, a significant number of MPs took the view that, whatever their personal view, they had to give effect to that vote. Dicey, on the other hand, conceived of the referendum as a purely negative weapon, unable to instigate change. Yes, if it is held after the event. But where it was held in advance, the referendum can effect change. This last reason in 5–07

[33] House of Lords Select Committee on the Constitution, *Referendums in the United Kingdom, 12th Report of Session 2009–2010*, para.62.

[34] House of Lords Select Committee on the Constitution, *Referendums in the United Kingdom, 12th Report of Session 2009–2010*, para.94.

[35] House of Lords Select Committee on the Constitution, *Referendums in the United Kingdom, 12th Report of Session 2009–2010*, para.140.

[36] Of course, the opposite occurred in 2016, when a number of MPs who still believed the UK should remain within the EU voted in favour of the legislation that authorised giving notice of the UK's intention to withdraw.

particular saw the 1997 devolution referendums being held before legislation was introduced to Parliament.[37] Holding the referendum before Parliament legislates is not without its difficulties either. The primary argument is that the people need to have a clear idea of what they are voting for. That line of argument led to some calls in the early stage of the Scottish independence referendum debate for a second vote after the terms of secession had been agreed. The same arguments were made as the UK negotiated its exit from the EU. There has been no consistent practice in the UK. Reform of the electoral system for the House of Commons was put to the people before legislation had been passed whereas, as we have seen, the people of Wales were asked about conferring legislative competence on the Welsh Assembly only after Parliament had enacted the necessary measures. What can perhaps be drawn from the UK's experience is that the more politically controversial the issue, the more likely it is that the people's view, in principle, will be sought before Parliament debates the issue and the detail.

5–08 The UK's experience of the referendum also raises an interesting question about the need for, and the appropriateness of, a turnout threshold to legitimise the referendum and the result.[38] A threshold can be a response to two questions: when is the turnout so low that the result should have no authority; and, especially in relation to constitutional issues, when is the result sufficiently clear to sanction the proposed change? As we have seen, a threshold has only once been used in the United Kingdom, in the 1978 devolution referendums where 40 per cent of those eligible to vote had to vote in favour of devolution for the proposals to be implemented. That was an example of a voter-registered threshold, linked as it was to the number of registered voters and not the number of votes cast. On an 80 per cent turnout a 40 per cent requirement needs 50 per cent of those voting to support the proposal. But if turnout falls to 60 per cent, two-thirds of those voting must vote in favour. The threshold of success therefore varies according to the turnout. Where the referendum concerns an issue of constitutional change or importance, a voter-registered threshold requirement can be justified so as to ensure the measure attracts sufficiently broad support within the population. Imagine the result of the Scottish independence referendum had been different and 55 per cent of those voting had voted in favour of independence but this time on a turnout of only 65 per cent. Would 35.8 per cent of Scots voting for independence have been regarded as a sufficient majority to end the Union? At the very least, it would have risked a bitter argument as to what the effect of the result actually was. Arguably events following the 2016 referendum vouch that 37.4 per cent of the registered electorate voted to leave the EU. Whilst the result was quickly accepted by leading politicians as clear and decisive, it did little to settle the issue. Such a threshold requirement can, however, also serve to depress turnout: failing to vote is a tantamount to a "no" vote. Such a threshold requirement therefore risks artificially lowering the turnout. It can also lead to problems after the vote where an overwhelming number of those voting supported a measure only for it to fall by having narrowly

---

[37] That this was the main reason for holding the referendum before, and not after, the legislation passed through Parliament was made clear by Tony Blair in his memoirs: Blair, *A Journey* (London: Hutchison, 2010), p.252.

[38] See Tierney, *Constitutional Referendums: The Theory and Practice of Republican Deliberation* (2012), pp.271–278; Bogdanor, *The New British Constitution* (2009), pp.192–194.

missed the threshold requirement.[39] Most states, therefore, eschew a voter-registered threshold requirement. As we have seen, so too has the United Kingdom for all subsequent referendums.

But turnout in those subsequent referendums (save only the polls in 2014, which was especially high, and 2016), in particular the 1998 referendum on the establishment of the Greater London Authority and the 2011 referendum on the transfer of limited legislative competence to the Welsh Assembly (34 per cent and 35.6 per cent, respectively), raise the question of whether a threshold related to a minimum percentage of the registered electorate voting is appropriate. The 1998 and 2011 results translate as 24.5 per cent and 22.6 per cent, respectively, of the electorate in each of those referendums actually voting in favour of the proposal. As Tierney explains, turnout threshold is common throughout European countries that use the referendum as part of their constitution. Only a handful of countries have no such threshold requirement and they are very much the exception.[40] Had a 50 per cent turnout threshold been set for each referendum that has been held in the UK, there would be no Mayor of London, Wales would have an Assembly (just) but without legislative competence and reform of the voting system for the House of Commons would have failed at the first hurdle. Yet in each case the validity of the result was not questioned because of the turnout.

Of course, there is nothing magic about achieving a 50 per cent turnout. All that demonstrates is half of the population care sufficiently about the question that is being asked of them to express their opinion. If a simple majority is sufficient to "win" a referendum with a 50 per cent turnout threshold, the victory is still achieved with little more than a quarter of the electorate positively supporting the measure. Again, the significance of the issue probably plays a major role. If the choice is the style of garden design for the city centre (as it was in Aberdeen in 2012) ought it really to be blocked because so few people engaged with the issue? Whether to leave the EU, or to change currency, on the other hand, has much longer-term consequences. As a result, there is a stronger case for ensuring that the proposed change has sufficient support from the electorate before proceeding.[41] After all, the very fact a referendum has been called indicates that the legislature consider is at least prudent to seek specific approval from the people direct. It should, of course, be hoped that in those circumstances a turnout threshold becomes academic. If a referendum is reserved for genuinely important constitutional issues, assuming the electorate have been properly informed of not only the arguments for and against but why the issue is important, the electorate ought to be willing to engage in direct democracy and express their view. Recognising that the Scottish independence referendum was of unique character, it did demonstrate the levels of public engagement that can be achieved when the people are aware of the importance and significance of the issue. One lesson from the 2016 referendum, however, might be about what the consequence of a particular result is. As became painfully apparent afterwards,

[39] Imagine, for example, a 40% threshold had been set for Leave to succeed in 2016 so that despite winning the popular vote, they lost the referendum. Far from settle the issue, the referendum would have inflamed it.

[40] Tierney, *Constitutional Referendums: The Theory and Practice of Republican Deliberation* (2012), p.272.

[41] Once whatever threshold has been passed, however, that the result is close (for example, Wales in 1997 and, arguably, the 2016 EU referendum) is no real reason to reject the result.

whilst a binary choice had been presented to the electorate, it was not a question that admitted of only two possible answers. As we discussed in Ch.1, determining what the people meant from their binary choice was tortious and acrimonious process.

The referendum and the sovereignty of Parliament

5–09 A referendum result cannot, legally, bind Parliament. As we have already seen, on an orthodox understanding of the constitution, the UK Parliament retains the power to make or unmake any law. And that orthodoxy was reaffirmed by the Supreme Court shortly after the 2016 referendum.[42] The people having expressed their view on the matter in a referendum does not qualify that power. Of course, the result of a referendum may act as a *political* limitation on Parliament's ability to legislate on a particular matter (and we saw such political consequences play out in the aftermath of the 2016 referendum). But Parliament has long had political or other non-legal limitations on its legislative options. None of them detract from its legal supremacy. However, the greater the recourse to the referendum, the greater the strain that parliamentary sovereignty is likely to come under. The UK remains a representative democracy. As we saw in Ch.4, above, the role of the elected representative is as much "trustee" as it is "representative", and they are not always (indeed may rarely be) required to vote in line with the views of the majority of their constituents. But where the people have been consulted directly, the case for their elected representative (having agreed, in the first place, to consult the people) declining to follow the expressed will of the people is, at best, thin. However, in *Moohan*, Lord Neuberger (with whom the other justices in the majority agreed), in the context of considering the consequence of a "yes" vote in the Scottish independence referendum, said that Members of Parliament would not be bound to vote so as to give effect to the result but instead would have been "free, indeed constitutionally bound, to vote as they saw fit".[43] If that would be true of a UK-wide referendum (and there is no reason to doubt that, on the current understanding of parliamentary sovereignty, it would be), then that may well preserve Parliament's ability to reject the result of a referendum. But should Parliament ever vote so as to deny effect to the views expressed in a referendum, in the absence of some compelling justification, inordinate strain would undoubtedly be placed on the continuing doctrine of parliamentary sovereignty.

REGULATION OF REFERENDUMS

Introduction

5–10 Despite the fact that only a handful of referendums have ever been held, detailed provision was made about them in 2000. Part VII of the Political Parties, Elections and Referendums Act 2000 introduced detailed rules on who may

[42] *R (Miller and another) v Secretary of State for Exiting the European Union* [2017] UKSC 5; [2018] A.C. 61 at [20]–[23].
[43] *Moohan, Petitioner* [2014] UKSC 67; 2015 S.L.T. 2 at [47].

participate in a referendum campaign, the funding of such a campaign and the conduct of any vote. Part VII of the 2000 Act applies to any referendum "held, in pursuance of any provision made by or under an Act of Parliament, on one or more questions specified in or in accordance with any such provision".[44]

Consequently, the Scottish independence referendum did not fall within the scope of the Act (called, as it was, by the Scottish Parliament). A poll held under s.64 of the Government of Wales Act 2006 (which allows the Welsh Ministers to hold a poll to ascertain the views of the Welsh public on how any of its powers should be exercised) is also excluded from the scope of the Act.[45] Specific provisions are made for these referendums. What follows is a brief overview of the main provisions of PPERA that would apply to a referendum that is called by the UK Parliament.

Preliminaries

The provisions of the Political Parties, Elections and Referendums Act 2000 begin to apply even before the legislation authorising a referendum has been enacted. Where the Bill proposing the referendum specifies the wording of the question that will be posed, the Electoral Commission is required to publish a statement of any views that it has as to the proposed question's intelligibility. That statement should be published, in such manner as the Commission may determine, as soon as practicable after the Bill is introduced.[46] An equivalent procedure is to be followed when the wording of the question is to be determined by secondary legislation.[47] An Act that sanctions the holding of a referendum should also prescribe a "referendum period".[48] During the "referendum period" controls on the spending of "permitted participants" apply. It is important, therefore, to understand who these controls apply to. 5–11

Permitted participants and campaign funding

Regulation of the campaign, and in particular its funding, is tied to the concept of the "permitted participant".[49] A "registered party" can make a declaration to the Commission stating the referendum to which it relates and the outcome that the party proposes to campaign for. An individual or certain legal entities listed in s.54 of the PPERA can also notify the Commission of their intention to campaign 5–12

[44] Political Parties, Elections and Referendums Act 2000 (PPERA) s.101(2).

[45] PPERA s.101(3).

[46] PPERA s.104(2).

[47] PPERA s.104(3)–(6).

[48] PPERA s.102. For the 2011 referendum on the proposed change to the voting system for the House of Commons the "referendum period" began on the day the Parliamentary Voting System and Constituencies Act 2011 was passed (16 February 2011) and ended on the day of the referendum (5 May 2011): Sch.1 para.1. For the 2016 EU referendum, the "referendum period" was required to be no less than 10 weeks and it ended on the day of the referendum (23 June 2016): Sch.1, para.1 of the European Union Referendum Act 2015. In the event, the "referendum period" commenced on 15 April 2016 (which was about two and a half months after the operative provisions of the 2015 Act came into force).

[49] PPERA s.105. Slightly modified provision was made for the EU referendum: European Union Referendum Act 2015 Sch.1, para.2.

in a referendum and the outcome they propose to campaign for.[50] A declaration by a registered party or a legal entity must identify the person responsible for compliance with the financial controls that are imposed. The Commission is required to maintain a register of declarations and notifications.[51] The Commission has the power to designate certain permitted participants as "organisations to whom assistance is available".[52] Where there are only two possible outcomes to a referendum, the Commission may only designate one permitted participant as representing those campaigning for the outcome in question.[53] Where there are more than two possible outcomes, the Secretary of State may, having consulted the Commission, specify the possible outcomes in relation to which permitted participants may be designated by the Commission.[54] A permitted participant may apply for designation by the Commission and such an application must be made within 28 days of the start of the referendum period.[55] The Commission must make its decision within 14 days of the end of that 28 day period. The referendum can be held no earlier than 28 days after the period for the Commission to make its decision has expired.[56] Where there is only one application to represent a particular outcome, the Commission shall designate that applicant unless it appears that they do not adequately represent those campaigning for that outcome.[57] Where there is more than one applicant to represent a particular outcome, the Commission shall designate the applicant that appears to them to represent to the greatest extent those campaigning for that outcome.[58] The participants designated by the Commission shall each receive a grant, of the same amount, not exceeding £600,000.[59]

That narrative is the statutory basis on which a referendum campaign ends up with an "official" "yes" campaign and an "official" "no" campaign (or, "remain" and "leave" as was the case in 2016). The ordinary political parties will normally make a declaration to the Commission so that they can participate in the campaign. But they are unlikely to be the "official" campaign for any particular outcome. A particular, one off, organisation is likely to be formed for that purpose. Referendum questions do not normally divide neatly along party lines[60] that make "official" campaigns on either side a better vehicle by which to ensure there is a coherent campaign for both sides of the argument. It also allows fund raising to be done in the name of the campaign and not the party, which allows those that may have no political loyalty to the party (or parties) leading the

---

[50] Those entities are: a company registered under the Companies Act 2006 or another Member State and carrying out business in the UK; a trade union; a building society; a limited liability partnership; a friendly society; or an unincorporated association (PPERA ss.54(2)(b) and (d)–(h) and 106(4)(b)). That list was included to extend charities and Scottish partnerships for the EU referendum.

[51] PPERA s.107.

[52] PPERA s.108.

[53] PPERA s.108(2).

[54] PPERA s.108(3).

[55] PPERA s.109(1) and (2).

[56] PPERA s.103.

[57] PPERA s.109(4).

[58] PPERA s.109(5).

[59] PPERA s.110. That provision was disapplied for the EU referendum (s.110 as substituted for the purposes of that referendum by the European Union Referendum Act 2015 Sch.1, para.11(2)(a)(ii)).

[60] That, for the purposes of the EU referendum, is a euphemistic understatement.

campaign they support to participate without feeling they are supporting, financially or otherwise, a political party they do not.

Once participants have registered with the Commission, and the referendum period has begun, they become subject to PPERA's financial controls. These controls are set out in Ch.2 of Pt VII and come in three parts: incurring costs associated with the referendum; spending limits; and receiving donations. Starting with costs incurred, PPERA defines "referendum expenses" as expenses that fall within Pt 1 of Sch.13[61] and incurred for referendum purposes.[62] Various anti-avoidance provisions are made in s.112 to prevent circumvention of the spending limits.[63] The Act then imposes controls on permitted participants incurring referendum expenses. It is an offence for any referendum expenses to be incurred without the consent of the responsible person (who was identified to the Commission at the time of registration) or a person authorised, in writing, by the responsible person.[64] Similarly, it is an offence to make a payment (of whatever nature) in respect of any referendum expenses that has been, or will be, incurred unless it is made by the responsible person or a person authorised, in writing, by the responsible person.[65] Any payment of more than £200 must be supported by an invoice or receipt and where the payment is made by a person authorised by the responsible person, it is an offence if that persons fails to provide the responsible person with the invoice or receipt and notification that they have made the payment as soon as possible after it has been made.[66] Any claim for payment incurred in respect of referendum expenses by a permitted participant during the referendum period must be submitted to the responsible person (or a person authorised by them to incur the expenses) within 30 days of the end of the referendum period.[67] It must be paid within 60 days of the end of the referendum period.[68] It is an offence to contravene either of these periods, although leave can be sought from the court to extend them. Such leave may only be granted if for any special reason it is appropriate to do so.[69] 5–13

Financial limits apply during the referendum period to any individual or body who is not a permitted participant. If they did not, there would be no incentive to register with the Commission and incur the reporting obligations that follow. That

[61] There are eight categories set out in Pt 1 of Sch.13: referendum campaign broadcasts, advertising of any nature; unsolicited material addressed to electors; certain promotional material; market research or canvassing for the purposes of ascertaining voting intentions; provision of services and facilities in relation to press conferences or other dealings with the media; transport by any means of persons to any place with a view to obtaining publicity in connection with a referendum campaign; and rallies and other events, including public meetings (but not party conferences) with a view to obtaining publicity in connection with the campaign.

[62] PPERA s.111(2). "For referendum purposes" means, read short, promoting or procuring a particular outcome (s.111(3)).

[63] PPERA s.112, which concerns "notional referendum expenses", for example, where employees are made available to a campaign or where property is transferred for a discount of more than 10% of its market value.

[64] PPERA s.113(1) and (2).

[65] PPERA s.114(1) and (4).

[66] PPERA s.114(2)–(4).

[67] PPERA s.115(1).

[68] PPERA s.115(2).

[69] PPERA s.115(3)–(5). Where the entitlement to payment is disputed, nothing in s.115 prevents an action for payment of any sums that are claimed to be due: s.116.

limit is currently £10,000 and it is an offence to incur expenses in excess of it.[70] Where the expenses are incurred by a body, the offence is committed by both the body and any person who knew, or ought reasonably to have known, that expenses would be incurred in excess of the limit.[71] So far as permitted participants are concerned, the bodies designated under s.108 (in other words, the "official" campaigns) may incur no more than £5,000,000 of referendum expenses during the referendum period (albeit that was increased to £7,000,000 for the purposes of the EU referendum).[72] The limit imposed on political parties is tied to their share of the vote at the previous UK general election. The relevant limits are these[73]:

Relevant % at last election	**Limit**	**Limit for EU referendum**
Greater than 30%	£5,000,000	£7,000,000
More than 20% but not more than 30%	£4,000,000	£5,500,000
More than 10% but not more than 20%	£3,000,000	£4,000,000
More than 5% but not more than 10%	£2,000,000	£3,000,000
Not more than 5% or no relevant %	£500,000	£700,000

For any other person or body that notified the Commission the limit is £500,000 (increased to £700,000 for the EU referendum). These limits apply to UK wide referendums. Where a referendum falls within the scope of the PPERA but only relates to part of the UK, the Secretary of State shall prescribe the necessary limits by order.[74] It is again an offence to exceed these limits.[75] For a political party, the offence is committed by the responsible person and any deputy treasurer (assuming they knew, or ought reasonably to have known, that the limit would be exceeded) and the party itself.[76] For other permitted participants, the offence is committed by the responsible person (again assuming they had the necessary knowledge) and the body itself.[77]

---

70 PPERA s.117(1)–(2).

71 PPERA s.117(3)–(4).

72 PPERA s.118 and Sch.14 para.1(2). The increase was said to be an uprating of the levels to account for inflation since 2000, when PPERA was enacted: European Union Referendum Act 2015, explanatory notes para.64.

73 PPERA s.118 and Sch.14 para.1(2)(b).

74 PPERA s.118 and Sch.14 para.2(2).

75 A number of investigations have been undertaken by the Electoral Commission in relation to spending during the EU referendum, as a result of which several penalties have been imposed. Further details are available at: *https://www.electoralcommission.org.uk/who-we-are-and-what-we-do/our-enforcement-work/investigations* [Accessed 14 May 2020].

76 PPERA s.118(2)(a).

77 PPERA s.118(2)(b).

Donations to political parties are regulated in the normal manner (which is set out in Pt IV of the PPERA).[78] For those individuals and bodies that are permitted participants but not registered political parties, special provision is made.[79] These rules, which need not be rehearsed here, broadly replicate the scheme in place for political parties. For example, the definition of "permissible donor" is the same, the de minimis threshold of £500 is retained and the reporting requirements are almost identical. Irrespective of which set of rules govern the receipt of donations, for all permitted participants that incur any referendum expenses during the referendum period, detailed returns must be submitted to the Commission within six months of the end of the referendum period.[80] Where the referendum expenses incurred by a permitted participant exceeded £250,000, the return to the Commission must be accompanied by a report prepared by a qualified auditor.[81] Various offences are committed by failing to comply with the requirement to make a return to the Commission.

The campaign

The Political Parties, Elections and Referendums Act 2000 goes on to make a **5–14**
number of particular provisions in relation to the conduct of the campaign. First, it restricts the material that can be published by any Minister of the Crown, government department or local authority in the 28 days immediately before the referendum.[82] The restrictions do not prevent any of these bodies answering specific requests for information, the issuing of press notices or publishing information concerning the holding of the poll. It does prohibit, however, the publication of any material that puts arguments for or against the referendum question or is in any way designed to encourage voting at the referendum. The purpose of the restriction is clear. The government will invariably have a position on any referendum (and particular local governments may take a contrary view from that of the central government). Indeed, depending on the question posed, the very future of the government may depend on the result (as was the case in 2016). The government is invariably in a much stronger position, in terms of the resources available to it and its access to the media, than other bodies that may be campaigning. Restricting its activities in the four weeks before a vote is probably the minimum measure necessary to level the playing field. Next, the PPERA requires that no material wholly or mainly relating to the referendum may be published during the referendum period unless it complies with certain stipulated requirements.[83] In short, such material must include the name and address of the printer of the material, the promoter of the material, and any person on behalf of whom the material is being published. It is an offence to not comply with these requirements. Finally, broadcasters are prohibited from carrying any referendum campaign broadcast made by any person or body not designated by the

[78] Outlined at para.4–20, above.

[79] PPERA s.119 and Sch.15.

[80] PPERA ss.120–124. For the EU referendum, a permitted participant whose referendum expenses did not exceed £10,000 (and a declaration to that effect was given to the Electoral Commission within three months of the end of the referendum period): PPERA s.120A.

[81] PPERA s.121.

[82] PPERA s.125.

[83] PPERA s.126.

Commission under s.108 (in other words, only the "official" campaigns may make a referendum campaign broadcast).[84] This duty, taken with the broadcasters' existing duty of impartiality, is designed to ensure that each side of the campaign has equal access to free airtime for referendum broadcasts.

5–15 In relation to the vote itself, it is conducted under the supervision of the Chief Counting Officer. The Chief Counting Officer shall be the chairperson of the Commission. They shall appoint a counting officer for each relevant area in Great Britain.[85] The Secretary of State is empowered to make such orders as they consider expedient in relation to the conduct of the referendum. Before making such an order, however, they shall consult the Commission. They may not make any order in relation to matters for which specific provision has been made in another enactment.[86]

Scotland

5–16 Separate provision, in the form of the Referendums (Scotland) Act 2020, has now been made to regulate any referendums held in pursuance of provisions made by or under an Act of the Scottish Parliament. Like the PPERA, detailed provision is made in respect of the franchise, voting, the campaign and finance. And the detailed rules are in large respect the same. The last referendum that was sanctioned by the Parliament was, of course, the 2014 independence referendum. For that vote, the Scottish Independence Referendum Act 2013 contained very similar provision, again largely mirroring the PPERA. The purpose of the 2020 Act is to have a detailed framework for the regulation of any future referendums sanctioned by the Scottish Parliament, thereby allowing any legalisation that calls a referendum to be shorter and more focused. In the absence of any current proposals for a further referendum,[87] the provisions of the 2020 Act will sit on the shelf until such a poll is called. Given the limited differences to the PPERA framework, the 2020 Act is not considered further.

---

[84] PPERA s.127. For the EU referendum, no referendum campaign broadcasts were permitted.

[85] PPERA s.128.

[86] PPERA s.129.

[87] Recognising the current impasse between the UK and Scottish Governments on whether a further s.30 Order would be granted to hold a second independence referendum.

CHAPTER 6

Parliaments

Since 1 July 1999, the Scottish Parliament has exercised legislative competence in the increasing sphere of devolved competence. It is a competence that is shared with the Westminster Parliament. The Scotland Act 1998 is explicit on that point.[1] Outwith that sphere, the Westminster Parliament retains exclusive legislative competence. In particular, terms of devolution are reserved to Westminster thus the Scottish Parliament remains subordinate to it.[2] 6–01

There are significant differences between the Westminster Parliament and the Scottish Parliament, which go beyond the differences in their legislative competences. Westminster is a bicameral legislature, the Scottish Parliament unicameral. Westminster and Scottish parliamentary committees have different functions (perhaps most prominently, the committees of the Scottish Parliament have a power to initiate legislation, which the Westminster committees do not yet share). But there are also many similarities and parallels between the two institutions. Both perform the same general functions of a representative, law-making body in a "parliamentary system": the enactment of legislation, the provision of a government and the sustaining of that government in office, and the important function of holding the government and other public authorities to account on behalf of the public as a whole. The rules and procedures governing both bodies have much in common, in so far as those applicable in Scotland often represent a statutory rendering of the conventions that have grown up at Westminster. The same is true in matters of privilege and standards, in that both bodies have jurisdiction to regulate their own procedures and the conduct of their members. The two Parliaments are therefore considered side by side, highlighting the distinctions between them where such exist, but noting also what they have in common where that is the case.

---

[1] Scotland Act 1998 ("SA 1998") s.28(7). The extent to which Westminster may enact legislation for Scotland the subject matter of which falls within the definition of devolved competence is regulated for the present by the so called "Sewel convention", whereby Westminster will not normally enact such legislation without first obtaining the consent of the Scottish Parliament: see para.2–11, above.

[2] SA 1998 s.28(7); *AXA General Insurance Co Ltd v Lord Advocate* [2011] UKSC 46; 2012 S.C. (U.K.S.C.) 122, per Lord Reed at [146].

LIFE OF PARLIAMENT

Westminster

6–02 The life of a Parliament at Westminster begins when the Sovereign exercises her prerogative to summon it to meet. By convention, the Queen exercises this prerogative following a general election. Parliament must meet in the subsequent years of its life to approve the appropriation of monies for the provision of public services and perform its other constitutional functions. It was, until 2011, for the Queen to dissolve Parliament. This was done on the advice of the Prime Minster and had to be done no later than five years after the previous general election.[3] In practice, Parliament was dissolved before this time, usually during its fourth year. The Fixed-term Parliaments Act 2011 removes that prerogative power.[4] The first UK general election after the passing of that Act was held on 7 May 2015[5] and future elections should ordinarily have been held on the first Thursday of May every five years.[6] The Prime Minister can, by statutory instrument, delay the election date by up to two months.[7] There are two mechanisms by which an earlier election can be called. Both lie in the hands, in theory at least, of the House of Commons and not the Prime Minister or the Sovereign. First, the House of Commons can pass a motion that there shall be an early general election. Such a motion requires a two-thirds majority in the House of Commons.[8] Second, an early general election can be prompted by a vote of no confidence in the government. This only requires a simple majority and shall trigger an election only if a motion of confidence is not then passed within 14 days.[9] Where an election is held in such circumstances, and the poll takes place before the first Thursday in May, the next general election is on the first Thursday in May in the fourth calendar year following the election. Where such a poll takes place after the first Thursday in May, the next election takes place in the fifth calendar year following the election (again on the first Thursday in May).[10] Such early elections were intended to be the exception. They have, however, been the norm. Following the 2015 election, the next election took place on 8 June 2017, the House of Commons having resolved that there should be an early election. That meant the next general election was due to take place on 5 May 2022. But this time the government was unable to pass the necessary motion under the 2011 Act. Instead, Parliament passed the Early Parliamentary General Election Act 2019,

---

[3] Parliament Act 1911 s.7.

[4] Fixed-term Parliaments Act 2011 s.3(2); see generally M. Ryan, "The Fixed-term Parliaments Act 2011" [2012] P.L. 213; R. Brazier, "A small piece of constitutional history" (2012) 128 L.Q.R. 315 and R. Craig, "Restoring Confidence: Replacing the Fixed-Term Parliaments Act 2011" (2018) 81 M.L.R. 480.

[5] Fixed-term Parliaments Act 2011 s.1(2).

[6] Fixed-term Parliaments Act 2011 s.1(3).

[7] Fixed-term Parliaments Act 2011 s.1(5); the reason for this provision lies in ensuring sufficient flexibility to deal with a situation such as the foot and mouth outbreak that promoted Tony Blair to delay the 2001 election by a month so as to deal with the crisis.

[8] Fixed-term Parliaments Act 2011 s.2(1).

[9] Fixed-term Parliaments Act 2011 s.2(3).

[10] Fixed-term Parliaments Act 2011 s.1(4). Compare with the provisions of the Scotland Act 1998: where an "extra-ordinary general election" (e.g. one that follows a vote of no confidence in the Scottish Government) does not interrupt the normal four year parliamentary cycle.

thus by-passing the two-thirds requirement of the 2011 Act. As a result, a poll took place on 12 December 2019. Applying the 2011 Act, a poll is next scheduled for 2 May 2024.

The case for Parliament to operate on a fixed-term basis had long been made. Both Labour and the Liberal Democrats went in to the 2010 election with a manifesto promise to legislate for a fixed-term Parliament. The advantage of a fixed-term Parliament, or so the argument goes, is primarily in restricting the power of the executive to call an election at a time of their choice. Prior to the 2011 Act, the decision rested with the Prime Minister alone, which allowed the election to be held on a date that would maximise the political advantage to the government. Given the circumstances in which the 2017 General Election was called, it is doubtful whether the 2011 Act has done anything to curb this particular executive advantage. Fixing the length of Parliament also allows for the better planning of the legislative programme and, especially in times of coalition, can offer stability and security to the government. How real these benefits are had been questioned before the events that led to the 2017 and 2019 elections.[11] In 2010, a fixed-term Parliament was important to the junior members of the coalition (the Liberal Democrats) so that the Prime Minister could not end the coalition at will (and at a time that gave him the greatest political advantage). Whether one is a supporter of fixed-term Parliaments or not, there are a number of criticisms that can be levelled at the 2011 Act. Why, for example, was a five-year period chosen? Under the Parliament Act 1911 that was the *maximum* length of a Parliament, but in practice most lasted for less than four years. Four years was selected as the appropriate length of time between elections for devolved legislatures (although that has since been increased to five) and is the most common period in other European countries. A five-year cycle also meant that the 2015 election would fall on the same day as elections to the Scottish Parliament. The 2011 Act addressed that problem by extending the then current session of the Scottish Parliament by a year.[12] That, however, only delayed the problem until 2020 when the elections would have again clashed. As we shall see shortly, the Scottish Elections (Dates) Act 2016 kicked that particular can down the road for a few years, by deferring (unnecessarily, it turned out, given the 2017 general election was called) the next Scottish Parliament election until 2021 (it having been due in 2020).[13] Furthermore, the 2011 Act leaves no residual power for the sovereign to dissolve Parliament. The Queen retains such a residual function, which could only be appropriately used in exceptional circumstances, in relation to Canada, Australia and New Zealand, but not now in relation to the United Kingdom. Why that decision was taken is not at all clear. However, the greatest criticism that can be levied at the 2011 Act is that is has done little to actually fix the term of Parliament. In 2017, the House of Commons voted in favour of an early election. That it would be asked to do so was announced from the steps of Downing Street and came as a surprise to most. Politically, it proved

---

[11] Brazier, "A small piece of constitutional history" (2012) 128 L.Q.R. 315, 316–317; V. Bogdanor, *The Coalition and the Constitution* (Oxford: Hart, 2011), Ch.6.

[12] Fixed-term Parliaments Act 2011 s.4; similar provision is made for Wales and Northern Ireland so as to avoid elections to those legislatures being held on the same day as an election to the UK Parliament (s.5 of the 2011 Act).

[13] With respect to the Welsh Assembly, the problem has been solved by increasing that body's term from four to five years (Wales Act 2014 s.1).

impossible to resist the Prime Minister's desire to go to the country. Yet, it was, just as before the 2011 Act, at a time of her choosing and no doubt at time believed, wrongly as it turned out, to be to her advantage. Again, in 2019, an early election was called. But this time, the 2011 Act showed its other flaw: it locked a government into office who had no majority in the House of Commons and no support for its flagship policy. Because the government could not garner two-thirds support for an election, and in the absence of a confidence motion being laid, it could not go to the country. That impasse was only resolved when Parliament legislated, in the form of the Early Parliamentary General Election Act 2019, to by-pass the requirements of the 2011 Act entirely. The 2011 Act was meant to remove the doubt surrounding the timing of an election and provide a degree of stability. Measured against that standard, the 2011 Act cannot be regarded as a success. That is not to suggest that fixed-term Parliaments are in themselves objectionable; they are not. But the 2011 Act represents another bit of rushed and piecemeal reform of the constitution that is likely to need reconsidered.

The Queen's Speech takes place early on in a newly summoned Parliament, and at the commencement of subsequent parliamentary sessions of the Parliament. It marks the formal opening of each new session following the summoning or re-summoning of Parliament. Sessions[14] usually run for about 12 months from November to November, although there is no legal requirement that they should. A session is brought to an end either by the dissolution of Parliament or by its prorogation. The significance of prorogation is that it suspends all parliamentary business until the next session (which may begin the following day). In particular, public Bills which do not complete their parliamentary stages before the end of the session lapse and must start again in the session following (although there is now provision for the carrying over of government legislation from one session to the next with the agreement of the House of Commons).[15] Accordingly, the significance is not in the fact Parliament does not sit (as would be the case in a recess) but that no parliamentary business can be transacted and Bills which have not completed their journey through Parliament fall. In 2017, the UK Government confirmed that the Session was to last for two years to facilitate the legislation necessary to give effect to the UK's exit from the European Union.[16] As a result, the longest parliamentary session in centuries began. It was believed to have been brought to an end in September 2019, when Parliament was thought to have been prorogued. It, as we have seen, had not been.[17] The Session finally concluded, without all of the Brexit-related legislation having been passed, when it was dissolved in preparation for the December 2019 election.

---

[14] A "Session" of the UK Parliament is usually a year but a "Session" of the Scottish Parliament is the entire period (usually four, but currently five, years) between elections.

[15] In Scotland, because a parliamentary session lasts the life-time of the Parliament, Bills have the full remaining spread of the parliamentary cycle following their introduction in which to complete their parliamentary stages.

[16] See: *https://www.gov.uk/government/news/government-to-confirm-two-year-parliament-to-deliver-brexit-and-beyond* [Accessed 15 May 2020].

[17] See para.1–21, above.

Holyrood

The life cycle of the Scottish Parliament is fixed by the Scotland Act 1998. It begins on a date falling within the period of seven days beginning with the day immediately after that on which the poll at a general election was held.[18] Ordinarily, it will end with its dissolution with a view to a general election being held on the first Thursday in May of the fourth calendar year following that in which the previous ordinary general election was held.[19] Should the first Thursday in May be unsuitable for some reason unsuitable, the Presiding Officer of the Scottish Parliament may propose an alternative date, no earlier than one month before and no later than one month after the first Thursday in May, to the Queen, and the Queen may[20] then by proclamation dissolve the Parliament, require the poll to be held on the date proposed and require the new Parliament to meet within the period of seven days beginning with the date of the poll. A Scottish general election cannot be held on the same day as a UK general election.[21] As we have seen, a clash becomes inevitable because of the fixed, five-year term of the UK Parliament. In the absence of any early UK general election, the next clash is due to happen in 2042. A clash had been due in 2020. In the event, that was avoided by the 2017 UK election. But before that had happened, the Scottish Parliament passed the Scottish Elections (Dates) Act 2016 that deferred the Scottish election to 2021 (and thus again extended the parliamentary term to five years). That legislation remains in force despite the 2017 election removing its reason for being. Given it was passed to avoid a clash that will now not take place, it might be thought that it should be repealed and the Scottish Parliament revert to its prescribed four-year cycle. Yet that has not been done and there has was never suggestion it should be done. When a clash does arise, it will be for the Scottish Ministers to specify the day that the election will take place on.[22] The original proposal from the Smith Commission placed a limit on that discretion: it would have required the Scottish general election to be held no less than two months before and no more than six months after the date on which the election should otherwise be held.[23] That proposal did not make its way into the 2016 Act. It is surprising that this discretion was vested in the Scottish Ministers. As we have just seen, it is the Presiding Officer, under s.2(5) of the Scotland Act 1998, that has the power to propose a variation to the planned 6–03

[18] SA 1998 s.2(3)(b). For the purposes of calculating the seven-day period, Saturday and Sunday, Christmas Eve and Christmas Day, Good Friday, a Scottish bank holiday or a "day appointed for public thanksgiving or mourning" are to be disregarded: s.4.

[19] SA 1998 ss.2(3)(a). If the election is to be held on the first Thursday in May, the Parliament must be dissolved at the beginning of the "minimum period" ending with the date of the poll. The "minimum period" is specified in accordance with orders made under s.12, which confers power on the Secretary of State to make provision about Scottish elections.

[20] Here, "may" not "shall" (cf. SA 1998 s.2(3)(a)). Presumably this is to preserve an element of discretion on the Queen's part as the ultimate safeguard against abuse (although it is significant that it is the Presiding Officer, not the First Minister, who is charged with proposing an alternative date), but it presents another odd contrast with the Fixed-term Parliaments Act 2011 that divested the Queen of any discretion in the dissolution of Parliament.

[21] Scotland Act 1998 s.(2A)(a), inserted by Scotland Act 2016 s.5(3).

[22] Scotland Act 1998 s.2(2B).

[23] HM Government, *Scotland in the United Kingdom: An enduring settlement* (The Stationery Office, 2015) para.1.4, *https://www.gov.uk/government/uploads/system/uploads/attachment_data/file/397079/Scotland_EnduringSettlement_acc.pdf* [Accessed 18 May 2020].

date of scheduled election.[24] It is even more surprising that the discretion confers considerable latitude upon the executive in relation to the timing of an election where a clash is scheduled. Although no limits are expressed in the Scotland Act, some must be implicit. For example, the power to select an alternative should not be capable of extending the life of the Parliament by years (or, perhaps, materially curtailing it). It must also be implicit that the alternative date will be chosen so that opposition parties have adequate time to properly prepare. In other words, it should be exercised in a manner consistent with the fundamental features of the Scotland Act 1998: that the Parliament is a representative assembly, chosen by the electorate at elections that should ordinarily be held at four-yearly intervals, to serve a democracy govern by the rule of law. But such limits as there are will be for the common law to determine, in the same way that the common law would recognise limitations on an otherwise unfettered discretion held by the executive.

Section 3 of the Scotland Act makes provision for extraordinary general elections. Where no fewer than two-thirds of the total number of MSPs (that is, at least, 86 MSPs) vote in favour of a resolution that the Parliament be dissolved, the Presiding Officer must propose a date for the holding of an election and the Queen may, by proclamation, dissolve the Parliament, require an extraordinary general election to be held on the date proposed and enjoin the new Parliament to meet within seven days of the date of the poll.[25] An extraordinary general election may also be required where the Parliament fails to nominate one of its members for appointment as First Minister within 28 days of a general election, or of the resignation or death of an incumbent First Minister, or of the incumbent First Minister ceasing to be an MSP otherwise than by virtue of a dissolution of the Scottish Parliament.[26] In any of these situations, if the extraordinary election is held within the six month period prior to the first Thursday in May, and an ordinary election was due to take place on the latter date, the ordinary election will not be held.[27]

COMPOSITION

The Sovereign

6–04 As we have seen, the Sovereign has an important, if formal, role to play in the dissolution and summoning of the Westminster and Scottish Parliaments. But the Sovereign is also a component part of the Westminster Parliament—"the King, Lords and Commons assembled"—in that Acts of Parliament are Acts of the Queen in Parliament, and must receive Royal Assent in order to become law.[28]

[24] Of interest, the Presiding Officer retains the power to propose a variation, subject to the same limits, to the date chosen by the Scottish Ministers: Scotland Act 1998 s.2(5ZA).

[25] SA 1998 s.3(1)(a) and (2)(b).

[26] SA 1998 s.3(1)(b); and see also s.46.

[27] SA 1998 s.3(3). This does not affect the year in which the subsequent ordinary general election will be held: s.3(4).

[28] By convention, of course, the Sovereign never refuses Royal Assent. The last time this happened was in the reign of Queen Anne, and even then seems to have been on the advice of her ministers. Royal Assent is different from Queen's Consent. The latter is required when the subject matter of the

The Queen is not part of the Scottish Parliament even in this formal sense, but Royal Assent is nonetheless necessary in order that a Bill passed by the Parliament may become an Act of the Scottish Parliament.[29]

Westminster

House of Lords

"No one shall be a member of the House of Lords by virtue of a hereditary peerage."

At a stroke (promptly qualified), s.1 of the House of Lords Act 1999 did away with what was widely accepted as an indefensibly undemocratic blemish on British constitutional arrangements. But it has to be put in its historical context: in 1911 the powers of the House of Lords to block legislation approved by the House of Commons were curtailed by the Parliament Act, the long title of which declared: **6–05**

> "it is intended to substitute for the House of Lords as it at present exists a Second Chamber constituted on a popular instead of hereditary basis, but such substitution cannot be immediately brought into operation."

A century on, the wait continues.[30] Perhaps the most that could be said for the historic right of hereditary peers to sit and vote in the House of Lords was that they offered some form of counterweight to the "elective dictatorship" flowing from the command of a majority in the House of Commons. But it was not a particularly compelling argument for retention of the hereditary principle: if nothing else, there was a question about how even-handed a counterweight the hereditary peers actually were.

The House of Lords remains in a transitional state, pending final reform. There are about 790 peers in total, comprising about 650 life peers,[31] 26 Lords Spiritual (being bishops and archbishops of the Church of England) and 92 hereditary peers exempted from the effects of the 1999 Act. Members of the judiciary (be

---

Bill before Parliament touches upon the Queen's prerogatives or certain personal property interests of the Queen (or, in some cases, the Prince of Wales, where his Consent is required). It is ordinarily a formality and is signified in each House by a Privy Counsellor (who is invariably also a minister of the Crown) at the appropriate point in the legislative process. For more detail, see Erskine May, *Parliamentary Practice*, 25th edn, para.9.6 (available online at: *https://erskinemay.parliament.uk/section/6542/queens-consent-on-bills/* [Accessed 15 May 2020].

[29] SA 1998 s.28(2)–(4).

[30] See C. Ballinger, *The House of Lords 1911–2011: A Century of Non-Reform* (Oxford: Hart, 2012).

[31] The Life Peerages Act 1958 provided for the conferment of life peerages on men and (for the first time) women with the right to sit and vote in the Lords. Life peers have helped to mitigate, if not remove, the political imbalance in the upper house; and, to the extent that life peerages are conferred in recognition of outstanding public service and/or expertise in particular fields, have brought to the House of Lords a rather wider range of experience and specialism than tends to exist in the Commons. But as appointees, life peers have no obviously greater claim to democratic legitimacy than hereditary peers.

they former Lords of Appeal in Ordinary[32] or other members of the judiciary) are now disqualified from sitting and voting in the House of Lords.[33] Following the enactment of the 1999 Act, the government appointed a Royal Commission under the chairmanship of Lord Wakeham to consider and make recommendations on the changes needed to bring about a fully reformed and modernised second chamber.[34] The Wakeham Commission reported in January 2000.[35] It recommended no substantial changes to the functions of the House of Lords or to the balance of power between the two Houses of Parliament, but dealt in detail with the question of the composition of a reformed upper house. In essence, Wakeham favoured a mixed membership of about 550, consisting of elected "regional members" and members appointed on the nomination of an independent statutory appointments commission charged with securing a "broadly representative" chamber. Some one-fifth of the members of this reformed House of Lords would sit on the cross-benches; the remaining, politically affiliated members would be required to reflect the voting preferences expressed at the most recent general election. The government endorsed Wakeham's recommendations, but its attempts to take them forward have run repeatedly into the sand.[36] Having undertaken to allow a free vote in Parliament on the composition of a reformed House of Lords in its manifesto for the 2005 general election, the government published a further White Paper in February 2007 in order to provide a framework within which such a vote might take place.[37] On 7 March 2007 a series of votes were held in the House of Commons on various reform options.[38] The House of Commons voted in favour of *both* a fully elected House of Lords and an 80 per cent elected House. A week later, the House of Lords voted against all of the proposals other than a wholly appointed House. The impasse continued. Despite this, a further Green Paper was published in July 2007, restating the government's commitment (now under Gordon Brown's leadership) to complete reform[39] and each of the three main parties went into the 2010 general election with manifestos containing commitments to complete the reform of the House of Lords. It was therefore unsurprising that the coalition agreement that followed the

---

32 The House of Lords judicial function (save as in so far as it retains jurisdiction to determine peerage claims: *Erksine May Parliamentary Practice*, edited by M. Jack, 24th edn (London: LexisNexis Butterworths, 2011), pp.182–183) was abolished on the creation of the Supreme Court on 1 October 2009.

33 Constitutional Reform Act 2005 s.137.

34 For the government's own thoughts on the matter, see HM Government, *Modernising Parliament: Reforming the House of Lords* (The Stationery Office, 1999) Cm.4183.

35 Royal Commission on the Reform of the House of Lords, *A House for the Future* (The Stationery Office, 2000) Cm.4534.

36 The government set out its proposals in a further White Paper, HM Government, *The House of Lords: Completing the Reform* (The Stationery Office, 2001) Cm.5291, which was then the subject of public consultation. The crucial outcome of that consultation process was the rejection, by almost 90% of respondents, of the government's proposal for a predominantly appointed second chamber. The government thereupon handed the matter over to Parliament; but the joint committee of both Houses of Parliament established in 2002 and charged with finding a way through to the next stage of reform met with no more success. A further, fruitless, public consultation took place in 2003–2004 on the proposals contained in yet another White Paper, Department for Constitutional Affairs, *Constitutional Reform: Next Steps for the House of Lords* (The Stationery Office, 2003) CP14/03.

37 HM Government, *The House of Lords: Reform* (The Stationery Office, 2007) Cm.7207.

38 They were: fully appointed House of Lords; fully elected; 20% elected; 40% elected; 50% elected; 60% elected; and 80% elected.

39 HM Government, *The Governance of Britain* (The Stationery Office, 2007), Cm.7170.

election contained a pledge to bring forward proposals for a wholly or mainly elected House of Lords. In 2012, the House of Lords Reform Bill was introduced by the Deputy Prime Minister, Nick Clegg.[40] The Bill proposed a mainly elected (80 per cent) chamber, with members elected for a 15 year term by means of proportionate representation.[41] There would eventually be 360 elected members, 90 appointed members, 12 Lords Spiritual and any "ministerial members".[42] The Bill only made it to the second reading in the House of Commons. In the face of increasing opposition in the House of Commons (primarily from Conservative backbench MPs), the government announced in August 2012 that it would not proceed with the Bill.[43] As a result, the only reforming legislation that was passed during the 2010–2015 Parliament was the House of Lords Reform Act 2014. But this did not contain substantive change to the structure and composition of the House. Rather, it made provision for members of the House of Lords to resign, for them to cease to be Members of the House if they failed to attend during a parliamentary session and their removal from the House upon conviction of a "serious offence" (an offence for which a period of imprisonment in excess of a year was imposed).

The task of reforming the House of Lords is not to be underestimated.[44] It is much easier to propose questions than identify solutions. How do you constitute the House of Lords on a popular basis without threatening the primacy of the House of Commons? Assuming some form of proportionate representation was employed for any elections to the House of Lords, and assuming the first past the post system continued to be employed by the House of Commons, that would probably give rise to a second chamber that was more representative of the views of the electorate.[45] How, on democratic grounds, could the House of Commons then claim a mandate to exercise the powers of the Parliament Acts if its legislation was rejected? More fundamentally, would it continue to be appropriate that the executive be drawn principally from the House of Commons? If the

---

[40] A draft Bill had been published a year earlier (HM Government, *House of Lords Reform Draft Bill* (The Stationery Office, 2011), Cm.8077, *https://www.gov.uk/government/uploads/system/uploads/attachment_data/file/229020/8077.pdf* [Accessed 15 May 2020]) which was then considered by a joint committee of the two Houses (Joint Committee on the Draft House of Lords Reform Bill, *Draft House of Lords Reform Bill, Report Session 2010–12* (The Stationery Office, 2012), HL Paper 284–I, HC 1313–I, *http://www.publications.parliament.uk/pa/jt201012/jtselect/jtdraftref/284/284i.pdf* [Accessed 15 May 2020]). There was no consensus from the joint committee with an alternative report being published by 12 of the committee's members. The government accepted the majority of the recommendations of the joint committee: HM Government, *Government Response to the Report of the Joint Committee on the Draft House of Lords Reform Bill* (The Stationery Office, 2012), Cm.8391, *https://www.gov.uk/government/uploads/system/uploads/attachment_data/file/228718/8391.pdf* [Accessed 15 May 2020].

[41] The system proposed was the closed list system of proportionate representation (which is currently used to elect "regional members" of the Scottish Parliament and for elections to the European Parliament). Under the proposal, the United Kingdom would be divided into 12 electoral regions (Scotland, Wales and Northern Ireland each representing a single region).

[42] Achieving a House in that form would take 15 years as 120 elected members would be returned at each general election (cl.4) and those elections would take place on the same day as elections to the House of Commons (cl.3).

[43] This led to allegations by the Deputy Prime Minster (that were denied by the Prime Minister) that the Conservative Party had broken the coalition agreement.

[44] For a further discussion, see V. Bogdanor, *The New British Constitution* (Oxford: Hart, 2009), Ch.6.

[45] We have seen the problems facing the first past the post system in Chs 1 and 4, above.

House of Commons moves to a system of proportionate representation, what system should be employed to prevent the House of Lords mirroring the composition of the Commons? If the House of Lords is to be appointed (in whole or in part), who makes the appointments? On what basis? For what term? What, if any, element of the House of Lords should be democratically elected? All of these are difficult questions. And they all defy an answer unless reform of the House of Lords goes hand in hand with wider constitutional reform. But the continuing irony is that whilst the undemocratic nature of the House of Lords (in particular the remaining hereditary element) remains objectionable in a modern democracy, it actually performs the role expected of an upper chamber to a reasonably good standard.[46]

House of Commons

6–06 At present, 650 MPs sit in the House of Commons, of whom 59 represent Scottish constituencies. Prior to the 2005 general election, there were 72 Scottish MPs. The reduction in their number constitutes the then government's response to what is dubbed the "West Lothian question"[47]—namely, whether it can be right that Scottish MPs should retain the ability to vote on legislation intended to apply only to England and Wales[48] when English and Welsh MPs have forfeited that ability in relation to matters devolved to a Scottish Parliament. Reducing Scottish representation at Westminster mitigates, but does not go to the root of, the problem. Arguably, only a shift to a federal model of constitutional organisation could provide a long-term solution.[49] Plainly, so long as Westminster continues to enact legislation for the whole of the UK, an appropriate level of Scottish representation must be maintained. It is not obvious, however, that the West Lothian question can be dismissed as an incidental, and ultimately minor, untidiness occasioned by devolution.[50] As further powers are devolved to Scotland, the case for addressing it becomes stronger. As we shall see shortly, changes have been made to the Standing Orders of the House of Commons to try and address this issue. How effective they will be remains unknown.

---

[46] The difficulties similar to those inherent in reforming the House of Lords have arisen in Canada, which has a Senate modeled on the House of Lords. The Supreme Court of Canada has recently considered the constitutionality of various options for reforming the Canadian Senate. It offers an interesting discussion of similar issues to those that have arisen in the United Kingdom: *Reference re Senate Reform* [2014] S.C.C. 32.

[47] So called because it was articulated in the debates on the earlier Scotland Bill in the 1970s by Tam Dalyell, then MP for West Lothian.

[48] Occasionally with decisive effect, as where the government's majority is secured by its Scottish MPs.

[49] A. Olowofoyeku, "Decentralising the United Kingdom: The federal argument" (1999) 3 Edin. L.R. 57.

[50] During the debates on the Scotland Bill in the late 1970s, an amendment was tabled that would have provided for the taking of a second vote in such circumstances (the idea being that, in the meantime, the Scottish MPs could be persuaded to abstain). The government of the day rejected the idea as a "constitutional imbecility", but it has resurfaced in the current debate and something like it may in the longer run require to be adopted.

Holyrood

The Scotland Act 1998 provides that there shall be 129 Members of the Scottish Parliament.[51] Seventy three of these are elected by the familiar "first past the post" or simple majority method in each of the constituencies from which, until the 2005 general election, Scottish MPs were returned (with Orkney and Shetland split into two separate constituencies). The remaining 56 members are elected in accordance with the "additional member" system of proportional representation from each of the eight European parliamentary constituencies provided for by the European Parliamentary Constituencies (Scotland) Order 1996[52] (although for European elections these have now been supplanted by the electoral system provided for by the European Parliamentary Elections Act 2002, under which Scotland constitutes a single region for the purposes of electing its eight MEPs). Thus seven regional members are returned from each region.[53] 6–07

ELIGIBILITY AND DISQUALIFICATION

The conditions of eligibility to stand for election to the House of Commons and the Scottish Parliament were considered in Ch.4, above.[54] As we saw, those conditions were broadly the same. The provisions differ, however, as to the consequences of disqualification. At Westminster, a person claiming that an individual disqualified by virtue of the House of Commons Disqualification Act 1975 has been elected to the House of Commons may apply to the Judicial Committee of the Privy Council for a declaration to that effect under s.7. The Judicial Committee may direct that the issue be tried in the High Court of England and Wales, the Court of Session or the High Court of Northern Ireland, depending on the location of the constituency in question; if so, the decision of that court is final. In Scotland, if a disqualified person is elected to the Scottish Parliament either as a constituency or a regional member, their election is void and their seat vacant.[55] Where a person becomes disqualified during the currency of their membership, they ceases to be an MSP and their seat falls vacant accordingly.[56] Where an MSP becomes disqualified on grounds of bankruptcy, their seat is not automatically vacated but they do become ineligible to participate in the proceedings of the Parliament and may lose other rights and privileges incidental to membership. In any of these situations, the Parliament may by resolution elect to disregard the member's disqualification under s.16(4) of the Scotland Act, if it considers that the ground of disqualification has been removed or that it is proper to disregard any disqualification incurred by the member.[57] Anyone who believes that a person is or has become disqualified from 6–08

[51] SA 1998 s.1 and Sch.1.

[52] European Parliamentary Constituencies (Scotland) Order 1996 (SI 1996/1926).

[53] For an account of the process governing elections to the Scottish Parliament, see paras 4–06—4–09, above.

[54] See para.4–14, above.

[55] SA 1998 s.17(1).

[56] SA 1998 s.17(2).

[57] But no such resolution may be adopted where an election petition has been presented in respect of the member, or where the disqualification has been established in election petition proceedings or

membership of the Scottish Parliament may apply to the Court of Session for a declarator to that effect.[58] It should be noted that the jurisdiction of the Court of Session in this respect extends to all possible grounds of disqualification, not merely, as with the Judicial Committee of the Privy Council, those arising from the House of Commons Disqualification Act 1975.

FUNCTIONS OF PARLIAMENTS

6–09 The Westminster and Scottish Parliaments alike have three essential functions: to provide and sustain a government in office; to make law; and to hold the executive to account.[59] The first of these we touched on in Ch.2, above, in the context of the constitutional conventions (or, in Scotland, statutory rules) surrounding the appointment and resignation of governments; we revisit the matter in the next chapter. Suffice to say here that the democratic legitimacy of a government in a parliamentary system depends upon its ability to command the continuing confidence of the House of Commons or Scottish Parliament as the case may be. That confidence withdrawn, the government must fall. Under the Scotland Act 1998 the First Minister (s.45(2)) and his or her ministers (s.47(2)(c)) must resign if a motion of no confidence is passed in relation to the Scottish Government.[60] An extraordinary general election will then follow only if the Parliament fails to nominate one of its number as First Minister within 28 days of that resignation (s.3(1)(b)). So far as Westminster is concerned, the matter is now, as we have seen, regulated by the Fixed-term Parliaments Act 2011. Where a motion of no confidence is passed in the government, a general election follows *if* a motion of confidence is *not* passed in a new government within 14 days. Both

---

proceedings under SA 1998 s.18. Mental illness is no longer a ground to suspend a member's participation in the work of the Parliament: Mental Health (Discrimination) Act 2013.

[58] SA 1998 s.18. The procedure provides an alternative mechanism for challenging a person's election to the election petition procedure laid down by the Representation of the People Act 1983, with the possible advantage that, whereas election petitions must be presented within 21 days of the contested election, there is no comparable time limit on proceedings under s.18. However, the jurisdiction of the court under s.18 is excluded if an election petition has already been presented; it is also excluded if the Scottish Parliament has adopted a resolution under s.16(4) to disregard a member's disqualification.

[59] Plainly that is not an exhaustive account. There are other parliamentary functions, such as the regulation of internal procedures and the supervision of parliamentary standards; and as elected representatives MPs and MSPs have a variety of functions in relation to their constituents and constituencies.

[60] The Scotland Act 1998 makes no provision for the possibility that, for 28 days and the period leading up to and immediately following an extraordinary general election, there would be no Scottish Government at all. It is open to the Parliament within that 28-day period to resolve that it should be dissolved, which would trigger the duty of the Presiding Officer under s.3(1)(a) to recommend to the Queen a date for an extraordinary election. But such a resolution requires the support of at least two-thirds of the total number of MSPs, and if the political complexion of the Parliament is such that it is unable within 28 days to nominate a replacement First Minister, it may be equally unfavourable to securing a resolution for dissolution. At Westminster, a government which loses a vote of confidence continues in office de facto on a caretaker basis during the currency of the election period, and arguably some such arrangement would require to be made in Scotland in the circumstances envisaged here; but there is no basis for it in the Scotland Act.

Parliaments, therefore, have provisions that delay the calling of an election in order that an attempt can be made to form an alternative government before resort is had to an unscheduled election.

The primary legislative function of the Parliaments we examine later in this chapter. There is of course a salient difference between the UK and Scottish Parliaments in this respect, in that while the legislative competence of the former is traditionally understood to be subject to no legal limits, the legislative competence of the latter is restricted in terms of the Scotland Act 1998.[61] It should not necessarily be assumed, however, that the legislative sovereignty of the Westminster Parliament means that it is wholly unfettered. True it is that a government in command of a reliable majority in the House of Commons may secure the enactment of legislation that is in some sense disagreeable or offensive to popular (or elite) sentiments. Nonetheless, a process, more or less protracted, must be followed in order to obtain the seal of parliamentary approval, and if the process provides no guarantee as to the substance of the legislative outcomes, it offers a measure of procedural protection the importance of which, in structuring and confining the will of the executive, is often overlooked.[62]

The role of the Parliaments in holding the executive to account is frequently **6–10** disparaged. As we shall see in Ch.7, below, there is certainly scope for doubting the adequacy of the convention of ministerial responsibility to Parliament as a mechanism for securing accountability for the exercise of political power. Much is made, for example, of the persistent failure of ministers to resign in response to departmental wrongdoing or error, as if this were a vital component of the concept. The emphasis on resignation flows from the fact that, as a matter of nineteenth century practice, before the emergence of the modern party system and the consolidation of government control over the legislature, Parliament could and sometimes did force the resignation of a minister or ministry in whose fitness for office it had lost confidence. Nowadays, such events are vanishingly rare.[63] But however ephemeral the sanction attaching to ministerial responsibility, the expectation that ministers should answer to Parliament, and account as fully and clearly as possible for their and their departments' actions and decisions, even to the extent of acknowledging errors where errors are made, remains very much alive. Not only that, but ministers do appear before Parliament and parliamentary committees, do subject themselves to questioning, and do not routinely mislead Parliament in the process (even if their answers may be evasive or at least less comprehensive than parliamentarians would like). To be sure, difficulties remain in "investigating the facts, agreeing on the application of the convention [of ministerial responsibility] to the facts, and enforcement",[64] difficulties that are attributable, at least in part, to what has been justly described as "the intense inefficiency of our parliamentary system".[65] The tabling of parliamentary questions, for example, is not an especially efficient means of eliciting information; and parliamentary debates are frequently notable only for the

---

[61] As we shall see, there are also significant differences between the two Parliaments in relation to legislative procedures.

[62] See K.D. Ewing and C.A. Gearty, *The Struggle for Civil Liberties: Political Freedom and the Rule of Law in Britain, 1914–1945* (Oxford: Oxford University Press, 2000), pp.12 and 13.

[63] The last time the government lost a vote of confidence was in 1979.

[64] I. Leigh, "Secrets of the Political Constitution" (1999) 62 M.L.R. 298.

[65] D. Judge, "Parliament in the 1980s" (1989) 60 *Political Quarterly* 400.

absence of any meaningful debate. But the convention of ministerial responsibility is not the only mechanism, nor even the only parliamentary mechanism, of accountability. Parliamentary committees both at Westminster and Holyrood provide a more exacting forum for the scrutiny of the executive than the parliamentary floor. Their fact finding capacities may have been blunted in the past, and their effectiveness unduly dependent on ministerial co-operation, but the first of these at least may have been enhanced by the enactment of freedom of information legislation, the utility of which is in no sense confined to pressure groups and busybodies.

LEGISLATIVE PROCESSES

Westminster

6–11 At Westminster, proposals for legislation (known as "Bills") are either public, private or hybrid.[66] Private bills provide for the conferment of special powers, benefits or exemptions on a person or body of persons in excess of or in conflict with the general law. There are two categories of public Bills. First, there are government Bills.[67] All government sponsored legislation is enacted by means of public Bills. Government Bills are introduced by the relevant minister. Second, there are private members' Bills. Public bills introduced by any other Member fall into this category. Often thought of as referring to Bills introduced by backbench MPs, private members' Bills also include any Bill introduced by the opposition parties. In other words, they are "non-government" Bills. There is no procedural distinction between the different categories of public Bills. However, in the House of Commons, all Bills are not equal and very limited time is made available for private members' Bills. Accordingly, any private members' Bill that is at all controversial has very limited chance of passing into law.[68]

6–12 A government Bill first comes to the formal notice of Parliament at first reading, although its contents may have been more or less extensively trailed in advance of that.[69] First reading is a purely formal stage, after which the Bill is

[66] *Erskine May Parliamentary Practice* (2019) describes hybrid Bills as "public bills which are considered to affect specific private or other local interests, in a manner different from the private or local interests of other persons or bodies of the same category" (para.30.57: *https://erskinemay.parliament.uk/section/5576/proceedings%20on%20hybrid%20bills/* [Accessed 9 July 2020]). After second reading, a hybrid Bill is sent to a select committee. If petitions objecting to the Bill are received, the committee deals with it in much the same way as a private Bill; if not, the Bill is recommitted to a standing committee or Committee of the Whole House and dealt with as a public Bill. An example is the Channel Tunnel Rail Link Act 1996. The only hybrid Bill to be enacted by the Scottish Parliament is the Forth Crossing Act 2011.

[67] For a detailed account of the entire legislative process, see Cabinet Office, *Guide to Making Legislation* (The Stationery Office, 2014) *https://www.gov.uk/government/uploads/system/uploads/attachment_data/file/328408/Guide_to_Making_Legislation_July_2014.pdf* [Accessed 15 May 2020].

[68] *Erskine May Parliamentary Practice* (2011), pp.525–526.

[69] In addition to established forms of pre-legislative consultation, such as the publication of White Papers or Royal Commission reports, the government has, since 1997, published draft Bills where possible in order to facilitate pre-legislative scrutiny by the appropriate select committee. The House of Commons Select Committee on Modernisation has recommended that where it is not possible to produce a draft Bill, the government should instead submit detailed policy proposals for

printed and published. Explanatory notes now ordinarily accompany a government Bill[70] and an "impact assessment" is now required.[71] A Bill can be introduced into either House, with the exception of "money Bills"[72] that must originate in the House of Commons.[73] We will illustrate the passage of a Bill based on it having been introduced in the Commons.[74] At second reading, the principles of the Bill are considered. If the Bill is passed (and it is rare for a government Bill to be denied a second reading), the Bill proceeds to committee. If, following line by line scrutiny, the Bill is amended in committee, it is reprinted as amended and "reported" to the Commons. At third reading, the Bill is debated in final form, and thereafter proceeds to the House of Lords. Procedure in the Lords is much the same as the Commons, except that Bills are normally considered by a Committee of the Whole House after second reading, amendments may be made at third reading as well, in committee and at report, and there is no provision in the Lords for curtailing debate. In the Commons, by contrast, the minister responsible for a Bill may move an allocation of time, or guillotine, motion to fix the time available for its remaining stages, and increasing use is also being made of programme motions, whereby the whole progress of the Bill through the Commons is timetabled in advance.[75]

If the Lords make no amendments to the Bill, it may be sent forward at once for Royal Assent.[76] If amendments are made, the Bill returns to the Commons, which may agree to the amendments, substitute amendments of its own or reject the amendments outright. In the latter two cases, the Bill is sent back to the Lords with the Commons' reasons. As a rule, the Lords acquiesce in the wishes of the Commons; but from time to time, they stand their ground. The Bill will then be batted back and forth between the two Houses until some form of compromise is reached, as usually happens. If, exceptionally, the two Houses fail to reach agreement within the parliamentary session, the Bill will lapse. Where such failure is attributable to insoluble differences between the two Houses, the Parliament Acts 1911 and 1949 provide for the will of the Commons to prevail over that of the Lords. The House of Lords may delay a public Bill for one session (other than a Bill certified by the Speaker of the House of Commons as a money Bill, which may be sent forward for Royal Assent if at the end of one

---

pre-legislative scrutiny: House of Commons Select Committee on Modernisation, *Modernisation of the House of Commons: A Reform Programme, Second Report of Session 2001–02* (The Stationery Office, 2002) HC 1168–I.

[70] Following the recommendation in the House of Commons Select Committee on Modernisation, *Second Report of Session 1997–98* (The Stationery Office, 1997) HC 389.

[71] Cabinet Office, *Guide to Making Legislation*, pp.110–115.

[72] As a result of the Parliament Act 1911 removing the House of Lords power to block or amend such Bills.

[73] As a general rule, more controversial Bills are likely to be introduced in the House of Commons. Bills that implement law reform or Law Commission proposals are ordinarily introduced in the House of Lords. Any Bill where the government may wish to resort to the Parliament Acts to ensure its passage must be introduced in the House of Commons.

[74] See *Erskine May Parliamentary Practice* (2019), Chs 27–29 for the detailed rules and procedure relating to the passage of a public Bill.

[75] While sensible in principle, in practice programme motions often have the effect of seriously constraining the time available for proper scrutiny of the detail of a Bill in committee. See Cabinet Office, *Guide to Making Legislation*, pp.184–188.

[76] Even major Bills—as witness, e.g. the Anti-Terrorism, Crime and Security Act 2001—may complete their parliamentary stages in a matter of days.

month the Lords have failed to pass it), but it is open to the Commons to revive the measure in the following session, bypass the Lords and proceed directly to Royal Assent.

Three Acts of Parliament were enacted under the procedure contained in the 1911 Act as originally enacted: the Government of Ireland Act 1914, the Welsh Church Act 1914 and the Parliament Act 1949 itself, which reduced the length of the Lords' delaying power from two years to one. The amended procedure was not then used until the enactment of the War Crimes Act 1991. The Labour Government of 1997–2001 had to resort twice to the procedure, to secure the enactment of the European Parliamentary Elections Act 1999 and the Sexual Offences (Amendment) Act 2000. It was also required to secure the enactment of the Hunting Act 2004, which was then the subject of legal challenge in *R. (on the application of Jackson) v Attorney General*.[77] The claimant's argument was that the Parliament Act 1911 did not permit the enactment of a statute amending its own terms, as the Parliament Act 1949 did, without the consent of the Lords. Since the 1949 Act was enacted without the consent of the Lords, it was accordingly invalid, and the statutes enacted under the Parliament Acts procedure since, including the Hunting Act, were likewise invalid. The argument depended upon the proposition that legislation enacted under the 1911 Act was a species of delegated legislation in the sense that, by its terms, the King, Lords and Commons had delegated to the King and Commons the power, in specified circumstances, to enact Acts of Parliament without the Lords' consent. If that were correct, then it followed that the legislative power conferred upon the King and Commons by s.2(1) of the 1911 Act could not be enlarged by them in the absence of clear statutory words authorising them to do so. This was simply a consequence of ordinary principles of statutory interpretation.

The House of Lords, sitting as a panel of nine, rejected the argument.[78] Sections 1 and 2 of the 1911 Act identified legislation enacted in accordance with its terms as "Acts of Parliament", an expression:

> "used, and used only, to denote primary legislation . . . The 1911 Act did, of course, effect an important constitutional change, but the change lay not in authorising a new form of sub-primary parliamentary legislation but in creating a new way of enacting primary legislation."[79]

In any event, it was not possible to characterise the 1911 Act as a "delegation" of legislative power: " . . . the overall object of the 1911 Act was . . . to restrict, subject to compliance with specified statutory conditions, the power of the Lords to defeat measures supported by a majority of the Commons"[80] in the context of an unprecedented constitutional crisis. Accordingly, it was open to Parliament, constituted as King and Commons, to rely on the 1911 Act for the purposes of

---

[77] *R. (on the application of Jackson) v Attorney General* [2005] UKHL 56; [2006] 1 A.C. 262.

[78] It had previously been rejected by the Divisional Court (*R. (on the application of Jackson) v Attorney General* [2005] EWHC 94 (Admin)) and, albeit on different grounds, by the Court of Appeal (*R. (on the application of Jackson) v Attorney General* [2005] EWCA Civ 126; [2005] Q.B. 579).

[79] *R. (on the application of Jackson) v Attorney General* [2005] UKHL 56; [2006] 1 A.C. 262, per Lord Bingham at [24].

[80] *R. (on the application of Jackson) v Attorney General* [2005] UKHL 56; [2006] 1 A.C. 262, per Lord Bingham at [25].

enacting the amending 1949 Act, and since the 1949 Act was a valid Act of Parliament, so too were the statutes subsequently enacted in accordance with its terms.

Special provision has now been made, in the Standing Orders of the House of Commons, to deal will be Bills that concern subjects that have been devolved and accordingly affect only England (or England and Wales).[81] Immediately after the 2014 referendum result, the then Prime Minister undertook, amongst other things, to implement "English votes on English laws" (EVEL). That topic then featured prominently in the 2015 general election campaign, especially when opinion polls suggested that the SNP would increase their representation at Westminster (to the point that in one poll the possibility of the SNP taking *all* of the Scottish constituencies was suggested). Superficially attractive, the idea of "English votes on English laws" is this: when the House of Commons debates and is then asked to pass legislation that would only apply to, and impact upon, England, only MPs representing English constituencies should be permitted to vote on the matter. What could be wrong with that? Nothing, in principle; it is, after all, just another way of describing devolution. But "English votes on English laws" was not a call for a devolved English legislature. It was a call for changes in House of Commons procedure for particular Bills. When that becomes clear, it does not take long to realise a range of problems could arise. For example, what are "English laws"? In a system of asymmetric devolution, identifying matters that are exclusively English is no mean feat. It is a problem that would only intensify if further power were transferred to Scotland but not to Wales and Northern Ireland. Remembering that the UK Parliament retains the power to legislate on devolved matters, if a Bill was presented that only concerned Scotland and that covered reserved matters, ought only Scottish MPs to vote on the matter? Why not? How would "English only" Bills be determined? We will return to that in a moment. But what would be the status of an Act passed on the EVEL procedure? It would appear that it is to be treated as a "normal" Act of Parliament as there is nothing on the face of an Act passed using that procedure which indicates that only English MPs participated in the final legislative stages.[82] That may appear surprising for two reasons. First, what if, as a matter of fact, the provisions of the Act did impact on Scottish (or Welsh, or Northern Irish) law? It ought to be inconceivable that this would be done deliberately, but it is possible as a result of an oversight or a failure to appreciate the impact of the provision and the proper scope of any reservation. The traditional view is that any procedural deficiency in the passage of an Act does not affect the validity of an Act.[83] Looking to the parliamentary roll, the Act bears to have been passed by the House of Commons. But in fact, that would only be partially correct. The second reason concerns the protection of fundamental human rights. Each of the devolved legislatures has their competence defined by reference to Convention Rights.[84] To the extent that any provision they adopt is incompatible with a Convention right, it is "not law". Acts passed by Westminster, on the other hand, remain law (and remain 6–13

[81] Standing Orders of the House of Commons, Rules 83J–83O.

[82] For example, the Preamble to the Housing and Planning Act 2016 (the first Bill to be passed using EVEL) is in standard terms.

[83] *Edinburgh & Dalkeith Railway v Wauchope* (1842) 8 Cl. & F. 710.

[84] Scotland Act 1998 s.29(2); Government of Wales Act 2006 s.103(6); Northern Ireland Act 1998 s.6(2).

enforceable) despite an incompatibility with a Convention right having been found.[85] Why should a measure passed by the House of Commons by only English MPs benefit from that protection? Put another way, it produces the curious result that the fundamental human rights of those living in England appear to have a lower standard of protection than the other parts of the UK.[86]

What of the formation of a government in a House of Commons now that "English votes on English law" has arrived?[87] By convention (there being no detailed law that regulates the selection of Prime Minster and the formation of a government) the Prime Minster is the person best able to command the support of a majority in the House of Commons. What if that person changes when Scottish MPs are left out of account? That raises the prospect of different party leaders being in a position to command a majority on different issues. It being the UK Parliament, and the UK Government, it may be assumed that the Prime Minister should be the person best able to command the support of a majority of MPs when all are included. But if that is correct, and the non-English MPs are excluded from voting on devolved issues (for example, most aspects of health[88]), the Prime Minister may be lacking a majority on those issues. Indeed, if the Prime Minister represents a non-English constituency, they may themselves be unable to vote on what could be a flagship policy of their own government. Could that give rise to a convention that the Prime Minister represents an English constituency? An equivalent convention probably exists in relation to portfolios that have been devolved.[89] But it would likely be objectionable to the other parts of the UK if there was now an expectation that the Prime Minister represent an English constituency.

6–14 Despite the problems that could arise under EVELs, the House of Commons amended their Standing Orders so as to makes this constitutional change. Under the provisions adopted, a Bill certified as falling within the EVEL provision must be considered by a Grand Committee consisting only of English (or, where appropriate, England and Welsh) MPs before the Third Reading in the House of

[85] Human Rights Act 1998 s.4. The best illustration is the continuing disenfranchisement of serving prisoners that we have just discussed and which is considered further in para.11–13.

[86] As Lord Rodger of Earlsferry explained in *Somerville v Scottish Ministers* [2007] UKHL 44; 2008 S.C. (H.L.) 45 at [94]: "The Scotland Act confers wide, but nevertheless limited, powers on the Scottish Parliament and the Scottish Executive. Essentially, the limitations on the powers of both institutions are similar. In particular, it is beyond the competence of either to do anything that is incompatible with Convention rights . . . The limitation also affords protection to the Conventions rights of all those who are affected by the acts of the institutions. This is important since the changes brought about by the Scotland Act are actually intended to benefit people by improving the government of Scotland." The same must surely be true of any change introduced to give effect to "English votes for English laws".

[87] Election results thus far have rendered these concerns, for now, academic: *https://commonslibrary.parliament.uk/parliament-and-elections/devolution/english-votes-for-english-laws-after-ge2017/* [Accessed 15 May 2020].

[88] For a practical example, see the NHS Funding Bill that was considered by the House of Commons in January/February 2020, which progressed under the EVEL procedure. But even this was controversial as it was argued by some SNP MPs that the Bill had a direct impact upon the Barnett funding formulae.

[89] The appointment of Dr (now Lord) John Reid as Health Secretary in June 2003 was controversial as Dr Reid represented a Scottish constituency and health had been more or less fully devolved to the Scottish Government. There has been no subsequent appointment of this nature.

Commons. As we have seen earlier,[90] the democratic case for some sort of qualification on the ability of Scots (and, where appropriate, Welsh) MPs voting in Westminster on matters that have been devolved is unanswerable. There is one particular part of the detail worth highlighting. Rule 83J requires that the Speaker shall, before the Second Reading, consider every public Bill presented by the government and certify any Bill, or clause within a Bill, that, in the Speaker's opinion, relates exclusively to England or to England and Wales and is within devolved competence. As we shall see shortly, what is and is not within devolved competence can be a question that divides the very sharpest legal minds.[91] It also provides a stark contrast with certificates given by the Presiding Officers of the devolved institutions about the competence, or otherwise, of the legislation before them: those certificates have no legal value whatsoever.[92] Not only, therefore, is the Speaker charged with resolving the precise boundaries of the devolution settlement, their task is further complicated by r.83J(6) that introduces a de minimis qualification to that boundary: "the Speaker shall treat any clause or schedule whose only effects are minor or consequential effects outside the area in question as relating exclusively to that area". These provisions have not yet been tested. When that inevitably happens, they risk politicising the limits of devolution and raising the justiciability of any decision by the Speaker. Ultimately, the limits of devolution are a question of law (more particularly, a question of the proper interpretation of the respective devolution statutes). That being so, Lord Nicholls comments in *Jackson v Attorney General* come to mind:

> "This question of statutory interpretation is properly cognisable by a court of law even though it relates to the legislative process. Statutes create law. The proper interpretation of a statute is a matter for the courts, not Parliament. This principle is as fundamental in this country's constitution as the principle that Parliament has exclusive cognisance (jurisdiction) over its own affairs."[93]

If that is correct, it arguably renders the Speaker's certificate justiciable and liable to prompt a direct conflict with art.9 of the Claim (and Bill) of Rights. That seems a high price to pay to resolve the "West Lothian" question. It is also surprising that a change of such potential constitutional significance could be made by an amendment to the Standing Orders of the House of Commons.

There are a number of procedures whereby an MP may introduce a private **6–15** members' Bill. Shortly after the start of each new parliamentary session, a ballot is held among backbench MPs to determine priority in the use of the time set aside for private members' business; in practice, only the first 20 names in the ballot have a realistic chance of seeing their Bills through to the statute books.[94] Private members' Bills have precedence over government business on 13 Fridays

---

[90] See para.6–06, above.

[91] For example, consider the judgments in *Martin v Most* [2010] UKSC 10; 2010 S.C. (UKSC) 40, and in particular the forthright terms of Lord Rodger's dissent, to see just how difficult some of the issues can be.

[92] *Imperial Tobacco v Lord Advocate* [2012] UKSC 61; 2013 S.C. (U.K.S.C.) 153 at [7] (Lord Hope of Craighead).

[93] *Jackson v Attorney General* [2005] UKHL 56; [2006] 1 A.C. 262 at [51].

[94] Assuming they have a Bill. A common practice is for MPs to wait to see where they are placed in the ballot and then choose between the draft Bills proffered them by interest groups or, indeed, the government, if it has been unable to find time for a measure in its own programme for the session.

in each session.[95] Ten minute rule Bills may be introduced on a motion under standing orders, seeking leave to present a Bill to the Commons, and "ordinary presentation" Bills may be introduced by MPs under standing orders in the same way as a government Bill.[96] Similar procedures apply in the House of Lords, although with this difference: a private members' Bill from the Lords cannot be proceeded with, or even printed, in the Commons until an MP has indicated a willingness to take it up, whereas, when a Commons private members' Bill is sent up to the Lords, it is deemed already to have had a first reading and is printed at once (although a peer must still be found to pilot it through its stages in the Lords).

Making it through to the statute books is not the only criterion of success for a private members' Bill.[97] Some are introduced to publicise a cause, or to prompt the government to take action. But many are introduced with the aim and intention of changing the law, and have proved an important means of achieving this, particularly in areas of social or moral controversy that cross party lines and where governments are unwilling to risk their own hard-pressed legislative time. The abolition of the death penalty, and reform of the law on abortion and homosexuality, for example, were brought about by private members' Bills.

6–16 Private legislation, designed to obtain special rights or privileges over and above those provided by the general law, is introduced by parliamentary agents acting on behalf of the prospective beneficiary. Since the powers sought may interfere with the rights and interests of others, who might therefore wish to object, the promoters of a private Bill must comply with requirements concerning publicity and notification.[98] Subject to that, and provided the Bill is otherwise competent and in proper form, private Bills go through essentially the same stages as public Bills. After second reading,[99] the Bill will be sent either to an opposed Bill committee or unopposed Bill committee, depending on whether objections have been lodged. In either case, the committee sits in a quasi-judicial capacity to determine whether the case for having the provision sought by the Bill is established; if it finds that it is not, the Bill is effectively thrown out. If, however, the committee finds the Bill to be acceptable, it reports accordingly (together with any amendments it may have made). The Bill is then read for a third time, and if it is passed it proceeds to the other House where it undergoes much the same process once again.

6–17 A special procedure applies to the enactment of private legislation intended solely for application in Scotland that relates to matters reserved to Westminster by the Scotland Act 1998.[100] Under the Private Legislation Procedure (Scotland)

[95] House of Commons Standing Orders r.14(9).

[96] But such Bills cannot be presented until the ballot Bills have been presented and set down for second reading, which is likely to exhaust the time available for private members' business.

[97] The success rate in that sense is variable. In some sessions, only a handful of private members' Bills are enacted into law; in others, upward of 20.

[98] *Erskine May Parliamentary Practice* (2019), Ch.42 ("Preliminary Proceedings in Both Houses on Private Bills").

[99] Whether a private Bill commences in the Commons or the Lords is determined by the Commons' Chairman of Ways and Means and the Lord Chairman of Committees. As a rule, private Bills promoted by local authorities or those raising complex issues commence in the Lords.

[100] Private Legislation Procedure (Scotland) Act 1936. The procedure has not been invoked since 2000 and the procedure is no longer explain in the current edition *Erskine May* (the most recent edition with an account of the procedure is the 22nd edn, 1997, Ch.41). Private legislation on

Act 1936, the promoter lodges a petition for a provisional order with the Secretary of State, on or before 27 November or 27 March in any year. Petitions objecting to the order sought must be received by 23 January or 24 May, whichever follows the date of submission of the petition for the order. The Secretary of State may grant or refuse the petition, or may order that an inquiry be held. The Commissioners of Inquiry sit in Scotland and follow the procedure of an opposed Bill committee; if they recommend that the order be granted, the Secretary of State may so grant it, with or without modifications. A provisional order granted by the Secretary of State, whether or not following an inquiry, then requires to be confirmed by Parliament.[101]

Holyrood

The Scotland Act requires that the proceedings of the Parliament be regulated by standing orders,[102] and in places specifies the content of standing orders,[103] but beyond this the Parliament is free to adopt such procedures as it chooses. The rules relating to the legislative procedure are presently contained in Chs 9 and 9A of the standing orders (relating respectively to public Bills and private Bills). In total, the standing orders provide for no fewer than 12 different species of Scottish legislation.[104] Rules 9.2–9.13A of the standing orders lay down general rules applicable to all public Bills introduced in the Parliament, except to the extent that the special rules set out in rr.9.14–9.16 and 9.17A–9.21 are inconsistent with the general rules in relation to particular types of Bill. In that event, the special rules prevail to the extent of the inconsistency. 6–18

Government Bills are the most important type of Bill in numerical terms, being Bills introduced by a member of the Scottish Government in order to carry forward the government's legislative agenda. The rules make provision for the form and manner of introduction of government Bills, and for the lodging of various accompanying documents. These are: a written statement by the Scottish Minister in charge of the Bill stating that, in their view, its provisions are within the competence of the Parliament[105]; a written statement signed by the Presiding Officer, indicating whether, in their view, the provisions of the Bill would be within the competence of the Parliament and, if in their view they would not be, their reasons[106]; a memorandum on delegated powers; a financial memorandum and policy memorandum; explanatory notes summarising the purposes and effects of the Bill; and (if the Bill contains provisions charging expenditure on the

---

devolved matters in Scotland naturally falls now to be enacted by the Scottish Parliament itself: see SA 1998 s.36(3)(c), Scottish Parliament Standing Orders Ch.9A, and see also para.6–16.

[101] By virtue of SA 1998 s.94, where any pre-devolution enactment requires an order to be confirmed by Act of Parliament or approved by way of special procedure (as to which see the Statutory Orders (Special Procedure) Act 1945), and the order-making power is one which passed to the Scottish Ministers under s.53 on 1 July 1999, the power to confirm falls to be exercised by the Scottish Parliament.

[102] SA 1998 s.22.

[103] See SA 1998 Sch.3.

[104] Namely, government Bills, members' Bills, committee Bills, budget Bills, Scottish Law Commission Bills, consolidation Bills, codification Bills, statute law repeals Bills, statute law revision Bills, emergency Bills, private Bills and hybrid Bills.

[105] SA 1998 s.31(1).

[106] SA 1998 s.31(2).

Scottish consolidated fund) a report signed by the Auditor General for Scotland setting out their views on whether the charge is appropriate. Once the Bill and its accompanying documents have been lodged with the Clerk to the Parliament, it is the job of the clerk to arrange for their printing and publication. The substantive part of the legislative process then gets underway.

At stage one, the Parliamentary Bureau[107] refers the Bill to the committee within whose remit its subject matter falls.[108] The committee considers the general principles of the Bill, often taking evidence from experts and interested parties, and, in the case of a government Bill, the accompanying policy memorandum. Having done so, it reports to the Parliament on whether the general principles of the Bill should be agreed. The Parliament is not bound by the committee's recommendation. If the Parliament does approve the general principles, the Bill proceeds to stage two, where it undergoes detailed scrutiny by the committee or lead committee in charge of it.[109] Bills may be amended at stage two, and any MSP may lodge amendments for the committee's consideration following the completion of stage one. If at the end of stage two the Bill has been amended, it is reprinted in amended form. Further amendments may be lodged at stage three, at which point the Parliament decides whether to pass or reject the Bill.[110] If there is a division at stage three on whether the Bill is passed, the result will be valid only if at least one-quarter of the total number of MSPs vote, whether for or against or to abstain. If the result of the division is not valid, the Bill is deemed to be rejected.

6–19 Space precludes detailed consideration of all the other species of Scottish legislation, but it is worth noting the rules applicable to members' Bills, committee Bills, emergency Bills and private Bills.[111] Members' Bills are the equivalent in Scotland of private members' Bills at Westminster, although again the applicable procedural rules differ considerably. Any MSP who is not a Scottish Minister may introduce up to two members' Bills in any one session (bearing in mind that in the Scottish Parliament, the term "session" denotes the full (ordinarily) four year cycle of the Parliament, not each year within that cycle). The MSP proposing a member's Bill must notify their proposal by lodging it with the clerk, setting out their name, the short title of the Bill and a brief summary of its purposes. The notice is published in the Business Bulletin, which signifies the start of a "consultation period" and the proposal is sent to the committee within whose remit the proposal falls. Once the consultation period

[107] The bureau is comprised of the Presiding Officer, a representative of each political party having five or more MSPs in the Parliament, and the representative of any group formed by MSPs representing parties with fewer than five MSPs in the Parliament (provided that the group itself numbers at least five MSPs). It has responsibility for organising the business of the Parliament: see Scottish Parliament Standing Orders Ch.5.

[108] If the subject matter of the Bill falls within the remit of more than one committee, the Parliamentary Bureau will move that one be designated lead committee on the Bill. The other committee(s) report to the lead committee, which must take its (or their) views into account in preparing its report for the Parliament.

[109] Unless the Parliamentary Bureau successfully moves that stage two be taken by a different committee or by a Committee of the Whole Parliament.

[110] There is no need, unlike in relation to protected subject-matter, for the minister responsible for the Bill or the Presiding Officer to restate his or her view on whether the amended Bill is within the Parliament's legislative competence.

[111] Note that the Scottish Parliament's tax varying power, as provided for by SA 1998 Pt IV, is exercisable by way of resolutions rather than primary legislation.

has concluded, the final proposal must, within one month, attract the support of at least 18 other MSPs for the Bill to be introduced. Thereafter it is subject to the same procedure as a government Bill.

Committee Bills are an innovation: each of the Parliament's committees may make a proposal for a Bill relating to a competent matter falling within its remit. A proposal for a committee Bill consists of a report to the Parliament setting out the committee's recommendations for legislation, together with an account of why the legislation is needed. The committee may, but need not, append to its report a draft Bill.[112] If the Parliament agrees to the proposal, the committee convenor may instruct that a Bill be drafted (if necessary) and may subsequently introduce the Bill in the Parliament. The subsequent stages of the Bill are the same as those applicable to government Bills, except at stage one with the Bill being referred to the Finance Committee to consider and report on the financial memorandum. The need for report on the Bill's general principles is, understandably, dispensed with.

The very first Act of the Scottish Parliament[113] was an emergency Bill. These are a species of government Bill in relation to which a member of the Scottish Government or a junior Scottish Minister moves that it be treated as an emergency Bill. If agreed, the Bill is referred directly to the Parliament at stage one for consideration of its general principles and a decision on whether these are agreed; stage two is taken by a Committee of the Whole Parliament; and the final vote at stage three is taken immediately thereafter. Unless the Parliament decides otherwise, all of the stages of an emergency Bill must be taken on the day on which the Parliament agrees to treat it as such.

As to private legislation, and as at Westminster, the role of the Parliament is not merely to legislate but also to arbitrate between the competing private interests of the promoter of the legislation and any objectors. The Parliament has considered 16 private Bills so far in its lifetime.[114] The applicable procedures, which are contained in Ch.9A of the standing orders, must therefore be both parliamentary and quasi-judicial in nature. The promoter must submit a text of the Bill, together with a substantial amount of supporting documentation,[115] to the clerk at least three weeks before the proposed date of introduction.[116] The promoter must also comply with requirements for notification and advertisement of the Bill in order to draw it to the attention of potential objectors. The Bill is introduced when it is formally lodged with the clerk. Any person, body corporate or unincorporated association may lodge objections to the Bill, within 60 days of

[112] The Parliament has established a Non-Government Bills Unit to assist MSPs, committees and the promoters of private legislation in the drafting and formatting of Bills.

[113] Mental Health (Public Safety and Appeals) (Scotland) Act 1999. See also, more recently, the Senior Judiciary (Vacancies and Incapacity) (Scotland) Act 2006.

[114] Many have concerned railways or tram lines. Full details are available on the Parliament's website, Scottish Parliament, "Private Bills", *https://www.parliament.scot/parliamentarybusiness/Bills/29669.aspx* [Accessed 15 May 2020].

[115] This includes a statement by the Presiding Officer on legislative competence; explanatory notes; a promoter's statement and memorandum; and, where the Bill seeks to authorise the construction or alteration of certain classes of works or the compulsory acquisition of land or buildings, various maps and plans, a book of reference and an environmental statement.

[116] This in order to allow the clerk to arrange for the distribution of copies of the Bill and supporting documentation to "partner libraries" throughout Scotland.

its introduction, if it would adversely affect their private interests.[117] A Private Bill Committee is convened following introduction of the Bill to consider its provisions and report to Parliament. It will have up to five members, and although the normal rules on party political balance do not apply to its composition, it may not include among its number any MSP who resides in, or represents, a constituency falling wholly or partly within the area which would be affected by the Bill. The Bill is then subject to a three-stage process. At the preliminary stage, the committee considers the general principles of the Bill and whether these should be agreed. It may take evidence from the promoter or his legal representatives, and should certainly do so if it is minded to recommend that the Bill be rejected. If, following the committee's preliminary stage report, the Parliament agrees to the general principles of the Bill, it proceeds to the consideration stage, which falls into two parts. In the first, quasi-judicial, part, the committee hears evidence on the Bill and the objections to it. On completion of this part, the committee prepares a report giving its decisions on the objections considered, with reasons where appropriate. In the second part, the committee sits in a legislative capacity to consider and dispose of amendments to the Bill.[118] At the final stage, at which further amendments are competent, the Parliament votes on whether or not to pass the Bill.[119] As with other enactments of the Scottish Parliament, the Presiding Officer may not send the Bill as passed forward for Royal Assent until after the expiry of the four week period during which the Law Officers or Secretary of State may intervene in terms of ss.33 or 35 of the Scotland Act.

6–20 A new category of legislation was introduced by the Scotland Act 2016.[120] There are now four types of provision that the Scottish Parliament can only pass if a super-majority is reach. They are any provision of a Bill that would modify, or confer a power to modify, any of the following: (a) the persons entitled to vote as electors at an election for membership to the Parliament; (b) the system by which members of the Parliament are returned; (c) the number of constituencies, regions or any equivalent electoral area; and (d) the number of members to be returned for each constituency, region or equivalent electoral area (collectively referred to as "protected subject-matter").[121] It is for the Presiding Officer to certify, "after the last time when a Bill may be amended but before the decision whether to pass or reject it", whether any provision of the Bill relates to a protected subject-matter.[122] Where such a certificate is made, s.31A of the Scotland Act 1998 is engaged:

---

[117] The Private Bill Committee charged with consideration of the Bill has a discretion to admit late objections where reasonable cause is shown for the delay, but not beyond the expiry of the preliminary stage.

[118] If substantial amendments are made, the promoter is expected to produce revised or supplementary explanatory notes.

[119] Only one private Act of the Scottish Parliament was enacted in the 1999–2003 Parliament. Seven private Acts were enacted, out of a total of 60, in the 2003–2007 Parliament. A further five have been enacted in the period 2008–2015. Four have been enacted in the current, 2016–2019, session.

[120] See, generally, Reid, "Elections and Super-Majorities: Simply Another Staging Post?" (2016) 20 Edin L.R. 367.

[121] Scotland Act 1998 s.31(5), inserted by Scotland Act 2016 s.11.

[122] Scotland Act 1998 s.31(2A), inserted by Scotland Act 2016 s.11. That decision can be referred to the Supreme Court by the Law Officers: Scotland Act 1998 s.32A.

> "If the Presiding Officer states under section 31(2A) that in his view any provision of a Bill relates to a protected subject-matter, the Bill is not passed unless the number of members voting in favour of it at the final stage is at least two-thirds of the total number of seats for members of the Parliament."

In other words, at least 86 MSPs would have to vote in favour of such a measure. The need for a super-majority for these provisions is obvious. Given they relate to the very composition of the Parliament, and in the absence of a revising chamber, putting them beyond the reach of a government returned with an overall majority is a sensible precaution. Two other questions arise from these provisions. First, although the concept of a super-majority is not new to the Scotland Act 1998,[123] it does beg the question why only these issues were put beyond a simple majority of the Parliament. For example, given the central importance of the independence of the judiciary to the rule of law, why is a super-majority not required for the removal of a Court of Session judge?[124] That sort of anomaly suggests that a more comprehensive review of the circumstances in which a super-majority should be required. Second, the timing of the Presiding Officer's assessment of the legislation is different from their general assessment of competence. Unlike their assessment of legislative competence, it is not made until the Bill is unamendable. That makes sense because it requires them to assess the actual provisions the Parliament are being asked to pass. But it would also make sense to require them to assess legislative competence at that point too. If they were required to do so, the mess that arose in *Salvesen v Riddle* may well have been avoided.[125]

At Westminster and Holyrood alike, there is concern about the capacity of existing procedures to cope with the pressures placed on them. It is arguable, as is implicit in many of the recommendations made by the Modernisation Committee of the House of Commons, that the only way of alleviating the strain on legislative procedures is to move much of the debate over the policies and principles of legislative proposals back to the pre-legislative stage, so that at least the main outstanding areas of disagreement are focused for the legislative process proper. In this respect, the greater willingness of government north and south of the border to engage in greater pre-legislative consultation is an important advance, although it is fair to say that the Scottish Parliament has made better efforts to institutionalise public participation in the legislative process, via the practice of committees of taking evidence on the general principles of Bills at stage one.[126] The problems of overload may not yet have manifested themselves quite as seriously at Holyrood as at Westminster, but it is still noticeable that much the greater part of legislative time is spent on government bills, contrary to an expectation in the early days that more legislation would emanate from **6–21**

[123] For example, s.3(1) of the 1998 Act requires a two-thirds majority to dissolve the Parliament and call an early general election.

[124] cf. Scotland Act 1998 s.95.

[125] *Salvesen v Riddell* [2013] UKSC 22; 2013 S.C. (U.K.S.C.) 236 (on which, see para.6–33, below). See also: D.J. Carr, "Not Law (but not yet effectively not law)" (2013) 17 Edin. L.R. 370. and D.J. Carr, "Not Law" (2012) 16 Edin. L.R. 410

[126] This is not to say that external perspectives will not influence the legislative process at Westminster, for MPs and peers alike draw on the views expressed to them by interested groups and parties in their contributions to legislative debate; the difference, however, is that in Scotland that participation is direct rather than filtered through the medium of elected members.

committees or members.[127] At Westminster, there is widespread disquiet that the advance programming of major Bills precludes proper scrutiny of their finer points; on more than one occasion in recent years, large numbers of amendments tabled for consideration in committee have had to be abandoned for simple lack of time. This matters, for to the extent that much of the parliamentary time devoted to legislation is (quite properly) spent on government Bills, the legislative process provides as much an opportunity for holding the government to account as questions and debates.

LEGISLATIVE COMPETENCE

Introduction

6–22 In relation to the legislative competence of the Westminster Parliament, there is little to add the earlier discussion of the supremacy, or sovereignty, of Parliament.[128] If there are things Westminster would not do on moral or political grounds, there are nevertheless no legal limitations, as the law is traditionally understood, on its ability to enact whatever primary legislation it chooses.[129] The focus of this section is therefore on the legislative competence of the Scottish Parliament, which is limited in terms of s.29(2) of the Scotland Act. A number of mechanisms exist to ensure, so far as possible, that the Scottish Parliament does not stray outwith the bounds of its competence. Most of these operate at the pre-Assent stage, i.e. before a Bill becomes an Act of the Scottish Parliament on the signifying of Royal Assent. However, it follows from the fact that an Act, or provision of an Act, "is not law"[130] if it is outside the legislative competence of the Parliament that its validity may be questioned after it has been enacted and entered into force. A question of this sort may be raised as a "devolution issue" in terms of s.98 and Sch.6 of the Scotland Act 1998 or a "compatibility issue" in terms of s.288ZB of the Criminal Procedure (Scotland) Act 1995.

It is worth noting the terms of s.29(2) in full:

> "(2) A provision is outside [the legislative competence of the Scottish Parliament] so far as any of the following paragraphs apply—
> (a) it would form part of the law of a country or territory other than Scotland, Scotland,

[127] This expectation was founded on the recommendations of the Consultative Steering Group on the Scottish Parliament, established in advance of devolution to consider parliamentary procedures, geared towards the achievement of (among other things) "power-sharing" in the new Parliament. This was felt to imply if not equality as between executive and non-executive Bills, at least greater priority for the latter than they have in fact received.

[128] See paras 3–02—3–08, above.

[129] The caveat reflects the comments of the First Division of the Inner House in *AXA General Insurance Co Ltd v Lord Advocate* [2011] CSIH 31; 2011 S.C. 662 at [67]: "There can accordingly be seen to be an as yet unresolved issue at the highest judicial level as to whether an Act of the UK Parliament could, in any circumstances, be open to challenge in the courts." We have discussed the current debate around this issue in Ch.3, above. Separately, secondary legislation has always been subject to judicial review as to its competence, the constitutional justification for review of such legislation has most recently been explained by the Supreme Court in *R (on the application of the Public Law Project) v Lord Chancellor* [2016] UKSC 39; [2016] A.C. 1531 at [21]–[28].

[130] SA 1998 s.29(1).

(b) it relates to reserved matters,
(c) it is in breach of the restrictions in Schedule 4,
(d) it is incompatible with any of the Convention rights or in breach of the restriction in section 30A[131],
(e) it would remove the Lord Advocate from his position as head of the it would remove the Lord Advocate from his position as head of the systems of criminal prosecution and investigation of deaths in Scotland."

The reference to extraterritorial effect in subpara.(a) must be understood in light of s.126(1), whereby the term "Scotland" includes "so much of the internal waters and territorial sea of the United Kingdom as are adjacent to Scotland". The reservation in relation to the functions of the Lord Advocate in subpara.(e) reflects the perceived need to secure his or her independence as public prosecutor and head of the system of investigation of deaths in Scotland, even though the Lord Advocate ceased on devolution to be a member of the UK Government and became instead a member of the Scottish Government. The principal restrictions on the competence of the Scottish Parliament, however, are those contained in s.29(2)(b)–(d): reserved matters, the protection of certain enactments from modification by the Scottish Parliament, and compatibility with the Convention rights and s.30A, which concerns "retained EU law". That concept was introduced to reflect the UK's departure from the European Union. By s.12 of the European Union (Withdrawal) Act 2018, the UK Parliament amended the Scotland Act 1998 so as to insert s.30A and a general reservation in respect of retained EU law.[132]

A prior question has now been resolved by the Supreme Court: when is competence tested? Is it at the time the Bill was passed or at the point it is challenged? In *UK Withdrawal from the European Union (Legal Continuity)(Scotland) Bill Reference*, the Supreme decided it was the latter.[133] In that case, which was the first pre-Assent reference by a Law Officer in relation to a Scottish Bill, in the period between the reference and the hearing in the Supreme Court, the UK Parliament had passed its own continuity legislation which was, in some respects, inconsistent with the Scottish Bill.[134] The Supreme Court explained that it was "satisfied that, when addressing the questions in the reference as to whether the Scottish Bill would be within legislative competence, this court must have regard to how things stand at the date when we decide those questions".[135] That conclusion was reached having regard to the wording of s.33 of the Scotland Act 1998, which makes provision for a pre-Assent reference to the Supreme Court. It allows the UK Government, at the hand of its law officers, to refer a Scottish Bill to the Supreme Court and, in the time before the case is heard, persuade the UK Parliament to legislate so as to defeat the proposed Bill. The circumstances in which the UK Government would act in such a way would be extremely rare, but that it can serves to underscore the continuing supremacy of the Westminster legislature. Aside from references under s.33 of the Scotland Act 1998, the competence of legislation would fall to be determined at the time it is challenged. That appears plain from the language for s.29(2) of the Scotland Act **6–23**

[131] Instead of s.30A of the Scotland Act 1998, the restriction used to be in relation to EU law.
[132] See para.6–26, below.
[133] [2018] UKSC 64; 2019 S.C. (UKSC) 13.
[134] The European Union (Withdrawal) Act 2018.
[135] [2018] UKSC 64; 2019 S.C. (UKSC) 13 at [92].

1998, for example, "it is [*note the present tense*] incompatible with any of the Convention rights". Given the content and meaning of the Convention rights, as well as the list of reserved matters and the restrictions in Sch.4, change over time, it is possible for a provision that was once within the legislative competence of the Parliament to pass outwith that competence. Accordingly, as time goes by, it may be necessary to review the content of the Scottish statute book to ensure that what has been passed by the Scottish Parliament remains law.

Reserved matters

6–24 The list of matters reserved to the exclusive competence of the Westminster Parliament is contained in Sch.5 to the Scotland Act, which is arranged in three parts.[136] Part I sets out a number of "general reservations" under six headings.[137] Part II sets out a number of "specific reservations" grouped under 11 headings.[138] Part III contains five paragraphs of general provisions relating primarily to the reservation of certain public bodies.

A provision of an Act of the Scottish Parliament will fall foul of this restriction if it "relates to" one of the reserved matters specified in Sch.5. Section 29(3) provides that:

> "the question whether a provision of an Act of the Scottish Parliament relates to a reserved matter is to be determined, subject to subs.(4), by reference to the purpose of the provision, having regard (among other things) to its effect in all the circumstances".[139]

In *Martin v Most* Lord Walker described the phrase "relates to" as:

> "familiar in this sort of context, indicating more than a loose or consequential connection, and the language of section 29(3), referring to a provision's purpose and effect, reinforces that".[140]

---

[136] Under SA 1998 s.30, the list may be modified by Order in Council as necessary or expedient (as was done, for example, to confer competence to hold the independence referendum). See para.1–03.

[137] The constitution (including the Crown, but not Her Majesty's prerogative and other executive functions, or functions exercisable by any person acting on behalf of the Crown; the Union of the Kingdoms of Scotland and England; the UK Parliament; and the continued existence of the High Court of Justiciary and the Court of Session); the registration and funding of political parties; foreign affairs (with the important exception of "observing and implementing international obligations, obligations under the Human Rights Convention and obligations under EU law"); the civil service of the state; defence; and treason.

[138] Financial and economic matters; home affairs; trade and industry; energy; transport; social security; regulation of the professions (though not the legal profession); employment; health and medicines; media and culture; and miscellaneous matters including judicial remuneration and equal opportunities. It should be noted that few of these headings are comprehensive, and many of the reservations are subject to exceptions.

[139] SA 1998 s.29(4), provides that a provision which would not otherwise relate to reserved matters but which modifies Scots private law or Scots criminal law as either applies to reserved matters shall be treated as "relating to" reserved matters (and thus invalid) unless its purpose is to make the law in question "apply consistently to reserved matters and otherwise".

[140] *Martin v Most* [2010] UKSC 10; 2010 S.C. (U.K.S.C.) 40 at [49]. That approach was endorsed by Lord Hope in *Imperial Tobacco Ltd v Lord Advocate* [2012] UKSC 61; 2013 S.C. (U.K.S.C.) 153 at [16]. That approach has the benefit of expanding the scope of devolved competence given the adoption of a "reserved powers model". What the court is talking about is more than a "loose or

It is clear, however, that some ancillary impact on reserved matters is not to be taken as fatal to the validity of the provision. This emerges from para.3 of Sch.4, which provides that modifications of the law on reserved matters are permissible so long as they are:

> "(a) incidental to, or consequential on, provision made (whether by virtue of the Act in question or another enactment) which does not relate to reserved matters; and (b) do not have a greater effect on reserved matters than is necessary to give effect to the purpose of the provision".

Moreover, s.101 provides that, where a provision of an Act of the Scottish Parliament[141] could be read in such a way as to be outside competence, that provision is to be read "as narrowly as is required for it to be within competence, if such a reading is possible, and is to have effect accordingly". As this implies, those acting under Acts of the Scottish Parliament will themselves need to consider whether its provisions require to be "read down" to avoid a conflict with reserved matters, for the legality of their own actings, if not the validity of the Act, may otherwise be vulnerable to challenge. The validity of the Act can be saved by a narrow reading; the actions taken under it, if outwith the scope of that reading, cannot.

There is a separate issue here, to which we shall have cause to return. Some incidental or consequential impact on reserved matters is permitted, provided it does not have a greater effect on reserved matters than is necessary to give effect to the purpose of the provision. The question is: who decides whether the effect on reserved matters is greater than necessary? Of course, the initial judgment is for the promoters of the legislation and the Scottish Parliament itself (and indeed for those who have a locus to initiate pre-Assent challenges to the competence of a Bill). But when the court comes to consider that judgment, what is the nature of its role? In the human rights context, a distinction has been drawn between primary and secondary judgments.[142] If the court's function is one of reviewing the reasonableness of the legislative choice, then it makes merely a secondary judgment. The court makes a primary judgment if it decides for itself whether the legislative choice is incompatible with human rights. It would appear that here, as in the human rights sphere, the court must make a primary judgment. It must determine at what point the effect of a provision on reserved matters becomes "greater than necessary" and then ask whether the Scottish Parliament went 6–25

consequential connection" to the reservation. But this line of reasoning was applied by the Supreme Court in *Re Recovery of Medical Costs for Asbestos Disease (Wales) Bill* [2015] UKSC 3; [2015] 2 W.L.R. 481 at [25] to the equivalent provision of the Government of Wales Act 2006 (s.108(7)). Wales then operated on a "transferred powers model" (it having moved to a "reserved powers model" as a result of the passage of the Wales Act 2017) with the result that this interpretation *narrows* the scope of devolution requiring as it does more than a "loose and consequential connection" to the devolution. That was a 3:2 split decision and, but for the effect of the Wales Act 2017, may well been revisited by the Supreme Court. It is a decision that appears to fall foul of Lord Neuberger's warning that, although the same language may be used in the different devolution statutes, the court should be careful about interpreting each statute the same: *Attorney General v National Assembly for Wales Commission* [2012] UKSC 53; [2013] 1 A.C. 792 at [50].

[141] Or of a Bill before the Scottish Parliament, or of subordinate legislation made by a member of the Scottish Government.

[142] R. Clayton and H. Tomlinson, *The Law of Human Rights* (Oxford: Oxford University Press, 2000), paras 5.122–5.124 and 5.133.

beyond that point. In the human rights sphere, the courts grant a certain latitude to the legislature, identifying the area within which, consistently with human rights, it has a free choice. But in relation to the reserved/devolved boundary the issue seems sharper. Intuitively, one would have thought a particular legislative choice has greater than necessary effect on reserved matters or it does not; a line must be drawn, not points on a spectrum, and it is to be drawn by the courts.

Enactments protected from modification

6–26 Schedule 4 to the Scotland Act complements the reservation of specified matters to Westminster by s.29 and Sch.5 and preserves certain existing legislation from modification by the Scottish Parliament,[143] including the Scotland Act itself so far as it prescribes the principal features of the devolution settlement. Exempted from this general prohibition are modifications to a number of specified sections of the Scotland Act, most of which relate to the statutory versions of the privileges enjoyed by the Houses of Parliament at Westminster and thus have to do with the Scottish Parliament's internal procedures.

Retained EU law

6–27 The Scottish Parliament cannot make laws that are inconsistent with retained EU law. That restriction was introduced by s.12 of the European Union (Withdrawal) Act 2018, which inserted s.30A into the Scotland Act 1998. For present purposes, the critical provisions are:

> "(1) An Act of the Scottish Parliament cannot modify, or confer power by subordinate legislation to modify, retained EU law so far as the modification is of a description specified in regulations made by a Minister of the Crown.
>
> (2) But subsection (1) does not apply to any modification so far as it would, immediately before exit day, have been within the legislative competence of the Parliament, …"

There then follows provision as to how, and when, such regulations may be made.[144] In short, the objective was to ensure that the legislative competence of the Parliament was the same immediately following departure from the EU. This reservation inevitably engages how wider legislative provision for the retention of EU law operates and that is discussed in Ch.10.

---

[143] The statutes or statutory provisions protected from modification include arts 4 and 6 of the Union with Scotland Act 1706 and of the Union with England Act 1707, so far as they relate to freedom of trade; Private Legislation Procedure (Scotland) Act 1936; European Communities Act 1972 s.1 and Sch.1; and Human Rights Act 1998.

[144] For example, the power is time-limited in that any such regulations must be made within two years of exit day (31 January 2022), although regulations made before that date remain in force after it: s.30A(7)–(8) of the Scotland Act 1998.

Convention rights

The Convention rights are those fundamental human rights enshrined in the European Convention on Human Rights that have been incorporated into the legal orders of the UK by the Human Rights Act 1998.[145] The Human Rights Act did not enter fully into force until 2 October 2000. Section 129(2) of the Scotland Act therefore provided for the Human Rights Act to be treated as if it were in force for the purpose of certain provisions of the Scotland Act, namely those relating to the devolved competence of the Scottish Parliament and Scottish Government, proceedings under the Act involving human rights questions and the definition of devolution issues.[146] The consequence of this was that the Scottish Parliament and Scottish Government were bound by the Convention rights for over a year before they became binding on other Scottish public authorities and on governmental bodies and public authorities south of the border.[147] **6–28**

Common law

It is now established that there are, in addition to the limits imposed by s.29(2), common law limits on the competence of the Scottish Parliament.[148] However, it would only be in rare and exceptional circumstances that the Parliament would transgress these limits. Any such review is not on the traditional common law grounds of irrationality/unreasonableness but could only be justified where the Parliament had legislated so as to abrogate fundamental rights (in which case the Convention rights limit to its competence ought to be engaged) or otherwise to secure the rule of law.[149] It ought to be a rare occurrence that a common law challenge is stateable, let alone successful. A Bill cannot be reviewed on a pre-Assent reference under s.33 of the Scotland Act 1998 on common law grounds.[150] **6–29**

CONTROLLING LEGISLATIVE COMPETENCE

We have so far considered the statutory, and now also common law, limits on the Scottish Parliament's legislative power. We turn now to consider the enforcement of those limits. There are three parts to this: first, the measures in place to ensure that only Bills that are within the Parliament's competence are presented for Royal Assent; second, the procedures for challenging any measure, which despite **6–30**

[145] Human Rights Act 1998 s.1 and Sch.1.

[146] SA 1998 ss.29(2)(d), 57(2) and (3), 100, 126(1) and Sch.6.

[147] The Convention rights became binding on the Lord Advocate on 22 May 1999, and on the Scottish Parliament and other members of the Scottish Government on 1 July 1999.

[148] *AXA General Insurance Co Ltd v Lord Advocate* [2011] UKSC 46; 2012 S.C. (U.K.S.C.) 122. See also: *Attorney General v National Assembly for Wales Commission* [2012] UKSC 53; [2013] 1 A.C. 792.

[149] *AXA General Insurance Co Ltd v Lord Advocate* [2011] UKSC 46; 2012 S.C. (U.K.S.C.) 122, per Lord Reed at [153].

[150] "United Kingdom Withdrawal from the European Union (Legal Continuity) (Scotland) Bill Reference" [2018] UKSC 64; 2019 S.C. (UKSC) 13 at [26].

those pre-Assent checks, reaches the statute book; and finally, the judicial approach to policing those limits that will include a discussion of the remedies available to the court.

Pre-assent checks

6–31 The Scotland Act provides for a number of devices designed to ensure, prior to the passage of a Bill into law, that it is within the Parliament's competence. In the case of government Bills, the member of the Scottish Government in charge of the Bill must, on or before its introduction in the Parliament, state that in their view the provisions of the Bill would be within the competence of the Parliament.[151] In the case of all Bills, the Presiding Officer must, on or before the introduction of a Bill, decide whether or not, in their view, its provisions would be within the competence of the Parliament and state their decision.[152] The form of these statements of competence and the manner in which they are to be made are provided for in rr.9.2 and 9.3 of the Standing Orders of the Scottish Parliament. It is an anomaly of the present system that no similar statement need be made once any amendments have been made to the Bill.[153] In *Salvesen v Riddle*, discussed below, amendments to the Agricultural Holdings (Scotland) Bill rendered certain of its provisions beyond the competence of the Parliament.[154] A requirement on the Presiding Officer and/or the responsible minister to restate their view on the competence of the Bill once it was in final form would not necessarily prevent a repeat of *Salvesen* but ought to reduce the risk of it happening.

Naturally, the views of the Scottish Ministers and/or Presiding Officer are not conclusive of the issue of competence,[155] and the Bill may yet have a variety of further hurdles to clear. If the Bill is passed by the Scottish Parliament, it is for the Presiding Officer to send it forward for Royal Assent.[156] But s.32(2) of the Scotland Act provides that they may not so submit it at any time during which the Advocate General, Lord Advocate or Attorney General is entitled to refer the Bill to the Supreme Court under s.33; where such a reference has been made but not

[151] SA 1998 s.31(1).

[152] SA 1998 s.31(2). A negative statement by the Presiding Officer would not, however, block the Bill's further progress. It is, in practice, very persuasive. See, for example: the ill-fated Civil Appeals (Scotland) Bill (which sought to abolish the right to appeal to what was then the House of Lords); the Presiding Officer stated that, in his view, the Bill was outside the Parliament's competence and its parliamentary process ended shortly thereafter (*Official Report*, 20 December 2006). But it did not prevent the consideration of the European Union (Legal Continuity) (Scotland) Bill, where the Lord Advocate appeared in the Chamber to explain why, in his view, and contrary to the view stated by the Presiding Officer, the Bill was within the legislative competence of the Parliament (*Official Report*, 13 December 2018).

[153] cf. the requirement placed on the Presiding Officer by s.31(2A) of the Scotland Act 1998. See para.6–17, above.

[154] See the discussion at para.6–33, below.

[155] See the speech of Lord Hope in *A v Scottish Ministers* [2001] UKPC D5; 2002 S.C. (P.C.) 63 at [7]: "... they are no more than statements of opinion, which do not bind the judiciary"; see also Lord Reed in *Imperial Tobacco Ltd v Lord Advocate* [2012] CSIH 9; 2012 S.C. 297 at [59]–[64] and *Imperial Tobacco v Lord Advocate* [2012] UKSC 61; 2013 S.C. (UKSC) 153 at [7] (Lord Hope of Craighead).

[156] SA 1998 s.32(1).

disposed of; or where the Secretary of State has made an order under s.35 of the Act prohibiting the Presiding Officer from submitting the Bill for Royal Assent.[157]

A reference may be made under s.33 at any time during the four week period commencing with the passing of the Bill by the Parliament, although the Law Officers may notify the Presiding Officer that they do not intend to make a reference.[158] In that event (subject to a s.35 order) the Presiding Officer may send the Bill for Royal Assent at once. If a reference is made in relation to a Bill, the Scottish Parliament may choose simply to wait until the reference is disposed of one way or the other. If the Supreme Court finds that the provisions of the Bill are within the powers of the Parliament, then the Presiding Officer may submit it for Royal Assent without further ado. If it does not so find, the Bill cannot be sent forward for Royal Assent in unamended form. The Parliament may in that event reconsider the Bill in a form designed to rectify the problems of the earlier version.[159] A reference to the Supreme Court may, of course, take some time to dispose of. This is particularly likely to be the case where the Bill raises some question of compatibility with EU law. Although the Supreme Court may competently deal with such a question itself, it may elect to refer the matter on to the Court of Justice for the European Union for a preliminary ruling under art.267 of the Treaty on the Functioning of the European Union.[160] In that event, the Scottish Parliament has the right under s.34[161] to resolve that it wishes to reconsider the Bill before the references (i.e. to the Supreme Court and to the Court of Justice of the European Union) are decided.[162] If it does so resolve, the Presiding Officer will notify the Law Officers accordingly and the person who made the reference must request its withdrawal. The Parliament may then consider and vote on an altered version of the Bill that seeks to accommodate the concerns that gave rise to the original reference. Even if the Bill is passed in its amended form, however, it may still be the subject of a second reference by a Law Officer, should one of them remain unsatisfied as to its competence. Only one such reference has to date been made under the Scotland Act: the United Kingdom Withdrawal from the European Union (Legal Continuity) Bill that resulted in a limited finding that provisions of the Bill were beyond the competence of the Parliament.[163] As similar power exists under the Government of Wales Act 2006 and since the Welsh Assembly has exercised legislative functions, the Attorney General has exercised his equivalent power and made three such references to the Supreme Court, including the very first legislative measure of the Welsh Assembly. Only one reference has resulted in a finding that the legislative provision was beyond the Assembly's legislative competence.[164]

---

[157] This latter is not a control over the competence of a Bill, but is considered here since it is grouped with the controls on competence within the scheme of the Scotland Act 1998.

[158] An equivalent power is conferred on the Law Officers in respect of a pre-Assent reference in respect of the protected subject-matter boundaries: s.32A of the Scotland Act 1998.

[159] SA 1998 s.36(4).

[160] See para.10–20, below.

[161] In the event of the United Kingdom leaving the European Union, s.34 of the Scotland Act 1998 will be repelled by the European Union (Withdrawal) Act 2018

[162] The procedures for such reconsideration are contained in the Parliament's Standing Orders r.9.9

[163] [2018] UKSC 64; 2019 S.C. (UKSC) 13. See para.1–16.

[164] *Attorney General v National Assembly for Wales Commission* [2012] UKSC 53; [2013] 1 A.C. 792; *Re Agricultural Sector (Wales) Bill* [2014] UKSC 43; [2014] 1 W.L.R. 2622 both held the

6–32 The power of the Secretary of State to intervene under s.35 is quite different from the reference power conferred on the Law Officers by s.33. In making a reference, the Law Officers are raising questions of legislative competence in relation to a Bill ("does the Parliament have the power to pass this law?"). An intervention by the Secretary of State has nothing to do with the legislative competence of the Scottish Parliament as such, despite the position of s.35 in the scheme of the Scotland Act. Thus, even if a Bill is within the competence of the Scottish Parliament, the Secretary of State may make a s.35 order preventing its submission for Royal Assent in two situations: where it contains provisions that he has reasonable grounds to believe would be incompatible with any international obligations of the UK or with the interests of defence or national security; or where it contains provisions that modify the law as it applies to reserved matters and that he has reasonable grounds to believe would have an adverse effect on the operation of the law as it applies to reserved matters. As with the Law Officers, the Secretary of State may not exercise this power if he has notified the Presiding Officer that he does not intend to make an order under s.35. Subject to that, he may make such an order at any time during the four week period commencing with the passing of the Bill by the Parliament; within four weeks of any subsequent approval of the Bill in amended form; or within four weeks of a reference to the Supreme Court being decided or otherwise disposed of. The order must be laid before both Houses of the Westminster Parliament and is subject to annulment by resolution of either House.

Devolution and compatibility issues

6–33 It follows from the fact that a provision in an Act of the Scottish Parliament "is not law" if it is outwith the boundaries of legislative competence prescribed by s.29 of the Scotland Act that, even where a Bill has survived pre-Assent scrutiny, received Royal Assent and entered into force, its validity remains open to challenge.[165] Such a challenge normally constitutes a devolution issue in terms of para.1(a) of Sch.6:

> "a question whether an Act of the Scottish Parliament or any provision of an Act of the Scottish Parliament is within the legislative competence of the Parliament".

It must be raised and resolved in accordance with the rules laid down by Sch.6. That position has been amended in relation to criminal proceedings. Where, in criminal proceedings, a challenge is raised based on an alleged incompatibility with EU law or Conventions rights, it is to be treated as a "compatibility issue" as

---

respective provisions were within competence. The third challenge saw the Supreme Court split 3:2, with the Recovery of Medical Costs for Asbestos Disease (Wales) Bill (which was designed to allow the NHS to recover the costs of treating the effects of asbestos related diseases for former employers and insurers) was outwith the legislative competence of the Welsh Assembly: *Re Recovery of Medical Costs for Asbestos Disease (Wales) Bill* [2015] UKSC 3; [2015] A.C. 1016. The reference was made not because the Counsel General doubted the competence of the measure (he argued for in the Supreme Court) but because a challenge by insurance companies was inevitable and he wanted to avoid years of litigation as the case made its way through the courts.

[165] See *A v Scottish Ministers* [2001] UKPC D5; [2003] 2 A.C. 602 and *Adams v Scottish Ministers*, 2003 S.C. 171.

opposed to a devolution issue.[166] A compatibility issue must be resolved in accordance with the rules laid down in ss.288ZB and 288AA of the Criminal Procedure (Scotland) Act 1995.[167] The important distinction between a compatibility issue and a devolution issue is that the Supreme Court may only determine the compatibility and not the overall case (whereas it can do the latter where a devolution issue arises). As the Supreme Court explained:

> "It is important to understand the nature of the jurisdiction exercised by this court under section 288AA of the 1995 Act. The court does not sit as a criminal appeal court exercising a general power of review … the powers of the Supreme Court are exercisable only for the purpose of determining the compatibility issue … When it has determined the compatibility issue, the Supreme Court must remit the proceedings to the High Court."[168]

In that way, the High Court of Justiciary retains its place at the apex of the criminal court system in Scotland.

Under Pt II of Sch.6, proceedings for the determination of a devolution issue may be instituted by the Advocate General or the Lord Advocate, but devolution issues may equally be raised, either by way of claim or defence, by any person. So, for example, a person might seek judicial review of an Act of the Scottish Parliament in the Court of Session on the grounds that it is outside the competence of the Parliament, or, when charged with a criminal offence, plead the invalidity of the legislation under which they are charged or of the decision to prosecute them.

While only the Supreme Court has jurisdiction to pronounce on the competence of Scottish legislation prior to its receiving Royal Assent, a devolution issue or compatibility issue may be raised in any proceedings before a court or tribunal. However, a tribunal from which there is no right of appeal must refer a devolution issue that arises before it to the Inner House of the Court of Session. Other tribunals, and any court other than the Supreme Court or a court consisting of three or more judges of the Court of Session, may do so. In criminal matters, a court other than a court consisting of two or more judges of the High Court of Justiciary may refer a compatibility issue arising in proceedings before it to the High Court. Where a devolution issue is raised before either the Court of Session or the High Court (that is, where it does not come before them on a reference from an inferior court) or a compatibility issue is raised before the High Court, the court may choose to refer the issue to the Supreme Court for resolution. In any event, an appeal against a determination by the Inner House of the Court of Session of a devolution issue lies to the Supreme Court. Similarly, there is a right of appeal to the Supreme Court in respect of a determination of both a devolution issue and a compatibility issue by a court consisting of two or

---

[166] SA 1998 Sch.6 para.1 (as amended by the Scotland Act 2012 s.36(4)). Where the vires of an Act of the Scottish Parliament is challenged on grounds other than incompatibility with EU law or Convention rights, it remains a "devolution issue" and determined in accordance with Sch.6. On compatibility issues, see: A Page, *Constitutional Law of Scotland*, paras 9–15—9–30.

[167] For more background, see the Consultation on Compatibility Issues undertaken in January 2018, available at: *http://www.scotland-judiciary.org.uk/Upload/Documents/CompatibilityissuesconsultationpaperReviewofsections34to37oftheScotlandAct2012.pdf* [Accessed 18 May 2020].

[168] *Macklin v HMA* [2015] UKSC 77; 2016 S.C. (U.K.S.C.) 47 at [11] (Lord Reed).

more judges of the High Court of Justiciary, but only with the leave of the High Court or, failing that, with special leave from the Supreme Court itself.[169] Paragraph 37 of Sch.6 provides that any power to make provision for regulating the procedure before any court or tribunal shall include the power to make provision in relation to devolution issues.

Judicial review of competence

6–34 Where the competence of a provision of an Act of the Scottish Parliament is challenged, essentially three questions fall to be answered: (a) what, applying the ordinary rules of statutory interpretation, does the provision mean; (b) read in that way, does the provision fall within the legislative competence of the Parliament; and (c) if the answer to question (b) is "no", can the provision be read narrowly enough so as to bring it within the competence of the Parliament?[170] If the answer to that final question is "no" a declaration that the provision is "not law" should follow. The question of remedy then arises. Following a declaration that a provision is "not law", the legislature should normally be afforded an opportunity to correct the problem, especially where there may be follow-on consequences for other parts of a legislative scheme. With that in mind, where the court decides that a provision of an Act of the Scottish Parliament is not within the legislative competence of the Parliament, the court is empowered to:

> "make an order—
> (a) removing or limiting any retrospective effect of the decision, or
> (b) suspending the effect of the decision for any period and on any conditions to allow the defect to be corrected".[171]

It is helpful to illustrate these issues with some examples.[172] First, we will consider the case of *Martin v Most*, where the Supreme Court had to consider the boundary of reserved matters and, in particular, when a provision "relates to" a reserved matter. Second, we will consider the first successful civil challenge to the competence of a legislative provision of the Scottish Parliament. Finally, we will look at the first pre-Assent reference of a Scottish Bill. But before that, the Supreme Court has set down a number of principles that apply when considering whether a provision of an Act of the Scottish Parliament is within legislative competence. It is there that we shall begin.

---

[169] Prior to the entry into force of the Scotland Act 1998, there was no right of appeal in Scots criminal cases beyond the High Court of Justiciary.

[170] SA 1998 s.101. Where the question is one of compatibility with Convention rights, the question should be answered under s.3 of the Human Rights Act 1998 (which requires that much the same exercise be undertaken): *DS v HM Advocate* [2007] UKPC D1; 2007 S.C. (P.C.) 1; *Salvesen v Riddell* [2013] UKSC 22; 2013 S.C. (U.K.S.C.) 236.

[171] SA 1998 s.102. For a general discussion about suspending the effect of judicial decisions, see: J Morgan, "'O Lord make me pure—but not yet': granting time for the amendment of unlawful legislation" (2019) 135 LQR 585.

[172] For a review of the various legislative competence challenges, see C.M.G. Himsworth and C.M. O'Neill, *Scotland's Constitution: Law and Practice*, 3rd edn (Haywards Heath: Bloomsbury Professional, 2015) paras 14.24–14.26. See also: Lazarowicz and McFadden, *The Scottish Parliament: Law and Practice* (EUP, 2018), Ch.9.

In *Imperial Tobacco Ltd v Lord Advocate* (which was an unsuccessful challenge to the ban on the display of tobacco or smoking related products and the ban on cigarette vending machines) Lord Hope set out three principles that should be followed when determining a challenge to the competence of a legislative provision of the Scottish Parliament.[173] They were: **6–35**

(1) Any question of competence must be determined by applying the particular rules that have been set out in s.29 of, and Schs 4 and 5 to, the Scotland Act 1998. It was not for the court to express a view on whether an issue was better legislated for by Holyrood or Westminster. The respective spheres of responsibility had been determined by the UK Parliament. Decisions based on federal systems were of limited assistance. It is important to remember that a provision may have a devolved purpose but nevertheless be outside competence.[174]

(2) The system of rules laid down by the Scotland Act 1998 "must, of course, be taken to have been intended to create a system for the exercise of legislative power by the Scottish Parliament that was coherent, stable and workable", but that is not a principle of construction. The rules in Scotland Act 1998 are to be interpreted in the same way as any other Act of Parliament.[175]

(3) Describing the Scotland Act 1998 as a "constitutional statute" offers no guide as to its proper interpretation. It is, within carefully prescribed limits, a generous settlement of legislative authority. There is no presumption that a provision of an Act of the Scottish Parliament is inside, as opposed to outside, competence.[176]

A few years later, in the first challenge to the legislative competence of a measure of the Welsh Assembly, Lord Hope restated those principles[177] and they have since been followed by the Supreme Court.[178] Most recently, in the *UK Withdrawal from the European Union (Legal Continuity) (Scotland) Bill Reference*, the Supreme Court summarised is case law on the approach to competence challenges. The passage is worth setting out in full:

> "Since the Scottish Parliament commenced its work on 2 July 1999, the courts have had occasion to interpret the law by which it is governed. The main principles may be summarised as follows. The powers of the Scottish Parliament, like those of Parliaments in many other constitutional democracies, are delimited by law. The Scottish Parliament is a democratically elected legislature with a mandate to make laws for the people of Scotland. It has plenary powers within the limits of its

[173] *Imperial Tobacco Ltd v Lord Advocate* [2012] UKSC 61; 2013 S.C. (U.K.S.C.) 153.

[174] *Imperial Tobacco Ltd v Lord Advocate* [2012] UKSC 61; 2013 SC (U.K.S.C.) 153 at [13]. On the last point, Lord Rodger illustrated it in *Martin v Most* [2010] UKSC 10; 2010 S.C. (U.K.S.C.) 40 at [76]: the Scottish Parliament may have the devolved competence to alter the sentencing powers of the lower courts but if it does so in a manner than infringes Convention rights, the measure will be beyond competence.

[175] *Imperial Tobacco Ltd v Lord Advocate* [2012] UKSC 61; 2013 S.C. (U.K.S.C.) 153 at [14].

[176] *Imperial Tobacco Ltd v Lord Advocate* [2012] UKSC 61; 2013 S.C. (U.K.S.C.) 153 at [15].

[177] *Attorney General v National Assembly for Wales Commission* [2012] UKSC 53; [2013] 1 A.C. 792 at [78]–[81].

[178] *Re Agriculture Sector (Wales) Bill* [2014] UKSC 43; [2014] 1 W.L.R. 2622, per Lord Reed at [5]–[6].

> legislative competence. But it does not enjoy the sovereignty of the Crown in Parliament; rules delimiting its legislative competence are found in s.29 of and schs 4 and 5 to the Scotland Act, to which the courts must give effect. And the UK Parliament also has power to make laws for Scotland, a power which the legislation of the Scottish Parliament cannot affect (Scotland Act, s.28(7)). The Scotland Act must be interpreted in the same way as any other statute. The courts have regard to its aim to achieve a constitutional settlement and therefore recognise the importance of giving a consistent and predictable interpretation of the Scotland Act so that the Scottish Parliament has a coherent, stable and workable system within which to exercise its legislative power. This is achieved by interpreting the rules as to competence in the Scotland Act according to the ordinary meaning of the words used."[179]

As we saw earlier, in the same case, the Supreme Court confirmed that legislative competence falls to be assessed at the time the challenge is heard as opposed to the time at which the impugned measure was passed.[180]

6–36 Against that background we turn to *Martin v Most*. This case concerned the maximum sentence that could be imposed for certain road traffic offences. Those sentences had been increased by s.45 of the Criminal Proceedings etc. (Reform) (Scotland) Act 2007, that being an Act of the Scottish Parliament. The competence of that provision was challenged on the basis that it related to a reserved matter, namely the Road Traffic Offenders Act 1988. The question divided the Supreme Court 3:2 (with Lord Hope and Lord Rodger failing to agree on the outcome of a Scottish appeal for the first time in their period together on the highest court).[181] That division of opinion, and the final outcome of the appeal, is closely linked to the particular statutory provisions in dispute in that case and whether it was a rule that was special to a reserved matter. For present purposes, that disagreement can be set to one side. It is possible to identify some helpful guidance about how the reserved matters boundary is to be policed so far as s.29(2)(b) is concerned (a point on which the Justices all agreed). A provision is outside competence if it "relates to" (s.29(2)(b)) a reserved matter and a whether a provision "relates to" a reserved matter is to be "determined… by reference to the purpose of the provision, having regard (among other things) to its effect in all the circumstances" (s.29(3)).[182] Lord Walker explained what he understood that phrase to mean:

> "Section 29(2)(b) prohibits legislation by the Scottish Parliament that 'relates to' reserved matters. That is an expression which is familiar in this sort of context, indicating more than a loose or consequential connection, and the language of sec 29(3), referring to a provision's purpose and effect, reinforces that."[183]

---

[179] *United Kingdom Withdrawal from the European Union (Legal Continuity) (Scotland) Bill Reference* [2018] UKSC 64; 2019 S.C. (UKSC) 13 at [12].

[180] *United Kingdom Withdrawal from the European Union (Legal Continuity) (Scotland) Bill Reference* [2018] UKSC 64; 2019 S.C. (UKSC) 13 at [92]. See para.6–23, above.

[181] For a fuller analysis of this case, see C. Himsworth, "Nothing Special About That? *Martin v HM Advocate* in the Supreme Court" (2010) 14 Edin. L.R. 487.

[182] The court had to consider other questions as well, in particular the application of s.29(4) and para.2(3) of Sch.4 (was the rule of Scots criminal law that the Act sought to modify "special to a reserved matter"). They are complex issues (which have not been made any easier by the decision is *Most* accordingly Lord Rodger: [149]) which we are not going to explore for present purposes.

[183] *Martin v Most* [2010] UKSC 10; 2010 S.C. (U.K.S.C.) 40 at [49].

That guidance has since been endorsed by the Supreme Court on a number of occasions.[184] Lord Rodger explained that the clearest indication of the purpose of a provision will usually come from a report that gave rise to the legislation or of one of the committees of Parliament but very often the purpose will be clear from its context within the Act in question.[185] At the end of that paragraph, Lord Rodger doubted whether a clear example of an unlawful provision would come before the courts because of the pre-legislative measures that are in place. That observation conveniently brings us on to the case of *Salvesen v Riddell*.

Salvesen v Riddell[186] was the first successful civil challenge to an Act of the Scottish Parliament and was based on an incompatibility with art.1 of the First Protocol to the European Convention on Human Rights. It concerned s.72 of the Agriculture Holdings (Scotland) Act 2003. That provision related to the right to buy certain agricultural tenancies and sought to regulate any purported termination of such a tenancy. The background to the legislation is complicated and it is unnecessary to explain it in detail. For present purposes it is enough to note that on 3 February 2003 S had served a notice the effect of which was to terminate his lease to R on 28 November 2008. He expected to obtain vacant possession of the property on that date. However, the 2003 Act struck at any purported termination notice that was served on or after 22 September 2002. To that extent the legislation was retrospective. That provision was not set out in the White Paper that preceded the Bill nor the Bill as introduced into the Parliament (and thus certified by the responsible minister and the Presiding Officer as within the Parliament's competence). It was the result of a government amendment and was said to be an "anti-avoidance" measure to prevent landlords avoiding the more favourable (to tenants) regime that the 2003 Act was going to introduce. Had the notice been served after 30 June 2003, the 2003 Act offered acceptable protections for landlords in the same position as S. The consequence for S, however, was that rather than receive vacant possession on 28 November 2008, on 12 December 2008 R served notice under the 2003 Act exercising his "right to buy". The Land Court upheld R's position. The provisions of the 2003 Act that allowed that turn of events were subsequently held to be beyond the competence of the Scottish Parliament. The declaration that the offending provision was not law was originally made by the Inner House, on appeal from the Scottish Land Court (where the point had not arisen) and was upheld by the Supreme Court.[187] The case is significant as it highlights a complete failure of the pre-Assent safeguards that are designed to prevent legislation beyond the competence of the Scottish Parliament reaching the statute book: it was "hard not to see this provision as having been designed to penalise landlords in this group 6–37

[184] *Imperial Tobacco Ltd v Lord Advocate* [2012] UKSC 61; 2013 S.C. (U.K.S.C.) 153, per Lord Hope at [16]; *Re Recovery of Medical Costs for Asbestos Disease (Wales) Bill* [2015] UKSC 3; [2015] A.C. 1016, per Lord Mance at [25].

[185] *Martin v Most* [2010] UKSC 10; 2010 S.C. (U.K.S.C.) 40 at [75].

[186] *Salvesen v Riddell* [2013] UKSC 22; 2013 S.C. (U.K.S.C.) 236.

[187] *Salvesen v Riddell* [2013] UKSC 22; 2013 S.C. (U.K.S.C.) 236. See the case note by D.J. Carr, "Not Law (but not yet effectively not law)" (2013) 17 Edin. L.R. 370. The Inner House decision is reported at *Salvesen v Riddell* [2012] CSIH 26; 2013 S.C. 69. On that decision, see: D.J. Carr, "Not Law" (2012) 16 Edin. L.R. 410; M.M. Combe, "Human Rights, Limited Competence and limited partnerships: *Salvesen v Riddell*", 2012 S.L.T. (News) 193.

retrospectively" and was accordingly discriminatory[188]; the difference in treatment between landlords who served notice before and after 30 June 2003 had "no logical justification"[189]; s.72 did not pursue an aim that was reasonably related to the aim of the legislation as a whole[190]; and there was no way in which the clear and plain language of the 2003 Act could be read in such a way as to bring it within the legislative competence of the Parliament.[191] In those circumstances, it was surprising that none of the pre-Assent checks raised any concerns over the lawfulness of s.72 of the 2003 Act.

That brought the court to the question of remedy. In the Supreme Court Lord Hope observed that:

> "the finding of incompatibility ought not to extend any further than is necessary to deal with the facts of this case, and it is important that accrued rights which are not affected by the incompatibility should not be interfered with".[192]

Such an approach demonstrates that some care will be required when forging the appropriate remedy. As we have already noted, s.102 of the Scotland Act allows the court to remove or vary the retrospective effect of its decision and/or suspend the effect for a period to allow the defect to be varied. Lord Hope declined to limit the retrospective effect of the decision, but went to hold that:

> "Decisions as to how the incompatibility is to be corrected, for the past as well as the future, must be left to the Parliament guided by the Scottish Ministers."[193]

In this particular case, that led the Supreme Court to suspend the effect of their decision for 12 months, whilst granting permission for the Lord Advocate to return (to the Court of Session) to seek an extension of that period if necessary.[194] The question of remedy did not arise in *Martin* but Lord Hope considered it on an obiter basis. Again, he would have suspended the effect of a finding of incompatibility for two months to allow it to be corrected but also removed any retrospective effect of the decision (not surprising perhaps given it related to criminal sentences that may have been imposed and already served in full).[195] Any remedy will obviously have to be tailored to the specific circumstances, but it appears the court will normally be prepared to suspend any declarator that a

---

188 *Salvesen v Riddell* [2013] UKSC 22; 2013 S.C. (U.K.S.C.) 236, per Lord Hope of Craighead at [42].

189 *Salvesen v Riddell* [2013] UKSC 22; 2013 S.C. (U.K.S.C.) 236, per Lord Hope of Craighead at [44].

190 *Salvesen v Riddell* [2013] UKSC 22; 2013 S.C. (U.K.S.C.) 236, per Lord Hope of Craighead at [44]

191 *Salvesen v Riddell* [2013] UKSC 22; 2013 S.C. (U.K.S.C.) 236, per Lord Hope of Craighead at [47].

192 *Salvesen v Riddell* [2013] UKSC 22; 2013 S.C. (U.K.S.C.) 236, per Lord Hope of Craighead at [51].

193 *Salvesen v Riddell* [2013] UKSC 22; 2013 S.C. (U.K.S.C.) 236, per Lord Hope of Craighead at [57].

194 *Salvesen v Riddell* [2013] UKSC 22; 2013 S.C. (U.K.S.C.) 236, per Lord Hope of Craighead at [57].

195 *Martin v Most* [2010] UKSC 10; 2010 S.C. (U.K.S.C.) 40 at [43].

provision is "not law" for at least a limited period so as to allow the Parliament an opportunity to address the consequences of the court's decision.[196]

Finally in this trilogy, we come to *UK Withdrawal from the European Union (Legal Continuity) (Scotland) Bill Reference*.[197] As we saw in Ch.1, this Bill was referred to the Supreme Court by the Advocate General for Scotland prior to Royal Assent to determine its competence. A range of challenges were advanced by the UK Government, most of which were unsuccessful. But before the reference was determined, the UK Parliament enacted the European Union (Withdrawal) Act 2018. That Act amended the Scotland Act 1998 so as to include itself in the list of enactments protected from modification by the Scottish Parliament.[198] That resulted in any provisions of the Scottish Bill that were inconsistent with the 2018 Act being rendered beyond competence and "not law". It was to prove fatal to the Bill. As we have just seen, the Supreme Court helpfully summarised its approach to competence challenges. Two other points of note were established by the case. First, the court had to decide when competence was assessed: when the Bill was passed by the Parliament or when competence was determined by the court? Unsurprisingly, the court held it was the latter. Competence is not a once and for all assessment. The most obvious example is the requirement Scottish legislation be compatible with Convention rights. The meaning and understanding of those Convention rights evolves: the Convention is a living instrument.[199] Accordingly, what is compatible with the Convention today may be incompatible with it at a later date. The same is true of protected legislation and reserved matters (both Schs 4 and 5 can be amended). If competence had fallen to be assessed at the time of enactment, over time the statute book could come to house provisions that the Parliament could not now competently enact. Such a result would have been inconsistent with the intention underlying s.29 of the Scotland Act 1998. The second point that the Supreme Court addressed was the difference between enactments that are protected under Sch.4 and general reservations under Sch.5. At para.51, the Court explained: 6–38

> "When the UK Parliament decides to reserve an entire area of the law to itself, it does so by listing the relevant subject-matter in sch.5. When it has not taken that step, but has protected a particular enactment from modification by including it in sch.4, it is not to be treated as if it had listed the subject-matter of the enactment in sch.5. Where the only relevant restriction on the legislative power of the Scottish Parliament is the protection of an enactment from modification under sch.4, the Parliament has the power to enact legislation relating to the same subject-matter as the protected enactment, provided it does not modify it. Without attempting an exhaustive definition, a protected enactment will be modified by a later enactment, even in the absence of express amendment or repeal, if it is implicitly amended, disapplied or repealed in whole or in part. That will be the position if the later enactment alters a rule laid down in the protected enactment, or is otherwise in conflict with its unqualified continuation in force as before, so that the protected

---

[196] The result of *Salvesen v Riddell* was the Agricultural Holdings (Scotland) Act 2003 Remedial Order 2014, which itself was subject to (unsuccessful) challenge: *McMaster v Scottish Ministers*, 2018 S.C. 546. For a discussion of the background, see: K. Shields, "*McMaster v Scottish Ministers*—the tenant farmers case" [2017] J.R. 113.

[197] *United Kingdom Withdrawal from the European Union (Legal Continuity) (Scotland) Bill Reference* [2018] UKSC 64; 2019 S.C. (U.K.S.C.) 13.

[198] European Union (Withdrawal) Act 2018 Sch.3, para.21.

[199] *Tyrer v United Kingdom* (1979–80) 2 E.H.R.R. 1. See also: para.11–03, below.

> enactment has to be understood as having been in substance amended, superseded, disapplied or repealed by the later one."[200]

That passage confirms the difference between a general reservation under Sch.5 (which reserves an entire subject area) and a specific reservation under Sch.4 (which protects particular enactments). In relation to enactments included in Sch.4, the Scottish Parliament has competence to legislate on the same topic so long as the effect of that legislation is not to empty the protected enactment of its substance.

PARLIAMENTARY COMMITTEES

6–39 In any institution, it is impracticable to expect all of its work to be done by the institution meeting in plenary session. Delegation to committees is therefore necessary, but it is also desirable, since committees charged with specific remits develop an expertise in their fields that enables the institution as a whole better to perform its functions. At Westminster, a distinction is drawn between general and select committees[201]; at Holyrood, the committees of the Scottish Parliament combine the functions of the two (and have other functions besides).

Westminster

6–40 General committees are appointed afresh by the House of Commons Committee of Selection as and when required and must reflect the party political balance in the Commons as a whole. They fall into four categories: public Bill committees, which are appointed to consider public Bills and which can now take evidence in relation to the provisions of the Bill from external witnesses and experts; those appointed to consider subordinate legislation; those appointed to consider EU documents; and the grand committees of Scotland, Wales and Northern Ireland.[202] They are used primarily as a means of accommodating business that would otherwise have to take place in the Chamber. The chair of a general committee is appointed by the Speaker. Select committees[203] are appointed for the life of each Parliament, and fall into five categories:

(a) domestic committees;
(b) scrutiny committees;
(c) internal committees, which oversee aspects of the House's procedures and practices;
(d) the departmental select committees; and

---

200 *United Kingdom Withdrawal from the European Union (Legal Continuity) (Scotland) Bill Reference* [2018] UKSC 64; 2019 S.C. (UKSC) 13 at [51].

201 General committees were known, until the 2006–2007 session, as standing committees.

202 House of Commons Standing Orders r.84. See also: *Erskine May*, 25th edn, para.39.1 (*https://erskinemay.parliament.uk/section/6038/introduction-to-general-committees-in-the-house-of-commons/* [Accessed 9 July 2020]).

203 See: *Erskine May*, 25th edn, para.38.1 (*https://erskinemay.parliament.uk/section/5880/introduction-to-select-committees-in-the-house-of-commons/* [Accessed 9 July 2020]).

(e) the committees charged with supervision of the work of the main officers of Parliament.

Although select committees have been a feature of parliamentary life for many years, the present structure of departmental select committees dates back only to 1979. They are charged with examining the expenditure, administration and policy of "their" departments of state and associated public bodies. They have been criticised for failing to alter the nature of the relationship between Parliament and government. Such criticism is not altogether fair. Unlike the congressional committees in the United States, they are neither constituted nor staffed so as to allow them to be systematic in their scrutiny, and though they have the power to "send for persons, papers and records", they cannot compel the attendance of witnesses or the production of documents. Their investigations are therefore dependent upon ministerial co-operation to a significant extent. Even so, as the Select Committee on Procedure concluded in 1990, the new select committees provided "a far more vigorous, systematic and comprehensive scrutiny of ministers' actions and policies than anything that went before".[204] Since the committees are constituted to reflect political balance in the House as a whole, voting can split along party lines; but it is not an invariable practice. Some committees if not others have shown willing to challenge the government (possibly at some cost to any ministerial aspirations their members may harbour). Outwith the category of departmental select committees, furthermore, the Select Committees on Procedure, Public Accounts and Public Administration have done much valuable work on constitutional fundamentals in an effort to improve Parliament's capacity to hold the executive to account.[205] The role of select committees has been strengthened in recent years. The House as a whole now elects the chairs of most of the select committees, with members being elected by their respective parliamentary groups.[206] The Prime Minister now appears before the Liaison Committee of the House of Commons three times a year and a Backbench Business Committee has been established with the power to schedule business in the Commons chambers on days set aside for non-government business. Select committees have undertaken some well-publicised and high-profile investigations in recent years: the Culture, Media and Sport Committee's report on phone hacking[207]; the Treasury Committee's reports into the banking crisis; and the Foreign Affairs Committee's report into the Iraq war decision[208] all

---

[204] House of Commons Select Committee on Procedure, *The Working of the Select Committee System: Second Report from the Select Committee on Procedure, Session 1989–90* (The Stationery Office, 1990) HC 19–I.

[205] See, e.g. House of Commons Procedure Committee, *Parliamentary Questions, Third Report of Session 2001–02* (The Stationery Office, 2002), HC 622; Select Committee on Public Administration, *Ombudsman Issues, Third Report of Session 2002–03* (The Stationery Office, 2003) HC 448, which excoriates the government for failing to make good its pledge to introduce legislation to reform the ombudsman system and for obstructing the work of the Parliamentary Commissioner; and the series of reports produced by the same committee in recent years on ministerial accountability.

[206] House of Commons Standing Orders r.122B. Chairs are now also subject to term limits, being the greater of two consecutive Parliament's (which will now ordinarily be 10 years) or 8 years (r.122A).

[207] House of Commons Culture, Media and Sport Committee, *News International and Phone-hacking, Eleventh Report of Session 2010–12* (The Stationery Office, 2012) HC 903.

[208] House of Commons Foreign Affairs Committee, *The Decision to go to War in Iraq, Ninth Report of Session 2002–03* (The Stationery Office, 2003) HC 813.

spring to mind. These committees, however, remain under-resourced as compared to the government departments they are trying to monitor. These high-profile reports aside, it open to doubt just how effective the committees can be at holding the government to account.[209]

Holyrood[210]

6–41 At Holyrood, the committees were expected to have a more important role to play, in large part due to the absence of a second chamber. The rules on the committees of the Scottish Parliament are contained in Ch.6 of the Parliament's standing orders. These require the Parliament to establish and maintain a number of mandatory committees. They are: the Standards, Procedures and Public Appointments Committee; the Finance Committee[211]; the Public Audit Committee; the European and External Relations Committee[212]; the Equalities Committee; the Public Petitions Committee; and the Delegated Powers and Law Reform Committee.[213] The remit of each of the mandatory committees is prescribed in the Parliament's standing orders.[214] These committees are established for the whole session of the Parliament.[215] The Parliament may also, on a motion of any member or from the Parliamentary Bureau, establish subject committees. These committees vary (their names at least) from one parliamentary session to the next. The following subject committees currently exist: Committee on the Scottish Government Handling of Harassment Complaints; Economy, Energy and Fair Work Committee; Education and Skills Committee; Environment, Climate Change and Land Reform Committee; Health and Sports Committee; Justice Committee; Justice Sub-Committee on Policing; Local Government and Communities Committee; Rural Economy and Connectivity Committee; Social Security Committee; and Solicitors in the Supreme Courts of Scotland (Amendment) Bill Committee. The remit of each of these committees, and their duration, is determined by the Parliament.[216] Each committee, other than a private Bill committee, is required to have between 5 and 15 members. The Parliamentary Bureau is charged with drawing up a provisional list of members for each committee, having regard to party political balance and preferences

---

[209] See the discussion in Himsworth and O'Neill, *Scotland's Constitution: Law and Practice* (2015), para.10.9. See also the report by the UCL Constitution Unit on the work of select committees by Meg Russell and Meghan Benton, *Selective Influence: The Policy Impact of House of Commons Select Committees*, June 2011 (available at: *https://www.nuffieldfoundation.org/wp-content/uploads/2019/11/Selective20Influence_the20policy20impacty20of20house20of20commons20select20committees.pdf* [Accessed 22 May 2020]).

[210] See also: A Page, *Constitutional Law of Scotland*, paras 4–52—4–68; Lazarowicz and McFadden, *The Scottish Parliament: Law and Practice* (EUP, 2018), pp.68–78.

[211] This Committee currently also deals with culture and the constitution (which would otherwise fall to a subject committee).

[212] This Committee currently also deals with culture and tourism (which would otherwise fall to a subject committee).

[213] Scottish Parliament Standing Orders r.6.1(5).

[214] Scottish Parliament Standing Orders rr.6.4–6.11.

[215] Scottish Parliament Standing Orders r.6.12(1).

[216] Scottish Parliament Standing Orders rr.6.1(3) and 6.12(2).

expressed by MSPs, which must then be approved by the Parliament. The Parliament must also approve any changes to a committee's remit or membership.[217]

The functions of the parliamentary committees are extensive. Each is empowered to examine such matters within its remit as it may deem appropriate, or as may be referred to it by the Parliament or another committee, and report to Parliament thereon. Each is charged, within its remit, with considering the policy and administration of the Scottish Government (including financial proposals and administration), any proposal for legislation (whether before the Scottish Parliament or the Westminster Parliament), and any relevant European legislation or international convention. They may consider the need for reform of the law and to that end may initiate legislative proposals. In the latter respect, their impact has been slight. Only three committee Bills have been enacted by the Parliament.[218] But in general terms, it is fair to say that the greater part of the Parliament's work is done through its committees, and the verdict of civil society (if not of the often hostile Scottish media) on their performance to date has been broadly favourable.[219] The values identified by the Consultative Steering Group as underpinning the Parliament's work—public participation, accountability and power sharing—may have an aspirational flavour, but the committees have to a significant extent succeeded in capturing them. More recently, the Calman Commission was supportive of the Holyrood committees but raised some concern about their effectiveness at holding the government to account.[220]

PARLIAMENTARY PRIVILEGE

Westminster

The privileges of the Westminster Parliament are rooted in the law and custom of Parliament. At the opening of each new Parliament, the Speaker formally claims from the Crown for the Commons "their ancient rights and privileges", namely: freedom of speech; freedom from arrest; the exclusive right to regulate their composition; and exclusive jurisdiction over their internal affairs. The Houses of Parliament also assert an exclusive jurisdiction over the existence and extent of their privileges and over breaches of privilege and contempts of Parliament, which has in the past provoked confrontation with the courts. 6–42

Article 9 of the Bill of Rights 1689 provides that:

[217] Scottish Parliament Standing Orders r.6.3.

[218] The Interests of Members of the Scottish Parliament Bill (from the Standards and Public Appointments Committee), the Scottish Parliamentary Commissions and Commissioners etc. Bill (Review of the Scottish Parliamentary Corporate Body Supported Bodies Committee) and the Scottish Parliamentary Pensions Bill (Scottish Parliamentary Pension Scheme Committee).

[219] Procedures Committee of the Scottish Parliament, *Third Report 2003 (Session 1), The Founding Principles of the Scottish Parliament: the Application of Access and Participation, Equal Opportunities, Accountability and Power Sharing in the Work of the Parliament* (The Stationery Office, 2003) SPP 818. Perhaps the main source of disquiet about the committees stemmed from the tendency to go into private session rather more routinely than the public interest in transparency might warrant.

[220] Report of the Calman Commission, Commission on Scottish Devolution, *Serving Scotland Better: Scotland and the United Kingdom in the 21st Century* (The Stationery Office, 2009), Ch.6.

> "the freedom of speech and debates or proceedings in Parliament ought not to be impeached or questioned in any court or place out of Parliament".

This confers on members of both Houses an immunity from civil and criminal liability in respect of words spoken during debates or in the course of parliamentary proceedings (although members may expose themselves to the disciplinary jurisdiction of the House itself). The precise scope of the privilege is unclear owing to the inexact nature of the term "proceedings in Parliament" but was considered by the Supreme Court in *R. v Chaytor*.[221] In that case, a number of MPs were charged with false accounting in relation to parliamentary expenses that they had claimed. Each pled that the Crown Court lacked jurisdiction to hear the case, it being excluded by art.9 of the Bill of Rights. Had that argument been upheld, it would have produced the unsatisfactory outcome that MPs accused of offences associated with their expenses claims were immune from prosecution in the ordinary courts and could only be dealt with by Parliament. That would be unlikely to inspire public confidence.[222] The appellants' claim of privilege was unanimously rejected by the Supreme Court (sitting as a panel of nine Justices). The first point the court confirmed was that it was for the court, nor Parliament, to determine the limits of art.9.[223] The court then went on to explain why art.9 required to be read narrowly:

> "There are good reasons of policy for giving article 9 a narrow ambit that restricts it to the important purpose for which it was enacted—freedom for Parliament to conduct its legislative and deliberative business without interference from the Crown or the Crown's judges. The protection of Article 9 is absolute. It is capable of variation by primary legislation, but not capable of waiver, even by Parliamentary resolution. Its effect where it applies is to prevent those injured by civil wrongdoing from obtaining redress and to prevent the prosecution of members for conduct which is criminal."[224]

Given the breadth of the protection that art.9 affords, the court was persuaded that its ambit should be restricted to the core business of Parliament. Submitting claims for expenses was "an incident of the administration of Parliament; it is not part of the proceedings of Parliament".[225] Accordingly, art.9 did not prevent the trial proceeding. The appellants had a second argument. They also sought to rely on a different privilege: what was said to be the exclusive cognisance of Parliament. In short, they argued, that it was for Parliament to deal with the alleged (and subsequently proved) wrongdoing, not the courts. As Lord Rodger explained, not since 1667 had the House claimed exclusive cognisance in a case where a member was alleged to have committed an ordinary crime in the House

---

[221] *R. v Chaytor (David)* [2010] UKSC 52; [2011] 1 A.C. 684.

[222] Query whether the appellants, if dealt with by Parliament, could then have complained under art.6 of the European Convention on Human Rights? Parliament would hardly be a "fair and impartial tribunal", made up, as it would be, of political friends and political foes. The "fair minded and informed observer" may have a "reasonable apprehension" of bias. Indeed, there may be evidence of actual bias. For discussion of a similar argument in relation to the Scottish Parliament, see N.S. Ghaleigh, B. Kemp and P. Reid, "Politics as a Profession: Electoral Law, Parliamentary Standards and Regulating Politicians" [2012] P.L. 658.

[223] *R. v Chaytor* [2010] UKSC 52; [2011] 1 A.C. 684, per Lord Phillips at [15].

[224] *R. v Chaytor* [2010] UKSC 52; [2011] 1 A.C. 684, per Lord Phillips at [61].

[225] *R. v Chaytor* [2010] UKSC 52; [2011] 1 A.C. 684, per Lord Phillips at [62].

or its precincts.[226] Furthermore, unlike the privilege that arises under art.9, the privilege of exclusive cognisance can be waived by the House.[227] The fact the House authorities had co-operated with the investigation that led to the charges and the failure by the Speaker to step in and assert privilege all suggested that the House did not consider the matter to fall within its exclusive cognisance.[228] The argument was disposed of by Lord Rodger thus:

> "... the mere fact that the House *could* treat the matter as one of contempt does not mean that the House *must* do so, On the contrary, if the conduct in question would also constitute an offence under the ordinary criminal law of England, then the individual can be prosecuted in the criminal courts in the usual way. The jurisdiction of the House to deal with the matter overlaps with the jurisdiction of the ordinary courts to deal with it as a criminal offence. In short, the matter does not fall within the exclusive cognisance of Parliament."[229]

Accordingly, the trials were allowed to proceed and in due course a number of MPs were convicted and sentenced to periods of imprisonment.

As the Supreme Court explained, the most significant effect of the privilege of freedom of speech is the absolute immunity enjoyed by MPs in the law of defamation, which rests on the notion that MPs should be able to speak freely in Parliament without any fear that what they say might later be used against them in court. This is not to say that a Member of Parliament cannot be sued in defamation at all; in respect of their utterances outwith the meaning of "proceedings in Parliament", they are as liable to be sued as anybody else.[230] Neither does it mean that no reference whatsoever may be made in court to parliamentary proceedings. Since 1980, the House of Commons has permitted reference to be made in court to *Hansard* and published reports of parliamentary committees. In *Pepper v Hart*,[231] the House of Lords (in its judicial capacity) held that, in interpreting ambiguous legislation, the courts might properly have regard to clear ministerial statements made during the passage of the legislation through Parliament. The courts have also established the practice of examining ministerial statements made in Parliament when considering applications for judicial review of the legality of ministerial decisions. Section 13 of the Defamation Act 1996 enables MPs to waive their privilege in order to pursue an action in defamation. In 2011, the privilege of freedom of speech attracted headlines when it was used to name two individuals who were said to have obtained "super-injunctions" to prevent publication of affairs they were said to have had. One individual was named in the House of Lords and shortly thereafter the injunction (which was not in fact a "super-injunction") was discharged. The other was named in the House of Commons but that did not lead to the injunction **6–43**

---

226 *R. v Chaytor* [2010] UKSC 52; [2011] 1 A.C. 684, per Lord Rodger at [117].

227 *R. v Chaytor* [2010] UKSC 52; [2011] 1 A.C. 684, per Lord Phillips at [63].

228 *R. v Chaytor* [2010] UKSC 52; [2011] 1 A.C. 684, per Lord Rodger at [123].

229 *R. v Chaytor* [2010] UKSC 52; [2011] 1 A.C. 684, per Lord Rodger at [108] (emphasis in the original); see also Lord Phillips at [81].

230 Although even here it is not possible to fortify one's case against an MP with reference to remarks he has made in Parliament, or rely on these to prove malice: see *Church of Scientology of California v Johnson-Smith* [1972] 1 Q.B. 522 QBD; *Prebble v Television New Zealand Ltd* [1995] 1 A.C. 321 PC (New Zealand).

231 *Pepper (Inspector of Taxes) v Hart* [1993] A.C. 593.

(which, again, was not "super") being discharged.[232] The constitutional propriety of freedom of speech being used in this way so as to substitute the view of an MP or a peer on whether an individual should be named for that of a High Court judge is dubious. In the case of the court, each party is protected by the right of appeal. The same is not true when a member of the legislature has taken matters into their own hands.[233]

It is not only parliamentary proceedings that attract the protection of the privilege, but also the publication of parliamentary proceedings. This was established by the Parliamentary Papers Act 1840, the enactment of which followed one of the great confrontations between Parliament and the courts over the existence and extent of parliamentary privilege. In *Stockdale v Hansard*,[234] it was held that privilege did not extend to the publication by *Hansard* of a report by the Inspectors of Prisons, which referred to an indecent book, published by Stockdale, found circulating in Newgate Prison. By resolution, the House of Commons responded by asserting its "sole and exclusive jurisdiction to determine upon the existence and extent of its privileges".[235] It added that the institution or prosecution of any action bringing the privileges of Parliament into discussion or decision by a court outwith Parliament itself constituted a breach of privilege "and renders all parties concerned therein amenable . . . to the punishment consequent thereon".[236] The 1840 Act gave statutory force to the Commons' view of what the law was, making clear that the protection of absolute privilege from civil and criminal proceedings extended to papers published under the authority of Parliament as certified by an officer of either House. Qualified privilege applies to the publication of fair and accurate reports of parliamentary proceedings and papers, so that there will be no liability in defamation without proof of malice.[237]

6–44 The privilege of freedom from arrest protects members from civil arrest, but not from arrest in connection with criminal offences. Since the abolition of imprisonment for debt in the nineteenth century, it has had little practical

---

[232] *CTB v News Group Newspapers Ltd* [2011] EWHC 1334 (QB).

[233] That, and other issues, arising from the episode are considered in P. Johnson, "What can the press really say? Contempt of court and the reporting of parliamentary proceedings" [2012] P.L. 491. The same approach was returned to by Lord Hain, in October 2018, named a prominent businessman as being the subject of allegations of bullying and sexual harassment (an injunction having been obtained to prevent publication of a story about those allegations). A complaint to the House of Lords Standards Commissioner was not upheld: *https://www.parliament.uk/documents/lords-commissioner-for-standards/The_conduct_of_LordHain.pdf* [Accessed 22 May 2020].

[234] *Stockdale v Hansard* (1837) 2 Mood & R. 9.

[235] H.C.J. 418 (1837).

[236] Stockdale subsequently obtained judgment against *Hansard*, but the two holders of the office of the Sheriff of Middlesex were imprisoned by order of the Commons for attempting to enforce the judgment. The court dismissed their application for habeas corpus on the basis that it could not go behind the Speaker's warrant to the effect that the two men were guilty of a breach of privilege and contempt of Parliament: *Sheriff of Middlesex Case* (1840) 11 Ad. & El. 273. They were later released by the Commons upon undertaking not to execute any orders of the court against *Hansard*, which in turn led to their being imprisoned by the courts for contempt of court.

[237] But while the 1840 Act resolved the differences between Parliament and the courts over this aspect of freedom of speech, it did not resolve the basic jurisdictional conflict over who it is, Parliament or the courts, that has the last word over the existence and extent of privileges when claimed.

significance.[238] The importance of the exclusive right to regulate its own composition has also been attenuated by the transfer of the right of the Commons to determine the result of disputed parliamentary elections to the ordinary courts.[239] The Houses of Parliament do retain the right to determine whether a person is disqualified from membership of either House, as when, in 1960, the House of Commons declared vacant the seat of Tony Benn MP after he succeeded to a viscountcy on the death of his father and barred him from the House. This jurisdiction is not, however, exclusive, as a person claiming that an individual disqualified from membership of the House of Commons by virtue of the House of Commons Disqualification Act 1975 has been elected to the Commons may apply under s.7 of the Act to the Judicial Committee of the Privy Council for a declaration to that effect.[240]

The privilege consisting of Parliament's exclusive right to control its own proceedings and to regulate its internal affairs without interference from the courts remains significant. It was on this basis that the ordinary courts declined to intervene in the celebrated case of *Bradlaugh v Gossett*.[241] Mr Bradlaugh, an atheist who had been refused the opportunity of taking the oath required before an MP may sit,[242] contested the legality of a resolution of the House of Commons to exclude him and sought an injunction to restrain the serjeant-at-arms from enforcing that resolution. The court held it had no jurisdiction to pronounce on the matter. It is also on the grounds of this privilege that the courts decline to investigate alleged procedural defects in the legislative process when the validity of an Act of Parliament is challenged. As we have seen,[243] the effect of the "enrolled Bill rule" is that a court of law can do no more than look to the Parliamentary Roll:

> "... if from that it should appear that a bill has passed both Houses and received the Royal Assent, no court can inquire into the mode in which it was introduced into Parliament, nor into what was done previous to its introduction, nor what passed in Parliament during its progress."[244]

If the enactment of legislation, whether public or private, has been obtained by fraud or other impropriety, or in contravention of the standing orders of Parliament, only Parliament can rectify matters by repealing the measure in question.

---

238 However, collateral privileges flow from the basic principle underlying freedom from arrest, namely the right of Parliament to the uninterrupted attendance and services of its members, such as the exemption of MPs from jury service and from citation to attend court as witnesses.

239 See now the Representation of the People Act 1983 Ch.2 Pt III and para.4–28, above.

240 Curiously, this jurisdiction was not transferred to the Supreme Court. The Judicial Committee may direct that the issue be tried in the High Court of England and Wales, the Court of Session or the High Court of Northern Ireland, depending on the location of the constituency in question; if so, the decision of that court is final.

241 *Bradlaugh v Gossett* (1884) 12 Q.B.D. 721 QBD.

242 This in the days before provision was made allowing MPs to make a solemn affirmation: see now the Oaths Act 1978.

243 See para.3–02, above.

244 *Edinburgh and Dalkeith Railway v Wauchope* (1842) 8 Cl. & F. 710 HL, per Lord Campbell. See also *British Railways Board v Pickin* [1974] A.C. 765, in which the House of Lords eschewed any jurisdiction to inquire into parliamentary procedures.

6–45 The Houses of Parliament retain a jurisdiction to deal with breaches of privilege and contempts of Parliament. "Contempt of Parliament" is a generic term to cover any offences punishable by Parliament, namely conduct offensive to the authority and dignity of the Houses or, as Erskine May puts it[245]:

> "Any act or omission which obstructs or impedes either House in the performance of its functions, or which obstructs or impedes any member or officer of such House in the discharge of his duty, or which has a tendency, directly or indirectly, to produce such results."[246]

The term "contempts" therefore includes breaches of privilege, that is, the infringement of any of the specific privileges noted above. The distinction between the two may be important, however, for while the Houses of Parliament cannot extend the scope of their own privileges and questions of the existence and extent of privilege may be addressed by the courts, the list of possible contempts remains open and the courts cannot question the causes of committal for contempt. Established examples of contempt include: disorderly conduct within the precincts of Parliament; the obstruction of members going to or coming from the Houses; bribery, corruption and other species of dishonesty; and refusal to give evidence before parliamentary committees. The most high-profile, and recent, contempt found by the House of Commons was held to have been committed by the government. By means of a humble Address[247] on 13 November 2018, the government was required to publish the full advice provided by the Attorney General to the Cabinet concerning the EU Withdrawal Agreement. Requiring the publication of a Law Officer's advice went against convention and, in the event, the government published only a summary of that advice. On 4 December 2018, the House of Commons passed a motion finding the government in contempt for having failed to publish the advice called for in the humble Address.[248]

The fact that certain conduct is found to constitute contempt does not mean that Parliament will take any further action against the contemnor. The House of Commons resolved in 1978 only to use its powers of punishment when:

> "satisfied that to do so is essential to provide reasonable protection for the House, its members or its officers, from such improper obstruction or attempt or threat of obstruction as is causing or is liable to cause substantial interference with the performance of their respective functions".

---

[245] *Erskine May Parliamentary Practice* (2019), para.15.2: *https://erskinemay.parliament.uk/section/4991/contempts/* [Accessed 18 May 2020].

[246] For a discussion of the full range of powers that Parliament has, see: *Erskine May Parliamentary Practice* (2019), paras 11–30—11–33 ("Punishment of Members"); pp.254–258 ("Misconduct of Members or Officers"); and Ch.5 ("Rules governing the conduct of Members of both Houses and the disclosure of financial interests"), especially paras 5–21—5–25, concerning the House of Commons, ("Complaints and investigations") and, concerning the House of Lords, paras 5–39—5–44 ("Enforcement").

[247] A little known about procedure until it was used in these circumstances. See: *Erskine May*, (2019), para.9.10: *https://erskinemay.parliament.uk/section/6548/addresses-to-the-crown/* [Accessed 9 July 2020].

[248] Hansard, 4 December 2018, Col.731. Of course, that the government lost such a vote is as much a reflection of its lack of majority. Perhaps more surprising is that having lost such a vote, a confidence vote did not follow and the government, despite having been found in contempt, carried on in office.

Nevertheless, the range of penalties at the theoretical disposal of the House is considerable. A member may be expelled or suspended; members or "strangers" may be admonished or reprimanded at the Bar of the House. Persons may be committed for contempt by the High Court of Parliament, without recourse to the ordinary courts, and the House retains a power, last used in 1880, of imprisonment (although curiously it has no power to impose fines).[249] As we saw in relation to *R. v Chaytor*, where the conduct that constitutes the contempt also amounts to a crime, Parliament's jurisdiction to punish the contempt is co-existent with the court's jurisdiction to deal with the criminal conduct.

As to the House of Lords, Erskine May comments that "the Lords enjoy their privileges simply because of their immemorial role in Parliament as advisers of the Sovereign".[250] Just as much as the House of Commons, the House of Lords claims the exclusive right to be the judge of its own privileges and the power to punish breaches of privilege and contempts, although issues of privilege arise less frequently in the Upper House. The privilege of peerage confers immunity from civil arrest.[251] Article 9 of the Bill of Rights 1689 applies equally to the Lords as to the Commons in protecting freedom of speech. The House of Lords is master of its own affairs and decides, through the Committee for Privileges, the right of newly created peers to sit and vote and on claims to old peerages.[252] Lastly, the Lords have the power to commit a person for contempt and, unlike the Commons, also have a power to fine and to order security to be given for good conduct.[253] **6–46**

Many of these privileges may appear archaic, but their underlying rationale remains broadly sound, as attested by the provision made in the Scotland Act to extend aspects of parliamentary privilege as developed at Westminster to the Scottish Parliament. Even so, as part of the general drive to modernise the workings of Parliament, a joint committee consisting of members of the House of Lords and of the House of Commons was established in July 1997 to review the law and practice of parliamentary privilege at Westminster and to make recommendations. The committee, chaired by Lord Nicholls of Birkenhead (then a Law Lord), published its first report in April 1999.[254] The joint committee's approach to its task was informed by the following considerations: **6–47**

> "The overall guiding principle is that the proper functioning of Parliament lies at the heart of a healthy parliamentary democracy. It is in the interests of the nation as a

---

[249] It is questionable now whether it would be consistent with the international obligations of the UK under the Convention for either House of Parliament to resort to its penal jurisdiction. It is not merely that the procedures of the Houses may lack compatibility with art.6 (particularly the right to be tried before an independent and impartial tribunal) but also that, in so far as the categories of contempts are not closed, imposition of criminal liability could be regarded as contrary to art.7, which prohibits the retrospective creation of criminal offences. See, generally, *Demicoli v Malta* (1991) 14 E.H.R.R. 47.

[250] *Erskine May Parliamentary Practice* (2019) para.12–2: *https://erskinemay.parliament.uk/section/4571/lords-privileges-of-parliament-and-of-peerage/* [Accessed 9 July 2020].

[251] See *Stourton v Stourton* [1963] 1 All E.R. 606.

[252] In the *Wensleydale Peerage Case* (1856) 5 H.L. Cas. 958, the House of Lords decided that the life peerage created for the judge Sir James Parke did not entitle him to sit in Parliament. The Appellate Jurisdiction Act 1876 authorised the appointment of Lords of Appeal in Ordinary carrying with it a right to sit and vote in the Lords, while the Life Peerages Act 1958 provided for the conferment of life peerages on men and women with the right to sit and vote.

[253] Although here again, it seems unlikely that such power would ever now be used: see para.6–40.

[254] Joint Committee on Parliamentary Privilege, *First Report of the Joint Committee on Parliamentary Privilege* (The Stationery Office, 1999) HL 43–I, HC 214–I.

> whole that the two Houses of Parliament should have the rights and immunities that they need in order to function properly. But the protection afforded by privilege should be no more than Parliament needs to carry out its functions effectively and safeguard its constitutional position. Appropriate procedures should exist to prevent abuse and ensure fairness. Thus the thread running through this report involves matching parliamentary privilege to the current requirements of Parliament and present-day standards of fairness and reasonableness."

In that light, the committee made a number of recommendations for change. It favoured abolition of existing privileges only in a few cases.[255] Otherwise, its proposals generally involved clothing existing privileges in statutory form or removing more glaring anachronisms. Thus, it recommended the enactment of legislation confirming the traditional view of art.9 of the Bill of Rights as a blanket prohibition on the examination of parliamentary proceedings in court, subject to specific and limited exceptions,[256] clarifying the meaning of the term "proceedings in Parliament", and replacing the provisions of the Parliamentary Papers Act 1840 with legislation in comprehensible form. It also called for the replacement of s.13 of the Defamation Act 1996 with new provision enabling the House, rather than an individual member, to waive privilege in court proceedings (and not merely those involving defamation). It favoured the introduction of new statutory offences of bribery and corruption, but noted that, since the prosecution of such offences would inevitably impact upon art.9, any prosecution should be subject to the consent of the Attorney General or Lord Advocate. The right of each House to administer its internal affairs within its precincts should be confined to activities directly and closely related to proceedings in Parliament and:

> "Parliament should no longer be a statute-free zone in respect of Acts of Parliament relating to matters such as health and safety and data protection. In future, when Parliament is to be exempt, a reasoned case should be made out and debated as the legislation proceeds through Parliament".

While each House should retain its disciplinary and penal jurisdiction over its own members, the disciplinary procedures of both Houses should be revised to bring them into line with contemporary standards of fairness, including rights guaranteed by the European Convention on Human Rights. Parliament's jurisdiction over contempts committed by strangers should be transferred to the courts, although Parliament should retain a residual jurisdiction including a power to admonish in non-contentious cases. None of these proposals, however, have been enacted into law.

---

[255] The joint committee recommended abolition of freedom from arrest in civil cases and of the collateral privilege exempting members from citation to attend court as witnesses (although it considered that citations should not be issued against members without the prior approval of a judge).

[256] Such as that established by *Pepper v Hart* [1993] A.C. 593.

Holyrood[257]

The Scottish Parliament and its members do not enjoy the same range of privileges as obtain at Westminster, and such "privileges" as they have are, like the Parliament itself, derived from the Scotland Act 1998. The Act extends two aspects of the privilege of free speech to the Scottish Parliament, its members and officers. First, by virtue of s.41, any statement made in proceedings of the Parliament and the publication under the authority of the Parliament of any such statement is absolutely privileged in the law of defamation. Even if an MSP makes a defamatory statement maliciously, or with the intention of injuring the reputation of the object of the statement, they cannot be held liable in respect of it (although, as at Westminster, he may fall foul of the disciplinary jurisdiction of the Parliament itself). Second, by virtue of s.42, certain proceedings of the Scottish Parliament—namely, parliamentary proceedings in relation to a Bill or subordinate legislation—are shielded from criminal liability for contempt of court. A fair and accurate report of such proceedings, provided it is made in good faith, is similarly protected. This immunity is narrower than that which obtains at Westminster: it would appear, for example, that contemptuous utterances made in the course of a general debate in the Scottish Parliament could result in the prosecution of the speaker.[258] However, para.1 of Sch.3 requires standing orders to make provision for the prevention of conduct constituting contempt of court and to lay down a sub judice rule. This finds its expression in standing order r.7.3(2), which requires that members do not conduct themselves in a manner that would constitute a criminal offence or contempt of court, and r.7.5, which prevents members from making reference to any matter in relation to which legal proceedings are active. It is therefore unlikely that many instances of contemptuous behaviour will arise from the proceedings of the Scottish Parliament. Like members of the Westminster Parliament, MSPs are exempt from jury service, but by virtue of s.85 of the Scotland Act, rather than freedom from arrest and its associated privileges. No immunity from arrest, either criminal or civil, is extended to MSPs by the Scotland Act. **6–48**

The aspect of parliamentary privilege that finds the most echoes in the Scotland Act is that of exclusive cognisance of internal affairs. The underlying rationale for this privilege is not dissimilar to that found in art.9 of the Bill of Rights: namely, to prevent outside interference, and specifically interference by the courts, with the proceedings of the Parliament. Absent such privileges, the ordinary work of the Parliament could be obstructed by the commencement of legal challenges to its activities. The Scotland Act, therefore, provides that the validity of any proceedings of the Scottish Parliament is unaffected by any vacancy in its membership[259] or by the participation of a member who is subject to disqualification.[260] The validity of any act of the Presiding Officer or either of his or her deputies is unaffected by any defect in the officer's or their election,[261]

---

[257] See also: A. Page, *Constitutional Law of Scotland*, paras 4–69—4–73.

[258] As compared to the examples we noticed above, where members of the Westminster Parliament relied upon privilege to reveal the identity of individuals otherwise protected by an injunction (a step that would otherwise have constituted a contempt of court).

[259] SA 1998 s.1(4).

[260] SA 1998 s.17(5).

[261] SA 1998 s.19(7).

and the validity of an Act of the Scottish Parliament is unaffected by any invalidity in the proceedings of the Parliament leading to its enactment.[262]

6–49 The courts have largely acquiesced in Westminster's assertion of exclusive jurisdiction over its internal affairs, and that there are still good reasons for this is reflected in these provisions of the Scotland Act. It is important to note, however, that the jurisdiction of the ordinary courts is not wholly excluded in relation to the internal workings of the Scottish Parliament. Certain aspects of its internal affairs are governed by the Scotland Act itself, or by subordinate legislation made under it, or by Scottish legislation required to be enacted by the Scotland Act. The rules on members' interests are an example. In *Whaley v Lord Watson of Invergowrie*,[263] the petitioners sought interim interdict to restrain Mike Watson MSP from proceeding further with the Protection of Wild Mammals (Scotland) Bill, on the grounds that he was in breach of the rules against paid advocacy. Lord Johnston refused the petitioners' motion, partly on the basis that the grant of the remedy would intrude upon the exclusive competence of the Parliament to regulate its own affairs. But, as the First Division subsequently made clear, that competence is not exclusive. The rules on members' interests were then contained in a statutory instrument made pursuant to the Scotland Act. Accordingly they were legal rules, enforceable as such by the ordinary courts.[264] The fact that the Standards Committee of the Scottish Parliament had a parallel jurisdiction to scrutinise alleged breaches of the rules on members' interests did not affect the point, nor was the court in any way bound by the fact that the Standards Committee had rejected a complaint that Mr Watson had breached the rule against advocacy.

A further issue raised by *Whaley* concerned the effect of s.40(3) and (4) of the Scotland Act. These provide that in any proceedings against the Scottish Parliament, the court shall not make an order for suspension, interdict, reduction or specific performance (or other like order) but may instead pronounce a declarator. Similarly, in any proceedings against an MSP, the Presiding Officer or their deputies, any member of the staff of the Parliament or the parliamentary corporation, the court may make no coercive order, but must confine itself to a declarator, if the effect of making a coercive order would be to give relief against the Parliament that is prohibited by s.40(3). In *Whaley*, it was argued that the court could not grant interdict against Mike Watson MSP because the effect of doing so would be to interdict the Parliament from proceeding with the Protection of Wild Mammals (Scotland) Bill. As the First Division held, however:

> "Section 40(4) of the 1998 Act is designed to prevent parties from obtaining in substance remedies affecting the Parliament which they could not obtain in proceedings against the Parliament. It follows that subsection (4) applies where proceedings for some legal wrong could lie against the Parliament. In the present

---

[262] SA 1998 s.28(5). See also s.50, which provides that the validity of any act of a member of the Scottish Government or of a junior Scottish Minister is unaffected by any defect in his nomination by the Parliament or, as the case may be, in the Parliament's agreement to his nomination; and s.69(3), which makes similar provision in respect of any procedural defects in the appointment of the Auditor General for Scotland.

[263] *Whaley v Lord Watson of Invergowrie*, 2000 S.C. 340.

[264] The position would have differed if the petition had raised a question of compliance with the standing orders, which do not require to be cast in legislative form and which are in fact contained in a resolution of the Parliament.

> case . . . the petitioners seek to interdict the first respondent from breaching Article 6 of the members' interests order—a wrong which could be committed only by a member and which could never be committed by the Parliament itself . . . In other words, any interdict against the first respondent could not have the effect of interdicting a wrong by the Parliament."[265]

So, for example, even if there were a compelling argument that the Scottish Parliament was proposing to enact legislation trespassing upon reserved matters, the court could not restrain it from proceeding by way of interdict. Nor could it interdict the printing and publication of the Bill by the Clerk to the Parliament, because that would effectively amount to an interdict against the Parliament proper. But coercive remedies are competent against members and officers of the Scottish Parliament where s.40(3) is not implicated, even though their grant may involve some disruption to the Parliament's internal affairs.

Finally, there are certain parallels to be drawn between the inherent jurisdiction enjoyed by the Houses of Parliament at Westminster as the High Court of Parliament and the conferment of specific powers on the Scottish Parliament in relation to witnesses, evidence and discipline. Section 22 of the Scotland Act provides for the regulation of parliamentary proceedings by standing order, and gives effect to Sch.3, which specifies how certain matters are to be dealt with by standing orders. Among the matters that Sch.3 requires standing orders to cover are the withdrawal from a member of the Parliament of their rights and privileges.[266] But while, as such, the Scottish Parliament has an independent disciplinary jurisdiction over its members,[267] it does not, by contrast to Westminster, have an autonomous penal jurisdiction, either over members or strangers. Sections 22 and 23 provide for the power of the Parliament to compel the attendance of witnesses and the production of documents, the exceptions to and modalities surrounding that power, and for the creation of summary offences of refusing or failing without statutory justification or reasonable excuse to attend or co-operate as required. The Houses of Parliament at Westminster, as the High Court of Parliament, have powers in relation to compelling attendance and the production of evidence similar to those of the ordinary courts, and have jurisdiction to deal with any breaches of privilege or contempts involved in non-compliance with their requirements. These provisions of the Scotland Act provide a statutory statement of the extent to which the Scottish Parliament is to have an equivalent jurisdiction, and it should, in particular, be noted that criminal offences under these provisions will be triable in the ordinary courts, but not before the Parliament itself. Similarly, an MSP who takes part in any parliamentary proceedings in contravention of the rules on the registration of financial interests or the rules against paid advocacy will be guilty of a criminal offence punishable by a fine, but again triable by the ordinary courts rather than the Parliament. 6–50

265 *Whaley v Lord Watson of Invergowrie*, 2000 S.C. 340, per Lord President Rodger at p351.

266 This is provided for by the Standing Orders r.1.7, in the following terms: "The Parliament may, on a motion of the Standards Committee, withdraw from a member his or her rights and privileges as a member to such extent and for such period as are specified in the motion".

267 For a discussion of the Parliament's disciplinary jurisdiction, see: Ghaleigh, Kemp and Reid, "Politics as a Profession: Electoral Law, Parliamentary Standards and Regulating Politicians" [2012] P.L. 658.

STANDARDS

Westminster[268]

6–51 On several occasions in the past century, the House of Commons has had cause to inquire into possible contempts of Parliament, breaches of privilege and other species of un-parliamentary conduct connected with links between a member's parliamentary role and outside financial (or equivalent) interests. A public register of members' interests was established in 1975. It proved insufficient to prevent the various misdemeanours that finally, in 1994, prompted the establishment of a Committee on Standards in Public Life:

> "to examine current concerns about standards of conduct of all holders of public office, including arrangements relating to financial and commercial activities, and to make recommendations as to any changes in present arrangements which might be required to ensure the highest standards of probity in public life".

The committee published its first report, concerning the holding by MPs of paid outside interests, in May 1995. The report acknowledged the widespread loss of public confidence in the probity of MPs, but found no evidence of "a growth in actual corruption". What it did find was that almost 70 per cent of MPs, not including the Speaker and ministers, had some form of financial relationship with outside bodies, ranging from company directorships and consultancies with lobbying firms and trade associations to sponsorship agreements with trade unions. The committee did not recommend the introduction of an outright ban on outside financial interests, taking the view that this would deter otherwise eligible and well qualified people from seeking election to the House of Commons, "... a Parliament composed entirely of full-time professional politicians would not serve the best interests of democracy". It did, however, recommend the establishment of a new Select Committee on Standards and Privileges and the appointment of a Parliamentary Commissioner for Standards, who would supervise compliance with a new Code of Conduct for MPs and report to the select committee on alleged breaches. It called for a specific prohibition on paid advocacy and the adoption of rules requiring members to deposit with the Commissioner for Standards, and thereby make available for public inspection, any agreements with bodies outside Parliament relating to the provision of services by them in their capacity as MPs, together with details of the remuneration received from any such employment. More generally, the committee set out seven general principles that were to be taken to govern all aspects of public life.[269] The House of Commons endorsed both the statement of principles and the specific recommendations of the committee in a free vote in November 1995, at the same time approving a resolution banning paid advocacy. The House subsequently approved a new Code of Conduct for MPs in July 1996.[270] It was enforced by the Select Committee on Standard and Privileges and

[268] See P. Leopold, "Standards of Conduct in Public Life" in J. Jowell and D. Oliver (eds), *The Changing Constitution*, 7th edn (Oxford: Oxford University Press, 2011) Ch.15.

[269] Namely selflessness, integrity, objectivity, accountability, openness, honesty and leadership.

[270] The current version of the code was adopted on 7 January 2019, House of Commons, "Code of Conduct" (The Stationery Office, 2015), HC 1882, *https://publications.parliament.uk/pa/cm201719/*

after repeating the seven principles of conduct in public life, it set out eight rules dealing with matters such as general conduct, acceptance of gifts, lobbying and advocacy and registration of gifts. When in doubt, members were exhorted to seek the advice of the Parliamentary Commissioner for Standards. The Commissioner was also responsible for maintaining the Register of Members' Interests. Registrable interests include any pecuniary interest or other material benefit that a member receives and which might reasonably be thought by others to influence their actions, speeches or votes in Parliament, or actions taken in their capacity as an MP.[271] A proposal to make it an offence to fail to register a financial interest (as it is for MSPs) was dropped during the passage of the Parliamentary Standards Act 2009.[272]

Although the House of Lords did not come under the same sort of pressure as the House of Commons over standards of conduct, peers nevertheless adopted a code of conduct modelled on that applicable to MPs and containing the seven principles of public life, and a new Register of Lords' Interests requiring registration by peers of all relevant interests.[273]

None of that prevented the expenses scandal that hit Westminster in 2009. As **6–52**
we have already seen, some parliamentarians ended up in prison as a result of false expenses claims. Others simply appeared ludicrous, for example, the claim made for a duck pond! Using the freedom of information legislation, journalists sought, and were eventually given, details of the expenses claimed by parliamentarians.[274] The first report of the Committee on Standards in Public Life had noted a widespread loss of trust in parliamentarians in the late-1990s. In the aftermath of the expenses scandal, their standing fell even further. A number of reforms were introduced to try and arrest the decline and restore public trust and confidence in their representatives. First, the Parliamentary Standards Act 2009[275] was hurried through Parliament (and was promptly amended by the Constitutional Reform and Governance Act 2010). That Act concerned only the House of Commons[276] and established a new body corporate known as the Independent Parliamentary Standards Authority.[277] The Authority is now

cmcode/1882/1882.pdf [Accessed 19 April 2020]. It is meant to be reviewed by the Parliamentary Commissioner for Standards once in each Parliament (that was not possible in the unexpectedly short 2015–2017 Parliament).

[271] The code of conduct divides registrable interests into the following 10 categories: directorships; remunerated employment, office, profession, etc.; the provision of services to clients where the services arise out of the member's position as an MP; sponsorships; gifts, benefits and hospitality in the UK exceeding a specified value; overseas visits; overseas benefits and gifts exceeding a specified value; land and property other than the member's personal residence(s) (or those of a spouse) that generate an income; shareholdings; and miscellaneous relevant interests not caught by any of the specific categories.

[272] See N. Parpworth, "The Parliamentary Standards Act 2009: A Constitutional Dangerous Dogs Measure?" (2010) 73 M.L.R. 262, 276.

[273] The code of conduct took effect on 31 March 2002.

[274] Only after a complaint to the Information Commissioner, which was then upheld by the High Court: *Corporate Officer of the House of Commons v Information Commissioner* [2008] EWHC 1084 (Admin); [2009] 3 All E.R. 403.

[275] Parpworth, "The Parliamentary Standards Act 2009: A Constitutional Dangerous Dogs Measure?" (2010) 73 M.L.R. 262.

[276] Parliamentary Standards Act 2009 s.2.

[277] Parliamentary Standards Act 2009 s.3; see *http://www.parliamentarystandards.org.uk* [Accessed 18 May 2020].

responsible for the salaries of MPs (both determining what they should be and their payment). Leaving the fixing of MPs' salary to an independent body ought to have been an uncontroversial step. When the Authority determined that MPs should receive a 10 per cent pay rise following the 2015 general election, however, the political parties united to denounce the decision. Given public sector pay rises were capped at 1 per cent at the time the response was not surprising. If transferring MPs' pay to an independent body was meant to take the sting out of it, the move failed spectacularly. The Authority's other key function is the administration of the MPs expenses scheme. The Authority also has a compliance officer who may conduct an investigation if they have reason to believe that any MP has been paid an amount under the expenses scheme that should not have been allowed.[278] Making a false or misleading claim under the expenses claim is also an offence punishable by a fine and/or a period of up to 12 months' imprisonment.[279] At the time of writing, further amendments to the Code are under consideration in response to a series of allegations of bullying, harassment and sexual harassment. That led to some amendments in July 2018[280] and the work of the Committee on Standards, in conjunction with Parliamentary Commissioner for Standards, is ongoing.

The Independent Parliamentary Standards Authority works closely with the Parliamentary Commissioner for Standards.[281] The work of the Parliamentary Commissioner for Standards is overseen by the Standards Committee, who are also responsible for investigating specific complaints alleging a breach of the code of conduct.[282] Exceptionally, and without precedent, the Standards Committee has, since 2013, had at least two (and no more than three) lay members.[283] A separate committee, the Privileges Committee, now deals with any matters of privilege that are referred to it by the House of Commons.[284]

Holyrood

6–53 Certain provisions concerning the maintenance and enforcement of standards[285] in the Scottish Parliament are contained in the Scotland Act itself. Section 39 deals with members' interests.[286] Broadly, it reflects the rules laid down in the House of Commons following the first report of the Committee on Standards in Public Life. In addition, it requires provision to be made by or under an Act of the Scottish Parliament for a register of members' interests to be published and made

---

[278] Parliamentary Standards Act 2009 s.9.

[279] Parliamentary Standards Act 2009 s.10.

[280] Largely to reflect the adoption of an Independent Complaints and Grievance Policy. See generally: *Erskine May*, 25th edn, para.5.2 (available at: *https://erskinemay.parliament.uk/section/6326/bullying-and-harassment-background/* [Accessed 27 May 2020]) and para.5.23 (*https://erskinemay.parliament.uk/section/6350/icgs-investigations/* [Accessed 27 May 2020]).

[281] See the Joint Statement of the Parliamentary Commissioner for Standards, the Chief Executive of the Independent Parliamentary Standards Authority and the Independent Parliamentary Standards Authority Compliance Officer (20 January 2015), *http://www.parliament.uk/documents/pcfs/IPSA-Joint-Statement.pdf* [Accessed 27 May 2020].

[282] House of Commons Standing Orders r.149.

[283] House of Commons Standing Orders r.149A.

[284] House of Commons Standing Orders r.148A.

[285] Lobbying is now separately and specifically regulated: Lobbying (Scotland) Act 2016.

[286] "Member" includes the law officers, whether or not they are also MSPs.

available for public inspection. It specifies that contraventions of the provisions made pursuant to it shall constitute criminal offences punishable on summary conviction by a fine not exceeding level five on the standard scale.

The provisions required by s.39 was made on an interim basis by the Secretary of State under the Scotland Act 1998 (Transitory and Transitional Provisions) (Members' Interests) Order 1999.[287] The matter is now governed by the Interests of Members of the Scottish Parliament Act 2006 (as amended by the Interests of Members of the Scottish Parliament (Amendment) Act 2016). Section 1 of the 2006 Act provides for the establishment of a statutory Register of Interests of Members of the Scottish Parliament. The Act then makes provision in connection with "registrable interests", namely registrable financial interests falling within the eight categories set out in the Schedule.[288] The maintenance of the register is the responsibility of the Clerk to the Parliament, who shall arrange for its publication and shall make it available for public inspection. Within 30 days of taking the oath of allegiance or making a solemn affirmation, a member must lodge with the clerk a written statement giving details of their registrable interests or, as the case may be, declaring that they have none. In addition, they must give details of registrable interests that are no longer held if:

> "after taking account of all the circumstances, that interest is reasonably considered to prejudice, or to give the appearance of prejudicing, the ability of the member to participate in a disinterested manner in the proceedings of the Parliament".[289]

Further provision is made for late registration, voluntary registration, and for deletion of spent entries from the register. The 2006 Act then makes provision in connection with "declarable interests". A member has a declarable interest in any matter if they have or had a registrable financial interest in the matter that appears in their entry on the register. A member is required to declare, orally or in writing as the Parliament may determine, the existence of a declarable interest before taking part in any proceedings of the Parliament relating to the matter in question. The prohibition on paid advocacy is continued, as required by s.39(4) of the Scotland Act 1998. Finally, the 2006 Act provides for the sanctions that shall attach to breaches of its terms. As noted, s.39 of the Scotland Act requires that such breaches shall constitute criminal offences. In addition, the member concerned may be excluded from proceedings of the Parliament, or otherwise prevented or restricted from participating in such proceedings, for such period as the Parliament may determine.

Apart from the rules on the registration and declaration of financial and other interests and the prohibition on paid advocacy, MSPs are also constrained to abide by the terms of the Code of Conduct for Members of the Scottish 6–54

[287] Scotland Act 1998 (Transitory and Transitional Provisions) (Members' Interests) Order 1999 (SI 1999/1350). See O. Gay, "The Regulation of Parliamentary Standards after Devolution" [2002] P.L. 422; D. Woodhouse, "Delivering Public Confidence: Codes of conduct, a step in the right direction" [2003] P.L. 511 (contrasting the regulatory regime adopted in Scotland favourably with that which obtains at Westminster).

[288] Namely, remuneration; related undertakings (essentially, unremunerated directorships or partnerships); election expenses; sponsorship; gifts; overseas visits; heritable property; and interests in shares.

[289] Interests of Members of the Scottish Parliament Act 2006 s.2(3). Where subsequent registrable interests are acquired, they must also be notified to the clerk within 30 days.

Parliament. The code is drafted and reviewed by the Standards, Procedures and Public Appointments Committee. The current iteration (the seventh edition) was adopted in January 2020.[290] It makes provision in relation to the registration and declaration of interests and the rule against advocacy, general conduct and conduct in the Chamber, the regulation of cross-party groups and lobbying. Like the standing orders, but unlike the rules on members' interests, it represents a non-statutory form of self-regulation, alleged breaches of which will be investigated and dealt with primarily, if not exclusively, by the Parliament itself rather than by the courts. It has yet to be determined whether breaches of the standing orders or Code of Conduct are justiciable or not. While distinguishing their legal form from that of the Members' Interests Order in *Whaley*, the First Division was careful to avoid stating in terms that the court would have no jurisdiction over the Parliament's non-statutory regulatory devices. The standing orders, at least, are adopted under authority of s.22 of the Scotland Act, Sch.3 of which requires that specified provision be made therein.

6–55 The Code of Conduct is enforced by the Commissioner for Ethical Standards in Public Life in Scotland ("the Commissioner"). This office was created on 1 April 2011 when the Scottish Parliamentary Commissions and Commissioners etc. Act 2010 came into force.[291] It abolished the then existing office of Scottish Parliamentary Standards Commissioner but the new Commissioner simply assumed the same powers and responsibilities. The Commissioner is independent of the Parliament, the Scottish Government and the Parliamentary Corporation. That independence is secured in two ways: the Commissioner is appointed for a single non-renewable term of eight years and can only be removed from office by the Scottish Parliament on a motion supported by two-thirds of all MSPs.[292] The functions of the Commissioner are essentially two-fold: he or she investigates any complaint that a member[293] has breached any of the "relevant provisions"; and reports to the Parliament on the outcome of any such investigation. The "relevant provisions" are the Code of Conduct for MSPs, the Standing Orders of the Parliament and the 2006 Act.[294] The Commissioner makes no determination as to whether any provision has been breached: that is a matter for the Parliament to determine after the Commissioner has reported.[295] In the first instance, the Commissioner's report is submitted to the Standards, Procedures and Public Appointments Committee[296] who are free to reach their own conclusion on the facts or direct the Commissioner to carry out any further investigations.[297] Having considered the matter, the committee then present their report to the

[290] Scottish Parliament, "Code of Conduct for Members of the Scottish Parliament, Edition 7" (Scottish Parliament, 2020), *https://www.parliament.scot/Parliamentaryprocedureandguidance/CCEd07Rev02202007.pdf* [Accessed 19 April 2020].

[291] See P. Reid, "Public Standards in Scotland: A Rubik's Cube?" (2012) 16 Edin. L.R. 229.

[292] Scottish Parliamentary Commissions and Commissioners etc. Act 2010 s.9.

[293] Defined by Scottish Parliamentary Standards Commissioner Act 2002 s.20, to include the Scottish Law Officers, whether or not MSPs; and former MSPs and Law Officers (although the reach of this will be limited by the requirement in s.6(5)(c) that complaints be made within one year of the conduct in question).

[294] Scottish Parliamentary Standards Commissioner Act 2002 s.3.

[295] Scottish Parliamentary Standards Commissioner Act 2002 s.9.

[296] Scottish Parliament Standing Orders r.3A.4

[297] Scottish Parliamentary Standards Commissioner Act 2002 s.10.

Parliament who again are free to reach their own conclusion. The ultimate decision on whether a member has breached any of the relevant provisions therefore rests with the Parliament.

There is, however, a catch. The Commissioner is required to follow any directions given to them by the Parliament.[298] One of those directions requires them to suspend their investigation and report the matter to the procurator fiscal where they are satisfied that the member under investigation has committed the conduct complained about and this conduct would amount to a criminal offence.[299] That direction, read together with s.17 of the 2006 Act and s.39(6) of the Scotland Act 1998, has the effect that whenever the Commissioner comes to the view that an MSP may have breached the rules on registration of an interest, they must refer the matter to the procurator fiscal *before* reporting to the Standards, Procedures and Public Appointments Committee. Thus, despite the statutory scheme leaving the final decision on whether or not a breach has occurred to the Parliament, where the Commissioner comes to the view that there has been a breach, the question will necessarily be referred for the procurator fiscal to consider whether criminal proceedings should be instigated. The consequences for an MSP's career of being so referred are likely to be fatal.

So it proved with Wendy Alexander. A brief account of her demise highlights a **6–56** number of flaws in the current system.[300] In the autumn of 2007 Wendy Alexander was elected the leader of the Scottish Labour Party. She was elected unopposed. Nonetheless she ran a campaign and raised funds for that purpose. Those donations were subject to the Electoral Commission's then reporting requirements in terms of the Political Parties, Elections and Referendums Act 2000 and Alexander made a "voluntary" return at the end of the campaign.[301] In the course of writing "thank you" letters to contributors to her campaign Alexander noticed one of the donors, Mr Green, had a Jersey address. That was potentially significant: she was only allowed to receive donations from "permissible donors" and for an individual that meant they had to be on the electoral register.[302] It transpired Mr Green was not a permissible donor and the time to return the donation under the 2000 Act had expired. The Electoral Commission launched an investigation to determine what, if any action, should be taken against Alexander. For present purposes, we are interested in what the Scottish parliamentary authorities did. Alexander had not registered any of the donations to her campaign in the Register of Members' Interests. Under the 2006 Act Alexander was obliged to register any gift in excess of 1 per cent of her salary as an MSP (then £520).[303] That obligation was independent of the

---

[298] Scottish Parliamentary Standards Commissioner Act 2002 s.4(2).

[299] Scottish Parliamentary Standards Commissioner Act 2002 (Procedures, Reporting and Other Matters) Direction 2020 para.15. *http://www.parliament.scot/Parliamentaryprocedureandguidance/Directions.pdf* [Accessed 19 April 2020].

[300] For a more detailed account of this episode and the issues it gave rise to, see Ghaleigh, Kemp and Reid, "Politics as a Profession: Electoral Law, Parliamentary Standards and Regulating Politicians" [2012] P.L. 658.

[301] It was voluntary because under the Political Parties, Elections and Referendums Act 2000 at that time, any donation under £1,000 did not need to be registered and all donations to the Alexander campaign fell below that level: s.62(11). The limit has since been raised to £1,500 (Political Parties and Elections Act 2009).

[302] Political Parties, Elections and Referendums Act 2000 s.54(2)

[303] Members of the Scottish Parliament Act 2006 s.5.

reporting requirements under the Political Parties, Elections and Referendums Act 2000. A complaint was lodged by an SNP researcher with the Commissioner about Alexander's failure. Having investigated the complaint the Commissioner concluded that Alexander should have registered the donations. This was contrary to the advice Alexander had received from the parliamentary clerks. Things got worse for Alexander. First, in response to the Commissioner's conclusion that the donations should have been registered, she made a voluntary entry in the Register of Members' Interests. In doing so, she issued a press release advising that this had been done "in light of an opinion received from [the Commissioner]".[304] That triggered a fresh complaint: this time alleging that Alexander had breached the MSPs Code of Conduct by disclosing the existence of a complaint that was under investigation by the Commissioner.[305] Second, the Commissioner referred the matter to the procurator fiscal in terms of the direction.

Skipping to the conclusion of this sorry saga highlights the problems with the system. Having considered the Commissioner's report on the first complaint, the Standards, Procedures and Public Appointments Committee, by a majority, held that the donations should have been registered, presented their report to the Parliament and moved that it be approved and that Alexander be suspended for one sitting day.[306] After an acrimonious and fairly partisan debate, the Parliament refused to pass the motion.[307] Being an MSP, Alexander even had a vote: unsurprisingly, she voted against the motion. But the result was the Parliament, who under the Act is the only arbiter of whether there has been a breach of the relevant provisions, found that Alexander had not breached the rules. By this time she had already been referred to the procurator fiscal by the Commissioner and two months before the vote had resigned as leader of the Scottish Labour Party. As to the complaint about disclosing the existence of the Commissioner's investigation, that was rejected by the Standards, Procedures and Public Appointments Committee.[308]

This was not a particularly satisfactory episode for the Parliament. A political career had been ruined over a £950 donation that the politician had forfeited, which led to alleged failings that were ultimately not upheld. This was done in a fairly partisan atmosphere and just serves to underscore the point that self-regulation (now regarded as unacceptable for most other professions) is unlikely to secure public confidence in politics as a profession.

---

304 The full background facts to this issue are set out in Annex A to the Scottish Parliament Standards, Procedures and Public Appointments Committee, *7th Report, 2008 (Session 3), Complaint against Wendy Alexander MSP* (Scottish Parliament, 2008) SP Paper 150.

305 The relevant provision of the code was para.9.1.4.

306 Scottish Parliament Standards, Procedure and Public Appointments Committee, *6th Report, 2008 (Session 3), Complaint against Wendy Alexander MSP* (Scottish Parliament, 2008) SP Paper 142.

307 Scottish Parliament, *Official Report*, cols 10577–10579 (4 September 2008).

308 Scottish Parliament Standards, Procedures and Public Appointments Committee, *7th Report, 2008 (Session 3), Complaint against Wendy Alexander MSP*.

SCOTTISH AFFAIRS AT WESTMINSTER

It remains to consider the machinery provided at Westminster for the consideration of Scottish affairs. For many years prior to devolution, special arrangements were made for the handling of Scottish business in the House of Commons, through time set aside for Scottish questions, the establishment of the Scottish Grand Committee, Scottish standing committees and the Select Committee on Scottish Affairs. Unsurprisingly, devolution entailed some reassessment of these arrangements.[309] The Select Committee on Procedure recommended, and the House by resolution accepted, that the range of questions that might properly be put to ministers in the Scotland Office should be formally reduced to include only those matters for which they retained responsibility,[310] and that the time available for Scottish questions be reduced. The latter was given effect in November 1999, since when Scottish questions have taken place once every four weeks, lasting for 30 minutes.[311] **6–57**

The Scottish Grand Committee, which consists of the full complement of Scottish MPs, was retained following devolution (despite a recommendation to the contrary from the Select Committee on Procedure) because, as the government pointed out:

> "there will still be occasions after devolution where members representing constituencies in Scotland... will want to have debates on reserved matters for which time cannot be found on the floor of the House".

The Grand Committee has not met, however, since 2003.[312]

The Scottish Affairs Select Committee is appointed by the House of Commons to examine the expenditure, administration and policy of the Scotland Office (including (i) relations with the Scottish Parliament and (ii) administration and expenditure of the offices of the Advocate General for Scotland [but excluding individual cases and advice given within government by the Advocate General]). Up to 11 MPs may be appointed to serve on it (not all of whom need represent Scottish constituencies).

---

[309] House of Commons Select Committee on Procedure, *Procedural Consequences of Devolution, Fourth Report of Session 1998–99* (The Stationery Office, 1999) HC 185.

[310] Corresponding provision is made in Scottish Parliament Standing Orders r.13.3.3.

[311] Naturally MPs remain free to table questions for written answers.

[312] There are also Grand Committees for Wales and Northern Ireland. They last met in 2018 and 2013, respectively.

CHAPTER 7

Governments

INTRODUCTION

7–01 As with parliaments, so too with governments: within the sphere of devolved competence, the Scottish Government is the government of Scotland[1]; outwith that sphere, the UK Government continues to exercise executive authority north of the border. "Executive authority" is a concept of some complexity. Other than, perhaps, their width, there is no difficulty with the statutory powers of executive institutions—ministers of the Crown, central government departments, the Scottish Administration and the penumbra of executive agencies, local and other public authorities operating to greater or lesser degree at arm's length from central or devolved government. Subtler questions arise, however, in relation to the non-statutory powers of governmental institutions, often (if not wholly accurately) referred to as "the prerogative". Explaining the nature of the prerogative requires something of a historical inquiry into the nature of that entity in which (if not whom) the prerogative is vested, namely the Crown. Broader, and still controversial, questions arise about the extent to which prerogative powers are, or should be, subject to judicial control. The scheme of this chapter is therefore as follows. We begin with a consideration of the sources of executive power in a general sense. We then move on to an account of the institutional structure of executive government as that relates to Scotland. At one time, such an account would have been relatively straightforward, in so far as it involved a reasonably clear demarcation between the executive powers of central and local government.[2] Now, however (and leaving local government to a later chapter), executive authority is exercised at a variety of levels and in a variety of institutional settings. This is not simply a consequence of devolution, but also of what might be termed the "marketising" of the state. Particularly in the last 40 years, efforts have been made to improve the efficiency of government[3] by repackaging or reallocating aspects of executive authority to entities better able (in theory) to capture the efficient practices of the private sector. In some

[1] Although, as we shall see, the powers of the Scottish Ministers go beyond that sphere in various ways, particularly in that s.63 of the Scotland Act 1998 makes provision for the transfer of functions exercisable in or as regards Scotland by a Minister of the Crown to the Scottish Ministers. This goes beyond the provision made in s.53 for a general transfer to the Scottish Ministers of ministerial functions exercisable within devolved competence, which transfer occurred on 1 July 1999.

[2] Although there has always been a Scottish dimension to the government of the UK, which may be said to cut across this distinction.

[3] Some commentators detect ulterior motives in this process, and it is fair to say that marketisation, in its various guises, has tended to be at the expense of the powers of local authorities and at some cost too to accountability for the exercise of executive power.

respects, as with privatisation and contracting out, the reallocation is clear, and the question that remains is whether and to what extent we should, nevertheless, continue to regard the powers and functions thus reallocated as public functions. In others, as with executive agencies, the change is less obvious, being internal to the orthodox structure of government, but similar issues arise about the adequacy of political and legal controls over their powers.

THE CROWN AND THE PREROGATIVE

Introduction

7–02 "The Crown" is not just a "piece of jewelled headgear under guard at the Tower of London".[4] It is a synonym for the central executive government of the United Kingdom; it is the name in which executive acts of the government are carried out.[5] Whilst much of what the Crown does in the sense of governing is now regulated by statute[6], that is not the Crown's only source of power. It also has its prerogative powers. As Dicey explained:

> "The prerogative is the name for the remaining portion of the Crown's original authority, and is therefore … the name for the residue of discretionary power left at any moment in the hands of the Crown, whether exercised by the Queen herself or by her Ministers. Every act which the executive government can lawfully do without the authority of an Act of Parliament is done in virtue of this prerogative."[7]

Just as when Dicey was writing, the prerogative is a residual source of power. As Lord Reid put it, "[t]he prerogative is really a relic of a past age, not lost by disuse, but only available for a case not covered by statute".[8] Earlier in the same case, Lord Reid noted that it was "not easy to discover and decide the law regarding the royal prerogative and the consequences of its exercise".[9] It is a historical exercise by which how the claimed power has been used in previous times is uncovered and its modern application determined.[10] In our discussion of the prerogative, we will approach it in three stages. First, we will consider how

[4] *Town Investments Ltd v Department of the Environment* [1978] A.C. 359 HL, per Lord Simon at p.397.

[5] *Town Investments Ltd v Department of the Environment* [1978] A.C. 359, per Lord Diplock at pp.380–382.

[6] Statute can obviously confer powers upon the Crown to act. But the Crown is only bound by the terms of a statute if Parliament must have intended the Crown to be bound (*R (Black) v Secretary of State for Justice* [2017] UKSC 81; [2018] A.C. 215 at [37]). That is not as stringent a test as was previously applied (where the Parliamentary intention was expected to be express or a necessary implication): *Lord Advocate v Dumbarton District Council* [1990] 2 A.C. 580. That is now read subject to *Black* and, in particular, the discussion at [2017] UKSC 81; [2018] A.C. 215 at [22]–[37].

[7] A.V. Dicey, *The Law of the Constitution*, 8th edn (London: 1915) p.425. Dicey at p.424 also described the prerogative as "a term which has caused more perplexity to students than any other expression referring to the constitution"! See also, C.R. Munro, *Studies in Constitutional Law*, 2nd edn (London: Butterworths, 1999) Ch.8.

[8] *Burmah Oil Co (Burma Trading) Ltd v Lord Advocate*, 1964 S.C. (HL) 117 at p.122.

[9] *Burmah Oil Co (Burma Trading) Ltd v Lord Advocate*, 1964 S.C. (HL) 117 at p.120.

[10] That being so, Sedley's historical account of the prerogative is commended: Sedley, *Lions Under the Throne: Essays on the History of English Public Law* (CUP; 2015), Ch.6.

prerogative powers are recognised. Second, we will look at how their exercise is controlled. Finally, on a related note, we will examine the Crown Proceedings Act 1947 that has practical consequences for litigating against the Crown.

Recognising a prerogative

To start with, it is important to understand that there can be no such thing as a "new" prerogative power. It is, as Lord Diplock put it: **7–03**

> "350 years and a civil war too late for the Queen's courts to broaden the prerogative. The limits within which the executive government may impose obligations or restraints on citizens in the United Kingdom without any statutory authority are now well settled and incapable of extension."[11]

The residual nature of the prerogative is a necessary consequence of the legislative supremacy of Parliament: as the ultimate source of law, on the orthodox understanding of our constitution, it must be the source of new powers. It falls to the courts to determine whether a claimed prerogative exists and, if so, the scope of, or boundaries to, that power.[12]

That it is for the courts to determine whether a prerogative power exists was determined as far back as 1610 and the *Case of Proclamations* where Sir Edward Coke declared "the King hath no prerogative, but that which the law of the land allows him".[13] In that case, the King had sought by way of royal proclamation to disapply legislation passed by Parliament. The court refused to recognise that the King had such a power. Nor can a recognised prerogative power be exercised in a manner that is contrary to statute. That is because the scope of a prerogative power is limited by any statute that covers the same terrain. It is a necessary consequence of the sovereignty of Parliament that it is open to Parliament to curtail or abrogate a prerogative, however well established.[14] So, where Parliament has expressed its will on an area that had previously been the subject of prerogative powers, those powers necessary fall into abeyance.[15] Put another way, if there is a statutory scheme that prescribes the way the government should

[11] *British Broadcasting Corporation v Johns (Inspector of Taxes)* [1965] Ch. 32, per Diplock LJ at 79. Lord Browne-Wilkinson made the same point in *R. v Secretary of State for the Home Department, Ex p. Fire Brigades Union* [1995] 2 A.C. 513 at p.552: "the constitutional history of this country is the history of the prerogative powers of the Crown being made subject to the overriding powers of the democratically elected legislature as the sovereign body".

[12] *Cherry and others v Advocate General for Scotland* [2019] UKSC 41; 2019 S.L.T. 1143 at [35]. *R (Bancoult) v Secretary of State for Foreign and Commonwealth Affairs* [2008] UKHL 61; [2009] A.C. 453 at [69] (Lord Bingham).

[13] *Case of Proclamations* (1610) 12 Co Rep 74 at p.76. That was a point which was captured in the Claim (and, in England and Wales, Bill) of Rights of 1689. As Sedley explains, it was probably established some time before that and Coke simply built upon the work of his predecessors: Sedley, *Lions Under the Throne: Essays on the History of English Public Law* (CUP; 2015), p.127.

[14] It would equally be open to Parliament to legislate to reverse the effect of a particular exercise of the prerogative but otherwise level the power in place. That, for example, was one of the arguments made by the government in the Prorogation case, where it was pointed out that Parliament could have, but did not, legislate to reverse the effect of the Order in Council proroguing Parliament.

[15] *Burmah Oil Co (Burma Trading) Ltd v Lord Advocate*, 1964 S.C. (HL) 117 at p.122.

act, recourse cannot be made to a supposed prerogative power. In *Attorney-General v De Keyser's Royal Hotel*, the government sought to do just that.[16] In the course of the First World War, the Crown purported to take possession of a hotel to headquarter certain military personnel. The owners of the hotel then sought rent, failing which compensation under the Defence Act 1842. The government answered that claim by asserting that the hotel had been occupied under a prerogative power to take possession of property for the defence of the realm and that prerogative carried with it, when exercised, no right to compensation. That claim was rejected by the House of Lords. Could the prerogative power (assuming it existed[17]) be relied upon to avoid the statutory entitlement to compensation? No. As Lord Atkinson explained:

> "It would be useless and meaningless for the legislature to impose restrictions and limitations upon, and to attach conditions to, the exercise by the Crown of the powers conferred by statute, if the Crown were free at its pleasure to disregard these provisions, and by virtue of its prerogative do the very thing the statutes empowered it to do."[18]

For so long as there was a statutory basis on which the government could act, with whatever protections or compensations Parliament had prescribed, any prerogative to the same effect was suspended (or, as it is sometimes put, has lapsed pro tanto).[19] But in the absence of a clear parliamentary intention to abolish the prerogative power, it is only in abeyance; should the statute be repealed, the prerogative power would remerge.[20] In addition to statutory limits on the scope of prerogative powers, there are common law limits too (including limits drawn by reference to common law constitutional principles).[21] If a purported exercise of a prerogative power impedes or frustrates the operation of a common law constitutional principle, it must have a reasonable justification. In other words, the boundary of a prerogative now also has a rather blurred edge: a prerogative power will be recognised to the extent it impedes or frustrates a common law constitutional principle but only if that interference has a reasonable justification.[22]

7–04 So, it is well established that it is for the courts to recognise and define the boundaries of a prerogative power. What, then, are the recognised prerogatives? In 2004, the House of Commons Public Administration Select Committee reviewed the operation of the prerogative and, in their report, recognised the following important examples of the prerogative: the making and ratification[23] of

---

[16] [1920] A.C. 508.

[17] Whether such a prerogative did in fact exist did not have to be decided in *De Keyser's* but the issue came back to the House of Lords in *Burmah Oil*, above, where it was held that compensation was payable where property was taken by the Crown under prerogative powers.

[18] [1920] A.C. 508 at p.539. Lord Parmoor was to similar effect at p.575.

[19] [1920] A.C. 508 at p.554 (Lord Moulton).

[20] *Burmah Oil Co (Burma Trading) Ltd v Lord Advocate*, 1964 S.C. (HL) 117 at p.161 (Lord Pearce).

[21] *Cherry and others v Advocate General for Scotland* [2019] UKSC 41; [2020] A.C. 373; 2019 S.L.T. 1143 at [38].

[22] *Cherry and others v Advocate General for Scotland* [2019] UKSC 41; [2020] A.C. 373; 2019 S.L.T. 1143 at [49]. See further: para.1–23, above and para.7–08, below.

[23] Ratification of international treaties is now subject to the Constitutional Reform and Governance Act 2010 which requires that a treaty be laid before both Houses of Parliament for a period of 21 sitting days during which both Houses may resolve that the treaty should not be ratified. That Act

international treaties; conduct of diplomacy, including the recognition of states, the appointment of ambassadors and UK relations with any given state; governance of British overseas territories; deployment and use of the armed forces overseas and the declaration of war[24]; use of the armed forces within the UK to assist the police; organisation of the civil service[25]; grant and revocation of passports; and grant of honours.[26] Whilst these are prerogatives of the Crown, they in fact vest in ministers and the Sovereign has no role in their exercise. In their 2004 report, the Public Administration Select Committee also made the case for putting the remaining prerogative powers on a statutory footing (and thereby at least putting them into abeyance). Not only would that, it was argued, aid transparency, but it would also allow limitations, where appropriate, to be placed on the exercise of the power.[27] In 2007, the government appeared to accept the thrust of the Committee's report[28] but only limited legislative action has followed.

There is a second set of prerogative powers that are recognised, the exercise of which the Sovereign is said to have a continuing role in respect of. These are said to be the "personal prerogative" of the Sovereign (that is, the Queen is personally involved in their exercise). It is often said that the Queen has three rights, "... the right to counsel, the right to encourage and the right to warn".[29] That is largely true and that is where it ends: she reigns, but she does not rule. It has been argued, however, that the personal prerogatives could in principle be exercised without reference to her ministers.[30] Those personal prerogatives would include: the appointment of the Prime Minister; the appointment and dismissal of ministers; prorogation of Parliament; and Royal Assent to legislation.[31] Each is heavily regulated by convention, which has led to the suggestion that the Sovereign exercises any personal choice in respect of them being said to be both wrong and **7–05**

simply encapsulates in legislation the position that, by virtue of convention (the Ponsonby Convention), had existed since at least 1924. For an explanation of the emergence of the Ponsonby Convention, see *R (on the application of Miller and another) v Secretary of State for Exiting the European Union* [2017] UKSC 5; [2018] A.C. 61 at [59].

[24] Whilst the army and air force are maintained by statute, the navy exists by virtue of the prerogative.

[25] This too was placed on a statutory footing by the Constitutional Reform and Governance Act 2010.

[26] House of Commons Public Administration Select Committee, *Taming the Prerogative: Strengthening Ministerial Accountability to Parliament* (HC 442).

[27] The Committee was most exercised by the power to engage in armed conflict without parliamentary approval (p.16). As we saw in Ch.2, approval is now sought from the House of Commons by way of convention. In 2016, the government specifically ruled out putting that convention on a statutory footing, citing amongst other reasons, the ability to respond quickly and without the threat of legal action (HC Deb, vol 608 col 11WS (18 April 2016; Secretary of State for Defence))

[28] Ministry of Justice, *The Governance of Britain* (Cm 7170 2007).

[29] W. Bagehot, *The English Constitution* (1867). For discussion of the significance of these three rights, see, e.g. Mitchell, "The Royal Prerogative in Modern Scots Law" [1957] P.L. 304; R. Brazier, *Constitutional Practice: The Foundations of British Government*, 3rd edn (Oxford: Oxford University Press, 1999).

[30] W.I. Jennings, *Cabinet Government*, 3rd edn (Cambridge: Cambridge University Press, 1959), p.394; V. Bogdanor, *The Monarchy and the Constitution* (Oxford: Clarendon Press, 1995), p.75.

[31] Prior to the passing of the Fixed-Term Parliaments Act 2011, that list would have included the dissolution of Parliament. That matter is now regulated by statute.

dangerous.[32] The most common source of speculation is around the first of the personal prerogatives (the appointment of the Prime Minister). To what extent could the Queen find herself exercising a personal choice in the event, for example, of a hung Parliament? Based on events of both 2010 and 2017, the answer appears to be "none". In 2010, the politics of the election result resolved themselves in such a way that there was a clear and obvious choice of Prime Minister.[33] That was in part due to the defeated incumbent remaining in office for a number of days after the result, ensuring that the Queen was not left without a Prime Minister whilst the would-be coalition partners agreed the terms on which they would share power. In 2017, things were even more straightforward. The incumbent Prime Minister may have lost her parliamentary majority at the ballot box but it was clear that nobody else was better placed to form an administration. She continued in office and a confidence and supply agreement was struck with one of the smaller parties. The other topics on which there is occasional speculation is when the Sovereign could properly refuse her consent to legislation.[34] That prompted some speculation in the summer of 2019 as Parliament threatened to pass legislation concerning Brexit that did not accord with the government's policy. The speculation was no more than that, but it did draw attention to the final stage of our legislative process: the Assent of the Monarch. There can be no royal "veto" based on the personal views or beliefs of the Sovereign.[35] Nor is it realistic to talk of the Sovereign withholding consent where a Bill is said to offend basic principles of the constitution. In such a circumstance, the protection of the constitution must properly be a matter for the courts, who have "the responsibility of upholding the values and principles of our constitution and making them effective."[36] If that is correct, it would be far preferable for the court to take a view on whether such a Bill could properly be enacted (which may require the various obiter comments about the limits on Parliament's legislative authority to be tested)[37] as opposed to the Sovereign unilaterally taking a view on the matter. In reality, there are few examples of the Sovereign exercising a personal choice in respect of what are said to be her personal prerogatives. That is because, by convention, the Sovereign may only act on the advice of her ministers. In previous editions of this book, it was said that those ministers were answerable to Parliament for such advice and thus any

---

[32] R. Blackburn, "Monarchy and the Personal Prerogatives" [2004] P.L. 546. See also, R. Blackburn, "The Royal Assent to Legislation and a Monarch's Fundamental Human Rights" [2003] P.L. 205.

[33] Which is exactly what Blackburn suggested would happen in responding to the "reams of academic speculative theorising" on when and how the Queen would get involved in mediating competing claims for the keys to Downing Street: Blackburn, "Monarchy and the Personal Prerogatives" [2004] P.L. 546, 552. On the formation of the 2010 coalition, see: V. Bogdanor, *The Coalition and the Constitution* (Oxford: Hart, 2011), Ch.2.

[34] For example, A. Twomey, "The refusal or deferral of royal assent" [2006] P.L. 580.

[35] See Blackburn's discussion of the constitutional crisis in Belgium in 1990 when King Baudouin, a devote Catholic, refused to sign a Bill legalising abortion: Blackburn, "The Royal Assent to Legislation and a Monarch's Fundamental Human Rights" [2003] P.L. 205. Royal Assent was last refused by Queen Anne, albeit apparently on the advice of her Ministers.

[36] *Cherry and others v Advocate General for Scotland* [2019] UKSC 41; [2020] A.C. 373; 2019 S.L.T. 1143 at [39].

[37] On which, see paras 3–13—3–14, above.

controls were political and not legal "in the sense they are reviewable by the courts".[38] That, as we noted in Ch.1 and which will return to in a moment, can no longer be said to be the case.

The first major constitutional battle of the Brexit process concerned the scope of prerogative power in respect of the conduct of foreign affairs, in particular the power to withdraw from an international treaty. In short, could prerogative power be used to notify the United Kingdom's intention to leave the European Union (and thereby start the process of withdrawing from the international treaties which establish it)? As the Supreme Court explained: **7–06**

> "Subject to any restrictions imposed by primary legislation, the general rule is that the power to make or unmake treaties is exercisable without legislative authority and that the exercise of that power is not reviewable by the courts."[39]

That general rule is simply a manifestation of the dualist theory of international law, which, as we discussed earlier, the United Kingdom subscribes.[40] In other words, international treaties entered into by the United Kingdom, without more, only have effect in international law. To enter into domestic law requires a positive act of incorporation, without which such treaties give rise to no legal rights or obligations in domestic law.[41] If it were otherwise, a treaty concluded by the executive could, without further action, create rights and obligations in domestic law and thereby permit the executive, by exercising a prerogative power, to alter domestic law. That, as we have just seen, is precisely what Sir Edward Coke said the Crown could not do in exercise of the prerogative.[42] Thus, the prerogative power to make and unmake treaties is tolerable only because it cannot create a domestic effect without further steps being taken. Law making is reserved to Parliament (and those authorised by Parliament). It was against that background the Supreme Court had to determine whether giving notice under art.50 TEU of the UK's intention to leave the EU would necessarily result in a change to domestic law. If it did, prior parliamentary approval would be required because the treaty making or breaking prerogative could not be used to prompt such a result. As we saw in Ch.1, the majority of the court concluded that parliamentary authority was required to give the notice and the prerogative power could not be relied upon.[43] However controversial the *Miller* case was, when boiled down to its constitutional fundamentals it was fairly simple: would what the government proposed to do result in a change to domestic law? If so, parliamentary authority (that is, an Act of Parliament) was required. Far from being controversial (in a constitutional sense, at least), the result was an assertion of the orthodox view on the treaty-making prerogative and an application of the basic principles of the separation of powers.

---

38 3rd edn, para.7–02. The same point was made at para.5–02 of the 2nd edn.

39 *R (on the application of Miller and another) v Secretary of State for Exiting the European Union* [2017] UKSC 5; [2018] A.C. 61 at [55].

40 See para.2–12, above.

41 *Moohan v Lord Advocate*, 2015 S.C. (U.K.S.C.) 1 at [29].

42 *Case of Proclamations* (1610) 12 Co Rep 74 at p.76.

43 See para.1–14, above.

Control of prerogative powers

7–07 In a sense, claiming the power to recognise the existence and scope of a prerogative power is a form of control over it. That, as we have seen, was established centuries ago. It was only comparatively recently, on the other hand, that the courts asserted a right to review the exercise of an established or recognised prerogative. It was not until the decision of the House of Lords in *Council of Civil Service Unions v Minister for the Civil Service* that such a jurisdiction was authoritatively established.[44] As Lord Scarman put it:

> "... if the subject matter in respect of which prerogative power is exercised is justiciable, that is to say if it is a matter upon which the court can adjudicate, the exercise of the power is subject to review in accordance with the principles developed in respect of the review of the exercise of statutory power ... Today, therefore, the controlling factor in determining whether the exercise of prerogative power is subject to judicial review is not its source but its subject matter."[45]

It is important to be clear what we are talking about at this point. So far as recognising the existence of a prerogative power and, if it exists, the extent of the power, subject matter is irrelevant and there is no issue of justiciability. The existence and scope of a prerogative is a question of law and thus it is clearly a matter that falls within the jurisdiction of the court to determine. What Lord Scarman addressed was the role of the court when the existence and scope of a prerogative is not in doubt but a challenge is mounted to how that power has been exercised within its accepted limits. It is at that point the court must have regard to the subject matter and whether it properly has jurisdiction to determine the lawfulness of the exercise of the prerogative power. That is because some questions simply do not admit of a legal answer. For example, whether to enter into an international treaty or not[46] or to declare war or to purchase nuclear weapons[47] are all matters for which the court is simply not equipped to assess the propriety of the decision. They are matters that properly fall to the political arena to control.[48]

But where the subject matter does not preclude review by the courts, judicial review is available in the normal way. In *R v Home Secretary, Ex p. Fire Brigades*

[44] *Council of Civil Service Unions v Minister for the Civil Service* [1985] A.C. 374. A power of judicial review had been asserted by some judges in earlier cases, notably by Lord Denning MR in *Laker Airways Ltd v Department of Trade* [1977] Q.B. 643 CA (Civ Div). See also *R. v Criminal Injuries Compensation Board, Ex p. Lain* [1967] 2 Q.B. 864 QBD, often regarded as the first instance of judicial review of the prerogative. Certainly the Court of Appeal treated the scheme for compensating victims of violent crime as established "under the prerogative" (it is now statutory), but "anyone may set up a trust or other organisation to distribute money, and for the government to do so involves no unique prerogative power": H.W.R. Wade and C.F. Forsyth, *Administrative Law*, 11th edn (Oxford: Oxford University Press, 2014), p.180.

[45] *Council of Civil Service Unions v Minister for the Civil Service* [1985] A.C. 374 at p.407.

[46] For example, *R v HM Treasury, Ex p. Smedley* [1985] QB 657; *R v Secretary of State for Foreign and Commonwealth Affairs, Ex p. Rees-Mogg* [1994] QB 552.

[47] For example, *Lord Advocate's Reference (No.1 of 2000)*, 2001 S.C.C.R. 296.

[48] It is for the court to determine what is and is not justiciable. The list is not set in stone and the possibility of that which was once considered non-justiciable becoming justiciable cannot be excluded. See: Sedley, *Lions Under the Throne: Essays on the History of English Public Law* (CUP; 2015), p.141.

Union the issue was whether the government could render a statutory scheme, which had not yet been brought into force, redundant by setting up a different scheme using the Crown's prerogative powers.[49] The answer was no. It was no answer for the government to say that it intended to invite Parliament to repeal the statutory scheme. That, the House of Lords explained, would be to pre-empt Parliament's decision on the matter.[50] The prerogative required to be exercised in a manner consistent with the fulfilment of the government's statutory duty.

At this point it is convenient to consider the last big Brexit-related constitutional battle: the Prorogation case.[51] As we discussed in Ch.1, that case arose out of the purported prorogation of Parliament in September 2019. It therefore concerned one of the "personal" prerogatives of the Sovereign. Objection was taken to the prorogation because, it was said, Parliament should be sitting, and thereby scrutinising the government, in the run up to the then Brexit deadline of 31 October 2019. At first instance in both Edinburgh and London,[52] the court refused to intervene. But in the Inner House of the Court of Session it was held that the advice to the Queen had been motivated by an improper purpose (stymying Parliamentary scrutiny of the executive) and accordingly the prorogation was unlawful.[53] The Supreme Court agreed with the Inner House that the prorogation was unlawful but for slightly different reasons. It is instructive to dwell on their reasoning for a moment. For the government, the argument was the decision to prorogue Parliament was not justiciable: the Prime Minister's advice to the Queen did not raise any legal question on which the court could properly adjudicate and rather than being reviewable by the court, the Prime Minister was answerable to Parliament for the advice he tendered. There was some support for that argument from the *GCHQ* case, where Lord Roskill had mentioned the dissolution of Parliament as one of the prerogative powers whose exercise was non-justiciable.[54] That argument had found favour with the High Court and within the Outer House of the Court of Session. The circumstances surrounding the prorogation also offered it some support. At the time of prorogation, Parliament was in its longest session since 1653, during which there had been a change of Prime Minister, so there was an interest in bringing the session to an end. Separately, the prorogation was approved by the Privy Council on 28 August 2019 and provided for Parliament to be prorogued between 9 and 12 September until 14 October 2019 so there was time to sit prior to 31 October 2019. Prior to prorogation Parliament did sit and it passed the European Union (Withdrawal) (No.2) Act 2019 (an Act which ran contrary to the government's key policy that the UK would leave the EU on 31 October 2019, deal or no deal). The House of Commons also refused two motions by the Prime Minister for an early general election under the Fixed Terms Parliament Act 2011 and passed a humble address demanding disclosure of information about the prorogation decision. But what Parliament did not do, and which it could have done, was to reverse the 7–08

[49] [1995] 2 A.C. 513.

[50] [1995] 2 A.C. 513 at p.552 (Lord Brown-Wilkinson).

[51] *Cherry and others v Advocate General for Scotland* [2019] UKSC 41; [2020] A.C. 373; 2019 S.L.T. 1143 ("the Prorogation case").

[52] *Cherry and others v Advocate General for Scotland* [2019] CSOH 70 (in Edinburgh) and *R (on the application of Miller) v Prime Minister* [2019] EWHC 2381 (QB); [2019] ACD 136 (in London).

[53] *Cherry and others v Advocate General for Scotland* [2019] CSIH 49.

[54] *Council of Civil Service Unions v Minister for the Civil Service* [1985] A.C. 374 at p.418.

prorogation decision. Finally, the number of sitting days due to be lost was modest because of a planned recess for the political party conference season. Put shortly, Parliament had managed to achieve many things before it was prorogued, most of which were in the face of opposition from the government, but it had not sought to reverse the prorogation. That being so, having not sought to reverse the prorogation itself, why was it necessary for the court to intervene? Indeed, given a very high stakes game of political poker was being played out, why was it appropriate for the court to intervene? The Supreme Court did not accept that it was being asked to review the exercise of an established prerogative. For the court, it was being asked to rule on the boundary between the prerogative and the operation of constitutional principles (in this case, the sovereignty of Parliament and responsible government).[55] Once that was established, all the factors relied upon by the government as pointing towards the issue being non-justiciable melt away:

> "no question of justiciability, whether by reason of subject matter or otherwise, can arise in relation to whether the law recognises the existence of a prerogative power, or in relation to its legal limits. Those are by definition questions of law. Under the separation of powers, it is the function of the courts to determine them."[56]

We have discussed the process of reasoning that led to that conclusion in Ch.1. For present purposes, it is instructive to consider how the court went about determining the boundary issue it had identified.

The limit on the power of prorogation (that being the justiciable issue) was expressed as follows:

> "a decision to prorogue Parliament (or to advise the monarch to prorogue Parliament) will be unlawful if the prorogation has the effect of frustrating or preventing, without reasonable justification, the ability of Parliament to carry out its constitutional functions as a legislature and as the body responsible for the supervision of the executive. In such a situation, the court will intervene if the effect is sufficiently serious to justify such an exceptional course."[57]

So, the court had to examine the justification offered for recommending the prorogation of Parliament. That, however, seems to risk collapsing the two different and distinct issues that the court had earlier recognised: (a) does a prerogative exist and, if so, what is its extent; and (b) can its exercise within its limits be reviewed by the court?[58] What the court appeared to do was consider how the prerogative had been exercised so as to determine what the limits of the prerogative were. Having reviewed the limited information put before them as to why (in the sense of reason, rather than motive) the Prime Minister had acted as he had, the court held:

> "It is impossible for us to conclude … that there was any reason—let alone a good reason—to advise Her Majesty to prorogue Parliament for five week … We cannot

[55] [2019] UKSC 41; [2020] A.C. 373; 2019 S.L.T. 1143 at [52].
[56] [2019] UKSC 41; [2020] A.C. 373; 2019 S.L.T. 1143 at [36].
[57] [2019] UKSC 41; [2020] A.C. 373; 2019 S.L.T. 1143 at [50].
[58] [2019] UKSC 41; [2020] A.C. 373; 2019 S.L.T. 1143 at [35].

speculate, in the absence of further evidence, upon what such reasons might have been. It follows that the decision was unlawful."[59]

Cast in those terms, it again looks a little artificial to say that the court was determining the boundary of the prerogative power rather than reviewing its exercise. But the opposite conclusion, that there were no justiciable limits to the prerogative power to prorogue was dangerous. As Professor Craig explained:

> "It would have meant that the principle of parliamentary sovereignty was recast, such that although there were no limits, procedural or substantive, to Parliament's power, these could only be exercised at the grace and favour of the executive, which could prorogue Parliament for whatsoever reason it wished, with no recourse to legal oversight."[60]

Whilst the government argued that there were practical reasons (e.g. the need for an annual extension of the Armed Forces Act 2006 and Parliament's authorisation of expenditure) why the power to prorogue was limited, relying entirely upon political controls presumes the current political norms persist. Given the period of turmoil that has recently been endured, vesting the ultimate protection of Parliament's ability to sit in the legal, rather than the political, sphere of the constitution has certain attractions.[61]

Care must be taken in trying to extrapolate too much from what was an exceptional case (decided at exceptional speed[62]). But it appears to take its place alongside cases such as *UNISON*,[63] *Privacy International*[64] and others that have asserted the role of the common law in securing adherence to constitutional values and, in particular, the central role of the rule of law.[65] Against that backdrop, it is less surprising that the Supreme Court was not prepared to recognise an unlimited power of prorogation, vested in the executive and unreviewable by the courts. And assuming the distinction between the existence and content of a prerogative power and its exercise has not been completely collapsed by the Prorogation case, it at least suggests that justiciability arguments will be met with greater scepticism than may have previously been the case.

---

59 [2019] UKSC 41; [2020] A.C. 373; 2019 S.L.T. 1143 at [61].

60 P. Craig, "The Supreme Court, prorogation and constitutional principle" [2020] P.L. 248 at p.277. See also [2019] UKSC 41; [2020] A.C. 373; 2019 S.L.T. 1143 at [42].

61 But not for all: e.g. T. Endicott, "Making constitutional principles into law" (2020) 136 L.Q.R. 175; M. Loughlin, "A note on Craig on Miller; Cherry" [2020] P.L. 278. Indeed, the result in the Prorogation case is arguably contrary to the approach to the prerogative contended for by Lord Reed (the joint author of the court's judgment in the Prorogation case) in *Miller (No.1)* where he said: "For a court to proceed on the basis that if a prerogative power is capable of being exercised arbitrarily or perversely, it must necessarily be subject to judicial control, is to base legal doctrine on an assumption which is foreign to our constitutional traditions." [2017] UKSC 5; [2018] A.C. 61 at [240]. How that is squared with what is said at para.42 of the Prorogation case is not, as Loughlin highlights, explained.

62 The case was argued over three days (17–19 September 2019) and the judgment was handed down on 24 September 2019.

63 *R (on the application of UNISON) v Lord Chancellor* [2017] UKSC 51; [2017] 3 W.L.R. 589.

64 *R (on the application of Privacy International) v Investigatory Powers Tribunal* [2019] UKSC 22; [2019] 2 W.L.R. 1219.

65 On common law constitutional principles, see paras.3–14, above.

The Crown Proceedings Act 1947

7–09 It is convenient to consider the Crown Proceedings Act 1947 at this point. Although the 1947 Act is principally concerned with defining the liability of the Crown in tort and delict in respect of acts committed by its servants or agents, s.21 also reserved the immunity from injunction and specific performance enjoyed by the Crown in England at common law and extended its application to Scotland. In any civil proceedings against the Crown, the court cannot make an order for implement or grant interdict but instead may grant a declarator of the rights of the parties. Furthermore, s.21 provides that the court cannot grant any interdict or make any order against an officer of the Crown if the effect of doing so would be to grant relief against the Crown that would not have been obtained in proceedings directly against the Crown. In practice, therefore, s.21 prevents the court granting interdict or making an order for specific performance against a minister of the Crown, a member of the Scottish Government or any other officer of the Crown.

7–10 That seems clear enough. In *R. v Secretary of State for Transport, Ex p. Factortame Ltd (No.2)*, however, the House of Lords was obliged as a matter of EU law to extend injunctive relief against the Crown where necessary to protect EU law rights.[66] Subsequently, in *M v Home Office*,[67] the House of Lords held the Home Secretary in contempt of court for disregarding an injunction requiring the Home Secretary to arrange for the immediate return to the jurisdiction of M, a Zairean asylum seeker. The injunction was granted as an emergency measure during the night, when it became apparent that, in breach of an undertaking to the court, the Home Secretary had countermanded arrangements to keep M in Britain. The following morning the judge discharged the injunction on the grounds that the authority of *Factortame* entitled him to grant injunctive relief against the Crown only where necessary to protect EU law rights, which were not here in issue. Nevertheless, during the currency of the injunction—a presumptively valid order of the court—the Home Secretary had ignored it. Giving the leading speech, Lord Woolf held that the reference in s.21 of the 1947 Act to "civil proceedings" was not apt to include proceedings for judicial review, so that the jurisdiction to grant injunctive relief in such proceedings, even where no question of EU law arose, was unimpaired.

7–11 Following *M v Home Office*, the question arose whether interdict was now to be regarded as available to restrain unlawful acts by the Secretary of State for Scotland or those acting on their behalf.[68] The Second Division held that it was not. The plain effect of s.21 had been to exclude interdict and implement in civil proceedings against the Crown. *M v Home Office*, having turned substantially on aspects of English procedure, was not authoritative as to the meaning of s.21 in Scotland. The question was revisited in *Davidson v Scottish Ministers*.[69] There it was argued that a coercive order might competently be issued against the Scottish

---

[66] *R. v Secretary of State for Transport Ex p. Factortame Ltd (No.2)* [1991] 1 A.C. 603. Necessarily this involved recognition in Scotland that relief by way of interdict, interim or perpetual, would require to be granted against the Crown, despite s.21 of the 1947 Act, in like circumstances: see *Millar & Bryce Ltd v Keeper of the Registers of Scotland*, 1997 S.L.T. 1000.

[67] *M v Home Office* [1994] 1 A.C. 377.

[68] *McDonald v Secretary of State for Scotland*, 1994 S.C. 234.

[69] *Davidson v Scottish Ministers*, 2002 S.C. 205.

Ministers where, in light of the Human Rights Act 1998, the applicant's Convention rights were in issue. The Extra Division held that the right to an effective remedy for breaches of Convention rights did not entitle a litigant to a remedy of their choice and that appeals to the rule of law as requiring coercive orders to be granted against the Crown were to no purpose unless means were shown of construing the plain language of s.21 in that way. The applicant appealed to the House of Lords.[70] It was pointed out that, in light of *M v Home Office* and *McDonald v Secretary of State for Scotland*, s.21 of the 1947 Act applied with different effects north and south of the Border (contrary to the usual presumption that Parliament intends a UK-wide provision to have a UK-wide meaning). There was nothing to indicate that the draftsman had intended such a distinction to obtain. In any event, it could not be justified. The House of Lords agreed, holding that references to "civil proceedings" in s.21 were to be read as excluding proceedings invoking the supervisory jurisdiction of the Court of Session in respect of acts or omissions of the Crown or its officers. Accordingly, in proceedings for judicial review, the remedies of interdict and implement may now competently be sought against the emanations of the Crown in Scotland. Similarly, where the Scottish Ministers breach an undertaking that has been given to the court in the context of such proceedings, it is open to the court to hold the ministers in contempt.[71]

UK GOVERNMENT

Prime Minister, Cabinet and Ministers of State

The appointment of the government is a prerogative act, and we have already noted many of the constitutional conventions surrounding this. The Queen is obliged by convention to appoint as Prime Minister the person who appears best able to command the confidence of the House of Commons and the Prime Minister then advises the Queen whom to appoint to ministerial office in their government, which advice she must, by convention, follow. Identification of the Prime Minister is normally clear as the electoral system for the House of Commons is designed to produce a majority government. In 2010, however, it was several days after the election before it became apparent that David Cameron would be in a position to form a government. The lack of any formal rules surrounding the appointment of the Prime Minister means that there is little to govern the succession to the office in the event the Prime Minister is unable to discharge its functions (either temporarily or through their untimely demise[72]). Some Prime Ministers have chosen to appoint a Deputy Prime Minister (for example, John Prescott was Deputy Prime Minister to Tony Blair, Nick Clegg to David Cameron). The most recent incumbents have not (although Boris Johnston 7–12

[70] *Davidson v Scottish Ministers* [2005] UKHL 74; 2006 S.C. (H.L.) 41.

[71] *Beggs v Scottish Ministers*, 2005 1 S.C. 342; *Smith v Scottish Ministers* [2015] CSOH 15; 2015 S.L.T. 131.

[72] The last Prime Minister to die in office was Lord Palmerston in 1865 and it was 11 days before his successor, Lord John Russell, was appointed. Where the Prime Minister has resigned, they have generally stayed in office until a successor has been identified.

nominated the Foreign Secretary, Dominic Rabb, as First Secretary of State[73]). It perhaps matters little. The Cabinet Manual is silent on the status of Deputy Prime Minister.[74] And it does not necessarily follow that the demise of the Prime Minister would see the nominated Deputy replace them. In the Cameron Government of 2010–2015, the Deputy Prime Minister was the leader of the junior coalition party. It is at least conceivable that had any successor, even on an interim basis, would have been identified from within the Conservative Party. The short point is that there are no conventions governing the succession where the office of Prime Minister unexpectedly becomes vacant. But it is to be expected that a political solution would quickly be found so that the Queen was not required to exercise any personal choice.[75]

For as long as they retain the confidence both of the Commons and of their party (or, at least, their Cabinet), the powers of the Prime Minister are considerable indeed, not only by virtue of being in charge but also because, for practical purposes, the principal prerogatives of the Crown vest in them. Perhaps curiously, the office of Prime Minister receives little statutory recognition, and indeed received none at all prior to the enactment of the Chequers Act 1918. But they are very much a creature of constitutional convention, as also is the Cabinet. There are no legal rules in any Act of Parliament governing the composition, procedures and functions of the Cabinet.[76] As an institution, it emerged and developed in the late eighteenth century, and in the nineteenth century at least functioned very much as a collegiate body, likened by one former Prime Minister to a company's board of directors. Yet by 1963, according to one Cabinet Minister of the day, the Cabinet, like the Sovereign, had become a dignified rather than effective element of the constitution.[77] At first blush, that seems unsurprising. Government has grown immensely in volume, intensity and complexity, yet the Cabinet continues to meet weekly and is no larger now than it was a century ago. It is true that much of its work is now delegated to cabinet committees, but this in itself may function to disperse power away from the Cabinet proper.[78] In Crossman's view, however, the consequence of the decline of cabinet government was an increase in the power of the Prime Minister, since the

---

[73] The Cabinet Manual (at para.3.12) describes that position thus: "A minister may be appointed First Secretary of State to indicate seniority. The appointment may be held with another office. The responsibilities of the First Secretary of State will vary according to the circumstances."

[74] The limit of what the Cabinet Manual says (at para.3.11) is: "The title of Deputy Prime Minister is sometimes given to a senior minister in the government, for example the deputy leader of the party in government or the leader of a smaller party in a coalition."

[75] For a fuller discussion of this issue, see: P. Norton, "A temporary occupant of No.10? Prime Ministerial succession in the event of the death of the incumbent" [2016] P.L. 18.

[76] Apart from the fact that the Ministerial and Other Salaries Act 1975 restricts the number of salaried Cabinet posts to 20. See now, however, the Cabinet Manual that was prepared at the request of Prime Minister Brown to bring together in a single document the laws, conventions and rules that affect the operation of and procedures of government. The current iteration of the manual is HM Government, *The Cabinet Manual: A guide to laws, conventions and rules on the operation of government* (The Stationery Office, 2011) *https://www.gov.uk/government/uploads/system/uploads/attachment_data/file/60641/cabinet-manual.pdf* [Accessed 1 June 2020]. The manual is a valuable source of information on the functioning of government generally.

[77] R. Crossman, *British Government*. Crossman was not the only Cabinet Minister to hold this view.

[78] The Ministerial Code states that matters that are solely the responsibility of an individual minister, or which do not significantly engage the collective responsibility of ministers, need not be taken either to Cabinet or even to committee. The job of committees is described in terms of settling issues

institutional mechanisms and constitutional conventions that once served a genuinely collegiate body, namely the conventions of confidentiality and collective responsibility, came to serve the Prime Minister instead.

The "presidential" style of leadership adopted by recent Prime Ministers may support Crossman's thesis, but it can be overstated. The extent of prime ministerial power seems very much a function of circumstances. If the premierships of Mr Blair and Mrs Thatcher might fairly be described as "presidential", the manner of Mrs Thatcher's fall from office, and the intervening premiership of Mr Major, indicate that there is more to central government than prime ministerial power alone. Moreover, as has been said, a focus on the Prime Minister obscures the point that "departments enjoy a greater degree of autonomy within the executive branch than is commonly acknowledged . . . by reason of the fact that their functions are vested directly in them".[79]

This autonomy is reinforced by the convention of individual ministerial responsibility to Parliament, whereby the minister must answer for the actions of their department and associated public authorities.[80] The implication of this—and it may be to state the obvious—is that central government is a far more complex organism than it is sometimes depicted. One does not need to be an avid student of political economy to perceive that executive power is distributed far more widely than the inner circle of Prime Minister and Cabinet; in practice, much of it reposes with ministers, officials and the web of agencies and public bodies beyond that.

Ministers are appointed by the Queen on the advice of the Prime Minister and hold office at Her Majesty's pleasure. By convention, ministers must be members either of the House of Commons or of the House of Lords. Section 2 of the House of Commons Disqualification Act 1975 provides that no more than 95 ministers may sit and vote in the House of Commons, and Sch.1 to the Ministerial and Other Salaries Act 1975 places limits on the total number of ministerial salaries that may be paid at any one time. These provisions are practical restrictions on the Prime Minister's powers of patronage, but there is no upper limit as such to the total number of ministers that may be appointed provided the excess are peers and/or unpaid. Peers as ministers are a necessary consequence of the statutory provisions and it is not at all uncommon for a political ally of the Prime Minister to be elevated to high ministerial office following the conferment of a life peerage.[81] **7–13**

---

brought before them at that level, or, if a decision of the full Cabinet is absolutely necessary, clarifying the issues and identifying the points of disagreement.

[79] T. Daintith and A. Page, *The Executive in the Constitution: Structure, Autonomy and Internal Control* (Oxford: Oxford University Press, 1999), pp.29 and 30.

[80] It may also be reflected in the conclusions reached by the Cabinet Secretary, having conducted a review at the Prime Minister's request in 1998, that cross-departmental issues were often not well handled.

[81] It is safe to say that by convention the Prime Minister requires to be a member of the House of Commons. The last peer to serve as Prime Minister was Lord Salisbury, who left office in 1902 (his nephew, Arthur Balfour, led the House of Commons and took the title of First Lord of the Treasury, which is normally held by the Prime Minister themselves). It appears that, following the resignation of Neville Chamberlain in May 1940, the King's preference for his replacement was Lord Halifax, but it became clear that Labour MPs would refuse to serve under Halifax in a wartime coalition Cabinet. Since the House of Commons controls supply, the Chancellor of the Exchequer and the Treasury Ministers also require to be Members of the House of Commons, but the position with regard to the

Some ministerial offices have a much longer historical pedigree than that of the Prime Minister. The office of the Lord Chancellor can be traced back to the thirteenth century; the office of Secretary of State emerged in England during the Tudor period, and from the eighteenth century two or more Secretaries of State were customarily appointed, dividing responsibility for home affairs and the colonies on the one hand and foreign affairs on the other. A Secretary of State for War was first appointed in 1794, and since then further Secretaryships of State have been created, merged and abolished as needs arise and lapse. The oldest government departments, such as the Treasury and the Home Office, are creatures of the prerogative; more modern manifestations of governmental activity may owe their origins to statute. Where new departments are created, the modern practice is to create by way of the prerogative a new Secretary of State, to whom functions are transferred by order made under the Ministers of the Crown Act 1975.[82] Once functions are vested in a Secretary of State, however, there is no need for further transfer orders when the distribution of functions between Secretaries is altered, for in law the office of Secretary of State is "in commission", one and indivisible, with the consequence that any one Secretary of State may act for or carry out the functions of any other.[83] In practice, however, each Secretary of State will normally confine themselves to the performance of functions related to the workings of their department.

Ministers are defined by s.8(1) of the Ministers of the Crown Act 1975 as the holders of "any office in Her Majesty's Government in the United Kingdom", a definition plainly apt to include the Secretaries of State, who head up government departments and sit in the Cabinet. Below Cabinet ministers in rank are Ministers of State, who share in the administration of departments and often have specific portfolios of their own. Their powers are largely statutory,[84] but as agents of the Crown they "can do anything an ordinary person can do provided that there is no statute to the contrary and Parliament has voted the money".[85]

7–14 Parliamentary secretaries assist with the parliamentary work of a department and may have some limited administrative responsibilities. They are appointed by their ministerial chiefs with the written approval of the Prime Minister rather than by the Queen, and, as this implies, they are neither ministers nor members of the government.

---

other high offices of state may be more equivocal. Lord Carrington served as Foreign Secretary from 1979–82, and Lord Young as Secretary of State for Trade and Industry from 1987–89, so it probably cannot be said that there is any convention preventing the appointment of peers as senior non-Treasury Ministers if political realities permit.

[82] It is also common practice, when creating a new department, to incorporate it, usually as a corporation sole, so that it may hold property, enter into contracts, sue and be sued in its own name rather than in the name of the Crown: see Daintith and Page, *The Executive in the Constitution: Structure, Autonomy and Internal Control* (1999), pp.32 and 33.

[83] This is reflected in statutory drafting practice, which refers simply to "the Secretary of State", meaning "any one of Her Majesty's Principal Secretaries of State". See *Agee v Secretary of State for Scotland*, 1977 S.L.T. (Notes) 54.

[84] Again, drafting practice is to refer to "the Minister of the Crown" generically rather than specifically.

[85] Cabinet Office, *Agency Chief Executives Handbook* (The Stationery Office, 1996), para.16; and see Daintith and Page, *The Executive in the Constitution: Structure, Autonomy and Internal Control* (1999), pp.34 and 35. This is known as the "Ram doctrine": see HM Government, *The Cabinet Manual: A guide to laws, conventions and rules on the operation of government*, para.3.31

Scottish dimension to the UK Government

With the handover of powers from the UK Government to the Scottish Government on 1 July 1999, the Scottish Office[86] was renamed the Scotland Office. The ministers working within it at present are the Secretary of State for Scotland and a parliamentary under-secretary. Alongside the Scotland Office there is the Office of the Advocate General for Scotland (the UK Government's legal advisor on Scots law). It is important to note that, as well as ensuring the continuing representation of Scottish interests within the UK Government, the Secretary of State for Scotland has a number of powers under the Scotland Act 1998. Following the transfer of competence over elections, the Secretary of State now has a limited role in relation to the timing of certain election[87] and provision has recently been made to permit the Scottish Ministers to borrow funds that are required over and above the Scottish consolidated fund from the Secretary of State.[88] Perhaps the most significant power is in relation to Scottish legislation and acts of the Scottish Government. As to the first, s.35 confers on the Secretary of State the power to make an order preventing the Presiding Officer from sending a Bill passed by the Scottish Parliament for Royal Assent if the Bill contains provisions that they have reasonable grounds to believe would be incompatible with any international obligations of the UK or with the interests of defence or national security, or which modify the law as it applies to reserved matters in a way that they have reasonable grounds to believe would have an adverse effect on the operation of the law in relation to reserved matters. Such an order may be made at any time within the four week period commencing with the passing of the Bill, and must be laid before both Houses of the Westminster Parliament. As to the second, the Secretary of State may by order made under s.58 direct the Scottish Government not to take action where they have reasonable grounds to believe that such action would be incompatible with any international obligations of the UK, or to act where they have reasonable grounds to believe such action to be necessary to give effect to any such obligations.[89] Section 58 also entitles the Secretary of State to revoke subordinate legislation made by the Scottish Government where one or more of the conditions for the exercise of the power under s.35 are met. 7–15

Since the Scotland Act 1998 devolved most of the issues falling within the responsibility of the Lord Advocate and Solicitor General for Scotland, it was considered appropriate that they should cease to be ministers of the Crown in the UK Government and become members of the Scottish Government. But the UK Government continues to require advice from time to time on matters of Scots law and devolution issues arising under the Scotland Act, as it may also require to be represented in litigation arising out of the devolution settlement.[90] With that in

[86] As established in 1885; the original Secretary for Scotland assumed the full status of Secretary of State in 1926 (although the office did not attract a salary commensurate with those of other Secretaries of State until 1937).

[87] Scotland Act 1998 s.12A.

[88] Scotland Act 1998 ss.66 and 66A.

[89] This may include a requirement that the Scottish Government introduce a Bill in the Scottish Parliament.

[90] L. Clark, "Three Years On: The Role of the Advocate General for Scotland", 2002 S.L.T. (News) 139.

mind, the Scotland Act established the new ministerial office of Advocate General for Scotland.[91] Apart from their role in relation to litigation and legal advice, the Advocate General has the power under s.33, in common with the Lord Advocate and Attorney General, to refer to the Supreme Court the question whether the provisions of a Bill passed by the Scottish Parliament are within its competence. They are also entitled, by virtue of s.98 and Sch.6, to institute proceedings for the determination of a devolution issue.

The Civil Service

7–16 In the background of the discussion so far has been the administrative machine that allows government to implement its policy: the Civil Service. The Civil Service is politically neutral with the result that when the government changes following a general election, the civil servants remain the same. Until recently, the Civil Service was established on a non-statutory basis, although it was regulated to some extent by orders in council, which are a form of legislation. Calls had long been made to place the Civil Service on a statutory footing, with the Blair Government of 1997 having made a joint commitment with the Liberal Democrats to introduce a Civil Service Bill.[92] Whilst a draft Bill was published in 2004, enacting it was never a sufficient priority to command the necessarily parliamentary time. The Constitutional Reform and Governance Act 2010 has, however, finally put the Civil Service on a statutory footing (but done little else to reform it). The 2010 Act applies to the Civil Service (except for the security services, Government Communications Headquarters ["GCHQ"] and the Northern Ireland Civil Service) (s.1). A Civil Service Commission is established and it has responsibility for overseeing the recruitment of civil servants (ss.2 and 11–14). Management of the Civil Service is entrusted to the Minister for the Civil Service (who is invariably the Prime Minister) (s.3(1)), although management of the Diplomatic Service is entrusted to the Secretary of State (s.3(2)).[93] The management powers conferred on the Minister for the Civil Service and the Secretary of State include the power to make appointments (s.3(3)) and both are required to publish codes of conduct for the Civil Service and the Diplomatic Service respectively (ss.5 and 6).[94] Separate civil service codes may be published for those civil servants who serve the Scottish and Welsh Governments (s.5(2)).[95] Although some statutory basis for the Civil Service is welcomed, the 2010 Act represents fairly modest progress.

---

[91] Scotland Act 1998 s.87.

[92] Summarised by G. Drewry, "The Executive: Towards Accountable Government and Effective Governance?" in J. Jowell and D. Oliver, *The Changing Constitution*, 7th edn (Oxford: Oxford University Press, 2011), pp.207–209.

[93] As is drafting practice, the generic "the Secretary of State" is used in the Act but in practice, of course, it is the Foreign Secretary that is responsible for the Diplomatic Service.

[94] The Civil Service code is available at *https://www.gov.uk/government/publications/civil-service-code/the-civil-service-code* [Accessed 29 April 2020] and the Diplomatic Service code is available at *http://civilservicecommission.independent.gov.uk/wp-content/uploads/2014/06/Diplomatic-Code.pdf* [Accessed 29 April 2020].

[95] The Scottish Code is available at *https://www.gov.scot/publications/civil-service-code/* [Accessed 29 April 2020].

Under the 2010 Act the Minister for the Civil Service is also obliged to publish a "special advisors code" (s.8).[96] That requirement is part of the first statutory regulation of special advisors, a role that has grown in importance under recent governments.[97] Whilst career civil servants are apolitical, special advisors are appointed personally by a minister (that appointment being approved by the Prime Minister) and whose appointment ends either when the minister that appointed them ceases to hold office or the day following a general election (s.15). The Minister for the Civil Service is required to lay a report before Parliament annually about the special advisors (including the number of advisors and their cost) advising the government (s.16).[98] These measures were all introduced against a background of growing concern about the number and influence of such advisors. Although the existence of such advisors was nothing new, they doubled in number under the first Blair Government. In 2001 the Public Administration Select Committee recognised that the special advisors were an "established part of government" but that the role had to be put on a "firmer footing".[99] Arrangements were reviewed again in 2012 by the same committee and a number of further recommendations made.[100] In particular, the committee expressed concern that, while the price of having a special advisor was that the minister was *responsible* for the advisor's management and conduct (as opposed to being *accountable* for the actions of their civil servants), that responsibility remained "more theoretical than actual".[101] Ministerial responsibility is considered further in a moment.

Reinventing government

An account of departmental government is hardly a complete depiction of the organisation of the modern executive. Much, even most, of the work of government is in fact conducted at some distance from the ministerial core, as the result of what has been termed a "quiet revolution" in public administration.[102] It is a revolution often associated with the Thatcher Governments of the 1980s, and it is certainly true that much of its initial impetus stemmed from the Thatcherite drive to roll back the frontiers of a state regarded as bloated and inefficient. But 7–17

[96] See Cabinet Office, Code of Conduct for Special Advisors (The Stationery Office, December 2016), *https://www.gov.uk/government/publications/special-advisers-code-of-conduct* [Accessed 29 April 2020], which includes a model contract for such advisors. The Scottish Government also has the power to appoint special advisors, details of which are available at: *https://www.gov.scot/publications/special-advisers-code-of-conduct-and-model-contract/* [Accessed 29 April 2020].

[97] For a comprehensive review of the role of the special advisor, see: B. Yong and R. Hazell, *Special Advisors: who they are, what they do and why they matter* (Oxford: Hart, 2014).

[98] An equivalent obligation is imposed on the First Ministers of Scotland and Wales: s.16(2) and (3).

[99] House of Commons Public Administration Select Committee, *Special Advisor: Boon or Bane? Fourth Report of Session 2000–01* (The Stationery Office, 2001) HC 293, para.81.

[100] House of Commons Public Administration Select Committee, *Special advisers in the thick of it, Sixth Report of Session 2012–13* (The Stationery Office, 2012) HC 134.

[101] House of Commons Public Administration Select Committee, *Special advisers in the thick of it, Sixth Report of Session 2012–13*, paras 90–91.

[102] M. Hunt, "Constitutionalism and the Contractualisation of Government in the United Kingdom" in M. Taggart (ed), *The Province of Administrative Law* (Oxford: Hart, 1997), Ch.4.

"new public management" in its various guises has become an international phenomenon, and in no sense is it (at least any longer) the preserve of the political right wing.

The commitment of the Conservative Governments of the 1980s and 1990s to rolling back the state manifested itself most prominently in the privatisation of state-owned industries. Within the government machine itself, freezes were imposed on civil service pay and recruitment and businessmen were brought in to advise on improving efficiency and effectiveness in the public sector. But, despite the government's best efforts at reinventing government and the transfer of over half of the state trading sector to private ownership, the level of public expenditure at the end of the 1980s was not noticeably different from its level in 1979: a near-doubling in real terms of welfare expenditure during the period kept the state's toll on annual gross domestic product at between 35 per cent and 40 per cent, where it remains yet. As the eighties gave way to the nineties, and the Thatcher administration was replaced by that of John Major, the reinvention of government began to focus less on the simple, if crude, objective of making government smaller and more on making what there was work better. This new approach was already in evidence by the close of the Thatcher years with the introduction of executive agencies and the emergence of private sector solutions to the perceived problems of government.

7–18 Executive agencies were spawned by the 1988 report *Improving Management in Government: The Next Steps*.[103] Having reviewed the organisation of the civil service and the way in which public services were provided, the authors of the report recommended that a complete separation be made between policy making functions and service delivery functions. The latter, covering an estimated 95 per cent of civil service activity, should be devolved to executive agencies instead of being (inefficiently) undertaken within the traditional structure of Whitehall departments. The government accepted the recommendations and required all departments to review their activities in order to assess their suitability for hiving off to agencies. The rigour of the procedure intensified in 1991 with the introduction of "market testing".[104] This required departments to scrutinise particular functions and ask themselves, first, whether a particular function could be abolished; if not, whether it could be privatised; if not, whether its performance could be contracted out to a private company; and if not, whether it could be hived off to an executive agency. Only if the answer to all of these questions was "no" might things stay as they were.

As the *Next Steps* report had predicted, some 90 per cent of civil servants now work for agencies.[105] Each agency operates within the terms of a "framework document" that establishes the respective responsibilities of the relevant minister and agency chief executive (who may be a civil servant but may equally be recruited from the private sector). The framework document also prescribes

---

[103] K. Jenkins, K. Caines and A. Jackson, *Improving Management in Government: The Next Steps* (HMSO, 1988). See the discussion by Drewry in "The Executive: Towards Accountable Government and Effective Governance?" in *The Changing Constitution* (2011), pp.196–201.

[104] Cabinet Office, *Competing for Quality* (HMSO, 1991) Cm.1730.

[105] Cabinet Office, *List of Ministerial Responsibilities* (The Stationery Office, 2019) Pt IV lists 35 executive agencies for which UK Government Ministers are responsible. That is a significant reduction (from 90 in 2001). Executive agencies falling within the competence of the devolved administrations are now answerable to those administrations.

performance and financial targets, plus the operating arrangements for the agency. Initially, and in theory at least, the chief executive answered to the minister for their agency's operational efficiency and performance in implementing the policies settled by the minister; the minister, in turn, answered to Parliament for the agency's work and for the policies they had formulated. Now, the accountability of agencies to Parliament is more direct: written parliamentary questions are referred, where appropriate, to agency chief executives; agencies are subject to the jurisdiction of the Parliamentary Commissioner for Administration; and chief executives routinely appear before departmental select committees to answer for their operational effectiveness. Proposals to make chief executives directly responsible to select committees were, however, rejected.[106]

The framework agreements between minister and agency are not contracts, nor could they be: agencies have no identity or legal personality separate from that of their parent departments. But they are intended to work like contracts and, as the *Next Steps* report envisaged, have brought about a fundamental shift in civil service thinking and working practices. The essence of that shift lies in the preference it represents for "marketised" solutions, modelled on the practices of the private sector, to public sector problems: " . . . contract has replaced command and control as the paradigm of regulation".[107] The ideas underpinning the reinvention of the state are now mainstream, and any notion that a Labour Government would halt or reverse these reforms was rapidly scotched after the 1997 election. On the contrary, Labour then wholeheartedly endorsed the process and took it further, as part of its wider drive to modernise the machinery of government. As it saw the matter: **7–19**

> "Most of the old dogmas that haunted governments in the past have been swept away . . . Better government is about much more than whether public spending should go up or down, or whether organisations should be nationalised or privatised. Now that we are not hidebound by the old ways of government, we can find new and better ones."[108]

In 2010, however, the coalition government took steps to arrest the seemingly endless expansion of non-governmental departments. The Public Bodies Act 2011 gave ministers wide ranging powers to abolish, merge or otherwise modify the constitution of a large number of bodies. Under the coalition government's policy, a body should only exist at arm's length from government if it performs a technical function, its activities require political neutrality or it needs to act independently to establish facts. Where none of those tests are met, the activity should now be undertaken by a body that is democratically accountable at either national or local level. The result of this policy has been the review of the activities of over 900 bodies. As a result of the abolition of over 200 bodies and the merger of 170 more the total number should fall to approximately 600.

---

[106] See Treasury and Civil Service Select Committee, *The Role of the Civil Service, Fifth Report of 1993–94* (HMSO, 1994), HC 27, making the proposal and *The Civil Service: Taking Forward Continuity and Change* (HMSO, 1995) Cm.2748 rejecting it.

[107] Hunt, "Constitutionalism and the Contractualisation of Government in the United Kingdom" in *The Province of Administrative Law* (1997), p.12.

[108] White Paper, *Modernising Government* (HMSO, 1999) CM 4310.

GOVERNMENT OF SCOTLAND

7–20 It is well, when speaking of the government of Scotland post-devolution, to be careful with terminology. Just as at the UK level the functions of government are in no sense confined to the ministerial core, so too in Scotland executive authority does not repose in the Scottish Government alone. The "Scottish Government" refers to the nucleus of Scottish Government, namely the First Minister, the ministers appointed by her and the two Law Officers, collectively referred to as "the Scottish Ministers".[109] The Scottish Government in this sense is the central component of the wider "Scottish Administration", which also includes junior Scottish Ministers, non-ministerial office holders and civil servants appointed to the staff of the Scottish Administration.[110] But the UK Government, as considered above, remain relevant to the government of Scotland, whilst, at a lower level, there is the layer of Scottish public authorities exercising executive authority at arm's length from the ministerial core.

Scottish Government[111]

7–21 The UK model of parliamentary government is replicated in Scotland, although the 1998 Act casts the conventions that surround the formation of governments at the UK level in statutory form. Like the Prime Minister, then, the First Minister is appointed by the Queen from among the members of the Scottish Parliament; like the Prime Minister, they hold office at Her Majesty's pleasure.[112] They may resign their office at any time, and must do so if the Parliament resolves that the Scottish Government no longer enjoys the confidence of the Parliament.[113] Although the Queen carries out the formal task of appointment, she will act (the Scotland Act does not in terms require this, but it is plainly the intention) on the nomination of the Parliament as communicated to her by the Presiding Officer, and the Parliament must make its nomination within 28 days of a Scottish general election, the resignation of an incumbent First Minister, the office falling vacant for a reason other than resignation, or of the First Minister ceasing to be an MSP other than by virtue of a dissolution of the Parliament.[114] If the 28 day period expires without a nomination being made, s.3(1)(b) requires the Presiding Officer

[109] Scotland Act 1998 s.44. A person appointed to ministerial office in the UK Government may not be a member of the Scottish Government, or vice versa. The current crop of Scottish Ministers include those styled "Cabinet Secretaries" and the ministerial core has adopted the name "Scottish Cabinet", although there is no legal foundation for this.

[110] Scotland Act 1998 s.126(7). The non-ministerial office holders are defined by s.126(8) as the Registrar General for Births, Marriages and Deaths for Scotland, the Keeper of the Registers of Scotland and the Keeper of the Records of Scotland.

[111] Until the Scotland Act 2012 came into force, what is now called the "Scottish Government" was known (in legislation at least) as the "Scottish Executive". In fact, the Scottish Executive had "rebranded" itself at the Scottish Government in the autumn of 2007, *http://www.scotland.gov.uk/News/Releases/2007/09/31160110* [Accessed 3 June 2020].

[112] Scotland Act 1998 s.45(1).

[113] Scotland Act 1998 s.45(2).

[114] Scotland Act 1998 s.46(2). Note that, whereas at Westminster an incumbent Prime Minister who wins a second general election simply continues in office without being reappointed, s.46(2)(a) seems clearly to envisage the re-nomination and reappointment of a victorious First Minister, even though they will in no sense have vacated the office. Provision is made in the Standing Orders of the Scottish Parliament for the nomination and election of the First Minister (rr.4.1 and 11.10).

to propose to the Queen a date for the holding of an extraordinary general election, the result of which may produce a party balance in the Parliament more conducive to the nomination of one of its members to be First Minister.[115]

Once the First Minister has been appointed, it falls to them under s.47 of the Scotland Act to appoint the other members of the Scottish Government and the junior Scottish Ministers. The Scottish Ministers, like the First Minister, must be members of the Scottish Parliament and their appointment must meet with the formal approval of the Queen. The First Minister may not, however, seek Her Majesty's approval for any ministerial appointment "without the agreement of the Parliament".[116] Once appointed, the Scottish Ministers hold office at Her Majesty's pleasure (which is to say that they are, in theory, dismissible at will by the Queen). They may in any case be removed from office at any time by the First Minister, with no requirement of parliamentary agreement. A minister who ceases to be an MSP (otherwise than by reason of a dissolution of the Parliament) ceases also to be a minister. Otherwise, a minister may resign at any time of their own choosing, and must do so if the Parliament resolves that the Scottish Government no longer enjoys the confidence of the Parliament. Junior Scottish Ministers are appointed by the First Minister under s.49, again with the approval of the Queen and the agreement of the Parliament as signified in accordance with standing orders, in order to assist the Scottish Ministers in the exercise of their functions. The conditions of tenure of office for junior Scottish Ministers are the same as those for the Scottish Ministers proper.

The Law Officers

The position of the Law Officers differs in significant ways. The offices of Lord Advocate and Solicitor General for Scotland are of some antiquity in Scottish government, the one dating back to the fourteenth century and the other to the sixteenth century. After the Anglo-Scottish union of 1707, the Lord Advocate became a member of the new government of Great Britain, and from 1746 (in which year the office of Scottish Secretary was abolished, not to be revived until the end of the nineteenth century) they assumed general ministerial responsibility for the government of Scotland in addition to their traditional legal duties. As members of the UK Government, the position of the Scottish Law Officers was somewhat anomalous. The normal constitutional convention requiring Her Majesty's Ministers to be members either of the House of Commons or of the House of Lords did not apply to them, although it did become customary to confer on the Lord Advocate a life peerage if they were not already a peer or an MP. Nonetheless, their ministerial responsibilities were extensive. They represented the Crown before the Scottish courts, advised the government on issues of 7–22

[115] There is no provision to prorogate this period, but see the decision of the House of Lords in *Robinson v Secretary of State for Northern Ireland* [2002] UKHL 32; [2002] N.I. 390 where the election of the First Minister and Deputy First Minister was upheld despite the time limit (in that case, six weeks: Northern Ireland Act 1998 s.16(8)) having been breached.

[116] As to the means by which the Parliament's approval is to be signified, see r.4.6 of the Standing Orders. Note that there is nothing in the Scotland Act 1998 to dictate to the First Minister how many ministers they must appoint or what their portfolios should be (the only "named" members of the Scottish Government, the First Minister apart, being the Lord Advocate and the Solicitor General for Scotland).

Scots law, controlled the system of public prosecutions in Scotland and were in charge of the drafting of Bills applying to Scotland. Many of the functions relating to law reform and the machinery of justice that for England and Wales were performed by the Lord Chancellor were in Scotland vested in the Lord Advocate.

Matters relating to Scots criminal law and procedure, the criminal justice system and the Scottish courts were prime candidates for devolution, and, as these encompassed most of the responsibilities of the Scottish Law Officers, it was deemed appropriate that they should cease to be ministers in the UK Government and become instead members of the Scottish Government. This is provided for by the Scotland Act, although, as noted, the position of the Law Officers remains special and distinctive in a number of respects. Under s.48, it is now for the First Minister to recommend to the Queen the appointment of a person as Lord Advocate or Solicitor General (formerly, the Queen made the appointments on the advice of the Prime Minister). As with the Scottish Ministers and junior Scottish Ministers, the First Minister must secure the agreement of the Parliament before forwarding the names of their recommended candidates for appointment to Her Majesty. It is to be noted, however, that with the Law Officers it is the Queen who makes the appointments; she does not, as with the Scottish Ministers, simply approve the appointments made by the First Minister. Similarly, the First Minister cannot remove either of the Law Officers from office at their own discretion: only the Queen may do this when the First Minister so recommends with the agreement of the Parliament. This greater security of tenure than is enjoyed by other members of the Scottish Government is a reflection of the greater constitutional significance of the Law Officers' role in the administration of justice in Scotland, with a correspondingly greater need for a degree of independence on the Law Officers' part. The independence of the Lord Advocate is further secured by a number of provisions scattered throughout the Scotland Act. Section 48(5), for example, states in terms that:

> "any decision of the Lord Advocate in his capacity as head of the systems of criminal prosecution and investigation of deaths in Scotland shall continue to be taken by him independently of any other person."

Section 29 limits the legislative competence of the Scottish Parliament so that it cannot remove the Lord Advocate from their position as head of the systems of criminal prosecution and investigation of deaths. Again, the general transfer of ministerial functions provided for by s.53 does not apply to the "retained functions" of the Lord Advocate (that is, those functions exercisable by them immediately before they ceased to be a minister of the Crown and other statutory functions conferred on them alone after they ceased to be a minister of the Crown). In all of these ways, then, the Scotland Act seeks to preserve the traditional autonomy enjoyed by the Law Officers in the discharge of their responsibilities.

Powers of the Scottish Government

Section 52(1) of the Scotland Act provides that "statutory functions may be conferred on the Scottish Ministers by that name". As devolution has taken root, the greater part of the Scottish Government's functions has begun to find its source in Acts of the Scottish Parliament and Scottish statutory instruments. Acts of the Westminster Parliament will in certain areas continue to confer functions on the Scottish Ministers. Otherwise, many of the Scottish Government's executive powers are founded on existing UK legislation, and to a lesser extent on executive powers rooted in the prerogative and the common law. The logic of devolution required not only that legislative competence over devolved matters be transferred from Westminster to the Scottish Parliament, but also that executive competence in these matters (and others) move from ministers in the UK Government to the Scottish Ministers. 7–23

At one level, this was accomplished by a general transfer of ministerial functions (statutory or prerogative) exercisable within devolved competence, effected on 1 July 1999, by operation of s.53 of the Scotland Act.[117] To that extent, therefore, the devolved competence of the Scottish Ministers is co-extensive, in principle, with the legislative competence of the Scottish Parliament.[118] But s.63 then provides for the transfer of additional functions "exercisable by a Minister of the Crown in or as regards Scotland". These are functions the subject matter of which falls outside the legislative competence of the Scottish Parliament. The Parliament accordingly has no power to alter or abrogate such functions, although the Scottish Ministers are answerable to the Parliament for the manner of their exercise.

Retained EU law and Convention rights

Compatibility with EU law was, and compatibility with retained EU law is now, a condition of the validity of Acts of the Scottish Parliament by virtue of s.29 of the Scotland Act, and by virtue of s.54, as reinforced by s.57(2), it is a condition of the legality of acts of members of the Scottish Government. During the United Kingdom's membership of the EU, the relevance of EU law to Scottish legislation and executive decision making went further than this. While Sch.5 of the Scotland Act reserves to Westminster competence over foreign affairs, including relations with the EU and European institutions, "observing and implementing . . . obligations under EU law" are expressly exempted from the scope of that reservation.[119] Thus the Scottish Parliament had a degree of positive competence in relation to the implementation in Scotland of EU law obligations. 7–24

[117] The concept of "devolved competence" for the purposes of s.53 is defined by reference to the definition of legislative competence contained in the Scotland Act 1998 s.29.

[118] Under the Scotland Act 1998 s.56, however, a number of statutory powers contained in pre-1998 enactments (mostly involving grant making and funding powers) continue, despite the terms of s.53, to be exercisable by a minister of the Crown concurrently with the Scottish Ministers. The list of jointly exercisable powers may be extended by subordinate legislation. Provision is also made for the joint exercise of powers in relation to bodies, offices or office holders whose responsibilities touch on both reserved matters and devolved matters.

[119] A similar exception is made to the general reservation in respect of the UK's international obligations.

From the end of the implementation period (which is, at the time if writing, due to end on 31 December 2020[120]), competence will be defined by reference to "retained EU law".[121]

7–25 As provided for by s.29 in relation to the legislative competence of the Scottish Parliament, by s.54 in relation to the devolved competence of the Scottish Government and as explicitly reinforced by s.57(2):

> "... a member of the Scottish Government has no power to make any subordinate legislation, or to do any other act, so far as the legislation or act is incompatible with any of the Convention rights."

Section 57(3) then provides that subs.(2) does not apply to an act of the Lord Advocate in prosecuting any offence, or in their capacity as head of the systems of criminal prosecution and investigation of deaths in Scotland, "which, because of subsection (2) of section 6 of the Human Rights Act 1998, is not unlawful under subsection (1) of that section". Section 6 of the Human Rights Act makes it unlawful for a "public authority" to act in a manner inconsistent with Convention rights unless, in terms of subs.(2), they are unable to act in any other way because of the terms of the primary or subordinate legislation pursuant to which they are acting.[122]

Intergovernmental relations

7–26 Only part of the story emerges from a consideration of the Scotland Act and the formal structures that are in place to regulate the government of Scotland. It is equally important to understand how the Scottish and UK Governments work together on a day-to-day basis. That relationship has evolved since the inception of devolution. It is inevitably tied to the prevailing political climate: between 1999 and 2007 there was a Labour led coalition in Edinburgh and a majority Labour Government in London. Since then, however, there is has been a nationalist government in Edinburgh that has so far had to work with a Labour Government, then a Conservative led coalition and now a majority Conservative Government. The politics of the respective governments inevitably play a significant part in their relationship. And Brexit, at points, placed inordinate strain on the relationship. Despite those political difference, the need for good working relations between the Edinburgh and London governments remains.

Relations are governed by a memorandum of understanding and various "concordats". [123] The original memorandum of understanding, adopted in

[120] During the "implementation period", the European Communities Act 1972 is for certain purposes deemed to remain in force despite its general repeal on 31 January 2020 (s.1A of the European Union (Withdrawal) Act 2018). For present purposes, competence continues to be defined by reference to EU law. For the detail of how that worked, see para.7–20 of the 3rd edn of this book.

[121] Scotland Act 1998, s.57(4), as amended by the European Union (Withdrawal) Act 2018.

[122] See, generally, I. Jamieson, "The Relationship between the Scotland Act and the Human Rights Act", 2001 S.L.T. (News) 43.

[123] For discussion, see: R. Rawlings, "Concordats and the Constitution" (2000) 116 L.Q.R. 257; A. Scott, "The Role of Concordats in the New Britain: Taking Subsidiarity Seriously" (2001) 5 Edin. L.R. 21.

2001,[124] set out the main principles on which inter-governmental relations would be conducted: communication and consultation, co-operation, exchange of information, statistics and research, and confidentiality.[125] The memorandum of understanding is a "statement of political intent" that was "binding in honour only". A number of further agreements supplement the memorandum of understanding. These include an agreement on the Joint Ministerial Committee and concordats on co-ordination of financial assistance to industry, international relations, statistics and, when it was relevant, EU policy issues (but that did not include Brexit). Although relations between Whitehall and the various devolved administrations would normally be done on a bilateral basis, the Joint Ministerial Committee was established consisting of the UK Government and the Scottish, Welsh and Northern Irish Ministers. Its terms of reference included: considering non-devolved matters that impinge on devolved responsibilities (and vice versa); to consider devolved matters if it is beneficial to discuss their respective treatment in different parts of the UK; to keep the arrangements for liaison between Whitehall and the devolved administrations under review; and to resolve disputes. The Joint Ministerial Committee was expected to meet once a year. In fact, there was no meeting of the committee between 2003 and 2008, when they resumed at the request of the Scottish First Minister.[126] Meetings are now irregular, with the last one being held in December 2018. There are also Joint Ministerial Committee sub-committees, which are attended by ministers holding relevant policy responsibilities. In recent years, the only active sub-committees have been those concerning Europe and EU negotiations. The respective Secretaries of State were also given responsibility for "the promotion of good relations" between the UK Government and their respective devolved administration.

Assessing the impact of the memorandum of understanding and accompanying concordats in practice is difficult. The House of Lords Select Committee on the Constitution have doubted their usefulness.[127] At the Joint Ministerial Committee meeting in December 2014 it was agreed, having regard to the fundamental changes in the constitutional landscape since the memorandum of understanding was originally prepared in 2000, that work would be commissioned on a revised memorandum of understanding.[128] That suggests that the various administrations found the memorandum of understanding to be of some continuing use. But no revised memorandum has been forthcoming.

---

[124] A new memorandum of understanding was published in October 2013, but the key provisions remain much the same.

[125] HM Government, *Memorandum of Understanding and Supplementary Agreements between the United Kingdom Government, Scottish Ministers, the Cabinet of the National Assembly for Wales and the Northern Ireland Executive Committee* (The Stationery Office, 2001) Cm.5240.

[126] House of Commons Justice Committee, *Devolution: A Decade On, Fifth Report of Session 2008–09* (The Stationery Office, 2009) HC 529, para.4.28.

[127] House of Lords Select Committee on the Constitution, *Devolution: Inter-Institutional Relations in the United Kingdom, Second Report of 2002–03* (The Stationery Office, 2002) HL Paper 28, para.38.

[128] Communiqué following meeting of the Joint Ministerial Committee on 15 December 2014, *https://www.gov.uk/government/news/joint-ministerial-committee-communique-december-2014* [Accessed 3 June 2020].

GOVERNMENT ACCOUNTABILITY[129]

7–27 Accountable government, like respect for the rule of law, is one of the hallmarks of a democratic society, and serves to distinguish it from a totalitarian state. As Lord Carnwath explained in *Miller (No.1)*:

> "No less fundamental to our constitution [than the principle of Parliamentary sovereignty] is the principle of Parliamentary accountability. The executive is accountable to Parliament for its exercise of the prerogative, including its actions in international law. That account is made through ordinary Parliamentary procedures."[130]

That Lord Carnwath was dissenting as to the result does not detract from the soundness of his observations in respect of the principle of parliamentary accountability. It was a theme that the Supreme Court returned to in the Prorogation case:

> "Ministers are accountable to Parliament through such mechanisms as their duty to answer Parliamentary questions and to appear before Parliamentary committees, and through Parliamentary scrutiny of the delegation legislation which ministers make. By these means, the policies of the executive are subjected to consideration by the representatives of the electorate, the executive is required to report, explain and defend its action, and citizens are protected from the arbitrary exercise of executive power."[131]

In part, it was said, that principle required the purported prorogation of September 2019 to be set aside. Thus, whilst government accountability to Parliament is often seen through the prism of political debates in the House of Commons, it should not be forgotten that those debates are the manifestation of a fundamental constitutional principle. And those debates are not simply political theatre. As the Supreme Court went on to remind us: "[t]he Government exists because it has the confidence of the House of Commons. It has no democratic legitimacy other than that".[132] That process of accountability is the mechanism by which the House of Commons can determine its confidence in the government, and thereby clothe it with legitimacy.

Accountable government is often described as having two dimensions, explanatory and amendatory—the first implying an obligation to answer for and justify policies adopted and decisions taken, the second an obligation to acknowledge deficiency and error, where necessary, and to undertake to put things right (which may or may not involve a change in the responsible personnel).[133] The former is at least as important as the latter, although a

---

[129] In the latter phases of the Brexit process, the House of Commons asserted itself over the government in a manner that was unprecedented (and which went some way beyond enforcing "accountability"). That episode is discussed in Ch.1 and, briefly, in Ch.3. What follows is a more conventional account of how government is expected to account to Parliament.

[130] *R (Miller and another) v Secretary of State for Exiting the European Union* [2017] UKSC 5; [2018] A.C. 61 at [249].

[131] *Cherry and others v Advocate General for Scotland* [2019] UKSC 41; 2019 S.L.T. 1143 at [46].

[132] *Cherry and others v Advocate General for Scotland* [2019] UKSC 41; 2019 S.L.T. 1143 at [55].

[133] C. Turpin, "Ministerial Responsibility" in J. Jowell and D. Oliver (eds), *The Changing Constitution*, 4th edn (Oxford: Oxford University Press, 2000), Ch.5.

tendency to focus on blame and sanction may obscure this. Plainly, in any democracy, the government will have the support of only a portion of the people to whom it is ultimately answerable via the ballot box. Not everyone will share its ideological persuasion, nor agree with its particular policies. But where a government accepts in good faith an obligation to explain itself and justify its actions (which implies at least that thought has been given to alternative means of pursuing its policy goals) it is easier to accept its choices; to that extent, accountable government is conducive to cohesion. In the same way, accountability reduces the risks of governmental fallibility. A government that feels obliged to account for its actions is the more likely to think things through properly in the first place, and although mistakes will inevitably be made—either because a policy is intrinsically flawed, or because it is poorly implemented—accountability in its amendatory form should ensure that they are rectified.

There is more than one way in which accountable government may be **7–28**
secured, and one may well obtain a better sense of the extent to which it is achieved in the UK by focusing less on the defects of particular mechanisms and more on the adequacy of all the mechanisms taken together. As noted, in the final analysis, a government is accountable to the people through periodic elections. If this control is sporadic and, often, blunted by the vagaries of the electoral process, it is nonetheless occasionally effective.[134] That apart, ongoing political accountability is traditionally held to be secured by parliamentary scrutiny of the executive, which rests on the constitutional doctrines of collective and individual ministerial responsibility to Parliament. We have touched on these doctrines already. Collective ministerial responsibility denotes the responsibility of all members of a government for all of its policies. However those policies are arrived at, it is the duty of each government minister publicly to defend them, and if a particular minister cannot do so then, by convention, they should resign.[135] Individual ministerial responsibility, by contrast, denotes the responsibility of each minister for everything that is done in their name by their department. In keeping with the traditional ideas of the anonymity and impartiality of the Civil Service, the minister takes the credit for departmental successes; the corollary is that they should take the blame for departmental failures, even where they are not directly and personally implicated therein. Again, the sanction attaching to individual ministerial responsibility—that which gives the doctrine its teeth—is said to be resignation. In practice, of course, loss of office is not the automatic consequence either of a breach of collective ministerial responsibility or of departmental failure. In the former case, while the minister who is unable to support a particular aspect of government policy may step down, and while the Prime Minister or First Minister may simply dismiss them, political considerations may militate against dismissal if the recalcitrant minister is not otherwise minded to go. In the latter case, we have already seen that departmental

[134] As in the 1997 general election, the result of which was as much a verdict on the outgoing Conservative administration as a mandate for its New Labour successor.

[135] In terms of both the Ministerial Code and the Scottish Ministerial Code, upholding the principle of collective responsibility is one of the key duties of a minister. Indeed, in Scotland, where coalition governments were expected to be the norm, the principle of collective responsibility assumed on even greater importance than at Westminster: see B.K. Winetrobe, "Collective responsibility in devolved Scotland" [2003] P.L. 24.

wrongdoing is rarely attended by a ministerial resignation.[136] In neither case, in normal circumstances, is Parliament likely to be in a position to enforce the sanction by withdrawing its confidence, either from a particular minister or the ministry as a whole.

But the ephemeral nature of the sanction does not deprive the doctrine of ministerial responsibility of all its force. There are numerous mechanisms, at Westminster and Holyrood alike, designed to facilitate parliamentary scrutiny of the executive. Questions are tabled by MPs and MSPs for oral or written answers. Motions and debates provide a means of requiring a minister to appear and give an account. The parliamentary committees, moreover, furnish a specialised and systematic forum for control at various levels, through their pre-legislative and post-legislative scrutiny of executive measures and inquiries undertaken into matters falling within their respective remits. Considered in isolation, the adequacy of all of these devices is open to question. A key reason for this relates to the availability of information to Parliament. Political accountability cannot function unless information about the activities of governmental bodies is provided to Parliament and parliamentary committees. By and large, that information is in the hands of the government, which is therefore in a position to control its dissemination. Parliamentary questions, motions and debates may seek to elicit information, but are an inherently inefficient way of doing so. Ministers may and do refuse to answer questions on a variety of grounds. As for parliamentary committees, while they provide a sharper focus on governmental activity, their efficacy too is limited by their reliance on ministerial co-operation, deficiencies in the provision of information, their inherently party political make-up and the restrictions placed on the candour of officials appearing before them. Specific inquiries may be illuminating on occasion, but committees are not well suited to the ongoing audit of the departments they monitor. In all of these ways, the ability of parliamentary institutions to secure accountability is diminished.

7–29 The reinvention of government has also heightened concern about the reach of parliamentary control. That reinvention involved drawing a distinction between the functions of policy making and policy execution, the latter of which is increasingly performed, whether by executive agencies, non-departmental public bodies or external contractors, at some distance from the ministerial core. It has been said, in light of these developments, that while the minister remains accountable to Parliament for the delivery as well as the formation of government policy, they are only properly responsible for the latter.[137] On this reckoning, responsibility can only properly attach where a minister is themselves culpable, either in the sense of being personally implicated in a serious departmental error or in the sense that they knew or should have known what was amiss. Beyond

[136] Both the Ministerial Code and Scottish Ministerial Code make clear, however, that an individual minister may only remain in office for so long as they retain the confidence of the Prime Minister or First Minister as the case may be.

[137] This distinction between the general accountability of ministers and their personal responsibility is not necessarily of recent provenance: something like it appears, for example, in the so called Maxwell-Fyfe guidelines, laid down by the Home Secretary in his response to the findings of the public inquiry into the disposal of land at Crichel Down in 1954: see *Hansard*, HC Vol.241, cols 1290 and 1291 (20 July 1954).

that, "pure vicarious headrolling is not required".[138] In principle, this seems unobjectionable: responsibility should be commensurate with the degree of power and control actually possessed. But in the reconfigured constitutional structure, it has led to the tactical employment by ministers of a distinction between policy and operational matters, which implies that the minister can be expected to know nothing about the latter.[139] What the distinction has allowed is the deflection of blame, away from the minister and on to officials, and constitutional accountability to Parliament is diminished, not enhanced, if the extent of the minister's duty to Parliament is to turn up and condemn the agency or quango charged with implementation.[140]

The parliamentary and academic criticism of this reworking of ministerial responsibility was amply justified by the instrumental way in which ministers applied the policy/operational distinction. That distinction presupposes clarity and certainty in the division of roles where neither exists to any marked extent. It also led to major blind spots in parliamentary scrutiny, in so far as agency chief executives were no freer than other civil servants to attend select committees and give evidence unencumbered by ministerial directions. But it may be that what was (and is) needed is a conscious adjustment to the modern constitutional landscape. Professor Woodhouse[141] suggests that, within this environment, the political accountability of ministers would be better captured by focusing on their role responsibility rather than causal responsibility in a simplistic sense. On that view, there is no reason why the Home Secretary should fall on their sword because a prison warder leaves a cell door open. But their general supervisory responsibility for ensuring, so far as possible, that such things do not occur should be acknowledged explicitly:

> "Ministers are . . . responsible for seeing that mechanisms are in place to provide them with the necessary and correct information so that they can respond to problems, if appropriate by taking direct control, and account to Parliament and the public. They are also responsible for ensuring that their departments have adequate human and financial resources to implement government policies, that those appointed as heads of executive agencies are suitably qualified, and that there are systems or procedures in place which minimise the dangers of errors being made. Such . . . 'positive' responsibilities . . . are supplemented by 'negative' responsibilities, so that the failure of ministers to intervene, when they should have done so, is not an appropriate excuse; neither is not knowing that something has happened when they should have known."[142]

Systemic operational failures should therefore be seen as engaging the responsibility (not merely the accountability) of the minister, either because they **7–30**

[138] G. Marshall (ed), *Ministerial Responsibility* (Oxford: Oxford University Press, 1989) p.11.

[139] D. Woodhouse, "The Reconstruction of Constitutional Accountability" [2002] P.L. 73, 75. In fact, the evidence suggests that ministers concern themselves far more with operational matters than the distinction implies. Moreover, the flaws in a policy are likely to become apparent only when the policy is put into operation.

[140] For example, the fall out between the then Home Secretary Michael Howard and the Director General of the Prison Service, Derek Lewis, over responsibility for prison security. This episode is more fully discussed by Drewry in "The Executive: Towards Accountable Government and Effective Governance?" in *The Changing Constitution* (2011), pp.203–205.

[141] Woodhouse, "The Reconstruction of Constitutional Accountability" [2002] P.L. 73, 75.

[142] Woodhouse, "The Reconstruction of Constitutional Accountability" [2002] P.L. 73, 78.

have failed to ensure that an agency is staffed and funded sufficiently to perform its allotted task,[143] or because they have failed to step in to arrest and correct maladministration. According to Woodhouse, recent practice suggests that this lesson is being absorbed in governmental circles.[144] The duties of ministers to account to Parliament and be held to account have been committed to paper, both at the Scottish and UK levels, in the latter case reflecting the terms of resolutions adopted by both Houses of Parliament.[145] But at least as important as recognising (if recognition it be) that ministerial responsibility does not stop with settling on a policy and charging others with its implementation is the insistence on the provision to Parliament of information.[146] The Scott Inquiry[147] into the sale of defence equipment to Iraq rightly identified this as the key to improved lines of political accountability. The entry into force of the Freedom of Information Act 2000 and the Freedom of Information (Scotland) Act 2002 has institutionalised the routine disclosure of official information and should make possible more effective scrutiny of government decision-making than has been possible in the past.

Nor should the legal accountability of ministers be neglected. The development of the law of judicial review may be seen in part as a response to the inadequacies of political channels of accountability. Even before the entry into force of the Human Rights Act 1998, the courts were able to insist that governmental powers were exercised lawfully, rationally and fairly, with appropriate regard to the fundamental rights of the citizen; now, all statutory powers fall to be read and given effect consistently with the Convention rights and may be the subject of declarations of incompatibility should this be impossible.[148] This growth in judicial review has been a source of considerable concern for the government and led to proposed reform of the procedure.[149] Between 1998 and 2012 the number of applications for judicial review (in England and Wales) rose from 4,500 to 12,400 (the bulk of the increase being accounted for by immigration claims). But the proposal to limit access to the

---

143 As was the case with the establishment of the Child Support Agency, in the view both of the Parliamentary Commissioner for Administration and the House of Commons Select Committee on Social Services.

144 Under reference to the inquiries into the sale of arms to Iraq (Inquiry into the Export of Defence Equipment and Dual-Use Goods to Iraq and Related Prosecutions, *Report of the Inquiry into the Export of Defence Equipment and Dual-Use Goods to Iraq and Related Prosecutions* (HMSO, 1996), HC 115), the failure to notify changes to the rules of entitlement to inherit a deceased spouse's state earnings related pension (Select Committee on Public Administration, *Administrative Failure: Inherited SERPS, Fifth Report of 1999–2000* (The Stationery Office, 2000), HC 433) and the supply of military equipment to Sierra Leone; and to the ministerial response to the Passport Agency crisis in the summer of 1999.

145 The text of which is set out by Drewry in "The Executive: Towards Accountable Government and Effective Governance?" in *The Changing Constitution* (2011), p.205.

146 Both ministerial codes stress that it is of "paramount importance that ministers give accurate and truthful information" to Parliament and require ministers to be as open as possible with Parliament and the public, refusing to disclose information only when it would be in the public interest to do so.

147 Inquiry into the Export of Defence Equipment and Dual-Use Goods in Iraq and Related Prosecutions, *Report of the Inquiry into the Export of Defence Equipment and Dual-Use Goods in Iraq and Related Prosecutions*.

148 Acts of the Scottish Parliament that cannot be read and given effect consistently with the Convention rights are of course invalid and may be struck down.

149 Ministry of Justice, *Judicial Review: Proposals for Further Reform* (The Stationery Office, 2013) Cm.8703.

courts for review of executive acts was widely criticised as an assault on the rule of law and the government pulled back from some of the more radical proposals. Finally, devolution itself has contributed in an important way to improving the accountability of government. By breaking government down into smaller parts and subjecting it to the control of separate parliaments or assemblies, devolution may well have made the attainment of political accountability more manageable and achievable.

CHAPTER 8

Courts, Tribunals and the Judiciary

INTRODUCTION

8–01 Put at its simplest, the function of the courts is to adjudicate on and determine disputes of fact and law, meaning the law as laid down in and under statutes and the common law as expounded and applied by the courts themselves. The performance of this function is in no sense confined to professional judges sitting in the civil and criminal courts, but falls also to the many members (lay and legally qualified) of the tribunal system.[1] Tribunals have long been part of the system of administrative justice, but since their restructuring just over a decade ago they have developed an increased, and increasing, prominence in the justice system. Courts and tribunals, between them, provide the adjudicative service by which the law is enforced; not just between private individuals but, and perhaps more importantly, between private individuals and the state. As Lord Bingham identified, the core of the rule of law requires "all persons and authorities within the state, whether public or private, should be bound by and entitled to the benefit of laws publically made, taking effect (generally) in the future and publicly administered in the courts".[2] When that is understood, it can be seen that the system of courts and tribunals are an essential component of the rule of law.[3] Their importance rests not only in resolving the individual disputes brought before them (important though that it is for the parties concerned) but the existence of an independent and properly accessible enforcement mechanism is the background against which society generally operates and in which respect for the law generally prevails. As Lord Reed explained:

---

[1] The system of tribunals in the United Kingdom was significantly reviewed, and streamlined, by the Tribunals, Courts and Enforcement Act 2007. For a discussion of the system introduced by the 2007 Act, see: M. Elliott and R. Thomas, "Tribunal Justice, *Cart*, and Proportionate Dispute Resolution" (2012) 71(2) C.L.J. 297. Similar reforms have now been introduced to Scotland (Tribunals (Scotland) Act 2014). The tribunal system is considered at paras 8–06—8–14, below.

[2] T. Bingham, *The Rule of Law*, p.37; see also Ch.1

[3] Or, as the Supreme Court put it in *R (on the application of UNISON) v Lord Chancellor* [2017] UKSC 51 there is a "constitutional right of access to justice: that is to say, access to the courts (and tribunals…)" (at [65]). Lord Sumption made the same point in *R (on the application of Privacy International) v Investigatory Powers Tribunal* [2019] UKSC 22; [2019] 2 W.L.R. 1219 at [182]: "A right of access to a court or similar judicial body to review the lawfulness of administrative or executive acts is an essential part of the rule of law". Finally, in *R (on the application of Miller and another) v Secretary of State for Exiting the European Union* [2017] UKSC 5; [2018] A.C. 61 at [18]: "The UK is a constitutional democracy framed by legal rules and subject to the rule of law. The courts have a constitutional duty fundamental to the rule of law in a democratic state to enforce rules of constitutional law in the same way as the courts enforce other laws."

> "But the value to society of the right of access to the courts is not confined to cases in which the courts decide questions of general importance. People and business need to know, on the one hand, that they will be able to enforce their rights if they have to do so, and, on the other hand, that if they fail to meet their obligations, there is likely to be a remedy against them. It is that knowledge which underpins everyday economic and social relations. That is so, notwithstanding that judicial enforcement of the law is not usually necessary, and notwithstanding that the resolution of disputes by other methods is often desirable."[4]

Just as it is the existence of an efficient system for the detection of crime and the prosecution of offenders that ensure general compliance with the criminal law, it is an accessible, cost effective, dispute resolution system that ensures that the laws enacted by Parliament, and in particular the rights and benefits conferred, and obligations imposed, on individuals are meaningful. If contesting an administrative decision to withdraw a particular benefit would cost more in legal fees than the benefit was worth, the incentive to ensure a proper decision is taken in the first place risks fading. So, at the root of the courts and tribunals system is a desire to ensure that there is an accessible, efficient and cost-effective system by which rights can be vindicated and obligations enforced.

Because an independent court system underpins the rule of law, and, as Lord Reed explained, the basic operation of society, it is important that society has confidence in that system. It is the need for such confidence that underlies the principle (which has been described, repeatedly, as a constitutional principle) that justice is administered by the courts in public.[5] It goes back to the old question: who guards the guards? If the courts guard the rule of law, who ensure the courts do that properly? The answer is the requirement that the court discharge their functions in public and, in the modern era, before the press and other media who can report on their proceedings. That carries with it a requirement that those covering and reporting upon court proceedings must be properly informed about those proceedings. For that reason, generally, documents lodged with the court (such as pleadings and notes of argument) should be made available to the media if requested. It is a principle that is not without qualification, and being a common law principle the extent to which it can be qualified is a matter for the courts.[6] In short, where the interests of justice require some or all of the proceedings to be withheld from the public (whether indefinitely or only whilst they are pending), the principle may be qualified.[7]

There is, however, another critical component to ensure the courts and tribunals system can effectively discharge its function and protect the rule of law:

---

[4] *R (on the application of UNISON) v Lord Chancellor* [2017] UKSC 51 at [71]. In fact, paras [66]–[89] deserve being read in their entirety for a full and robust explanation of the importance of a properly accessible system of courts and tribunals. The context of that case was a significant (and, the Supreme Court held, unlawful) increase in the fees to raise proceedings before the Employment Tribunals. The effect of the increase on the availability of the Employment Tribunal was such that it offended the constitutional principle of access to the courts and was thus unlawful at common law.

[5] *A v Secretary of State for the Home Department* [2014] UKSC 25; 2014 S.C. (UKSC) 151 at [23]–[26]; *Kennedy v Information Commissioner* [2015] A.C. 455; *Dring v Cape Intermediate Holdings Ltd* [2019] UKSC 38; [2019] 3 W.L.R. 429.

[6] *A v Secretary of State for the Home Department* [2014] UKSC 25; 2014 S.C. (UKSC) 151 at paras.23 et seq.

[7] See, for example, *A v Harrower* [2017] HJCAC 91; 2018 J.C. 93.

those courts and tribunals must be, and must be seen to be, independent of both the parties to the dispute and the state. As Lord Bingham again explained:

> "The constitution of a modern democracy governed by the rule of law must … guarantee the independence of judicial decision-makes, an expression I use to embrace all those making decisions of a judicial character … In short, [decision-makers] must be independent of anybody or anything which might lead them to decide issues coming before them on anything other than the legal and factual merits of the case as, in the exercise of their own judgment, they consider them to be."[8]

It is ensuring a sufficient appearance of independence from the other aspects of the state that informed both the creation of the Supreme Court (in place of the Judicial Committee of the House of Lords) and the restructuring of the tribunal system, both of which are discussed below. And as will become apparent, securing that independence requires decision-makers to have sufficient security of tenure, remuneration and, in certain circumstances, to stand aside and allow a colleague to determine the case before them. With the advent of devolution, and the incorporation of the European Convention on Human Rights into domestic law, the courts have acquired a new and explicitly "constitutional" jurisdiction that has focused attention on the judicial role and on the relationship of the judiciary with other organs of the state.[9] And as we saw in earlier chapters, the proper limit of the courts' role repeatedly arose during the Brexit process.

COURTS

Though the legal system of Scotland is distinct from that of England and Wales and that of Northern Ireland, the Scottish judiciary is not, at least in its upper echelons, exclusively Scottish. Since 1 October 2009, the UK Supreme Court has sat at the apex of the Scottish judicial system in civil matters.[10] That court does not, however, sit at the head of the criminal justice system. The High Court of Justiciary remains the court of final appeal for criminal matters in Scotland.[11] The UK Supreme Court has inherited the jurisdiction previously vested in the Judicial Committee of the Privy Council as the final court of appeal on devolution issues **8–02**

[8] T. Bingham, *The Rule of Law*, pp.91–92

[9] See S. Tierney, "Constitutionalising the Role of the Judge: Scotland and the new order" in A.E. Boyle et al (eds), *Human Rights and Scots Law* (Oxford: Hart, 2002), Ch.5.

[10] Leave to appeal is now required to appeal to the Supreme Court: Court of Session Act 1988 s.40. The requirement for leave was introduced as part of the Courts Reform (Scotland) Act 2014 (s.117). Prior to that, an appeal could be taken as of right (assuming two advocates, or solicitors with extended rights of audience, signed off the appeal as reasonable). In the first instance, permission must be sought from the Inner House. In certain circumstances, if that application is refused, it may be renewed to the Supreme Court. Unlike England (where the High Court can certify a point that can then be appealed direct to the Supreme Court, bypassing the Court of Appeal), there can be no appeal against any decision of a Lord Ordinary (s.40(5) of the 1988 Act). Permission may only be granted where the case raises an arguable point of law of general public importance that ought to be considered by the Supreme Court at that time (s.41(3) of the 1988 Act; more commonly known as "the second appeals test").

[11] *McInnes (Paul) v HM Advocate* [2010] UKSC 7; 2010 S.C. (U.K.S.C.) 28, per Lord Hope of Craighead at [5]; *Fraser (Nat Gordon) v HM Advocate* [2011] UKSC 24; 2011 S.C. (U.K.S.C.) 113, per Lord Hope of Craighead at [11].

under s.98 and Sch.6 of the Scotland Act 1998 and, now, compatibility issues under the Criminal Procedure (Scotland) Act 1995, as well as the jurisdiction to determine "pre-Assent references" made in respect of Bills passed by the Scottish Parliament by one of the Law Officers.[12] That devolution jurisdiction, when exercised in the context of a criminal case, has proved politically controversial and prompted some ill-advised and intemperate remarks by members of the Scottish Government.[13] We will return to that shortly.

8–03 The UK Supreme Court was created by Pt 3 of the Constitutional Reform Act 2005.[14] It replaced the Appellate Committee of House of Lords thereby removing the final court of appeal from Parliament and, it was said by the government of the day, completing the separation of powers. The jurisdiction of the Judicial Committee of the Privy Council, in matters of Scots, English and Welsh and Northern Irish law, and questions about the various devolution settlements, was also transferred to the new court.[15] Whether it was entirely necessary was a matter of debate, but the removal of the judicial function of the House of Lords had probably become inevitable by the middle of the first decade of the new century.[16] Whatever the strengths of the competing arguments, on 30 July 2009, the Appellate Committee of the House of Lords delivered their final judgments and come 1 October 2009, the judges that in July had been Lords of Appeal in Ordinary were sworn in as Justices of the Supreme Court.[17] Despite its name, the

---

[12] Scotland Act 1998 s.33. Only one reference in relation to Scottish legislation has been made: *UK Withdrawal from the European Union (Legal Continuity) (Scotland) Bill* [2018] UKSC 64; 2019 S.C. (UKSC) 13 (which was, as a result of subsequent Westminster legislation, largely outwith competence)—see para.6–38, above. In Wales, however, a number of early references were made (with mixed results): *Attorney General v National Assembly for Wales Commission* [2012] UKSC 53; [2013] 1 A.C. 792 (concerning provisions in relation to Welsh by-laws that were held to be within legislative competence); *Attorney General for England and Wales v Counsel General for Wales* [2014] UKSC 43; [2014] 1 W.L.R. 2622 (concerning the validity of the Agricultural Sector (Wales) Bill which was held to be within competence); and *Recovery of Medical Costs for Asbestos Diseases (Wales) Bill, Re* [2015] UKSC 3; [2015] A.C. 1016 (a pre-emptive reference by the Welsh Law Officer in anticipation of a subsequent challenge; the relevant provisions were held to be outwith competence).

[13] See the coverage of the then Justice Secretary's comments following the Supreme Court's decision in *Fraser*. For example, D. Leask, "MacAskill threat to end Supreme Court funding" (1 June 2011) *http://www.heraldscotland.com/news/crime-courts/macaskill-threat-to-end-supreme-court-funding-macaskill-threat-to-end-supreme-court-funding.13900094* [Accessed 30 March 2020].

[14] In language reminiscent of s.1(1) of the Scotland Act 1998, s.23(1) of the 2005 Act declares: "There is to be a Supreme Court of the United Kingdom"; see paras 6–02 and 6–03 of the second edition of this work for details of the Appellate Committee of the House of Lords and the Judicial Committee of the Privy Council.

[15] The territorial jurisdiction of the Judicial Committee is otherwise unaffected. It has physically moved location from Downing Street to the Supreme Court building in Parliament Square. See the rather curious proposal to breathe fresh life into the Judicial Committee so far as the United Kingdom was concerned in the (now discarded) House of Lords Reform Bill, which was introduced in Parliament on 11 July 2012. Clause 36 would have vested jurisdiction to resolve disputes about disqualification from the reformed House in the Privy Council and not the Supreme Court. The explanatory notes shed no light on why that choice was made. The Privy Council does, however, retain some specific statutory jurisdictions, for example determining disputed claims to a baronetcy: *In the matter of the Baronetcy of Pringle of Stichill* [2016] UKPC 16.

[16] On the "construction" of a new Supreme Court, as well as the case for such a court, see: A Le Seuer (ed.), *Building the UK's New Supreme Court* (Oxford: OUP, 2004).

[17] Constitutional Reform Act 2005 ("the 2005 Act") s.24; all other than Lord Neuberger, who had been appointed as Master of the Rolls, assumed office as a Justice of the Supreme Court. Lord Neuberger did, however, return to the Supreme Court, as its President, in October 2012.

UK Supreme Court reigns supreme throughout the land in relation to only one type of case: a devolution matter. In those cases, the decision of the Supreme Court is binding in all legal proceedings and binds all courts, other than the Supreme Court itself.[18] In all other cases, a decision of the Supreme Court is to be regarded as a decision of a court of the part of the United Kingdom that gave rise to the appeal.[19] Thus a decision in an appeal from the Court of Appeal in London is formally binding only in England and Wales. In practice, however, in areas where the law of the other jurisdictions of the United Kingdom is broadly the same, or is based upon an Act of Parliament that applies throughout the United Kingdom, a decision of the Supreme Court is in effect binding.[20]

The continuing role of the Supreme Court in Scots law, in particular, the extent to which it impacts on criminal law, has been something that the Scottish Government of Alex Salmond gave much thought. Both Professor Neil Walker and Lord McCluskey were commissioned to produce reports, the former being a more wide ranging consideration of the question of the final appellate jurisdiction in Scots law,[21] and the latter focusing on the relationship between the High Court and the Supreme Court in criminal cases.[22] This led to an amendment to the Scotland Act 1998 to carve out certain criminal proceedings from the definition of "devolution matters".[23] The Scotland Act 2012 introduced the following words to the end of para.1 of Sch.6 to the 1998 Act (which defines a devolution matter):

> "But a question arising in criminal proceedings in Scotland that would, apart from this paragraph, be a devolution issue is not a devolution issue if (however formulated) it relates to the compatibility with any of the Convention rights or with EU law of—
> (a) an Act of the Scottish Parliament or any provision of an Act of the Scottish Parliament,
> (b) a function,
> (c) the purported or proposed exercise of a function, or
> (d) a failure to act."[24]

Where such issues arise, they must now be dealt with as "compatibility issues" under the Criminal Procedure (Scotland) Act 1995. A "compatibility issue" is defined as:

> "a question, arising in criminal proceedings, as to—
> (a) whether a public authority has acted (or proposes to act)—

---

[18] 2005 Act s.41(3); "devolution matter" is defined in s.41(4) of the 2005 Act.

[19] 2005 Act s.41(2).

[20] For example, the response to the Supreme Court decision in (the Scottish appeal) *Montgomery v Lanarkshire Health Board* [2015] UKSC 11; 2015 S.C. (UKSC) 63 was accepted as restating the law throughout the United Kingdom. The case for such uniformity is even more compelling in relation to constitutional questions, where it would be little short of absurd if the different jurisdictions of the United Kingdom could come to different views on important points of the UK constitution (see, for example, the point made by the Divisional Court in *Miller v Secretary of State for Exiting the European Union* [2016] EWHC (Admin) 2768 at [19].

[21] Walker, *Final Appellate Jurisdiction in the Scottish Legal System* (The Stationery Office, 2010).

[22] Lord McCluskey et al, *Final Report of Review Group: Examination of the Relationship Between the High Court of Justiciary and the Supreme Court in Criminal Cases* (Scottish Government, 2011).

[23] On "devolution issues" more generally, see para.6–33.

[24] Scotland Act 2012 s.36(4).

(i) in a way which is made unlawful by section 6(1) of the Human Rights Act 1998, or
(ii) in a way which is incompatible with EU law, or
(b) whether an Act of the Scottish Parliament or any provision of an Act of the Scottish Parliament is incompatible with any of the Convention rights or with EU law".[25]

Where such an issue arises, the procedures to be followed are set out in s.288ZB and s.288AA of the 1995 Act.[26] A compatibility issue can be referred to the Supreme Court by the High Court. Alternatively, an appeal lies to the Supreme Court, but only with the permission of either the High Court or the Supreme Court.[27] The Supreme Court only has jurisdiction to determine the compatibility issue. Once it has done so, the case must be returned to the High Court to proceed as appropriate.[28] That provision broadly reflects the procedure followed in *Fraser v HM Advocate* where the Supreme Court allowed the appeal but remitted the case to the High Court to determine whether permission should be granted to bring fresh proceedings and formally quash the conviction.[29] It may be thought to be largely symbolic: the London court does not actually, for example, quash a conviction because of an incompatibility; that is done by the High Court of Justiciary when the case is returned (but that court has no choice in the matter). But in the aftermath of the decisions in *Cadder* and *Fraser*, symbolism had become fairly important. The "compatibility issues" provisions came into effect on 22 April 2013.[30]

8–04 The Court of Session and the High Court of Justiciary are together known as the Supreme Courts of Scotland, with a network of sheriff and Justice of the Peace courts operating below them. So far as the civil courts in Scotland are concerned, they have recently undergone a significant restructuring.[31] Prior to the reforms made by the Judiciary and Courts (Scotland) Act 2008, each sheriff principal was responsible for his or her own sheriffdom, whereas the Lord President was responsible for the Supreme Courts of Scotland. The Lord President is now the head of the Scottish Judiciary.[32] Scotland's supreme civil court is the Court of Session, which can trace its roots back to the first half of the sixteenth century. Its jurisdiction is both original and appellate and extends over the whole of Scotland, in contrast to that of the sheriff courts. It is composed of the Lord President and Lord Justice Clerk, together with the Senators of the

---

[25] Criminal Procedure (Scotland) Act 1995 s.288ZA(2), as inserted by the Scotland Act 2012 s.34(3).

[26] Inserted by ss.35 and 36(6) of the Scotland Act 2012, respectively.

[27] Criminal Procedure (Scotland) Act 1995 s.288AA(5).

[28] Criminal Procedure (Scotland) Act 1995 s.288AA(2) and (3); s.288ZB(6) and (7).

[29] *Fraser v HM Advocate* [2011] UKSC 24; 2011 S.C. (U.K.S.C.) 113, per Lord Hope at [43].

[30] Scotland Act 2012 (Commencement No.3) Order 2013 (SI 2012/6). A report was published in September 2018 of the group that was established, and led by the Lord Justice General, to review the operation of the compatibility issue provisions that were introduced by the Scotland Act 2012. No major changes were recommended. The report is available at: *http://www.scotland-judiciary.org.uk/Upload/Documents/ScotlandActReview2012CompatabilityissuesReportSeptember2018.pdf* [Accessed 05 June 2020].

[31] Courts Reform (Scotland) Act 2014.

[32] Judiciary and Courts (Scotland) Act 2008 s.2(1); in short, this places the Lord President at the head of all Scottish judges that sit in Scottish courts, other than those that are Justices of the UK Supreme Court. He (and the office has always been held by a man) is also Head of the Scottish Tribunals: Tribunals (Scotland) Act 2014 s.2 (see para.8–10, below).

College of Justice or Lords of Session, as the Court of Session judges are collectively known,[33] and has the power both at common law and under statute to regulate its own procedure by way of Act of Sederunt. Scotland's supreme criminal court is the High Court of Justiciary, and it is perhaps supreme in a truer sense than the Court of Session, for there is no right of appeal beyond the High Court sitting as an appellate body[34] except, as we have seen, in respect of what are now called compatibility issues, which can be determined by the UK Supreme Court. All judges of the High Court (the Lords Commissioners of Justiciary) have, since 1887, also been judges of the Court of Session. The head of the High Court is the Lord Justice General, an office that, since 1836, has been held by the Lord President of the Court of Session. It has exclusive jurisdiction to try the most serious crimes, known as the pleas of the Crown, and concurrent jurisdiction with the sheriff court to try less serious crimes when a trial on indictment by solemn procedure (i.e. before a judge and jury of 15) is deemed appropriate by the prosecutor.[35] It was empowered to sit as an appellate court in 1926, the normal quorum being three,[36] and it too has power to regulate its own internal procedure by way of Acts of Adjournal.

The sheriff courts, which go back at least as far as the twelfth century, are presently regulated by the Sheriff Courts (Scotland) Acts 1907 and 1971, as updated and amended by the Courts Reform (Scotland) Act 2014 ("the 2014 Act"). The jurisdiction of a sheriff, although confined in the main to their particular districts, is extensive, encompassing both civil and criminal matters.[37] In civil cases, the sheriff court has *exclusive* competence in all causes worth less than £100,000.[38] Scotland is divided into six sheriffdoms, each headed by a sheriff principal; each sheriffdom, bar one,[39] is then subdivided into sheriff court districts based on the principal towns within the sheriffdom. For each district, there is at least one sheriff, the total number depending on the level of work involved. In general, the territorial jurisdiction of a sheriff is restricted to their **8–05**

---

[33] The maximum number of Court of Session judges that may now be appointed, including the Lord President and Lord Justice Clerk, is 35: Court of Session Act 1988 s.1 (increased from 34 by the Maximum Number of Judges (Scotland) Order 2016). Temporary judges may also be appointed to sit in the Court of Session in terms of the Law Reform (Miscellaneous Provisions) (Scotland) Act 1990 s.35. There are, at the time of writing, 13 such temporary judges: *http://www.scotland-judiciary.org.uk/Upload/Documents/ListofTemporaryJudgesJanuary2019.pdf* [Accessed 5 June 2020]. Such temporary judges must now be current or former judicial officer holders; the practice of appointing senior members of the Bar was ended by Lord President Gill: *http://www.scotland-judiciary.org.uk/Upload/Documents/GuidanceTempJudges6Feb2013.pdf* [Accessed 5 June 2020].

[34] Criminal Procedure (Scotland) Act 1995 s.124.

[35] A prosecution will be brought in the High Court if a sentence of more than five years' imprisonment is sought, since the sheriff courts may only imprison convicted persons for up to five years. Where a sheriff considers that a sentence of five years is inadequate following conviction in the sheriff court, they may remit the case to the High Court for sentence.

[36] Criminal Procedure (Scotland) Act 1995 ss.103 and 104. Where an appeal is taken against sentence only, it is normally heard by only two judges.

[37] Broadly, the civil jurisdiction of the sheriff courts covers small claims, summary causes and ordinary causes, the distinction between the three depending on the value of the claim involved. In criminal matters, the sheriff has jurisdiction to try all crimes other than the pleas of the Crown and may conduct trials in accordance with summary or solemn procedure (i.e. in the latter case, with a jury).

[38] s.39 of the 2014 Act.

[39] Glasgow and Strathkelvin, which only sits at Glasgow Sheriff Court (making it one of the busiest courts in Europe).

particular district or sheriffdom. That had the effect that certain orders, for example an interdict, would have effect only within the sheriffdom. That was one of the issues addressed by the 2014 Act, with a sheriff now having power to grant an interdict having effect beyond the boundary of his or her sheriffdom.[40] The 2014 Act also introduced, for the first time, "all-Scotland" jurisdiction for the sheriff court in certain circumstances. Under s.41 of the 2014 Act the Scottish Ministers can now confer "all-Scotland" jurisdiction upon specified sheriff courts in relation to specific issues. Only one such jurisdiction has thus far been created: Edinburgh Sheriff Court now has all-Scotland jurisdiction in relation to personal injury claims.[41] That court also has the power (previously reserved to the Court of Session) to hear civil jury trials.[42]

The judiciary immediately above and below the sheriff court was also reformed by the 2014 Act. By s.5 of the 2014 Act, the office of summary sheriff was created. The appointment process is similar to that of a sheriff (Her Majesty makes the appointment on the recommendation of the First Minister). A summary sheriff has both civil and criminal jurisdiction. Schedule 1 prescribes the civil jurisdiction of a summary sheriff, which includes a wide range of family and child law cases and simple procedure proceedings.[43] In relation to criminal matters, there is a general conferral of the jurisdiction and powers that a sheriff has under the Criminal Procedure (Scotland) Act 1995, but that is then immediately restricted to summary matters.[44] Jurisdiction has also been conferred upon summary sheriffs in relation to fatal accident inquiries.[45]

Appeals from a sheriff (or a summary sheriff) now lie with the newly created Sheriff Appeal Court. That court was established by the 2014 Act[46] and replaced the previous right of appeal to the sheriff principal.[47] The Sheriff Appeal Court has "all such powers as are, under the law of Scotland, inherently possessed by a court of law" to allow it to discharge its jurisdiction and give effect to its decisions.[48] Unlike decisions of the sheriffs principal that were binding only within the sheriffdom of the sheriff principal concerned, decisions of the Sheriff Appeal Court are binding on any sheriff (including summary sheriff) or justice of the peace anywhere in Scotland.[49] They are also binding upon the Sheriff Appeal Court itself, unless it has convened as a larger bench.[50] Each sheriff principal is

---

[40] s.84 of the 2014 Act, read with s.40 of the 2014 Act (the latter being the more general jurisdictional provision for the sheriff court).

[41] All-Scotland Sheriff Court (Sheriff Personal Injury Court) Order 2015/213.

[42] Pt 3, Ch.1 of the 2014 Act. Note that, unlikely solemn criminal proceedings, a civil jury consists of 12.

[43] See also: s.44 of the 2014 Act.

[44] s.45(2)–(3) of the 2014 Act. A summary sheriff can take some formal steps in relation to solemn proceedings but nothing of substance (s.45(3)).

[45] Inquiries into Fatal Accidents and Sudden Deaths etc. (Scotland) Act 2016 s.38.

[46] s.46 of the 2014 Act.

[47] s.109 of the 2014 Act. Some enactments still confer a right of appeal to the Sheriff Principal and that jurisdiction generally endures. In those cases, a right of appeal lies to the Court of Session and not the Sheriff Appeal Court (s.114 of the 2014 Act).

[48] s.47(3) of the 2014 Act.

[49] s.48(1) of the 2014 Act.

[50] s.48(1)(c) of the 2014 Act. That suggests that in time, when a decision of the Sheriff Appeal Court is challenged in a subsequent case, a larger bench of the Sheriff Appeal Court may convene rather than remitting the appeal to the Court of Session.

automatically an appeal sheriff.[51] In addition, the Lord President may appoint sheriffs, who have held office as such for at least five years, to be appeal sheriffs.[52] In practice, this is a part-time appointment. There is no limit on the number of appeal sheriffs that can be appointed.[53]

An appeal lies from the Sheriff Appeal Court to the Court of Session. It is, however, restricted. Only a final judgment can be appealed and then only with the leave of the Sheriff Appeal Court, failing which, the permission of the Court of Session.[54] The requirement that it be a final judgement is significant. In practice, it means that a defender who insists upon their preliminary plea at debate and, whether having won or lost before sheriff, happens to lose the argument before the Sheriff Appeal Court, there is no further right of appeal. That absolute prohibition seems unnecessary and, in novel cases, liable to create absurd results. For example, a defender could be fixed by the Sheriff Appeal Court with a finding that a duty of care was owed in novel circumstances and there would be no right to appeal to the Inner House unless a proof was run and lost before the sheriff. That is not consistent with the efficient determination of the case. If *Donoghue v Stevenson* were to have arisen for the first time now, it would never have made the Supreme Court as the exclusive jurisdiction of the sheriff would have required it to be raised there and no appeal beyond the Sheriff Appeal Court would have been permitted without a proof. A limited right to seek permission to appeal to the Court of Session would have seemed more reasonable.

More local still are the justice of the peace courts, established by Pt 4 of the Criminal Proceedings etc. (Reform) (Scotland) Act 2007, which also provided for the previous network of district courts.[55] The jurisdiction of a justice of the peace is limited to minor offences and certain local administrative matters. Whilst the justice is (legally) lay, they sit with a legally qualified clerk when hearing cases.

TRIBUNALS[56]

Introduction

Sitting alongside the traditional court system is a developing tribunal system. **8–06**
Tribunals have two primary advantages over the court system: they can adapt their procedures to the particular type of dispute that they determine and they can develop an experience and specialism in particular areas that the judiciary in mainstream courts could not. A particular benefit is their membership. Whilst many have a legally qualified member (in the UK system, referred to as a tribunal judge but in Scotland as a legal member), they often have non-legal members. So,

---

[51] s.49 of the 2014 Act.

[52] s.50(1) and (3) of the 2014 Act.

[53] s.50(2) of the 2014 Act. A sheriff can be removed from office as an appeal sheriff by the Lord President so long as he has the consent of a majority of the sheriffs principal (s.50(7)). Removal from the office of appeal sheriff under that provision does not affect that person's continuing appointment as a sheriff (s.50(8)).

[54] s.113(1) of the 2014 Act.

[55] Criminal Proceedings etc. (Reform) (Scotland) Act 2007 s.64.

[56] This section benefitted greatly from a lecture given by the Rt. Hon. Lady Smith, President of the Scottish Tribunals, to the Faculty of Advocates on 28 April 2018.

for example, the tax tribunal may have an accountant and the social security tribunal a medical member. That flexibility in membership brings a breadth of experience a conventional court would never possess. Primarily, tribunals determine appeals by citizens against a decision of the state (in relation to entitlement to benefits, liability for tax or immigration status). But they deal with a range of other matters too (and their jurisdiction is expanding). Whilst tribunals, in many instances, lack the formality of courts, they adhere to the same core value: determination of a right by an independent and impartial decision-maker. Before turning to examine the current tribunal structure, it is helpful first to sketch out the history that led to where we are now.

Legislative history

8–07 When the welfare state was born in the early years of the twentieth century, it required to be administered. How was entitlement to the new benefits to be determined? The individual value of the benefits meant the courts were not a realistic forum to resolve such matters. Nor were the courts seen as a suitable environment, there being concern that early decisions had undermined the objection of the welfare reforms.[57] As a result, a range of tribunals emerged. By the 1950s, it was considered necessary to review the operation of the tribunal system with a view to bringing some consistency to the procedures they followed and ensuring an overall cohesion to the structure. In 1957, the Franks Committee, who had been charged with that task, reported.[58] The Committee started from the proposition that tribunals should be considered as adjudicators rather than administrators.[59] In other words, putting it in separation of powers language, they were part of the judiciary rather than the executive. From that, it necessarily flowed that hitherto rights of appeal to the minister were unsustainable. A system that would allow for an appeal from a first instance tribunal to an appellate tribunal was envisaged and there should be no attempt to oust the court's judicial review jurisdiction. Legally qualified chairs, appointed by the Lord Chancellor, were proposed. The recommendations of the Franks Committee were largely implemented in the Tribunals and Inquiries Act 1958, which was, in due course, replaced by the Tribunal and Inquiries Act 1992. Tribunals took on a much more judicial appearance.

In 2000, the then Lord Chancellor commissioned a fresh review of the tribunals system. Under the chairmanship of Sir Andrew Leggatt, it produced a report the following year that urged far-reaching reform.[60] The main problem that Leggatt sought to remedy was the absence of anything that could properly be called a tribunal system. Instead, there were a range of different tribunals, many of which shared the same or similar practices and rules but which did not operate under the one umbrella. The creation of a Tribunals Service, independent of the Lord Chancellor's department, was recommended and a single, two-tier system,

---

[57] For the historical development in further detail, see P. Craig, *Administrative Law*, 8th edn (Sweet & Maxwell, 2016), paras 2–017—2–020 and 9–005—9–012.

[58] *Report of the Committee on Administrative Tribunals and Enquiries* (1957), Cmnd.218.

[59] *Report of the Committee on Administrative Tribunals and Enquiries* (1957), Cmnd.218 at paras 40–42.

[60] Report on the Review of Tribunals by Sir Andrew Leggatt, *Tribunals for Users—One System, One Service*, 16 August 2001.

with different divisions within each tier, was suggested. That would result in a single route of appeal: from the first tier to the second tier and, in limited circumstances, a further appeal to the courts. With that appeal route, which led to the courts, it was suggested that left no place for judicial review. A High Court judge should be appointed as the Senior President of the Tribunals System, with each division having its own president. After an extensive period of consultation, most of Leggatt's recommendations found themselves enacted in the Tribunals, Courts and Enforcement Act 2007. As we shall see in a moment, the exclusive of judicial review did not make it into the Act.

Structure of the tribunals

At present, there are two tribunal structures operating within Scotland.[61] Under the 2007 Act, there is the UK tribunal system and under the 2014 Act there is a Scottish tribunal system that follows broadly the same structure. The root of the division between the two systems can be found in the Scotland Act 1998: matters that are reserved under that Act fall within the UK tribunal system and all other matters (i.e. those that have been devolved[62]) would fall within the Scottish system. The Scottish tribunal system is in a developmental phase and it continues to have new jurisdictions conferred upon it. **8–08**

UK tribunal structure

The tribunal system created by the 2007 Act has the following key characteristics: **8–09**

(a) Two generic tribunals were created: the First-tier Tribunal ("the FTT") and the Upper Tribunal ("the UT"). The UT is generally an appellate tribunal for the FTT.
(b) All existing, and any future, tribunals were intended to be fitted into this general structure. To accommodate that, each was to consist of a range of "chambers". There are currently four chambers to the UT: Administrative Appeals Chamber; Tax and Chancery Chamber; Immigration and Asylum Chamber; and the Lands Chamber. There are currently seven chambers to the FTT: War Pensions and Armed Forces Compensation Chamber; Social Entitlement Chamber; Health, Education and Social Care Chamber; General Regulatory Chamber; Tax Chamber; Immigration and Asylum Chamber; and the Property Chamber.[63]

---

[61] That is a slight over-simplification. There are other tribunals which fall outside the tribunal structure established by the 2007 Act and the 2014 Act (e.g. the Lands Tribunal) but for present purposes, attention is focused on the general framework that has been put in place. At the time of writing, plans were in place to transfer a number of other tribunals into the unified structure but the timescale for implementation has been repeatedly extended.

[62] As is explained at para.6–22, to talk of matters being devolved is slightly misleading: everything is devolved other than that which has been specifically reserved.

[63] That structure is best illustrated, and the jurisdiction of each chamber explained, in the diagram at: *https://www.judiciary.uk/wp-content/uploads/2012/05/tribunals-chart-updated-9-October-2019.pdf* [Accessed 8 June 2020].

(c) Tribunal rules are set by the Tribunal Procedure Committee.[64] That has ensured a greater consistency in approach between the various chambers. The rules require to further the objectives specified in s.22(4) of the 2007 Act, namely: that justice is done; the system is accessible and fair; proceedings are handled quickly and efficiently; rules are both simple and simply expressed; and, where appropriate, responsibility is conferred on members of the FTT or UT for ensuring that proceedings before them are handled quickly and efficiently.[65] The practical result is a set of procedures that are simpler, more flexible and without all the formality of the court processes.

(d) There are a number of mechanisms for checking the decisions made by the FTT and UT. First, both the FTT and UT are permitted to review their own decisions.[66] That can be done by the FTT or UT on its own initiative or on the application of a person who would otherwise have a right of appeal. The FTT may correct accidental errors in the decision (or a record of the decision), amend the reasons given for a decision or set the decision aside.[67] Where the decision is set aside, the FTT must either re-decide the matter or refer it to the UT.[68] Where the UT decides to set aside its decision, it must re-decide the matter itself.[69] The power to review should be used sparingly and only where the original decision was clearly wrong.[70] Second, and more conventionally, there is a right of appeal. From the FTT, there is a right of appeal to the UT on a point of law.[71] That right is subject to obtaining permission from the FTT, failing which the UT.[72] Like the right of review, there are certain prescribed decisions against which an appeal does not lie.[73] Where the UT finds there was an error of law, it has a *discretion* to set aside the decision of the FTT.[74] In other words, if an error does not invalidate the decision of the FTT it can be allowed to stand. An appeal against the UT lies to the Court of Session (or, in England and Wales and Northern Ireland, the respective Courts of Appeal).[75] Again, permission is required from the UT, failing which the court.[76] Where permission is sought to appeal a decision of the UT that is itself a decision on an appeal from the FTT, the test for granting permission is the "second appeals test", namely, that the proposed appeal would raise some important point of principle or practice or that there is some other compelling reason for the

---

[64] 2007 Act s.22. The detailed process for making the rules is contained in sch.5 to the 2007 Act.

[65] On the characteristics of tribunals generally, see M.H. Dewart, *The Scottish Legal System*, 6th edn, (Bloomsbury Professional, 2019), para.4.30.

[66] 2007 Act, ss.9 and 10. There are a few limited exclusions prescribed by s.11(5).

[67] ss.9(4) and 10(4) of the 2007 Act.

[68] s.9(5) of the 2007 Act.

[69] s.10(5) of the 2007 Act.

[70] *R (on the application of RB) v First-tier Tribunal (Review)* [2010] UKUT 160 (AAC); [2010] M.H.L.R. 192, as approved by the Supreme Court in *R (on the application of Modaresi) v Secretary of State for Health* [2013] UKSC 53; [2013] 4 All E.R. 318 at [11].

[71] s.11 of the 2007 Act.

[72] s.11(3) of the 2007 Act.

[73] s.11(5) of the 2007 Act.

[74] s.12(2) of the 2007 Act.

[75] ss.13(1) and (12) of the 2007 Act.

[76] s.13(3) of the 2007 Act.

court to hear the appeal.[77] What is meant by an error of law and the second appeals test are considered further below.

(e) A judicial review jurisdiction has been conferred upon the UT.[78] In certain circumstances the Court of Session can be required, and in a wider set of circumstances it has a discretion, to transfer a judicial review petition to the UT.[79] In practice, this rarely happens.[80] When exercising this jurisdiction, the UT has the same powers, and must apply the same principles, as the Court of Session would have when determining an application to its supervisory jurisdiction.[81]

Scottish tribunal structure

In Scotland, the tribunal structure was reshaped by the Tribunals (Scotland) Act 2014. It adopts the same two-tier approach of the UK tribunals. There is a First Tier Tribunal ("the SFTT") and an Upper Tribunal ("the SUT"). Currently only the SFTT is split into chambers.[82] Generally, the Scottish tribunals deal with matters that have not been reserved to Westminster under the devolution settlement. In other words, they deal with matters within devolved competence. As that has expanded, the tribunal has had to expand (e.g. the devolution of income tax powers necessitated the Tax Chamber). Whilst the Lord President is the head of the Scottish Tribunals, there is a President of the Scottish Tribunals, who is appointed by the Lord President, and who has practical responsibility for Scottish Tribunals.[83] The guiding principle for the Scottish Tribunals is set out in s.12(3) of the 2014 Act: **8–10**

> "The principle is the need for proceedings before the Scottish Tribunals—
> (a) to be accessible and fair, and
> (b) to be handled quickly and effectively."

Sheriffs are ex officio members of the SFTT.[84] Sheriffs (but not part-time sheriffs) are also ex officio members of the SUT, as are judges of the Court of Session.[85] Otherwise, membership of the tribunals (it can be ordinary, that is lay, legal or judicial members) is by appointment and the criteria is prescribed by the 2014 Act.[86] Similar provision is made to allow certain judicial review cases to be transferred from the Court of Session to the SUT.[87] A duty equivalent to that imposed by s.1 of the Judiciary and Courts (Scotland) Act 2008 is imposed with

[77] So far as appeals to the Court of Session are concerned, s.13(6A), read with s.13(7) of the 2007 Act.
[78] 2007 Act s.15.
[79] 2007 Act s.20.
[80] No orders have yet been made which would require a mandatory transfer to the UT.
[81] 2007 Act s.21.
[82] The SFTT consists, at the time of writing, of the General Regulatory Chamber, Health and Education Chamber, Housing and Property Chamber, the Social Security Chamber and the Tax Chamber.
[83] The first, and current, President of the Scottish Tribunals is the Rt. Hon. Lady Smith.
[84] s.17(1) of the 2014 Act.
[85] s.17(2) of the 2014 Act.
[86] s.32 of and Schs 3 and 5 to the 2014 Act.
[87] Tribunals (Scotland) Act 2014 s.57.

respect to members of the tribunals.[88] Provision is made to appeal a decision of the SUT to the Court of Session. Such an appeal must be on a point of law and with the permission of the SUT or, where that has been refused, the Court of Session. Permission will only be granted where there are "arguable grounds for the appeal".[89] Nothing is said of judicial review in the Act, but it is to be expected that it will remain available with respect to un-appealable decisions of the Upper Tribunal for Scotland. At the time of writing, the process of transferring existing tribunals into the Scottish structure is ongoing.[90]

Other tribunals

8–11 Not all tribunals are within the structure outlined above. The most obvious anomaly remains the Employment Tribunal, which remains outside the new tribunal system. In Scotland, the Mental Health Tribunal and the Lands Tribunal are the two most obvious examples. Plans are in place for those each to be transferred into the Scottish tribunals, but a firm date is not available at the time of writing. There are yet other bodies that exercise adjudicative functions that remain wholly independent of the tribunals structure. For example, the Medical Practitioners Tribunal, which is responsible for the determination of regulatory complaints against doctors, is an independent body that plays no part of the tribunals structure. Most other professional regulators are in the same position.

Appeals and judicial review

8–12 Ultimately, the tribunal system (whether the UK or the Scottish system) links back into the court structure. It does so in two ways. First, there is an inbuilt appeal route from the tribunal to the court. Second, as an "inferior court or tribunal", they are subject to the supervisory jurisdiction of the court.[91] In relation to both, however, restrictions are imposed on resort to the court so that the aim of the tribunal system to provide a quick, cost effective and fair decision cannot be thwarted by resort to conventional litigation (with the costs, and often delays, that comes with it).

Appeals to the court

8–13 As we have just seen, an appeal on a point of law lies to the Court of Session (or, where appropriate, the Court of Appeal). That right is subject to two significant restrictions. First, an appeal is restricted to a point of law. Most obviously, that excludes an appeal that simply challenges the findings of fact. But, as is discussed in Ch.15 in more detail, if the error of fact is glaring enough, it can properly be considered a point of law.[92] Such cases are, however, rare. What constitutes a question of law, in the context of an appeal from the tribunals, can

[88] Tribunals (Scotland) Act 2014 s.3.

[89] Tribunals (Scotland) Act 2014 s.48.

[90] For the current position, see: *https://www.gov.scot/policies/access-to-justice/tribunals-system/* [Accessed 5 June 2020].

[91] On judicial review generally, see Ch.14.

[92] See para.15–05 and cases discussed therein.

also be controversial. In *R (Jones) v First-tier Tribunal* the Supreme Court explained that, to some extent, where a particular statutory scheme had been entrusted to the tribunals, they should be allowed to develop guidance on the meaning and application of the scheme, under the supervision of the UT.[93] Part of that supervisory role required the UT to ensure a consistency in the application of any scheme. And it was not for the appellate courts to interfere unnecessarily:

> "A pragmatic approach should be taken to the dividing line between law and fact, so that the expertise of tribunals at the first tier and that of the Upper Tribunal can be used to best effect. An appeal court should not venture too readily into this area by classifying issues as issues of law which are really best left for determination by the specialist appellate tribunals."[94]

Second, before permission to appeal is granted, it is necessary to satisfy the second appeal test. For permission to be granted, the proposed appeal requires to raise some important point of principle or practice or that there is some other compelling reason for the court to hear the appeal. Those ideas were explained by Lord Hope in *Eba*:

> "Underlying the first of these concepts [some important point of principle or practice] is the idea that the issue would require to be one of general importance, not one confined to the petitioner's own facts and circumstances. The second [some other compelling reason] would include circumstances where it was clear that the decision was perverse or plainly wrong or where, due to some procedural irregularity, the petitioner had not had a fair hearing at all."[95]

It has been said that it will be a rare case that will satisfy that test.[96] That is because it is not enough for an appellant to show that something has gone wrong in their case. They must show either that it has gone very badly wrong so that they did not have a fair hearing or what did go wrong would affect cases beyond their own. It would be a concern if mistakes like that were anything other than rare. What the test does bring is a degree of finality that, when the guiding principle of the tribunals is recalled, is generally a good thing.[97] To those that object that it risks leaving erroneous decisions standing, the answer is in the principle that "a system of law, while it can guarantee to be fair, cannot guarantee to be infallible".[98]

---

[93] [2013] UKSC 19; [2013] 2 A.C. 48 at [41] (Lord Carnwath).

[94] [2013] UKSC 19; [2013] 2 A.C. 48 at [16] (Lord Hope).

[95] *Eba v Advocate General for Scotland* [2011] UKSC 29; 2012 S.C. (U.K.S.C.) 1 at [48] (Lord Hope).

[96] *EP v Secretary of State for the Home Department* [2014] CSIH 30; 2014 S.C. 706 at [26] (Lady Smith).

[97] For some discussion of the need for finality, through the prism of civil disputes, see: Lord Dyson, *Time to call it a day: some reflections on finality and the law*, 14 October 2011, available at: *https://www.supremecourt.uk/docs/speech_111014.pdf* [Accessed 5 June 2020].

[98] *R. (on the application of Cart) v Upper Tribunal* [2011] QB 120 at [36] (Sedley LJ).

Judicial review of the tribunal

8–14 It was proposed by the Leggatt Review that express provision be made to exclude judicial review of un-appealable decisions of the Upper Tribunal.[99] That was not done.[100] In neither the 2007 Act nor the 2014 Act did the legislature attempt to exclude the jurisdiction (to have done so would have required the very clearest of language[101]). Instead the UT was designated a "superior court of record" but despite arguments by the government to the contrary, that did nothing to exclude judicial review.[102] It might asked why judicial review is necessary where an appeal process that feeds into the court system (at appellate level) has been provided for by the legislature. The short answer is to prevent the tribunal becoming a legal island as a result of refusals to grant permission to appeal against decisions where something has obviously gone wrong in the UT or the law has been developed by the tribunals in a way that undermined its overall coherence.[103] But unfettered access to the courts, by means of judicial review, would risk undermining the benefits of the tribunal system and, in particular, the guiding principle set out in the 2014 Act (so far as the Scottish Tribunals are concerned). As Lord Brown put it in *Cart*:

> "The rule of law is weakened, not strengthened, if a disproportionate part of the courts' resources is devoted to finding a very occasional grain of wheat on a threshing floor full of chaff."[104]

The solution settled upon by the Supreme Court was to recognise that unappealable decisions of the UT were subject to judicial review. But permission should only be granted where the same conditions are met for the granting of leave to appeal from the Upper Tribunal: there is some important point of principle or some other compelling reason.[105] By that means, the filter that controls access to the court system is the same, whether the access point is a right

---

[99] Review of Tribunals, *Tribunals for Users: One System, One Service*, para.6.30–6.34.

[100] Standing what was said in *R (on the application of Privacy International) v Investigatory Powers Tribunal* [2019] UKSC 22; [2019] 2 W.L.R. 1219 at [144] by Lord Carnwath, is must now be considered doubtful whether such a provision would be effective. See further, para.14–03.

[101] See: *R. (on the application of Cart) v Upper Tribunal* [2011] UKSC 28; [2012] 1 A.C. 663 at [37] (Lady Hale). See also, on attempts to oust the jurisdiction of the court to review the actions of a tribunal, *R (on the application of Privacy International) v Investigatory Powers Tribunal* [2019] UKSC 22; [2019] 2 W.L.R. 1219. Whether the Scottish Parliament could oust the jurisdiction of the Court of Session is unclear.

[102] Tribunal, Courts and Enforcement Act 2007 s.3(5). This is a term that is unknown to the law of Scotland. For the reasons set out by Laws LJ in the Divisional Court in *R. (on the application of Cart) v Upper Tribunal* [2010] EWCA Civ 859; [2011] Q.B. 120 at [30]–[31] designation as a "superior court of record" did not exclude the Upper Tribunal from the court's judicial review jurisdiction.

[103] *R. (on the application of Cart) v Upper Tribunal* [2011] UKSC 28; [2012] 1 A.C. 663 at [43] (Lady Hale). *R (on the application of Privacy International) v Investigatory Powers Tribunal* [2019] UKSC 22; [2019] 2 W.L.R. 1219 at [99] (Lord Carnwath).

[104] *R. (on the application of Cart) v Upper Tribunal* [2011] UKSC 28; [2012] 1 A.C. 663 at [100]. See also: *Eba v Advocate General for Scotland* [2011] UKSC 29; 2012 S.C. (U.K.S.C.) 1 at [49] (Lord Hope) and *EP v Secretary of State for the Home Department* [2014] CSIH 30; 2014 S.C. 706 at [26] (Lady Smith).

[105] *Eba v Advocate General for Scotland* [2011] UKSC 29; 2012 S.C. (U.K.S.C.) 1, per Lord Hope at [48]; this decision should be read with the decision of the Supreme Court in *R. (on the application of Cart) v Upper Tribunal* [2011] UKSC 28; [2012] 1 A.C. 663 (both appeals were heard together and

of appeal under the legislation or judicial review of an unappealable decision. That prevents judicial review being used to circumvent the overall aim of the legislation. In practice, it is not enough to point to a mistake in the decision below. Any mistakes will be expected to have consequences beyond the individual case before it will justify the court becoming involved. Judicial review of the First Tier Tribunal (be it UK or Scotland) is rarely likely to be competent given the right of appeal to the Upper Tribunal.[106]

JUDICIARY

Introduction

An independent and impartial judiciary is a basic component of the rule of law. **8–15**
By "judiciary" we no longer mean simply the judges that staff our courts. As we have just seen, a vast swath of decisions is in fact taken in tribunals rather than courts. But to have confidence in the adjudicative process, it is important users have confidence that the decision maker was free from external pressures and acted in a fair manner. And it is not just the parties to any particular dispute that need that confidence. As we saw at the start of this chapter, a functioning judicial system is of benefit to the whole of society and thus the whole of society must have confidence in the system that is in place. That independence and impartiality is readily accepted. In what follows, we consider the structures in place to ensure that they are secured.

Judicial independence

"Independence of a tribunal is required" explained Lord Carswell in *Kearney v* **8–16**
HM Advocate:

> "in order that the public, seeing this, may feel confident in its ability to decide cases without any influence from the Executive being brought to bear or any feeling that it needs to have regard to the views or wishes of the Executive in reaching its decisions."[107]

It is well established in the jurisprudence of the European Court of Human Rights that the way in which judges are appointed, their term of office and security of tenure, their mode of remuneration and the presence or absence of guarantees against outside pressure are all factors relevant to the question of whether the tribunal presents a sufficient appearance of independence.[108] But it would be wrong to think that the importance of judicial independence only arrived with art.6 of the European Convention on Human Rights. It had long been recognised and protected by the common law. The structural independence of the Scottish

---

advised on the same day). See also: *SA v Secretary of State for the Home Department* [2013] CSIH 62; 2014 S.C. 1 and *EP v Secretary of State for the Home Department* [2014] CSIH 30; 2014 S.C. 706.

[106] On the need to exhaust alternative remedies, see para.14–07, below.

[107] *Kearney (Arthur) v HM Advocate* [2005] UKPC D1; 2006 S.C. (P.C.) 1 at [62].

[108] *Findlay v United Kingdom* (1997) 24 E.H.R.R. 221 at p.73.

judiciary has been reinforced in recent years by the Judiciary and Courts (Scotland) Act 2008 and the Courts Reform (Scotland) Act 2014. Both give the Lord President, and the sheriffs principal, responsibility for securing the efficient disposal of business within the courts for which they are responsible.[109]

The Judiciary and Courts (Scotland) Act 2008 placed an obligation upon a number of people, including the First Minister, the Lord Advocate, the Scottish Ministers and Members of the Scottish Parliament, to "uphold the continued independence of the judiciary".[110] This statutory obligation ought not to have been necessary as the importance of an independent judiciary in securing the rule of law in a democratic society should have been obvious to those that fall within the ambit of s.1 of the 2008 Act. Yet the constitutionalising of the courts' role in modern society has increased the occasions where the courts are forced into a position where conflict with the executive appears inevitable. And that was true long before Gina Miller had ever presented an application for judicial review. Respect for the importance of an independent judiciary normally prevents the executive from publically criticising judicial decisions that have gone against them. It is not always the case. To take one example: a series of decisions from the High Court in immigration cases in the early part of this century culminated in an unprecedented outburst by the then Home Secretary, David Blunkett. In response to a decision by the High Court that six asylum seekers were entitled to receive support from the National Asylum Support Service despite having failed, in the view of Home Office officials, to have claimed asylum as soon as was "reasonably practicable"[111] led the Home Secretary to declare he was "fed up" with a situation where "Parliament debates issues and the judges then overturn them".[112] He then stated his view that the judge, Collins J, had got it wrong. On the back of this Collins J found the unwelcome focus of the media's attention.[113]

As Lord Irvine LC put it, speaking extrajudicially:

> "But what about when the court disagrees with the executive? In a democracy under the rule of law, it is not mature to cheer the judges when a win is secured and boo them when a loss is suffered."[114]

It is not only the executive that can be perceived as threatening the independence of the judiciary. They are, however, in a privileged position. Not only do they have ready access to the media but they are involved in the appointment of the judiciary and are responsible for their remuneration. Accordingly, more formal mechanisms are in place to secure the independence of the judiciary from the executive in both of those regards. We will now discuss each of those in turn.

[109] Judiciary and Courts (Scotland) Act 2008 ("the 2008 Act") s.2; 2014 Act ss.27–29.

[110] 2008 Act s.1(1).

[111] *R (on the application of Q) v Secretary of State for the Home Department* [2003] EWHC 195 (Admin).

[112] *The Times*, 20 February 2003.

[113] See the discussion in A. Bradley, "Judicial Independence Under Attack" [2003] P.L. 397; the Court of Appeal upheld the majority of Collins J decision (*R (on the application of Q) v Secretary of State for the Home Department* [2003] EWCA Civ 364; [2004] Q.B. 36) but were not subject to similar comment or coverage. As we saw in Ch.1, whatever spotlight was turned on Collins J, it was nothing compared to that focused on the Divisional Court in *Miller (No.1)*.

[114] Lord Irvine of Lairg, "The Impact of the Human Rights Act: Parliament, the Courts and the Executive" [2003] P.L. 308, 323.

Judicial appointments

Judicial appointments in the United Kingdom were traditionally a matter for the executive, although in Scotland steps were taken, within the limits imposed by the Scotland Act, to introduce a measure of independence and transparency into the process.[115] Judicial appointments are now regulated by statute and designed to ensure that the role of the executive in such appointments is minimised and the process is sufficiently transparent. The appointment of Justices of the Supreme Court is regulated by the Constitutional Reform Act 2005 (as amended by the Tribunal and Enforcement Act 2007 and the Crime and Courts Act 2013). There are to be no more than the equivalent of 12 full-time Justices of the Supreme Court, each appointed by the Queen.[116] One of the Justices may be appointed to be the president of the court and another to be the deputy president.[117] A person is not qualified to be a justice unless they have held high judicial office for a period of at least two years, have satisfied the judicial appointments eligibility condition on a 15-year basis or have been a qualifying practitioner for a period of at least 15 years.[118] "High judicial office", for the purposes of Scotland, means a judge of the Court of Session[119] and a "qualifying practitioner" is one who is an advocate or a solicitor with rights of audience before both the Court of Session and the High Court of Justiciary.[120] Selection is by a commission convened by the Lord Chancellor.[121] That commission, which must have no fewer than five members, is ordinarily chaired by the President of the Supreme Court.[122] It must have a representative of the judicial appointment boards from each part of the United Kingdom.[123] Originally the Deputy President was also a member of the commission, but, as a result of changes introduced by the Crime and Courts Act 2013, the President is required to nominate another senior judge from anywhere within the United Kingdom to sit with him on the commission (and that judge cannot be a fellow Justice of the Supreme Court).[124] Where the commission is convened to recommend a person for appointment as President of the Court, the President is not to be a member of the commission and it is to be chaired by 8–17

[115] See "Judicial Appointments Reform", 2001 S.L.T. (News) 101. Put shortly, before the First Minister put forward any recommendation for appointment to judicial office, he took the advice of a Judicial Appointments Board established in 2002 with the functions of advertising posts, interviewing candidates and drawing up a shortlist of candidates considered suitable for particular appointments.

[116] 2005 Act s.23(2); the Crime and Courts Act 2013 (Sch.13) amended the 2005 Act so as to provide that the Supreme Court shall consist of not more than the full time equivalent of 12 judges and thereby allow for some form of part time working or job sharing by justices. The 2005 Act also makes provisions for appointment of acting judges (s.38) drawn from the supplementary panel (s.39) or from the ranks of Appeal Court judges in England and Wales and Northern Ireland or the Inner House of the Court of Session (s.38(8)).

[117] 2005 Act s.23(5).

[118] 2005 Act s.25(1).

[119] 2005 Act s.60(2).

[120] 2005 Act s.25(2); note the requirement to have rights of audience before both of the supreme courts of Scotland; rights of audience before only one of them is now sufficient to qualify a solicitor advocate for appointment to the Court of Session bench: 2008 Act s.21.

[121] 2005 Act ss.26–27 and Sch.8.

[122] 2005 Act, s.27(1A).

[123] 2005 Act, s.27(1B).

[124] Crime and Courts Act 2013 s.20 and Sch.13, Pt 1, para.4.

non-legally-qualified member.[125] As originally enacted, the commission reported to the Lord Chancellor, who had a limited right to veto a selection or require the commission to reconsider its selection.[126] Now, the name of the person selected by the commission is given to the Prime Minister, who has no option but to recommend the appointment of that individual to the Queen.[127] The sole selection criterion is merit,[128] although the commission making the selection must ensure that the justices of the court, between them, have "knowledge of, and experience of practice in, the law of each part of the United Kingdom".[129] In the House of Lords this translated into a convention that there was ordinarily two Scottish Law Lords and one Northern Irish Law Lord. Thus far, that convention has continued in the Supreme Court.[130] Since 2013, it has been the practice of the Supreme Court to have a justice (an ad hoc member if necessary) with experience in Welsh law when considering devolution matters from Wales.[131]

8–18 Judicial appointments in Scotland are now regulated by a combination of the Scotland Act 1998 and the Judiciary and Courts (Scotland) Act 2008. The Lord President of the Court of Session and the Lord Justice Clerk are appointed by the Queen on the advice of the Prime Minister, although s.95(2) of the Scotland Act provides that the Prime Minister shall not recommend to the Queen the appointment of any person who has not been nominated by the First Minister, and before making any nomination, the First Minister must establish a selection panel in accordance with Sch.2 of the 2008 Act.[132] That panel is responsible for recommending to the First Minister individuals suitable for appointment to the vacant post.[133] The First Minister may not make a nomination under s.95(2) of the Scotland Act until that selection panel has made a recommendation.[134] The criteria for selection is "solely on merit" but the selection panel must also be satisfied that the candidate is "of good character".[135] All other judicial appointments in Scotland (both permanent and part-time) now pass through the hands of the Judicial Appointments Board for Scotland, which was placed on a statutory footing by the 2008 Act.[136] The Board is independent of the Scottish Government and, although judges of the Court of Session, sheriffs principal and

125 2005 Act, s.27(1C) as inserted by Crime and Courts Act 2013 s.20 and Sch.13, Pt 1, para.4.

126 2005 Act ss.28–31. Those provisions were repealed by the Crime and Courts Act 2013, Sch.13(1), para.7.

127 2005 Act s.26(3).

128 2005 Act s.27(5).

129 2005 Act s.27(8).

130 The vacancy that arose following the untimely death of Lord Rodger of Earlsferry was filled by the Scottish judge Lord Reed and the vacancy created by the retirement of Lord Hope of Craighead was filled by another Scot, Lord Hodge. The Northern Irish Justice, Lord Kerr, has served on the court since is beginning.

131 A policy announced by the President of the Supreme Court in a speech to the Institute of Government on 18 June 2013, *http://www.supremecourt.uk/docs/speech-130618.pdf* [Accessed 5 June 2020] at para.20, and which has been adhered to when considered challenges to legislative acts of the Welsh Assembly: see, for example, *Re Agricultural Sector (Wales) Bill* [2014] UKSC 43; [2014] 1 W.L.R. 2622 where the Lord Chief Justice of England and Wales, Lord Thomas sat as an ad hoc justice. Lord Lloyd-Jones is now a permanent member of the court.

132 2008 Act s.19(2).

133 2008 Act s.19(3).

134 2008 Act s.19(4).

135 2008 Act s.20.

136 2008 Act s.9 and Sch.1.

sheriffs are still appointed by the Queen on the recommendation of the First Minister,[137] an individual cannot be recommended by the First Minister to the Queen unless the Board has recommended their appointment to the office in question.[138] The Board consists of judicial (one Court of Session judge, one sheriff principal and one sheriff), legal (one advocate and one solicitor) and lay members. The number of lay members must be equal to the number of judicial and legal members and the chairman of the board must be a lay member.[139] The Board is charged with recommending to the Scottish Government suitable candidates for appointment to judicial office. The selection criterion is the same as that for the Lord President and Lord Justice Clerk: solely on merit, with the board being satisfied that the individual is of good character.[140] Subject to that criteria, the Board is to have regard to the need to encourage diversity amongst the judiciary.[141] Recommendations are made to the relevant minister who can decide not to accept a recommendation. Where the minister does so, they must give the Board reasons for that decision and the Board must reconsider its recommendation. It can, however, recommend the same individual again.[142]

The 2008 Act does not alter the statutory criteria of eligibility for appointment to judicial office. To be appointed a sheriff principal, sheriff or summary sheriff, a candidate must have been legally qualified as a solicitor or advocate for at least 10 years.[143] The same condition of eligibility applies to the appointment of a person as a part time sheriff (or summary sheriff). This was created in light of the abolition by s.7 of the Bail, Judicial Appointments etc. (Scotland) Act 2000 Act of the office of temporary sheriff following the decision of the High Court of Justiciary in *Starrs v Ruxton*.[144] Under art.19 of the Treaty of Union of 1707, appointments to the Court of Session bench are governed by a requirement of at least five years' standing as a member of the Faculty of Advocates. In 1990, eligibility was extended to sheriffs principal or sheriffs who have held office as such for a continuous period of at least five years, and also to solicitors who have enjoyed rights of audience in either the Court of Session or High Court of Justiciary for at least five years.[145] It is for the Lord President and Lord Justice Clerk, with the consent of the Scottish Ministers and after such consultation with the judges as is appropriate, to make any appointments to the Inner House.[146] **8–19**

It is hard to assess the extent to which the introduction of a statutory appointments process has improved the standing of the judiciary. Whilst greater transparency in the process is to be welcomed, there is limited evidence to say one way or the other whether it has made a qualitative difference. Such research **8–20**

---

[137] Scotland Act 1998 s.95(4). See: *https://www.judicialappointments.scot* [Accessed 5 June 2020].
[138] 2008 Act s.11(1) and Scotland Act 1998 s.95(5).
[139] 2008 Act Sch.1 paras 3–4.
[140] 2008 Act s.12.
[141] 2008 Act s.14.
[142] 2008 Act s.11.
[143] At that time prescribed by Sheriff Courts (Scotland) Act 1971 s.5 but see now s.14 of the Courts Reform (Scotland) Act 2014.
[144] *Starrs v Ruxton*, 2000 J.C. 208.
[145] Law Reform (Miscellaneous Provisions) (Scotland) Act 1990 s.35(1), as amended by s.21 of the 2008 Act. Those provisions are now contained in s.20A of the 2008 Act (as inserted by s.123 of the Courts Reform (Scotland) Act 2014.
[146] Court of Session Act 1988, s.2(6). The Scottish Ministers must be satisfied that the business of the Inner House requires a vacancy to be filled before giving their consent (s.2(8)).

as there is has been done by the Judicial Appointments Board itself. The Board commissioned an external evaluation of itself in 2009 that surveyed the legal profession in Scotland for its views and perceptions of the judicial appointments process. The objective was two-fold: to understand the make-up of the population that is eligible for appointment to judicial office and to understand the factors that encourage or deter eligible candidates from applying.[147] No firm conclusions were drawn from the survey, but it did provide the Board with a better understanding of the composition of the pool of eligible candidates. In relation to diversity, however, there has been an increase in the number of women appointed to the Court of Session bench, but still only 10 of the 35 current Senators are women.

Tenure and pay

8–21 At common law, it was presumed that a judicial office was held *ad vitam aut culpam* ("for life or until blame").[148] Statute now provides that judicial office holders shall retire at the age of 70, albeit there is provision for a judge to continue to sit on a part-time basis, as a retired judge, until the age of 75.[149] Justices of the Supreme Court hold office "during good behaviour" and may be removed only on the address of both Houses of Parliament.[150] Judges of the Court of Session (and the Chairman of the Scottish Land Court) may be removed by the Queen, on the recommendation of the First Minister, if they have been found to be unfit for office on account of inability, neglect of duty or misbehaviour.[151] On the same grounds, a sheriff can be removed from office by the First Minister.[152] To secure the independence of the judiciary, strict procedures are prescribed before a judicial office holder can be removed from office.[153] These procedures are designed to insulate the judiciary, so far as possible, from political pressures and the threat of removal for political reasons. We have already seen how tempting it can be for politicians to launch attacks upon the judiciary. It is important that the judiciary should have nothing to fear. Chapter 5 of Pt 2 of the Judiciary and Courts (Scotland) Act 2008 now makes provision for the procedures to be followed before a judge of the Court of Session may be removed from office. This fulfilled the requirement of the Scotland Act, initially met by

[147] MVA Consultancy for the Judicial Appointments Board for Scotland, *Continuous Improvement: An Analysis of Scotland's Judicial Appointments Process* (Edinburgh: MVA Consultancy, 2009) *http://www.judicialappointmentsscotland.org.uk/Publications/Research_Projects2/Continuous_Improvement_An_Analysis_of_Scotland_s_Judicial_Appointments_Process_-_Volume_1_-_October_2009__final_.pdf* [Accessed 5 June 2020].

[148] *Mackay and Esslemont v Lord Advocate*, 1937 S.C. 860.

[149] Judicial Pensions and Retirement Act 1993 s.26; Judiciary and Courts (Scotland) Act 2008 s.20E; Courts Reform (Scotland) Act 2014 s.12; Constitutional Reform Act 2005 s.39.

[150] 2005 Act s.33. They may resign at any time (and the President and Deputy President can resign from that office without resigning as a Justice): s.35.

[151] Scotland Act 1998 s.95(6)–(8).

[152] Courts Reform (Scotland) Act 2014 s.25.

[153] As the Supreme Court of Canada put it in *Valente v The Queen* [1985] 2 S.C.R. 673; (1985) 24 D.L.R. (4th) 161 at p.31: "The essence of security of tenure . . . is a tenure, whether until an age of retirement, for a fixed term, or for a specific adjudicative task, that is secure against interference by the Executive or other appointing authority in a discretionary or arbitrary manner."

statutory instrument, to make such provision.[154] The 2008 Act also made provision for shrieval office holders that have since been replaced by fresh provisions in the Courts Reform (Scotland) Act 2014.[155]

The First Minister is required to constitute a tribunal to investigate and report on whether a judicial office holder is unfit to hold that office where the Lord President requests that they do so or in such other circumstances as the First Minister themselves thinks fit, having first consulted the Lord President.[156] Where a tribunal is constituted to investigate and report upon a judge of the Court of Session it shall consist of two members who have held high judicial office[157] (at least one of whom shall be, or have been, a judge of the Court of Session),[158] an advocate or a solicitor of at least 10 years' standing and an individual who has never held high judicial office and has never been an advocate or a solicitor.[159] Where a tribunal is constituted to investigate and report on the holder of shrieval office, it shall consist of one member who is a qualifying member of the Judicial Committee of the Privy Council (who shall chair the tribunal and have a casting vote),[160] one member who holds the same shrieval office as the person under investigation, and an advocate or a solicitor of at least 10 years' standing and an individual who has never been a qualifying member of the Judicial Committee of the Privy Council, nor held shrieval office nor ever been an advocate or a solicitor.[161] The selection of members of such a tribunal is to be made by the First Minister with the consent of the Lord President, unless it is the Lord President under investigation, in which case the consent of the Lord Justice Clerk must be obtained.[162] Where the Lord President has requested that a tribunal be constituted, they may suspend the person who is to be subject to investigation from office until they order otherwise.[163] This power is in addition to the Lord President's power under s.34 of the 2008 Act to suspend a judicial officer holder where it is necessary for the purpose of maintaining public confidence in the judiciary. The tribunal may, prior to reporting to the First Minister, recommend that the person subject to their investigation be suspended.[164] Where the First Minister receives such a recommendation, they have a discretion as to whether to suspend the person under investigation.[165] The tribunal has the power to compel the attendance of any person to give evidence or to produce documents in their 8–22

[154] Scotland Act 1998 s.95(8); Scotland Act (Transitory and Transitional Provisions) (Removal of Judges) Order 1999 (SI 1999/1017).

[155] 2014 Act ss.21–25, replacing the provisions that were made by the s.40 of the 2008 Act. There is now a process for handling complaints against the judiciary which are now handled in accordance with the Complaints about the Judiciary (Scotland) Rules 2015.

[156] 2008 Act s.35(1); 2014 Act s.21(1) and (2); references to the 2008 Act relate to the provisions that concern judges of the Court of Session (including the Lord President and the Lord Justice Clerk) or the Chairman of the Scottish Land Court whereas references to the 2014 Act relate to the provisions that concern holders of shrieval office.

[157] As defined by s.60(2) of the 2005 Act.

[158] 2008 Act s.35(7).

[159] 2008 Act s.35(4).

[160] 2014 Act s.21(7).

[161] 2014 Act s.21(4).

[162] 2008 Act s.35(8); 2014 Act s.21(6).

[163] 2008 Act s.36(1); 2014 Act s.22(2).

[164] 2008 Act s.36(3); 2014 Act s.22(4).

[165] 2008 Act s.36(5); 2014 Act s.22(5).

possession or under their control[166] and the procedure to be followed by such a tribunal may be prescribed by Act of Sederunt.[167] Having concluded their investigation the tribunal must submit a written report to the First Minister, which must then be laid before the Scottish Parliament, setting out the conclusions of the tribunal and their reasons for reaching those conclusions.[168] Where the tribunal has concluded that a holder of shrieval office is unfit to hold that office, the First Minister may then remove that person by order made by statutory instrument.[169] A similar conclusion in relation to a temporary judge of the Court of Session empowers the First Minister to remove that person from office.[170] Where a judge of the Court of Session has been found by the tribunal to be unfit to hold that office, the First Minister may recommend to the Queen that the individual be removed from office, but only after the Scottish Parliament, on the First Minister's motion, has resolved that she should make such a recommendation.[171]

8–23 What was not provided for, at least prior to the enactment of the Senior Judiciary (Vacancies and Incapacity) (Scotland) Act 2006, was the maintenance of the orderly conduct of judicial business in circumstances where either of Scotland's two senior judges, the Lord President and the Lord Justice Clerk, was incapacitated, or either office was vacant by reason of death, resignation or removal. As the administrative functions of the Lord President increased, it became more important to ensure continuity at the senior end of the judiciary. The illness of the then Lord President, Lord Hamilton, in 2006 saw emergency legislation, in the form of the Senior Judiciary (Vacancies and Incapacity) (Scotland) Act 2006, introduced in the Scottish Parliament. The Bill completed its parliamentary process in a single day. That Act has since been repealed and its provisions broadly replicated in Ch.2 of Pt 2 of the 2008 Act. In the event of incapacity, the 2008 Act makes provision for a written declaration to that effect to be given to the First Minister by a majority of the total number of judges of the Inner House of the Court of Session.[172] That starts a procedure that is triggered automatically in the event of a vacancy arising. Where the Lord President is unable to act, or their office is vacant, their functions shall be carried out by the Lord Justice Clerk, and those of the Lord Justice Clerk shall, in turn, be carried out by the senior Inner House judge. Provision is also made in s.6 of the 2008 Act for a situation in which neither the Lord President nor the Lord Justice Clerk is able to act by reason of incapacity or an event giving rise to a vacancy. The special procedures are brought to an end either by a vacancy being filled in the ordinary way, or, in the case of incapacity, by a majority of the total number of judges of the Inner House judges giving a written declaration to the First Minister to the effect that they are satisfied that the incapacity has been overcome.

166 2008 Act s.37(1); 2014 Act s.23(1).
167 2008 Act s.37(5); 2014 Act s.23(5). No such Act of Sederunt has yet been made.
168 2008 Act s.38; 2014 Act s.24.
169 2014 Act s.25.
170 2008 Act s.39.
171 Scotland Act 1998 s.95(7).
172 Where that declaration concerns the Lord President, the judges making such a declaration must include the Lord Justice Clerk (s.4(4)). The converse is true: any declaration concerning the Lord Justice Clerk must include the Lord President (s.5(4)).

The tenure of those appointed to judicial office on a temporary basis caused some problems after devolution. Tenure of judicial office is clearly a necessary adjunct of judicial independence, and although Parliament may (and does) override the presumption of the common law, any limitations on tenure must not be such as to undermine the appearance of a tribunal's independence.[173] Thus in *Starrs v Ruxton*,[174] the High Court of Justiciary held that, although the initial appointment of temporary sheriffs by the executive was not inherently objectionable, the brevity of their term of office (only one year), coupled with the power (albeit unused) under s.11 of the Sheriff Courts (Scotland) Act 1971 to recall a temporary sheriff's commission and the practice of appointing permanent sheriffs from the pool of temporary sheriffs, was fatal to the compatibility of the system with the right to a fair hearing before an independent and impartial tribunal under art.6 of the Convention. This caused significant practical difficulties at the time. The Lord Advocate, in whose name all prosecutions are brought, was required by s.57(2) of the Scotland Act 1998 to act in a manner that was compatible with Convention rights. Bringing, or continuing, a prosecution before a temporary sheriff was not so compatible. The Lord Advocate, or the local procurator fiscals on his behalf, therefore had no power to continuing criminal prosecutions before temporary sheriffs. A similar challenge to temporary judges in the High Court of Justiciary, who were appointed for a three year term, failed in *Kearney v HM Advocate*[175] as did a challenge to temporary judges in the Court of Session in *Clancy v Caird*.[176] As Lord Sutherland made clear in *Clancy*, there is no inherent objection to a fixed term appointment: **8–24**

> "... [T]here can be no objection per se to the appointment of judges for a fixed term, provided that during that period there is security of tenure which guarantees against interference by the executive in a discretionary or arbitrary manner."[177]

Both as a matter of fact and law, temporary judges of the Court of Session do enjoy security of tenure during their term of office. Their independence and impartiality on that ground, at least, was therefore unimpeachable. The decision in *Starrs* led to the commissions of all temporary sheriffs being revoked and provision made in the Bail, Judicial Appointments etc. (Scotland) Act 2000 for their replacement by a new body of part-time sheriffs.[178] Those provisions are now found in the Courts Reform (Scotland) Act 2014. Part-time sheriffs, the

---

[173] For the approach of the European Court of Human Rights to this question, see *Campbell v United Kingdom* (1984) 7 E.H.R.R. 165. The test is an objective one: whether there are grounds for reasonable apprehension that the tribunal is not independent. On that basis, the court held a prison board of visitors to constitute an independent and impartial tribunal, even though its members were appointed for fixed terms of three years and were as a matter of law removable from office. The court accepted, however, that as a matter of fact if not of law the government treated members as irremovable during their terms of office.

[174] *Starrs v Ruxton*, 2000 J.C. 208.

[175] *Kearney v HM Advocate* [2005] UKPC D1; 2006 S.C. (P.C.) 1.

[176] *Clancy v Caird*, 2000 S.C. 441.

[177] *Clancy v Caird*, 2000 S.C. 441 at [6].

[178] Sheriff Courts (Scotland) Act 1971 s.11A (as inserted by Bail, Judicial Appointments etc. (Scotland) Act 2000 s.7).

number of which was previously capped at 80,[179] sit for between 20 and 100 days in any one year and they are appointed for a five-year term, which is ordinarily renewable.[180]

It is not only the security of a judge's tenure that underpins their independence. The terms of their remuneration are also relevant to the question. The Act of Settlement of 1700, which was incorporated into Scots law by the Treaty of Union, provides that judicial salaries must be "ascertained and established"—in other words, not subject to executive discretion. The remuneration of Court of Session judges, sheriffs principal, sheriffs, members of the Lands Tribunal for Scotland and the Chairman of the Scottish Land Court is reserved to Westminster by para.L1 of Sch.5 to the Scotland Act, but payment of the salaries thus fixed is charged on the Scottish consolidated fund.[181] Parliamentary authority for the payment of judicial salaries is deemed to be permanent and does not require to be reviewed and renewed each year.[182] During their term of office, a judge's salary may be increased, but it may not be reduced.[183]

Judicial impartiality

8–25 Closely related to the idea of judicial independence is judicial impartiality.[184] Impartiality is fundamental to the integrity of the judicial role. If a judge has an interest of some kind in the outcome of proceedings before them, they must decline jurisdiction to decide the matter (or at the very least disclose their interest to the parties, so that the parties can decide whether to waive any objection). As Lord Hewart CJ famously put it, it is "of fundamental importance that justice should not only be done but should manifestly and undoubtedly be seen to be done".[185] The great difficulty in this area, as the more recent case law illustrates, is identifying at what point a judge's personal opinions, beliefs, relationships (personal or professional) cross the line into disqualifying bias. The devolution settlement and the incorporation of the Convention into national law have conferred on the judiciary a crucially important, and politically sensitive,

---

179 Sheriff Courts (Scotland) Act 1971 s.11A(5). That provision, along with the rest of the 1971 Act, was repealed by the 2014 Act.

180 2014 Act ss.8 and 9.

181 In relation to shrieval office holders, see 2014 Act s.16(13).

182 Note, however, that in terms of the 2014 Act s.16, part time sheriffs are paid by the Scottish Ministers, at a rate determined by them, out of moneys earmarked for the Justice Department of the Scottish Government.

183 2005 Act s.34(4) (for Justices of the Supreme Court).

184 They are separate and distinct concepts although not always readily differentiated. See, for example, the discussion in *Starrs v Ruxton*, 2000 J.C. 208, per Lord Prosser at [232] ("The two concepts appear to me to be inextricably interlinked, and I do not myself find it useful to try and separate the one from the other"); and per Lord Reed at [252]–[253] ("I do not regard it as necessary to attempt an exhaustive definition of the concepts of independence and impartiality or to define the distinction between them") and the judgement of Lord Carswell in *Kearney v HM Advocate* [2005] UKPC D1; 2006 S.C. (P.C.) 1 at [56]–[64].

185 *R. v Sussex Justices, Ex p. McCarthy* [1924] 1 K.B. 256 at p.259. For a comparative discussion, see S. Sedley, "When should a judge not be a judge?" (2011) 22 *London Review of Books*. Available online at: *https://www.lrb.co.uk/the-paper/v33/n01/stephen-sedley/when-should-a-judge-not-be-a-judge* [Accessed 5 June 2020].

jurisdiction that places a higher premium than ever on their impartiality.[186] The former Lord Chancellor, Lord Mackay of Clashfern, adverted to this when, looking ahead to the adoption of a human rights charter in the United Kingdom and the consequent involvement of judges in "political" decision making, he remarked:

> "The question which would then be asked, and to which an answer could not be postponed indefinitely, is whether the introduction of such a political element into the judicial function would require a change in the criteria for appointing judges, making the political stance of each candidate a matter of importance as much as his or her ability to decide cases on their individual facts and the law applicable to those facts. Following on from that is the question of how confidence in judicial independence and impartiality can be maintained, and whether their appointment should be subjected to political scrutiny of the sort seen in the United States."[187]

The very debate reveals the special value we place, and have always placed, on the impartiality of the judiciary. It is for this reason that judges are disqualified from membership of the House of Commons and Scottish Parliament.[188] Similarly, convention requires a judge to dissociate themselves from party political matters.[189] A previous political career, whether as MP, MSP or Law Officer, is no bar to judicial appointment, although in certain situations, for example where a judge is called upon to rule judicially on the meaning and effect of legislation that they drafted or that, as Lord Advocate or Solicitor General, they promoted during its parliamentary passage, they will be unable to sit compatibly with art.6 of the Convention.[190] **8–26**

It is well established that where a judge has a direct pecuniary or proprietary interest in the outcome of a case before them, they are automatically disqualified from sitting.[191] Thus in *Dimes v Proprietors of the Grand Junction Canal*,[192] the Lord Chancellor was held to be disqualified from affirming a judgment of the **8–27**

---

[186] It has been argued that human rights protection, at least, does not draw the courts into matters of political controversy: the judicial role here is simply to define the sphere within which legislature and executive have a free hand. "[Rights] may not be submitted to the vote; they depend on the outcome of no elections", per Jackson J, *Virginia State Board of Education v Barnette* (1943) 319 U.S. 624. But it is difficult to reconcile this view with the very real controversy ignited by the Supreme Court's own pronouncements on issues such as abortion (*Roe v Wade* (1973) 410 U.S. 113), homosexuality (*Bowers v Hardwick* (1986) 478 U.S. 186; *Lawrence v Texas* (2003) 539 US 558), gay marriage (*Obergefell v Hodges* Unreported, 26 June 2015, US Supreme Court) and affirmative action (*Califano v Goldfarb* (1977) 430 U.S. 199; *Gratz v Bollinger* (2003) 539 US 244).

[187] Lord Mackay of Clashfern, quoted in R. Clayton and H. Tomlinson, *The Law of Human Rights* (Oxford: Oxford University Press, 2000), para.1.57.

[188] See House of Commons Disqualification Act 1975 s.1(1)(a) and the Scotland Act 1998 s.15(1)(a).

[189] On this basis, a Court of Session judge felt obliged to resign from a committee set up by the Leader of the Opposition in 1968 to formulate Conservative policy on the constitutional future of Scotland. Subsequently, in 1977, a sheriff was dismissed from office after using his judicial office as a platform for the promotion of his political beliefs.

[190] *Davidson v Scottish Ministers (No.2)*, 2005 1 S.C. (H.L.) 7.

[191] See, e.g. *R. v Rand* (1866) L.R. 1 Q.B. 230 QB; *R. v Camborne Justices, Ex p. Pearce* [1955] 1 Q.B. 41 QBD.

[192] *Dimes v Proprietors of the Grand Junction Canal* (1852) 3 H.L. Cas. 759. There is a de minimis exception to this otherwise strict rule. For example, see the statement by the Supreme Court that justices with not ordinarily disclose small shareholdings: Supreme Court, "Disclosure of small shareholdings", *https://www.supremecourt.uk/procedures/disclosure-of-small-shareholdings.html* [Accessed 5 June 2020].

Vice Chancellor in favour of the canal company by virtue of his substantial shareholding in the company. The categories of automatic disqualification were extended by the decision of the House of Lords in *R. v Bow Street Metropolitan Stipendiary Magistrate, Ex p. Pinochet Ugarte (No.2)*,[193] overturning the earlier decision of the House of Lords in which it was held by a 3:2 majority that Senator Pinochet, as a past Head of State, enjoyed no immunity from arrest and extradition in respect of alleged crimes against humanity. Lord Hoffmann (who agreed with the speeches of Lord Nicholls and Lord Steyn, but who gave no separate reasons for holding that Pinochet was not entitled to immunity) turned out to be a director and chairman of Amnesty International Charity Ltd, while his wife had worked for Amnesty's International Secretariat since 1977. Amnesty International had sought, and been granted, leave to intervene in the first appeal to the House of Lords. In overturning that decision, Lord Browne-Wilkinson held:

> "[Although] the cases have all dealt with automatic disqualification on the grounds of pecuniary interest, there is no good reason in principle for so limiting automatic disqualification. The rationale of the whole rule is that a man cannot be judge in his own cause. In civil litigation the matters in issue will normally have an economic impact; therefore a judge is automatically disqualified if he stands to make a financial gain as a consequence of his own decision in the case. But if, as in the present case, the matter at issue does not relate to money or economic advantage but is concerned with the promotion of the cause, the rationale disqualifying a judge applies just as much if the judge's decision will lead to the promotion of a cause in which the judge is involved together with one of the parties."[194]

In such cases there is no scope of fine distinctions and Lord Hewart CJ's famous dictum applies with its full force: disqualification is automatic and nothing more requires to be proved.[195] If the judge proceeds to decide nevertheless, their decision cannot stand.

This rule against bias also comes into play, even though the judge is not interested in the outcome or otherwise acting as a judge of their own cause, where for some other reason there are grounds for suspicion about their impartiality. The test is now settled. The task of the court is, first, to ascertain all the circumstances that have a bearing on the suggestion that a judge has an appearance of bias. The question is then whether a fair minded and informed observer, having considered the facts, would conclude that there was a real possibility that the judge was biased.[196]

---

[193] *R. v Bow Street Metropolitan Stipendiary Magistrate, Ex p. Pinochet Ugarte (No.2)* [2000] 1 A.C. 119.

[194] *R. v Bow Street Metropolitan Stipendiary Magistrate, Ex p. Pinochet Ugarte (No.2)* [2000] 1 A.C. 119 at [135B].

[195] *R. v Bow Street Metropolitan Stipendiary Magistrate, Ex p. Pinochet Ugarte (No.2)* [2000] 1 A.C. 119, per Lord Browne-Wilkinson at [133B].

[196] *Porter v Magill* [2001] UKHL 67; [2002] 2 A.C. 357, per Lord Hope at [95]–[103].

Yet while the test is simple to state, the subject of impartiality remains uncommonly resistant to classification and definition.[197] Those difficulties are considered further in Ch.15 where they are discussed in the context of grounds for judicial review.

[197] In *Locabail (UK) Ltd v Bayfield Properties Ltd* [2000] Q.B. 451 CA (Civ Div), while declining to list the factors that might give rise to an apprehension of bias, the Court of Appeal was at pains to stress that it could not "conceive of circumstances in which an objection could be soundly based on the religion, ethnic or national origin, gender, age, class, means or sexual orientation of the judge. Nor, at any rate ordinarily, could an objection be soundly based on the judge's social or educational or service or employment background or history, nor that of any member of the judge's family; or previous political associations; or membership of social or sporting or charitable bodies; or Masonic associations; or previous judicial decisions; or extra-curricular utterances (whether in textbooks, lectures, speeches, articles, interviews, reports or responses to consultation papers); or previous receipt of instructions to act for or against any party, solicitor or advocate engaged in a case before him, or membership of a [professional body]". Four joined appeals were considered by the Court of Appeal in *Locabail*; the outcome in one of those appeals, *Timmins v Gormley*, is not readily reconcilable with the tenor of the quoted passage. In Scotland, see *Hoekstra v HM Advocate (No.1)*, 2000 J.C. 387; 2000 S.L.T. 605.

CHAPTER 9

Local Government

INTRODUCTION

It is an unusual parliamentary session, at Westminster and Holyrood alike, that does not see the enactment of at least one measure of greater or lesser significance relating to local government. This rash of legislation reflects a process aptly described by Professor Loughlin as a "politicisation and juridification" of relations between central and local government.[1] If that relationship is less characterised, now, by antagonism on the one hand and resistance on the other, it is nevertheless profoundly different from the traditional model, wherein the essential autonomy of local government was taken not only as given but as necessary to the health of the constitution.[2] Loughlin identifies four key features of that traditional model. The first was multifunctionality: local authorities were charged with the performance of a diverse range of functions, allocated to them not necessarily because, on an abstract economic analysis, they were the institutions best placed efficiently to perform them, but because their role was shored up by the features of local accountability, via the election of local councillors, and a degree of financial independence through their ability to raise local taxes. In keeping with these features of multifunctionality, representation and financial autonomy was the fourth: the conferment of broad discretionary powers on local authorities, which left them largely "free to decide on the precise pattern of the services which they delivered and even to redefine the nature of the services they provided".[3] 9–01

Local authorities were not, in this scenario, merely local agents for the implementation of central government policy. Within their accepted spheres of competence, they enjoyed a substantial degree of freedom. Why then did this model break down?

At risk of oversimplification, the root cause was money. The share of national wealth consumed by local government increased five-fold in the period between

---

[1] M. Loughlin, "The Restructuring of Central-Local Government Relations" in J. Jowell and D. Oliver (eds), *The Changing Constitution*, 4th edn (Oxford: Oxford University Press, 2000), Ch.6 and I. Leigh "The Changing Nature of Local and Regional Democracy" in J. Jowell and D. Oliver (eds), *The Changing Constitution*, 7th edn (Oxford: Oxford University Press, 2011), Ch.9.

[2] This viewpoint was captured by the Royal Commission on Local Government in England, *Report of the Royal Commission on Local Government in England* (HMSO, 1969) Cmnd.4040 ("the Redcliffe-Maud Report") in the following terms: "It is only by the combination of local representative institutions with the central institutions of Parliament, Ministers and departments, that a genuine national democracy can be sustained."

[3] Loughlin, "The Restructuring of Central-Local Government Relations" in *The Changing Constitution* (2000), p.140.

1890 and 1970. Over the same period, local authorities lost responsibility for income-generating trading activities, such as the local provision of utilities, whilst assuming responsibility for the delivery of welfare state services such as public housing and education. The costs associated with this, since they could not be met locally, required to be met by central government grants. As the financial dependency of the localities on the centre increased, so the latter could legitimately claim to take a closer interest in what local authorities were doing with the funds. For much of the post-war period, characterised by economic growth and a general political consensus on the virtues of the welfare state, the emerging tensions could be concealed. When, in the 1970s, economic growth faltered, the tensions became inescapably apparent. The Labour Governments of the time sought to address the public expenditure crisis through the well-established methods of consensus and dialogue, with little if any success. The election of the Conservative Government in 1979 marked the real watershed in central-local government relations, for this was a government committed not only to controlling public expenditure but also to a "rolling back" of the state in all its guises and a fundamental reappraisal of the assumptions that had underpinned the welfare state. The unwillingness of local government to co-operate with the centre in the pursuit of its objectives led central government to resort to what was, after all, always at its disposal: the sovereignty of Parliament. Disregarding the conventional restraints and understandings that had previously characterised central-local government relations, the Conservative administrations of the eighties and nineties progressively replaced with a prescriptive, regulatory framework the facilitative legislative framework within which local government was accustomed to working. Whole tiers of local government were simply swept away.[4] Short of that, local authorities were subjected to a battery of new duties in the interests of efficiency, some of which required the wholesale transfer of local authority functions to the private sector,[5] others of which imposed on local government a range of "market-mimicking" disciplines.[6] The central government vision for local government involved:

> "a formal separation between service specification and service provision, requiring service provision to be achieved through market competition, and altering the governmental function to the residual one of planning only for services that the market cannot provide."[7]

---

[4] As with the abolition of the Greater London Council and the metropolitan borough councils in England in 1986, and, in Scotland, with the replacement of the regional and district councils by a single tier of unitary local authorities pursuant to the Local Government etc. (Scotland) Act 1994 ("the 1994 Act").

[5] As with the compulsory competitive tendering regime, introduced, initially, by the Local Government, Planning and Land Act 1980 and subsequently, in fortified form, by the Local Government Act 1988.

[6] See, e.g. Local Government Act 1988 s.35, which required district auditors in Scotland to undertake "value for money" audits to ensure that local authorities had made "proper arrangements for securing economy, efficiency and effectiveness in [their] use of resources".

[7] Loughlin, "The Restructuring of Central-Local Government Relations" in *The Changing Constitution* (2000), p.157.

It was an impoverished vision, and one understandably resented by local authorities of all political stripes.[8] As the House of Lords Select Committee on Relations between Central and Local Government noted in 1996, its pursuit had damaged if not destroyed the older idea of mutually tolerant partnership between the centre and the localities:

> "This we believe will severely impair the ability of local government to respond to changing economic and social circumstances. [The Conservative legislation] will seriously dilute the legitimacy of local authorities, their institutional, administrative and political capacity and their ability to offer effective local services. They will also seriously diminish the accountability and responsiveness of government to the community at a time of growing social and economic stress."[9]

Many of the recommendations made by the select committee were picked up by the Labour Party in advance of its election victory in 1997, and informed its first major White Paper on local government.[10] But Labour was in no sense bent on restoring the status quo ante. Explicitly or implicitly, its programme for local government accepted many of the elements of the Conservative reforms. It remained wedded to strict financial controls. Under the guide of "modernising" the management, performance and accountability of local authorities, it confined the discretion of local authorities in relation to their own internal organisation and introduced new, overarching codes on ethical standards. It insisted on local authorities working in partnership with a variety of other agencies, whether public, private or voluntary in character. In the latest round of legislative initiatives, then, there remained a strong sense that central government still cannot bring itself to trust local authorities. **9–02**

Whatever the ills bedevilling local government in Scotland, however, it lies within the competence of the Scottish Parliament, now, to address them. All matters relating to local government, and most of the functions of local authorities, fall within the devolved competence of the Parliament as defined by Sch.5 to the Scotland Act 1998.[11] In anticipation of devolution, the Secretary of State for Scotland established a Commission on Local Government and the Scottish Parliament, charged with considering how to build the most effective relations between local government and the Scottish Parliament and Executive, and how local authorities might best make themselves responsive and democratically accountable to the communities they serve. The commission, chaired by Sir Neil McIntosh, reported in June 1999.[12] Its recommendations ranged widely, including: the establishment of formal working relationships between local authorities on the one hand and MSPs and the Scottish Executive

---

[8] For an overview, see S. Jenkins, *Accountable to None: The Tory Nationalisation of Britain* (London: Hamish Hamilton, 1995).

[9] House of Lords Select Committee on Relations between Central and Local Government, *Rebuilding Trust* (HMSO, 1996) HL 97.

[10] HM Government, *Modern Local Government: In touch with the People* (The Stationery Office, 1998) Cm.4014.

[11] Previously, the franchise for local government elections was reserved to Westminster. That reservation was, however, removed by the Scotland Act 2016 (s.3), when a general competence to determine the franchise in Scotland was conferred on the Scottish Parliament.

[12] Commission on Local Government and the Scottish Parliament, *Moving Forward: Local Government and the Scottish Parliament* (The Stationery Office, 1999) (the McIntosh Report).

on the other; the conferment on local authorities of a statutory power of general competence; the introduction of a four-year term for local authorities and a system of proportional representation for local elections; the establishment of an independent inquiry into local government finance; and various changes to the way in which local authority business is conducted. Many of these proposals have been taken forward in some way, and are discussed further below. Perhaps inevitably, legislative initiatives to date have tended to have much in common with similar initiatives at Westminster (although there are significant differences of approach in some respects). It remains to be seen whether, in the future, central-local government relations in Scotland, and indeed models of local government, will develop along lines distinct from those which obtain south of the border.

STRUCTURE OF SCOTTISH LOCAL GOVERNMENT[13]

9–03 The present structure of local government in Scotland is the product of the Local Government etc. (Scotland) Act 1994, which took full effect on 1 April 1996. Prior to that, Scottish local government was organised on two basic levels, with nine regional councils and 53 district councils (together with three all-purpose islands councils representing Orkney, Shetland and the Western Isles). The regional/district split was founded in the recommendations of the Royal Commission chaired by Lord Wheatley, which was appointed to inquire into the structure of local government in Scotland and which reported in 1969.[14] The touchstones of the Wheatley Report were that the structure of local government should be such as to enable local authorities to play "a more important, responsible and positive part in the running of the country", equipping them to deliver public services effectively, ensuring proper accountability for the exercise of their powers to the local electorate and securing, so far as possible, the participation of local people in decision-making. With these objectives in mind, Wheatley rejected the idea of a single tier of all-purpose local authorities in favour of a two tier system, wherein regional authorities would take responsibility for major strategic services and district councils would take charge of more "local" services. Little altered, the Wheatley recommendations were enacted into law by the Local Government (Scotland) Act 1973, much of which remains in force.

In 1991, however, the Secretary of State for Scotland announced the government's intention to replace this structure with a single tier system of unitary authorities. Widespread opposition to the government's plans counted for nought, and the proposals were duly enacted in the 1994 Act. The net result was

---

[13] See also C.M.G. Himsworth, *Local Government Law in Scotland* (Edinburgh T.&T. Clark, 1995); C.M.G. Himsworth, "Local Government in Scotland" in A. McHarg and T.J. Mullen (eds), *Public Law in Scotland* (Edinburgh: Avizandum, 2006); *Stair Memorial Encyclopedia, Reissue: Local Government* (London: LexisNexis).

[14] Royal Commission on Local Government in Scotland, *Report of the Royal Commission on Local Government in Scotland* (HMSO, 1969) Cm.4150 (the Wheatley Report).

the present, single layer of 32 unitary local authorities.[15] Certain functions were removed from local authority control altogether.[16] Arrangements were also put in place for the establishment of joint boards and other forms of joint arrangements between the new authorities. Such arrangements are not new—the 1973 Act makes provision for them, as amended by the 1994 Act—but the 1994 reorganisation brought about a significant expansion in their use, principally because many of the new authorities are too small in size to assume individual responsibility for particular functions in their areas. In some cases, joint arrangements are mandatory under the 1994 Act.[17] In others, it is for the local authorities to decide whether they wish to enter into joint arrangements, but it should be noted that where the Scottish Ministers consider that any functions should be discharged jointly by particular authorities, and that those authorities have failed to make any, or satisfactory, arrangements for the joint discharge of those functions, they may by order establish a joint board for those purposes after consulting the authorities in question.[18] The provisions in relation to joint arrangements are of interest, for they (or more accurately, the inevitable and acknowledged extension in their use) sit oddly with the rationale for abolishing the dual tiers of local government in the first place. The government's case for shifting to a single tier of unitary authorities rested on the claims that the two tiers created confusion in the public mind about who was responsible for what, encouraged duplication of functions and hence waste, and were apt to generate friction between local authorities and hence delay and inefficiency. It is not obvious how the institution of a single tier of unitary authorities coupled with a proliferation of joint arrangements was supposed to address any of these problems, if problems they were.[19]

---

[15] Which left Scotland "in terms of average population per elected council . . . about the most locally under-represented nation in Western Europe": see D. Wilson and C. Gane, *Local Government in the United Kingdom*, 3rd edn (Basingstoke: Macmillan, 1998).

[16] Water and sewerage functions were vested in three new water authorities pursuant to Pt II and Schs 7–11 of the Act (and see now the Water Industry (Scotland) Act 2002, which transferred the functions of the three water authorities to a single body, Scottish Water). Responsibility for the children's reporter system passed to the new Scottish Children's Reporter Administration pursuant to Pt III and Sch.12 of the Act; and responsibility for the promotion of tourism transferred to new area tourist boards established and appointed by the Secretary of State (or, now, the Scottish Ministers) (but see now the Tourist Boards (Scotland) Act 2006).

[17] The Scottish Ministers have the power under s.27 of the 1994 Act to establish joint boards to discharge the functions of two or more valuation authorities. Responsibility for structure planning under the Town and Country Planning (Scotland) Act 1997 is to be exercised in the context of "structure plan areas" designated by the Scottish Ministers, which may cover the area of more than one planning authority. In that event, the planning authorities concerned are to perform their function in accordance with such joint arrangements as they may adopt under ss.56–58 of the Local Government (Scotland) Act 1973 ("the 1973 Act").

[18] See s.20 of the 1994 Act, which inserts new ss.62A–62C into the 1973 Act for these purposes.

[19] Jean McFadden criticises joint arrangements on the further ground that, since they "tend to be officer-led rather than member-led, and since members [of joint boards] are appointed by their councils rather than directly elected, they lack democratic legitimacy and direct accountability to the electorate": *Stair Memorial Encyclopaedia, Reissue: Local Government*, para.447.

LOCAL AUTHORITIES—MEMBERSHIP AND ELECTIONS

9–04 Unless disqualified by virtue of the Local Government (Scotland) Act 1973 or any other enactment, a person is entitled to stand for election as a member of a local authority if they have attained the age of 18,[20] is a British subject, citizen of the Irish Republic or is a qualifying foreign national,[21] and is not subject to any legal incapacity, provided (this in contrast to parliamentary elections) they can show a relevant local connection. That is established where the person is a registered local government elector in the area of the authority, or the occupier (whether as owner or tenant) of any land or other premises in the area during the whole of the 12-month period preceding the election, or has their principal or only place of work in the area during that same period, or is resident in the area throughout that time.[22] This general entitlement to seek election is then subject to a number of grounds of disqualification. A person whose estate has been sequestrated by a court in Scotland or who has been adjudged bankrupt elsewhere than in Scotland is disqualified,[23] as is a person who has been convicted anywhere in the British Islands[24] of a criminal offence carrying a sentence of not less than three months' imprisonment at any time in the five years preceding their nomination or election,[25] and a person who is disqualified under Pt III of the Representation of the People Act 1983.[26] Section 31A of the 1973 Act, as inserted by s.7 of the Local Governance (Scotland) Act 2004, provides that a person elected as a member of a local authority who is also the holder of "any paid office or employment or other place of profit in the gift or disposal of the authority" is disqualified from remaining a member if they fail, prior to the "relevant day",[27] to resign from that office, employment or place of profit. The rule is intended to preserve the important distinction between members and officers of local authorities, but has the effect of excluding from membership of their own local authority not only senior managers and policy advisers but also staff in technical or manual occupations. More broadly still, a person who holds a "politically restricted post" in any local authority in Great Britain is disqualified from becoming a member of any other local authority.[28] Where it is claimed that a

---

[20] The age restriction was reduced from 21 to 18 by s.8 of the Local Governance (Scotland) Act 2004, which amends s.29 of the 1973 Act.

[21] The concept of a "qualifying foreign national" is a product of the Scottish Elections (Franchise and Representation) Act 2020 (s.3), which was introduced in consequence of the UK's departure from the EU.

[22] 1973 Act s.29.

[23] 1973 Act s.31(1)(b) and (2).

[24] That is, anywhere in the UK, the Republic of Ireland, the Channel Islands or the Isle of Man.

[25] 1973 Act s.31(1)(c).

[26] 1973 Act s.31(1)(d). This includes disqualification following conviction in respect of corrupt or illegal election practices.

[27] "Relevant day" is defined as "the day first occurring after that on which the person elected a member of the local authority was, under the local elections rules, declared to be so elected (no account being taken of a day which is a Saturday or Sunday or Christmas Eve, Easter Monday, or a bank holiday in Scotland . . . or a day appointed for public thanksgiving or mourning in Scotland".

[28] Local Government and Housing Act 1989 s.1. This provision is based on the recommendations of the Widdicombe Committee of Inquiry into Local Authority Business, *Report of the Committee of Inquiry into Local Authority Business* (HMSO, 1986) Cm.9797 and survived a challenge to its compatibility with art.10 of the European Convention on Human Rights, in *Ahmed v United Kingdom* (1995) 20 E.H.R.R. CD72 and (2000) 29 E.H.R.R. 1. See, generally, McFadden, *Stair Memorial*

disqualified person is, or is seeking to become, a member of a local authority, proceedings may be brought before the sheriff principal under s.32 of the 1973 Act. The participation of a disqualified person in any proceedings of the council or its committees does not, however, affect the validity of any decisions taken therein.[29]

As to the timing of local government elections, in 2002, and in accordance with the recommendation of the McIntosh Report, four-year terms were introduced for local government, with elections being synchronised with Scottish parliamentary elections.[30] Further change was to come, however. As we saw in Ch.4, above, from 2007 the single transferrable vote system was introduced for local government elections.[31] Then, in 2009, the link with the Scottish parliamentary elections was broken. The Scottish Local Government (Elections) Act 2009 required the next local government elections to be held in 2012, then in 2017 and thereafter every four years. The result was intended to be that local government elections will now be held midway through the term of the Scottish Parliament. But when the Scottish Parliament (again) moved to a five-year session (as it has done permanently now), the date was again changed. So, the next local government election will be in 2022.[32] When the Scottish Elections (Reform) Bill passes into law, local authority elections will also move to a five-year cycle.[33]

LOCAL GOVERNMENT POWERS

Local authorities have no inherent powers to undertake functions of their own choosing. They are creatures of statute, and everything that they do must find its source in law.[34] This is the ultra vires rule, and the restraint that it imposes on local authorities should not be lightly discounted. It is true that many local government powers and functions are cast in broad discretionary terms, but even where this is so the courts will insist that the powers are not exercised for purposes ulterior to those envisaged by the statute, or on the basis of irrelevant considerations, or in an unreasonable manner. **9–05**

An important aspect of local authorities' functions, which may be seen as distinct from their role in providing, or facilitating the provision of, public

Encyclopaedia, Reissue: Local Government, paras 245 and 256; for criticism, see G.S. Morris, "Local Government Workers and Rights of Political Participation: Time for a change" [1998] P.L. 25.

29 1973 Act ss.33 and 43.

30 Scottish Local Government (Elections) Act 2002. This was perhaps not unwise, for the claims of local government to democratic legitimacy appear somewhat thin when local election turnouts habitually fail to rise above 25% of the local electorate.

31 See para.4–11, above.

32 1994 Act, s.3(1C), inserted by the Scottish Elections (Dates) Act 2016.

33 Scottish Elections (Reform) Bill, cl.2(1).

34 And not merely in the words of a statute alone. The common law grounds for judicial review—illegality, procedural impropriety and irrationality—provide a further level of legal constraint, as do such other jurisprudential innovations as the extension to local authorities of a fiduciary duty to local taxpayers in the use and management of their funds: see *Bromley LBC v Greater London Council* [1983] 1 A.C. 768 HL, followed in Scotland by the Inner House in *Commission for Local Authority Accounts in Scotland v Stirling DC*, 1984 S.L.T. 442.

services, relates to their powers to make subordinate legislation for their areas.[35] The nature of these measures varies. At one end of the spectrum, there are rules that are primarily administrative in character, such as orders made for the regulation of public processions under s.63 of the Civic Government (Scotland) Act 1982 (as amended by s.71 of the Police, Public Order and Criminal Justice (Scotland) Act 2006), structure and development plans drawn up under the Town and Country Planning (Scotland) Act 1997, and strategies as adopted, for example, under s.89 of the Housing (Scotland) Act 2001 and s.1 of the Antisocial Behaviour etc. (Scotland) Act 2004. The adoption of such rules, plans and strategies may be authorised or required by statute, and statute (or regulations made thereunder) may similarly prescribe or guide their content. Even non-statutory guidance or statements of policy published by a local authority may have a rule-like effect in certain circumstances, as where, for example, it provides the foundation for a legitimate expectation in judicial review proceedings, or for a finding of maladministration by the Scottish Public Services Ombudsman where it is said that the local authority has failed to follow its own criteria. At the other end of the spectrum are the numerous statutory provisions authorising local authorities to make byelaws for their areas.[36] In addition to the more specific powers contained in such statutes as the Civic Government (Scotland) Act 1982 and the Local Government and Planning (Scotland) Act 1982, there is a general byelaw-making power in s.201 of the Local Government (Scotland) Act 1973, which provides that a local authority "may make byelaws for the good rule and government of the whole or any part of its area and for the prevention and suppression of nuisances therein". It should be noted, however, that, quite apart from the limitations imposed on a local authority's byelaw-making power by the ultra vires rule, any byelaw adopted by the authority must first be confirmed by the Scottish Ministers (or such other confirming authority as the relevant legislation may specify). At least one month before the local authority applies to the Scottish Ministers for confirmation, it must give public notice of its intention to do so and advise members of the public of their right to object to the byelaw proposed.[37] The Scottish Ministers may, having considered any objections received, confirm the byelaw, with or without modifications, or refuse to confirm it.[38]

9–06 Where byelaws are duly adopted, the responsible local authority is obliged to review them at intervals not exceeding 10 years, to ensure that they are updated or revoked as necessary.[39] Where the authority proposes to revoke any byelaw, it must comply with the procedures as to advance publicity prescribed by s.202 of the 1973 Act. All local authorities are required to keep a register of byelaws containing a description of each byelaw and any offences or penalties attaching to

---

[35] This power is distinct again from the power of local authorities to promote or oppose private legislation. By virtue of s.82(1) of the Act 1973 a local authority may promote or oppose any private legislation where it is satisfied that it is expedient to do so, and may defray the expenses incurred in so doing. The decision to promote or oppose must be authorised by resolution of the council adopted in accordance with s.82(2) of the 1973 Act. For private legislative procedures, see paras 6–12—6–14, above.

[36] See, generally, McFadden, *Stair Memorial Encyclopaedia, Reissue: Local Government*, paras 276–301.

[37] Failure to follow these procedures would itself entitle the Court of Session to reduce the byelaw.

[38] 1973 Act s.202.

[39] 1973 Act s.202A.

it, its dates of confirmation and coming into force and the date on which it was last renewed. The register is open to public inspection free of charge, although a reasonable charge may be made for providing certified copies of byelaws.[40] The Civic Government (Scotland) Act 1982, as well as amending the rules and procedures relating to byelaws, also introduced a new form of subordinate legislation known as "management rules".[41] Unlike byelaws, management rules may be made by a local authority without the further approval of the Scottish Ministers, although the local authority must give public notice of its intention to adopt particular rules and accord to objectors the right to make representations before bringing the rule into effect (if this is what the authority decides to do). But management rules may only be made for the purpose of regulating the use of, and the conduct of persons on or in "land or premises which are owned, occupied or managed by the authority or are otherwise under its control and to which the public have access, whether on payment or not".[42]

Where an "authorised officer" of the local authority reasonably believes that a person is breaching or has breached the terms of a management rule, they may exclude or expel that person from the land or premises.[43] The local authority may make exclusion orders effective for up to one year in the case of persistent offenders.[44] Failure to comply with an exclusion order, or with an instruction to leave (or not to enter) land or premises, is a criminal offence.[45]

Over and above their functionally specific powers and duties, local authorities **9–07**
have a variety of powers that may be described as ancillary or subsidiary.[46] Some of these are reasonably precise in their terms, such as the power conferred by s.83(3) of the 1973 Act to make contributions to charitable funds, appeals and the like. Others are (at least on their face) more permissive, although even the latest additions to the legislative corpus do not go so far as to confer on local authorities a power of general competence.[47] One such power is contained in s.69 of the 1973 Act.[48] This provides that:

> "a local authority shall have the power to do anything (whether or not involving the expenditure, borrowing or lending of money or the acquisition or disposal of any property or rights) which is calculated to facilitate, or is conducive or incidental to, the discharge of any of their functions".

It is, in fact, nothing more than a statutory statement of the common law position in relation to the ultra vires rule,[49] and was for a long time widely understood as a generous enabling power. That belief was exploded by the decision of the

---

40 1973 Act s.202B.

41 Civic Government (Scotland) Act 1982 ss.112–118.

42 Civic Government (Scotland) Act 1982 s.112(1).

43 Civic Government (Scotland) Act 1982 s.116.

44 Civic Government (Scotland) Act 1982 s.117

45 Civic Government (Scotland) Act 1982 s.118

46 For a comprehensive survey, see McFadden, *Stair Memorial Encyclopaedia, Reissue: Local Government*, paras 315–356.

47 Such as was recommended not only by the McIntosh Report but also by the Wheatley Report before that.

48 The corresponding provision in England and Wales, the Local Government Act 1972 s.111, is in identical terms.

49 As Lord Selborne LC put it in *Attorney General v Great Eastern Railway Co* (1880) 5 App. Cas. 473 at 478, the doctrine of ultra vires "ought to be reasonably, and not unreasonably, understood and

House of Lords in *Hazell v Hammersmith and Fulham LBC*.[50] There, the local authority had entered into "interest rate swap" contracts with financial institutions.[51] It purported to do so on the basis of s.111 of the Local Government Act 1972, assuming that swaps could legitimately be entered into as being incidental to their borrowing powers. The House of Lords disagreed. It was for a local authority, acting prudently in accordance with its fiduciary duty to local taxpayers, to determine at the time of borrowing money whether it would be able to afford interest payments thereon. Speculating on the capital markets was neither conducive nor incidental to that function. Interest rate swap contracts were therefore ultra vires and void.[52] This is not to say that the ultra vires rule always operated against the interests of local authorities. In the *Credit Suisse* cases, the Court of Appeal held that agreements between the local authorities and the bank, whereby the authorities undertook to guarantee the borrowings of companies established by the authorities in purported performance of their functions, were ultra vires and unenforceable by the bank.[53]

The ramifications of these decisions went beyond the immediate financial consequences for local authorities and banks. Previously, local authorities had been regarded as low risk counterparties by financial and commercial institutions. That perception changed sharply for the worse, putting at risk the drive by central government to encourage (if not force) the contracting-out of service delivery and other forms of public/private partnership.

9–08 The government responded to this on a number of fronts. One of the first enactments of the Labour Government elected in 1997 was the Local Government (Contracts) Act 1997 that, while it does not abrogate the ultra vires rule in its application to local government contracts, significantly mitigates the risks associated with it. Its aim, in the words of the minister responsible for piloting it through the House of Commons, was:

> "to make explicit the power of a local authority to enter into contracts of the sort envisaged in public/private partnership schemes . . . and to provide a safe harbour, by protecting contractors and lenders, if an authority is later found to have entered into an arrangement which is invalid".

Section 1(1) makes clear the power of a local authority to enter into contracts with others for the provision of, or in order to make available, assets or services or both (whether or not together with goods) for the purposes of, or in connection

---

applied, and whatever may fairly be regarded and incidental to, or consequential upon, those things which the legislature has authorised ought not (unless expressly prohibited) to be held by judicial construction to be ultra vires".

[50] *Hazell v Hammersmith and Fulham LBC* [1992] 2 A.C. 1 HL. In Scotland, see to similar effect *Morgan Guaranty Trust Co of New York v Lothian RC*, 1995 S.C. 151.

[51] It was far from being alone in this. Following the decision of the House of Lords in *Hazell*, over 200 actions were commenced, both by local authorities and banks, to recover sums paid under contracts held in *Hazell* to be ultra vires the local authorities.

[52] See also *McCarthy & Stone (Developments) Ltd v Richmond upon Thames LBC* [1992] 2 A.C. 48 HL and, in Scotland, *SPH (Scotland) Ltd v City of Edinburgh Council* Unreported 25 June 2003 Outer House. For the consequences of *Hazell* on the law of unjust enrichment, see *Morgan Guaranty Trust Co. of New York v Lothian RC*, 1995 S.C. 151 and (in England) *Kleinwort Benson Ltd v Lincoln City Council* [1999] 2 A.C. 349 HL.

[53] *Crédit Suisse v Allerdale BC* [1997] Q.B. 306 CA (Civ Div) and *Credit Suisse v Waltham Forest LBC* [1997] Q.B. 362 CA (Civ Div).

with, the discharge of their functions. Where a local authority enters into such a contract, it has the power also to enter into a contract with a financial institution, where the latter makes a loan or provides any other form of finance to a party to the primary contract other than the local authority itself.[54] The Act then establishes a certification mechanism in respect of such contracts. Provided the certification requirements[55] are met by the local authority (and they are not especially rigorous), the validity of the certified contract cannot be questioned in any private law proceedings. It remains possible in public law proceedings for the court to hold the contract unlawful, but the court may order that the unlawful contract continue to have effect. Even if the contract is set aside, agreed contractual "discharge terms" will apply to determine compensation due, unless these too are ultra vires (or none have been agreed). In that event, statutory damages terms apply. In the context of certified contracts, therefore, the risks of invalidity are placed firmly on the shoulders of local authorities.

But contract is only one means through which local authorities may perform their functions. Broader enabling powers have also been enacted. The Local Government in Scotland Act 2003 proclaims itself in its long title as an Act "to provide anew about the way in which local authorities discharge their functions".[56] The three main parts of the Act make provision for the achievement by local authorities of "best value" in their delivery of public services, the introduction of a duty of "community planning" and for a power to advance community well-being. The duty to secure best value is a duty to pursue "continuous improvement in the performance of [local authority] functions",[57] which in turn is defined in terms of maintaining an appropriate balance between the quality of performance and the costs of performance, both to the authority and to persons paying, fully or partly, for the services provided. In striking that balance, the authority must have regard to efficiency, economy, effectiveness and equal opportunities.[58] At the same time, Pt 1 relaxes certain of the restrictions imposed on local authorities' contracting powers[59] and on their powers to enter into trading arrangements for the provision of goods and services.[60] Moreover, with the formal introduction of best value, the compulsory competitive tendering

[54] Local Government (Contracts) Act 1997 s.1(2).

[55] Local Government (Contracts) Act 1997 s.3(2)(a)–(g).

[56] The equivalent legislation south of the border is the Local Government Act 1999 and the Local Government Act 2000 Pt I (as amended by the Localism Act 2011). In many respects, the 1999 Act, 2000 Act and 2003 Act simply take forward, and give legislative force to, what was already taking place as a matter of local government or audit practice.

[57] Local Government in Scotland Act 2003 (2003 Act) s.1(1) and (2).

[58] 2003 Act s.1(3) and (4). Not only that, but the local authority must also perform its functions in relation to best value in such a way as to contribute to the achievement of sustainable development.

[59] Namely, the restrictions contained in the Local Government Act 1988 s.17(5)(a), (b) and (d), which prohibit local authorities from taking into account specified "non-commercial considerations" when deciding whether and on what terms to enter into contracts. It should be noted that these restrictions are not abrogated entirely, as was contended for in some quarters, but only in the circumstances defined in s.7(2)(a)–(c) of the 2003 Act. The restrictions in respect of non-commercial considerations elsewhere in s.17(5) of the 1988 Act are unaffected.

[60] 2003 Act ss.8 and 9 (the latter being not yet in force). Note that in terms of the Local Authorities (Goods and Services) Act 1970, a local authority is obliged, before entering into any trading arrangement thereunder, to consider whether the arrangement will be likely to improve or promote the well-being of either or both of its area and persons living in that area.

regime contained in the Local Government Act 1988 is abolished.[61] It is to be noted, however, that, whereas the compulsory competitive tendering regime only ever applied to around one-fifth of local authority functions, the duty to secure best value applies across the board. To that extent alone, its implications for local authorities are the more profound.

9–09 Monitoring compliance with s.1 falls to the Controller of Audit and the Accounts Commission for Scotland.[62] On receipt of a report from the controller alleging failure by a local authority to comply with its duties, the commission may direct the controller to carry out further investigations or state its findings, with or without a preliminary hearing. On receipt of the commission's findings, the authority concerned is obliged to consider those findings at a meeting of the council and to notify the commission of any remedial action it proposes to take.[63]

9–10 Part 2 made provision in relation to community planning. It was the duty of each local authority to initiate, maintain and facilitate a "community planning process".[64] The object of this process was to institutionalise consultation between the local authority, all public bodies responsible for providing public services in its area, and such community bodies and other bodies or persons as appropriate, in planning for the provision of, and providing, those public services.[65] Apart from local authorities themselves, health boards, the Police Service of Scotland, the Scottish Fire and Rescue Service, Scottish Enterprise, Highlands and Islands Enterprise and Strathclyde Passenger Transport Executive are required to participate in community planning.[66] Under s.19, local authorities and their community planning partners may request the Scottish Ministers to establish by order corporate bodies to "co-ordinate and further" community planning. Monitoring compliance with the duty of community planning is shared between the local authorities themselves,[67] the Scottish Ministers[68] and the Accounts Commission for Scotland.[69] Part 2 was repelled and replaced by Pt 2 of the Community Empowerment (Scotland) Act 2015, which placed community planning on a firmer statutory footing but followed the same broad structure.

---

[61] 2003 Act s.60(1)(e) and (f).

[62] 2003 Act s.3.

[63] 2003 Act s.5. For the further enforcement powers vested in the Scottish Ministers, see below.

[64] 2003 Act s.15(1).

[65] For definition of "public bodies" and "community bodies", see 2003 Act s.15(4). The statutory objective of the successor scheme is: "improvement in the achievement of outcomes resulting from, or contributed to by, the provision of services" delivered by the local authority or a range of other public bodies (s.4(2) of the Community Empowerment (Scotland) Act 2015).

[66] 2003 Act s.16(1). This list may be amended by the Scottish Ministers. See now: Community Empowerment (Scotland) Act 2015 s.14 and Sch.1.

[67] Presumably the discharge of their duty to report from time to time under s.17(1) of the 2003 Act is intended to provide an opportunity for self-assessment.

[68] In addition to their power to issue guidance about community planning under s.18 of the 2003 Act and to adopt regulations governing the form, content and frequency of reports provided under s.17(1), the Scottish Ministers have the power under s.17(8) to call for reports and information from local authorities about the implementation by them of community planning, together with their wider enforcement powers under Pt IV of the Act.

[69] The Accounts Commission for Scotland has the power under s.1(1) of the Local Government Act 1992 to direct the publication of information about local authorities' standards of performance in such a way as to "facilitate the drawing of conclusions" about the discharge of their community planning functions.

Part 3 concerns the power to advance well-being, the nearest the legislation comes to conferring a power of general competence.[70] Under s.20(1), a local authority has the power "to do anything which it considers is likely to promote or improve the well-being of (a) its area and persons within that area; or (b) either of those". 9–11

The power includes: power to incur expenditure; give financial assistance to any person; enter into agreements or arrangements with any person; co-operate with, facilitate or co-ordinate the activities of any person; exercise functions on behalf of any person; or to provide staff, goods, materials, facilities, services or property to any person.[71] On the face of this, there would seem to be few forms of innovation in service delivery that would now fall foul of the ultra vires rule. But it is not quite that generous. First, s.22(1) provides that nothing in s.20 is to be taken as enabling a local authority to do anything that, by virtue of a "limiting provision", it is unable to do.[72] Second, a local authority may not by virtue of s.20 do anything that would "unreasonably duplicate" something that a person other than the local authority is obliged or empowered to do pursuant to its statutory functions. Third, it can only be used in a manner that is consistent with the local authorities' other statutory duties.[73] In short, then, Pt 3 restates, albeit in relaxed form, the ultra vires doctrine. Perhaps for that reason, it is not attended by the usual raft of provision for ministerial monitoring and audit: whether a local authority has acted properly within the scope of its powers under s.20 will be, at least ultimately, a question for the courts.

However, Pt 4 makes overarching provision for enforcement of the duties created by Pts 1–3. Among other things, it confers on the Scottish Ministers the power to issue "preliminary notices" and, thereafter, "enforcement directions" where it appears to the Scottish Ministers that a local authority has "significantly exceeded its power under section 20".[74] As with the enforcement powers conferred on the Scottish Ministers in relation to best value, accounting and community planning by ss.23 and 24, these are open to the objection that they allow the executive to dictate to an elected authority what it must do and how it must do it. But the objection to ss.26 and 27 goes further. They authorise the Scottish Ministers to determine questions of vires, which are questions of law, and an authority to which an enforcement direction is given is under a duty to comply with it.[75] Further, in issuing an enforcement direction, the Scottish Ministers may require the authority to take such action as is specified in the direction "being action calculated to remedy or prevent the recurrence of its significant excess of power".[76] It would, at least in principle, be open to an 9–12

---

[70] Pursuant to the enactment of the power to advance well-being, essentially obsolete powers, including aspects of the power contained in s.83 of the Local Government (Scotland) Act 1973 (the general power of local authorities to incur expenditure) and ss.171A–171C of that Act (the power of local authorities to promote economic development in their areas) are repealed: see 2003 Act s.60(1).

[71] 2003 Act s.20(2).

[72] "Limiting provision" is defined as a provision in any enactment which expressly prohibits or prevents a local authority from doing something or which limits its powers in that respect. Mere absence of positive authority is not to be taken as a prohibition in this sense: 2003 Act s.22(2) and (3).

[73] *Portobello Park Action Group Association v City of Edinburgh Council*, 2013 S.C. 184 at paras [39]–[42].

[74] 2003 Act ss.26 and 27.

[75] 2003 Act s.27(7).

[76] 2003 Act s.27(1).

authority to resist such a direction on the basis that, if its action is intra vires, there is no legal basis for the direction, and if it is ultra vires, it is simply *void ab initio* (and unlikely to give rise to any liability to pay compensation to any person). Presumably if a local authority were to resist an enforcement notice in this way, it would fall to the Scottish Ministers to bring proceedings for an order requiring the authority to comply with its duty. But the right of the Scottish Ministers must depend on the validity of their own direction, and the court could not decide that without inquiring into the nature of the local authority's alleged breach of s.20. In that regard, moreover, a court is not confined to finding a given act or decision to be ultra vires only when the excess of competence is "significant".

It becomes apparent that, while there is much in the 2003 Act that is genuinely enabling, it falls a long way short of according autonomy to local authorities within the limits of the law. At all times, local authorities are required to have regard to guidance and regulations promulgated by the Scottish Ministers under the Act. The choices made by local authorities in the exercise of their functions in relation to best value, community planning and the promotion of well-being may exceptionally be subject to judicial oversight, but they are routinely subject to ministerial oversight and audit control, both of which are reinforced by the rigorous reporting requirements laid on local authorities by the Act. In significant respects, the regime contained in the 2003 Act is more prescriptive and interventionist than the regime contained in the Local Government Acts 1999 and 2000 south of the border. Is this acceptable because the centre is now more local? No doubt, via the Scottish Government and Accounts Commission and thence the Scottish Parliament, all of this may be said to enhance the accountability of local authorities for the performance of their functions to the public. But there is a strong sense here that this accountability is but a by-product of, and secondary to, the consolidation of central control and supervision over the activities of local government in Scotland.

ORGANISATION OF LOCAL AUTHORITY BUSINESS

9–13 Within the UK and Scottish Governments, executive decisions are taken by ministers, who answer for their decisions to Westminster or the Scottish Parliament. The organisation of local authority business is quite different, ". . . there is no source of executive authority other than the council itself".[77] But while the functions of local authorities are vested in the council for each local government area, it would obviously be impracticable for the full council to take every decision. Except where statute provides otherwise, therefore, the council may delegate its functions to committees, subcommittees, joint committees[78] or officers of the councils, though not to a single councillor.[79]

[77] Committee of Inquiry into Local Authority Business, *Report of the Committee of Inquiry into Local Authority* Business, para.5.2.

[78] Bearing in mind that committees must reflect the political balance of the full council.

[79] See, generally, 1973 Act s.56. Local authorities are not permitted to delegate major financial decisions, defined by s.56(6) as functions with respect to determining the level of council tax for their area and borrowing money. Note also s.82 of the 1973 Act, which requires the decision to promote or oppose private legislation to be taken by the full council. A number of statutory provisions also

Local authorities are accorded a good deal of latitude as to how they carry out their business. They are required to hold a first meeting within 21 days of a local election, at which they must elect a convenor and, if they wish, a depute convenor.[80] Thereafter, it is largely up to individual authorities how often they hold meetings.[81] It is also, subject to the restrictions already noted, for each authority to decide whether and to what extent it wishes to delegate functions to committees and officers, and on the particular model of delegation it wishes to adopt. There is no longer any requirement that particular committees be established. Again, it is for the council to provide for the conduct and procedures of committee meetings through standing orders of its own choosing.[82]

9–14 At various times, thought has been given to the adoption of different models of organising local authority business. The Maud Committee recommended that each local authority should appoint a management board of five to nine councillors, to which all other committees would be answerable.[83] The Widdicombe Committee considered three different models—the management board, the ministerial model and the separation of powers model based on an elected or appointed executive—but found none of them to be sufficiently advantageous to justify a departure from prevailing practice. The government revisited the issue in its 1998 White Paper.[84] In England and Wales, this was followed by a further round of consultation on new forms of governance for local authorities,[85] which led in turn to the provision contained in Pt II of the Local Government Act 2000.[86] This provides for the adoption by English and Welsh

require certain reports to be considered by the full council, in the interests of publicity: see, e.g. Ethical Standards in Public Life etc. (Scotland) Act 2000 s.18, which requires the written findings of the Standards Commission to be considered at a meeting of the full council; and 2003 Act s.5, which requires a local authority, on receipt of a report by the Accounts Commission for Scotland on its compliance with the duty to secure best value, to consider the report at a meeting of the council and notify the commission of the remedial steps it proposes to take. Interestingly, like provision in the Local Government (Scotland) Act 1975 s.29, in relation to consideration of reports by the Commissioner for Local Administration in Scotland, is repealed by the Scottish Public Services Ombudsman Act 2002.

[80] 1994 Act s.4. There is no statutory definition of the functions of a convenor or depute convenor, other than in para.3 of Sch.7 to the 1973 Act, which states that the convenor (or depute convenor) shall chair meetings of the council. At meetings where a vote is taken, the convenor or depute convenor has a casting vote in the event of a tie. In Aberdeen, Dundee, Edinburgh and Glasgow the convener of the council is known as the "Lord Provost".

[81] Apart from the requirement to hold a first meeting within 21 days of the election, the only other requirement is that a local authority should hold as many meetings as it thinks necessary. Schedule 7 to the 1973 Act makes provision in relation to the calling and conduct of meetings, but broadly it is for each council to regulate its own practice by way of standing orders. The usual pattern is for meetings of the full council to be held every four or six weeks, with a summer recess and Christmas break.

[82] 1973 Act s.62. The Local Government and Housing Act 1989 s.20, confers on the Scottish Ministers the power to prescribe standing orders to be adopted by local authorities, but the power has never been used. For the legal effect of standing orders, see *R. v Hereford Corp, Ex p. Harrower* [1970] 1 W.L.R. 1424 DC.

[83] Committee of Inquiry into the Management of Local Government, *Report of the Committee of Inquiry into the Management of Local Government* (HMSO, 1969) Cm.4840 (the Maud Report).

[84] HM Government, *Modern Local Government: In touch with the People*.

[85] Department of the Environment, Transport and Regions, *Local Leadership, Local Choice* (The Stationery Office, 1999), Cm.4298 and Welsh Office, *A Stronger Voice for Local People: Consulting on the Draft Local Government Bill* (The Stationery Office, 1999).

[86] Separate provision was made in relation to London in the Greater London Authority Act 1999.

local authorities of "executive arrangements" under which certain functions of the local authority become the responsibility of the executive.[87]

9–15 Section 11 gives authorities a choice as to the form of their executive arrangements between three options: an elected mayor, acting with two or more councillors appointed to the executive by them (the "mayor and cabinet" model); a councillor elected as executive leader by the council, acting with two or more councillors appointed by them or by the authority (the "leader and cabinet" model); or an elected mayor acting with an officer of the authority appointed by the council (the "mayor and council manager" model). Sections 13–17 then make provision for the denomination of executive functions. Consulting in Scotland, the McIntosh Commission found little support for any of these alternatives to the status quo.[88] As the commission noted, however, if Scottish local authorities do not have formal executives, majority groups constitute something very similar. In effect, many decisions of a local authority are in no sense taken in public meetings, but agreed in private meetings of the controlling group on the council. The McIntosh Committee, therefore, recommended that councils should review their procedures with a view to ensuring that policy proposals and matters for decision are subject to open debate, and that the council is able to scrutinise the majority group and hold it properly to account for its decisions. The Scottish Ministers chose to take this forward not by introducing legislation along the lines of Pt II of the Local Government Act 2000, but by requiring councils to review their organisational structures and appointing an advisory panel to assist them in that task. The panel reported in 2001.[89] All but three of Scotland's 32 local authorities undertook reviews of their internal structures, and all but three of those made some changes, involving either a streamlining of their existing committee systems, the introduction of formal executives or the adoption of devolved structures of decision-making.

So far as the organisation of local authority business in Scotland is concerned, then, statutory regulation is relatively light. Two areas into which statute does intrude, however, relate to public access to local authority meetings and to the policing of standards of conduct. As to the first, statutory rights of access to council meetings were accorded initially only to the press.[90] Substantially extended rights of access, for press and public, were provided for by the Public Bodies (Admission to Meetings) Act 1960, which applied to meetings of the full council and to education committees; this was extended again by the Local Government (Scotland) Act 1973 to all committee (but not subcommittee) meetings. The current law is contained in the Local Government (Access to Information) Act 1985, which inserted into the 1973 Act a new Pt IIIA and a new Sch.7A. It requires, first, that public notice of the time and place of all meetings, including meetings of committees and subcommittees, be posted at the offices of a local authority at least three clear days in advance or, that failing, at the time the meeting is called. Second, it provides that meetings of the council and any

[87] Local Government Act 2000 s.10.

[88] Commission on Local Government and the Scottish Parliament, *Moving Forward: Local Government and the Scottish Parliament*.

[89] Leadership Advisory Panel, *Scottish Local Government's Self-Review of its Political Management Structures: Report of the Leadership Advisory Panel* (Scottish Executive, 2001) ("the MacNish Report").

[90] Local Authorities (Admission of the Press to Meetings) Act 1908.

committee and subcommittee shall be open to the public. This general rule is then qualified in a number of ways. The council (or committee) has the power to exclude where necessary to prevent or suppress disorderly conduct.[91] It may also, acting by formal resolution, exclude the public from a meeting during consideration of an item of business that is likely to involve disclosure of "exempt information".[92] There is no provision for challenging a resolution to exclude, although it is in principle subject to judicial review and in one case the Court of Appeal apparently assumed that the exclusion of the public pursuant to an unlawful resolution would render invalid the subsequent proceedings and any decision taken therein.[93] Section 50A(2) of the 1973 Act further provides that the public must be excluded from a meeting during consideration of an item of business that is likely to involve disclosure of confidential information.[94] The right of access to meetings is then reinforced by provision for access to documents relating to meetings. Before a meeting, copies of the agenda, the report for the meeting and any background papers must be made available for public inspection at the offices of the local authority.[95] A reasonable number of copies of the agenda and reports must be made available at the meeting itself for use by members of the public,[96] and after the meeting copies of the minutes, the agenda and any reports provided to members must be retained for six years and made available for public inspection.[97] All this accounted for, it should also be noted that the Freedom of Information (Scotland) Act 2002 now imposes on local authorities extensive statutory duties in relation to the disclosure of information held by them, both as a matter of routine publication and on request.

As to the probity of local councillors, the old patchwork of provision for controlling standards in public life has largely been replaced by the Ethical Standards in Public Life etc. (Scotland) Act 2000.[98] The Prevention of Corruption Act 1906 extended (and extends) to local councillors, and certain other species of unethical behaviour constitute criminal offences under the Local Government (Scotland) Act 1973.[99] Beyond that, the 1973 Act together with the Local Government and Housing Act 1989 made provision for a register of interests, and **9–16**

[91] 1973 Act s.50A(8).

[92] 1973 Act s.50A(4). The categories of exempt information are defined in Sch.7A, and include: information relating to individual employees, tenants, clients and other recipients of benefits from the authority; information concerning contracts of the authority; information relating to the prevention or investigation of crime; and legal advice given to the authority. "Information" is defined to include "an expression of opinion, any recommendations and any decision taken": s.50K(1).

[93] *R. v Liverpool City Council, Ex p. Liverpool Taxi Fleet Operators' Association* [1975] 1 All E.R. 379 QBD, a case involving the Public Bodies (Admission to Meetings) Act 1960.

[94] "Confidential information" has a special meaning for these purposes, being confined by s.50A(3) of the 1973 Act to information provided by a government department on terms that forbid its disclosure to the public, and information the disclosure of which is prohibited by or under any enactment or by order of the court.

[95] 1973 Act s.50D.

[96] 1973 Act s.50B.

[97] 1973 Act s.50D. Where the minutes fail to provide a fair and coherent record of the proceedings, on account of removal of any references to "exempt information", the authority is required instead to make available a summary version of the record of the meeting. Background documents must also be retained and made available for inspection, but only for a period of four years following the meeting.

[98] In England and Wales, less onerous provision is made in the Local Government Act 2000 Pt III.

[99] See, e.g. 1973 Act s.38(2), which makes it a criminal offence to fail to declare an interest in a contract.

s.31 of the 1989 Act authorised the Secretary of State (or, post-devolution, the Scottish Ministers) to adopt a code of conduct by which all councillors undertake to be bound. The regulatory gap is obvious: on the one hand, a number of criminal offences dependent on the criminal standard of proof; on the other, a code, breach of which carries no formal sanction other than anything the member's party, the authority or the local electorate might happen to mete out. In its third report, the Committee on Standards in Public Life described the situation as wholly insufficient to secure public confidence in the probity of local government, and recommended the adoption of a national code of ethical standards to be enforced at local level.[100]

The matter being devolved, the Scottish Government took over responsibility for consulting on these proposals, and came up with a framework for ethical standards differing from the committee's recommendations in two important ways. First, it extended the scope of the code beyond local government to include also "devolved public bodies". Second, it rejected the idea of local enforcement in favour of a national standards commission, charged with investigating complaints concerning breaches of the new codes of conduct. This framework is reflected in the 2000 Act.[101] The Scottish Ministers are charged with issuing a mandatory code of conduct for local councillors,[102] including provision about the registration and declaration of their interests and their ineligibility to participate in council business affecting those interests,[103] together with a model code of conduct for members of devolved public bodies containing a mixture of mandatory and optional provisions so that individual public bodies have some scope for tailoring the model code to suit their particular circumstances.[104] Every local authority and devolved public body is required by s.7 to set up, maintain and make available for public inspection a register of members' interests. Section 8 and Sch.1 then provide for the establishment of the Standards Commission for Scotland and the remainder of Pt 2 is devoted to the conduct of investigations where breaches of the codes of conduct are alleged to have taken place.

9–17 Section 9 and Sch.2 originally provide for the appointment of a chief investigating officer, who takes responsibility for the initial investigation of complaints made to the commission. Those functions have since been transferred to the Commissioner for Ethical Standards in Public Life in Scotland.[105] The commission may issue general directions to the commissioner relating to the performance of their functions, but may not direct them as to how they conduct particular investigations.[106] Investigations must be carried out in confidence, so

---

[100] Committee on Standards in Public Life, *Third Report—Standards of Conduct in Local Government in England, Scotland and Wales* (The Stationery Office, 1997) CM.3702–1.

[101] See, generally, D.W. Cobb, "Shutting the Door or Cleaning the Stable? The Ethical Standards in Public Life etc (Scotland) Act 2000", 2001 S.L.T. (News) 205.

[102] Standards Commission for Scotland, *The Councillors' Code of Conduct*, 3rd edn (Scottish Government, 2010) *http://www.gov.scot/Publications/2010/12/10145144/0* [Accessed 8 June 2020].

[103] Ethical Standards in Public Life etc. (Scotland) Act 2000 ("the 2000 Act") s.1. "Interests" are defined by s.1(8) to include "pecuniary and non-pecuniary interests".

[104] 2000 Act s.2. Devolved public bodies are required to submit their individual codes of conduct for the approval of the Scottish Ministers within time limits stipulated by order made under s.3.

[105] Scottish Parliamentary Commissions and Commissioners etc. Act 2010. The functions were transferred via the Public Standards Commissioner for Scotland (Public Service Reform (Commissioner for Ethical Standards in Public Life in Scotland etc.) Order 2013 (SSI 2013/197)).

[106] 2000 Act s.10.

far as possible, and should normally be completed within three months.[107] The commissioner has the same powers as the Court of Session to require the attendance and examination of witnesses and the production of documents,[108] although no one may be compelled to give evidence or produce documents that they could not be compelled to give or produce in civil proceedings in the Court of Session. Therefore, it might be open for a witness to claim, say, confidentiality or privilege in relation to particular documents. Conceivably, the commissioner could treat such a claim as obstruction, which entitles them to certify the matter to the Court of Session. The Court of Session may in turn treat the matter as a contempt of court. On conclusion of an investigation, it is for the commissioner to decide whether or not to report to the Standards Commission.[109] If they are minded to report that the subject of the investigation has breached the applicable code of conduct, they must first give the subject a copy of their proposed report and accord them an opportunity to make representations thereon. But it should also be noted that the commissioner may or, if so directed by the commission, must submit an interim report on an investigation in progress, and that the commission may on receipt of such a report suspend from office the member concerned for a period not exceeding three months (which may, however, be renewed).[110] The commission may only exercise the power of suspension where satisfied that the further conduct of the investigation is likely otherwise to be prejudiced or (more broadly) that it would be in the public interest to do so. The commission is not required to hold a hearing before imposing a suspension, although the subject of the interim report must be given an opportunity to make representations on its contents.

Where the commissioner submits a final report under s.14 of the Act, the commission may decide to take no further action, direct them to conduct further investigations or hold a hearing.[111] If a hearing is held, it must be conducted by at least three members of the commission, and the individual whose conduct is being considered is entitled to be heard, either in person or through a representative (legal or otherwise), but, that apart, the procedure to be followed at the hearing is for the commission itself to determine.[112] The commission has the power to require the attendance of any person to give evidence and the production of documents, and is expressly authorised to examine witnesses on oath. Failure to attend a hearing, give evidence or produce documents, without reasonable excuse, is a criminal offence. At the conclusion of a hearing, the members of the commission must state their findings in writing and provide copies to the subject of the inquiry, the council or body concerned, any other person the commission considers should receive a copy, and any other person **9–18**

[107] Where it appears that the investigation will take longer to complete, the chief investigating officer must notify the commission, the individual subject to the investigation and the relevant authority or body of that fact: 2000 Act s.12(5).

[108] "Documents" includes information held by means of a computer or in any other electronic form: 2000 Act s.13(5).

[109] 2000 Act s.14.

[110] 2000 Act s.21.

[111] For a list of hearings, and their outcomes, see Standards Commission for Scotland, "Concluded Investigations Referred from CES", *http://www.standardscommissionscotland.org.uk/cases/case-list* [Accessed 9 July 2020].

[112] 2000 Act s.17.

who pays a "reasonable charge" for a copy.[113] The findings, adverse or otherwise, must be considered at a full meeting of the council.

9–19 Where the commission's verdict is that the applicable code of conduct has been breached, it has a number of possible sanctions at its disposal. It may: censure the member concerned, but otherwise take no action; suspend that person, for a period not exceeding one year, from all or specified meetings of the council or body; or (in the case of a councillor) disqualify them from being, or being nominated for election as, or being elected as a councillor, for a period of up to five years.[114] A person who is found to have contravened a code of conduct and/or upon whom a sanction is imposed under s.19 may appeal to the sheriff principal within 21 days of the relevant decision.[115] The grounds for appeal, in the case of an appeal against a finding of breach of the code, are: that the commission's finding was based on an error of law; that there was procedural impropriety in the conduct of the hearing; that the commission has acted unreasonably in the exercise of its discretion; or that the facts found to be proved by the commission do not support its decision. The grounds for appeal in the case of an appeal against the imposition of a sanction are narrower: that the sanction was excessive, or that the commission has acted unreasonably in the exercise of its discretion. In the first case, the sheriff principal may confirm or quash the verdict of the commission, or quash the decision and remit the matter to the commission for reconsideration. In the second case, they may confirm or quash the sanction, or quash it and either substitute a different sanction or remit the matter to the commission. There is a further right of appeal from the decision of the sheriff principal to the Court of Session.

[113] 2000 Act s.18. The section makes no provision for releasing the report in confidence or in redacted form, even though s.17 permits the commission to conduct hearings in private if it considers that this would be in the public interest.

[114] 2000 Act s.19. It is worth noting that both disqualification and suspension under s.21 could present problems for a local authority in terms of securing the necessary political balance on its committees, and could even deprive a majority group of its overall control of the council.

[115] 2000 Act s.22.

CHAPTER 10

The UK and the European Union

INTRODUCTION

On 31 January 2020, the United Kingdom ceased to be a member of the European Union. That brought to an end the UK's 47-year membership of what has become the EU. The UK is the first, and so far only, country to leave the EU, but the effects of membership of the EU will continue to be felt in domestic law for some time to come. Indeed, as we saw in Ch.3, EU membership may have left an indelible mark upon the constitution of the UK. At the time of writing, the UK is in the "implementation period": it has left the EU but in almost all respects it continues to be treated as a member of the EU.[1] That implementation period is due to end on 31 December 2020. But even then, the body of EU law that existed on 31 January 2020 has, as we shall see, been largely imported into domestic law. Accordingly, some understanding of the structure and functioning of the EU is likely to remain important for some time to come. Against that background, this chapter comes in two parts: the European and the domestic. First, there is a broad overview of the institutions of the EU, the form of legislation that is passes and the main ways in which EU law impacts on Member States.[2] In the second part, we look at the European Union from the domestic perspective and consider the legislative arrangements that were, and are now, in place to regulate the UK's relationship with the EU and EU law. **10–01**

THE EUROPEAN UNION

The evolution of the European Union

To understand the Europe of today it is necessary to understand the process of evolution that has taken place. "Europe" as it is today (subject to the Brexit) came into being on 1 December 2009 with the entry into force of the Treaty of Lisbon. But the foundations of today's Union were laid in the early 1950s. The initial steps towards European integration were taken in 1952 when the European Coal and Steel Community ("the ECSC") was formed. Six nations (France, (the **10–02**

[1] The main difference being it no longer participates in any of the institutions of the EU.

[2] The substance of EU law has always been beyond the scope of this work. Many texts are devoted to that subject, or more frequently one particular aspect of it. For general texts covering EU law see, for example D.A.O. Edward and R.C. Lane, *European Union Law* (Cheltenham: Edward Elgar, 2013); A. O'Neill, *EU Law for UK Lawyers* (Oxford: Hart, 2011), or P. Craig and G. De Burca, *EU Law: Text, Cases and Materials*, 5th edn (Oxford: Oxford University Press, 2011).

Federal Republic of) Germany,[3] Italy, Belgium, the Netherlands and Luxembourg) signed the Treaty of Paris. This was not an ordinary international treaty. It created a super-national body with independent institutions having the power to bind the Member States. In creating this "Community" the Member States transferred some of the powers normally exercised by sovereign states but for specific and defined purposes and for a limited period of time.[4] A number of institutions were created: a High Authority was the main executive institution with decision-making power and responsibility for implementing the aims of the Treaty; an Assembly consisting of delegates from national parliaments, which exercised essentially supervisory powers; a Council, consisting of one representative from each Member State; and a court charged with the interpretation and application of the Treaty. That structure is very similar to what we see in the European Union of today.

After aborted attempts to form a European Defence Community and a European Political Community (foundering on French anxieties about German rearmament), discussions continued between the ECSC Member States about how to progress the project of European integration. Those discussions led to the foundation of two further communities in March 1957: the European Economic Community ("the EEC") and the European Atomic Energy Community ("the EAEC"). These treaties entered into force on 1 January 1958 and were, unlike the time limited ECSC, for an "unlimited duration".[5] The two new treaties followed the same scheme as the ECSC Treaty: there was an Assembly consisting of delegates from national parliaments, a Council and a court. The High Authority was, in the two new communities, known as the Commission. From the inception of the EEC and the EAEC, the three communities shared a single assembly and a single court. In 1967, the Councils of the respective communities were merged and the ECSC High Authority and the EEC and EAEC Commissions came together to form the Commission of the European Communities. Although there remained three legally distinct Communities, they each now shared the same institutions and the distinctions began to blur.

In economic terms, the European Communities were a conspicuous success. In parallel to the European Communities, seven other countries formed the European Free Trade Association ("the EFTA") in 1960.[6] Four of the EFTA members, however, sought membership of the Communities twice during the 1960s. A third attempt led to a Treaty of Accession being signed by Denmark, Ireland, Norway and the UK in January 1972. In that event, the Norwegian people declined membership in a referendum resulting in Norway failing to ratify the Treaty. The remaining countries did ratify the Accession Treaty and, as a result, became members of the three Communities on 1 January 1973. The 1970s ended with reform of the Assembly. Until that point, it comprised of delegates

---

[3] Following German reunification in 1990, the Democratic Republic of Germany became part of the Communities without any amendment to the then existing treaties or a separate accession agreement. The consequence of the reunification of Germany was a significant increase in the Communities' territory and an additional 16 million people within its boundaries.

[4] European Coal and Steel Community Treaty art.97: the ECSC was formed for 50 years and therefore expired, naturally, on 24 July 2002.

[5] European Economic Community Treaty art.240; European Atomic Energy Community Treaty art.208.

[6] The seven were: Denmark, Norway, Austria, Portugal, Switzerland, Sweden and the UK.

appointed by the respective parliaments of the Member States and it possessed limited powers.[7] Direct elections to what was now called the European Parliament took place for the first time in 1979. With direct election came at least some level of democratic legitimacy and thus a claim for greater powers. Those powers were to come over the following years. The 1980s started with the accession of Greece, who became the tenth Member State of the Communities, and the secession of Greenland. Although Greenland remained part of Denmark, in 1979 Greenland acquired the power to opt out of Danish treaty obligations and, following a referendum in 1982, did just that in relation to the Communities.[8] In 1985, five Member States entered into the Schengen agreement, the effect of which was the removal of border controls between their respective countries.[9] The work needed to implement the agreement was such that it was 10 years before the system came fully into force. On 1 January 1986 the Communities grew to 12 in number with the accession of Spain and Portugal.

That year, 1986, was, however, more noteworthy in the evolution of the Union for the adoption by the Member States of the Single European Act. Signed in February 1986, it came into force on 1 July 1987 and committed the Member States to an ambitious timetable to complete the "internal market" by the end of 1992. The Single European Act revived the integrationist momentum in the Communities. In addition to the commitment to the internal market, the Single European Act made important amendments to the legislative procedures of the Communities. These enhanced the role of the European Parliament and an amendment to the EEC Treaty allowed qualified majority voting (in place of unanimity) in an increased number of areas in the Council of Ministers. A new Court of First Instance was created to assist the Court of Justice, the Parliament was given a veto over the accession of new Member States and the Communities acquired an extended competence that now reached into economic and monetary union, social policy, social and economic cohesion and the environment.

The Single European Act produced significant momentum for further **10–03** integration. Plans for economic and monetary union were developed alongside plans for deeper political integration. The result was another treaty: the Treaty on European Union, more commonly known as the Maastricht Treaty. The Maastricht Treaty was politically controversial.[10] It was also subject to legal challenge in a number of Member States[11] and was initially rejected by the Danes

---

[7] It had two main powers, both of them rightly regarded as "nuclear options": it could require the Commission, en masse, to resign and it could reject the budget prepared by the Commission. Otherwise, the Assembly was limited to trying to call the Commission to account where it considered that to be necessary.

[8] The result was the Communities lost over 50% of its territory but less than 0.1% of its population.

[9] The original Schengen countries were Belgium, the Federal Republic of Germany, France, Luxembourg and the Netherlands.

[10] For one account of the trouble it caused the Major Government, see: K. Clarke, *Kind of Blue: A Political Memoir* (MacMillan, London: 2016), pp.309–315.

[11] In the UK, those challenges came in the form of applications to the courts for interdict (in Scotland) and injunction (in England and Wales): *Monckton v Lord Advocate*, 1995 S.L.T. 1201 and *R. v Secretary of State for the Foreign and Commonwealth Office, Ex p. Rees-Mogg* [1994] Q.B. 552 DC, respectively.

in a referendum.[12] The Maastricht Treaty created the "European Union" and adopted the "three pillar" structure for the Union. The first of the three pillars was the existing Communities. The Communities were flanked by the other two pillars: a common foreign and security policy and co-operation on justice and home affairs. This unwieldy structure reflected the tension at the heart of the European Union between integration and intergovernmentalism. The Communities pillar was, as ever, a genuinely super-national structure that bound the Member States in ever-widening areas—a "new legal order of international law" as the Court of Justice put it.[13] The Maastricht Treaty also made a number of important changes to the treaties that founded the Communities, in particular the EEC Treaty. These included the renaming of the EEC as the European Community ("the EC"), the conferral of a number of new competences, the creation of citizenship of the EU and provision for achieving economic and monetary union and the adoption of a single currency. The other two pillars were, on the other hand, much more akin to traditional creations of international law. Neither of these pillars had supremacy over national laws nor direct effect.[14] The Maastricht Treaty also elevated the concepts of proportionality and subsidiarity to the status of general principles of Community law.[15] Their elevation ought to have provided some reassurance to those concerned about the pace and direction of European integration. Proportionality requires the Communities' institutions to go no further than is necessary to achieve the objectives of the treaties; subsidiarity requires that legislative and administrative action be taken at the most appropriate level, be it European, national or regional level. The other important aspect of the Maastricht Treaty was its endorsement of the concept of "variable geometry" or differential integration. This was intended to permit Member States to move towards integration at different speeds in difference contexts[16] and respond to the tension that existed, and continues to exist, amongst the Member States about their differing vision as to how far the project of European integration should go.[17] The difficulties with this multifaceted conception of the EU were reflected in the provision made in the Maastricht Treaty for a further intergovernmental conference in 1996 to consider "to what

[12] The Treaty was initially rejected by Danes in a referendum by the narrowest of margins (there was less than 1% in it) but following a number of undertakings at the Edinburgh Summit in December 1992, the Treaty was approved by the Danish people the following year.

[13] *NV Algemene Transport- en Expeditie Onderneming van Gend en Loos v Nederlandse Administratie der Belastingen* (C-26/62) [1963] E.C.R. 1 at p.12.

[14] Both supremacy and direct effect were key characteristics of the Communities and are discussed more fully below at paras 10–26—10–27. Supremacy has also been discussed in the context of its consequences for the sovereignty of the Westminster Parliament (at para.3–09).

[15] Proportionality is discussed in Ch.11 (in relation to human rights) and Ch.15 (in relation to judicial review). So far as EU law is concerned, proportionality has significant differences. See *R. (on the application of Lumsdon) v Legal Services Board* [2015] UKSC 41; [2016] A.C. 697 at [22]–[82].

[16] For general discussion, see D. Curtin, "The Constitutional Structure of the European Union: A Europe of bits and pieces" (1993) 30 C.M.L. Rev. 17; S. Weatherill, "The Provisions on Closer Co-operation" in D. O'Keeffe and P. Twomey (eds), *The Legal Issues of the Amsterdam Treaty* (Oxford: Hart, 1999), Ch.2.

[17] That lack of agreement on the vision for the future of Europe (closer integration along a federal model or an economic union that respects the sovereignty of the Member States) has rendered the EU an "essentially contested concept" (Z. Bankowski and E.A. Christodoulidis, "The European Union as an Essentially Contested Project" (1998) 4(4) E.L.J. 341).

extent the policies and forms of co-operation introduced by this Treaty may need to be revised". The product of that further conference was a further treaty: the Treaty of Amsterdam.

The Treaty of Amsterdam was signed in October 1997. Before turning to consider that, in attempt to maintain some degree of chronology, three other developments should be noted. First, the European Economic Area ("the EEA") came into being on 1 January 1994. The EEA consisted of the EU Member States on the one hand and six of the now seven Member States of the EFTA.[18] Second, in 1994 a further accession treaty was agreed, this time with Austria, Finland, Sweden and, for a second time, Norway. Each country held a referendum to ratify their accession to the EU and, for a second time, the Norwegian people rejected membership. There were no such difficulties in the other accession countries who duly joined the EU on 1 January 1995.[19] Finally, as noted above, the Schengen agreement (which removed border checks between the signatory countries) became fully operational on 26 March 1995 and by now its signatories had expanded from five to nine.[20] Returning to the Treaty of Amsterdam, it modified the three pillar structure of the EU and made further changes to the Communities. The role of the European Parliament was further enhanced with an extension of the "co-decision" legislative procedure into new areas. In the Council of Ministers, qualified majority voting was extended. The EC acquired further competences, many transferred from the third pillar, including visas, asylum, immigration and other policies related to free movement of persons. On a practical level, the biggest impact the Treaty of Amsterdam had was the renumbering of all the EC and Maastricht Treaty articles, which caused no end of confusion.[21] The Treaty of Amsterdam was met with a rather muted reception, perhaps because it failed to grapple with the pressing issue of constitutional and institutional reform that was necessary before further expansion of the Union. Those issues were again deferred to another intergovernmental conference and another treaty. 10–04

The Treaty of Nice was signed on 26 February 2001. It sought to ready the Union for expansion beyond its then membership of 15. The power of veto was removed for almost all matters and the weighting of votes in the Council and the allocation of seats in the European Parliament amongst the Member States were determined. The structure and jurisdiction of the Court of Justice was also amended. After initially being rejected by the Irish people in a referendum, it was

---

[18] The EFTA Member States were by now Austria, Norway, Sweden and Switzerland (who remained from the time the United Kingdom was a member) along with Finland, Iceland and Liechtenstein. The Swiss people rejected the European Economic Area Treaty in a referendum and as a result it was only the other six EFTA members that joined the EEA.

[19] The consequence of their accession was the EFTA element of the recently created EEA was reduced to three: Iceland, Liechtenstein and Norway.

[20] Spain, Portugal, Greece and Italy, although only the first two implemented the agreement when it became operational in 1995. The membership has grown further and now includes all EU Member States (with the exception of Ireland, who have not signed; Bulgaria, Croatia, Cyprus and Romania are obliged by the terms of their accession agreements to join but have not yet implemented the agreement), together with four non-Member States (Iceland, Liechtenstein, Norway and Switzerland). The United Kingdom has never signed the agreement.

[21] The result being that both article numbers were invariably used, for example art.234 (ex art.177).

approved at the second attempt and entered into force on 1 February 2003.[22] Given, as we shall see, the Treaty of Nice has been superseded, the most significant and lasting decision to come out of the intergovernmental conference that gave rise to the Treaty was the adoption, by way of a solemn proclamation, of the Charter of Fundamental Rights that had been drafted at the request of the European Council meeting in Cologne in July 1999.[23] The Charter contained many familiar rights, in language that was similar, and in places identical, to the rights set out in the European Convention on Human Rights. But it went further and set out a number of social and economic rights,[24] which were afforded the same status as more traditional fundamental rights.[25] Having been "solemnly proclaimed", the Charter had no legal effect, it did not bind the Member States and it did not confer any rights on EU citizens. As such "soft law" has the habit of doing, it hardened over time and the Charter has now been adopted by the Member States, giving it the same legal force as the treaties.[26]

The Treaty of Nice served its primary function and enabled the EU to expand and admit a further 10 members on 1 May 2004[27] taking the membership to 25. Accession treaties were agreed with Bulgaria and Romania the following year and they joined on 1 January 2007. Breaking the chronology slightly, the most recent country to join the EU was Croatia, who joined the Union on 1 July 2013, bringing the membership to 28 at the time the UK left.[28]

10–05 Returning to the chronology, in February 2002, under the chairmanship of former French President Giscard d'Estaing, a "constitutional convention" was convened. In the summer of 2003, the convention agreed the text of a draft "Treaty establishing a Constitution for Europe". The draft constitution sought to bring together the various Treaties of the Communities and the Union in a single text. The proposed text was submitted to the President of the Council on 18 July 2003. After a series of intergovernmental conferences and several rounds of negotiation the final version of the Treaty Establishing a Constitution for Europe was signed in Rome on 29 October 2004. Signing the Treaty, it would transpire, was the easy bit. To enter into force the Treaty, like all previous European treaties, required to be ratified by each of the Member States in accordance with their own constitutional procedures. As with Maastricht, judicial challenges

---

22 For the sake of completeness, it should be noted that between the signing of the Treaty of Nice and its coming into force, the very first Treaty, which founded the ECSC, expired on 24 July 2002 and brought that Community to an end. Much of its work was absorbed by the EC.

23 The Charter is considered in more detail below at para.10–30, below. See also, Edward and Lane, *European Union Law* (2013), paras 6.114–6.118; O'Neill, *EU Law for UK Lawyers* (2011), paras 6.55–6.98.

24 For example, rights to collective bargaining (art.28), social security (art.34) and healthcare (art.35).

25 arts 51 and 52 of the Charter.

26 See para.10–31 below and *Kucukdeveci v Sweden* (C-555/07) [2010] E.C.R. I-365.

27 The new members were: the Czech Republic, Estonia, Cyprus, Latvia, Lithuania, Hungary, Malta, Poland, Slovakia and Slovenia.

28 At the time of writing there are five "candidate countries" for membership of the EU. "Candidate countries" are those countries that are in the process of integrating EU laws into their domestic law. This is a change from the initial accessions, which provided a post-accession period of alignment. All admissions since (and including) the 2004 group of 10 have followed this pre-alignment model. The current "candidate countries" are: Albania, Montenegro, Serbia, the former Yugoslav Republic of Macedonia and Turkey. Two more countries are "potential candidate countries" meaning they have sought membership but do not yet fulfil the membership criteria. Those counties are Bosnia and Herzegovina and Kosovo.

followed in a number of Member States, none of which were successful.[29] Initially, ratification went smoothly. By the spring of 2005 nine Member States had ratified the constitution, including Spain where the electorate had supported ratification by an overwhelming majority in a referendum.[30] Referendums were due, however, in nine more Member States.[31] First, in May 2005, the French people rejected the constitution by a margin of 55:45 (on a 70 per cent turnout). A few weeks later, the Dutch public also rejected the constitution, this time by a margin of 62:38 (on a 62 per cent turnout). Despite ratification by Estonia, Latvia, Luxembourg (after a positive referendum result) and Malta,[32] the French and Dutch electorate had effectively killed the constitution. The remaining referendums that had been promised by Member States (including the United Kingdom) were postponed and it was accepted that the anticipated date for the constitution to come into force (1 November 2006) was now unachievable. But the end of the constitution did not mark the end of the desire to reform the Union. In 2007 the Council agreed to hold another intergovernmental conference with a view to producing a fresh treaty that would draw heavily on the aborted constitution. The product of that conference was the Lisbon Treaty, which was signed on 13 December 2007.

The Lisbon Treaty entered into force on 1 December 2009. Much of the **10–06** content of the failed constitution was reflected in the Treaty but some of the more inflammatory provisions were excluded, such as provision on the flag and anthem of the EU and an express declaration of the supremacy of EU law.[33] The most significant difference between the constitution and the Lisbon Treaty was the structure adopted. Whereas the constitution would have resulted in a single document, the Lisbon Treaty reverts to the traditional formula of amending the existing treaties, albeit extensively. Articles 1 and 2 of the Lisbon Treaty list the changes to the EU and EC Treaties.[34] What was previously the EC Treaty was now to be known as the Treaty on the Functioning of the European Union (TFEU) and the heavily amended Maastricht Treaty was styled the Treaty establishing the European Union (TEU). The key points to note include: the Union "replace[d] and succeed[ed] the European Community"[35]; the Union

[29] In the United Kingdom, an attempt was made to prevent a Bill being introduced to Parliament to give effect to the Treaty: *R. (on the application of Southall) v Secretary of State for Foreign and Commonwealth Affairs* [2003] EWCA Civ 1002; [2003] 3 C.M.L.R. 18. For references to challenges in other Member States, see Edward and Lane, *European Union Law* (2013), para.1.50.

[30] The other countries that had ratified the constitution were Austria, Belgium, Cyprus, Greece, Hungary, Italy, Lithuania and Slovenia.

[31] It perhaps betrays the political sensitivity of the constitution in a number of countries that so many referendums were held when only Ireland was obliged by its constitution to hold one. The Dutch referendum was the first such plebiscite in its history.

[32] The parliaments of Germany, Finland and Slovakia had also approved the constitution and it was awaiting formal ratification by the president of each of those countries (in the case of Germany and Slovakia, after judicial challenges had been resolved).

[33] Of course, leaving these provisions out of the Treaty did nothing to change the fact that each of them existed and still exist.

[34] The list of amendments ran to well over 100 pages when the Lisbon Treaty was published in the *Official Journal*; [2007] OJ C306/1.

[35] art.1 TEU; thus ended the European Community but the EAEC remains in place and continues to be governed by its own Treaty.

acquired legal personality[36]; the pillar structure that was created by the Maastricht Treaty was largely removed with most of the third pillar (co-operation on justice and home affairs) absorbed by the Community form and common foreign and security policy brought within the Union; and there is no hierarchy between the TEU and TFEU and together they are known as "the Treaties".[37]

It is apparent from that brief canter through the history of the EU, that many of the tensions that surfaced in the Brexit debate in the UK (the pace of scale of integration and the extent of residual autonomy for Member States) reflected tensions that had long existed within the EU. Before turning to consider the institutions that form the EU and the legislative powers of the Union, a word on the terminology employed may be helpful. For ease of reference, the discussion that follows refers to "the EU" and "the Union" and should be taken to include the collective structures of the European Union. Similarly, the phrase "EU law" will be employed and should be taken to include that which falls within the jurisdiction of the Court of Justice of the European Union. Finally, reference to treaty articles will invariable be to the TFEU or the TEU as amended by the Treaty of Lisbon. Every effort has been made to update, where appropriate, references in any quotes from the case law of the court to the current treaty provision to avoid the need to work back through the previous treaties.

The institutions of the EU

10–07 Article 13 TEU provides that the institutions of the EU shall be: (a) the European Parliament; (b) the European Council; (c) the Council; (d) the European Commission; (e) the Court of Justice of the European Union; (f) the European Central Bank; and (g) the Court of Auditors. The Parliament and the Council are vested with the legislative (and budgetary) functions of the EU.[38] The European Council has no legislative functions; it is there to provide "the Union with the necessary impetus for its development".[39] The executive functions of the EU belong to the Commission,[40] which is responsible to the European Parliament[41] and judicial functions rest with the Court of Justice.[42] It can be seen, therefore, that the EU possesses the same key organs as a conventional nation state. To place the continuing impact of EU law in its proper context, an overview of the key institutions may be helpful.[43]

---

[36] art.47 TEU; this was significant in that it allowed the EU to enter international treaties in its own right.

[37] art.1 TEU; art.1(2) TFEU. The consolidated versions of the Treaties were published in the *Official Journal* in March 2010: [2010] OJ C83.

[38] arts 14(1) and 16(1) TEU.

[39] art.15(1) TEU.

[40] art.17(1) TEU.

[41] art.17(8) TEU.

[42] art.19(1) TEU.

[43] The European Central Bank and the Court of Auditors, along with other EU institutions such as the European Investment Banks and the Committee of the Regions, will not be discuss in this book. For a discussion of those institutions, see Edward and Lane, *European Union Law* (2013), Ch.4. The Lisbon Treaty also introduced two new (and, at the time, controversial) positions: a permanent president of the European Council (previously, the presidency of the European Council had rotated around the

The European Parliament

The European Parliament, based in Strasbourg, consists of members (MEPs) directly elected by the electorate of the 27 Member States. No Member State shall have fewer than six MEPs or more than 96.[44] The allocation of seats amongst the Member States is determined by the European Council, acting unanimously and on the initiative, and with the consent, of the European Parliament.[45] Members of the European Parliament are elected for a five year term.[46] They must be elected by direct universal suffrage in a free and secret ballot[47] using a system of proportional representation.[48] The majority of Member States function as a single constituency for the purposes of European elections. Whilst a member, the United Kingdom, along with Belgium, France, Italy and Ireland, was an exception in subdividing into constituencies. For the purposes of elections to the European Parliament, the United Kingdom was divided into 12 multi-member regions, with each region allocated between three and 10 MEPs depending upon its population.[49] Members of the European Parliament now receive a salary that is fixed at 38.5 per cent of the salary of a judge of the Court of Justice.[50] Prior to that system coming into force in 2009, an MEP was paid the equivalent of a member of their home parliament. That led to wide disparities between the salaries paid to MEPs of different Member States. Although candidates usually stand under the banner of their national party, once in Strasbourg they generally organise themselves according to pan-European groups. There are currently seven political groups in the European Parliament together with a small group of non-attached members.[51] These European political parties are required to "contribute to forming European political awareness and to expressing the will of the citizens of the Union".[52] To be recognised as a European political party, the party must meet the following conditions: it must have legal personality in the Member State in which its seat is located; it must be represented in one quarter of the Member States, either by MEPs or in the national or regional parliaments of 10–08

Member States on a six-monthly basis) and a High Representative of the Union for Foreign Affairs and Security Policy (there was no prior equivalent for this post). For a discussion of those roles, see para.10–08 of the 3rd edn of this work.

44 art.14(2) TEU. The number temporarily increased to 766 with the accession of Croatia in 2013 but was readjusted in advance of the European Parliamentary elections in May 2014.

45 art.14(2) TEU.

46 art.14(3) TEU.

47 art.14(3) TEU.

48 Decision 2002/772 amending the Act concerning the election of the representatives of the European Parliament by direct universal suffrage, annexed to Decision 76/787/ECSC, EEC, Euratom [2002] OJ L283/1; the decision further requires that either a list system is employed or the single transferrable vote system. In this context, see also art.223(1) TFEU.

49 Scotland, Northern Ireland and Wales each formed a separate region. England was then divided into nine regions. The smallest regions were Northern Ireland and the North East (both with three MEPs). The South East was the largest region, returning 10 MEPs.

50 Decision 2005/684 adopting the Statute for Members of the European Parliament [2005] OJ L262/1, art.10.

51 The current groupings, and their membership, can be found on the European Parliament's website, *https://www.europarl.europa.eu/about-parliament/en/organisation-and-rules/organisation/political-groups* [Accessed 2 June 2020].

52 art.10(4) TEU.

the Member States; it must conform with the founding principles of the EU; and it must have either participated in elections to the European Parliament or expressed a desire to do so.[53]

10–09 The European Parliament exists to ensure that EU citizens are directly represented at EU level.[54] Its powers have expanded, in particular following the introduction of direct elections. The Parliament has the power to adopt its own rules and procedures[55] and, unless otherwise provided for in the treaties, acts by simple majority of the votes cast.[56] The European Parliament performs five main functions. First, as explained below, it plays a role in the appointment, and then holding to account, of the Commission.[57] So far as the appointment of the Commission is concerned, however, that role is limited to approval en masse of the nominees. The inability to reject individual candidates leaves the Parliament with a fairly blunt axe. Second, the European Parliament plays an important role in relation to the EU budget. Responsibility for the EU budget is shared between the Parliament, the Council and the Commission.[58] Third, the European Parliament has general supervisory powers. The Commission is responsible to the Parliament.[59] The Parliament may, at the request of a quarter of its component members, set up a temporary committee of inquiry to investigate alleged contraventions or maladministration in the implementation of EU law.[60] The European Parliament can also receive petitions, addressing any matter within the EU fields, from any citizen of the EU or any natural or legal person residing or having its registered office in a Member State.[61] An ombudsman, empowered to receive complaints from any citizen of the EU or any natural or legal person residing or having its registered office in a Member State, concerning allegations of maladministration in the activities of the EU institutions, bodies, offices or agencies (with the exception of the Court of Justice acting in its judicial capacity), shall also be elected by the European Parliament.[62] The ombudsman is elected following each European Parliamentary election and holds office for the duration of the Parliament's term.[63] They are eligible for re-election.[64] Fourth, the European Parliament is required to consent to a number of EU decisions in areas of constitutional or political importance. These areas include: composition of, and method of election to, the European Parliament[65]; the conclusion by the EU of specified categories of agreements with third countries or international

[53] Regulation 2004/2003 on the regulations governing political parties at European level and the rules regarding their funding [2003] OJ L297/1 (as amended by Regulation 1524/2007 amending Regulation (EC) No.2004/2003 on the regulations governing political parties at European level and the rules regarding their funding [2007] OJ L343/5), art.3.

[54] art.10(2) TEU.

[55] art.232 TFEU.

[56] art.231 TFEU.

[57] See para.10–13, below.

[58] art.314 TFEU.

[59] art.17(8) TEU.

[60] art.226 TFEU.

[61] art.227 TFEU.

[62] art.228(1) TFEU.

[63] art.228(2) TFEU.

[64] art.228(2) TFEU.

[65] art.14(2) TEU and art.223 TFEU, respectively.

organisations[66]; the accession of new Member States[67]; the secession of existing Member States[68]; and a number of specific policies in relation to judicial co-operation in criminal matters.[69] Fifth, and finally, the European Parliament now plays an important role in the passage of EU legislation.[70]

The European Council

The European Council has met regularly since the 1970s but with the entry into force of the Lisbon Treaty it was formally recognised by the treaties.[71] The European Council (which must be distinguished from "the Council", which is discussed below) consists of the Heads of State, or of government, of the Member States,[72] together with the President of the European Council and the President of the Commission.[73] Meetings of the European Council have more colloquially been referred as "summit meetings" or "European summits". The European Council has no legislative function (unlike "the Council") but exists to "provide the Union with the necessary impetus for development" and to set the general political direction and priorities.[74] The European Council is required to meet twice every six months, or when the President convenes a special meeting.[75] Decisions of the European Council should be taken by consensus, unless the treaties require otherwise.[76] The President is required to report to the European Parliament after each meeting of the European Council.[77] Despite having no legislative function, the European Council has proved to be a useful forum for bringing the leaders of the Member States together on a regular basis. Discussion is not necessarily restricted to areas of EU competence and the European Council **10–10**

---

66 art.218(6) TFEU; in particular the European Parliament had to consent to the EU's accession to the European Convention on Human Rights (art.218(6)(a)(ii) TFEU) on which see para.12–38.

67 art.49 TEU.

68 art.50 TEU; although quite what would happen if the rest of the secession process had been successfully navigated only for the European Parliament to refuse to consent is another matter given the right of Member States to withdraw from the EU "in accordance with its own constitutional requirements".

69 For example, the formation of a European Public Prosecutors Office (art.86 TFEU) or the definition of certain criminal offences (art.83 TFEU).

70 The European Parliament is not a legislature in the sense that Westminster and Holyrood are considered as such. Instead, the legislative functions of the EU are shared between a number of institutions, one of which is the European Parliament. EU legislation is now passed by either the "ordinary legislative process" (see art.294 TFEU), which is the default option, or the "special legislative process" (see art.289 TFEU). For details of the legislative processes see, for example, Edwards and Lane, *European Union Law*, at paras 3–62—3–64.

71 art.13(1) TEU.

72 For example, the UK was represented by the Head of Government, the Prime Minister, as opposed to the Head of State, the Queen. France, however, would be represented by her President, the Head of State. Each Head of State/government can be assisted by a minister who may attend with them (art.15(3) TEU).

73 art.15(2) TEU.

74 art.15(1) TEU.

75 art.15(3) TEU.

76 art.15(4) TEU. Accordingly, a vote in the European Council is rare. The UK Prime Minister (David Cameron) forced a vote over the appointment of the new Commission President in June 2014. He lost the vote 26:2. The Prime Minister's report to Parliament following the European Council meeting can be found at: *Hansard*, HC Vol.583, cols 559–601 (30 June 2014).

77 art.15(6)(d) TEU.

provides a forum for the Member States to discuss areas of mutual concern and matters that are subject to intergovernmental co-operation. Decisions taken in the European Council are taken by the respective leaders in their capacity as representatives of the Member States. Any decision taken, therefore, is a decision of the Member States (and not of the Council). As a result, such decisions are immune from judicial review before the Court of Justice.[78]

The Council

10–11 The Council is a different creature and must be differentiated from the European Council. The Council, jointly with the European Parliament, is responsible for exercising the EU's legislative and budgetary functions.[79] The Council consists of representatives of each Member State, at ministerial level, who have the authority to commit the government of their Member State and to cast its vote.[80] The High Representative chairs the Council when it meets to discuss foreign affairs, otherwise the presidency of the Council is held by the Member States on the basis of equal rotation.[81] The order in which the Member States hold the presidency is determined by the European Council and by qualified majority.[82] The Council meets in different configurations depending upon the business to be discussed.[83] The configurations are determined by the European Council and by qualified majority.[84] There are currently 10 configurations of the Council.[85] The Council is, however, a single entity despite the configurations structure. Accordingly, legislative measures adopted by the Council make no mention of the specific configuration that adopted the measure. The Council is assisted in its work by a Committee of the Permanent Representatives of the Member States (more commonly referred to as "COREPER").[86] Permanent Representatives perform a function akin to an ambassador. The Committee of the Permanent Representatives of the Member States is responsible for preparing the work for all Council meetings and for ensuring the central rules and principles of the EU are observed.[87] Like the Council, the Committee of the Permanent Representatives of the Member States is chaired by the Permanent Representative (or their deputy) of the Member State that holds the presidency of the Council, save for the political and security committee, which is chaired be a representative of the High Representative.[88] The Committee of the Permanent Representatives of the

[78] *European Parliament v Council of Ministers of the European Communities* (C181/91 and C248/91) [1993] E.C.R. I-3685; [1994] 3 C.M.L.R. 317 at p.12.

[79] art.16(1) TEU.

[80] art.16(2) TEU. Not every Member State has to be represented at every meeting of the Council. A Member State can appoint another Member State as a proxy to vote on its behalf. However, a Member State cannot exercise more than one proxy (art.239 TFEU; Rules of Procedure of the Council arts 5 and 11).

[81] art.16(9) TEU.

[82] art.236 TFEU.

[83] art.16(6) TEU.

[84] art.236 TFEU.

[85] Details can be found at *https://www.consilium.europa.eu/en/council-eu/configurations/* [Accessed 2 June 2020].

[86] art.16(7) TEU; art.240(1) TFEU.

[87] art.240(1) TFEU; Rules of Procedure of the Council art.19(1).

[88] Rules of Procedure of the Council art.19(4).

Member States can set up, or approve, subcommittees or working parties to assist it with a view to carrying out certain preparatory work or studies as defined in advance.[89] In practice, these meetings, which are normally attended by civil servants from the appropriate field, are invaluable in assisting the Council in performing its core functions.

Voting in the Council is a complicated business. The Council can, in some areas, act by simple majority and in some other areas it must act unanimously.[90] The default rule, however, is that the Council can act by qualified majority.[91] Qualified majority voting weights each Member State's vote by reference to their population. The operation of the qualified majority voting system was altered significantly by the Lisbon Treaty. Since 1 November 2014 a qualified majority has been defined as "at least 55% of the members of the Council, comprising at least fifteen of them and representing Member States comprising at least 65% of the population of the Union".[92] **10–12**

A "blocking minority" must consist of at least four Member States otherwise a qualified majority shall be deemed to have been achieved.[93] Where not all Member States participate in a vote, the pre-1 November 2014 rules for such situations continue to apply, other than where the Council does not act on a proposal from either the Commission or the High Representative, in which case the required majority is 72 per cent of the Member States participating in the vote, representing not less than 65 per cent of the population of the participating Member States.[94]

The Commission

It is important to start by noting what the Commission is not. It is not the civil service of the EU. The Commission has a civil service that supports it work, but so too does the Council and the Parliament. The Commission, based in Brussels, is more than simply the executive arm of the EU. The Commission is charged with promoting the general interest of the EU and taking appropriate initiatives to that end.[95] In particular, the Commission is responsible for: ensuring compliance with the treaties and measures adopted pursuant to them; overseeing the application of EU law under the control of the Court of Justice; executing the budget and managing programmes; and the co-ordination of executive and management functions as laid down in the treaties.[96] In addition, the Commission has a significant legislative function. It alone has the power to initiate EU legislation under the ordinary legislative process.[97] Given the importance of this **10–13**

[89] Rules of Procedure of the Council art.19(3).
[90] An abstention, or an absence, does not prevent the Council acting unanimously: art.238(4) TFEU.
[91] art.16(3) TEU. Unlike votes requiring unanimity, an abstention or absence can affect the outcome as it is effectively a "no" vote.
[92] art.16(4) TEU.
[93] art.16(4) TEU.
[94] art.238(3) TFEU.
[95] art.17(1) TEU.
[96] art.17(1) TEU.
[97] art.17(2) TEU; art.289(1) TFEU.

institution, and the vast power it possesses under the treaties, it is critical to an appreciation of how the EU functions to understand how the Commission operates.

10–14 The Commission consists of a President and a number of Commissioners. These are independent of the Member States.[98] While the TEU provides that from 1 November 2014, the number of Commissioners (including the Commission President[99] and the High Representative) should correspond to two-thirds of the number of Member States,[100] the European Council has determined that the previous rule (that there was one Commissioner from each Member State) should continue. The Commission President is responsible for laying down guidelines within which the Commission is to work, determining the internal organisation of the Commission and appointing the Vice Presidents of the Commission (other than the High Representative, who holds office as a Vice President of the Commission ex officio).[101] They can also require the resignation of a Commissioner.[102] The appointment of the Commission President previously required the unanimous agreement of the Member States. The Lisbon Treaty amended that procedure so as to remove the right of a Member State to veto a nominee for the position.[103] The European Council must now, acting by qualified majority, propose to the European Parliament a candidate for the position of Commission President. If that candidate is not approved by the Parliament, the European Council shall propose a new candidate to the Parliament.[104] Commissioners are then nominated by the Council, "by common accord" with the President-elect.[105] Nominees are selected on the basis of suggestions made by the Member States. A nominee, whose independence shall be beyond doubt, should be chosen on the ground of their general competence and European commitment.[106] The proposed Commissioners, together with the (European Council) President and the High Representative, shall, as a collective, be subject to a vote of consent by the European Parliament.[107] If the Parliament consents, the Commissioners are then appointed by the European Council, acting by qualified majority.[108] Once appointed, the Commission's term of office is five years.[109] A Commissioner can be "compulsorily retired" by the Court of Justice,

---

[98] art.245 TFEU.

[99] This is the third "President" we have encountered. In an attempt to try to minimise confusion with the President of the European Council and the President of the Council, this President will be referred to as the "Commission President" throughout.

[100] art.17(5) TEU.

[101] art.17(6) TEU.

[102] art.17(6) TEU. They cannot require the High Representative to resign but they can trigger the process by which he or she may be removed. The High Commissioner may only be removed by the European Council, acting by qualified majority.

[103] As the UK Prime Minister learned to his cost in June 2014 when he was unable to prevent the nomination of former Luxembourg Prime Minister Jean Claude Juncker, see fn.76, above

[104] art.17(7) TEU.

[105] art.17(7) TEU.

[106] art.17(3) TEU.

[107] art.17(7) TEU.

[108] art.17(7) TEU.

[109] art.17(3) TEU.

on application by either the Council or the Commission, where the Commissioner no longer fulfils the conditions required for the performance of their duties or has been guilty of serious misconduct.[110]

The Commission acts by a simple majority of its members.[111] It is collegiate and dissent is not formally recorded.[112] The President allocates to each Commissioner responsibility for one or more areas of EU activity. The Commission is divided into departments, known as directorates-general, and of which there are currently 33. Each directorate-general is responsible for a different area of EU policy, for example climate change, energy, home affairs or trade. The portfolios of the directorates-general do not correspond exactly to the portfolios of the Commissioners and, as will be obvious from the fact that there are 33 directorates-general and only 27 Commissioners, one Commissioner may have responsibility for more than one directorate-general. Each directorate-general is divided into directorates, which are in turn divided into units. A director-general (akin to a permanent secretary in Whitehall) is responsible for each directorate-general and they work closely with the Commissioner responsible for the directorate-general.

Evidently, the Commission has a very broad range of responsibilities. With **10–15**
that comes significant power. The Commission plays a central role in the EU legislative process, in addition to which it exercises the executive functions of the EU. It has significant powers in relation to the adoption of subordinate legislation.[113] The Commission oversees the application of EU law and has the power to take enforcement action against Member States where they fail to comply with an EU obligation that is incumbent upon them.[114] The Commission also has the power to take enforcement action against legal or other persons, most notably in the sphere of competition law.[115] Finally, the Commission represents the EU at a number of different international organisations, in particular the World Trade Organisation.

The Commission is accountable to the European Parliament. In addition to its role in the appointment of the Commission, the Parliament may censure the Commission. A motion of censure requires a two-third majority of the votes cast, representing a majority of the component members of the European Parliament, to pass. Where such a motion is passed, the Commission, as a whole (including the High Representative), must resign.[116] Just as the Parliament's role in the appointment of the Commission is to support or reject the proposed Commissioners as a block, likewise the power to censure results in the removal of all of the Commissioners. It is therefore a fairly blunt instrument. The role of the European

[110] art.247 TFEU.
[111] art.250 TFEU.
[112] art.17(6)(b) TEU.
[113] These procedures are explained more fully in Edward and Lane, *European Union Law* (2013), paras 3.24–3.29.
[114] art.258 TFEU. In the first instance, the Commission must deliver to the Member State concerned a "reasoned opinion" and give the state an opportunity to submit its observations. If the Member State does not comply with the opinion within the period prescribed by the Commission, the Commission is empowered to bring the matter before the Court of Justice.
[115] For an explanation of the Commission's enforcement powers in the sphere of competition law, see Edward and Lane, *European Union Law* (2013), paras 13.89–13.108.
[116] art.234 TFEU. The censured Commission remain in office until their replacements have been appointed.

Parliament would be much enhanced if it had the option simply to censure an individual Commissioner.[117] Finally, the Commission is required to respond to questions put by the Parliament and its members.[118] The Commission has the right to attend all meetings of the Parliament and, at its request, to be heard.[119] This gives the Commission the opportunity to explain, or give an insight into, its thinking on legislative initiatives and timescales or other aspects of the EU law.

The Court of Justice of the European Union

10–16 Having formed the Commission with executive authority and rule-making powers, it was necessary to have a judicial mechanism to review the exercise of those powers. The formation of the Court of Justice in the founding Treaties was therefore the necessary corollary of the Commission. What is now the Court of Justice of the European Union has evolved as the Communities developed and the Union was formed. Under the Lisbon Treaty, the Court of Justice of the European Union (CJEU) is charged with "ensur[ing] that in the interpretation and application of the Treaties the law is observed".[120] The CJEU, in fact, comprises of two separate courts: the Court of Justice and the General Court.[121] We will concentrate on the first of those bodies, the Court of Justice.

10–17 The Court of Justice now comprises of 27 judges (one per Member State)[122] who are "assisted" by eleven advocates general.[123] Each of the judges and advocates general must be a person whose independence is beyond doubt, who possesses the qualifications for appointment to the highest judicial offices in their respective countries or be jurisconsult of recognised competence.[124] Appointment is for a (renewable) six year term.[125] To avoid the mass replacement of the court and to facilitate continuity in the membership of the court, the term of half of the judges and advocates general falls for renewal every three years.[126] Nominations for the court (which are usually made by the Member States) are now reviewed by a panel that produces a non-binding opinion on the suitability of the nominee for the office of judge or advocate general.[127] Having received the opinion of the panel, judges and advocates general are appointed by "common accord" of the governments of the Member States.[128] A judge may only be removed from office

[117] That said, the Parliament did play a central role in bringing about the resignation of the Santer Commission in March 1999. See, generally, V. Mehde, "Responsibility and Accountability in the European Commission" (2003) 40 C.M.L. Rev. 423.

[118] art.230 TFEU.

[119] art.230 TFEU.

[120] art.19(1) TEU.

[121] A third judicial body, the Civil Service Tribunal, which had been established in 2004, was dissolved on 1 September 2016 and its functions transferred to the General Court.

[122] art.19(2) TEU.

[123] art.19(2) TEU. Article 252 TFEU prescribes that there be eight advocates general but the Council, acting unanimously, is given the power to increase that number. They did so by Decision 2013/336 increasing the number of Advocates-General of the Court of Justice of the European Union [2013] OJ L179/92 with the result that the number of advocates general increased to nine with effect from 1 July 2013 and increased again to 11 from 7 October 2015, where it currently rests.

[124] art.19(2) TEU; art.253 TFEU.

[125] art.19(2) TEU; art.253 TFEU.

[126] art.253 TFEU; Statute of the Court of Justice art.9.

[127] art.255 TFEU.

[128] art.19(2) TEU; art.253 TFEU.

if the unanimous opinion of the judges and the advocates general is that they no longer fulfil the requisite conditions or meet the obligations of their office.[129] The judges of the court elect one of their number to serve as the president of the court for a term of three years.[130] Since 2012, a vice president has also been elected and they also serve a three year term.[131]

The court sits in three different formations. First, the court divides itself into a number of chambers. Each chamber consists of either three or five judges and each chamber is chaired by a president. The chamber presidents are elected by the judges from within their number. Presidents of the five-judge chambers are elected for three years. Presidents of the three-judge chambers are elected annually.[132] Second, the court may convene as the "Grand Chamber". The Grand Chamber comprises of 15 judges and is presided over by the President of the Court. It also includes the Vice President of the Court and three presidents of chambers of five judges. The court must sit as the Grand Chamber where a Member State or an EU institution that is a party to the case so requests.[133] Finally, the court may sit as the full court, which requires not less than 17 judges to be present. The court shall convene as the full court when, having heard the advocate general, the case is considered to be of exceptional importance or when hearing specified cases under the treaties.[134] Whatever the formation, the court only ever delivers a single judgment of the court; there are no dissenting or concurring opinions. Each case that is received by the court is assigned to a judge who is the "judge-rapporteur". They prepare a preliminary report and, on the basis of that report, the court, at a general meeting, determines which formation of the court should hear the case.

Each case is also assigned an advocate general. The advocates general are members of the court, who sit on the bench with the judges during oral hearings. The function of the advocate general is to "assist" the court.[135] After the oral hearing, the advocate general ordinarily prepares an "opinion" that is delivered in open court (and usually printed along with the report of the eventual judgment).[136] This is a "reasoned submission" on the case and is ordinarily more discursive than the judgment produced by the court (no doubt as a result of the necessary compromises made in drafting a single judgment of the court). Consequentially, although not an authoritative statement of EU law, an advocate general's opinion can be helpful in understanding the judgment of the court and they can assist the development of EU law more generally.

---

[129] Statute of the Court of Justice art.6; the same rule is applied to advocates general by art.8 of the Statute.

[130] art.253 TFEU.

[131] Statute of the Court of Justice art.9a. The functions of the Vice President are set out in Decision 2012/671 concerning the judicial functions of the Vice-President of the Court [2012] OJ L300/47.

[132] Statute of the Court of Justice art.16.

[133] Statute of the Court of Justice art.16.

[134] Statute of the Court of Justice art.16. The Statute of the Court of Justice art.16 currently requires the court to sit as the full court for cases brought under arts 228(2) (removal of the ombudsman), 245(2) and 247 (removal of a commissioner) and 286(6) (removal of a member of the Court of Auditors). The CJEU convened as the full court to hear the Art.50 reference in Case C-621/18 *Wightman and others v Secretary of State for Exiting the European Union* [2019] QB 199. See para.1–19.

[135] art.19(2) TEU.

[136] It is no longer necessary for the court to receive an opinion from the advocate general before giving judgment: art.252 TFEU

10–18 In terms of art.19(3) TEU, the role of the Court of Justice is three-fold: to rule on actions brought by a Member State, an institution[137] or a natural or legal person; to give preliminary rulings where requested to do so by the national courts of Member States; and to rule in other cases provided for in the treaties. Scratch below the surface and matters become more complicated than they first appear. The Court of Justice has made it clear that the EU is based on the rule of law and as such the court is entitled to review, when asked to do so, whether any EU measure conforms with the treaties and accordingly, where necessary, a natural or legal person may bring a direct action before the court.[138] There are essentially four categories of action that can be brought before the Court of Justice: direct actions; appeals[139]; preliminary references under art.267 TFEU; and opinions.[140] It is, however, appropriate to say a few words about the preliminary reference system, touching as it does on the relationship between the Court of Justice and national courts.

Article 267 TFEU provides:

> "The Court of Justice of the European Union shall have jurisdiction to give preliminary rulings concerning: (a) the interpretation of the Treaties; (b) the validity and interpretation of acts of the institutions, bodies, offices or agencies of the Union; Where such a question is raised before any court or tribunal of a Member State, that court or tribunal may, if it considers that a decision on the question is necessary to enable it to give judgment, request the Court to give a ruling thereon.
>
> Where any such question is raised in a case pending before a court or tribunal of a Member State against whose decision there is no judicial remedy under national law, that court or tribunal shall bring the matter before the Court."

The majority of cases that come before the Court of Justice arrive by means of an art.267 reference.[141] The reference procedure is not an appeal and while the parties to an action can request that the national court make a reference, it is ultimately a matter for the discretion of that court.[142] It is important to note the two functions that an art.267 reference can perform. First, the national court can request an opinion on the interpretation of EU law. This is an important

137 Under art.87 of the Transition Agreement between the EU and UK, the Commission is entitled to bring proceedings against the UK for any breach of its obligations prior to the end of the transition (implementation) period, or for certain breaches of the Withdrawal Agreement, for a period of four years from the end of the transition period. Note, that the agreement between the UK and EU talks of a "transition period" that is the same as the "Implementation Period" as defined in the European Union (Withdrawal Agreement) Act 2020.

138 *Parti Ecologiste Les Verts v European Parliament* (294/83) [1986] E.C.R. 1339; [1987] 2 C.M.L.R. 343 at p.23.

139 That is to say appeals from the General Court. There is no right of appeal to the Court of Justice from any national court. This can be contrasted with the European Court of Human Rights, which allows an individual to make an application provided they have exhausted their domestic remedies (European Convention on Human Rights art.35).

140 For details of the various categories of action, see, Edward and Lane, *European Union Law* (2013), paras 5.30–5.154; O'Neill, *EU Law for UK Lawyers* (2011), Chs 3 (preliminary references) and 4 (direct actions).

141 In 2019, for example, approximately two-thirds of the cases pending before the CJEU were preliminary references. In that year, 641 references were made (in 2009, that figure was 302). For more details, see: *Annual Report 2019: Judicial Activity*, CJEU (2020), available at: *https://curia.europa.eu/jcms/upload/docs/application/pdf/2020-05/qd-ap-20-001-en-n.pdf* [Accessed 15 June 2020].

142 *Willy Kempter KG v Hauptzollamt Hamburg-Jonas* (C-2/06) [2008] E.C.R. I-411 at [41].

mechanism by which the Court of Justice can ensure a uniform interpretation of EU law throughout the Union.[143] Second, the national court can request an opinion from the Court of Justice on the validity of an act of an EU institution or body. Given the restrictive rules on standing that limit the ability of individuals to challenge the validity of acts of the EU institutions,[144] this limb of the art.267 reference procedure provides an important mechanism by which the validity of such acts can be judicially reviewed. The point may be obvious, but it bears mentioning: the Court of Justice can only rule on questions of EU law. It cannot interpret national law,[145] it cannot advise if national law is compatible with EU law[146] and it cannot annul, set aside or strike down national law.[147] The rules of the various national courts prescribe the procedure for that court referring a question to the Court of Justice. But the question arises: when should a national court refer a question to the Court of Justice? Article 267 differentiates between national courts from which lies an appeal to a higher national court (these courts "*may*" refer a question) whereas a national court of last resort "*shall*" refer a question.[148] In reaching a decision on whether to refer a question to the Court of Justice, lower courts retain a discretion as to whether to make a reference. They may have regard to factors such as the importance of the issue or the likely expense and delay a reference would cause. It is open to a lower court to come to the view that it should give judgment itself and it would then become a matter for the appeal court to review. The lower courts are not prevented from making a reference by any national rules of precedence: it is open to the lower court to refer a question even where the higher court has ruled on the same point.[149] Having taken a decision to refer a question to the Court of Justice, the framing of the question is a matter for the court. The Court of Justice has issued guidance on the form and content for a preliminary reference that should, so far as possible, be

---

[143] *NV Algemene Transport- en Expeditie Onderneming van Gend en Loos v Nederlandse Administratie der Belastingen* (C-26/62) [1963] E.C.R. 1.

[144] art.263 TFEU. The rules on standing in such applications are discussed in O'Neill, *EU Law for UK Lawyers* (2011) paras 4.21–4.36. See also *Inuit Tapiriit Kanatami v European Parliament* (C-583/11 P) [2014] Q.B. 648 Grand Chamber, noted by A. Kornezov, "Locus standi of private parties in actions for annulment: has the gap been closed" [2014] C.L.J. 25.

[145] For example, the request made of it in *Kleinwort Benson Ltd v Glasgow City Council* (C346/93) [1996] Q.B. 57; [1995] E.C.R. I-615.

[146] *Groupement National des Negociants en Pommes de Terre de Belgique v ITM Belgium SA* (C-63/94) [1995] E.C.R. I-2467; *Wilson v Ordre des Avocats du Barreau de Luxembourg* (C-506/04) [2006] E.C.R. I-8613; [2007] 1 C.M.L.R. 7.

[147] If asked to do so, the court will answer by explaining whether EU law precludes the national law in question but it is for the national court to disapply a provision of national law.

[148] What exactly the national court of last resort is for Scotland was not as simple a question as might be expected. In civil matters, it is clearly the UK Supreme Court. But in criminal matters, it is probably the High Court of Justiciary, although a limited right of appeal, with leave, lies to the UK Supreme Court where a "compatibility issue" arises in terms of the Scotland Act 1998 (Sch.6 of that Act). A similar issue arose in England and Wales in cases where there is no right to apply to the UK Supreme Court for leave to appeal a decision of the Court of Appeal: *Chiron Corp v Murex Diagnostics Ltd (No.8)* [1995] All E.R. (E.C.) 88.

[149] *Rheinmuhlen-Dusseldorf v Einfuhri und Vorratsstelle fur Getreide und Futtermittel* (C-166/73) [1974] E.C.R. 33.

adhered to.[150] Once the reference has been made, proceedings before the national court should be sisted (stayed). The delay in receiving an answer can be considerable.[151]

Once the Implementation Period is finished, it will no longer be open to the British courts to refer questions to the Court of Justice of the European Union under art.267.[152] But as we shall see, the general retention of EU law as it stood when the UK left is bound to throw up questions as to the proper interpretation of those rules. That will now be a matter for domestic courts, guided (but not bound) by the decisions of the CJEU.[153]

10–19 The other EU court is the General Court (formerly known as the Court of First Instance). It was founded in 1988 to assist the Court of Justice in discharging its functions. It consists of two judges from each Member State,[154] but it is not served by advocates general.[155] The General Court's jurisdiction is now prescribed by art.256 TFEU. The General Court has first instance jurisdiction in all actions raised directly by natural and legal persons. With the exception of those reserved to the Court of Justice or delegated to a specialist court, the General Court hears proceedings raised in terms of arts 263 (review of the legality of legislative acts and various acts of the institutions), 265 (action by a Member State against an institution for failure of that institution to act),[156] 268 (compensation for damage in accordance with art.340 (action for damages against an institution)), 270 (staff disputes) and 272 (arbitration) TFEU. The decision of the General Court in these cases is appealable to the Court of Justice, but only on a point of law.[157] The General Court also has jurisdiction to hear appeals from the specialist courts.[158] The treaties enable the General Court to assume jurisdiction to hear preliminary references in terms of art.267 TFEU, but that has not yet been done. Finally, on 1 September 2016, when the Civil Service Tribunal was dissolved, the General Court assumed the jurisdiction that had previously vested in that body. That transfer coincided with the expansion of the General Court's membership (from one judge per Member State to two).

---

[150] Recommendations of the Court of Justice of the European Union to national courts and tribunals in relation to the initiation of preliminary ruling proceedings [2012] OJ C338/1.

[151] On the preliminary reference procedure generally see: A. Poole, "Arguing for and against references to the European Court of Justice", 2009 S.L.T. (News) 23; A. Arnull, "The Law Lords and the European Union: swimming with the incoming tide" (2010) 35 E.L. Rev. 57.

[152] European Union (Withdrawal) Act 2018 s.6(1). But references can be made during the Implementation Period and the CJEU will answer any references made before that period ends. See, art.86 of the Withdrawal Agreement (*Agreement on the withdrawal of the United Kingdom of Great Britain and Northern Ireland from the European Union and the European Atomic Energy Community* [2019] OJ CI384/1) ("the Withdrawal Agreement").

[153] European Union (Withdrawal) Act 2018 s.6(2): "a court or tribunal may have regard to anything done on or after IP competition day by the European Court...". See further: para.10–42, below.

[154] Although art.19(2) TEU provides that the General Court shall include "at least one judge per Member State" thus allowing the membership of the court to be extended if necessary.

[155] art.254 TFEU; Statute of the Court of Justice art.48. Provision is made in the Statute of the Court of Justice art.49 for one of the members of the court to discharge the functions of an advocate general but this rarely happens in practice.

[156] The actual formulation of that article is not a model of clarity in terms of its drafting and should be referred to for its full terms.

[157] art.256(1) TFEU.

[158] art.256(2) TFEU.

EU Legislation

That the EU has legislative functions is a unique characteristic amongst international bodies. The Member States have transferred to the EU the power to legislate in certain specified areas, which allows the EU institutions to take autonomous decisions within those spheres. The process by which EU legislation is enacted no longer involves the UK, but given the general retention of EU law, the different types of EU legislation will remain relevant for some time to come. Article 288 TFEU provides, "[t]o exercise the Union's competences, the institutions shall adopt regulations, directives, decisions, recommendations and opinions". Only regulations have general effect throughout the EU. Directives and decisions are binding (to differing degrees discussed below) on those to whom they have been addressed. Recommendations and opinions, however, have no binding force (but may have an indirect impact or influence on the interpretation of EU law). For present purposes, we shall focus on regulations and directives. **10–20**

Regulations

"A regulation shall have general application. It shall be binding in its entirety and directly applicable in all Member States."[159] The defining characteristic of a regulation is that their entry into force and application within the national legal orders of the Member States are wholly independent of any measure of reception into national law. In other words, they are directly applicable (not to be confused with direct effect, which is discussed below). Indeed, any purported implementation of a regulation into domestic law is not permitted: **10–21**

> "The direct application of a Regulation means that its entry into force and its application in favour of or against those subject to it are independent of any measure of reception into national law. By virtue of the obligations arising from the Treaty and assumed on ratification, Members States are under a duty not to obstruct the direct applicability inherent in Regulations and other rules of [EU] law. Strict compliance with this obligation is an indispensable condition of simultaneous and uniform application of [Regulations] throughout the [EU]."[160]

In short, a regulation becomes part of the Member States' legal systems without any further action on their part.[161] A consequence of this is that regulations are capable of conferring rights on individuals that can be enforced directly by them before national courts. This is a characteristic of the concept of direct applicability that is shared with the concept of direct effect (and discussed further below). Once adopted, regulations must be published in the *Official Journal*. They enter into force on the date specified in the notice, failing which on the twentieth day following publication of the notice.[162]

---

[159] art.288 TFEU.

[160] *Fratelli Variola SpA v Amministrazione Italiana delle Finanze* (C-34/73) [1973] E.C.R. 981.

[161] In the United Kingdom, a regulation was, of course, reliant upon the European Communities Act 1972 for its recognition in domestic law (*Thoburn v Sunderland City Council* [2002] EWHC 195 (Admin); [2003] Q.B. 151 at [59]).

[162] art.297 TFEU.

Directives

10–22 "A directive shall be binding, as to the result to be achieved, upon each Member State to which it is addressed, but shall leave to the national authorities the choice of form and methods."[163] In many ways a directive is what a regulation is not: it does not have general application and it calls for implementation at Member State level. Directives therefore give the EU a greater flexibility and are appropriate where harmonisation is required rather than uniformity. First, they do not need to be addressed to all Member States, therefore do not necessarily apply throughout the Union. Second, a directive leaves it to a Member State to decide how best to incorporate its requirements into domestic law, whereas a regulation must be capable of being dropped into the legal system of all the Member States. With such an enlarged Union, that is an increasingly challenging task. Despite this, directives are often so prescriptive that they leave Member States little room in practice when it comes to implementation.

Directives applying to all Member States must be published in the *Official Journal* and take effect in the same way as regulations. Directives normally then allow the addressee Member States a specified period of time in which to transpose the measures into national law. The obligation rests on the Member States and any internal constitutional difficulties (for example, the failure by a devolved or sub-national executive to implement a directive) is of no interest to the EU.[164] Although a directive does not require to be implemented until a certain date, after its publication Member States must refrain from adopting any measure that would prevent the objective of the directive being achieved[165] and the courts of the Member States must interpret domestic law, as far as possible, in light of the wording and purpose of a directive.[166] Directives normally require Member States to notify the Commission of the measures taken to implement them. Failure on the part of the Member State to implement a directive, at all or correctly, within that period may expose the state to enforcement action by the Commission and liability in damages for that breach of EU law.[167] Furthermore, individuals may be able to rely directly on the provisions of the directive in proceedings before the national courts where the directive satisfies the conditions for direct effect.[168]

Other forms of legislation

10–23 There are three other forms of legislation: decisions, recommendations and opinions. "A decision shall be binding in its entirety. A decision which specifies those to whom it is addressed shall be binding only on them."[169] Both regulations

---

163 art.288 TFEU.

164 For an explanation of the obligation resting on the Member States see *Commission v Netherlands* (C-144/99) [2001] E.C.R. I-3541 at [15]–[17] of Advocate General Tizzano's opinion.

165 *Inter-Environnement Wallonie ASBL v Region Wallonie* (C-129/96) [1997] E.C.R. I-7411; [1998] 1 C.M.L.R. 1057.

166 *Marleasing SA v La Comercial Internacional de Alimentacion SA* (C-106/89) [1990] E.C.R. I-4135.

167 *Francovich v Italy* (C-6/90) [1991] E.C.R. I-5357.

168 On direct effect of directives, see para.10–27, below.

169 art.288 TFEU.

and decisions are binding in their entirety. What distinguishes the two measures is that decisions are only addressed to a limited number of persons.[170] Since the Lisbon Treaty, a decision does not necessarily require an addressee but where it has one (and the addressee can be a Member State or a natural or legal person(s)) it is binding on them and only them. A decision without an addressee remains "binding in its entirety" but it is not clear on whom. Decisions are generally used to address specific issues or problems and where general measures, such as a regulation, would be inappropriate. In particular, decisions are used to notify breaches of EU law or determinations that state aid is incompatible with the common market. "Recommendations and opinions shall have no binding force."[171] The Council, and where specifically authorised by the treaties, the Commission and the European Central Bank, may adopt recommendations.[172] Recommendations are adopted following the procedure that is applicable to the subject matter at issue.[173] Because recommendations and opinions have no binding force, they cannot create legal rights nor can they have direct effect. Nevertheless, national courts are required to take notice of them, in particular when they may inform the interpretation of other provisions of EU law.[174] In recent years, greater use has been made of these measures as vehicles for the development of EU policy as the old stress on uniformity has given way (as it inevitably had to in such an enlarged Union) to a new emphasis on flexibility.

Hierarchy of EU norms

The Lisbon Treaty introduced, for the first time, a hierarchy of EU norms.[175] The treaties sit at the top of that hierarchy. Below them, a distinction is now drawn between "legislative acts", "delegated acts" and "implementing acts".[176] A legislative act is a regulation, directive or decision adopted by the European Parliament and the Council, on the recommendation of the Commission.[177] A legislative act may delegate to the Commission the authority to adopt non-legislative acts of general application "to supplement or amend non-essential elements of the legislative act".[178] The legislative act must explicitly define the objectives, content, scope and purpose of the delegation and the "essential **10–24**

[170] See *Yusuf v Council of the European Union* (T-306/01) [2005] E.C.R. II-3533; [2005] 3 C.M.L.R. 49 at [185]. Although the Grand Chamber allowed an appeal against this decision, they endorsed the Court of First Instance's (as it then was) discussion of the difference between regulations and decisions: *Kadi v Council of the European Union* (C-402/05 P) [2009] 1 A.C. 1225; [2008] E.C.R. I-6351 at [237]–[247].

[171] art.288 TFEU.

[172] art.292 TFEU.

[173] art.292 TFEU.

[174] *Grimaldi v Fonds des Maladies Professionnelles* (C-322/88) [1989] E.C.R. 4407; [1991] 2 C.M.L.R. 265 at p.18.

[175] The word "law" was used in the aborted EU Constitution and was replaced with "norm" come the Lisbon Treaty to avoid any federal connotations that may accompany the term "law"; on the hierarchy of EU norms generally, see P. Craig, "Delegated acts, implementing acts and the new Comitology Regulation" (2011) 36 E.L. Rev. 671.

[176] arts 289, 290 and 291 TFEU, respectively.

[177] art.289(1) TFEU. This is the "ordinary legislative" procedure and is discussed further at para.10–32, below.

[178] art.290(1) TFEU.

elements" of the legislative act may not be delegated.[179] The legislative act may also impose conditions on the delegation.[180] Any non-legislative act adopted under a delegated power must include the word "delegated" in its title.[181] Both legislative and non-legislative acts are legally binding EU acts. Member States are required to adopt "all measures of national law necessary" to implement such acts.[182] Where uniformity is required in the implementation of a legislative act, that act shall confer implementing powers (ordinarily) on the Commission.[183] An implementing measure adopted by the Commission must use the word "implementing" in its title.[184]

Impact of EU Law on domestic legal systems

10–25 We now turn to discuss some of the main principles of EU law that have a direct impact on the Member States and their relationship with the EU. There are four aspects of EU law that are considered: primacy of EU law; direct effect; state liability for damages; and the protection of fundamental rights.

Primacy of EU law

10–26 As we saw earlier long before the United Kingdom negotiated membership of the EU, the Court of Justice of the European Union had made it clear that EU law was a new and distinctive species of international law. Borne out of a modest dispute over an unpaid Italian electricity bill, the primacy of EU law was declared by the court in *Costa v ENEL*:

> "The transfer by the States from their domestic legal system to the Community legal system of the rights and obligations arising under the Treaty carries with it a permanent limitation of their sovereign rights, against which a subsequent unilateral act incompatible with the concept of the Community cannot prevail."[185]

Subsequently, the court went on to confirm that EU law in all its forms, not simply the treaties, prevails over national law, even where the conflicting national provision is constitutional in nature.[186] The court took the primacy of EU law to its logical conclusion in *Amministrazione delle Finanze dello Stato v Simmenthal SpA* where it held that a national court must:

> "apply Community law in its entirety and protect rights which the latter confers on individuals, and must accordingly set aside any provision of national law which may conflict with it, whether prior or subsequent to the Community rule".[187]

---

[179] art.290(1) TFEU.
[180] art.290(2) TFEU.
[181] art.290(3) TFEU.
[182] art.291(1) TFEU.
[183] art.291(2) TFEU.
[184] art.291(4) TFEU.
[185] *Costa v Ente Nazionale per l'Energia Elettrica (ENEL)* (C-6/64) [1964] E.C.R. 585 at p.14.
[186] *Internationale Handelsgesellschaft mbH v Einfuhr- und Vorratsstelle fur Getreide und Futtermittel* (C-11/70) [1970] E.C.R. 1125.
[187] *Amministrazione delle Finanze dello Stato v Simmenthal SpA* (C-106/77) [1978] E.C.R. 629.

Thus, national laws are not invalidated or struck down if inconsistent with EU law (unless national law prescribes that result)[188] but simply set aside and disapplied. Nonetheless, the rule as to the primacy of EU law has caused significant constitutional difficulties in a number of Member States. We have already seen, in Ch.3, the challenges it presented for the UK.[189] For now it is worth noting that the domestic constitutional implications for the UK of EU membership were not exhaustively resolved during the time of membership. As the Supreme Court explained in *R. (on the application of Buckingham CC) v Secretary of State for Transport*, were a provision of EU law to clash with a fundamental principal of the UK constitution, it would be for the British courts, applying domestic law, to resolve such a conflict: the answer is not to be found (exclusively at any rate) in the jurisprudence of the Court of Justice of the European Union.[190] That is an issue that may never need to be resolved now. But as we saw earlier, the mark left on the UK constitution by EU law, and in particular the doctrine of supremacy, is likely to be permanent.

Direct effect of EU law

The treaties always contained a mechanism for their enforcement through the right of the Commission or another Member State to bring issues of non-adherence before the Court of Justice. In one of the earliest cases to come before the court, however, judicial enforcement was to go a step further. In *NV Algemene Transport-en Expeditie Onderneming van Gend en Loos v Nederlandse* **10–27**

[188] For example, an Act of the Scottish Parliament was "not law" to the extent it is inconsistent with EU law (Scotland Act 1998 s.29(2)). That resulted, however, from a provision of the Scotland Act, an Act of the UK Parliament, and not a rule of EU law.

[189] It is not only the courts of the UK that struggled with the constitutional consequences of EU membership and the primacy of EU law. In France, the Conseil d'Etat at one time refused to question the validity of French legislation on the ground that it conflicted with Community law and declined to accept the doctrine of direct effect of directives (see, e.g. *Syndicat General de Fabricants de Semoules de France* [1970] C.M.L.R. 395; *Minister of the Interior v Cohn-Bendit* [1980] 1 C.M.L.R. 543) and has only relatively recently signalled its acceptance of the supremacy of Community law: P. Roseren, "The Application of Community Law by the French Courts from 1982 to 1993" (1994) 31 C.M.L. Rev. 315. The German constitution permits the transfer of sovereign powers to intergovernmental institutions, so to that extent the reception of the supremacy of EU law caused little difficulty. Less straightforward was the question of whether EU law could take priority over the inalienable fundamental rights enshrined in the basic law. Following the decision of the Court of Justice of the European Union in *Internationale Handelsgesellschaft*, the German Constitutional Court refused to renounce its right to uphold fundamental rights in German law even in the face of conflict with EU law (although it found on the facts of that case that no such conflict existed). Subsequently the German courts departed from this position, but in *Brunner v Treaty on European Union* [1994] 1 C.M.L.R. 57, the Constitutional Court, while confirming the legality of ratification of the Maastricht Treaty and acknowledging the primary responsibility of the European Court of Justice for the protection of fundamental rights, suggested that it retained the competence to perform this task if the European Court of Justice failed to do so adequately, and also asserted a right to review the legal instruments of the European institutions to ascertain whether they remained within the limits of the sovereign rights transferred to them.

[190] *R. (on the application of Buckingham CC) v Secretary of State for Transport* [2014] UKSC 3; [2014] 1 W.L.R. 324, per Lord Reed at [79] and per Lords Neuberger and Mance [203]–[205]. See also: P. Craig, "Constitutionalising constitutional law: HS2" [2014] P.L. 373. That of course differs from the scenario that presented itself to the House of Lords in *Factortame*, where the clash was between EU law and an "ordinary" Act of Parliament.

Administratie der Belastingen,[191] a reference for a preliminary ruling from a Dutch tax tribunal, the Court of Justice addressed the question of the effect, as a matter of Dutch domestic law, of what is now art.30 TFEU. The court held that, unlike most international treaties, which only create mutual obligations between the states that are party to the treaty, EU law imposed obligations and conferred legal rights on individuals as well. These rights would arise "not only when an explicit grant is made by the Treaty, but also through obligations imposed, in a clearly defined manner, by the Treaty on individuals as well as on member states and the Community institutions".

For a treaty article to have this direct effect of creating an enforceable individual right, the court held that the provision in question required to be clear, negative, unconditional, containing no reservation on the part of the Member State and independent of any national implementing measure. Since what is now art.30 TFEU satisfied these criteria, the applicants in *Van Gend en Loos* were able to invoke the protection of EU law in the proceedings before their national court.

Since then the doctrine of direct effect has expanded considerably, partly as a consequence of the Court of Justice applying the criteria for direct effect in a generous manner[192] and partly through the extension of the doctrine to other measures of EU law besides articles of the treaties and regulations. Decisions were held to be capable of having direct effect in 1970,[193] and in 1974 it was held that directives too could have direct effect and create enforceable individual rights.[194] There are, however, two important riders to note in relation to the direct effect of directives. First, it is only after the expiry of the time period allowed for implementation of the directive that its capacity for direct effect crystallises. That is because directives leave some discretion to national authorities in relation to implementation. That discretion would be meaningless if individuals could, at any time, rely directly on the terms of a directive in proceedings before national courts. However, it is equally important that, where the directive requires enforceable rights to be conferred on individuals, Member States should not be able to defeat that intention by implementing the directive erroneously or not implementing it at all within the time allowed. In other words, once the time limit for implementation has elapsed, the individual may rely directly on the provisions of the directive in legal proceedings (provided that the conditions for direct effect are satisfied, namely that it imposes upon the Member State a clear, precise and

[191] *NV Algemene Transport-en Expeditie Onderneming van Gend en Loos v Nederlandse Administratie der Belastingen* (C-26/62) [1963] E.C.R. 1, more commonly referred to as *Van Genden Loos*.

[192] For example *Defrenne v SA Belge de Navigation Aerienne* (SABENA) (C-43/75) [1976] E.C.R. 455, where the court held that the not particularly precise, nor negative, obligation in what is now art.157 TFEU (that "[e]ach Member State shall ensure that the principle of equal pay for male and female workers for equal work or work of equal value is applied") was capable of being directly effective (a view that neither the Commission nor the Member States appeared to share at the time).

[193] *Grad v Finanzamt Traunstein* (C-9/70) [1970] E.C.R. 825.

[194] *Van Duyn v Home Office* (C-41/74) [1974] E.C.R. 1337.

unconditional obligation intended to create rights for individuals).[195] National authorities cannot then plead their own mistake, tardiness or other shortcomings in their defence.[196]

Second, the CJEU has consistently held that directives cannot produce horizontal direct effect, that is legal rights enforceable as between private parties.[197] Since the justification for according direct effect to directives at all is largely rooted in the desire to bind Member States to the proper discharge of their EU obligations, it stands to reason that the institutions of the state should be caught by the direct effect of a directive. So they are, because directives are capable of producing vertical direct effects, or effects binding on the state. But this does not provide convincing justification for horizontal direct effect: private persons are not responsible for the proper implementation of directives into national law, and accordingly it would be unfair to expect them to suffer the consequences of the government's failings. There is force in this reasoning. But another species of unfairness flows from distinguishing between the horizontal and vertical direct effect of directives in this way. By virtue of the vertical direct effect of directives, public employees obtain rights against their employer the benefit of which is denied to the employees of private sector organisations. The court has repeatedly made it clear that where an individual is entitled to rely upon a directive against a Member State, it does not matter in what capacity the latter is acting.[198] The court has acknowledged that this state of affairs is less than ideal, but points out that it is easily avoided provided the Member States properly implement directives into national law. As we noted above, national courts are required to interpret domestic law, as far as possible, in light of the wording and purpose of a directive.[199] That gives directives a limited "indirect" effect. However, it was the court's ruling in *Francovich v Italy* that further incentivised Member States to properly and timeously implement directives.

State liability for damages

In *Francovich*,[200] individuals who had suffered loss due to the persistent non-implementation of a directive by the Italian authorities sued the Italian Government to make good the damage caused to them. The Italian court referred **10–28**

---

[195] *Becker v Finanzamt Munster-Innenstadt* (C-8/81) [1982] E.C.R .53; *Foster v British Gas Plc* (C-188/89) [1991] 1 Q.B. 405 [1990] E.C.R. I-3313.

[196] At the risk of stating the obvious, where a Member State has properly and timeously implemented a directive, normally no issue of direct effect can then arise: *Johnston v Chief Constable of the Royal Ulster Constabulary* (C-222/84) [1986] E.C.R. 1651. But the matter is one of substance, not form. If an otherwise properly implemented directive is not being applied by a Member State correctly so that the rights that should be conferred have not, in fact, been conferred, the directive itself can be founded upon if it meets the relevant criteria: *Marks & Spencer Plc v Customs and Excise Commissioners* (C-62/00) [2003] Q.B. 866; [2002] E.C.R. I-6325.

[197] *Marshall v Southampton and South West Hampshire AHA* (C-152/84) [1986] E.C.R. 723; *Faccini Dori v Recreb Srl* (C-91/92) [1994] E.C.R. I–3325 at p.20; *Dominguez v Centre Informatique du Centre Ouest Atlantique* (C-282/10) [2012] 2 C.M.L.R. 14 at [37].

[198] *Marshall v Southampton and South West Hampshire AHA* (C-152/84) [1986] E.C.R. 723 at p.49; *Foster v British Gas Plc* (C-188/89) [1991] 1 Q.B. 405 [1990] E.C.R. I-3313 at para.17; *Dominguez v Centre Informatique du Centre Ouest Atlantique* (C-282/10) [2012] 2 C.M.L.R. 14 at [38].

[199] See para.10–27, above; *Marleasing SA v La Comercial Internacional de Alimentacion SA* (C-106/89) [1990] E.C.R. I-4135.

[200] *Francovich v Italy* (C-6/90) [1991] E.C.R. I-5357.

to the Court of Justice the question of whether EU law recognised any principle of Member State liability in damages for failure to implement a directive. The court held that it did, provided that the directive was intended to confer rights on individuals (whether or not those rights also satisfy the criteria of direct effect); provided also that the content of the rights is capable of being identified from the provisions of the directive; and provided there was a causal link between the Member State's failure to fulfil its obligations and the loss sustained by the complainant. Subsequently, it was held that the *Francovich* doctrine was applicable to any breach by a Member State of EU law provided that the breach was "sufficiently serious".[201] The decisive criterion for proving a sufficiently serious breach of EU law is whether the Member State in question has "manifestly and gravely disregarded the limits on its discretion" imposed by EU law.[202] As EU law does not discriminate between the institutions of the Member States, in principle a liability in damages for breach of EU law can arise as a result of a judgment of the national court.[203] It will only be in truly exceptional circumstances that such a liability is likely to arise.[204] Despite the general retention of EU law following the UK's exit from the EU, *Francovich* damages are expressly excluded from that transfer and thus will no longer be available at the end of the implementation period.[205]

Conclusions

10–29 In all of these ways—sometimes, admittedly, on slender textual foundations—the Court of Justice has built up a body of law designed to be effective in securing uniform judicial protection between the Member States in areas falling within EU competence. In this regard, the court has been as powerful, if not more powerful, an engine of European integration than the Commission.

Protection of fundamental rights

10–30 A fourth front is opening up in which the Court of Justice of the European Union may further develop EU law. Fundamental (that is, human) rights are now a central tenet of EU law:

[201] *Brasserie du Pecheur SA v Germany* (C-46/93) [1996] Q.B. 404; [1996] E.C.R. I-1029; *R. v Secretary of State for Transport Ex p. Factortame Ltd (No.5)* [2000] 1 A.C. 524.

[202] See P. Craig, "Once More unto the Breach: the Community, the State and damages liability" (1997) 113 L.Q.R. 67; W. Van Gerven, "Bridging the Unbridgeable: Community and national tort Laws after *Francovich* and *Brasserie*" (1996) 45 I.C.L.Q. 507; T. Tridimas, "Liability for Breach of Community Law: Growing Up and Mellowing Down?" (2001) 38 C.M.L. Rev. 301. European Union institutions can also be found liable for damages for breach of EU law. See Edward and Lane, *European Union Law* (2013), para.5.96 and cases cited therein.

[203] *Kobler v Austria* (C-224/01) [2004] Q.B. 848; [2003] E.C.R. I-10239.

[204] *Kobler v Austria* (C-224/01) [2004] Q.B. 848; [2003] E.C.R. I-10239 at [51]–[59]. Examples would include a manifest disregard for the case law of the Court of Justice by the final court of appeal of a Member State or a blatant non-compliance with the obligation to make a preliminary reference.

[205] 2018 Act Sch.1, para.4.

> "Fundamental rights, as guaranteed by the European Convention for the Protection of Human Rights and Fundamental Freedoms and as they result from the constitutional traditions common to the Member States, shall constitute general principles of the Union's law."[206]

It was not always so. The original Treaties of the Communities made no reference to fundamental rights. It was the court, after an initial reluctance,[207] that "discovered" implicit in the EU legal order rights that broadly reflected those of the Member States: international human rights treaties that the Member States were party to supplied "guidelines" that should be followed[208] and the court drew "inspiration" from the constitutional traditions common to the Member States.[209] The most significant international treaty on human rights, common to all the Member States, is, of course, the European Convention on Human Rights. Prior to the Lisbon Treaty, the EU was not, and could not, be a party to the Convention.[210] Article 6(2) TEU now requires that the EU accede to the Convention.[211] A draft accession agreement was agreed between the EU and the Council of Europe in April 2013. That agreement was referred to the court for its opinion on whether it was compatible with EU law. An oral hearing took place in May 2014 and those Member States that participated, along with the EU institutions, supported the accession agreement. In June 2014, the advocate general gave his opinion that was, in effect, a qualified yes.[212] Against that background, it came as a surprise that the CJEU, in December 2014, issued its opinion and concluded that the accession agreement was *not* consistent with EU law.[213] That conclusion causes a number of problems: the EU cannot accede to the Convention until it has addressed the concerns raised by the court in its opinion.[214] The EU, however, remained bound by the terms of art.6(2) TEU and is thus under an obligation to accede to the Convention. In November 2019, negotiations formally resumed between the EU and the Council of Europe on the EU's accession to the Convention. The outcome of those discussions is awaited.

Failing to accede to the European Convention on Human Rights did not mean there was no human rights protection in EU law. On the contrary, the EU has its own document. The Charter of Fundamental Rights of the European Union ("the **10–31**

---

[206] art.6(3) TEU; art.2 TEU is to similar effect.

[207] For example, *Stork v High Authority of the European Coal and Steel Community* (C-1/58) [1959] E.C.R. 17.

[208] *Nold Kohlen- und Baustoffgrosshandlung v Commission of the European Communities* (C-4/73) [1974] E.C.R. 491 at p.13.

[209] *Kremzow v Austria* (C-299/95) [1997] E.C.R. I-2629.

[210] *Re Accession of the Community to the European Human Rights Convention* (Opinion 2/94) [1996] E.C.R. I-1759.

[211] The European Convention on Human Rights was previously open to signature by members of the Council of Europe. It was amended by Protocol No.14, art.17, which inserted a new art.59(2) to specifically allow the EU to accede to it.

[212] Opinion of the Court on the draft Accession Agreement of the European Union to the European Convention on Human Rights (Opinion 2/13), 13 June 2014, opinion of Advocate General Kokott, [2015] 2 C.M.L.R. 21.

[213] Opinion of the Court on the draft Accession Agreement of the European Union to the European Convention on Human Rights (Opinion 2/13), 18 December 2014, OJ C-62/2; [2015] 2 C.M.L.R. 21.

[214] It is perhaps worth noting that the court, as an EU institution, was part of the negotiation process for the accession agreement. During that process, a number of concerns raised by the court were addressed in the final agreement. The sheer number of objections now raised by the court to EU accession to the European Convention therefore came as a surprise.

Charter") was adopted by "solemn proclamation" in December 2000.[215] It was adopted not by the Member States but by the institutions of the EU. The Charter is wider in scope than most other fundamental rights treaties, covering socio-economic rights, such as the right of collective bargaining and action (art.28), fair and just working conditions (art.31) and healthcare (art.35), in addition to the more traditional fundamental rights. Where a right protected by the Charter corresponds to an equivalent right in the European Convention, the Charter right has the same meaning and scope as the Convention right.[216] That breadth of rights was obviously not to everyone's taste with the UK and Poland negotiating a protocol to the Charter to clarify its application in their respective legal systems.[217] Initially, at least, the Charter was of limited practical effect: it did not have the same status as the treaties and it was binding on Member States only when implementing EU law.[218] That changed with the Lisbon Treaty. Article 6(1) TEU now provides:

> "The Union recognises the rights, freedoms and principles set out in the Charter of Fundamental Rights of the European Union of 7 December 2000, as adapted at Strasbourg, on 12 December 2007, which shall have the same legal value as the Treaties."[219]

Thus, the Charter now has the same standing as the treaties. It features more regularly in judgments of the Court of Justice and has already been used on a number of occasions to strike down EU legislative measures for non-compliance.[220] The Supreme Court has confirmed that the Charter has direct effect in UK law and applies when the UK implements EU obligations.[221] The

---

[215] The full text was published in the Official Journal (Charter of Fundamental Rights of the European Union [2000] OJ C364/1) and is available online at: *http://www.europarl.europa.eu/charter/pdf/text_en.pdf* [Accessed 15 June 2020].

[216] art.52(3) of the Charter.

[217] Quite how much clarity it brought to matters is another question. The Charter did not extend the ability of British or Polish courts to any legislative or administrative acts inconsistent with fundamental rights and the socio-economic rights contained in Ch.IV of the Charter were declared not to create new justiciable rights. As a result of the decision of the Grand Chamber of the Court of Justice of the European Union in *R. (on the application of NS) v Secretary of State for the Home Department* (C-411/10) [2013] QB 102; [2012] 2 C.M.L.R. 9 at [119]–[122] and the High Court in *R. (on the application of AB) v Secretary of State for the Home Department* [2013] EWHC 3453 (Admin); [2014] 2 C.M.L.R. 22 at [11]–[14] any belief that the Protocol amounted to an opt-out was dispelled. On the Protocol generally see, O'Neill, *EU Law for UK Lawyers* (2011), paras 6.68–6.73.

[218] art.51(1) of the Charter.

[219] The Charter as originally proclaimed was adapted in anticipation of its elevation to the status of primary law. The adapted version, which makes few substantive changes, was published in the *Official Journal*: [2007] OJ C303/1.

[220] For example, and perhaps most controversially, in *Digital Rights Ireland Ltd v Minister for Communications, Marine and Natural Resources* (C-293/12), [2015] Q.B. 127 where the Data Retention Directive was struck down for non-compliance with arts 7 (respect for private and family life) and 8 (protection of personal data). The UK response to this decision was to enact emergency legislation to effectively reinstate the provisions of the directive: Data Retention and Investigatory Powers Act 2014 (which received Royal Assent within three days of its first reading in the House of Commons). That too has been held to be incompatible with the EU law: *R (on the application of Davis and others) v Secretary of State for the Home Department* [2015] EWHC 2092 (Admin); [2016] 1 C.M.L.R. 13. See further: para.12–12, below.

[221] *Rugby Football Union v Consolidated Information Services* [2012] UKSC 55; [2012] 1 W.L.R. 3333.

decision of the Employment Appeal Tribunal in *Janah v Libya*[222] gives an insight into the potential domestic consequences of the Charter. J claimed she had been unfairly dismissed from her post working at the Libyan embassy in London. Employment falls within the scope of EU law. Her claim was rejected by the Employment Tribunal on the basis it was barred by the State Immunity Act 1978. On appeal, the Employment Appeal Tribunal held that the relevant provisions of the 1978 Act were incompatible with J's right to a fair trial in terms of art.6 of the European Convention and art.47 of the Charter. So far as the European Convention issue was concerned, the 1978 Act could not be "read down" in terms of s.3 of the Human Rights Act 1998,[223] but it could be disapplied as incompatible with the Charter.[224] This gave rise to an acute issue in the UK: as we shall see in the next chapter, it was a careful and deliberate choice not to confer on the courts a power to disapply an Act of Parliament where it conflicted with a Convention right; where, however, such a Convention right also finds expression in the Charter, and the case falls within the sphere of EU law, the courts had exactly that power in terms of the European Communities Act 1972. That conclusion was upheld by the Court of Appeal[225] and the Supreme Court.[226] The exact interrelationship between the Charter, the European Convention on Human Rights, the Human Rights Act and the European Communities Act seemed destined to occupy the minds of the higher courts for some time. Whilst the European Union (Withdrawal) Act 2018 effected, as we will see in a moment, a general retention of EU law at the end of the Implementation Period, so far as the Charter is concerned, it has not been a part of domestic law since "exit day" (31 January 2020).[227]

The scope of the Charter should not, however, be over-emphasised: as art.51(2) of the Charter makes clear, it does not establish any new power or task for the Union, or modify the powers or tasks defined by the treaties. It therefore only applies within the sphere of EU law.[228] It remains too early to tell just how extensive an impact it will have.

---

222 *Benkharbouche v Embassy of Sudan; Janah v Libya* [2014] 1 C.M.L.R. 40; [2014] I.C.R. 169. See A Sanger, "The State Immunity Act and the right of access to the court" (2014) 73(1) C.L.J. 1.

223 On the operation of s.3 of the Human Rights Act 1998, see paras 11–07—11–10.

224 *Benkharbouche v Embassy of Sudan; Janah v Libya* [2014] 1 C.M.L.R. 40; [2014] I.C.R. 169 at [69].

225 *Benkharbouche v Embassy of Sudan; Janah v Libya* [2015] EWCA Civ 33; [2015] 2 C.M.L.R. 20.

226 *Benkharbouche v Embassy of Sudan; Janah v Libya* [2017] UKSC 62; [2019] A.C. 777, in particular, see [78].

227 European Union (Withdrawal) Act 2018 s.5(4).

228 Although that may be expanding beyond its bounds as traditionally understood. See *Zambrano v Office National de l'Emploi (ONEm)* (C-34/09) [2012] Q.B. 265; [2011] E.C.R. I-1177; I. Solanke, "Using the citizen to bring the refugee in, *Gerardo Ruiz Zambrano v Office National de l'Emploi (ONEM)*" (2012) 75 M.L.R. 101; A. Hinarejos, "Extending Citizenship and the Scope of EU Law" [2011] C.L.J. 309.

EU LAW IN THE UK

Introduction

10–32 We have already seen, in Ch.3, above, the impact of EU law on the doctrine of parliamentary sovereignty. Wrestling with issues like that is not unique to the UK and similar discussions can be found in the jurisprudence of supreme and constitutional courts throughout the EU.[229] We have also seen the special place that EU law had in the law of Scotland as one of the limitations imposed upon the competence of both the devolved Parliament and the Scottish Ministers. To an extent, that is all history now, but given the enduring impact of EU membership on the law, and in particular the constitution, of the UK, it is worth spending some time considering two of the primary legislative measures that gave effect to, and regulated, EU law in the UK: the European Communities Act 1972 and the European Union Act 2011. Thereafter, we will turn to the principle legislative vehicles that secured the UK's withdrawal from the EU: the European Union (Withdrawal) Act 2018 and the European Union (Withdrawal Agreement) Act 2020.[230]

European Communities Act 1972

10–33 The 1972 Act was the mechanism by which the UK acceded to the EU on 1 January 1973.[231] When the UK joined what was then the European Economic Community, effect had to be given to all existing EU law, as well as ensuring that future EU legislation could be effectively implemented in the UK. Furthermore, as we have seen, EU law also required that it was given precedence over any (and all) national law. Section 2(1) of the 1972 Act was designed to achieve those aims:

> "All such rights, powers, liabilities, obligations and restrictions from time to time created or arising by or under the Treaties, and all such remedies and procedures from time to time provided for by or under the Treaties, as in accordance with the Treaties are without further enactment to be given legal effect or used in the United Kingdom shall be recognised and available in law, and be enforced, allowed and followed accordingly; and the expression enforceable EU right and similar expressions shall be read as referring to one to which this subsection applies."[232]

Lord Denning described the effect of that provision in characteristically vivid terms:

> "The Treaty does not touch any of the matters which concern solely England and the people in it. These are still governed by English law. They are not affected by the Treaty. But when we come to matters with a European element, the Treaty is like an

[229] Edward and Lane, *European Union Law* (2013), para.6.19 and cases cited therein.

[230] For a fuller discussion of the process that led to the UK's departure from the EU, see Ch.1.

[231] The Treaty of Accession could not bring about that result because of the dualist nature of the UK: international treaties can only change the law of the UK when Parliament gives effect to them (*Attorney General for Canada v Attorney General for Ontario* [1937] A.C. 326 PC (Canada)). See para.2–12, above.

[232] European Communities Act 1972 s.2(1) (as amended).

> incoming tide. It flows into the estuaries and up the rivers. It cannot be held back, Parliament has decreed that the Treaty is henceforward to be part of our law. It is equal in force to any statute."[233]

In describing it as "equal in force" to any statute, Lord Denning may have underestimated the impact of the accession to the EU. As the House of Lords confirmed in *Factortame*, s.2(1) of the 1972 Act was authority to disapply inconsistent, and subsequently enacted, primary legislation.[234] As Lord Bridge explained:

> "If the supremacy within the European Community of Community law over the national law of Member States was not always inherent in the EEC Treaty it was certainly well established in the jurisprudence of the Court of Justice long before the United Kingdom joined the Community. Thus whatever limitation of its sovereignty Parliament accepted when it enacted the European Communities Act 1972 was entirely voluntary. Under the terms of the 1972 Act it has always been clear that it was the duty of a United Kingdom court, when delivering final judgment, to override any rule of national law found to be in conflict with any directly enforceable rule of Community law."[235]

Laws LJ, in *Thoburn v Sunderland City Council*, captured the impact of the 1972 Act well: "[i]t may be there has never been a statute having such profound effects on so many dimensions of our daily lives".[236] That was closer than Lord Denning to the view expressed by the Supreme Court in *Miller (No.1)*:

> "Many statutes give effect to treaties by prescribing the content of domestic law in the areas covered by them. The 1972 Act does this, but it does considerably more as well. It authorises a dynamic process by which, without further primary legislation (and, in some cases, even without any domestic legislation), EU law not only becomes a source of UK law, but actually takes precedence over all domestic sources of UK law, including statutes. This may sound rather dry or technical to many people, but in constitutional terms the effect of the 1972 Act was unprecedented."[237]

In any event, s.2(1) of the 1972 Act had the effect that the EU Treaties and EU legislation (as interpreted by the Court of Justice) became a direct source of UK law[238] and the EU Treaties and EU Regulations were directly applicable without further action on the part of the UK.[239] Section 2(2) was the other way in which EU law took effect in the UK. It conferred power on Her Majesty by Order in Council, or any designated minister, to make regulations for the purpose of implementing any EU obligation incumbent upon the UK (primarily, implementing a directive). Section 3 of the 1972 Act imposes an obligation on the courts to

---

233 *HP Bulmer Ltd v J Bollinger SA* [1974] Ch. 401 CA at p.418F.

234 *R. v Secretary of State for Transport, Ex p. Factortame Ltd* [1991] 1 A.C. 603.

235 *R. v Secretary of State for Transport, Ex p. Factortame Ltd* [1991] 1 A.C. 603 HL at pp.658–659.

236 *Thoburn v Sunderland City Council* [2002] EWHC 195 (Admin); [2003] Q.B. 151 at [62].

237 *R (on the application of Miller and other) v Secretary of State for Exiting the European Union* [2017] UKSC 5; [2018] A.C. 61 at [60].

238 *R (on the application of Miller and other) v Secretary of State for Exiting the European Union* [2017] UKSC 5; [2018] A.C. 61 at [62].

239 *R (on the application of Miller and other) v Secretary of State for Exiting the European Union* [2017] UKSC 5; [2018] A.C. 61 at [63].

determine any question of EU law "in accordance with the principles laid down by and any relevant decision of the European Court".[240]

As we saw in Ch.3, accession to the EU presented a formidable challenge to the classic understanding of parliamentary supremacy. The 1972 Act contains no plain declaration of the supremacy of EU law. Instead, the legislative effect of the primacy of EU law is to be found tucked away in the middle of s.2(4): "... any enactment passed or to be passed ... shall be construed and have effect subject to the foregoing provisions of this section". There it is: any enactment, which therefore includes an Act of Parliament, is to have effect subject to the provisions of EU law. Or, as the Supreme Court put it in *Miller (No.1)*:

> "although the 1972 Act gives effect to EU law, it is not itself the originating source of that law. It is ... the 'conduit pipe' by which EU law is introduced into UK domestic law. So long as the 1972 Act remains in force, its effect is to constitute EU law an independent and overriding source of domestic law."[241]

In other words, it was the UK domestic courts that resolved the tension between the orthodox view of parliamentary sovereignty and the supremacy of EU law. And they resolved it in favour of EU law.

European Union Act 2011

10–34 The 2011 Act was the subject of significant confusion.[242] It appears to have had two aims (perhaps out of concern that Lord Denning's "incoming tide" was closer to a tsunami?). First, it sought to introduce various "locks", both legislative and in the form of a referendum requirement, before certain changes could be made to numerous aspects of EU law. As we will see, and leaving aside the more general issues associated with the use of referendums in the United Kingdom (which are discussed in Ch.5, above), that had potentially profound constitutional implications. Second, it enacts what was originally billed by the then Foreign Secretary (William Hague) as a "sovereignty clause". Unlike the "locks", the "sovereignty clause" appeared to lurk at the opposite end of the spectrum in terms of constitutional significance.

The "locks"

10–35 Much of the 2011 Act was devoted to establishing a system that required parliamentary and/or popular approval before the UK could assent to, or implement, numerous EU decisions. The "referendum locks" were contained in ss.2–6 of the 2011 Act. These complicated provisions are not readily amenable to a brief summary,[243] but they did provide a comprehensive code that is not to be

240 That can be contrasted with the obligation in the Human Rights Act to "take into account" decisions of the Strasbourg court. See paras 11–05—11–06.

241 *R (on the application of Miller and other) v Secretary of State for Exiting the European Union* [2017] UKSC 5; [2018] A.C. 61 at [65].

242 See, for example, M. Gordon and M. Dougan, "The United Kingdom's European Union Act 2011; 'who won the bloody war anyway?'" (2012) 37 E.L. Rev. 3.

243 The more detailed analysis of the European Union Act 2011 by Professor Craig is commended: P. Craig, "The European Union Act 2011: Locks, Limits and Legality" (2011) 48 C.M.L. Rev. 1915.

construed expansively.[244] Section 2 provided that a treaty that amends either the TEU or the TFEU shall not be ratified unless it has been approved by Parliament and the "referendum condition" is met. The "referendum condition" required: (a) the Act providing for the approval of the treaty shall provide that the provision approving the treaty is not to come into force until a referendum has been held as to whether or not the treaty should be ratified; (b) such a referendum was held; and (c) the majority of those voting in the referendum were in favour of ratifying the treaty. Similar provision was made in s.3 for an equivalent approval process where the TEU and/or TFEU were amended in accordance with the simplified revision procedure in art.48(6) TEU. The referendum requirements of ss.2 and 3 were avoided where the treaty or decision does not fall within s.4 of the 2011 Act, or, in the case of s.3, where the "significance condition" is satisfied.[245] Section 4 is drafted in very broad terms and it would have been rare that a treaty or art.48(6) TEU decision did not fall within it.[246] Section 5 required a minister to lay a statement before Parliament confirming their view as to whether a treaty or decision falls within the scope of s.4 and their reasons for that conclusion. Section 6 then introduced another raft of decisions that required approval both by Parliament and in a referendum. A minister "may not vote in favour of or otherwise support" a decision that falls within s.6. Such decisions ranged from a decision under art.48(7) TEU to move to qualified majority voting[247] or various decisions in relation to EU common defence or the European Public Prosecutor's Office to a decision to adopt the euro.[248] The case for a referendum on the last was much more compelling than the first. Sections 7–10 then required statutory or parliamentary approval before a minister may approve, vote in favour of or otherwise support a range of EU decisions.[249]

Despite the referendum provisions never being invoked before the 2011 Act was, in substance, repealed, they are worth dwelling on for a moment. Leaving aside issues around the legality, as a matter of EU law, of a number of the provisions of the 2011 Act,[250] there are two main issues of domestic constitutional significance thrown up by the 2011 Act. The first is the requirement **10–36**

244 *Wheeler v Office of the Prime Minister* [2014] EWHC 3815; [2015] 1 C.M.L.R. 46 at [28]. The case is a useful illustration of some of the apparent gaps in the convoluted provisions in ss.2–6.

245 Section 3(4) of the 2011 Act provides: "The significance condition is that the Act providing for the approval of the decision states that— (a) the decision falls within section 4 only because of provision of the kind mentioned in subsection (1)(i) or (j) of that section, and (b) the effect of that provision in relation to the United Kingdom is not significant."

246 Three specific carve-outs are made in s.4(4): "A treaty or Article 48(6) decision does not fall within this section merely because it involves one or more of the following—(a) the codification of practice under TEU or TFEU in relation to the previous exercise of an existing competence; (b) the making of any provision that applies only to member States other than the United Kingdom; (c) in the case of a treaty, the accession of a new member State." As Craig points out, the language of this provision is complex and likely to be of limited practical significance. For example, accession treaties are often used to introduce other treaty amendments, thus the exception is unlikely to apply: Craig, "The European Union Act 2011: Locks, Limits and Legality" (2011) 48(6) C.M.L. Rev. 1915, 1923–1924.

247 See para.10–33, above.

248 The full list is set out in s.6(5) of the 2011 Act.

249 The matters covered by these sections are more fully explained by Craig, "The European Union Act 2011: Locks, Limits and Legality" (2011) 48 C.M.L. Rev. 1915, 1917–1920.

250 See Craig, "The European Union Act 2011: Locks, Limits and Legality" (2011) 48 C.M.L. Rev. 1915, 1928–1936.

that an Act of Parliament shall not come into force until such time as a referendum has been held. It may be argued that the 2011 Act changed the "manner and form" of legislation.[251] Did Parliament redefine itself, for matters falling within the 2011 Act, as a tricameral body consisting of Commons, Lords and the citizens?[252] On that argument, if Parliament were to pass an Act approving a treaty amendment or another decision that falls within the scope of the 2011 Act without holding a referendum and obtaining a positive result, the court should not recognise that Act as valid. There is some Commonwealth authority to support the "manner and form" argument.[253] As we saw in Ch.3 above, however, on a classic understanding of the doctrine of parliamentary sovereignty, Parliament cannot bind its successors. Thus, applying the orthodox view of sovereignty, it would be open to Parliament to dispense with the requirements of the 2011 Act in any particular case. It might be thought that the political cost of eliding the referendum requirement would be such that Parliament would never countenance such a thing. But the range of issues on which a referendum is now required is so vast. Take, for example, a proposed decision to adopt measures concerning unfair dismissal by the ordinary legislative process instead of the special legislative process in terms of art.153(2) TFEU. Section 6 of the 2011 Act required approval by Act of Parliament and by referendum before the minister could vote in favour of such a measure. No such referendum ever had to be held. Just as well, because you could only pity the party activists that have to drum up enthusiasm amongst the electorate to traipse to a polling station on a damp Thursday evening to cast their vote on that issue. And pity the Prime Minister who may have had to explain to Parliament that, after spending parliamentary time passing the necessary Act and tens of millions of pounds organising and winning a referendum, that the decision was not passed because, whilst the UK was organising its referendum, one or more Member States had changed their mind and the measure failed despite the British people giving it the thumbs up. So whilst the referendum "lock" may have been politically binding on issues such as adopting the single currency or any substantial revision of the treaties, for many of the matters caught within the scope of the 2011 Act, it may be (and probably should be) a requirement more honoured in the breach than in the observance.

The second issue of note was the form of referendum. There were no turnout thresholds and a simple majority of the votes cast was enough for ratification.[254] As we discussed in Ch.5, above, issues of legitimacy arise when the turnout in a referendum falls significantly. Low turnout would inevitably have been an issue of concern in relation to the 2011 Act. The "catch-all" manner in which it is drafted risked the British electorate being asked, at reasonably frequent intervals (at least for a country that had only ever had, at the time, two nationwide referendums) to express a view on fairly technical points of EU law. There is no need to repeat the points made earlier about the democratic legitimacy of a

[251] See, for example, I. Jennings, *The Law of the Constitution*, 5th edn (London: University of London Press, 1959) Ch.4.

[252] V. Bogdanor, "Imprisoned by a Doctrine: The Modern Defence of Parliamentary Sovereignty" (2012) 32 O.J.L.S. 179.

[253] See para.3–05, above.

[254] See ss.2(2)(c) and 3(2)(c) of the 2011 Act.

referendum result in such circumstances.[255] But there threatened to be a substantial political price to pay had the UK indulged in a series of referendums under the 2011 Act. How often would the other Member States have been prepared to put otherwise uncontroversial measures on hold for six months or so (and it is hard to envisage the necessary Act being passed and referendum held in less than six months)? And how would they have reacted when, after such a pause, the UK returns to the Council to explain that on a 20 per cent turnout, 51 per cent of the electorate voted against the proposal to adopt the ordinary legislative process in relation to that regulation concerning unfair dismissal? It is all moot now, but it is hard to see how the 2011 Act could ever have been a workable, long term, solution. Instead, sooner or later, it was bound to have been used a proxy for the in/out vote that was held in 2016. In that sense, the 2016 referendum, in some guise, was probably inevitable so long as the 2011 Act remained in place.

The "sovereignty clause"

Despite the constitutional implications of the "lock" provisions in the 2011 Act, it was what became s.18 of the Act that caused much of the debate as the Act made its way through Parliament. After various iterations, the form that was settled upon was this: 10–37

> "Directly applicable or directly effective EU law (that is, the rights, powers, liabilities, obligations, restrictions, remedies and procedures referred to in section 2(1) of the European Communities Act 1972) falls to be recognised and available in law in the United Kingdom only by virtue of that Act or where it is required to be recognised and available in law by virtue of any other Act."

As enacted, s.18 is simply a declaration of what the law is, and what it had always been understood to be:

> "It is important now to declare—*and it must be made plain*—that the provisions of article 119 of the EEC Treaty take priority over anything in our English statute on equal pay which is inconsistent with article 119. *That priority is given by our own law. It is given by the European Communities Act 1972 itself.*"[256] (Emphasis added.)

The counter-argument, that EU law contains the entrenchment of its own supremacy[257] and by importing EU law into domestic law Parliament thereby imported that entrenchment, was specifically rejected by the Divisional Court of

---

[255] See para.5–08, above.

[256] *Macarthys Ltd v Smith* [1981] Q.B. 180 CA (Civ Div) at p.200E–F; Lord Bridge made the same point in *R. v Secretary of State for Transport, Ex p. Factortame Ltd (No.2)* [1991] 1 A.C. 603 at p.659A: "Thus, whatever limitation of its sovereignty Parliament accepted when it enacted the European Communities Act 1972 was entirely voluntary. Under the terms of the Act of 1972 it has always been clear that it was the duty of a United Kingdom court, when delivering final judgement, to override any rule of national law found to be in conflict with any directly enforceable rule of [EU] law."

[257] *NV Algemene Transport- en Expeditie Onderneming van Gend en Loos v Nederlandse Administratie der Belastingen* (C-26/62) [1963] E.C.R. 1 and *Costa v ENEL* (C-6/64) [1964] E.C.R. 585.

the High Court in *Thoburn v Sunderland City Council*.[258] So quite why s.18 was required, other than as a political gesture, is unclear. It simply declares that the law is exactly what it had always been understood to be by the courts.[259] If, however, the "manner and form" argument in relation to the "locks" outlined above is correct, Parliament has limited its sovereignty in relation to ratification of EU Treaty amendments and other decisions. If it can limit its sovereignty in that field, why not others? If that is correct, as Bogdanor points out, it is somewhat paradoxical, and ironic, that in seeking to defend parliamentary sovereignty against "the Europeans", Parliament in fact surrendered it.[260]

EU Law post-membership: introduction

10–38 That, as we know, is almost all history now. Most of the 2011 Act has been repealed and what survives will soon be removed from the statute book. Likewise, the 1972 Act. The principle piece of legislation that now governs the status of EU law in the UK is the European Union (Withdrawal) Act 2018 ("the 2018 Act"). And for now, that Act has to be read alongside the European Union (Withdrawal Agreement) Act 2020 ("the 2020 Act"). Before turning to look at some of the detail of those Acts, it is helpful to introduce a few concepts that underlie the new legislative scheme.

First, there are two important dates in the exit process: "exit day" and "IP completion day". Exit day was 31 January 2020 at 23:00 and it was defined by the 2018 Act.[261] When the 2018 Act was passed, exit day was set as 29 March 2019 at 23:00 before being changed to 31 October 2019 at 23:00.[262] However unpalatable the change of date was for the Prime Minister of the day, they were changes that were required by the 2018 Act. That was because "exit day" had to coincide with the day and time at which the EU Treaties would cease to apply to the UK.[263] Exit day was significant because it marked the day on which the UK formally left the EU. But a second date is likely to have more practical consequence: "IP completion day". That is a date that was introduced by the 2020 Act and it marks the day on which the transitional (to use the language of the Withdrawal Agreement) or implementation (to use the language of the 2020 Act)

---

258 *Thoburn v Sunderland City Council* [2002] EWHC 195 (Admin); [2003] Q.B. 151 at [58]–[59].

259 *R (on the application of Miller and other) v Secretary of State for Exiting the European Union* [2017] UKSC 5; [2018] A.C. 61 at [66].

260 Bogdanor, "Imprisoned by a Doctrine: The Modern Defence of Parliamentary Sovereignty" (2012) 32 O.J.L.S. 179, 190.

261 2018 Act s.20(1).

262 European Union (Withdrawal) Act 2018 (Exit Day) (Amendment) (No.2) Regulations 2019 and European Union (Withdrawal) Act 2018 (Exit Day) (Amendment) (No.3) Regulations 2019. For a short spell there were two possible exit days depending upon whether the Withdrawal Agreement was approved: European Union (Withdrawal) Act 2018 (Exit Day) (Amendment) (No.1) Regulations 2019. See para.1–20, above for the context of those changes.

263 2018 Act, s.20(3)–(4). As originally enacted, the 2018 Act provided that a minister "may" by regulations amend the definition of "exit day" to coincide with the point at which the Treaties ceased to apply. That was changed to "must" by the European Union (Withdrawal) (No.2) Act 2019 (s.4(1)). Had it been otherwise, there was at least a risk of there being a gap when either the Treaties applied but the 1972 Act had been repealed (or the other way round). As it was, the change meant that the UK had, as a matter of European and domestic law, to cease being a Member State at a single point in time. See also, para.1–20, above.

period comes to an end.[264] It is currently fixed for 31 December 2020 at 23:00. Like exit day, a minister can, by regulations, vary the date. Unlike the exit day, which had to coincide with the day on which the Treaties ceased to apply to the UK, the 2020 Act only provides that a minister "may" amend the definition of IP completion day to ensure that the date and time specified in the definition coincide with the date and time the transition period set in the Withdrawal Agreement is to end.[265] It is hard to imagine why the two should not coincide, but the 2020 Act does not require that they should. If the transition period is to be extended, that should be done before 1 July 2020 and any extension can be for up to two years.[266]

Having considered the IP completion day, that necessarily begs the question: what is the implementation period? According to s.1A(6) of the 2018 Act, it is "the transition or implementation period provided for by Part 4 of the withdrawal agreement and beginning with exit day and ending on IP completion day".[267] Part 4 of the Withdrawal Agreement provides for a transition period.[268] As a general rule, during the transition period, EU law shall be applicable to and in the UK.[269] In case there was any doubt about what was intended by the continued application of EU law during this period, it is put beyond doubt in art.127(3): **10–39**

> "During the transition period, the Union law applicable pursuant to paragraph 1 shall produce in respect of and in the United Kingdom the same legal effects as those which it produces within the Union and its Member States, and shall be interpreted and applied in accordance with the same methods and general principles as those applicable within the Union."

In short, to the extent that EU law applies during the transition period, the UK is a Member State of the EU in all but name.[270] Whilst EU law continues to generally apply to the UK during the transition period, participation in the institutions is generally ended. For example, the UK no longer participates in the decision-making and governance of the bodies, offices and agencies of the EU, nor does it participate in any of the decision-making (nor does it attend meetings) of the institutions of the EU (e.g. the Commission or the Council).[271] The UK, however, remains subject to the jurisdiction of the Court of Justice and the Commission has the same enforcement powers in relation to the UK as it would for any Member State.[272] The UK is also bound by any obligations stemming from international agreements concluded by the EU, but, unless the UK is in its own right a member of any body set up by such agreements, it shall not participate in their work (unless, exceptionally, invited to do so by the EU).[273]

---

[264] 2020 Act s.39(1).
[265] 2020 Act s.39(4).
[266] art.132(1) of the Withdrawal Agreement.
[267] That provision was inserted by s.1 of the 2020 Act.
[268] art.126 of the Withdrawal Agreement.
[269] art.127(1) of the Withdrawal Agreement.
[270] And that is stated in terms in art.127(6): "Unless otherwise provided in this Agreement, during the transition period, any reference to Member States in the Union law applicable pursuant to paragraph 1, including as implemented and applied by Member States, shall be understood as including the United Kingdom."
[271] art.7(1) of the Withdrawal Agreement.
[272] art.131 of the Withdrawal Agreement.
[273] art.129(1)–(2) of the Withdrawal Agreement.

Furthermore, the UK may not act in a way that would be prejudicial to the EU's interests.[274] But the UK can enter into new international agreements, so long as they do not enter into force during the transition period.[275]

With those concepts in mind, we can now turn to look at the legislation. It is more convenient to start with the 2020 Act.

The European Union (Withdrawal Agreement) Act 2020

10–40 It was not until the December 2019 General Election shifted the parliamentary arithmetic in the government's favour that it was possible secure Parliament's agreement to the Withdrawal Agreement. Despite all the drama along the way, the 2020 Act became law with little fuss, such was the majority that the government now held. Once the Withdrawal Agreement had been ratified, it became necessary to the amend the 2018 Act that otherwise made no provision for a transitional period. That was done by s.1 of the 2020 Act that, as we have just seen, introduced the concept of the "Implementation Period". Whilst the language is different, it has exactly the same meaning as the "transition period", which is the phrase used throughout the Withdrawal Agreement.[276] Given the 2018 Act repealed the European Communities Act 1972 on exit day, provision had to be made for the continuing effect of EU law in accordance with the Withdrawal Agreement.[277] That has been done by providing that the 1972 Act, despite its repeal by s.1 of the 2018 Act, continues to have effect in domestic law so far as is necessary to give effect to the Withdrawal Agreement.[278] In a similar vein, all domestic legislation that was enacted to give effect to EU obligations prior to exit day ("EU-derived domestic legislation"[279]) continues to have effect in domestic law so far as is necessary to give effect to the Withdrawal Agreement.[280] In addition to that general saving of the 1972 Act to the extent necessary to honour the obligations of the Withdrawal Agreement, s.5 of the 2020 Act inserts a new s.7A into the 2018 Act. It provides:

> "**General implementation of remainder of withdrawal agreement**
> **7A.**—(1) Subsection (2) applies to—
> (a) all such rights, powers, liabilities, obligations and restrictions from time to time created or arising by or under the withdrawal agreement, and
> (b) all such remedies and procedures from time to time provided for by or under the withdrawal agreement,
>
> as in accordance with the withdrawal agreement are without further enactment to be given legal effect or used in the United Kingdom.
>
> (2) The rights, powers, liabilities, obligations, restrictions, remedies and procedures concerned are to be—
> (a) recognised and available in domestic law, and
> (b) enforced, allowed and followed accordingly.

[274] art.129(3) of the Withdrawal Agreement.
[275] art.129(4) of the Withdrawal Agreement.
[276] 2018 Act s.1A(6), inserted by s.1 of the 2020 Act.
[277] As we saw in para.10–33, it was clear that EU law derived its status from the 1972 Act.
[278] 2018 Act s.1A(2)–(3), inserted by s.1 of the 2020 Act.
[279] 2018 Act s.1B(7), inserted by s.2 of the 2020 Act.
[280] 2018 Act s.1B(2)–(3), inserted by s.2 of the 2020 Act.

> Every enactment (including an enactment contained in this Act) is to be read and has effect subject to subsection (2)."

In short, s.7A re-enacted the substance of s.2(1) of the 1972 Act and confers the same status upon the Withdrawal Agreement. As we saw in Ch.3, s.2(1) of the 1972 Act was said to have affected a constitutional revolution by limiting the power of Parliament to legislate contrary to EU law.[281] On the one hand, given the Withdrawal Agreement was intended to ensure the UK remained in effect a Member State for the transition period, it is little surprise that Parliament chose to recycle the language used in s.2(1) of the 1972 Act. But it is ironic (and perhaps a little surprising) that later in the 2020 Act, Parliament provided:

> "**Parliamentary sovereignty**
>
> **38.**—(1) It is recognised that the Parliament of the United Kingdom is sovereign.
>
> (2) In particular, its sovereignty subsists notwithstanding—
>
> ...
>
> (b) section 7A of [the 2018 Act]
>
> ...
>
> (3) Accordingly, nothing in this Act derogates from sovereignty of the Parliament of the United Kingdom."

Much like s.18 of the European Union Act 2011, this provision may have played well politically but it is doubtful what, if any, legal significance it could have. Given the parallels in language between s.7A of the 2018 Act and s.2(1) of the 1972 Act, it is hard to foresee the courts reaching a different conclusion on its effect.[282] And s.38(3) appears to be completely otiose, if Laws LJ in *Thoburn* is accepted as having accurately stated the constitutional position when he held that the scope and nature of parliamentary sovereignty ultimately rested in the hands of the court.[283] But it does highlight that, to the very end, membership of the EU caused a tension at the very heart of the constitution.[284]

The European Union (Withdrawal) Act 2018

Initially heralded as the "Great Repeal Bill", the 2018 Act gets to the point straight away, "The European Communities Act 1972 is repealed on exit day".[285] **10–41**

There then follows 193 pages of legislation, spread of over a further 24 sections and nine schedules that set about qualifying the effect that repeal of the 1972 Act would otherwise have had. As we have just seen, the provisions inserted by the 2020 Act all but undo the repeal of the 1972 Act for the duration of the transition/implementation period. But the main purpose of the 2018 Act is to cater

---

281 See para.3–10, above and H.W.R. Wade, "Sovereignty—Revolution or Evolution?" (1996) 112 L.Q.R. 568.

282 As to that conclusion, see para.10–33, above and in particular the passage from *R (on the application of Miller and other) v Secretary of State for Exiting the European Union* [2017] UKSC 5; [2018] A.C. 61 at [60].

283 *Thoburn v Sunderland City Council* [2002] EWHC 195 (Admin); [2003] QB 151 at [60].

284 Other provision was made by the 2020 Act in relation to, for example, immigration related issues, the recognition of professional qualification and the co-ordination of social security systems (see Pt 3 of the 2020 Act). Whilst important, those more technical provisions are not discussed in this work.

285 2018 Act s.1.

for the post-transition/implementation period. And the discussion that follows proceeds on the basis that period has ended.

The 2018 Act creates a body of law to be known as "retained EU law". In short, ss.2–5 of the 2018 Act go about copying over almost the entire body of EU law as it stands on IP completion day into domestic law. It is an attempt to freeze most of EU law as at exit day and import it into domestic law. That should result in certainty and legal continuity: all things being equal, the law should be the same the day after IP completion day. Retained EU law is made up of two components. First, there is "EU-derived domestic legislation".[286] That is more or less any enactment made under s.2(2) of the 1972 Act and any enactment "relating otherwise to the EU or the EEA".[287] Despite becoming part of the corpus that is retained EU law, EU-derived domestic legislation continues to be domestic law as an enactment of the same kind (i.e. if a provision is in an Act of Parliament it continues to have that status).[288] Next there is "direct EU legislation".[289] That is the body of EU law that had effect by virtue of s.2(1) of the 1972 Act (i.e. directly applicable provisions of the Treaties and most EU Regulations). It is now converted into domestic law so that it continues to apply post-transition/implementation period. It is, however, converted only in so far as operative immediately before exit day. In short, to be converted into domestic law the provision has to have been in force on exit day.[290] And it is only EU legislation that is available in an English language version that can be converted (and where it is available in multiple languages, only the English language version is converted).[291] Any remaining EU rights and obligations that do not fall within EU-derived domestic legislation and direct EU legislation are saved by s.4 of the 2018 Act. It provides for the retention of any rights, powers, liabilities, obligations, restrictions, remedies and procedures that were recognised in domestic law by virtue of s.2(1) of the 1972 Act and which are enforced, allowed and followed accordingly.[292] Most obviously, that will catch directly effective rights contained with EU treaties (i.e. those rights that are sufficiently clear, precise and unconditional as to confer rights directly).[293] The EU law that is retained under ss.2 and 3 is divided into either "retained direct principal EU legislation" or "retained direct minor EU legislation".[294] That distinction is relevant to how that retained legislation can be modified going forward. Retained direct principal EU legislation is specifically defined (and includes, for example, most EU Regulations) and any retained legislation that does not fall within that definition is retained direct minor EU legislation.[295]

---

[286] 2018 Act s.2(1).

[287] 2018 Act s.2(2). The "relating otherwise to the EU or the EEA" is designed to catch, for example, an Act of Parliament that contained cross-references to a definition contained in an EU instrument: Explanatory Notes, para.77.

[288] 2018 Act s.7(1).

[289] 2018 Act s.3(1).

[290] 2018 Act s.3(3).

[291] 2018 Act s.3(4). Other language versions remain available for use as an aid to the interpretation of the legislation.

[292] 2018 Act s.4(1).

[293] See para.10–27, above. An illustrative, and non-exhaustive, list of such rights is provided at para.94 of the Explanatory Notes.

[294] 2018 Act s.7(2)–(3).

[295] 2018 Act s.7(6).

There are, however, exceptions to this general retention of EU law and they are provided for in s.5. There are two general qualifications introduced there. First, the principle of the supremacy of EU law does not apply to any enactment or rule of law made on or after exit day.[296] But the principle of the supremacy of EU law does continue to apply so far as relevant to the interpretation of any provision or rule of law that pre-dates exit day.[297] In other words, the "normal" approach to implied repeal is restored: if Parliament now legislates in a way that is inconsistent with any aspect of retained EU law, that provision is not to be disapplied because of any inconsistency with retained EU law.[298] Second, the Charter of Fundamental Rights is expressly excluded from domestic law after exit day.[299] To the extent that the Charter only served to recognise and reaffirm existing rights that were already part of EU law, those rights ought to have entered domestic law as a result of the general retention of EU law. So, if a right recognised by the Charter was otherwise recognised, it will continue to be recognised.[300] Accordingly, the exclusion of the Charter is likely to make limited practical difference.[301]

Having retained the legislation, it was also necessary to retain the case law applying to, and interpreting, that legislation. Accordingly, s.6 introduces the concept of "retained case law", which comprises of two groups: "retained EU case law" and "retained domestic case law".[302] "Retained EU case law" means any principle laid down by, and any decisions of, the European Court,[303] as they had effect in EU law immediately before IP completion day and so far as they related to anything that now constitutes retained EU law. "Retained domestic case law" consists of any principles laid down by, and decisions of, a UK court, as they have effect immediately before IP completion day so far as they relate to retained EU law. That body of case law is supplemented by "retained general principles of EU law", which are the general principles of EU law, as they have effect in EU law immediately before IP completion day, and so far as they relate to retained EU law (and are not otherwise expressly excluded by the 2018 Act).[304] But note that whereas legislation and the treaties have been frozen as at exit day, retained case law is frozen as at IP completion day. **10–42**

Having retained that body of case law, what are domestic courts to do with it? And what should they do with decisions of the CJEU that come after IP completion day but which explain the correct interpretation of an EU measure that forms part of retained EU law? When faced with a question as to the validity, meaning or effect of retained EU law, the court is to decide the point (so far as that law is unmodified on or after IP completion day) in accordance with any retained case law and any retained general principles of EU law and having regard (amongst other things) to the limits, immediately before IP completion

[296] 2018 Act s.5(1).
[297] 2018 Act s.5(2).
[298] On implied repeal, see para.3–03, above.
[299] 2018 Act s.5(4).
[300] 2018 Act s.5(5).
[301] For a fuller consideration of the post-exit role of the Charter, see: M. Markakis, "Brexit and the EU Charter of Fundamental Rights" [2019] P.L. 82.
[302] 2018 Act s.6(7).
[303] That is, the Court of Justice: Interpretation Act 1978 Sch.1, read with s.21 of the 2018 Act.
[304] 2018 Act s.6(7).

day, of EU competences.[305] But retained case law is not binding on the Supreme Court (or, when sitting as a final court of appeal, the High Court of Justiciary) and it can be departed from by applying the same test those courts would apply when otherwise considering whether to depart from its own case law.[306] Accordingly, it will be open to the Supreme Court to develop retained EU law in a different direction from that taken by the Court of Justice in respect of the equivalent EU law. From that, the answer to the second question posed above becomes obvious. Decisions of the Court of Justice that post-date IP completion day do not bind domestic courts.[307] But the domestic courts are not required to shut their eyes to post-IP completion day events on the continent. They "may have regard to anything done on or after IP completion day by the European Court, another EU entity or the EU so far as it is relevant to any matter before the court or tribunal".[308] To that extent, it will remain necessary to keep appraised of developments in the EU and the jurisprudence of the Court of Justice.

10–43 It is inevitable that the import of such a large body of law will throw up a number of wrinkles. Most obviously, retained EU law, when it was drafted, was all predicated on the UK being a member of the EU and thus participating in the institutions and bodies of the Union. Accordingly, retained EU law will be littered with references to bodies the UK no longer participates in nor has access to. That will leave much of what has been retained making no sense. In the language of the 2018 Act, these issues are known as "deficiencies". And they are dealt with by s.8 of the 2018 Act, which provides:

> "**Dealing with deficiencies arising from withdrawal**
> **8.**—(1) A Minister of the Crown may by regulations make such provision as the Minister considers appropriate to prevent, remedy or mitigate -
> (a) any failure of retained EU law to operate effectively, or
> (b) any other deficiency in retained EU law,
> Arising from the withdrawal of the United Kingdom from the EU.
> …
> (5) Regulations under subsection (1) may make any provision that could be made by an Act of Parliament."

That provision confers a very wide legislative power upon the executive.[309] Perhaps somewhat ambitiously, the power conferred by s.8(1) expires two years after IP completion day (31 December 2022).[310] What constitutes "deficiencies" is set out in s.8(2)–(4). Those provisions do not lend themselves to easy summary, so it is simplest to set them out in full:

> "(2) Deficiencies in retained EU law are where the Minister considers that retained EU law—
> (a) contains anything which has no practical application in relation to the United Kingdom or any part of it or is otherwise redundant or substantially redundant,

---

305 2018 Act s.6(3).
306 2018 Act s.6(4)–(5).
307 2018 Act s.6(1).
308 2018 Act s.6(2).
309 In appropriate areas, this power can be exercised by the devolved administrations: s.11 of, and sch.2 to, the 2018 Act.
310 2018 Act s.8(8).

(b) confers functions on, or in relation to, EU entities which no longer have functions in that respect under EU law in relation to the United Kingdom or any part of it,

(c) makes provision for, or in connection with, reciprocal arrangements between –

(i) the United Kingdom or any part of it or a public authority in the United Kingdom, and

(ii) the EU, an EU entity, a member State or a public authority in a member State,

which no longer exists or are no longer appropriate,

(d) makes provision for, or in connection with, other arrangements which –

(iii) involve the EU, and EU entity, a member State or a public authority in a member State, or

(iv) are otherwise dependent upon the United Kingdom's membership of the EU or Part 4 of the withdrawal agreement,[311]

and which no longer exist or are no longer appropriate,

(e) makes provision for, or in connection with, any reciprocal or other arrangements not falling within paragraph (c) or (d) which no longer exist, or are no longer appropriate, as a result of the United Kingdom ceasing to be a party to any of the EU Treaties or as a result of either the end of the implementation period or any other effect of the withdrawal agreement,

(ea) is not clear in its effect as a result of the operation of any provision of sections 2 to 6 or Schedule 1,

(f) does not contain any functions or restrictions which—

(i) were in an EU directive and in force immediately before IP completion day (including any power to make EU tertiary legislation), and

(ii) it is appropriate to retain, or

(g) contains EU references which are no longer appropriate.

(3) There is also a deficiency in retained EU law where the Minister considers that there is—

(a) anything in retained EU law which is of a similar kind to any deficiency which falls within subsection (2), or

(b) a deficiency in retained EU law of a kind described, or provided for, in regulations made by a Minister of the Crown.

(4) But retained EU law is not deficient merely because it does not contain any modification of EU law which is adopted or notified, comes into force or only applies on or after IP completion date."

Not only is the legislative power conferred by s.8(1) broad, so too is the definition of the deficiencies in respect of which it may be exercised. A striking feature is the extent to which matters turn on the view of the minister. The power itself, in s.8(1), turns on what the minister "considers appropriate". And before it is necessary to engage in what is or is not a "deficiency", the minister may legislate if they consider there to be a failure of EU law to "operate effectively". So far as "deficiencies" are concerned, the whole definition is anchored around what the minister "considers" to be a problem and then further breadth is introduced by, for example, including not only redundant provisions but "substantially redundant" provisions too. Presumably it is again for the minister to form a view on whether something is substantially redundant.

[311] Pt 4 of the Withdrawal Agreement concerns the transition/implementation period.

Unsurprisingly, the breadth of this power caused concern as the legislation made its way through Parliament. As the House of Lords Constitution Committee noted:

> "We are concerned that applying a subjective test of 'appropriateness' to a broad term like 'deficiency' makes the regulation-making power in [the clause] potentially open-ended. However, requiring that ministers set out the 'good reasons' to use the power and that it is a 'reasonable course of action', as we recommend ... would ameliorate the subjective nature of 'deficiencies'."[312]

A necessity requirement was resisted by the government. But there are other limitations on the general power that has been conferred. Regulations made under s.8(1) of the 2018 Act cannot impose or increase taxation, make retrospective provision, create a relevant criminal offence, establish a public authority, amend, repeal or revoke the Human Rights Act 1998 or any subordinate legislation made under it, or amend or repeal the principle devolution statutes.[313] Schedule 7 to the 2018 Act makes provision for parliamentary scrutiny of the power conferred by s.8.[314] In particular, some regulations must be made using the affirmative procedure (for example, those that transfer an EU legislative power to a UK body or which create or widen the scope of a criminal offence).[315] Where the government propose to make regulations using the negative resolution procedure,[316] unless a declaration of urgency is made by the minister, the instrument must be laid before the House of Commons for "sifting".[317] This requires the minister to lay a statement before Parliament explaining why the negative procedure is appropriate and why it was chosen. Each House then has 10 sitting days within which to make recommendation as to the procedure to be used. If no recommendation is made, the minister may proceed to make the regulations. If either House makes a recommendation that the minister proceed by affirmative resolution, the minister may accept that recommendation. If it is not accepted, however, a statement must be laid before the House explaining why they do not agree with the recommendation. Of course, how effective any parliamentary oversight is will depend to some degree on how busy parliament is going to be. A substantial number of "deficiencies" will exist when retained EU law "goes live"

---

[312] Select Committee on the Constitution, European Union (Withdrawal) Bill, 9th Report of Session 2017–19, HL Paper 69, para.176. See also: *Bingham Centre for the Rule of Law, Briefing Paper: Parliament and the Rule of Law in the Context of Brexit (London: Bingham Centre for the Rule of Law, 2016)*, available at: *https://www.biicl.org/documents/1284_briefing_paper_-_parl_and_rol_in_brexit.pdf* [Accessed 15 June 2020] and J. Grogan, *Rights and remedies at risk: implications of the Brexit process on the future of rights in the UK* [2019] P.L. 683.

[313] 2018 Act s.8(7).

[314] For more detail, see Erskine May, *Parliamentary Practice*, 25th edn, at para.32.3 (*https://erskinemay.parliament.uk/section/5666/scrutiny-of-delegated-legislation-made-under-the-european-union-withdrawal-act-2018/* [Accessed 15 June 2020]).

[315] For details of the affirmative procedure (which requires positive approval by Parliament before the regulation is made), see Erksine May, *Parliamentary Practice*, 25th edn, at para.31.13 (*https://erskinemay.parliament.uk/section/5625/the-affirmative-procedure/* [Accessed 15 June 2020]).

[316] For details of that procedure (where a regulation is subject to annulment by resolution of either House of Parliament) see: Erksine May, *Parliamentary Practice*, 25th edn, para.31.15 (available at: *https://erskinemay.parliament.uk/section/5627/the-negative-procedure/* [Accessed 15 June 2020]).

[317] European Union (Withdrawal) Act 2018 Sch.7, para.3.

at the end of the transition/implementation period so it remains to be seen whether Parliament has sufficient capacity to properly exercise this supervisory function.

Those are the main provisions of the 2018 Act that seek to ensure continuity of the law following IP completion day. Detailed provision is made in relation to the devolution settlements, each of which had its competence delimited by reference to EU law.[318] Most significant is s.12 of the 2018 Act, which amends the Scotland Act 1998[319] so as to insert a new s.30A. So far as material for present purposes, this provides: **10–44**

> "**Legislative competence: restriction relating to retained EU law**
> **30A.**—(1) An Act of the Scottish Parliament cannot modify, or confer power by subordinate legislation to modify, retained EU law so far as the modification is of a description specified in regulations made by a Minister of the Crown.
> (2) But subsection (1) does not apply to any modification so far as it would, immediately before [exit day][320], have been within the legislative competence of the Parliament.
> ...
> (7) No regulations may be made under this section after the end of the period of two years beginning with exit day.
> (8) Subsection (7) does not affect the continuation in force of regulations made under this section at or before the end of the period mentioned in that subsection."

In short, leaving the EU should not impose any new limitation upon the competence of the Scottish Parliament (a point that caused some political concern during the exit process). But because the Scottish Parliament has a general competence over all matters unless they are specifically reserved, absent any regulations being made by a minister, the Scottish Parliament would have competence over all powers that previously vested in the EU. It is also curious that the power to make regulations is limited to two years from exit day (as compared, for example, to the power in s.8 that is limited to two years from IP completion day). In any event, before a minister can make such regulations the Scottish Parliament must have an opportunity to make a "consent decision".[321] The Scottish Parliament has 40 days within which to make such a decision. A refusal to consent does not prevent a minister from laying the regulations before the UK Parliament for approval.

---

[318] 2018 Act ss.10–12 and Schs 2 and 3.
[319] And the Northern Ireland Act 1998 and the Government of Wales Act 2006 to similar effect.
[320] An amendment changing that to IP completion day has, at the time of writing, not yet been brought into force. The amendment was made by Sch.5(2), para.18 of the 2020 Act.
[321] Scotland Act 1998 s.30A(3)–(4), as inserted by s.12 of the 2018 Act.

CHAPTER 11

Human Rights

INTRODUCTION

It has been said that if the twentieth century had a "big idea" at all, it was the idea of human rights.[1] More accurately, the "big idea" was the codification, at national and international level, of these rights. The post-war period was characterised by the emergence of a new international order in which, in response to the atrocities perpetrated during the Second World War and (in some cases) with a view to securing social and economic advancement, human rights featured prominently. The European Convention on Human Rights was a product of these times, adopted under the auspices of the Council of Europe and signed and ratified by the UK in 1951.[2] Unlike many other international treaties, the Convention provided a mechanism for its own enforcement in the European Court of Human Rights, which was established in 1958 following the acceptance by the requisite eight signatory states of its compulsory jurisdiction. The UK accepted the compulsory jurisdiction of the court in 1966, and granted its citizens the right of individual petition the same year.[3] 11–01

The consequences of this were two-fold. First, pressure grew for the adoption of a domestic bill of rights, whether by incorporation of the Convention into national law or otherwise.[4] At the same time, perhaps stung by the European Court's exposure of the deficiencies of the common law in defending individual freedom, the courts themselves began to develop, in various ways, a domestic human rights jurisprudence.[5] In order to understand the constitutional climate in which the Human Rights Act was eventually enacted in 1998, it is necessary to consider the nature and foundation of that jurisprudence, the development of which was part of a wider reappraisal of our constitutional traditions.

---

[1] R. Singh, *The Future of Human Rights in the United Kingdom: Essays on law and Practice* (Oxford: Hart Publishing, 1997), p.1.

[2] G. Marston, "The United Kingdom's Part in the Preparation of the European Convention on Human Rights" (1993) 43 I.C.L.Q. 819.

[3] Lord Lester, "UK Acceptance of the Strasbourg Jurisdiction: What really went on in Whitehall in 1965" [1998] P.L. 237.

[4] The argument for incorporation was never one of mere principle. In practical terms, it was difficult to see why, if British citizens were to have the benefit of the Convention rights at all, they should be obliged to resort to the European Court of Human Rights in Strasbourg to vindicate them.

[5] The initiative here was almost exclusively taken by the English courts. In Scotland, it was held in *Kaur v Lord Advocate*, 1980 S.C. 319, that the courts were not entitled to have regard to the Convention, whether as an aid to statutory construction or otherwise. This remained the position until the decision of the Inner House in *T, Petitioner*, 1997 S.L.T. 724.

PRE-INCORPORATION STATUS OF HUMAN RIGHTS

11–02 As we have seen, the UK adopts a "dualist" view of the relationship between international treaties and domestic law.[6] On this view, a treaty does not form part of national law unless and until incorporated into the law by legislation. That failing, the treaty cannot create rights or duties enforceable before the national courts.[7] The rationale for this is that the making of a treaty is an executive, not a legislative, act, and the government should not be permitted to burden citizens with obligations unsanctioned by Parliament.[8] This is not to say that the Convention was without legal effect in the domestic laws of the UK. In England at least, the courts had regard to the Convention rights as an aid to the construction of ambiguous statutory provisions, on the presumption that Parliament would not have intended to legislate inconsistently with the UK's treaty obligations.[9] Further, where legislation was enacted specifically to comply with the UK's obligations under the Convention, the courts sought to read and give effect to it consistently with the Convention rights.[10] By the same token, the Convention provided a guide to the development of the common law.[11] More broadly, the courts began to recognise fundamental rights as factors material to the lawful and rational exercise of discretion by administrative officials. In so doing, they fashioned a domestic human rights jurisprudence offering, by the time of incorporation of the Convention, a level of protection comparable to, if by no means co-extensive with, that accorded under the Convention proper.[12] This manifested itself in different ways. One technique was to develop (or rediscover) a robust principle of statutory construction, whereby, in the absence of clear and express provision to the contrary, Parliament was taken to authorise no interference with fundamental rights.[13] In other cases, the human rights dimension influenced the rigour with which the court would test the reasonableness of the decision. Thus, in *Bugdaycay v Secretary of State for the*

---

[6] And whether it should continue to do so in relation to issues of human rights has been disputed. See para.2–12, above.

[7] *JH Rayner (Mincing Lane) Ltd v Department of Trade and Industry* [1990] 2 A.C. 418 HL. That, of course, was at the core of the debate in *Miller (No.1)*, as discussed in Ch.1. For a debate about the issue, see: E. Bjorge, "Can unincorporated treaty obligations be part of English law?" [2017] P.L. 571.

[8] For criticism of this doctrine in relation to human rights treaties, see Lord Steyn, "Democracy Through Law" [2002] E.H.R.L.R. 723. See above.

[9] *Waddington v Miah* [1974] 1 W.L.R. 683 HL.

[10] *Re Lonrho Plc* [1990] 2 A.C. 154 HL at pp.208 and 209.

[11] *Derbyshire CC v Times Newspapers Ltd* [1993] A.C. 534 HL.

[12] See J. Munro, "Judicial Review, Locus Standi and Remedies: The impact of the Human Rights Act 1998" in A.E. Boyle et al (eds), *Human Rights and Scots Law* (Oxford: Hart, 2002), Ch.6.

[13] Lord Browne-Wilkinson made the case for this approach in "The Infiltration of a Bill of Rights" [1992] P.L. 397. The technique was applied, by Lord Browne-Wilkinson and others, in a number of important decisions, including *R. v Secretary of State for the Home Department, Ex p. Leech (No.2)* [1994] Q.B. 198 CA (Civ Div) (cf. in Scotland, *Leech v Secretary of State for Scotland*, 1993 S.L.T. 365); *R. v Secretary of State for Social Security, Ex p. Joint Council for the Welfare of Immigrants* [1996] 4 All E.R. 385 CA (Civ Div); *R. v Lord Chancellor, Ex p. Witham* [1997] 2 All E.R. 779 QBD; and *R. v Secretary of State for the Home Department, Ex p. Pierson* [1998] A.C. 539 HL. For more venerable authority, see *Pyx Granite Co Ltd v Ministry of Housing and Local Government* [1960] A.C. 260 HL.

Home Department,[14] where the applicant, an asylum seeker, sought judicial review of the Home Secretary's decision to deport him, Lord Bridge held:

> "The most fundamental of all human rights is the individual's right to life, and when an administrative decision under challenge is said to be one which may put the applicant's life at risk, the basis of the decision must surely call for the most anxious scrutiny."[15]

The effect of *Bugdaycay* was to prepare the way for the reception of something resembling the principle of proportionality.[16] As early as 1996, in appropriate cases, the courts were prepared to hold that "the more substantial the interference with human rights, the more the court will require by way of justification before it is satisfied that the decision is reasonable".[17]

HUMAN RIGHTS ACT 1998

Against that background, the Human Rights Act 1998 was enacted, entering into force on 2 October 2000, and bringing with it a significant change to the legal landscape in the UK.[18] The avowed purpose of the Human Rights Act was to "bring rights home" so as to allow UK citizens to rely upon the rights protected by the Convention before the domestic courts.[19] The Human Rights Act is almost unique in that it cuts across almost all areas of law.[20] The Act did this not by wholesale incorporation of the Convention but by creating a number of "Convention rights" in exactly the same terms as those protected by the **11–03**

[14] *Bugdaycay v Secretary of State for the Home Department* [1987] A.C. 514 HL.

[15] *Bugdaycay v Secretary of State for the Home Department* [1987] A.C. 514 at p.531. The "anxious scrutiny" doctrine, which essentially involves the substitution of orthodox *Wednesbury* review for a level of control approaching review for proportionality, was subsequently adopted in cases involving freedom of expression (see *R. v Secretary of State for the Home Department, Ex p. Brind* [1991] 1 A.C. 696 HL) and the right to respect for private life (see *R. v Ministry of Defence, Ex p. Smith* [1996] Q.B. 517 CA (Civ Div)), although in neither case to the advantage of the applicant.

[16] The differences between *Wednesbury* review and proportionality review are discussed in the speech of Lord Steyn in *R. (on the application of Daly) v Secretary of State for the Home Department* [2001] 2 A.C. 532 HL.

[17] *R. v Ministry of Defence, Ex p. Smith* [1996] Q.B. 517, per Lord Bingham MR at p.554. See in Scotland *Abdadou v Secretary of State for the Home Department*, 1998 S.C. 504. Conversely, the orthodox *Wednesbury* standard continued to apply in areas not impinging upon fundamental rights, particularly where the decision challenged involved questions of high economic or social policy: see, e.g. *R. v Secretary of State for the Environment, Ex p. Hammersmith and Fulham LBC* [1991] 1 A.C. 521 HL; *East Kilbride DC v Secretary of State for Scotland*, 1995 S.L.T. 1238.

[18] As we have seen, the Scotland Act 1998 had ensured that the effects of Convention rights had already been felt in Scotland.

[19] Home Office, *Rights Brought Home: The Human Rights Bill* (The Stationery Office, 1997), Cm.3782, *https://www.gov.uk/government/uploads/system/uploads/attachment_data/file/263526/rights.pdf* [Accessed 18 June 2020]; the UK was under no obligation to give domestic effect to the Convention: *James v United Kingdom* (1986) 8 E.H.R.R. 123 at 84; *Observer v United Kingdom* (1992) 14 E.H.R.R. 153 at 76; and *McCann v United Kingdom* (1996) 21 E.H.R.R. 97 at p.153.

[20] For an eloquent description of the effects of the Human Rights Act 1998, see Lord Rodger's comments at [179]–[185] in *Wilson v First County Trust Ltd (No.2)* [2003] UKHL 40; [2004] 1 A.C. 816 HL.

Convention.[21] It is a very skilfully crafted statute. It required to balance the continuing sovereignty of Parliament with the effective protection of the rights it contained, whilst allowing those rights to reflect the domestic context within which they would be relied upon. Added to that is the fact that the Convention is a living, and evolving, instrument: the scope of any particular article today may not be what it was yesterday.[22] The Human Rights Act is, as we have seen, a "constitutional statute" that, although not immune from express repeal, holds an elevated place in the constitution. Its status was best described by Lord Rodger of Earlsferry:

> "Although the Act is not entrenched, the Convention rights that it confers have a peculiar potency. Enforcing them may require a court to modify the common law. So far as possible, a court must read and give effect to statutory provisions in a way that is compatible with them. Rights that can produce such results are clearly of a higher order than the rights which people enjoy at common law or under most other statutes."[23]

In 2015, the Conservative Government was elected with a manifesto pledge to repeal the Human Rights Act and replace it with a "British Bill of Rights". That came to nothing as Brexit came to dominate the political agenda. The current government, however, is now committed to "updating" the 1998 Act. What exactly that entails is unknown.

11–04 Before turning to consider the key provisions of the Human Rights Act[24] it is appropriate to sound a note of caution. The Act, and the Convention rights it creates, despite Lord Rodger's elegant description, are secondary to the common law in relation to the protection of human rights. That is a point the Supreme Court has reminded the legal profession of more than once:

> "What we now term human rights and public law has developed through our common law over a long period of time... The growth of the state has presented the court with new challenges to which they have responded by a process of gradual adaption and development of the common law to meet current needs. This has always been the way of the common law and it has not ceased on the enactment of

---

[21] The articles of the Convention that are prescribed as "Convention rights" are arts 2–12 and 14, arts 1–3 of the First Protocol and art.1 of the Thirteenth Protocol, all read with arts 16–18 of the Convention (Human Rights Act s.1(1)). They have effect subject to any derogation or reservation by the UK (s.1(2)) and are set out in Sch.1. Section 1(4) provides that the Secretary of State may amend the Human Rights Act as necessary to reflect any Protocol to the Convention signed and ratified by the UK.

[22] *Tyrer v United Kingdom* (1979–80) 2 E.H.R.R. 1 was the first time the Strasbourg court acknowledged the idea, but it has since become firmly embedded in its case law. In the European Court on Human Rights, *Practical Guide to Admissibility Criteria* (Council of Europe/European Court of Human Rights, 2019: *https://www.echr.coe.int/Documents/Admissibility_guide_ENG.pdf* [Accessed 18 June 2020]), the court states: "As a living instrument, the Convention must be interpreted in light of present-day conditions" (at para.7).

[23] *Wilson v First County Trust Ltd (No.2)* [2003] UKHL 40; [2004] 1 A.C. 816 at [180]. Lord Rodger's description of the Human Rights at [179]–[184] is worth reading in its entirely.

[24] It is not possible to discuss the substance of any, let alone all, of the Convention rights. They are considered in a number of specialist texts, including: Lord Lester, Lord Pannick and J. Herberg, *Human Rights Law and Practice*, 3rd edn (London: Lexis Nexis, 2009); J.L. Murdoch, *Reed and Murdoch: Human Rights Law in Scotland*, 4th edn (Haywards Heath: Bloomsbury Professional, 2017); Wadham et al, *Blackstone's Guide to the Human Rights Act 1998*, 7th edn (Oxford: Oxford University Press, 2015).

> the Human Rights Act 1998, although since then there has sometimes been a baleful and unnecessary tendency to overlook the common law. It needs to be emphasised that it was not the purpose of the Human Rights Act that the common law should become an ossuary."[25]

With that note of caution ringing in our ears, we now turn to consider the specific provisions of the Human Right Act 1998.

Section 2: status of European Court of Human Rights jurisprudence[26]

Having defined (in s.1 and the Schedule to the Act) the Convention rights,[27] the Human Rights Act starts by explaining what regard domestic courts should have to decisions of the European Court of Human Rights in Strasbourg. Section 2(1) provides that domestic courts must "take into account" any decision of the European Court of Human Rights[28] "whenever made or given" so far as it is relevant to the question that is before the court. So decisions of the European Court of Human Rights are not binding on domestic courts.[29] However, domestic courts should, "[i]n the absence of special some circumstances . . . follow any clear and constant jurisprudence of the European Court of Human Rights".[30] That dicta has evolved into what has now become known as the "*Ullah* principle": **11–05**

> "It is of course open to member states to provide for rights more generous than those guaranteed by the Convention, but such provision should not be the product of interpretation of the Convention rights by national courts, since the meaning of the

[25] *Kennedy v Charity Commission* [2014] UKSC 20; [2015] A.C. 455, per Lord Toulson at [133]; Lord Mance made similar comments at [46]. A similar point was made by Lord Reed in *R. (on the application of Sturnham) v Parole Board* [2013] UKSC 23; [2013] 2 A.C. 254 at [29] and *R. (on the application of Osborn) v Parole Board* [2013] UKSC 61; [2014] A.C. 1115 at [54]–[63]. Those remarks considering further academic, and judicial, consideration of common law constitutional rights (as we touched on in Ch.3). For a fuller survey of that issue, see: M Elliott and K Hughes, *Common Law Constitutional Rights* (Hart Publishing, 2020).

[26] For an interesting discussion of this issue see, Lord Phillips, "Strasbourg Has Spoken" in A. Burrows, D. Johnston and R. Zimmermann, *Judge and Jurist: Essays in Memory of Lord Rodger of Earlsferry* (Oxford: Oxford University Press, 2013).

[27] Not every right in the European Convention on Human Rights is a "Convention right" for the purposes of domestic law. Regard should be had to the rights listed in the Schedule of the 1998 Act.

[28] Or an opinion or decision of the Commission or decision of the Committee of Ministers.

[29] This does nothing to the domestic rules of precedent: if a judge considers that a binding decision is inconsistent with European Court of Human Rights jurisprudence they must decide the case in accordance with the binding domestic authority. They can then, if appropriate, give leave to appeal. See: *Kay v Lambeth LBC* [2006] UKHL 10; [2006] 2 A.C. 465. That approach is illustrated in *AM (Zimbabwe) v Secretary of State for the Home Department* [2020] UKSC 17, where the appellant had presented no argument to the Tribunal under art.3 (he was complaining about health care provision should he be deported), but by the time the matter reached the Court of Appeal, the Strasbourg jurisprudence had moved on (*Paposhvili v Belgium* [2017] Imm LR 867). He again failed in the Court of Appeal. In the Supreme Court, however, their earlier decision (*N v Secretary of State for the Home Department* [2005] 2 A.C. 296) was departed from and the new line from Strasbourg adopted.

[30] *R. (on the application of Alconbury) v Secretary of State for the Environment, Transport and the Regions* [2001] UKHL 23; [2003] 2 A.C. 295, per Lord Steyn at [26].

> Convention should be uniform throughout the States party to it. The duty of national courts is to keep pace with the Strasbourg jurisprudence as it evolved over time: no more, but certainly no less."[31]

Lord Brown subsequently put his own twist on *R. (on the application of Ullah) v Special Adjudicator* when he explained the final sentence "could as well have ended: 'no less, but certainly no more'".[32] That approach to the Strasbourg jurisprudence has proved controversial,[33] but it allowed Lord Rodger to produce his memorably succinct judgment in *Secretary of State for the Home Department v AF (No.3)*: "Strasbourg has spoken, the case is closed".[34] That statement is not absolute. In *R. v Horncastle*, Lord Phillips explained the circumstances in which domestic courts can decline to follow Strasbourg jurisprudence:

> "The requirement to 'take into account' the Strasbourg jurisprudence will normally result in the domestic court applying principles that are clearly established by the Strasbourg court. There will, however, be rare occasions where the domestic court has concerns as to whether a decision of the Strasbourg court sufficiently appreciates or accommodates particular aspects of our domestic process. In such circumstances it is open to the domestic court to decline to follow the Strasbourg decision, giving reasons for this course. This is likely to give the Strasbourg court the opportunity to reconsider the particular aspect of the decision that is in issue, so that there takes place what may prove to be a valuable dialogue between the domestic court and the Strasbourg court."[35]

Horncastle was such a case (concerning the admissibility of hearsay evidence in criminal proceedings) where the Supreme Court refused to follow Strasbourg jurisprudence that did not stem from the Grand Chamber and that was not altogether clear.[36] That approach was explained further by Lord Neuberger in *Manchester City Council v Pinnock* where he said:

> "This court is not bound to follow every decision of the European court . . . Where, however, there is a clear and constant line of decisions whose effect is not inconsistent with some fundamental substantive or procedural aspect of our law, and whose reasoning does not appear to overlook or misunderstand some argument or point of principle, we consider that it would be wrong for this court not to follow that line."[37]

---

31 *R. (on the application of Ullah) v Special Adjudicator* [2004] UKHL 26; [2004] 2 A.C. 323, per Lord Bingham of Cornhill at [20].

32 *R. (on the application of Al-Skeini) v Secretary of State for Defence* [2007] UKHL 26; [2008] 1 A.C. 153 at [106].

33 See, for example R. Masterman, "Section 2(1) of the Human Rights Act 1998: Binding Domestic Courts to Strasbourg?" [2004] P.L. 725; J. Wright, "Interpreting Section 2 of the Human Rights Act: Towards an Indigenous Jurisprudence of Human Rights" [2009] P.L. 595; N. Bratza, "The Relationship between the UK Courts and Strasbourg" [2011] E.H.R.L.R. 505; Lord Irvine, "A British Interpretation of Convention Rights" [2012] P.L. 237. The controversy continues, as illustrated in the divide opinion in the Supreme Court in *R (Hallam) v Secretary of State for Justice* [2019] UKSC 2; [2020] A.C. 279.

34 *Secretary of State for the Home Department v AF (No.3)* [2009] UKHL 28; [2010] 2 A.C. 269 at [98].

35 *R. v Horncastle (Michael Christopher)* [2009] UKSC 14; [2010] 2 A.C. 373 at [11].

36 *R. v Horncastle* [2009] UKSC 14; [2010] 2 A.C. 373, per Lord Brown of Eaton-under-Heywood at [120].

37 *Manchester City Council v Pinnock* [2010] UKSC 45; [2011] 2 A.C. 104 at [48].

Those words should not be taken too literally: they are general guidelines.[38] But the Supreme Court has generally followed that approach, in particular in relation to prisoner voting rights.[39] Where there is a clear line of jurisprudence emanating from the Grand Chamber, then giving domestic effect to it should not be controversial:

> "A decision of the European Court of Human Rights is more than an opinion about the meaning of the Convention. It is an adjudication by the tribunal which the United Kingdom has by Treaty agreed should give definitive rulings on the subject."[40]

What of the situation where Strasbourg has yet to speak on the point? Is it for the Supreme Court to push the boundaries and expand the meaning and content of the Convention rights? Or should it await guidance from Strasbourg?

It has been held that it would be "highly undesirable" for the domestic courts to get "out of step" with the Strasbourg interpretation[41] and that the "wiser course" is to wait until the Strasbourg court has spoken.[42] That would appear to be the natural consequence of the "*Ullah* principle": no more, but certainly no less; no less, but certainly no more. Lord Brown explained, in *R. (on the application of Al-Skeini) v Secretary of State for Defence*, why it was important that domestic courts did not get ahead of the Strasbourg court: **11–06**

> "There seems to me, indeed, a greater danger in the national court construing the Convention too generously in favour of an applicant than in construing it too narrowly. In the former event the mistake will necessarily stand: the member state cannot itself go to Strasbourg to have it corrected; in the latter event, however, where Convention rights have been denied by too narrow a construction, the aggrieved individual *can* have the decision corrected in Strasbourg."[43]

---

[38] *R (Kaiyam) v Secretary of State for Justice* [2015] A.C. 1344 at [21]; *R (Hallam) v Secretary of State for Justice* [2019] UKSC 2; [2020] A.C. 279 at [89].

[39] *R. (on the application of Chester) v Secretary of State for Justice* [2013] UKSC 63; 2014 S.C. (U.K.S.C.) 25; [2014] A.C. 271, per Lord Mance at [27] and Lord Sumption at [121]. *Poshteh v Kensington and Chelsea RLBC* [2017] UKSC 36; [2017] A.C. 624 is an interesting example where the Supreme Court followed its own previous decision (*Ali v Birmingham City Council* [2010] UKSC 8; [2010] 2 A.C. 39) despite the Strasbourg court having gone against that decision (*Ali v United Kingdom* (2016) 63 E.H.R.R. 20) on the basis that decision was not a clear and constant line (it being a single decision from a Chamber) and the Supreme Court preferred to follow its own previous, and unanimous, decision pending review by the Grand Chamber ([2017] UKSC 36; [2017] A.C. 624 at [37]).

[40] *R. (on the application of Chester) v Secretary of State for Justice* [2013] UKSC 63; 2014 S.C. (U.K.S.C.) 25; [2014] A.C. 271, per Lord Sumption at [121]. In the same case, at [27], Lord Mance explained: "It would have then to involve some truly fundamental principle of our law or some most egregious oversight or misunderstanding before it could be appropriate for this court to contemplate an outright refusal to follow Strasbourg authority at the Grand Chamber level."

[41] *M v Secretary of State for Work and Pensions* [2006] UKHL 11; [2006] 2 A.C. 91, per Lord Nicholls at [29].

[42] *Ambrose v Harris* [2011] UKSC 43; 2012 S.C. (U.K.S.C.) 53, per Lord Hope of Craighead at [15], read with Lord Hope's comments in *Smith v Ministry of Defence* [2013] UKSC 41; [2014] A.C. 52 at [42].

[43] *R. (on the application of Al-Skeini) v Secretary of State for Defence* [2007] UKHL 26; [2008] 1 A.C. 153 at [106] (emphasis in the original). This was not a new statement and was consistent with earlier comments by the House of Lords: *R. (on the application of Clift) v Secretary of State for the*

If domestic decisions were to run ahead of the Strasbourg jurisprudence, short of legislating to reverse any particular decision, the UK would be stuck with the result. That, however, has given rise to what Lord Kerr described (in the course of his dissent in *Ambrose v Harris*)[44] as *Ullah*-type reticence.[45] *Ambrose* concerned the content of art.6, the right to a fair trial and in particular the issue of questioning of an accused person, before detention, without a solicitor present. Was that compatible with art.6(3)(c) of the Convention? The task for the Supreme Court, said Lord Hope, was to identify as best it could where the Strasbourg court stands on the issue but not to expand the scope of art.6 further than the Strasbourg jurisprudence justifies.[46] Lord Kerr disagreed:

> "I greatly doubt that Lord Bingham contemplated—much less intended—that his discussion of this issue [in *Ullah*] should have the effect of acting as an inhibitor on courts in this country giving full effect to Convention rights unless they have been pronounced upon by Strasbourg. I believe that, in the absence of a declaration by the European Court of Human Rights as to the validity of a claim to a Convention right, it is not open to courts of this country to adopt an attitude of agnosticism and refrain from recognising such a right simply because Strasbourg has not spoken."[47]

Lord Kerr, joined by Lord Wilson, was again prepared to adopt a construction that would have developed the meaning of the Convention beyond the point reached by the Strasbourg Court in *Moohan, Petitioner*.[48] As Lord Wilson put it:

> "[W]here there is no directly relevant decision of the ECtHR with which it would be possible (even if appropriate) to keep pace, we can and must do more. We must determine for ourselves the existence or otherwise of an alleged Convention right."[49]

But that was a minority view (this time because the majority held there was a "clear and consistent" line of authority that determined the question).[50] Most recently, Lord Kerr returned to this theme in *D v Commissioner of Police of the Metropolis*.[51] Having identified a number of cases where the "mirror principle" appeared to have been departed from,[52] Lord Kerr went on to say:

Home Department [2006] UKHL 54; [2007] 1 A.C. 484, per Lord Hope at [49] and *N v Secretary of State for the Home Department* [2005] UKHL 31; [2005] 2 A.C. 296, per Lord Hope at [25] and Lord Brown at [76].

44 *Ambrose v Harris* [2011] UKSC 43; 2012 S.C. (U.K.S.C.) 53.

45 *Ambrose v Harris* [2011] UKSC 43; 2012 S.C. (U.K.S.C.) 53 at [126].

46 *Ambrose v Harris* [2011] UKSC 43; 2012 S.C. (U.K.S.C.) 53 at [20].

47 *Ambrose v Harris* [2011] UKSC 43; 2012 S.C. (U.K.S.C.) 53 at [128]; Lord Kerr has developed these comments further when speaking extra-judicially, see *The UK Supreme Court: The Modest Underworker of Strasbourg?*, Clifford Chance lecture, 25 January 2012, *http://www.supremecourt.uk/docs/speech_120125.pdf* [Accessed 18 June 2020].

48 *Moohan, Petitioner* [2014] UKSC 67; 2015 S.C. (U.K.S.C.) 1 (prisoner voting case in relation to the Scottish independence referendum); see para.1–05, above.

49 *Moohan, Petitioner* [2014] UKSC 67; 2015 S.C. (U.K.S.C.) 1 at [105].

50 *Moohan, Petitioner* [2014] UKSC 67; 2015 S.C. (U.K.S.C.) 1, per Lord Hodge at [9]–[13].

51 [2018] UKSC 11; [2019] A.C. 196.

52 [2018] UKSC 11; [2019] A.C. 196 at [77]. The examples were *Rabone v Pennine Care NHS Trust* [2012] 2 A.C. 72 (positive obligation to protect the life of a mentally ill young women recognised despite an absence of Strasbourg authority) and *Surrey County Council v P* [2014] A.C. 896 (where Lord Neuberger suggested that in the absence of Strasbourg authority, reliance would be placed on principles that had been expressed by that court).

> "Reticence by the courts of the UK to decide whether a Convention right has been violated would be abnegation of our statutory under section 6 of HRA. This section makes it unlawful for a public authority, including a court, to act in a way which is incompatible with a Convention right.
>
> ...
>
> I would firmly reject the suggestion that the decision of this court on whether the respondents enjoy a right under the HRA to claim compensation against the appellant should be influenced, much less inhibited, by any perceived absence of authoritative guidance from ECtHR."[53]

Those observations were, however, obiter.

The unwillingness to develop Convention rights beyond the Strasbourg jurisprudence can appear difficult to reconcile with other features of the Convention rights system. First, the purpose of the Human Rights Act was to ensure domestic law provided a remedy for human rights violations.[54] It did this not by way wholesale incorporation of the Convention but by the creation of domestic law rights (called "Convention rights") that correspond to rights under the Convention. Being domestic rights, their interpretation is a matter for the domestic courts,[55] who should interpret them "like any other statute".[56] It also jars with the national authorities being viewed as the primary means of securing the rights protected by the Convention. The Convention is, as the Strasbourg Court has made clear, a living instrument, the interpretation of which evolves over time. That suggests that domestic courts ought to participate in that process of ensuring the Convention keeps pace with changes in society. That may, on occasion, require domestic courts to lead the Convention into new areas.[57] And in areas that the Strasbourg Court has left to fall within the "margin of appreciation", the domestic courts will have to reach their own view anyway (so uniformity through the contracting states is not inherent within the Convention).[58] Finally, it risks giving insufficient weight to the fact the Convention establishes minimum standards for rights protection: it represents the floor, not the ceiling.[59] But there are arguments the other way, not least the traditional rule of statutory construction whereby the court will try to interpret legislative provisions based on an international treaty in a way that does not put the UK in breach of those

---

[53] [2018] UKSC 11; [2019] A.C. 196 at [78]–[79].

[54] *Aston Cantlow and Wilmcote with Billesley Parochial Church Council v Wallbank* [2003] UKHL 37; [2004] 1 A.C. 546, per Lord Hope of Craighead at [44]; *R. (on the application of Quark Fishing Ltd) v Secretary of State for Foreign and Commonwealth Affairs* [2005] UKHL 57; [2006] 1 A.C. 529, per Lord Nicholls of Birkenhead at [34]; *R. (on the application of Al-Skeini) v Secretary of State for Defence* [2007] UKHL 26; [2008] 1 A.C. 153, per Lord Rodger of Earlsferry at [54].

[55] *Re McKerr* [2004] UKHL 12; [2004] 1 W.L.R. 807.

[56] *Re G (Adoption: Unmarried Couple)* [2008] UKHL 38; [2009] 1 A.C. 173, per Lord Hoffmann at [33]; cf. Lord Scott's comments in *R. (on the application of Animal Defenders International) v Secretary of State for Culture, Media and Sport* [2008] UKHL 15; [2008] 1 A.C. 1312 where at [44] he acknowledged that Convention right were domestic rights but they "are not merely part of domestic law".

[57] As appeared to be recognised by the majority in *Re G (Adoption: Unmarried Couple)* [2008] UKHL 38; [2009] 1 A.C. 173.

[58] *Re G (Adoption: Unmarried Couple)* [2008] UKHL 38; [2009] 1 A.C. 173, per Lord Hoffmann at [36].

[59] *Handyside v United Kingdom* (1976) 1 E.H.R.R. 737.

obligations.[60] Laws LJ, in a postscript to his judgment in *Children's Rights Alliance for England v Secretary of State for Justice*, called on the Supreme Court to revisit the *Ullah* principle in the hope that it may be reformed.[61] If they do, those who would advocate reform include the Lord Chancellor who was the architect of the Human Rights Act[62] and, to a lesser extent, a former President of the Strasbourg Court itself.[63]

Section 3: the interpretive obligation

11–07 Section 3 of the Act provides:

> "(1) So far as it is possible to do so, primary legislation and subordinate legislation must be read and given effect in a way which is compatible with the Convention rights."[64]

This is the "interpretive obligation" laid on the courts by the Act, and it is one of the Act's key provisions.[65] The interpretative obligation contained in s.3 is a strong one ("*must* be read . . . "[66]), but one that is only engaged when a legislative provision, interpreted in accordance with the ordinary canons of statutory interpretation, produces a result that is incompatible with a Convention right. The first task is always to ascertain the "ordinary" interpretation of a provision (in

---

[60] For a critique of the case for domestic courts going beyond the Strasbourg jurisprudence, see A. Kavanagh, *Constitutional Review under the UK Human Rights Act* (Cambridge: Cambridge University Press, 2009), pp.155–164.

[61] *Children's Rights Alliance for England v Secretary of State for Justice* [2013] EWCA Civ 34; [2013] H.R.L.R. 17 at [62]–[64]; see also Sir John Laws' third Hamlyn Lecture (J. Laws, *The Common Law Constitution* (Cambridge: Cambridge University Press, 2014)). On reform of the *Ullah* principle see M. Andenas and E. Bjorge, "*Ambrose*: is the *Ullah* principle wrong?" (2012) 128 L.Q.R. 319 and Masterman, "The Mirror Crack'd", UK Constitutional Law Association blog (13 February 2013), *http://ukconstitutionallaw.org* [Accessed 18 June 2020]; and S. Ghandhi, "*Al-Skeini* and the Extra-Territorial Application of the European Convention on Human Rights" in *Judge and Jurist: Essays in Memory of Lord Rodger of Earlsferry* (2013).

[62] Lord Irvine, "A British Interpretation of Convention Rights" [2012] P.L. 237.

[63] Bratza, "The Relationship between the UK Courts and Strasbourg" [2011] E.H.R.L.R. 505. Various judges have commented on the continuing debate in extra-judicial lectures, for example: Lady Hale, "*Argentoratum Locutum:* Is the Supreme Court Supreme?" (2012) 12 H.R.L.R. 65 and Lord Reed, "The Common Law and the ECHR" (Inner Temple, 11 November 2013.

[64] As noted in *Ghaidan v Godin-Mendoza* [2004] UKHL 30; [2004] 2 A.C. 557 (see, in particular, the speeches of Lord Steyn at [45]–[48] and Lord Rodger at [118]), this wording is modelled on the approach prescribed by the European Court of Justice for the interpretation of domestic measures by reference to European directives: see *Marleasing SA v La Comercial Internacional de Alimentacion SA* (C-106/89) [1990] E.C.R. I-4135. Note also Lord Irvine, "The Development of Human Rights in Britain under an Incorporated Convention on Human Rights" [1998] P.L. 221, in which the then-Lord Chancellor identified the interpretive techniques employed in EU cases as providing useful guidance on the proper role of the courts under the Human Rights Act 1998 s.3(1).

[65] s.3 in fact contains two obligations: to "read" legislation in a Convention compliant manner and to "give effect to" legislation in a Convention compliant manner. They are distinct obligations (*Ghaidan v Godin-Mendoza* [2004] UKHL 30; [2004] 2 A.C. 557, per Lord Rodger of Earlsferry at [107]). Although our primary focus here is how the court "reads" legislation, other public authorities (which are also required to apply s.3) will have to ensure not only their interpretation of legislation is in accordance with s.3 but that they "give effect" to it in a Convention-compliant manner.

[66] The obligatory nature of s.3(1) should be stressed. Whereas the courts empowered to make them have a discretion in relation to declarations of incompatibility, s.3(1) is, as Lord Millett observed in *Ghaidan v Godin-Mendoza* [2004] UKHL 30; [2004] 2 A.C. 557 at [59], "a command".

other words, to understand the intention of Parliament when enacting the provision). Only then can it be determined if it is necessary to invoke s.3.[67]

The function of the courts under s.3(1) remains interpretive, not quasi-legislative. Plainly, s.3(1) does not permit the courts altogether to rewrite statutory provisions in order to achieve compatibility with the Convention rights[68]; if it did, s.4 (which, as we shall see in a moment, provides for declarations of incompatibility) would be redundant. Equally plainly, it goes beyond the established principles of statutory construction, such as that which permits the courts to interpret ambiguous statutory provisions consistently with the Convention rights. Even if the meaning of a provision, construed according to the ordinary principles of interpretation, admits of no doubt, s.3(1) may nonetheless require that the provision be given a different meaning.[69] In *R. v Lambert*,[70] for example, the House of Lords accepted that the language of s.28(3) of the Misuse of Drugs Act 1971, in imposing on an accused person a legal or persuasive burden of proof of their innocence, conflicted with the presumption of innocence enshrined in art.6(2) of the Convention. It was possible to "rescue" the provision, however, by resorting to the interpretive obligation in s.3(1) and taking the word "proves" to mean "gives sufficient evidence", so converting a legal burden into a merely evidential one.

In *Ghaidan v Godin-Mendoza*, Lord Nicholls observed that, in enacting s.3, Parliament intended the courts to be able to modify the meaning and effect of legislation "to an extent bounded only by what is 'possible'".[71] Parliament had specifically rejected a "reasonableness" test for s.3 during the passage of the Human Rights Act. What s.3 provides is, in effect, "a strong rebuttable presumption in favour of an interpretation consistent with the Convention rights".[72] What is less clear is where the limits of "possibility" lie. As Lord Nicholls noted in *Re S (Children) (Care Order: Implementation of Care Plan)*, the Act reserves the amendment of primary legislation to Parliament: "By this means, the Act seeks to preserve parliamentary sovereignty. The Act maintains the constitutional boundary." Accordingly, "a meaning which departs substantially from a fundamental feature of an Act of Parliament is likely to have crossed the boundary between interpretation and amendment".[73]

---

[67] *S v L* [2012] UKSC 30; 2013 S.C. (U.K.S.C.) 20, per Lord Reed at [15]–[17].

[68] In this respect, s.3(1) may be contrasted with provisions in the constitutions of former British colonies in relation to laws incompatible with constitutional rights. Such provisions commonly authorise the courts to construe such laws "with such modifications, adaptations, qualifications and exceptions as may be necessary to bring them into conformity with the constitution", and clearly envisage the courts engaging in a quasi-legislative role: see *R. v Hughes (Peter)* [2002] UKPC 12; [2002] 2 A.C. 259.

[69] *R. v A (No.2)* [2001] UKHL 25; [2002] 1 A.C. 45, per Lord Steyn at [44]; *Ghaidan v Godin-Mendoza* [2004] UKHL 30; [2004] 2 A.C. 557, per Lord Nicholls at [30].

[70] *R. v Lambert (Steven)* [2001] UKHL 37; [2002] 2 A.C. 545.

[71] *Ghaidan v Godin-Mendoza* [2004] UKHL 30; [2004] 2 A.C. 557 at [32]. The same point had already been made by the House of Lords in *R. v A (No.2)* [2001] UKHL 25; [2002] 1 A.C. 45 at [44].

[72] *Ghaidan v Godin-Mendoza* [2004] UKHL 30; [2004] 2 A.C. 557, per Lord Steyn at [50].

[73] *Re S (Children) (Care Order: Implementation of Care Plan)* [2002] UKHL 10; [2002] 2 A.C. 291 at [37]–[40]. See also, e.g. *De Freitas v Permanent Secretary of Ministry of Agriculture, Fisheries, Land and Housing* [1999] 1 A.C. 69 PC (Antigua and Bermuda), per Lord Clyde at p.79; *Ghaidan v Godin-Mendoza* [2004] UKHL 30; [2004] 2 A.C. 557, per Lord Nicholls at [33] and Lord Rodger of Earlsferry at [115].

This is not to say that interpretive devices such as "reading down" to narrow the scope of a provision, or "reading in" supplementary words or phrases if necessary to secure compatibility, are excluded as impermissible amendments to the legislative language. The exercise is not purely linguistic, but purposive.[74] But s.3 does not go so far as to allow the courts to introduce into the operation of primary legislation rights and duties not sanctioned by Parliament. Neither does s.3 allow the courts to read and give effect to legislation in a way apt to have practical repercussions which the courts are ill equipped to evaluate. There may be several ways of reading and giving effect to a provision in order to achieve compatibility with the Convention rights. As the House of Lords repeatedly acknowledged,[75] the choice between them may well raise questions of social or economic policy or resource allocation requiring legislative, not judicial, resolution.

But while the limitations on the scope of the interpretive obligation are easily stated, their application is far from self-executing. *Ghaidan* provides a useful illustration. As amended, para.2 of Sch.1 to the Rent Act 1977 allowed the surviving spouse of a protected tenant of a dwelling house to succeed to the statutory tenancy on the tenant's death, if then living there. A person living with the original tenant as "his or her wife or husband" was treated as a spouse for these purposes. Mr Godin-Mendoza complained that the natural and ordinary meaning of this provision breached his rights under arts 8 and 14 of the Convention, since he was prevented from succeeding to the statutory tenancy of his late partner, with whom he had lived in a stable homosexual relationship for almost 20 years.

Applying s.3(1), the Court of Appeal read and gave effect to the provisions complained of so as allow the same sex partner of a deceased tenant to succeed to the statutory tenancy of the property in which both had lived.[76] The landlord appealed to the House of Lords. By a majority the House of Lords dismissed the appeal. There was no appreciable difference between the members of the court as to the scope of the interpretive function under s.3(1), and all were agreed that, as they stood, the relevant provisions of the Rent Act were incompatible with Mr Godin-Mendoza's Convention rights. The majority had no difficulty in interpreting para.2 of Sch.1 to the Rent Act as if it provided that a person, whether of the same or of the opposite sex, who was living with the original tenant in a long term relationship, was to be treated as the spouse of the original tenant. It mattered not (bearing in mind that s.3(1) involves a purposive approach to interpretation rather than semantic pedantry) that Parliament had started with the husbands and wives of deceased tenants and subsequently extended the

---

[74] Lord Steyn, in particular, was at pains to emphasise this in a number of speeches: *R. v A (No.2)* [2001] UKHL 25; [2002] 1 A.C. 45 at [45]; *Ghaidan v Godin-Mendoza* [2004] UKHL 30; [2004] 2 A.C. 557 at [39]. See to like effect, e.g. *Somerville v Scottish Ministers* [2006] CSIH 52; 2007 S.C. 140 at [49] and [54].

[75] In addition to *De Freitas v Permanent Secretary of Ministry of Agriculture, Fisheries, Land and Housing* [1999] 1 A.C. 69 and *Re S (Children) (Care Order: Implementation of Care Plan)* [2002] UKHL 10; [2002] 2 A.C. 291, see also *R. (on the application of Anderson) v Secretary of State for the Home Department* [2002] UKHL 46; [2003] 1 A.C. 837; *Bellinger v Bellinger* [2003] UKHL 21; [2003] 2 A.C. 467.

[76] Thereby departing from the earlier decision of the House of Lords in *Fitzpatrick v Sterling Housing Association Ltd* [2001] 1 A.C. 27 HL, that a same sex partner could only succeed to the less secure assured tenancy.

protection of the legislation to those who had lived with the deceased as if married. Since it was not necessary to be married to qualify for that protection, the fact that homosexuals could not then marry was not to be regarded as the critical factor excluding them from its scope. So, to hold involved no "judicial vandalism"[77] or violence to the legislative text. Lord Rodger expressed the matter in the following terms:

> "[The] key to what it is possible for the courts to imply into legislation without crossing the border from interpretation to amendment does not lie in the number of words that have to be read in. The key lies in a careful consideration of the essential principles and scope of the legislation being interpreted. If the insertion of one word contradicts those principles or goes beyond the scope of the legislation, it amounts to impermissible amendment. On the other hand, if the implication of a dozen words leaves the essential principles and scope of the legislation intact but allows it to be read in a way which is compatible with Convention rights, the implication is a legitimate exercise of the powers conferred by section 3(1)."

There is probably little in this passage with which Lord Millett, dissenting in *Ghaidan*, would disagree. Nonetheless, Lord Millett was unable to accept the interpretation favoured by the majority as a proper exercise of the interpretive function under s.3(1). Lord Millett accepted that s.3 required the court to:

> "take the language of the statute as it finds it and give it a meaning which, however unnatural or unreasonable, is intellectually defensible. It can read in and read down; it can supply missing words, so long as they are consistent with the fundamental features of the legislative scheme; it can do considerable violence to the language and stretch it almost (but not quite) to breaking point. The court must strive to find a possible interpretation compatible with the Convention rights. But it is not entitled to give it an impossible one, however much it would wish to do so. In my view, s.3 does not entitle the court to supply words which are inconsistent with a fundamental feature of the legislative scheme; nor to repeal, delete or contradict the language of the offending statute".[78]

The statutory provisions in question were concerned with spouses, or persons living together as husband and wife. A heterosexual couple could be married, or live together as husband and wife. A homosexual couple could not.[79] Lord Millett continued:

> "By what is claimed to be a process of interpretation of an existing statute framed in gender specific terms, and enacted at a time when homosexual relationships were not recognised by law, it is proposed to treat persons of the same sex living together as if they were living together as husband and wife and then to treat such persons as if they were lawfully married. It is to be left unclear as from what date this change in the law has taken place... Worse still, in support of their conclusion that the

---

[77] The expression is Lord Bingham's: see *R. (on the application of Anderson) v Secretary of State for the Home Department* [2002] UKHL 46; [2003] 1 A.C. 837 at [29].

[78] *Ghaidan v Godin-Mendoza* [2004] UKHL 30; [2004] 2 A.C. 557 at [67]–[68].

[79] The Bill that became the Civil Partnership Act 2004 was before Parliament during the hearing of the *Ghaidan* appeal. This creates a new legal relationship comparable to, but distinct from, marriage. Which statutes to amend by extending their reach to civil partners and persons living together as civil partners, and whether and to what extent the Act should be retrospective, were questions then being considered in the context of the legislative process, as Lord Millett pointed out.

existing discrimination is incompatible with the Convention, there is a tendency in some of the speeches of the majority to refer to loving, stable and long-lasting homosexual relationships. It is left wholly unclear whether qualification for the successive tenancy is confined to couples enjoying such a relationship or, consistently with the legislative policy which Parliament has hitherto adopted, is dependent on status and not merit."[80]

11–08 What is "possible" as a matter of interpretation is context specific and cannot be resolved in the abstract. The scheme of the Human Rights Act, and statements made to Parliament by ministers in the course of its enactment, make tolerably clear that declarations of incompatibility are (or were intended) to be a remedy of last resort, from which it follows that incompatibility with Convention rights, when it arises, is (or was intended) to be resolved by reliance on the interpretive obligation in most cases. But where the legislation has wide ranging implications, it will usually be appropriate to leave it to the legislature to determine these policy issues and enact fresh provision, rather than the court relying upon s.3 to "cure" the problem.[81] Where a curative interpretation is unachievable, the court will not suggest how the provision should be revised so as to achieve compatibility with Convention rights: that is a matter for Parliament.[82] But the proper limits of the interpretive function under s.3(1) are bound up with sensitivities as to the proper limits of the judicial role, for one thing, and with wider issues regarding the clarity and accessibility of the law, for another. Lord Abernethy alluded to these concerns in giving the opinion of the Registration Appeal Court in *Smith v Scott*.[83] In that case, the appellant submitted that s.3(1) of the Representation of the People Act 1983, which disenfranchises all persons serving a custodial sentence following conviction of a criminal offence (and which was held by the European Court of Human Rights to be incompatible with art.3 of the First Protocol to the Convention in *Hirst v United Kingdom (No.2)*)[84] could be rescued under s.3(1) of the Human Rights Act by reading in words to the effect that the disenfranchisement of a particular prisoner would depend on the

---

[80] *Ghaidan v Godin-Mendoza* [2004] UKHL 30; [2004] 2 A.C. 557 at [99]–[100]. Lord Millett added that Parliament's consideration of the scope of the Civil Partnership Act was, to that extent, foreclosed by the decision of the majority. Lord Millett's approach echoes that of the New Zealand Court of Appeal in *Quilter v Attorney General of New Zealand* [1998] 1 N.Z.L.R. 523, in which the court rejected the argument that the prohibition of discrimination in the Bill of Rights Act 1990 required it to reinterpret the provisions of the Marriage Act in such a way as to extend its scope to same sex couples. It should, however, be said that the Bill of Rights Act 1990 requires that any interpretation adopted by the courts must be "reasonable". As Lord Steyn noted in *Ghaidan* at [44], this model was available to the draftsman of the Human Rights Act but was, clearly, rejected in favour of the stronger obligation now contained in s.3(1).

[81] *Re S (Children) (Care Order: Implementation of Care Plan)* [2002] UKHL 10; [2002] 2 A.C. 291; *R. (on the application of Wright) v Secretary of State for Health* [2009] UKHL 3; [2009] 1 A.C. 739, per Baroness Hale of Richmond at [39].

[82] *R. (on the application of Wright) v Secretary of State for Health* [2009] UKHL 3; [2009] 1 A.C. 739, per Baroness Hale of Richmond at [39]. Although Lord Neuberger has recently suggested that in some circumstances a declaration should not be made without the court having expressed some idea about how it could be remedied: *R. (on the application of Nicklinson) v Ministry of Justice* [2014] UKSC 38; [2015] AC 657 at [127].

[83] *Smith v Scott* [2007] CSIH 9; 2007 S.C. 345.

[84] *Hirst v United Kingdom (No.2)* (2006) 42 E.H.R.R. 41. This is not an issue that has gone away and is considered at paras 4–13 above and 11–13 below.

discretion of the sentencing judge. The Registration Appeal Court rejected this argument in explicit terms: such an interpretation would:

> "depart substantially from a fundamental feature of the legislation. Without the benefit of consultation or advice, this Court would, in a real sense, be legislating on its own account, especially in view of the wide range of policy alternatives from which a 'possible' solution would require to be selected".[85]

The court further indicated that the approach to interpretation favoured by the majority in *Ghaidan* "appears to us to give rise to potentially significant difficulties in the consistent interpretation of legislation in the various courts which may have to apply it" and expressly reserved its opinion on the extent to which that approach might be followed and applied in the Scottish courts. Despite that note of caution having been sounded, *Ghaidan* remains the leading case on the application of s.3. And before parting with it, there is one final point to note: whilst our discussion has focused on how the court grapples with the interpretation of a statute, s.3 is not limited to the court. It applies to everyone else (in particular public authorities) who has cause to interpret and give effect to legislation.[86] That flows from the obligation imposed on all public authorities (including the court) to act in manner that is compatible with Convention rights.[87] That produces a final consequence: a party need not be a "victim"[88] to plead s.3; it is enough that he or she has sufficient standing to raise the case.[89]

A minister sponsoring a Bill in either House of Parliament must, prior to its second reading, make a statement to the effect that the provisions of the Bill are compatible with the Convention rights or that, although they are unable to make a statement of compatibility, the government nevertheless wishes the Bill to proceed.[90] A statement of compatibility is clear evidence, appearing on the face of an enactment, that it was not the intention of the legislature to violate Convention rights, and it was thought it might provide a strong incentive to the courts (whatever the subject matter of the legislation) to find means of construing the legislation consistently with the Convention.[91] They have had no such effect: **11–09**

---

[85] *Smith v Scott* [2007] CSIH 9; 2007 S.C. 345 at [27]

[86] *Ghaidan v Godin-Mendoza* [2004] UKHL 30; [2004] 2 A.C. 557, per Lord Rodger of Earlsferry at [106].

[87] Human Rights Act 1998 s.6; see para.11–14, below.

[88] See para.11–23, below.

[89] *R. (on the application of Rusbridger) v Attorney General* [2003] UKHL 38; [2004] 1 A.C. 357.

[90] Human Rights Act 1998 s.19. A statement to the effect that a Bill is outwith competence but the government wish to proceed in any event is rare (for example, ss.319 and 321 of the Communications Act 2003 that banned political adverts on TV—the European Court of Human Rights subsequently held the ban to be Convention compliant: *Animal Defenders International v United Kingdom* (2013) 57 E.H.R.R. 21). In the Scottish Parliament, the Presiding Officer must make a statement confirming whether or not in their view the provisions of any Bill introduced in the Parliament would be within the competence of the Parliament, which competence depends inter alia on compatibility with the Convention rights; and the Scottish Minister in charge of an Executive Bill must make a similar statement in respect of that Bill: Scottish Parliament Standing Orders rr.9.1 and 9.3(a).

[91] See Lord Irvine, "The Development of Human Rights in Britain under an Incorporated Convention" [1998] P.L. 221.

> "These statements may serve a useful purpose in Parliament . . . But they are no more than expressions of opinion by the minister. They are not binding on the court, nor do they have any persuasive authority."[92]

Since 1 January 2002, the explanatory notes issued to accompany Westminster Bills have given an outline of the government's views on compatibility, although falling short of the disclosure of its legal advice sought by some.[93] Where a Bill is amended such that the minister responsible for it forms the view that their statement of compatibility no longer holds true, it would be a breach of the Ministerial Code to present the Bill for Royal Assent without first informing Parliament of their revised view.[94] As to pre-incorporation enactments, there were indications of a tendency to examine parliamentary materials, on a rather broader basis than was countenanced by *Pepper v Hart*,[95] in order to ascertain the mischief against which the legislation was aimed and the legislature's reasons for adopting the enactment in the chosen form.[96] In *Wilson v First County Trust (No.2)*,[97] the Speaker of the House of Commons and the Clerk of the Parliament intervened to object to this use of *Hansard* as an encroachment upon art.9 of the Bill of Rights.[98] The House of Lords accepted that the Court of Appeal in that case had made inappropriate use of parliamentary material. Nevertheless, it was held that where the courts are assessing the compatibility of legislation with the Convention rights, it is necessary to identify the rationale for the legislation, an exercise that may involve reference to "additional background material". Such material may be found in published documents, such as government White Papers, or in statements made by ministers or members in either House of Parliament during debate on a Bill. In either case, if relevant, the courts are entitled to take it into account without "questioning" proceedings in Parliament, intruding into the legislative process or ascribing to Parliament the views expressed by a minister: "The court would merely be placing itself in a better position to understand the legislation".[99]

---

[92] *R v A (No.2)* [2001] UKHL 25; [2002] 1 A.C. 45, per Lord Hope of Craighead at [69].

[93] Lord Lester, "Parliamentary Scrutiny of Legislation" [2002] E.H.R.L.R. 432.

[94] Cabinet Office, *Guide to Making Legislation* (The Stationery Office, 2017), para.12.24 (available at: *https://assets.publishing.service.gov.uk/government/uploads/system/uploads/attachment_data/file/645652/Guide_to_Making_Legislation_Jul_2017.pdf* [Accessed 18 June 2020]).

[95] *Pepper v Hart* [1993] A.C. 593. For an explanation of the proper application of the rule in *Pepper v Hart*, see: D. Lowe and C. Potter, *Understanding Legislation: a practical guide to statutory interpretation* (Hart Publishing: 2018), paras 7.10–7.16.

[96] See, e.g. the Court of Appeal decision in *Wilson v First County Trust Ltd (No.2)* [2001] EWCA Civ 633; [2002] Q.B. 74. Having examined the legislative history of the Consumer Credit Act 1974, the Court of Appeal remarked that the parliamentary debates "tended to confuse rather than to illuminate" (at [36]), shedding no light on why Parliament thought it necessary to enact the provisions there in issue.

[97] *Wilson v First County Trust Ltd (No.2)* [2003] UKHL 40; [2004] 1 A.C. 816.

[98] This provides that the proceedings of Parliament shall not be impeached or questioned in any court or place outside Parliament.

[99] *Wilson v First County Trust Ltd (No.2)* [2003] UKHL 40; [2004] 1 A.C. 816, per Lord Nicholls at [64]. See also [140]–[144] per Lord Hobhouse. Lord Nicholls added that, in most cases, reference to *Hansard* was unlikely to prove useful. The same was said of the doctrine established in *Pepper v Hart*, but lawyers nonetheless feel obliged to trawl through *Hansard* in search of ministerial statements or other material that may shed some favourable light on the meaning of statutory provisions (thereby increasing the costs of litigation). Lord Steyn has argued that the only defensible application of *Pepper v Hart* arises in situations where the government states in Parliament that a

Wilson v First County Trust Ltd (No.2) also clarified one further matter relating to the reach of s.3(1) of the Human Rights Act. It is plain that the interpretive obligation applies to any enactment, whenever enacted. The courts cannot, however, apply a Convention-proofed interpretation of an enactment to acts or events that occurred prior to the coming into force of the Act. In other words, events prior to 2 October 2000 are not measured against an interpretation of a provision founded upon s.3. To that extent, the Human Rights Act does not have retroactive effect. This distance from the commencement of the Human Rights Act, and having regard to the various limitation periods that operate, this issue will now rarely arise. **11–10**

Section 4: declarations of incompatibility

If it is not possible to read and give effect to a statutory provision consistently with the Convention rights, then certain higher courts[100] may make a declaration of incompatibility in respect of the provision.[101] In relation to a provision of subordinate legislation, the same courts may make a declaration of incompatibility if satisfied that the provision is incompatible with a Convention right and that the parent statute (disregarding any possibility of revocation) prevents removal of the incompatibility.[102] For the purposes of the Human Rights Act, Acts of the Scottish Parliament constitute subordinate legislation.[103] However, a declaration of incompatibility under s.4 could never be appropriate in relation to a provision of an Act of the Scottish Parliament: as we saw in Ch.6, above, where such a provision is held to be incompatible with Convention rights it is ultra vires the Scottish Parliament and should be held to be "not law". [104] It will be obvious that s.3 and s.4 work very closely together. The more than can be achieved through s.3, the less s.4 will have to be deployed. As we will see in a moment, s.4 can leave an applicant with a somewhat pyrrhic victory so limiting the use of s.4 is not necessarily a bad thing. But the other side of the coin is that the more cases that are resolved using s.3, the fewer that are returned to Parliament to resolve using the remedial mechanism that is provided for in the Human Rights Act (s.10). It calls for a careful balance to be struck. **11–11**

statutory provision means one thing and subsequently contends for a different meaning in litigation: "*Pepper v Hart*: A re-examination" (2001) 21 O.J.L.S. 59.

[100] For Scottish purposes, the Supreme Court, the Courts Martial Appeal Court, the Court of Session and the High Court of Justiciary sitting otherwise than as a trial court: Human Rights Act 1998 s.4(5)(a) and (d).

[101] Human Rights Act 1998 s.4(2); the remedy is a discretionary one and the court may refuse to make a declaration even where satisfied the impugned provision is incompatible with Convention rights. For example, where a declaration has already been made by another court, there is unlikely to be any merit in issuing a second declaration: *R. (on the application of Chester) v Secretary of State for Justice* [2009] EWHC 2923 (Admin); [2010] H.R.L.R. 6 at [32]–[44].

[102] Human Rights Act 1998 s.4(4).

[103] Human Rights Act 1998 s.21. So too does "any order, rules, regulations, scheme, warrant, byelaw or other instrument made by a member of the Scottish Government... in exercise of prerogative or other executive functions of Her Majesty which are exercisable by such a person on behalf of Her Majesty".

[104] Scotland Act 1998 s.29; see para.6–24 above, See also: I. Jamieson, "The Relationship between the Scotland Act and the Human Rights Act", 2001 S.L.T. (News) 43.

11–12 Resort to s.4 "must always be an exceptional course"[105] and one that is available only after the court has first tried to remedy the problem using s.3.[106] Where a court is considering whether to make a declaration of incompatibility, the Crown is entitled to notice of the proceedings and thereafter to be joined as a party to the proceedings.[107] The Crown in this sense is defined to include a minister of the Crown (or any person nominated by them) and a member of the Scottish Government.[108] Where an incurable problem has been found, the granting of a declaration of incompatibility is a matter for the discretion of the court; the court is not obliged to make such a declaration.[109] But a declaration can be made even if it is not necessary in order to dispose of the case.[110] Where the offending provision has already been declared incompatible and the complaint is the failure to take remedial action, a further declaration is unlikely.[111] It is ordinarily not for the court to propose a solution to the incompatibility it is declaring,[112] but in exceptional circumstances that may be appropriate.[113] If a declaration of incompatibility is granted, however, it has no effect on "the validity, continuing operation or enforcement of the provision in respect of which it is given; and . . . is not binding on the parties to the proceedings in which it is made".[114]

The sovereignty of Parliament is thus preserved. Rather, a declaration under s.4 triggers the power in s.10 to take remedial action. It is important to note that it is only a power. The minister is not obliged to make a remedial order, nor need Parliament to enact amending legislation, although any failure to do so in

105 *Ghaidan v Godin-Mendoza* [2004] UKHL 30; [2004] 2 A.C. 557, per Lord Steyn at [50].

106 *Wilson v First County Trust Ltd (No.2)* [2003] UKHL 40; [2004] 1 A.C. 816, per Lord Nicholls at [14].

107 Human Rights Act 1998 s.5(1) and (2).

108 Thus it might be appropriate for a member of the Scottish Government to be joined as a party to proceedings relating to a pre-commencement enactment (as defined in the Scotland Act 1998 s.53(3)) where that enactment confers functions exercisable post-devolution by the Scottish Ministers, either by way of the general transfer of functions provided for by s.53 or by way of a transfer of functions pursuant to s.63.

109 "If the court is satisfied that the provision is incompatible with a Convention right, it *may* make a declaration of that incompatibility" (Human Rights Act 1998 s.4(2), emphasis added). *R (Steinfeld) v Secretary of State for International Development* [2018] UKSC 32; [2020] A.C. 1 at [56]–[57]. Whether to make a declaration can be controversial: see, for example, the differing views expressed by the Justices in *R (Nicklinson) v Ministry of Justice* [2014] UKSC 38; [2015] A.C. 652.

110 *R (Johnson) v Home Secretary* [2016] UKSC 56; [2017] A.C. 365.

111 *R. (on the application of Chester) v Secretary of State for Justice* [2013] UKSC 63; 2014 S.C. (U.K.S.C.) 25; [2014] A.C. 271, per Lord Mance at [39]. In that case, not only did the Supreme Court refuse to make a second declaration of incompatibility in relation to s.3 of the Representation of the People Act 1983, it also refused to make a declaration of incompatibility in relation to the near identically worded s.8 of the European Parliamentary Elections Act 2002.

112 *R. (on the application of Wright) v Secretary of State for Health* [2009] UKHL 3; [2009] 1 A.C. 739, per Baroness Hale of Richmond at [39].

113 *R. (on the application of Nicklinson) v Ministry of Justice* [2014] UKSC 38; [2014] 3 W.L.R. 200, per Lord Neuberger at [127]. Lord Wilson, in the same case (at [204]) said: "But a court will be of maximum assistance to Parliament in this regard if it not only identifies the factors which precipitate the infringement but articulates options for its elimination." *Nicklinson* was an exceptionally hard case concerning the proper interpretation of the Suicide Act 1961 and what, if any, right a person had to assisted suicide.

114 Human Rights Act 1998 s.4(6)(a) and (b).

response to a declaration of incompatibility will provide the aggrieved individual with a strong case to take to Strasbourg.[115] Ultimately, however, redress is political:

> "But the court has no role to sanction government for such failures. Under the Human Rights Act 1998 the minister has no obligation to act on a declaration of incompatibility. If he does not, the complainant's remedy is to take proceedings in Strasbourg... [and] failure by a member state of the Council of Europe to give effect to a decision of the European Court of Human Rights sounds at the political level; it is as such not amendable to sanctions in national courts."[116]

This perhaps highlights an aspect of what Ewing called the "futility" of the Human Rights Act.[117]

Where there is a desire to respond positively to a s.4 declaration, a remedial order may be made by Her Majesty in Council[118] or in accordance with the procedures prescribed by Sch.2. The ordinary procedure[119] requires the relevant minister of the Crown[120] to lay a draft of the remedial order before both Houses of Parliament after the expiry of a 60-day period commencing with the laying before both Houses of a document containing a draft of the proposed order and the "required information".[121] If, during the 60-day period, representations (including any parliamentary report or resolution) are made to the minister in relation to the proposed order, the minister must accompany the draft order laid under para.2(a) with a statement summarising the representations received and giving details of any changes made to the proposed order as a result thereof.[122] The draft order must then be approved by affirmative resolution of both Houses of Parliament within 60 days of its being laid in its final form.[123] Schedule 2 also provides for an urgent procedure, applicable in cases where the incompatible

[115] This power is also exercisable where, following an adverse decision of the European Court of Human Rights in proceedings against the UK, it appears that a provision of legislation is incompatible with an obligation of the UK arising under the Convention: Human Rights Act 1998 s.10(1)(b). In neither case need the power in s.10 be used; it may be preferable to remedy the defect identified by the Convention or a declaration of incompatibility by way of primary legislation enacted in the normal way.

[116] *R. (on the application of Chester) v Secretary of State for Justice* [2010] EWCA Civ 1439; [2011] 1 W.L.R. 1436, per Laws LJ at [27].

[117] K.D. Ewing, "The futility of the Human Rights Act" [2004] P.L. 829; K.D. Ewing, "The continuing futility of the Human Rights Act" [2008] P.L. 668; not that everybody agrees with Ewing: A. Lester, "The utility of the Human Rights Act: a reply to Keith Ewing" [2005] P.L. 249.

[118] By way of an Order in Council: Human Rights Act 1998 s.10(5).

[119] Human Rights Act 1998 Sch.2 para.2(a).

[120] That is, "the holder of an office in Her Majesty's Government in the United Kingdom": Ministers of the Crown Act 1975 s.8.

[121] Human Rights Act 1998 Sch.2 para.3(1). The "required information" is defined by para.5 as an explanation of the incompatibility that the proposed order seeks to remove, including particulars of the relevant declaration of incompatibility, funding or order, and a statement of the minister's reasons for proceeding under s.10 and for making an order in the terms proposed. It should be noted that the minister may only proceed under s.10 if they consider that there are "compelling reasons" for doing so (although it is inconceivable that their judgment in that matter could be challenged by way of judicial review).

[122] Human Rights Act 1998 Sch.2 para.3(2).

[123] In calculating the 60-day periods, no account is to be taken of any time during which Parliament is prorogued or dissolved, or both Houses are adjourned for more than four days: Human Rights Act 1998 Sch.2 para.6.

provision is contained in subordinate legislation that has been quashed, or declared invalid, by reason of its incompatibility with the Convention rights.[124] In such cases, the minister may make a remedial order with immediate effect, but then lay the order before Parliament and declare that, because of the urgency of the matter, it was necessary to proceed without the order first being approved in draft by both Houses. Representations may be made to the minister in relation to the order during the period of 60 days following its laying before Parliament, at the end of which period the minister must lay before Parliament a statement summarising the representations and giving details of any changes they consider appropriate to make to the original order in light thereof. If any changes are made, the minister must make a further remedial order replacing the original order. The order (original or replacement) ceases to have effect at the end of a 120-day period following the laying of the original order unless, during that time, both Houses of Parliament adopt resolutions approving it.[125]

11–13 The series of cases concerning the rights of convicted prisoners illustrates the limits of the Human Rights Act as a means by which to secure the protection of Convention rights. As we saw in Ch.4, above, s.3 of the Representation of the People Act 1983 previously[126] barred any convicted prisoner who is, at the time of an election, serving a period of imprisonment from voting. Such a blanket ban on prisoners voting has long been held to infringe art.3 of the First Protocol[127] to the Convention.[128] As a result, a declaration of incompatibility was made by the (Scottish) Electoral Registration Court in relation to s.3 of the 1983 Act in 2007.[129] There was, however, no political desire to amend the law so as to introduce a more proportionate ban. Indeed, when the matter surfaced again in 2011 the then Prime Minister told Parliament that the thought of enfranchising any serving prisoners made him feel physically ill and a proposed relaxation of the ban was overwhelmingly rejected by the House of Commons.[130] The matter returned to the Supreme Court in 2013 when a number of prisoners continued to

---

[124] Human Rights Act 1998 s.10(4) and Sch.2 para.2(b).

[125] But such lapse of the order will not affect the validity of anything previously done under it, or affect the power of the minister to make a fresh remedial order: Human Rights Act 1998 Sch.2 para.4(4).

[126] From 1 April 2020, those serving a sentence of less than 12 months are permitted to vote in Scottish elections. The bar on voting in Westminster elections endures. However, a compromise was reached with the Council of Europe whereby the bar on voting would be made clearer at the time of sentencing and those released on temporary licence would be entitled to vote (those changes to be introduced administratively) (HC Deb 2 November 2017, Vol.630, c.1007). That was accepted by the Council of Europe: Committee of Ministers, 1302nd meeting, 5–7 December 2017.

[127] For a summary of the general significance of art.3 of the First Protocol see Lord Collins' comments in *R. (on the application of Barclay) v Secretary of State for Justice* [2009] UKSC 9; [2010] 1 A.C. 464 at [52]–[59].

[128] *Hirst v United Kingdom (No.2)* (2006) 42 E.H.R.R. 41 Grand Chamber. It was not an unanimous decision and both the President, and the future President, of the court dissented. Despite that, the European Court of Human Rights has subsequently adhered to that line, despite repeated requests to depart from it: *Scoppola v Italy (No.3)* (2013) 56 E.H.R.R. 19, Grand Chamber; *Greens v United Kingdom* (2011) 53 E.H.R.R. 21; *McLean v United Kingdom* (2013) 57 E.H.R.R. SE8.

[129] *Smith v Scott* [2007] CSIH 9; 2007 S.C. 345. The matter was most recently considered by the Supreme Court in *Moohan, Petitioner* [2014] UKSC 67; 2015 S.L.T. 2 (a point on which the Supreme Court split 5:2).

[130] *Hansard*, HC col.493 (Vol.523) to 586 (10 February 2011) for a record of the debate.

complain about their inability to participate in elections.[131] There was nothing the Supreme Court was prepared to do: the ban could not be interpreted in a Convention-compliant manner under s.3[132]; it was for Parliament, using the remedial powers it has under s.10, to amend the legislation, and any further declarator would be pointless as Parliament had a draft Bill before it (although there was little prospect of it securing sufficient votes). This entire episode highlights the limits of the Human Rights Act, and thus the limits to the protection of fundamental human rights. However convicted prisoners may be regarded,[133] the Grand Chamber of the European Court of Human Rights has held that their fundamental human rights have been infringed and that finding has been accepted (however reluctantly) by the Supreme Court.[134] It is an infringement that was allowed to persist for over a decade. As Baroness Hale noted in *Chester*:

> "Democracy is about more than respecting the views of the majority. It is also about safeguarding the rights of minorities, including unpopular minorities."[135]

It is unlikely that a s.4 declaration that affected a majority of the electorate would go uncorrected by the legislature for so long. So it is always likely to be a minority group, and usually an unpopular minority, that will be the left with the pyrrhic victory that is a declaration that their fundamental human rights have been infringed, which has no effect on the continuing validity, operation or enforcement of the offending provision. Whether they be serving prisoners or terrorist suspects,[136] their rights ought to be treated equally:

> "... it is the purposes of all human rights instruments to secure the protection of the essential rights of members of minority groups, even when they are unpopular with the majority. Democracy values everyone equally even if the majority does not."[137]

---

[131] *R. (on the application of Chester) v Secretary of State for Justice* [2013] UKSC 63; 2014 S.C. (U.K.S.C.) 25; [2014] A.C. 271. Complaints were also founded upon alleged EU law rights and the identical ban under the European Parliamentary Elections Act 2002 (s.8) was also challenged.

[132] Given the range of possible options (discussed briefly in *R. (on the application of Chester) v Secretary of State for Justice* [2013] UKSC 63; 2014 S.C. (U.K.S.C.) 25; [2014] A.C. 271 by Lord Sumption at [114]) s.3 of the Human Rights Act was never likely to be suitable for an issue such as this.

[133] And the applicants in *Chester* appear to be individuals who were particularly unlikely to encourage any sympathy or be likely to benefit from any modified ban (see *R. (on the application of Chester) v Secretary of State for Justice* [2013] UKSC 63; 2014 S.C. (U.K.S.C.) 25; [2014] A.C. 271, per Baroness Hale at [87] and [99]).

[134] Lord Sumption, in particular, sets out why the Grand Chamber's decision may not be sound: *R. (on the application of Chester) v Secretary of State for Justice* [2013] UKSC 63; 2014 S.C. (U.K.S.C.) 25; [2014] A.C. 271 at [113]–[137].

[135] *R. (on the application of Chester) v Secretary of State for Justice* [2013] UKSC 63; [2014] A.C. 271; 2014 S.C. (U.K.S.C.) 25 at [88]. Lord Sumption did not accept that serving prisoners constituted a minority in that sense: "But the present issue has nothing whatever to do with the protection of minorities. Prisoners belong to a minority only in the banal and legally irrelevant sense that most people do not do the things which warrant imprisonment by due process of law" (*R. (on the application of Chester) v Secretary of State for Justice* [2013] UKSC 63; 2014 S.C. (U.K.S.C.) 25; [2014] A.C. 271 at [112]).

[136] As was the case in perhaps the most celebrated s.4 declaration: *A v Secretary of State for the Home Department* [2004] UKHL 56; [2005] 2 A.C. 68. See para.13–09, below for a discussion of that case.

[137] *Ghaidan v Godin-Mendoza* [2004] UKHL 30; [2004] 2 A.C. 557, per Baroness Hale of Richmond at [132].

That being so, it really ought not to have taken over a decade, and return trips to both London and Strasbourg, before an acceptable response to the declaration of the Scottish court in *Smith* was forthcoming.

Public authorities

11–14 So far, the provisions we have considered have been principally aimed at the court and how it secures the protection of Convention rights. Section 6 is, however, pivotal to the scheme of incorporation adopted by the Human Rights Act. It provides: "It is unlawful for a public authority to act in a way which is incompatible with a Convention right".[138] An "act" includes a failure to act but does not include a failure to introduce in, or lay before, Parliament a proposal for legislation or a failure to make any primary legislation or remedial order.[139] A public authority may only act in a manner that is incompatible with a Convention right when required to do so by primary legislation, or by secondary legislation made under it, and only then when the provision cannot be interpreted (pursuant to s.3) in a manner that is compatible with the Convention right in issue.[140] But given the strength of the obligation under s.3 to strive for a Convention-compliant interpretation of legislation, recourse to s.6(2) is rare.[141] Three points are immediately apparent. First, it is critically important to identify who or what falls within the meaning of the term "public authority" because, second, the Act does not, at least directly, regulate relations between private parties. Finally, it is necessary to understand the territorial scope of the Human Rights Act: does the s.6 prohibition apply to public authorities that operate outside the UK?

Section 6 of the Human Rights Act defines "public authorities" as follows:

> "(3) In this section 'public authority' includes—
> (a) a court or tribunal, and
> (b) any person certain of whose functions are functions of a public nature but does not include either House of Parliament or a person exercising functions in connection with proceedings in Parliament. . . .
>
> (5) In relation to a particular act, a person is not a public authority by virtue only of subsection 3(b) if the nature of the act is private."[142]

This definition is not exhaustive: it was not thought necessary to define expressly bodies that are "obviously" public authorities, but only to make clear that the term included bodies that might otherwise be thought to fall outwith its scope.[143] It follows that "standard" public authorities, such as local authorities and government departments, are bound by the duty to act in conformity with the Convention rights in respect of all their activities, whereas "functional" public authorities—bodies some of whose functions are "functions of a public

[138] Human Rights Act 1998 s.6(1).
[139] Human Rights Act 1998 s.6(6).
[140] Human Rights Act 1998 s.6(2).
[141] See para.11–07, above.
[142] Human Rights Act 1998 s.6(4) excluded the House of Lords acting in its judicial capacity from the definition of "Parliament". That provision was repealed by the Constitutional Reform Act 2005 as a consequence of the establishment of the Supreme Court.
[143] See R. Clayton and H. Tomlinson, *The Law of Human Rights* (Oxford: Oxford University Press, 2000), paras 5.05–5.08.

nature"—are bound only in the performance of those functions and not, by virtue of s.6(5), in respect of their private acts.[144] It is therefore key to understanding the breadth of the Human Rights Act that these two ideas ("functions of a public nature" and "nature of the act is private") are understood. Unsurprisingly, they have proved controversial.

During the passage of the Human Rights Bill through Parliament, the Home Secretary indicated that the means of distinguishing public from private functions should "relate to the nature and substance of the act, not to the form and legal personality".[145] It was also suggested that the way in which the courts—meaning, clearly, the English courts—have developed the concept of judicial review would offer valuable guidance.[146] Like s.6, the scope of judicial review in England turns on a distinction between public and private functions.[147] It has since been made clear by the House of Lords that the two are distinct.[148] The English jurisprudence could never be a complete guide, however, not least since s.2 of the Human Rights Act requires the courts to take account of the principles developed by the European Court of Human Rights, and that court has its own approach to what constitutes a public authority.[149] As has been said:

> "It is only by ensuring that Convention rights are respected throughout our legal system and at all levels of society that the state can avoid liability in Strasbourg for permitting such violations [of the Convention rights]. This is the purpose of the Human Rights Act and it explains the non-incorporation of Article 13.[150] Unlike judicial review, the purpose is not limited to protecting individuals against abuses of power by the state and governmental bodies. While the presence of a governmental

[144] This distinction between standard and functional public authorities was drawn by Clayton and Tomlinson, and was approved by the Court of Appeal in *Poplar Housing and Regeneration Community Association Ltd v Donoghue* [2001] EWCA Civ 595; [2002] Q.B. 48.

[145] *Hansard*, HC Vol.314, col.433 (17 June 1998).

[146] D. Pannick, "Who is Subject to Judicial Review and in Respect of What?" [1992] P.L. 1; *Aston Cantlow and Wilmcote with Billesley Parochial Church Council v Wallbank* [2003] UKHL 37; [2004] 1 A.C. 546, per Lord Hope of Craighead at [25]; *Poplar Housing and Regeneration Community Association Ltd v Donoghue* [2001] EWCA Civ 595; [2002] Q.B. 48, per Lord Woolf CJ at [65].

[147] Whether an function is "public" or "private" is not determinative of its susceptibility to review in Scotland; rather, the test is whether there is "a tripartite relationship between the person or body to whom the jurisdiction, power or authority has been delegated or entrusted, the person or body by whom it has been delegated or entrusted and the person or persons in respect of or for whose benefit that jurisdiction, power or authority is to be exercised": see *West v Secretary of State for Scotland*, 1992 S.C. 385, per Lord President Hope at p.413. The distinction between "public" and "private" may now be relevant, however, in relation to the question of standing to bring judicial review proceedings in Scotland: *AXA General Insurance Co Ltd v Lord Advocate* [2011] UKSC 46; 2012 S.C. (U.K.S.C.) 122; see para.14–04 below.

[148] *YL v Birmingham City Council* [2007] UKHL 27; [2008] 1 A.C. 95, per Lord Bingham at [12]. See also W. Wade and C. Forsyth, *Administrative Law*, 11th edn (Oxford: Oxford University Press, 2014), p.149

[149] See, e.g. *Chassagnou v France* (1999) 29 E.H.R.R. 615 at p.100.

[150] Article 13 enshrines the right to an effective remedy for breaches of the Convention rights. It is not a Convention right in terms of the Human Rights Act 1998 because (according to the government) it need not be: the fact of incorporation of the other Convention rights is sufficient to secure their effective protection in domestic law. But that is only true if the definition of public authorities under s.6 accurately reflects the scope of state responsibility in the Strasbourg Court for breaches by the state of its duty under art.1 of the Convention, to secure the Convention rights and freedoms to all within its jurisdiction, and in that regard "the state cannot absolve itself from responsibility by delegating its obligations to private bodies or individuals": *Costello-Roberts v United Kingdom* (1993) 19 E.H.R.R. 112 at p.27.

feature is probably conclusive of a body being a public authority within section 6, then, its absence should not be conclusive against it."[151]

11–15 In most cases, distinguishing public and private functions will present no problem. But at the margins, it becomes more controversial. If the nature of a function and not its form is crucial, are private schools and hospitals to be treated as public authorities, at least to the extent that they provide education and health care?[152] Are charities, because of the nature of charitable objects and the state support they enjoy in terms of the tax advantages flowing from charitable status?[153] Are commercial organisations that contract to perform or provide services on behalf of a standard public authority? Are trade unions and professional bodies, because their functions relate to freedom of association (and may raise other significant questions, as in relation to the conformity of their procedures to due process guarantees)? Are religious organisations, because their functions relate to freedom of conscience and expression?[154] In some cases, such questions have been disposed of with relative ease. In *Marcic v Thames Water Utilities Ltd*, for example, no point was even taken about whether the defendant, as a privatised utility, was a public authority for the purposes of s.6.[155] Again, in *R. (on the application of A) v Partnerships in Care Ltd*,[156] it was held that a private psychiatric hospital, registered as a mental nursing home under the Registered Homes Act 1984 and licensed to receive patients detained under the Mental Health Act 1983, was a public authority for the purposes of s.6. A, an NHS patient, had been placed in the hospital for treatment of a personality disorder. The hospital managers decided to cease offering such treatment. Keith J held that the relevant statutory duties were laid directly upon the hospital as a registered facility and that the hospital managers were a body upon whom important statutory functions relating to the provision of appropriate care and treatment had been devolved. There was a strong public interest in securing the proper discharge of such functions. For those reasons, it was appropriate to place the hospital within the scope of s.6.

11–16 Both decisions accord with the government's stated intention that privatised or contracted-out methods of delivering public services should not exclude the provider from the coverage of the Human Rights Act.[157] The Court of Appeal considered the issue in *R. (on the application of Heather) v Leonard Cheshire*

[151] K. Markus, "*Leonard Cheshire Foundation*: What is a Public Function?" [2003] E.H.R.L.R. 92, 96.

[152] The question assumes what is not necessarily the case, namely that the provision of education and health care involves, by definition, a public function. On this point, see, e.g. *Aston Cantlow and Wilmcote with Billesley Parochial Church Council v Wallbank* [2003] UKHL 37; [2004] 1 A.C. 546, per Lord Rodger of Earlsferry at [159]; *YL v Birmingham City Council* [2007] UKHL 27; [2008] 1 A.C. 95, per Lord Neuberger at [161]–[169]; and D. Oliver, "Functions of a public nature under the Human Rights Act" [2004] P.L. 329.

[153] See *RSPCA v Attorney General* [2001] 3 All E.R. 530 Ch Div.

[154] See *Aston Cantlow and Wilmcote with Billesley Parochial Church Council v Wallbank* [2003] UKHL 37; [2004] 1 A.C. 546.

[155] *Marcic v Thames Water Utilities Ltd* [2003] UKHL 66; [2004] 2 A.C. 42.

[156] *R. (on the application of A) v Partnerships in Care Ltd* [2002] EWHC 529 (Admin); [2002] 1 W.L.R. 2610.

[157] An intention no doubt born out of a desire to comply with the Strasbourg authority that did not allow liability under the Convention to be evaded by delegating public functions to private bodies. For example, *Costello-Roberts v United Kingdom* (1993) 19 E.H.R.R. 112.

Foundation.[158] The foundation ran a nursing home for the disabled. Residents were placed in the home by social services and health authorities pursuant to their statutory duties to provide accommodation to those in need of care and attention by reason of age, illness or disability, and to their power to make arrangements for such accommodation to be provided by third parties. The foundation decided to close the home and the residents applied for judicial review, arguing that the foundation was a public authority and that its decision was in breach of art.8. The Court of Appeal held that "the role that [the foundation] was performing manifestly did not involve the performance of public functions".[159] Its reasons for so holding were that there was no material difference between the services provided by the foundation to privately funded and publicly funded residents, yet it was only in respect of the latter that it was said to be performing public functions; the degree of public funding, while relevant, was not conclusive; the foundation was not standing in the shoes of the local authorities or exercising any statutory powers; and, save for an element of regulation by the Care Commission, there was insufficient control exercised by the local authority over the foundation. The approach taken by the Court of Appeal was concerningly narrow given the prevalence of contracting-out and other forms of public/private partnership as a means of public service delivery. A reassuring note was sounded by the House of Lords in *Aston Cantlow and Wilmcote with Billesley Parochial Church Council v Wallbank*,[160] where the House considered the approach to s.6(3). Without reference to *R. (on the application of Heather) v Leonard Cheshire Foundation*, let alone overruling it,[161] Lord Nicholls said:

> "Clearly there is no single test of universal application. There cannot be, given the diverse nature of governmental functions and the variety of means by which these functions are discharged today. Factors to be taken into account include the extent to which in carrying out the relevant function the body is publically funded, or is exercising statutory powers, or is taking the place of central government or local authorities, or is providing a public service."[162]

It appeared that the House of Lords was laying down a broad, functions-based, approach to "functions of a public nature".

[158] *R. (on the application of Heather) v Leonard Cheshire Foundation* [2002] EWCA Civ 366; [2002] 2 All E.R. 936.

[159] *R. (on the application of Heather) v Leonard Cheshire Foundation* [2002] EWCA Civ 366; [2002] 2 All E.R. 936 at [35].

[160] *Aston Cantlow and Wilmcote with Billesley Parochial Church Council v Wallbank* [2003] UKHL 37; [2004] 1 A.C. 546.

[161] *R. (on the application of Heather) v Leonard Cheshire Foundation* [2002] EWCA Civ 366; [2002] 2 All E.R. 936 was cited in argument before the House of Lords (as was an earlier decision of the Court of Appeal in *Poplar Housing and Regeneration Community Association Ltd v Donoghue* [2001] EWCA Civ 595; [2002] Q.B. 48), but not referred to in the judgment.

[162] *Aston Cantlow and Wilmcote with Billesley Parochial Church Council v Wallbank* [2003] UKHL 37; [2004] 1 A.C. 546 at [12]. See also Lord Hope at [41]. Lord Rodger at [160], suggested that "the essential characteristic of a public authority is that it carries out a function of government which would engage the responsibility of the United Kingdom before the Strasbourg organs".

11–17 The leading case on this matter is now *YL v Birmingham City Council.*[163] It was a case that concerned the duty of the council to provide accommodation to YL, an 84-year-old lady suffering from Alzheimer's. Under the National Assistance Act 1948, the council had a duty to make arrangements to provide YL with accommodation. Under s.26 of that Act, the council contracted an independent care home to accommodate YL. That home accommodated privately paying residents, but the majority had at least part of their fees paid by the council. YL was one such resident who had the majority of her fees met by the council. Six months after YL moved into the home, the company running the home purported to terminate its contract with YL. Proceedings were commenced on behalf of YL in which, inter alia, a declarator was sought that the company running the home were exercising public functions for the purposes of s.6 of the Human Rights Act. When the case reached the House of Lords, it divided their Lordships 3:2, with the majority holding that the company was not exercising public functions. Lord Scott summarised his reasons for so holding in the following terms:

> "Southern Cross is a company carrying on a socially useful business for profit. It is neither a charity nor a philanthropist. It enters into private law contracts with the residents in its care homes and with the local authorities with whom it does business. It receives no public funding, enjoys no special statutory powers, and is at liberty to accept or reject residents as it chooses (subject, of course, to anti-discrimination legislation which affects everyone who offers a service to the public) and to charge whatever fees in its commercial judgment it thinks suitable. It is operating in a commercial market with commercial competitors."[164]

Lord Mance shared those concerns, and appeared to be troubled by the distinction that would fall to be drawn between self-funding residents (who would not engage the Convention) and (part-) publicly funded residents (who would).[165] Likewise, Lord Neuberger recognised the force in the point that a person who would have a Convention rights claim if the service was provided by the council should not lose that simply because they have been contracted out. But that did not assist YL for a number of reasons. In particular, Lord Neuberger held that the council's duty was simply to *arrange* the provision of care, not to *provide* care so YL's was not a contracting out case.[166]

Lord Bingham and Baroness Hale dissented in forceful terms. Lord Bingham concluded his speech by saying:

> "When the 1998 Act was passed, it was very well known that a number of functions formerly carried out by public authorities were now carried out by private bodies. Section 6(3)(b) of the 1998 Act was clearly drafted with this well-known fact in mind. The performance by private body A by arrangement with public body B, and perhaps at the expense of B, of what would undoubtedly be a public function if

[163] *YL v Birmingham City Council* [2007] UKHL 27; [2008] 1 A.C. 95. For discussion of this case, see: S. Palmer, "Public, private and the Human Rights Act 1998: an ideological divide" [2007] C.L.J. 559; S. Choudhry, "Children in 'care' after *YL*—the ineffectiveness of contract as a means of protecting the vulnerable" [2013] P.L. 519.

[164] *YL v Birmingham City Council* [2007] UKHL 27; [2008] 1 A.C. 95 at [26].

[165] *YL v Birmingham City Council* [2007] UKHL 27; [2008] 1 A.C. 95 at [116]–[117].

[166] *YL v Birmingham City Council* [2007] UKHL 27; [2008] 1 A.C. 95 at [146]–[153].

> carried out by B is, in my opinion, precisely the case which section 6(3)(b) was intended to embrace. It is, in my opinion, this case."[167]

Lady Hale identified a number of important factors to be borne in mind when considering the reach of s.6(3)(b):

> "While there cannot be a single litmus test of what is a function of a public nature, the underlying rationale must be that it is a task for which the public, in the shape of the state, have assumed responsibility, at public expense if need be, and in the public interest."[168]

The fact that YL made some contribution to the cost of the home did not prevent her care being a "function of a public nature". National Health Service dental care, as Lady Hale pointed out, is still a function of a public nature despite those that can afford to do so paying for it.[169] Lady Hale concluded that applying the factors she had identified to YL, she had "no doubt" that Parliament intended her situation to fall within s.6(3)(b) and to the extent that the decision of the Court of Appeal in *R. (on the application of Heather) v Leonard Cheshire Foundation* suggested otherwise, it was wrong.[170]

Given the prevalence of contracting-out and other forms of public/private partnership as a means of public service delivery, the approach taken in *YL* matters. Whether the recipient of public services will be able to rely on their Convention rights should not turn on the happenstance of the identity and nature of the service provider. But that appears to be the practical result. By way of illustration, in *Ali v Serco Ltd*,[171] a failed asylum seeker challenged the lawfulness of her eviction from the property where she temporarily resided. That accommodation had been provided in accordance with the obligation imposed on the Secretary of State under s.95 of the Immigration and Asylum Act 1999. Serco, a private company, provided that accommodation on behalf of the Secretary of State. For other reasons, the challenge failed. But at first instance, the Lord Ordinary held that Serco was a public authority for the purposes of s.6 of the Human Rights Act.[172] That seems to accord perfectly with the expectations of the Home Secretary at the time the 1998 Act was passed.[173] Not so, said the Inner House:

> "The fundamental distinction, on this basis, is therefore between the entity that is charged with the public law responsibility, in that case a local authority, and the private operator who contracts with that entity to provide the service. The latter person operates according to private law obligations and responsibilities. The public law duty to provide care remains that of the entity with public law responsibility, in that case the local authority.
>
> ...
>
> The state cannot absolve itself of responsibility for such public law duties as the provision of accommodation to asylum seekers by delegating its responsibility to

167 *YL v Birmingham City Council* [2007] UKHL 27; [2008] 1 A.C. 95 at [20].
168 *YL v Birmingham City Council* [2007] UKHL 27; [2008] 1 A.C. 95 at [65].
169 *YL v Birmingham City Council* [2007] UKHL 27; [2008] 1 A.C. 95 at [72].
170 *YL v Birmingham City Council* [2007] UKHL 27; [2008] 1 A.C. 95 at [73].
171 *Ali v Serco Ltd* [2019] CSIH 54; 2019 S.L.T. 1335.
172 *Ali v Serco Ltd* [2019] CSOH 34; 2019 S.L.T. 463 at [32].
173 See fn.145, above.

> private bodies. If arrangements are made with a private company to provide accommodation, responsibility for the exercise of the public law duty is not delegated, but remains with the Home Secretary."[174]

Whilst that might be consistent with the majority view in *YL*, it simply highlights the criticisms that have been made of that decision. Whether a particular function is performed by a local authority directly or by a private company on a contracted-out basis, the function remains the same.[175] The fact that the identity of the body performing the function has changed is neither here nor there for the purposes of s.6 since, provided the function is of a public nature, the body is bound to act compatibly with the Convention rights, if only to that extent. The Inner House's emphasis on where the public law *duty* rests sits ill at ease with s.6's focus on the public nature of the *function* (in the case of *Ali*, the provision of accommodation which had clearly been transferred to Serco).[176] Criticism of *YL* has been extensive and attempts to amend the Human Rights Act to reverse its effects have failed.[177] As a result, the scope of this important provision of the Human Rights Act has been given a much narrower scope than was originally intended[178] and has left much uncertainty as to when the provider of a service will fall within the terms of the Act.

11–18 That brings us to the question of jurisdiction. This is an issue that will normally present no problem whatsoever: a public authority based in the UK, that operates in the UK and whose acts have effect in the UK obviously falls within the scope of s.6. What of those public authorities that operate furth of the UK? Events in Iraq have been the main vehicle through which this question has been considered. Can a solider on deployment in the desert of Iraq rely on their Convention rights? Does an Iraqi citizen detained by the UK Army have Convention rights under the Human Rights Act? The answers to these questions have generated much litigation and have required the Supreme Court to consider the territorial scope of the Act.

Acts of Parliament do not, unless the contrary intention appears, have effect beyond the UK.[179] Accordingly, the starting position is that the obligations imposed on public authorities are only intended to apply within the UK. The territorial scope of the Convention is set out in art.1: "The high contracting parties shall secure to everyone within their jurisdiction the rights and freedoms defined in section 1 of this Convention." Article 1 is not a Convention right under the Human Rights Act, but it does define the scope of the Act: the territorial scope

174 *Ali v Serco Ltd* [2019] CSIH 54; 2019 S.L.T. 1335 at [54]–[56].

175 P. Craig, "Contracting Out, the Human Rights Act and the Scope of Judicial Review" (2002) 118 L.Q.R. 551, 556.

176 Similarly, the reassurance that the Home Secretary "remains answerable" ([57]) for the discharge of the duty is likely to ring hollow: s.6 is designed to make rights effective and so the fact the Home Secretary may have to answer for an asylum seeker being removed from their property by the private party she has contracted with does not really leave that individual with a particularly effective right.

177 Joint Committee on Human Rights, *Legislative Scrutiny: Health and Social Care Bill, Eighth Report of Session 2007–08* (The Stationery Office, 2008), HL 46; HC 303. Wade and Forsyth, *Administrative Law* (2014), p.148.

178 The Secretary of State for Constitutional Affairs intervened in *YL* in support of her position.

179 L. Norbury and D. Bailey, *Bennion on Statutory Interpretation*, 7th edn (London: LexiNexis, 2019), para.4.2. However, there is the curious practice of specifying that an Act applies to Northern Ireland with the consequences that Acts that are silent on the point are taken to apply only to Great Britain.

of the Act was intended to be co-extensive with the territorial scope of the UK's obligations under the Convention.[180] Thus, to understand the scope of the Human Rights Act it is necessary to understand the scope of the Convention. This was recently considered by the Grand Chamber in *Al-Skeini v United Kingdom*.[181] At paras [131] and [132] of the judgment, the Grand Chamber explained:

> "131. A state's jurisdictional competence under article 1 is primarily territorial. Jurisdiction is presumed to be exercised normally throughout the state's territory. Conversely, acts of the contracting states performed, or producing effects, outside their territories can constitute an exercise of jurisdiction within the meaning of article 1 only in exceptional circumstances.
>
> 132. To date, the court in its case law has recognised a number of exceptional circumstances capable of giving rise to the exercise of jurisdiction by a contracting state outside its own territorial boundaries. In each case, the question whether exceptional circumstances exist which require and justify a finding by a court that the state was exercising jurisdiction extra-territorially must be determined with reference to the particular facts."

The Grand Chamber then discussed three distinct categories where extra-territorial jurisdiction could be found: state agent authority and control (for example, diplomatic staff working overseas)[182]; effective control over an area (for example, where a contracting state exercises some or all of the public powers ordinarily exercised by the government of that area)[183]; and the Convention legal space (for example, where the contracting state detains a foreign national overseas and holds them in a facility controlled by them).[184] In relation to that last category, the Grand Chamber went on to say:

> "It is clear that, whenever the state through its agents exercises control and authority over an individual, and thus jurisdiction, the state is under an obligation under article 1 to secure to that individual the rights and freedoms under section 1 of the

---

[180] *R. (on the application of Quark Fishing Ltd) v Secretary of State for Foreign and Commonwealth Affairs* [2005] UKHL 57; [2006] 1 A.C. 529, per Lord Nicholls of Birkenhead at [34]: "To this end the obligations of public authorities under sections 6 and 7 mirror in domestic law the treaty obligations of the United Kingdom in respect of corresponding articles of the Convention and its protocols. That was the object of these sections... Thus, and this is the important point for present purposes, the territorial scope of the obligations and rights created by sections 6 and 7 of the Act was intended to be co-extensive with the territorial scope of the obligations of the United Kingdom and the rights of victims under the Convention. The Act was intended to provide a domestic remedy where a remedy would have been available in Strasbourg. Conversely, the Act was not intended to provide a domestic remedy where a remedy would not have been available in Strasbourg."

[181] *Al-Skeini v United Kingdom* (2011) 53 E.H.R.R. 18; this was an appeal following the decision of the House of Lords in *R. (on the application of Al-Skeini) v Secretary of State for Defence* [2007] UKHL 26; [2008] 1 A.C. 153 in which the House had held that an Iraqi citizen that had died while in UK custody, and having been grossly mistreated by UK soldiers, was within the jurisdiction of the UK for the purposes of the Human Rights Act, whereas five civilians who had been shot in a range of circumstances (some of which were hotly disputed) where not within the jurisdiction of the UK.

[182] *Al-Skeini v United Kingdom* (2011) 53 E.H.R.R. 18 at [134]; see also *Bankoviœ v Belgium* (2001) 11 B.H.R.C. 435; (2001) 44 E.H.R.R. SE5 at [71].

[183] *Al-Skeini v United Kingdom* (2011) 53 E.H.R.R. 18 at [135].

[184] *Al-Skeini v United Kingdom* (2011) 53 E.H.R.R. 18 at [136]; the example given is based on the circumstances of *Al-Saadoon v United Kingdom* (2009) 49 E.H.R.R. SE11.

> Convention *that are relevant to the situation of that individual. In this sense, therefore, the Convention rights can be 'divided and tailored'*."[185]

The final part of that paragraph, in italics, is central to understanding jurisdiction in relation to persons detailed by a contracting state. In such circumstances (for example an insurgent detained in Iraq) the state would not be under an obligation to secure the detainee's right to respect for family life or freedom of association. They would, however, as a minimum, require to secure the detainee's art.2 (right to life) and art.3 (prohibition of torture) rights.

11–19 In relation to the Human Rights Act, the House of Lords and the Supreme Court have had cause to consider jurisdictional scope on a number of occasions.[186] However, the first time the Supreme Court had the opportunity to consider the issue with the benefit of the Grand Chamber's decision in *Al-Skeini* was in *Smith v Ministry of Defence*.[187] One of the issues for the Supreme Court was: do soldiers on active service abroad fall within the UK's jurisdiction for the purposes of the Convention (and thereby within the scope of the Human Rights Act)?[188] While the court was divided on the other issues, they were unanimous in the answer to this question. As service personnel are under the control and authority of the state they are within its jurisdiction. Accordingly, they can rely upon their rights under the Human Rights Act.[189] Important in that extension of the territorial scope of the Act was the Strasbourg Court's decision that the package of rights contained with the Convention can, contrary what had previously been held,[190] be divided and tailored to fit the particular circumstances.[191] What is clear from the discussion in *Smith* is that the duty imposed on a public authority under s.6 of the Human Rights Act is capable of applying beyond the shores of the UK and for the benefit of people that are not citizens of this country. That presents a new and different dimension to the deployment of the armed forces overseas on missions such as that undertaken in Iraq.

---

[185] *Al-Skeini v United Kingdom* (2011) 53 E.H.R.R. 18 at [137] (emphasis added).

[186] *R. (on the application of Gentle) v Prime Minister* [2008] UKHL 20; [2008] 1 A.C. 1356, was the government under a duty, in terms of art.2, to obtain reliable legal advice before committing soldiers to war? The soldiers were not within the jurisdiction of the UK at the relevant time (Lord Bingham at [8](3)) and, in any event, art.2 did not prohibit the government from participating in an invasion that was unlawful in international law (Lord Rodger at [39]); *R. (on the application of Smith) v Oxfordshire Assistant Deputy Coroner* [2010] UKSC 29; [2011] 1 A.C. 1, did a soldier operating outside his base in Iraq fall within the jurisdiction of the UK for the purposes of the Convention? Private Smith collapsed while working off base. He was rushed back to base but died soon after due to heat stroke. The House of Lords held (6:3) that the soldiers operating abroad did not fall within the scope of the Convention.

[187] *Smith v Ministry of Defence* [2013] UKSC 41; [2014] A.C. 52.

[188] Two other issues were before the Supreme Court that were both important and interesting, but beyond the scope of this book: what duty did the state owe to soldiers when procuring equipment to be used in the battlefield and the scope of the doctrine of combat immunity. For a discussion of both of those issues, see: G. Junor, "A soldier's (human) rights when fighting abroad: the Supreme Court decides", 2013 S.L.T. (News) 251; R. Mullender, "Military Operations, fairness and the British state" (2014) 130 L.Q.R. 28.

[189] *Smith v Ministry of Defence* [2013] UKSC 41; [2014] A.C. 52, per Lord Hope of Craighead at [52].

[190] *Bankovic v Belgium* (2001) 45 E.H.R.R. SE5.

[191] *Smith v Ministry of Defence* [2013] UKSC 41; [2014] A.C. 52, per Lord Hope of Craighead at [48]–[49].

The horizontal effect of the Human Rights Act

The Human Rights Act is drafted to have vertical effect: it applies directly only to the organs of the state and other bodies falling within the definition of public authorities. But its potential horizontal effect—its application to purely private relationships—is considerable. This comes about in two ways. First, the interpretative obligation laid on the courts by s.3 applies, as we have seen, to all legislation in any proceedings, not merely in proceedings involving a public authority.[192] Through the medium of existing statutory provisions, read and given effect in a manner compatible with the Convention rights, those rights may become binding as between private parties, and if it is not possible to read and give effect to a provision consistently with the Convention rights, a declaration of incompatibility may be made. Second, the fact that courts and tribunals are themselves "public authorities" for the purposes of the Human Rights Act means that it is unlawful for them to act incompatibly with the Convention rights. **11–20**

Different views have been expressed as to the effect of this. Sir William Wade argued that both the spirit of the Act and a literal construction of s.6 mean that, if a Convention right is relevant to proceedings before it, the court must decide in accordance with it, no less in a case between private parties than in a case against a public authority.[193] Sir Richard Buxton, on the other hand, insisted that the Convention creates rights only against the state (in its various manifestations) and that incorporation of the Convention rights did not change their content so as to render them enforceable against private parties.[194] Murray Hunt offers an intermediate position, in which the Convention rights will "pervade the law" but will fall short of creating wholly new private law causes of action.[195] In fact, the question of horizontal effect may be a subtler one than any of these accounts acknowledge.[196] Consider first the influence the Convention rights have on the development of the common law. Since that influence was making itself felt even prior to the enactment of the Human Rights Act, there is plainly no reason why the process should not continue. "Statutory horizontality"—bringing the Convention rights into play by means of the interpretative obligation—is plainly justified by the terms of s.3; to argue otherwise would be to deprive s.3 of a good deal of its meaning. In so far as public authorities may have powers to prevent breaches of the Convention rights, and may be liable under the Human Rights Act for failures to act as much as for their positive actions, a form of "intermediate horizontality" is created: if a private individual is not themselves bound to respect

---

[192] Subject, however, to the presumption against retrospectivity, as explained by the House of Lords in *Wilson v First County Trust Ltd (No.2)* [2003] UKHL 40; [2004] 1 A.C. 816, see especially the speech of Lord Rodger at [186]–[214].

[193] H.W.R. Wade, "Horizons of Horizontality" (2000) 116 L.Q.R. 217. See also, e.g. Lester, Pannick and Herberg, *Human Rights: Law and Practice* (2009), pp.54–65.

[194] R. Buxton, "The Human Rights Act and Private Law" (2000) 116 L.Q.R. 48. Both Wade and Buxton cite statements made by the Lord Chancellor during the parliamentary passage of the Human Rights Bill in support of their views. Given the inherent conflict between these statements, one of which cheerfully countenances horizontal effect and the other of which plainly does not, this would not seem to be a question amenable to resolution under the *Pepper v Hart* doctrine: see A.J. Bowen, "Fundamental Rights in Private Law", 2000 S.L.T. (News) 157.

[195] M. Hunt, "The 'Horizontal Effect' of the Human Rights Act" [1998] P.L. 423.

[196] See I. Leigh, "Horizontal Rights, the Human Rights Act and Privacy: Lessons from the Commonwealth" (1999) 48 I.C.L.Q. 57.

another's Convention rights, a public authority may be obliged to prevent them from actually violating them.[197] There is also authority for the proposition that a court must, in order to comply with s.6(1), conform its own procedures to the requirements of the Convention rights.[198] This would extend to what is termed "remedial horizontality", as seen where the court's decision to grant or withhold a remedy is determined by reference to the effect on the parties' Convention rights. Thus, in *Karl Construction Ltd v Palisade Properties Plc*,[199] Lord Drummond Young recalled an inhibition granted on the dependence of the action between the parties on the grounds that its grant was incompatible with the defender's rights under art.1 of the First Protocol to the Convention. Previously the remedy was granted as of right in actions for payment of a sum or for damages, where the pursuer had included a warrant for inhibition in their summons. The Rules of the Court of Session required only that the summons be intimated to the defender. But the effect of an inhibition, once granted, is draconian: it freezes the whole of the defender's heritable assets, so that they are unable to use or dispose of them; the grounds for recall are (or were) limited; and the defender has no right to be compensated for wrongful use of the diligence. While Lord Drummond Young accepted that inhibition pursued a legitimate aim (namely, furthering the administration of justice by ensuring that assets are available to satisfy any decree granted in the pursuer's favour), he did not find that it struck the requisite "fair balance" between the general interests of the public and the rights of individuals to the use and enjoyment of their property. In other words, it was disproportionate.

11–21 In fact, the Human Rights Act appears to have horizontal effect in every respect bar one: private individuals cannot sue one another for breaches of their Convention rights as such. Lady Hale summarised the position in *Cambell v MGN Ltd*:

> "The 1998 Act does not create any new cause of action between private persons. But if there is a relevant cause of action applicable, the court as a public authority must act compatibly with both parties' Convention rights."[200]

That case was one of a series in the early years of this century concerning the extent to which the common law conveyed a right to privacy. Article 8 of the Convention protects private and family life. To what extent did the common law,

---

[197] The analogy here is with the treatment of "positive obligations" arising under the Convention, i.e. those that require affirmative action by the state. Thus in *A v United Kingdom* (1998) 27 E.H.R.R. 611, the state was liable for failing to protect a child from punishment at the hands of his stepfather, which was held to amount to inhuman and degrading treatment contrary to art.3 (the stepfather was acquitted by a jury, which accepted his defence of "reasonable chastisement" in his prosecution for assault). But see the likely limits to any such liability: *Mitchell v Glasgow City Council* [2009] UKHL 11; 2009 S.C. (H.L.) 21 and *Michael v Chief Constable of South Wales* [2015] UKSC 2; [2015] A.C. 1732.

[198] Thus, in *R. (on the application of A) v Lord Saville of Newdigate* [2001] EWCA Civ 2048; [2002] 1 W.L.R 1249, the Court of Appeal held that the Bloody Sunday Inquiry had breached the art.2 rights (right to life) of former soldiers called to give evidence by requiring them to attend the tribunal in Londonderry to do so. For an unequivocal acceptance of procedural and remedial horizontality in Scotland, see *Newman Shopfitters Ltd v MJ Gleeson Group Plc*, 2003 S.L.T. (Sh. Ct) 83 at [40].

[199] *Karl Construction Ltd v Palisade Properties Plc*, 2002 S.C. 270. See also, now, *Advocate General for Scotland v Taylor*, 2004 S.C. 339 at [34]; *Gillespie v Toondale Ltd*, 2006 S.C. 304.

[200] [2004] UKHL 22; [2004] 2 A.C. 457 at [132].

and in particular the traditional remedy of breach of confidence, offer a similar protection? If it did not offer protection similar to that of art.8, a curious situation would arise where it would be unlawful for the state to publish a particular piece of information about an individual but not for another private individual (or entity, for example, a newspaper). Lord Hoffmann explained the point at para.50:

> "What human rights law has done is to identify private information as something worth protecting as an aspect of human autonomy and dignity. And this recognition has raised inescapably the question of why it should be worth protecting against the state but not against a private person. There may of course be justification for the publication of private information by private persons which would not be available to the state … but I can see no logical ground for saying that a person should have less protection against a private individual that he would have against the state for the publication of personal information for which there is no justification."[201]

Accordingly, in that case, the law of breach of confidence was developed so that some protection was afforded to the privacy of the claimants. But the court cannot create a new cause of action. That is illustrated by the circumstances of Mrs Wainwright and her son.[202] They were both strip-searched when visiting another of Mrs Wainwright's children in Leeds Prison. That child was being held on remand on a charge of murder but was suspected by the governor of dealing drugs inside the prison. His supplier was unknown and the governor directed that any visitor had to be strip searched. But the search of Mrs Wainwright and her son was not done in accordance with the prison rules. That caused then substantial distress and, so far as her (visiting) son was concerned, post-traumatic stress disorder. They claimed that their privacy had been infringed. But the action failed. As Lord Hoffmann explained, the common law did not recognise a general tort of invasion of privacy nor was it required to do so by the Convention.[203] In any event, whether to introduce such a general right would require "a detailed approach which can be achieved only by legislation rather than the broad brush of common law principle".[204] That final comment illustrates another aspect of this debate over horizontal application of the 1998 Act. Even where the court could, in principle, develop the common law (because a suitable existing remedy is available) it will not always be appropriate for the court to do so. Some questions are best left to the legislature.

The section 6(2) "defence"

Section 6(2) of the Human Rights Act disapplies s.6(1) in two situations: first, **11–22**
where a public authority could not, as the result of one or more provisions of primary legislation, have acted in any other way; or, second, where it was acting to give effect to or enforce statutory provisions that cannot be read and given effect in a manner compatible with the Convention rights. The first of these envisages a situation in which the public authority had no discretion at all, the second a situation in which such discretion as it had could not be exercised in

---

[201] [2004] UKHL 22; [2004] 2 A.C. 457 at [50].
[202] *Wainwright v Home Office* [2003] UKHL 53; [2004] 2 A.C. 406.
[203] [2003] UKHL 53; [2004] 2 A.C. 406 at [30]–[35].
[204] [2003] UKHL 53; [2004] 2 A.C. 406 at [33].

conformity with the Convention. If that is the case then, assuming the act in question did breach a Convention right, the only remedy open to the litigant will be a declaration of incompatibility.[205]

Given the flexibilities of language, one would have thought that a public authority would be able to say that such discretion as it had could not be exercised compatibly with the Convention in very few cases. This in turn would seem to imply that public authorities have their own role to play in securing observance with the Convention rights, by considering whether, in any particular case, the Convention rights are engaged and how this might influence the decision it proposes to reach. But it is important to remember that the protection of Convention rights is a results business: what matters is that the decision a public authority takes is Convention compliant, the process by which it reaches that decision is irrelevant. The House of Lords made this point forcefully in two cases. First, in *R. (on the application of Begum) v Governors of Denbigh High School*, the House of Lords held that the Court of Appeal had fallen into error by holding that an individual's Convention rights had been breached by a public authority who had simply omitted to have regard to them.[206] That case concerned the uniform policy adopted by a non-denominational state school. Since a high proportion of the pupils were Muslim, the policy allowed girls to wear the shalwar kameeze and a headscarf, in the school colours, rather than the standard uniform. The claimant, a 14-year-old pupil, wore the shalwar kameeze and headscarf without objection for her first two years at the school. She then claimed that she was obliged by her evolving religious beliefs to adopt the jilbab, a long, shapeless coat that more fully conceals the arms and legs. She appeared at the school thus attired and was sent home. She never returned to the school. She claimed that the school had violated her art.9 right to respect for her religious beliefs. The judge at first instance dismissed the claim. The Court of Appeal, without deciding whether as a matter of substance the uniform policy was incompatible with art.9, held that the school had breached her Convention rights by failing to reach its decision by a proper process of reasoning. The House of Lords disagreed. While domestic judicial review is normally concerned with the decision-making process rather than the merits of the actual decision, challenges based on Convention rights are different. As Lord Hoffmann put it:

> "In domestic judicial review, the court is usually concerned with whether the decision-maker reached his decision in the right way rather than whether he got what the court might think to be the right answer. But Article 9 is concerned with substance, not procedure. It confers no right to have a decision made in a particular way. What matters is the result."[207]

---

[205] The obvious drawback of this is that it has no effect on the validity, continuing operation or enforcement of the provision in respect of which it is made, and is not binding on the parties to the proceedings: see Human Rights Act 1998 s.4(6), and para.11–12, above.

[206] *R. (on the application of Begum) v Governors of Denbigh High School* [2006] UKHL 15; [2007] 1 A.C. 100.

[207] *R. (on the application of Begum) v Governors of Denbigh High School* [2006] UKHL 15; [2007] 1 A.C. 100 at [68]; see Lord Bingham at [29] to similar effect: "But the focus at Strasbourg is not and has never been on whether a challenged decision or action is the product of a defective decision-making process, but on whether, in the case under consideration, the applicant's Convention rights have been violated"; and Lord Nicholls at [68].

Shortly afterwards, in another case, this time concerning the licencing of sex shops in Belfast, Lord Hoffmann made the point even clearer:

> "Either the refusal infringed the respondent's convention rights or it did not. If it did, no display of human rights learning by the Belfast City Council would have made the decision lawful. If it did not, it would not matter if the councillor's had never heard of article 10 or the First Protocol."[208]

The result is that even where a public authority has no regard to the possible infringement of a person's Convention rights, but happens upon a Convention-compliant decision, there is no ground for complaint. In that regard, challenges founded on an alleged infringement of a Convention right differ markedly from common law judicial review of a public authority's decision.

Section 7: proceedings under the Human Rights Act

Section 7(1) of the Human Rights Act provides: **11–23**

> "A person who claims that a public authority has acted (or proposes to act) in a way which is made unlawful by section 6(1) may—
> (a) bring proceedings against the authority under this Act in the appropriate court or tribunal, or
> (b) rely on the Convention right or rights concerned in any legal proceedings but only if he is (or would be) a victim of the unlawful act."

Judicial review is the normal vehicle by which to raise an issue under s.7(1)(a).[209] To that end, s.7(3) and (4) provide that the test of standing to apply for judicial review in such cases is status as a victim of the act complained of. A person is a victim for the purposes of s.7(1) only if they would be a victim for the purposes of art.34 of the Convention.[210] To raise a challenge under the Human Rights Act, it is necessary to meet the test set in that Act, rather than the common law test for standing.[211] It is therefore necessary to understand what is required to be a "victim" of an act for the purposes of the Convention. That requires consideration of art.34 of the Convention.[212]

Article 34 provides that the European Court of Human Rights may receive applications from any person, non-governmental organisation or group of individuals claiming to be a victim or victims of a violation of one or more of the Convention rights. In relation to art.2, claims will be entertained from close relatives ("indirect victims") of a deceased.[213] Local authorities and other organs

---

208 *Belfast City Council v Miss Behavin' Ltd* [2007] UKHL 19; [2007] 1 W.L.R. 1420 at [13]; see also Lord Neuberger at [90].

209 But not all claims under the Human Rights Act must be by means of judicial review. For example, where damages are sought for infringement of Convention rights, it is perfectly competent to proceed by means of an ordinary action in the sheriff court: *Ruddy v Chief Constable, Strathclyde Police* [2012] UKSC 57; 2013 S.C. (U.K.S.C.) 126.

210 Human Rights Act 1998 s.7(7).

211 See paras 14–08—14–12, below for discussion of the test for standing.

212 See generally: Woolf et al, *De Smith's Judicial Review* (2018), paras 2–047—2–063; Wadham et al., *Blackstone's Guide to the Human Rights Act 1998* (2015), paras 4.16–4.28; and Murdoch, *Reed and Murdoch: Human Rights Law in Scotland*, 4th edn, paras 2.71–2.81.

213 *Rabone and other v Pennine Care NHS Trust* [2012] UKSC 2; [2012] 2 A.C. 72.

of the state (what would be "core" public authorities in terms of s.6) cannot institute proceedings.[214] But legal persons and other bodies, including companies, newspapers, churches, trade unions and political parties, may be able to rely directly on at least some of the Convention rights. Pressure groups are not necessarily excluded, provided that, in common with individual applicants, they can demonstrate a reasonable likelihood that the measure complained of will be or was applied to them or their members, and provided they have authority to act on behalf of their members, who must be identified.[215] The test applied by the Strasbourg Court in determining the scope of art.34 has been to ask whether the applicant was directly affected by the act or omission that is complained of. It is not necessary to show some financial loss or prejudice: that goes to the later question of just satisfaction and is irrelevant to the necessarily prior question of status as a victim.[216] So while the test of victimhood is narrower than the English test of "sufficient interest" it appears to be close to, although not absolutely coterminous with, the test introduced in Scotland by the Supreme Court in *AXA General Insurance Co Ltd v Lord* Advocate, which requires a petitioner to show that he or she is directly affected by a decision.[217]

But it should not be supposed that an active role for pressure groups in human rights litigation is excluded by the Human Rights Act. In Scotland and England alike it is open to them to fund, if not front, test cases in the human rights arena. More importantly, changes have been made to the rules of court north and south of the border to facilitate third party interventions in judicial review proceedings, whether or not involving human rights.[218] Rule 58.8A of the Rules of the Court of Session[219] provides that a person who is not directly affected by any issue raised in a petition for judicial review may nevertheless apply to the court for leave to intervene in the petition or in an appeal connected therewith. Where leave is granted, an intervention will normally take the form of a written submission, lodged with the court and copied to the parties, not exceeding 5,000 words in length, but the court may exceptionally allow longer written submissions to be made and may direct that it wishes to hear oral submissions from the intervener.[220] The Inner House has, however, adopted a very narrow reading of this rule that is unlikely to encourage applications (at appellate level at least).[221]

---

214 *Aston Cantlow and Wilmcote with Billesley Parochial Church Council v Wallbank* [2003] UKHL 37; [2004] 1 A.C. 546, per Lord Hope of Craighead at [46]. So, for example, a Health Board cannot be a "victim" (and thus cannot invoke art.6 if it is prosecuted): *Grampian University Hospitals NHS Trust v Napier*, 2004 J.C. 117.

215 See *Norris v Ireland* (1986) 8 E.H.R.R. CO75; and contrast *Open Door Counselling Ltd v Ireland* (1992) 15 E.H.R.R. 244.

216 *Ilhan v Turkey* (2002) 34 E.H.R.R. 36; *JM v United Kingdom* (2011) 53 E.H.R.R. 6.

217 *AXA General Insurance Co Ltd v Lord Advocate* [2011] UKSC 46; 2012 S.C. (U.K.S.C.) 122, per Lord Hope of Craighead at [63].

218 The rules of the European Court of Human Rights make comparable provision for public interest interventions.

219 Inserted by Act of Sederunt (Rules of the Court of Session Amendment No.5) (Public Interest Intervention in Judicial Review) 2000 (SSI 2000/317).

220 For the merits and demerits of "public interest" interventions, see S. Fredman, "Scepticism under Scrutiny" in T. Campbell, K.D. Ewing and A. Tomkins (eds), *Sceptical Essays on Human Rights* (Oxford: Oxford University Press, 2001), Ch.11; R. Charteris, "Intervention—in the Public Interest?", 2000 S.L.T. (News) 87.

221 *Sustainable Shetland v The Scottish Ministers* [2013] CSIH 116.

Proceedings under s.7(1) of the Human Rights Act must be commenced within one year of the date on which the act complained of took place.[222] That period is subject to any stricter time limit in relation to the procedures in question and so the year that is allowed in the Human Rights Act is reduced to three-months where proceedings are brought by way of judicial review.[223] There is, however, a discretion to extend the period where the court considers it equitable to do so in all the circumstances.[224] It is yet to be decided when time commences in relation to a continuing act, but it has been suggested, obiter, that it would run from the date on which the breach ended.[225] But a generous view should be taken to assessing the date on which the act complained of took place. In *O'Connor v Bar Standards Board*, the question was whether the prosecution of disciplinary proceedings was a single, continuing, act or a series of individual decisions (each of which would be subject to its own one-year time limit). In giving the judgment of the Supreme Court, Lord Lloyd-Jones explained the proper approach to s.7(5)(a) of the Human Rights Act: 11–24

> "The expression 'the date on which the act complained of took place' is apt to address a single event. However, the provision should not be read narrowly. There will be many situations in which the conduct which gives rise to the infringement of a Convention right will not be an instantaneous act but a course of conduct. The words of section 7(5)(a) should be given a meaning which enables them to apply to a continuing act of alleged incompatibility. While it is correct that section 7(5)(b) may often empower a court to grant an extension of time to bring proceedings in respect of a course of conduct which has extended over a period of longer than a year, leaving a claimant to have recourse to such a discretionary remedy is inappropriate. It cannot justify limiting the scope of section 7(5)(a). The primary provision in 7(5)(a) must be capable of providing an effective and workable rule for situations where the infringement arises from a course of conduct."[226]

It is clear, then, that the court should not lightly find that a claim has been brought out of time where the initial offending act gave rise to a continuing consequence.[227]

Where, in proceedings under s.7(1)(a) or (b) of the Human Rights Act, the court finds that the public authority respondent is acting, or proposes to act, in a manner made unlawful by s.6(1), it may grant "such relief or remedy, or make such order, within its powers as it considers just and appropriate".[228] In the context of judicial review, the Court of Session may make any order that could be made if sought in any action or petition, including an order for reduction, declarator, suspension, interdict, implement, restitution, payment (whether of

---

222 Human Rights Act 1998 s.7(5).

223 On the time-limits for judicial review, see paras 14–14—14–20, below.

224 Human Rights Act 1998 s.7(5)(b).

225 *A v Essex CC* [2010] UKSC 33; [2011] 1 A.C. 280, per Baroness Hale of Richmond at [113]. That would be consistent with what Lord Hope suggested in *Somerville v Scottish Ministers* [2007] UKHL 44; 2008 S.C. (H.L.) 45 at [51]. Lord Hope's comments in *Somerville* were recently approved by the Supreme Court in *O'Connor v Bar Standards Board* [2017] UKSC 78; [2017] 1 W.L.R. 4833 at [30].

226 *O'Connor v Bar Standards Board* [2017] UKSC 78; [2017] 1 W.L.R. 4833 at [23].

227 But note the caveat at [31] of the judgment, that basing a claim on a failure to act (e.g. a failure to reverse what is said to be the offending act) is unlikely attract sympathy as it could readily be used to circumvent the entire limitation scheme.

228 Human Rights Act 1998 s.8(1).

damages or otherwise) and any interim order.[229] It is now clear that s.21 of the Crown Proceedings Act 1947, which excludes the remedies of interdict and implement against the Crown (including, by virtue of Sch.8 to the Scotland Act 1998, the Scottish Ministers) in "civil proceedings", does not prevent the grant of either remedy in the exercise of the supervisory jurisdiction of the Court of Session on an application for judicial review.[230]

11–25 Section 8(2) of the Human Rights Act provides that damages may be awarded by a court having power to award damages or order the payment of compensation where a breach of the Convention rights is established.[231] But damages may only be awarded where such an award would be "just and appropriate": violation of one's Convention rights alone will not necessarily be sufficient.[232] Moreover, in deciding whether an award of damages is necessary to afford just satisfaction to the applicant, the court is required by s.8(3)(b) to consider the consequences of the award, which is likely to be regarded as calling attention to the risks of opening the floodgates to hundreds of other potential claims. Here as elsewhere, the court must take into account the principles applied by the European Court of Human Rights in deciding whether to award damages and, if so, in what amount. But the jurisprudence of the court in this respect has been justly criticised as inconsistent, opaque and premised upon unarticulated assumptions about the "value" of different types of application.[233] In their joint report on damages under the Human Rights Act, the Law Commission and Scottish Law Commission accepted that when the court awards damages, it seeks to restore the applicant to the position they would have been in but for the breach complained of.[234] But they were driven to remark upon the lack of principle in the case law of the court on the question of monetary redress. The report concluded that the entry into force of the Human Rights Act would involve little change to the law of damages in either jurisdiction, in that:

> "where the courts . . . have established appropriate levels of compensation for particular types of loss in relation to claims in tort or delict, it would seem appropriate for the same rules to be used in relation to a claim under the Human Rights Act."

11–26 In the event, the courts have proceeded in a different manner. In *R. (on the application of Greenfield) v Secretary of State for the Home Department*, Lord Bingham explained that the proper place to look for guidance on the appropriate level of damages was Strasbourg, not domestic authorities:

---

[229] Rules of the Court of Session r.58.13.

[230] *Davidson v Scottish Ministers* [2005] UKHL 74; 2006 S.C. (H.L.) 41. On the Crown Proceedings Act 1947, see para.7–09, above.

[231] Where damages are sought, that can be done by means of an ordinary action in the sheriff court: *Ruddy v Chief Constable, Strathclyde Police* [2012] UKSC 57; 2013 S.C. (U.K.S.C.) 126. On damages under the Human Rights Act generally, see Wadham et al, *Blackstone's Guide to the Human Rights Act 1998* (2015), paras 4.54–4.71.

[232] M. Amos, "Damages for Breach of the Human Rights Act 1998" [1999] E.H.R.L.R. 178; R. Clayton, "Damage limitation: the Courts and Human Rights Act Damages" [2005] P.L. 429.

[233] A.R. Mowbray, "The European Court of Human Rights' Approach to Just Satisfaction" [1997] P.L. 647.

[234] Law Commission and the Scottish Law Commission, *Damages under the Human Rights Act 1998* (The Stationery Office, 2000), Law Com. No.266; Scot. Law Com. No.180, Cm.4853.

"They are not inflexibly bound by Strasbourg awards in what may be different cases. But they should not aim to be significantly more or less generous than the court might be expected to be, in a case where it was willing to make an award at all."[235]

As Lord Bingham pointed out, the purpose of the Human Rights Act was not to provide a victim with a better remedy at home than they could get in Strasbourg; it was to provide them with the same remedy. Furthermore, a finding of violation will be an important part of any just satisfaction and damages will not ordinarily be necessary to encourage high standards of compliance with the Convention.[236] More recently, the Supreme Court has offered guidance to lower courts when assessing damages in a Human Rights Act case:

"First, at the present stage of the development of the remedy of damages under section 8 of the 1998 Act, courts should be guided, following *Greenfield*, primarily by any clear and consistent practice of the European court. Secondly, it should be borne in mind that awards by the European court reflect the real value of money in the country in question. The most reliable guidance as to the quantum of awards under section 8 will therefore be awards made by the European court in comparable cases brought by applicants from the UK or other countries with a similar cost of living. Thirdly, courts should resolve disputed issues of fact in the usual way even if the European court, in similar circumstances, would not do so."[237]

The consequence has been that rather than awards of damages under the Human Rights Act reflecting common law awards for similar complaints, damages are rarely awarded and when they are, tend to be significantly lower than would be expected at common law.

Sections 12 and 13: the press and religion

Sections 12 and 13 of the Human Rights Act have been described as the only blemishes on an otherwise beautifully drafted Act.[238] Nevertheless, they merit brief consideration. Section 12 applies if the court is considering granting any relief that, if granted, might affect the exercise of the Convention right to freedom of expression.[239] This was a matter of considerable public interest a few years ago following a spate of high profile "super injunctions" concerning, mainly, high profile footballers. It was also a matter of much misunderstanding: the real complaint was the granting of anonymised injunctions (where the applicants 11–27

---

235 *R. (on the application of Greenfield) v Secretary of State for the Home Department* [2005] UKHL 14; [2005] 1 W.L.R. 673 at [19].

236 *R. (on the application of Greenfield) v Secretary of State for the Home Department* [2005] UKHL 14; [2005] 1 W.L.R. 673 at [19].

237 *R. (on the application of Sturnham) v Parole Board* [2013] UKSC 23; [2013] 2 A.C. 254, per Lord Reed at [39].

238 *Wilson v First County Trust Ltd (No.2)* [2003] UKHL 40; [2004] 1 A.C. 816, per Lord Rodger of Earlsferry at [179].

239 Human Rights Act 1998 s.12(1). "Relief" does not include a blanket order such as that available under s.11 of the Contempt of Court Act 1981. Where such a blanket order is made, s.12 is not engaged, as no "relief" is being granted. Common law fairness, however, requires that a person affected by such an order can apply promptly for its recall: *A v Secretary of State for the Home Department* [2014] UKSC 25; 2014 S.C. (U.K.S.C.) 151.

name was withheld).[240] If the person against whom such an order is to be granted is neither present nor represented, such an order cannot be granted unless the court is satisfied that the applicant has taken all reasonably practicable steps to notify that person or there are compelling reasons why they should not be notified.[241] It is only in exceptional circumstances that an interdict should be granted where advance notice has not been given.[242] In any case, s.12(3) requires the court to be satisfied that "the applicant is likely to establish that publication should not be allowed" before granting a pre-trial order. "Likely" does not mean "more likely than not"; it means the prospects of success are sufficiently favourable to justify making an order in all the circumstances of the case.[243] Finally, the court must have "particular regard" to the importance of the right to freedom of expression, taking into account the public interest in the material concerned and the extent to which it is already in the public domain. Regard should also be had to any relevant privacy code.[244] In reality, these provisions make little difference. In *PJS v News Group Newspapers Ltd*, the claimant, who had a high public profile and was married to a celebrity who was also in the public eye, sought an order preventing publication of a story alleging his involvement in an adulterous relationship with two other people.[245] Whilst an interim injunction was obtained in England and Wales, details were published in the United States, Canada and Scotland. That resulted in his name and details of the story circulating freely on social media and the internet. When the newspaper returned to the Court of Appeal seeking discharge of the injunction, that court held that s.12 "enhances the weight" to be given to art.10 and discharged the injunction.[246] The Supreme Court disagreed: "each right has equal potential force in principle, and the question is which way the balance falls in the light of the specific facts and considerations in a particular case".[247] Accordingly, s.12 confers no priority upon art.10. Furthermore, the Supreme Court made clear that it is important to understand what the public interest in publication was (and the public interest, as a matter of law, in publishing a story such as this "is at the

[240] For example, see *CTB v News Group Newspapers Ltd* [2011] EWHC 1232 (QB). It also highlighted the territorial scope of an injunction/interdict: it applies within the jurisdiction of the court. That was significant in *CTB* as, whilst publication was restrained in England and Wales, the Glasgow-based *Sunday Herald* published the story anyway. More concerning was the Member of Parliament that, relying upon the privilege that attaches to statements made in Parliament, disclosed the identity of *CTB* in the House of Commons and thus thwarted the order that the court had been persuaded to grant having heard argument from both parties (see: P. Johnson, "What can the press really say? Contempt of court and the reporting of parliamentary proceedings" [2012] P.L. 491).

[241] Human Rights Act 1998 s.12(2).

[242] Committee on Super-Injunctions, *Report of the Committee on Super-Injunctions: Super-Injunctions, Anonymised Injunctions and Open Justice* (The Stationery Office, 2011), para.3.22.

[243] *Cream Holdings Ltd v Banerjee* [2004] UKHL 44; [2005] 1 A.C. 253. This approach was designed to give the court sufficient flexibility in cases where, for example, the consequences of disclosure may be particularly grave (per Lord Nicholls of Birkenhead at [22]).

[244] Human Rights Act 1998 s.12(4).

[245] *PJS v News Group Newspapers Ltd* [2016] UKSC 26; [2016] A.C. 1081. For a general discussion of this case, see: J. Rowbottom, *Holding back the tide: privacy injunctions and the digital media* (2017) 133 L.Q.R. 177 and O Butler, *Confidentiality and intrusion: building storm defences rather than trying to hold back the tide* [2016] CLJ 452.

[246] [2016] EWCA Civ 393; [2016] Fam. Law 962 at [40] (Jackson LJ).

[247] *PJS v News Group Newspapers Ltd* [2016] UKSC 26; [2016] A.C. 1081 at [51] (Lord Neuberger).

bottom end of the spectrum of importance").[248] Finally, the effect upon the family, in particular the children, of the claimant was a legitimate consideration (which had been given insufficient weight).[249] The result of all that is whatever s.12 says, it offers no priority to art.10 in practice.

Section 13 requires that "particular regard" be had to the Convention right of freedom of thought, conscience and religion (art.9) if a court's determination "might affect the exercise by a religious organisation (itself or its members collectively)" of that right.[250] Born out of a fear that the Human Rights Act may undermine the ability of the church to refuse to marry same sex couples,[251] this provision appears to have even less significance than s.12. Under the Convention, where art.9 is engaged, any restriction on that right would have to be justified under the Convention. Consequently, s.13 does not give art.9 any greater weight than it already had.[252]

The role of the courts in human rights litigation

The Human Rights Act has given the courts, in particular the Supreme Court (and the House of Lords before it), a much higher profile and has required it to intervene on matters that are at times the subject of considerable political controversy. These issues have ranged from the legality of the legislative and executive response to the threats presented in the post-9/11 world to the extent to which the government owe duties under the Human Rights Act to servicemen and women operating in a combat environment. The court's decisions have inevitably been controversial. Often cases require the court to balance competing interests and to assess the proportionality of any interference with a person or group's Convention rights. Proportionality as a concept was not introduced by the Human Rights Act, but it is a prominent feature in many decisions under the Act. Its application was recently explained by Lord Reed in *Bank Mellat v HM Treasury (No.2)*.[253] The passage merits repetition in full: **11–28**

> "An assessment of proportionality inevitably involves a value judgment at the stage at which a balance has to be struck between the importance of the objective pursued and the value of the right intruded upon. The principle does not however entitle the courts simply to substitute their own assessment for that of the decision-maker. As I have noted, the intensity of review under EU law and the Convention varies according to the nature of the right at stake and the context in which the interference occurs. Those are not however the only relevant factors. One important factor in relation to the Convention is that the Strasbourg court recognises that it may be less well placed than a national court to decide whether an appropriate balance has been struck in the particular national context. For that reason, in the Convention case law

---

[248] *PJS v News Group Newspapers Ltd* [2016] UKSC 26; [2016] A.C. 1081 at [24] (Lord Neuberger) and [52] (Lord Mance).

[249] *PJS v News Group Newspapers Ltd* [2016] UKSC 26; [2016] A.C. 1081 at [36] (Lord Mance); [53] (Lord Neuberger) and [72]–[78] (Lady Hale).

[250] Human Rights Act 1998 s.13(1).

[251] No person can be compelled to perform the marriage of a same sex couple: Marriage (Same Sex Couples) Act 2013 s.2.

[252] *R. (on the application of Amicus) v Secretary of State for Trade and Industry* [2004] EWHC 860 (Admin) at [41]. See the recent discussion by the Sheriff in *Apprentice Boys of Derry, Bridgeton v Glasgow City Council*, 2019 S.L.T. (Sh. Ct) 317 at [88]–[90].

[253] *Bank Mellat v HM Treasury (No.2)* [2013] UKSC 39; [2014] A.C. 700.

the principle of proportionality is indissolubly linked to the concept of the margin of appreciation. That concept does not apply in the same way at the national level, where the degree of restraint practised by courts in applying the principle of proportionality, and the extent to which they will respect the judgment of the primary decision maker, will depend on the context, and will in part reflect national traditions and institutional culture. For these reasons, the approach adopted to proportionality at the national level cannot simply mirror that of the Strasbourg court."[254]

Lord Reed went on to set out the structured approach that should be adopted by the court when it is called upon to make an assessment of the proportionality of a particular measure:

"...[I]t is necessary to determine (1) whether the objective of the measure is sufficiently important to justify the limitation of a protected right, (2) whether the measure is rationally connected to the objective, (3) whether a less intrusive measure could have been used without unacceptably compromising the achievement of the objective, and (4) whether, balancing the severity of the measure's effects on the rights of the person to whom it applies against the importance of the objective, to the extent that the measure will contribute to its achievement, the former outweighs the latter."[255]

The fourth question in particular appears apt to further politicise the court's role. Assessing whether the restriction on the individual's Convention rights is outweighed by the importance of the objective that is sought will often be a very political, and controversial, question.

11–29 Mention is made by Lord Reed of the related issue of the "margin of appreciation" (or "degree of respect") to be afforded by the courts to the legislature and executive. That raises the question as to when the court should decline to decide a point and hold that another branch of government is better placed or better qualified to make the assessment. In *R. (on the application of Countryside Alliance) v Attorney General* (which was a challenge to the hunting bans), Lord Bingham made the point this way:

"The democratic process is liable to be subverted if, on a question of moral and political judgment opponents of the Act achieve through the courts what they could not achieve in Parliament."[256]

---

[254] *Bank Mellat v HM Treasury (No.2)* [2013] UKSC 39; [2014] A.C. 700 at [71]. Although Lord Reed was dissenting on the application of the test in that particular case, his analysis of the concept of proportionality was endorsed by the majority: per Lord Sumption at [20]. It has subsequently been followed by the Supreme Court: *Gaughran v Chief Constable of the Police Service of Northern Ireland* [2015] UKSC 29; [2015] 2 W.L.R. 1303.

[255] *Bank Mellat v HM Treasury (No.2)* [2013] UKSC 39; [2014] A.C. 700 at [74]; see also Lord Sumption at [20]. In that analysis Lord Reed drew on Lord Clyde's seminal discussion of proportionality in *de Freitas v Permanent Secretary of Ministry of Agriculture, Fisheries, Land and Housing* [1999] 1 A.C. 69 at [80] and Dickson CJ's discussion in the Canadian Supreme Court in *R. v Oakes* [1986] 1 S.C.R. 103.

[256] *R. (on the application of Countryside Alliance) v Attorney General* [2007] UKHL 52; [2008] 1 A.C. 719 at [45]. See also *AXA General Insurance Co Ltd v Lord Advocate* [2011] UKSC 46; 2012 S.C. (U.K.S.C.) 122, per Lord Hope at [49] where speaking of the Scottish Parliament (but the point is more general) he said: "While the judges, who are not elected, are best placed to protect the rights of the individual, including those who are ignored or despised by the majority, the elected members of a legislature of this kind are best placed to judge what is in the country's best interests as a whole."

The balance is always a difficult one to strike, as Lord Brown's dissent in the same case demonstrates.[257] Questions of law, no matter how controversial, are always matters for the court. As Lord Hoffmann has explained:

> "In a society based upon the rule of law and the separation of powers, it is necessary to decide which branch of government has in any particular instance the decision-making power and what the legal limits of that power are. That is a question of law and must therefore be decided by the courts.
>
> This means that the courts themselves often have to decide the limits of their own decision-making power. That is inevitable. But it does not mean that their allocation of decision-making power to the other branches of government is a matter of courtesy or deference. The principles upon which decision-making powers are allocated are principles of law. The courts are the independent branch of government and the legislature and executive are, directly and indirectly respectively, the elected branches of government. Independence makes the courts more suited to deciding some kinds of questions and being elected makes the legislature or executive more suited to deciding others. The allocation of these decision-making responsibilities is based upon recognised principles. The principle that the independence of the courts is necessary for a proper decision of disputed legal rights or claims of violation of human rights is a legal principle. It is reflected in article 6 of the Convention. On the other hand, the principle that majority approval is necessary for a proper decision on policy or allocation of resources is also a legal principle. Likewise, when a court decides that a decision is within the proper competence of the legislature or executive, it is not showing deference. It is deciding the law."[258]

Identification of questions of law, as distinct from questions of policy lying within the proper province of legislative or executive action, is not a value-neutral matter, and it might appear that, as the judges have gained confidence in the exercise of a human rights jurisdiction, there has been a greater readiness to identify as legal questions issues that would once have fallen without question into the "political" sphere. In *Secretary of State for the Home Department v Rehman*, a case concerning the Secretary of State's decision that it was "conducive to the public good" to deport a person because of their involvement with a group associated with terrorist activities in Kashmir, Lord Hoffmann added a postscript to his speech (that was delivered shortly after the 9/11 attacks), explaining that those attacks were:

> "... a reminder that in matters of national security, the cost of failure can be high. This seems to me to underline the need for the judicial arm of government to respect the decisions of ministers of the Crown on the question of whether support for terrorist activities in a foreign country constitutes a threat to national security. It is not only that the executive has access to special information and expertise in these matters. It is also that such decisions, with serious potential results for the community, require a legitimacy which can be conferred only by entrusting them to persons responsible to the community through the democratic process. If the people

---

[257] *R. (on the application of Countryside Alliance) v Attorney General* [2007] UKHL 52; [2008] 1 A.C. 719 at [157]–[159].

[258] *R. (on the application of ProLife Alliance) v British Broadcasting Corp* [2003] UKHL 23; [2004] 1 A.C. 185 at [75]–[76].

> are to accept the consequences of such decisions, they must be made by persons whom the people have elected and whom they can remove."[259]

Lord Hoffmann's tone had changed by the time he delivered his speech in the *A v Secretary of State for the Home Department* case.[260] That case is discussed more fully in Ch.13, below. For now it is enough to note that it concerned the UK Government's decision to derogate from art.5 of the Convention (right to liberty) in the aftermath of 9/11, claiming there to be a "threat to the life of the nation" (no other signatory to the Convention took that view). Parliament then enacted provision for the detention of foreign terrorist suspects without trial and without limit of time.[261] Nine people detained under this provision challenged the lawfulness of their detention. The case came before a panel of nine Law Lords. The first question for the House of Lords was whether there was a "threat to the life of the nation". By a majority of 8:1, the House of Lords held that to be an assessment that was pre-eminently political and on which great weight should be accorded to the judgment of the executive and of Parliament and that the court should not interfere with it.[262] Lord Hoffmann, in a short speech that deserves to be read in full, dissented. "Nothing could be more antithetical to the instincts and traditions of the people of the United Kingdom" than the power that Parliament had conferred.[263] But he disagreed with his colleagues on the prior question of the threat faced by the UK:

> "This is a nation which has been tested in adversity, which has survived physical destruction and catastrophic loss of life. I do not underestimate the ability of fanatical groups of terrorists to kill and destroy, but they do not threaten the life of the nation. Whether we would survive Hitler hung in the balance, but there is no doubt that we shall survive Al-Qaeda. The Spanish people have not said that what happened in Madrid, hideous crime as it was, threatened the life of their nation. Their legendary pride would not allow it. Terrorist violence, serious as it is, does not threaten our institutions of government or our existence as a civil community."[264]

The other members of the panel (Lord Walker dissenting; Lord Hoffmann offered no view on the point) went on to quash the derogation on the basis it breached art.14, discriminating as it did so as only to apply to foreign nationals. The offending provision was, as a result, declared incompatible with arts 5 and 14 of the Convention. As we have already seen, a declaration under s.4 of the Human Rights Act did not assist the appellants secure their release. But Lord Hoffmann's dissent show how attitudes to the issue of deference can change and how significant a role the courts can now play.[265]

---

[259] *Secretary of State for the Home Department v Rehman* [2001] UKHL 47; [2003] 1 A.C. 153 at [62].

[260] *A v Secretary of State for the Home Department* [2004] UKHL 56; [2005] 2 A.C. 68.

[261] Anti-Terrorism, Crime and Security Act 2001 s.23.

[262] See, for example, *A v Secretary of State for the Home Department* [2004] UKHL 56; [2005] 2 A.C. 68, per Lord Bingham at [27]–[29].

[263] *A v Secretary of State for the Home Department* [2004] UKHL 56; [2005] 2 A.C. 68 at [86].

[264] *A v Secretary of State for the Home Department* [2004] UKHL 56; [2005] 2 A.C. 68 at [96].

[265] The Government did not welcome the decision with the then Home Secretary reasserting Parliament's right to be arbiter of what was necessary for the security of the country. See, for example, "Law lords 'simply wrong', says Straw", *The Guardian* (17 December 2014), *http://www.theguardian.com/uk/2004/dec/17/terrorism.immigrationpolicy* [Accessed 18 June 2020]. The recent

THE FUTURE OF THE HUMAN RIGHTS ACT

In 2015 a Conservative Government was elected with a commitment to repeal the Human Rights Act and to replace it with a "British Bill of Rights". By 2019, the manifesto pledge was to "update" the Act. Neither are new ideas.[266] No firm proposals have been made at the time of writing but the manifesto pledged to "... update the Human Rights Act and administrative law to ensure that there is a proper balance between the rights of individuals, our vital national security and effective government".[267] **11–30**

Previously, the desire had been to "break the link" between the Strasbourg court and domestic courts.[268] Whether that would be envisaged in any "update" is unknown. As we have seen, however, the Human Rights Act requires only that domestic courts "take account of" Strasbourg jurisprudence. Decisions of that court are not binding and the Supreme Court can, if appropriate, decline to follow them.[269] Domestic jurisprudence prescribes the circumstances in which it is appropriate to take that course (the *Ullah* principle), not the Convention or the Strasbourg Court. The courts have also repeatedly stressed that what the Human Rights Act created were *domestic* rights and that, before resort was had to Convention rights, the ordinary protections of the common law should be considered for there the answer will often be found. As Lord Reed explained in *R. (on the application of Osborn) v Parole Board*:

> "The values underlying both the Convention *and our own constitution* require that Convention rights should be protected by a detailed body of domestic law ... The Human Rights Act 1998 has however given domestic effect, for the purposes of that Act, to the guarantees described as Convention rights ... The importance of the Act is unquestionable. It does not however supersede the protection of human rights under the common law or statute, or create a discrete body of law based on the judgments of the European court. *Human rights continue to be protected by domestic law*, interpreted and developed in accordance with the Act when appropriate."[270]

The emphasis placed on the domestic (that is the common law) protection for fundamental rights suggests that the repeal or "updating" of the Human Rights Act may make little practical difference.

Substantial updating, let alone repeal, of the Human Rights Act would be far from straightforward. As we have seen when looking at the competences of the Scottish Parliament and Scottish Government, Convention rights (a term introduced by the Human Rights Act) are central to delimiting the competences of the devolved bodies. Significant change would also threaten to drive another **11–31**

decision in *R. (on the application of Nicklinson) v Ministry of Justice* [2014] UKSC 38; [2014] 3 W.L.R. 200 provides another illustration, this time not in the field of national security but assisted suicide, of the Justices having to wrestle with essentially moral issues.

[266] See, for example, Lord Bingham's defence of the Human Rights Act in 2010 when again the prospect of repeal appeared to be gathering political momentum: T. Bingham, "The Human Rights Act" [2010] E.H.R.L.R. 568.

[267] Conservative Party Manifesto (2019), p.48.

[268] Conservative Party Manifesto (2015), p.60.

[269] *R. v Horncastle* [2009] UKSC 14; [2010] 2 A.C. 373.

[270] *R. (on the application of Osborn) v Parole Board* [2013] UKSC 61; [2014] A.C. 1115 at [56]–[57] (emphasis added).

wedge between the Scottish and UK Governments, with the former apparently content with the current Convention rights system (reflected, as it was, in the draft constitution for an independent Scotland that was published in advance of the 2014 referendum). The Scottish Government has stated its continuing support for the Act, which makes it unlikely that the Scottish Parliament would pass a legislative consent motion agreeing to the repeal of the Human Rights Act. By convention, such a motion is required where Westminster proposes to legislate on a devolved matter or alter the terms of the devolution statutes.[271] Whilst the Human Rights Act is reserved (Sch.4 of the Scotland Act 1998), its substantial updating would likely require amendment of the Scotland Act 1998. Westminster may retain the legislative competence to enact such measures without the consent of the Scottish Parliament (s.28(7) of the Scotland Act 1998), so the refusal of the Scottish Parliament to pass a legislative consent motion would not present a legal bar to the repeal of the Human Rights Act. It would, however, present a significant political problem should the UK Government proceed to amend the terms of the devolution settlement against the wishes of the Scottish Parliament. Similar, if not more acute, problems arise in Northern Ireland where not only are Convention rights a feature of the devolved settlement, but the Belfast Agreement (which underpins much of the peace process) appears to bind the UK (as a matter of international law) to:

> "complete incorporation into Northern Ireland law of the European Convention on Human Rights (ECHR), with direct access to the courts, and remedies for breach of the Convention, including power for the courts to overrule Assembly legislation on grounds of inconsistency."[272]

If substantial updating of the Human Rights Act will require any part of that agreement to be revisited, it is certain to be a long and difficult process.

For now, however, the Human Rights Act remains in full force and we await the new government's proposals as to how their manifesto pledge will be implemented. While that is being considered, it is helpful to restate the two questions Lord Bingham asked some years ago of critics of the Human Rights Act: (a) which of the rights contained in the Act should be discarded? and (b) would you rather live in a country in which these rights were not protected by law?[273]

---

[271] Although, as the Brexit process illustrated, and as the Supreme Court confirmed in *Miller (No.1)*, the absent of legislative consent from the Scottish Parliament in no way prevents the Westminster Parliament from legislating as it wishes.

[272] Belfast Agreement, "Rights, Safeguards and Equality of Opportunity: Human Rights" (10 April 1998), para.2.

[273] T. Bingham, *The Rule of Law* (London: Allen Lane, 2010), p.84. Chapter 7 in its entirety should be read by anyone engaging in the debate on the future of the Human Rights Act.

CHAPTER 12

Citizen and the State

INTRODUCTION

Most citizens will live their lives in blissful ignorance of many of the other topics covered in this book. That there is a parliament, a government and courts will be known to them but they will rarely, if ever, have caused to enquire into how they operate and how they relate to each other. Few, if any, voters will care about the detail of electoral law beyond knowing how to vote in the system that is then in use and having a general confidence that the system is "fair". The Scottish independence referendum perhaps was an exception to this and represented an unprecedented engagement in a host of constitutional issues. But, as we saw earlier, constitutional law is not just about institutions and how they operate. It is also about the interaction between the citizen and the state, the governed and the governors. This is the level of constitutional law that is likely to engage most citizens. Granted that most law-abiding citizens may not take too close an interest in the police powers of arrest and detention, but most will have a view on when the state can monitor their communications or access their personal information. Similarly, many citizens will never take part in a public march or protest but will value the fact that such demonstrations of public opinion are permitted and will have a view on how they are policed. So in this chapter we focus on the different ways in which the citizen interacts with the state and the manner in which state power can (or should) be exercised over its citizens. This involves a review of a number of different topics: state powers of surveillance; police powers of arrest, detention, search and questioning; maintenance of public order; and the right to protest. But we will start with a brief comment on two issues that remain topical: immigration and access to information.[1] **12–01**

CITIZENSHIP

Who can come into the country, for how long and on what terms have been especially controversial questions in recent years. In particular, EU rules concerning free movement of people, which resulted in EU citizens[2] being exempt from the normal immigration rules, have proved especially controversial during the 2016 referendum campaign. The rules that regulate immigration and **12–02**

[1] From that list of issues, it will be obvious that a comprehensive review of any, let alone all, of those topics is beyond the scope of this book. Specialist texts will be referenced where appropriate.
[2] As well as members of the EEA States (Iceland, Liechtenstein, Norway and Switzerland).

asylum are now vast and its capacity to generate jurisprudence appears boundless.[3] We are only going to touch upon one small area: given constitutional law concerns the relationship between the state and its citizens, how does one acquire citizenship of the UK?[4]

The need for rules on citizenship really arises as a consequence of international law governing states. As a matter of public international law, it is for each state to determine its own rules on who are its citizens and nationals.[5] Since the entry into force of the British Nationality Act 1981 on 1 January 1983, there have been five means by which British nationality can be acquired: birth or adoption; by descent; registration; and naturalisation. A child born in the UK (which includes, for these purposes, the Channel Islands and the Isle of Man) or, since 2002, in a British Overseas Territory, qualifies for British citizenship if: (a) the parents are married and at least one is a British citizen or settled in the UK; (b) the parents are unmarried, but the mother, at least, is a British citizen or settled in the UK; or (c) at the time of birth one or both of the parents is a member of the armed forces.[6] The common law rule that birth in the UK was in itself sufficient to acquire citizenship was abolished by the 1981 Act.[7] "Settled" means "ordinarily resident" and not subject to any restriction under the Immigration Act 1971 on the period for which one may remain in the UK.[8] A person aged under 18 who is not a British citizen and is adopted in the UK becomes a British citizen on adoption if one or both of the adoptive parents is a British citizen. A child born outside the UK acquires British citizenship by descent if at least one parent is a British citizen (otherwise than by descent) or is abroad in the service of the Crown. The rules for acquiring citizenship through registration or naturalisation are complex and not infrequently changed. Reference should be made to specialist texts.

Citizenship carries with it a number of significant consequences. In some countries (but not now in the UK) it can render you bound to a period of national service. Citizenship is often a prerequisite to owning land, gaining employment, entering the civil service or obtaining certain political rights. "Aliens"[9] are subject to a number of restrictions (such as voting rights, membership of Parliament and appointment to civil or military office). In day-to-day life the most practical consequence of citizenship is the ability to obtain a British passport. It is a prerequisite to acquiring a British passport that the applicant has citizenship. A passport is not only important in allowing an individual to travel,[10]

---

[3] For further details, see M. Phelan and M.J. Gillespie, *Immigration Law Handbook*, 9th edn (Oxford: Oxford University Press, 2015).

[4] For a detailed accounts, see L. Fransman, *British Nationality Law*, 3rd edn (Haywards Heath: Bloomsbury Professional, 2011); *Macdonald's Immigration Law and Practice*, edited by I.A. Macdonald and R. Toal, 9th edn (London: Lexis Nexis, 2014).

[5] I. Brownlie, *Principles of Public International Law*, 7th edn (Oxford: Oxford University Press, 2008), pp.383–385.

[6] Borders, Citizenship and Immigration Act 2009 s.42.

[7] British Nationality Act 1981 s.1.

[8] See generally s.50 of the 1981 Act, as amended by the Nationality, Immigration and Asylum Act 2002.

[9] That is people who are not citizens of the Commonwealth or the Republic of Ireland nor a British protected person (see British Nationality Act 1981 s.50).

[10] Entering and leaving the UK is now a statutory entitlement for those that have a right of abode in the UK: Immigration Act 1971 s.1.

but also to obtain consular protection if necessary and to evidence their right of abode in the UK when re-entry is sought.[11] Issue, or refusal, of a passport is a prerogative power but is subject to judicial review.[12] If the Secretary of State refuses to issue a passport, cogent reasons must be provided in light of the obvious consequences such a decision has for a person's ability to travel.[13]

ACCESS TO INFORMATION[14]

"Information", explained Lord Mance, "is the key to sound decision-making, to accountability and development; it underpins democracy and assists in combatting poverty, oppression, corruption, prejudice and inefficiency."[15] But there are two sides to the access to information coin: freedom of information, which allows the public access to official information, and official secrets, which prevents the public access to official information. Governments have sought to protect "official" information for centuries, but a public right of access to such information is a relatively new, and important, development: **12–03**

> "Modern democratic government means government of the people by the people for the people. But there can be no government by the people if they are ignorant of the issues to be resolved, the arguments for and against different solutions and the facts underlying those arguments. The business of government is not an activity about which only those professionally engaged are entitled to receive information and express opinions. It is, or should be, a participatory process. But there can be no assurance that government is carried out for the people unless the facts are made known, the issues publicly ventilated. Sometimes, inevitably, those involved in the conduct of government, as in any other walk of life, are guilty of error, incompetence, misbehaviour, dereliction of duty, even dishonesty and malpractice. Those concerned may very strongly wish that the facts relating to such matters are not made public. Publicity may reflect discredit on them or their predecessors. It may embarrass the authorities. It may impede the process of administration. Experience however shows, in this country and elsewhere, that publicity is a powerful disinfectant. Where abuses are exposed, they can be remedied. Even where abuses have already been remedied, the public may be entitled to know that they occurred. The role of the press in exposing abuses and miscarriages of justice has been a potent and honourable one. But the press cannot expose that of which it is denied knowledge."[16]

Freedom of information legislation was introduced by the Blair Government, much to the regret of the Prime Minister.[17] The Freedom of Information Act 2000 **12–04**

---

[11] Immigration Act 1971 s.3(9).

[12] *R. v Secretary of State for Foreign and Commonwealth Affairs, Ex p. Everett* [1989] Q.B. 811 CA (Civ Div). On prerogative powers, see Ch.7, above.

[13] *R. (on the application of Ali) v Secretary of State for the Home Department* [2012] EWHC 3379 (Admin); *R. (on the application of Fayad) v Secretary of State for the Home Department* [2014] EWHC 2556 (Admin).

[14] See P. Birkinshaw, "Information: public access, protecting privacy and surveillance" in J.L. Jowell and C. O'Cinneide (eds), *The Changing Constitution*, 9th edn (Oxford: Oxford University Press, 2019), Ch.13.

[15] *Kennedy v Charity Commission* [2014] UKSC 20; [2015] A.C. 455 at [1].

[16] *R. v Shayler* [2002] UKHL 11; [2003] 1 A.C. 247, per Lord Bingham of Cornhill at [21].

[17] T. Blair, *A Journey* (London: Hutchinson, 2010), p.516

and the Freedom of Information (Scotland) Act 2002 are the legislative instruments that secure a general right of access to information held by public bodies in Scotland with the general purpose of creating openness in government.[18] They make broadly similar provision, with the 2000 Act relating to reserved functions and the 2002 Act relating to devolved functions. Both Acts came fully into effect on 1 January 2005. Since then, a number of stories owe their origins to this legislation: from the MPs expenses scandal in 2009, to how much it costs to police the Old Firm match, the public, and especially the press, have obtained hitherto unthinkable access to official documents.[19] As Lord Bingham explained, knowledge of the facts is a necessary prerequisite to holding the government to account (and knowing when, and for what, to hold them to account). For a detailed discussion of the operation of this legislation, reference should be made to specialist texts,[20] but for present purposes it is worth noting some of the key provisions of the legislation[21]:

1) Section 1 of the 2002 Act provides for a broad right to information held by Scottish public authorities (s.1(1)). A broad range of bodies (from the Scottish Ministers and the Parliament to the various health boards to a range of quangos) fall within the meaning of "Scottish public authority" (s.3; Sch.1).
2) That general entitlement to information is promptly qualified by a range of exemptions that are set out in Pt 2 of the Act. The production of information that would compromise national security (s.31), law enforcement (s.35), relations between the governments of the United Kingdom (s.28) or undermine the convention of the collective responsibility of the Scottish Ministers (s.30), to take a few examples, can be resisted. The limits of these exemptions are both important and controversial, with the court having recognised a general public interest in disclosure of information.[22] Provision is also made to allow repeated or vexatious requests to be refused (s.14).
3) The Scottish Information Commissioner ("the Commissioner") is responsible for promoting good practice by public authorities and enforcing the regime (s.43, Sch.2). Where a public authority refuses a request for information, an appeal lies to the Commissioner (s.47). If satisfied that the public authority ought to have provided the information requested, the Commissioner may issue an enforcement notice requiring the authority to take steps to comply with the request within a specified period (s.51). The First Minister has a limited right to veto an enforcement notice (s.52). Following the Supreme Court's decision in *R. (on the application of Evans)*

---

[18] *Beggs v Scottish Information Commissioner* [2015] CSIH 17; 2015 S.C. 520 at [26].

[19] Not every story has lived up to expectations: after a 10-year legal battle to obtain access to letters sent by Prince Charles to senior members of the government, culminating in the Supreme Court quashing the Attorney General's veto of the disclosure order (*R. (on the application of Evans) v Attorney General* [2015] UKSC 21; [2015] A.C. 1787), when the letters were finally released the only real question that was raised was why the government fought for so long to prevent that happening.

[20] For example, K. Dunion, *Freedom of Information in Scotland in Practice* (Dundee: Dundee University Press, 2012).

[21] The discussion that follows takes place under reference to the 2002 (Scottish) Act, but broadly equivalent provision is made under the 2000 Act.

[22] *Scottish Ministers v Scottish Information Commissioner* [2007] CSIH 8; 2007 S.C. 330 at [11].

v Attorney General, which dealt with the equivalent provision in the 2000 Act, any such veto will have limited use.[23] Failure to comply with an enforcement notice may be reported to the court, with the court empowered to treat any failure in the same way it would treat a contempt of court (s.53). An appeal, on a point of law, lies to the Court of Session against a determination by the Commissioner (s.56).[24]

On the other hand, there is the Official Secrets Act 1989. While the freedom of information legislation seeks to secure access to official documents, the Official Secrets Act has exactly the opposite objective. The 1989 Act is significantly narrower than its predecessor, s.2 of the Official Secrets Act 1911. That provision, however, had endured sustained and widespread criticism and it was increasingly difficult to enforce.[25] The 1989 Act replaced that provision and was intended to be more targeted. Its principal provisions are: **12–05**

1) The disclosure, without lawful authority, of any information relating to security and intelligence (s.1), defence (s.2) or international relations (s.3) is prohibited. An offence is committed by a member of the security and intelligence services, or any person who is notified that they are subject to the provisions of s.1 of the Act, by the simple act of disclosure (s.1(1)). A disclosure by a Crown servant or government contractor (defined in s.12) is an offence if it is a "damaging disclosure" (ss.1(3), 2(1) and 3(1)).
2) It is generally a defence to show that the accused did not know, and had no reasonable cause to believe, that the information disclosed related to security and intelligence, defence or international relations or, where applicable, had no reasonable cause to believe the disclosure would be damaging (ss.1(5), 2(3) and 3(4)).
3) A disclosure is "damaging" if it, as relevant: (i) damages, or would be likely to damage, the work of any part of the security services (s.1(4)); (ii) damages, or would be likely to damage, the capabilities of the armed forces or results in the loss of life or injury to members of the armed forces or serious damage to their equipment and/or installations, or endangers British interests abroad, including the safety of British citizens (s.2(2)); (iii) endangers, or would be likely to endanger, the interests of the UK abroad, seriously obstructs the promotion or protection by the UK of those interests or endangers the safety of UK citizens abroad (s.3(2)).
4) There is no defence available that any disclosure was in the public interest. To the extent that represents an interference with the art.10 right of freedom of expression, it is a justified interference (*R. v Shayler*).[26]

The 1989 Act, although narrower than its predecessor, still strikes at a wide range of material and covers a wide range of individuals. Prosecutions under the Act

---

[23] *R. (on the application of Evans) v Attorney General* [2015] UKSC 21; [2015] A.C. 1787.

[24] And from there, if necessary, to the Supreme Court. For example: *Common Services Agency v Scottish Information Commissioner* [2008] UKHL 47; 2008 S.C. (H.L.) 184 and *South Lanarkshire Council v Scottish Information Commissioner* [2013] UKSC 55; 2014 S.C. (U.K.S.C.) 1.

[25] For example, the jury's acquittal in *R. v Ponting* [1985] Crim. L.R. 318 in the face of a direction from the trial judge that effectively excluded the line of defence.

[26] *R. v Shayler* [2002] UKHL 11; [2003] 1 A.C. 247.

are, however, rare and hard to pursue successfully. Former members of the security services who wish to write and publish memoirs have to obtain permission to refer to information that would otherwise fall within the scope of the 1989 Act. The ordinary courts have no jurisdiction to judicially review (at least one founded on art.10 of the European Convention on Human Rights) a refusal to give such consent; jurisdiction belongs to the Investigatory Powers Tribunal.[27]

SURVEILLANCE[28]

12–06 The European Court of Human Rights has repeatedly made clear that an interference with protected rights will never be justifiable if it lacks a legal basis. The traditional premise of the common law, however, is that all is allowed except that which is specifically prohibited by law. The police as much as anybody else have had the benefit of this. What it meant in practice was that the police required no positive legal authority for their actions provided their actions did not amount to legal wrong. Hence in *Malone v United Kingdom*,[29] the claimant had no remedy before the domestic courts because the tapping of his telephone by the police was not unlawful, but he had a remedy before the Strasbourg Court because there was no positive legal basis for what the police had done.[30] Again in *R. v Khan*,[31] the entirety of the evidence against the accused consisted in tape recorded conversations obtained via a listening device installed by the police in the house of a suspect. Since the installation of the device was not unlawful, the trial judge ruled the evidence admissible and the accused was obliged to plead guilty. Again, the European Court found that the individual's right to respect for his private life under art.8 had been breached.[32]

The European Court of Human Rights first accepted surveillance techniques as constituting an interference with the rights protected by art.8 in *Klass v Germany*.[33] Any interference with that right must be, among other things,

---

[27] *R. (on the application of A) v Director of Establishments of the Security Service* [2009] UKSC 12; [2010] 2 A.C. 1.

[28] See generally *Renton and Brown's Criminal Procedure*, 6th edn (Edinburgh: W. Green), paras 5.21–5.29. For an overview and critique of recent developments, see: P. Birkinshaw, "Information: Public Access, protecting privacy and surveillance" in J. Jowell and C. O'Cinneide, *The Changing Constitution*, 9th edn (OUP, 2019).

[29] *Malone v United Kingdom* (1984) 7 E.H.R.R. 14.

[30] Telephone tapping was placed on a statutory footing by the Interception of Communications Act 1985, which was repealed and replaced by the Regulation of Investigatory Powers Act 2000.

[31] *R. v Khan (Sultan)* [1997] A.C. 558.

[32] *Khan v United Kingdom* (2000) 8 B.H.R.C. 310. Covert entry upon and interference with property by the police, Her Majesty's Revenue and Customs, the National Crime Squad and the National Criminal Intelligence Service was placed on a statutory footing by Pt III of the Police Act 1997. See also *Hewitt v United Kingdom* (1989) 67 D.R. 88, which exposed the absence of legal basis for secret surveillance activities and prompted the enactment of the Security Services Act 1989 and the Intelligence Services Act 1994; and *Govell v United Kingdom* (1997) 23 E.H.R.R. CD101, which exposed the absence of legal basis for intrusive surveillance activities and led to the enactment of the Regulation of Investigatory Powers Act 2000. In a number of respects, these powers have been supplemented by the anti-terrorist legislation considered in Ch.13, below (which, as there discussed, is not as strictly tailored to anti-terrorism as it might be).

[33] *Klass v Germany* (1978) 2 E.H.R.R. 214.

prescribed by law, which is to say that the act in question must have some basis in domestic law (not necessarily statutory) and be "accompanied by adequate and effective safeguards ... to protect against arbitrary interference".[34] In addition, the law must be sufficiently accessible and foreseeable, in the sense of being formulated with sufficient precision to enable one to foresee, with reasonable certainty, the consequences a given action may entail. This does not of course mean that potential subjects of surveillance require to be given advance warning of it, but the law must be sufficiently clear to give citizens:

> "an adequate indication of the circumstances in which and the conditions on which public authorities are empowered to resort to this secret and potentially dangerous interference with the right to respect for private life and correspondence."[35]

A statutory code that confers discretion on police officers is not necessarily inconsistent with the requirement of foreseeability, provided that the scope of the discretion and the manner of its exercise are prescribed with adequate clarity and provided that some form of ex post facto control is available.[36]

If surveillance activities are shown to have a legal basis in this sense, they then fall to be justified by reference to the countervailing public interests specified in art.8(2). Justification premised on the protection of national security or public safety is readily established in the jurisprudence of the court.[37] When considering whether surveillance (and other aspects of police activity) are necessary for the prevention of disorder and crime, the court looks to the seriousness of the interference with the protected right, the nature of the crime involved, and the presence or absence of a judicial warrant for the activity in question. Thus, an interference with privacy that could not be justified by reference to the public interest in preventing petty crime may well be justifiable where the relevant criminal activity is serious.[38] By the same token, where the extent of the interference is slight, the absence of prior judicial authorisation is unlikely to be fatal.

The Regulation of Investigatory Powers Act 2000[39] and its sister legislation in **12–07**
Scotland represented the most comprehensive attempt to date to place police intelligence on a proper statutory basis and to conform to the requirements of the Convention. The UK Act extends to Scotland, but in relation to the authorisation of surveillance activity, s.46 provides that no person may grant an authorisation if

---

[34] *Malone v United Kingdom* (1984) 7 E.H.R.R. 14 at 67 and 68.

[35] *Malone v United Kingdom* (1984) 7 E.H.R.R. 14 at 67. See also *Valenzuela Contreras v Spain* (1998) 28 E.H.R.R. 483 at 46, where the European Court of Human Rights sets out the minimum conditions to be met by a statutory code on telephone tapping.

[36] See *Silver v United Kingdom* (1983) 5 E.H.R.R. 347, where the court held that it was acceptable to limit the scope of discretionary powers, if not in the parent enactment itself, then in secondary legislation or guidance adopted under it.

[37] See, e.g. *Leander v Sweden* (1987) 9 E.H.R.R. 433, where the European Court of Human Rights found that internal terrorist activity amounted to a serious threat to national security, ample to justify the collection of information and maintenance of secret files on candidates for sensitive employment positions.

[38] Compare, for example, *McLeod v United Kingdom* (1998) 27 E.H.R.R. 493 and *Murray v United Kingdom* (1994) 19 E.H.R.R. 193.

[39] Regulation of Investigatory Powers Act 2000 ("RIPA 2000").

it appears that the proposed surveillance will take in place in Scotland.[40] In that case, the authorisation must be sought and granted under the Regulation of Investigatory Powers (Scotland) Act 2000 instead.[41]

The Regulation of Investigatory Powers (Scotland) Act 2000 is concerned only with covert surveillance,[42] of which there are three categories: directed surveillance; intrusive surveillance; and the conduct and use of covert human intelligence sources.[43] Directed surveillance is non-intrusive covert surveillance undertaken for the purposes of a specific investigation or operation, in a manner likely to result in obtaining private information about any person, whether or not they are the subject of the operation.[44] The term "private information" includes any information relating to the person's private and family life.[45] Intrusive surveillance is covert surveillance carried out in relation to anything taking place on residential premises or in any private vehicle,[46] which involves the presence of someone in the premises or vehicle, or which is carried out by means of a surveillance device.[47] Covert human intelligence sources are defined as persons who establish or maintain a personal or other relationship with another person for the covert purpose of facilitating the covert use of that relationship to obtain information or to provide access to information to another person.[48]

---

[40] Subject to RIPA 2000 s.46(2), which specifies the purposes for which an authorisation extending to Scotland may be granted under the UK Act. Such authorisations may be granted where necessary in the interests of national security or of the economic well-being of the UK, or on the application of, or to authorise conduct by, a member of either of the intelligence services (MI5 and MI6), Her Majesty's forces, the Ministry of Defence, the Ministry of Defence Police, the Commissioners of Customs and Excise, and the British Transport Police.

[41] Regulation of Investigatory Powers (Scotland) Act 2000 ("RIP(S)A 2000").

[42] "Surveillance" includes monitoring, observing or listening to persons, their movements, conversations or other activities or communications; recording anything so monitored, observed or listened to; and surveillance by or with the aid of surveillance devices: RIP(S)A 2000 s.31(2). It does not include, among other things, any entry on or interference with property or wireless telegraphy, which would be unlawful unless authorised under Pt III of the Police Act 1997. Such surveillance is "covert" if it is carried out in a manner calculated to ensure that the subjects are unaware that it is or may be taking place: RIP(S)A 2000 s.1(8).

[43] RIP(S)A 2000 s.1(1).

[44] RIP(S)A 2000 s.1(2). Note the saving in s.1(2)(c), for unauthorised surveillance of the sort that occurs when a police officer, observing a person acting suspiciously, follows the person to find out whether they are engaged in some criminal activity.

[45] RIP(S)A 2000 s.1(9). Since this definition is expressly non-exhaustive, it would presumably extend to other species of private information, such as information about a person's business affairs.

[46] RIP(S)A 2000 s.31(1) defines "residential premises" as "so much of any premises as is for the time being occupied or used by any person, however temporarily, for residential purposes or otherwise as living accommodation (including hotel or prison accommodation that is so occupied or used)" (but excluding any common parts of a building). "Private vehicle" is defined as any vehicle "used primarily for the private purposes of the person who owns it or of a person otherwise having the right to use it" (but excluding vehicles rented for a particular journey). In his annotations to the Act, Dr Alastair Brown makes the point that the confinement of intrusive surveillance to residential premises and private vehicles must presumably be deliberate, since authorisations under Pt III of the Police Act 1997 may be sought in relation to business premises, and the zone of privacy under art.8 of the European Convention, has been held to extend to offices: *Niemietz v Germany* (1992) 16 E.H.R.R. 523.

[47] RIP(S)A 2000 s.1(3) and (4).

[48] RIP(S)A 2000 s.1(7). A purpose is covert if and only if the relationship is conducted in a manner calculated to ensure that one of the parties is unaware of the purpose; and a relationship is used covertly, and information disclosed covertly, if and only if it is used or disclosed in a manner calculated to ensure that one of the parties is unaware of the use or disclosure: RIP(S)A 2000 s.1(8).

Section 5 of the Regulation of Investigatory Powers (Scotland) Act 2000 provides the legal basis for these activities. This provides that surveillance in any of the senses defined above shall be lawful for all purposes if it is conducted by a person in accordance with the terms of an authorisation granted under the Act. Authorisations should normally be in writing, but may be granted or renewed orally in any urgent case.[49] An authorisation will normally cease to have effect three months after its grant or latest renewal, unless it is an authorisation for the use of a covert human intelligence source, in which case the period is 12 months. Oral authorisations, or authorisations granted by a person entitled to grant them only in urgent cases, lapse after 72 hours.[50] An authorisation may be renewed by any person who would have been entitled to grant it as new at any time before it ceases to have effect, except where the application for renewal relates to the conduct and use of a covert human intelligence source.[51] An authorisation must be cancelled by the person who granted or last renewed it, if they are satisfied that the authorised conduct no longer satisfies the requirements of the Act.[52] **12–08**

The controls applicable to directed surveillance and the use of covert human intelligence sources are broadly similar. Either may be authorised by an officer having the rank of superintendent or above, or, in cases of urgency, inspector or above.[53] A person designated by reference to their rank in any police force as having power to grant authorisations may exercise that power only on the application of an officer in the same force.[54] In either case, an authorisation may only be granted if the granter is satisfied that surveillance of the type specified in the application is both necessary for certain specific purposes and a proportionate method of achieving the applicant's objectives. The specified purposes are the prevention and detection of crime, the prevention of disorder, the protection of public safety and the protection of public health.[55] In relation to an authorisation of the use of a covert human intelligence source, the granter must also be satisfied that arrangements exist for ensuring that an appropriate police officer is charged with day-to-day responsibility for dealing with the source and for the source's security and welfare, and that there will at all times be another officer of the same force charged with general oversight of the use made of the source and the maintenance of proper records.[56] Only conduct of the description specified in the

---

[49] RIP(S)A 2000 s.19(1).

[50] RIP(S)A 2000 s.19(3).

[51] In that case, the authorisation may only be renewed by a person who is satisfied that a review has been carried out of the use made of the source and the tasks given to and information obtained from the source since the authorisation was granted or renewed, and who has considered that review: RIP(S)A 2000 s.19(6), (7).

[52] RIP(S)A 2000 s.20.

[53] RIP(S)A 2000 ss.6(1), 7(1) and 8(1); and see also the Regulation of Investigatory Powers (Prescription of Offices etc., and Specification of Public Authorities) (Scotland) Order 2010 (SSI 2010/350) (as amended).

[54] RIP(S)A 2000 s.11(1). The provision has limited significance following the establishment of Police Scotland (cf. Police and Fire Reform (Scotland) Act 2012) as its effect is that a designated officer in Police Scotland can only grant an application from a constable or other officer of Police Scotland.

[55] RIP(S)A 2000 ss.6(3), and7(3).

[56] RIP(S)A 2000 s.7(2)(c) and 7(6).

authorisation, which is carried on in the circumstances and for the purposes of the investigation or operation therein identified, is clothed with legality by the authorisation.[57]

12–09 Intrusive surveillance is subject to stricter controls, representing as it does a greater invasion of individual privacy. It may be authorised only by the chief constable of Police Scotland (or any other senior officer of Police Scotland designated by the chief constable for the purposes of the Regulation of Investigatory Powers (Scotland) Act 2000),[58] and only then if they are satisfied that it is both necessary for the purpose of preventing or detecting serious crime[59] and a proportionate method of achieving that end.[60] The grant or cancellation of an authorisation for intrusive surveillance must be notified to a Judicial Commissioner[61] as soon as reasonably practicable, specifying such matters as may be prescribed by order of the Scottish Ministers.[62] A notice of the grant of an authorisation must state either that the approval of a commissioner is required before the authorisation can take effect, or that the case is one of urgency (giving reasons for this belief).[63] An urgent authorisation so notified takes effect from the time of its grant; in other cases, the authorisation takes effect only once the granter receives written notice of a commissioner's approval.[64] Where a commissioner is satisfied that, at the time an authorisation was granted, there were no reasonable grounds to believe that its grant was either necessary or proportionate, they may quash it with effect from the time of its grant or any renewal thereof, and if they are satisfied that there were no reasonable grounds for treating the case as urgent, they may likewise quash the authorisation as granted.[65] The chief constable may appeal to the Investigatory Powers Commissioner.[66] The incorporation of commissioners into this machinery reflects the jurisprudence of the European Court of Human Rights, and specifically its requirements that the powers of the state be subjected to a measure of judicial

---

[57] RIP(S)A 2000 ss.6(4) and 7(4). It does not necessarily follow, however, that conduct falling outwith the scope of the authorisation is, by definition, unlawful (at least as a matter of domestic law), or that evidence thereby obtained would be inadmissible. While the European Court of Human Rights takes a dim view of interferences with individual rights that lack a positive legal base, it has also held that evidence gathered in breach of a protected Convention right may be admitted provided the overall fairness of the trial is not thereby impaired: see *Schenk v Switzerland* (1988) 13 E.H.R.R. 242.

[58] Subject to RIP(S)A 2000 s.10(1A).

[59] "Serious crime" is defined as conduct constituting one or more offences for which an adult with no previous convictions could reasonably be expected to be sentenced to at least three years' imprisonment, conduct involving the use of violence, conduct resulting in substantial financial gain, or conduct by a large group of persons in pursuit of a common purpose: RIP(S)A 2000 s.31(6) and (7).

[60] RIP(S)A 2000 s.10(1) and (2). Section 10(3) expressly requires the chief constable to consider whether the information sought could reasonably be obtained by means other than intrusive surveillance.

[61] RIP(S)A 2000 s.13(1). Notification originally had to be made to a "Surveillance Commissioner" but the provision was amended by the Investigatory Powers Act 2016. A person may not be appointed a Judicial Commissioner unless they hold (or have held) "high judicial office" within the meaning of Pt 3 of the Constitutional Reform Act 2005.

[62] As to which, see the Regulation of Investigatory Powers (Notification of Authorisations) (Scotland) Order 2000 (SSI 2000/340).

[63] RIP(S)A 2000 s.13(3).

[64] RIP(S)A 2000 s.14.

[65] RIP(S)A 2000 s.15.

[66] RIP(S)A 2000 ss.16 and 17, as amended by the Investigatory Powers Act 2016.

control.[67] In addition to this, s.23 confers on persons aggrieved by any form of surveillance activity falling within its scope a right to complain to the Investigatory Powers Tribunal (established by s.65 of the UK Act),[68] provided that the conduct in question is believed to have taken place in relation to that person or any of their property, and to have taken place in "challengeable circumstances"[69] or circumstances in which authorisation should have been sought.

Interception of communications is now regulated by the Investigatory Powers Act 2016 (which repeals various aspects of RIPA). Its provisions are not free from controversy and it is the result of litigation over the previous regime for intercepting communications and, in particular, the retention of any communications data. We will turn to that controversy in a moment. But for now, it is helpful to sketch out the main provisions of the 2016 Act. The purpose of the 2016 Act is set out in s.1(1): "This Act sets out the extent to which certain investigatory powers may be used to interfere with privacy". Before using any of the powers conferred by the 2016 Act, a public authority *must* have regard to four factors: (a) whether what is sought to be achieved by the warrant, authorisation or notice could reasonably be achieved by other less intrusive means; (b) whether the level of protection to be applied in relation to any obtaining of information by virtue of the warrant, authorisation or notice is higher because of the particular sensitivity of that information; (c) the public interest in the integrity and security of telecommunication systems and postal services; and (d) any other aspects of the public interest in the protection of privacy.[70] Other factors that *may* be taken into account include: (a) the interests of national security or the economic well-being of the United Kingdom; (b) the public interest in preventing and detecting serious crime; (c) any other factors that are relevant to the proportionality or necessity of the conduct for which authority is sought; (d) the requirements of the Human Rights Act 1998; and (e) other requirements of public law.[71] It is an offence to intentionally intercept a communication in the course of its transmission[72] without lawful authority (assuming the interception is carried out in the UK).[73] A communication is intercepted if "the effect of the relevant act is to make any content of the communication available, at a relevant time, to a person who is not 12–10

---

[67] See, e.g. *Klass v Germany* (1978) 2 E.H.R.R. 214; *Funke v France* (1993) 16 E.H.R.R. 297.

[68] The Investigatory Powers Tribunal is the only tribunal before whom proceedings can be raised against any of the intelligence services or various other complaints arising out of anything that has been (or may have been) done pursuant to RIPA 2000 or RIP(S)A 2000. For more information on this tribunal's role and function, as well as a list of its decisions, see *http://www.ipt-uk.com* [Accessed 9 July 2020].

[69] RIP(S)A 2000 s.23(2). Surveillance takes place in challengeable circumstances if it is conducted, or purports to be conducted, pursuant to an authorisation issued under the RIP(S)A 2000 or under s.93 of the Police Act 1997 (authorisations to interfere with property or wireless telegraphy).

[70] 2016 Act, s.2(2).

[71] 2016 Act, s.2(4). Given the terms of the Human Rights Act 1998, and the obligations it imposes on public authorities (as discussed in Ch.11), it may be thought surprising that it is listed in the "may have regard to" category.

[72] By means of a public telecommunications system, a private telecommunications system or a public postal service (each of those being defined in ss.261–262 of the 2016 Act). In relation to private telecommunications, no offence is committed by a person who has a right to control the operation or use of the system or has the express or implied consent of such a person to carry out the interception (s.3(2)).

[73] 2016 Act s.3(1).

the sender or intended recipient of the communication".[74] "Lawful authority" is defined by s.6 and broadly means approval under the 2016 Act.

In relation to the interception of communications, warrants are governed by Pt 2, Ch.1 of the 2016 Act. There are three kinds of warrants that can be granted under that chapter: (a) targeted interception warrants; (b) targeted examination warrants; and (c) mutual assistance warrants.[75] Only an "intercepting authority" can apply for such a warrant.[76] The power to issue a warrant rests with the Secretary of State,[77] who must be satisfied that granting a targeted interception or a targeted examination warrant is necessary in the interests of national security, for the purposes of preventing or detecting serious crime or in the interests of the economic well-being of the UK so far as those interests are also relevant to the interests of national security.[78] Where a warrant is issued, it is subject to approval by the Judicial Commissioner.[79] Where the application for a warrant concerns communications to or from a "member of a relevant legislature",[80] the Secretary of State cannot issue the warrant without the approval of the Prime Minister.[81] Where the warrant targets communications that may be the subject of legal privilege, there must be "exceptional and compelling circumstances" for granting the warrant and enhanced safeguards in relation to the protection of such communications must be in place.[82] We will return to legal privilege in a moment. Enhanced protection is also required where journalistic material is the subject of a warrant.[83] Once granted, a warrant lasts for six months (or, if granted urgently, five working days).[84] An urgent warrant can be renewed for a further

---

74 2016 Act s.4(1). "Content" is, in turn, defined by s.261(6). The "relevant time" is any time while the communication is being transmitted and any time when it is stored in or by the system (whether before or after transmission) (s.4(4)). For the definition of "wireless telegraphy", see ss.116–117 of the Wireless Telegraphy Act 2006.

75 2016 Act s.15(1). Each is then explained and defined in the following subsections.

76 2016 Act s.18. So far as Scotland is concerned, the applicable "intercepting authority" is likely to be one of the head of an intelligence service; the Director General of the National Crime Agency; the chief constable of Police Scotland, the Commissioners for HMRC or the Chief of Defence Intelligence.

77 Unless the application is relevant to Scotland, in which case authority rests with the Scottish Ministers: s.19(4) and s.21 of the 2016 Act. A "relevant Scottish application" is defined in s.22.

78 2016 Act ss.19–20. In relation to the interests of the economic well-being of the UK, so far as those interests are also relevant to the interests of national security, that can only be engaged where the information considered necessary is information relating to the acts or intentions of persons outside the British Islands (s.20(4).

79 2016 Act s.23. In urgent cases, that approval can be retrospective (but must be sought within 3 working days): s.24.

80 Defined in s.26(3) of the 2016 Act to include either House of Parliament or any of the devolved legislatures.

81 2016 Act s.26(2).

82 2016 Act s.27(4). These provisions placed in statute provisions that were to be found in Codes of Practice under the RIP(S)A and RIPA schemes. That those productions had been left to Codes of Practice had been criticised: Joint Committee on the Draft Investigatory Powers Bill, Report, HL Paper 93; HC 651 (3 February 2016). Available at: *https://publications.parliament.uk/pa/jt201516/jtselect/jtinvpowers/93/93.pdf* [Accessed 22 June 2020]. Separately, such provision as made in the Codes had also been criticised. See, for example, the response of the Faculty of Advocates to the consultation on the news Codes under RIP(S)A: *http://www.advocates.org.uk/media/2561/final-faculty-response-rip-s-a-11-october.pdf* [Accessed 22 June 2020].

83 2016 Act ss.28–29.

84 2016 Act s.32. An urgent warrant is one which has been issued without the approval of a Judicial Commissioner (s.32(3)).

five working days; other warrants can be renewed for 30 days.[85] Such a renewal again requires approval by a Judicial Commissioner.[86] Where a warrant has been granted, it must be cancelled where the "appropriate person" (i.e. the person who granted it) considers that the warrant is no longer necessary or proportionate to what it sought to achieve.[87]

Before moving on, a comment on legal professional privilege is necessary. In amongst the detail of the legislation, the significance of the powers conferred by 2016 Act can be lost. They are well illustrated by considering its interrelationship with the law of legal professional privilege. It is a cornerstone of the rule of law that communications between a client and their lawyer are privileged: it cannot be overridden "by some supposedly greater public interest".[88] It is central to the functioning of this privilege that it is absolute: unless a client can have complete confidence that what they disclose to their lawyer is protected there will be an inevitable chilling effect.[89] Yet there is an obvious risk that, in monitoring communications of an individual, privileged material may also be intercepted. That risk is more significant where the subject of surveillance is in any sort of dispute with the government: the consequence being that their opponent in litigation potentially has access to their (thought to be) confidential discussions with their lawyers. Take, for example, a murder trial in the High Court. Invariably the accused has, through legal aid, only such assistance as the State has itself provided. If the State also has the ability to monitor an accused's exchanges with their lawyers, an already unbalanced fight takes on the appearance of an unfair fight. It is no answer, as was sometimes suggested, to say that any inadvertent interception of such privileged exchanges will not be relied upon in court. That they are available at all (to inform, for example, further investigations or trial strategy) is damage enough. If such surveillance is to be permitted at all (and it has been held to be in principle permissible[90]), it has to be such a rare occurrence that the possibility of it occurring does not destroy the right.[91] In February 2015, in the course of proceedings before the Investigatory Powers Tribunal, the UK Government conceded that from January 2010 the regime for interception, analysis, use, disclosure and destruction of legally privileged material was not in accordance with law for the purposes of art.8(2) of the Convention and therefore unlawful.[92] That regime was based on codes of practice issued under s.71 of the **12–11**

[85] 2016 Act s.33.

[86] 2016 Act s.33(7).

[87] 2016 Act s.39.

[88] *Three Rivers District Council v Bank of England* [2004] UKHL 48; [2005] 1 A.C. 610, per Lord Scott of Foscote at [25]. *R. v Derby Magistrates' Court, Ex p. B* [1996] A.C. 487: "It is a fundamental condition on which the administration of justice as a whole rests." W.G. Dickson, *A Treatise on the Law of Evidence in Scotland*, revised edition (Edinburgh: Clark, 1887) at para.1663 said: "By sacred and settled rule of law, communications between a party and his legal adviser regarding the subject of a suit depending or threatened are secure from disclosure." In support of that proposition, Dickson cited authority stretching back to the sixteenth century. It is a principle whose importance has not diminished with time.

[89] *Bolkiah v KPMG* [1999] 2 A.C. 222.

[90] *McE v Prison Service of Northern Ireland* [2009] UKHL 15; [2009] 1 A.C. 909.

[91] *McE v Prison Service of Northern Ireland* [2009] UKHL 15; [2009] 1 A.C. 909 at [51] (Lord Phillips)

[92] See *Belhaj v Security Services* (Case No.IPT/13/132-9/H) Unreported 26 February 2015 Investigatory Powers Tribunal. The case went on for a hearing on remedies (a particularly difficult issue where confirming or denying a breach also discloses the fact that surveillance was underway and

Regulation of Investigatory Powers Act 2000. The "additional safeguards" now found in s.27 of the 2016 Act in large part respond to the concerns arising from that case. Whether they are enough remains debatable.

12–12 Returning to the 2016 Act, detailed provision is now made for obtaining and retaining communications data and the bulk interception of communications. We will dwell on communications data for a few moments. The significance of communications data can be easily overlooked. It is often said, reassuringly, that the *content* of the communication is not retained just the date, time and place of, and the parties to, the phone call or email. That data can, however, be significant. In tracking, and thwarting, a terrorist plot, it may be essential to identify that person A and person B were in regular communication during a particular period and, possibly, being able to show where they were at the time of those communications. But suppose person A is a high-profile celebrity who is seeking treatment for a drug addiction. If person A sits on their smartphone replying to emails every week whilst waiting to be seen in the clinic, that communications data is sufficient to identify that person A regularly attends a particular location that can then be readily identified as a treatment clinic. In that scenario, the need for collecting that communications data is unclear. From the communications data that the service providers are required to retain, much can be understood about a person's life, including very sensitive personal information. The collection, retention and use of this data must also be set in the context of the "Wikileaks" scandal and the public concern over the mass collection of surveillance data.

In part motivated by such privacy concerns, there was considerable litigation over the need, originally found in an EU Directive,[93] for telecommunications companies to retain this data. Provision was made, by the UK, requiring such data to be retained for 12 months.[94] In April 2014, however, the Court of Justice of the European Union (CJEU) ruled that the Data Retention Directive was a disproportionate interference with the right to respect for private life and to the protection of personal data (arts 7 and 8 of the EU Charter of Fundamental Rights).[95] That resulted in the Directive being annulled, which in turn robbed the UK's implementing regulations of any legal basis and required their repeal. To ensure that communications data could continue to be retained, the Data Retention and Investigatory Powers Act 2014 was passed (completing its parliamentary passage in just three days). It more or less re-enacted in primary legislation what had previously been contained in the 2009 Regulations. Unsurprisingly, the 2014 Act was subject to challenge and the important parts of the 2014 Act were held to be incompatible with EU law and the EU Charter of

---

would breach the government's "neither confirm nor deny policy"). That determination (*Belhaj v Security Services* [2015] UKIPTrib 13_132-H) is available at *http://www.ipt-uk.com/docs/ABDEL_HAKIM_BELHADJ_Final.pdf* [Accessed 22 June 2020].

[93] Directive 2006/24 on the retention of data generated or processed in connection with the provision of publicly available electronic communications services or of public communications networks and amending Directive 2002/58/EC [2006] OJ L105/54. That Directive was implemented in the UK by the Data Retention (EC Directive) Regulations 2009 (SI 2009/859).

[94] Data Retention (EC Directive) Regulations 2009 (SI 2009/859) reg.5. The directive required that data be retained for not less than six and not more than 24 months (reg.6).

[95] *Digital Rights Ireland Ltd v Minister for Communications, Marine and Natural Resources* (C-293/12) [2015] Q.B. 127; [2014] 3 C.M.L.R. 44.

Fundamental Rights.[96] The Court of Appeal was less convinced and a number of questions were referred to the CJEU seeking clarity on the scope of its ruling in the *Digital Rights* case.[97] In December 2016, the Grand Chamber of the CJEU delivered its judgment answering the reference.[98] It held that the 2014 Act fell within the scope of EU law (itself a controversial question given the EU had no competence over national security) and then gave a very strict judgment that made the general and indiscriminate retention of communications data almost impossible. It was obvious that material aspects of the 2014 Act were incompatible with EU law and the Charter. When the case returned to the Court of Appeal, s.1 of the 2014 Act (which contained the power to require the retention of communications data) was declared inconsistent with EU law.[99]

In the meantime, the government announced its intention to bring forward an Investigatory Powers Bill to "modernise the law on communications data". This was to include "better equipping" law enforcement and intelligence agencies and filling gaps in the respective abilities to build the necessary intelligence and evidence. The existing law has been criticised by the Intelligence and Security Committee.[100] This followed on from criticism of the Regulation of Investigatory Powers Act 2000 ("RIPA is not fit for purpose") by the Home Affairs Select Committee[101] and in June 2015 the Independent Reviewer of Terrorism Legislation called for a complete overhaul of the legislative basis for surveillance and data retention.[102] That Bill was to become the Investigatory Powers Act 2016, which we have discussed above. But that did not bring litigation to an end. In April 2018, Pt 4 of the 2016 Act (which provides for the retention of communications data) was found by the High Court to be incompatible with EU law and the government was given until 1 November 2018 to amend the Act.[103] The court was concerned that access to retained data was not restricted to combating "serious crime" and that access to such data was not subject to prior approval by a court or other independent body. Regulations were duly made to address the concerns of the court.[104]

This whole episode illustrates the challenge the law faces in adapting to developing technology. Communications data is doubtless of considerable

---

[96] *R (on the application of Davis and others) v Secretary of State for the Home Department* [2015] EWHC 2092 (Admin); [2016] 1 C.M.L.R. 13. The effect of that decision was suspended until 31 March 2016 to allow the government time to consider how to respond. On disapplying or suspending such declarations (which is also a common approach in devolution challenges) see: J. Morgan, "'O Lord make me pure—but not yet': granting time for the amendment of unlawful legislation" (2019) 135 L.Q.R. 585.

[97] *R (on the application of Davis and others) v Secretary of State for the Home Department* [2015] EWCA Civ 1185; [2017] 1 All E.R. 62.

[98] The case was joined with another from Sweden: *Telez Sverige AB v Post-och telestyrelsen* (Joined Cases C-203/15 and C-698/15) [2017] QB 771.

[99] *R (Watson) v Secretary of State for the Home Department* [2018] EWCA Civ 70; [2018] QB 912.

[100] Intelligence and Security Committee of Parliament, *Privacy and Security: A modern and transparent legal framework* (The Stationery Office, 2015) HC 1075.

[101] House of Commons Home Affairs Committee, *Regulation of Investigatory Powers Act 2000, Eight Report of Session 2014–15* (The Stationery Office, 2014) HC 711.

[102] D. Anderson, QC, *A Question of Trust: Report of the Investigatory Powers Review* (The Stationery Office, 2015).

[103] *R (on the application of National Council for Civil Liberties (Liberty)) v Secretary of State for the Home Department* [2018] EWHC 975 (Admin); [2019] QB 481.

[104] Data Retention and Acquisition Regulations 2018.

assistance to law enforcement agencies and would be of interest to many others. But as we saw above, much can be pieced together about someone's life from knowing who they call or email, from where they call or email and when they do so. Striking the balance remains controversial and as technology continues to develop, the extent to which the state can use those developments for surveillance of its citizens is bound to remain controversial.[105]

ARREST AND DETENTION

Introduction

12–13 Where surveillance is concerned, the individual may never be aware that their privacy has been invaded, or may become aware only after the interference has ceased. But there is no ignoring the deprivation of liberty involved in arrest or detention, which is why art.5 of the Convention provides as follows:

> "No-one shall be deprived of his liberty save in the following cases and in accordance with a procedure prescribed by law: . . . (c) the lawful arrest or detention of a person effected for the purpose of bringing him before the competent legal authority on reasonable suspicion of having committed an offence or when it is reasonably considered necessary to prevent his committing an offence or fleeing after having done so."

The right to liberty carries with it a number of ancillary rights, as set out in art.5(2)–(5): the right to be informed promptly and in a language one understands of the reasons for one's arrest and of any charge against one; the right to be brought promptly before a judge where arrested or detained in connection with a criminal matter; the right to be brought to trial within a reasonable time or to be released pending trial[106]; and the right to compensation where arrested or detained in a manner incompatible with art.5.[107] The Strasbourg Court has described the right to liberty as being at the heart of any political system that

[105] For a general discussion, see: M. White, "Data retention: serious crime or a serious problem?" [2019] PL 633.

[106] Hence the Bail, Judicial Appointments etc. (Scotland) Act 2000, Pt 1 of which made provision for bail to be granted even in serious cases, where previously it had been unavailable.

[107] This right to compensation for continued detention has proved controversial in recent years, with a series of challenges by prisoners serving indeterminate sentences who complain that they are not in a position to satisfy the parole board that they are suitable for release because of a failure to provide them with access to the necessary treatments and/or courses during their detention. See, for example, *R. (on the application of Kaiyam) v Secretary of State for Justice* [2014] UKSC 66; [2015] A.C. 1344; *R. (on the application of Sturnham) v Parole Board for England and Wales* [2013] UKSC 23; [2013] 2 A.C. 254; *James v United Kingdom* (2013) 56 E.H.R.R. 12. In *Kaiyam* the Supreme Court refused to follow the Strasbourg Court and hold that a breach of art.5 in these circumstances required the release of the prisoner (as that would require the release of someone the parole board were not yet satisfied was safe to release) and thus an award of damages was appropriate. The approach taken in *Kaiyam* was departed from by the Supreme Court in *Brown v Parole Board for Scotland*, 2018 S.C. (U.K.S.C.) 49, but the high threshold for showing a breach of art.5 was reiterated. Where an award has been made, it has tended to be in the hundreds of pounds.

purports to abide by the rule of law.[108] Whether a person has been deprived of their liberty in any particular case is treated by the court as a function not merely of the duration of the period in which the person was subject to restraint but also of the type, manner and effects of that restraint. It is the substance of the act and not its form that is crucial.[109]

We have already noted the approach of the Strasbourg Court to the question whether a given interference with fundamental rights is prescribed by, or in accordance with, the law. In addition, any arrest or detention must conform to the substantive standards prescribed by art.5(1)(c). So, for example, an arrest not founded on a reasonable suspicion would not constitute a lawful arrest. What is "reasonable" turns very much on what is known to the arresting officer at the material time, but the test is an objective one.[110] Scots law previously recognises two forms of apprehension by the police: "arrest" (whether at common law or under statute) and "detention" (under the Criminal Procedure (Scotland) Act 1995). The continuing need for these two methods of apprehension was doubted.[111] They have been swept away and the Criminal Justice (Scotland) Act 2016 now provides the statutory basis on which a person may be arrested without a warrant.[112] A very limited power to detain a person (whilst certain details are confirmed) endures. 12–14

The 2016 Act followed on from a review of Scottish criminal law and practice carried out by Lord Carloway in 2011. [113] That review arose from the fallout of a series of Supreme Court decisions concerning the rights of a person detained under the 1995 Act. Prior to the Supreme Court's decision in *Cadder v HM Advocate*,[114] a person detained under the 1995 Act had no right to consult a 12–15

---

[108] *Winterwerp v Netherlands* (1979) 2 E.H.R.R. 387 at 37. Note that art.5 of the European Convention, relates only to the fact of detention, not to the conditions thereof. The treatment of persons held in detention is covered by art.3, which prohibits torture and inhuman or degrading treatment or punishment: see in that regard, e.g. *Napier v Scottish Ministers* [2002] U.K.H.R.R. 308.

[109] Difficulties of definition can arise at the margins, as seen in *Goodson v Higson*, 2002 S.L.T. 202. See also: *Secretary of State for the Home Department v JJ and others* [2007] UKHL 45; [2008] 1 A.C. 385 where the compatibility of control orders with art.5 was considered by the House of Lords and the circumstances in which they would amount to a deprivation of liberty explained.

[110] Thus, there was a breach of art.5 in *Fox v United Kingdom* (1990) 13 E.H.R.R. 157, where the applicants had been arrested under s.11(1) of the Northern Ireland (Emergency Provisions) Act 1978. Section 11(1) conferred a power of arrest on a constable in respect of "any person whom he suspects of being a terrorist". In *McKie v Chief Constable for Northern Ireland* [1985] 1 All E.R. 1, this was held by the House of Lords to involve a subjective test: whether the officer had such a suspicion, and whether it was honestly held. The issue before the European Court of Human Rights was not whether s.11(1) itself breached art.5 but whether there was, in the circumstances, sufficient evidence to give rise to a reasonable suspicion. The court found there was not, from which it follows that any power of arrest, common law or statutory, may only be exercised lawfully, in light of the Human Rights Act 1998, where there are "facts or information that would satisfy an objective observer that the person concerned may have committed the offence" (*Fox v United Kingdom* (1990) 13 E.H.R.R. 157 at 32).

[111] The Carloway Review, *The Carloway Review, Report and Recommendations* (Scottish Government, 2011), para.5.0.4.

[112] Certain exceptions persist, for example the arrest of a prisoner unlawfully at large (Prisons (Scotland) Act 1989 s.40). The full list is set out in s.57A of the 2016 Act. On arrest under the 2016 Act and more generally, see: Renton and Brown, *Criminal Procedure*, 6th edn, paras 6–11—6–22.

[113] The Carloway Review, *The Carloway Review, Report and Recommendations, http://www.scotland.gov.uk/About/Review/CarlowayReview* [Accessed 22 April 2020].

[114] *Cadder v HM Advocate* [2010] UKSC 43; 2011 S.C. (U.K.S.C.) 13.

solicitor, only to have the fact of their detention intimated to a solicitor.[115] Detention, at that time, could last for no more than six hours and with no ability to defer the start of that time, obvious practical difficulties would have arisen (particularly in rural communities) in providing a right for a suspect to consult a solicitor before the police could interview them. That was not the motive behind the absence of a right to consult a solicitor, as Lord Rodger explain in *Cadder*:

> "... s.15 of the 1995 Act deliberately deprives the suspect of any right to take legal advice before being questioned by the police, in the hope that, without it, he will be more likely to incriminate himself during questioning."[116]

That gave Scots law a problem with art.6 of the European Convention for the Grand Chamber of the Strasbourg Court had, in *Salduz v Turkey*, held that:

> "[I]n order for the right to a fair trial to remain sufficiently 'practical and effective' article 6(1) requires that, as a rule, access to a lawyer should be provided as from the first interrogation of a suspect by the police, unless it is demonstrated in light of the particular circumstances of each case that there are compelling reasons to restrict this right. Even where compelling reasons may exceptionally justify denial of access to a lawyer, such restriction—whatever its justification—must not unduly prejudice the rights of the accused under article 6. The rights of the defence will in principle be irretrievably prejudiced when incriminating statements made during police interrogation without access to a lawyer are used for a conviction."[117]

The High Court of Justiciary (sitting as a bench of seven) declined to follow *Salduz*, pointing to the range of other protections that Scots law afforded to accused persons so as to secure their right to a fair trial.[118] That approach was rejected by the Supreme Court. What *Salduz* did was to provide a right against "self-incrimination" and the other protections relied upon by the High Court (many of which went beyond what the European Convention on Human Rights would require) were not sufficient to protect that particular right. Indeed, as Lord Rodger explained, Scots law was "the very converse" of what Strasbourg required.[119] It was therefore a breach of art.6, and thus unlawful, for the prosecution to rely on evidence obtained during an interview where the suspect had not been afforded the opportunity to consult a solicitor.[120]

That gave rise to a number of problems. Leaving aside the political controversy it provoked, the practical issue for the prosecuting authorities was reassessing numerous cases to determine whether they had a sufficiency of

---

[115] A person arrested on any criminal charge did have (and continues to have) the right to consult with a solicitor: s.17 of the Criminal Procedure (Scotland) Act 1995.

[116] *Cadder v HM Advocate* [2010] UKSC 43; 2011 S.C. (U.K.S.C.) 13 at [90]–[91].

[117] *Salduz v Turkey* (2009) 49 E.H.R.R. 19 at [55]. Lord Rodger explains (at [67]) that this right could be traced back to the Strasbourg Court's decision in *Saunders v United Kingdom* (1997) 23 E.H.R.R. 313.

[118] *HM Advocate v McLean (Duncan)* [2009] HCJAC 97; 2010 S.L.T. 73.

[119] *Cadder v HM Advocate* [2010] UKSC 43; 2011 S.C. (U.K.S.C.) 13 at [93], but see Lord Rodger's discussion of the evolution of Scots law on this point at [73]–[93].

[120] Under the Terrorism Act 2000 "safety interviews" may be conducted without a solicitor being present where the urgency of the situation demands it. Such interviews have been held to be Convention-compliant: *Ibrahim v UK* (2015) 61 E.H.R.R. 9 (a decision of the Fourth Section, which has been appealed to the Grand Chamber). See also: M. Seet, "Suspected Terrorists and the Privilege Against Self-Incrimination" [2015] CLJ 208.

evidence without such interviews. Eight hundred and sixty seven cases could not proceed as a result.[121] Two other questions arose from the decision: how early in the process does a person have to be informed of their right to speak to a lawyer and can such a person waive their right to consult a lawyer (and if so, how)? The first question troubled the Supreme Court, particularly as a result of comments made by the President of the Strasbourg Court in his concurring opinion in *Salduz*, where it was suggested that the obligation should begin from the moment a suspect was detained.[122] As Lord Hope pointed out in *Cadder*, having regard to the fact that a person could be detained under s.14 of the 1995 Act at any time of day or night anywhere in the country, urban or rural, the best that could ever be achieved was the presence of a solicitor within a short time after the person's arrival at a police station.[123] Even that may be difficult in particularly remote locations. In *Ambrose v Harris*, the Supreme Court confirmed that the obligation to provide access to a solicitor began when a person has been effectively restrained to the point that they have no option but to remain with the police.[124] That will necessarily depend on the particular circumstances: being questioned having been stopped at the side of the road was not enough, but having been handcuffed and searched after a quantity of heroin was found was sufficient. In relation to waiver, that question returned to the Supreme Court in *HM Advocate v Jude* where the court confirmed that there was no absolute rule that an accused must receive legal advice before they can be held to have effectively waived their right of access to a solicitor.[125] Before any waiver can be effective, however, the accused must have been given an indication of the broad nature and the gravity of the offence they were suspected of[126] and their status as a suspect must be clear.[127] But the very practical concern was one of time. Detention under the 1995 Act was for a period of six hours that started immediately and could not be interrupted. As a result, the time available to the police to actually question a detained person would often be seriously curtailed and the utility of detaining someone undermined. Against that background, the 2016 Act came into being and with it the whole process of taking someone into custody and questioning them was overhauled.

Arrest

Section 1 of the 2016 Act sets out a constable's power of arrest without a warrant. It provides: 12–16

"Power of a constable

[121] See Crown Office and Procurator Fiscal Service, "Crown review of cases after *Cadder v HMA*", *https://www.copfs.gov.uk/foi/responses-we-have-made-to-foi-requests/42-responses2012/392-how-many-cases-were-abandoned-or-suspended-as-a-result-of-cadder* [Accessed 23 July 2020].

[122] *Salduz v Turkey* (2009) 49 E.H.R.R. 19, per Judge Bratza at [O-I2].

[123] *Cadder v HM Advocate* [2010] UKSC 43; 2011 S.C. (U.K.S.C.) 13 at [37]. Lord Rodger made much the same point at [70].

[124] *Ambrose v Harris* [2011] UKSC 43; 2012 S.C. (U.K.S.C.) 53.

[125] *Jude (Raymond) v HM Advocate* [2011] UKSC 55; 2012 S.C. (U.K.S.C.) 222.

[126] *R v HM Advocate* [2012] HCJAC 165; 2013 S.C.C.R. 164. Detailed specification of the offences is not, however, required: *GM v HM Advocate* [2013] HCJAC 26; 2013 S.C.C.R. 176.

[127] *Renton and Brown's Criminal Procedure Legislation*, para.A4–33.

1.—(1) A constable may arrest a person without a warrant if the constable has reasonable grounds for suspecting that the person has committed or is committing an offence.

(2) In relation to an offence not punishable by imprisonment, a constable may arrest a person under subsection (1) only if the constable is satisfied that it would not be in the interests of justice to delay the arrest in order to seek a warrant for the person's arrest.

(3) Without prejudice to the generality of subsection (2), it would not be in the interests of justice to delay an arrest in order to seek a warrant if the constable reasonably believes that unless the person is arrested without delay the person will—

(a) continue committing the offence, or
(b) obstruct the course of justice in any way, including by—
(i) seeking to avoid arrest, or
(ii) interfering with witnesses or evidence.

(4) For the avoidance of doubt, an offence is to be regarded as not punishable by imprisonment for the purpose of subsection (2) only if no person convicted of the offence can be sentenced to imprisonment in respect of it."

A constable has no power to arrest a person without a warrant other than that conferred by s.1.[128] There are a few points to note. First, whether an offence is punishable by imprisonment is not a question of whether that particular person would be imprisoned if convicted; the question is whether a custodial sentence would be available (and all common law offences can attract a custodial sentence). Second, whether an arrest was wrongful will turn on whether it was reasonable for the arresting officer to believe it was justified. As we have just noted, art.5 of the Convention requires that the reasonableness of the arresting officer's belief be judged objectively. The domestic courts have not, in the past, tended to inquire too closely into the objective strength or weakness of the suspicion an arresting officer claims to have harboured at the relevant time; rather, provided it is shown that the suspicion was honestly held, it is for the accused to prove that the suspicion was unreasonable.[129] It has now been held (albeit in relation to the previous provisions for detention under s.14 of the 1995 Act) that it is necessary for the arresting officer themselves to have a reasonable suspicion; it is not acceptable that they rely upon the instruction of a senior officer without some understanding of the basis on which the senior officer formed the view that arrest was justified.[130] There is no reason to expect a different approach under the 2016 Act. Third, traditionally, arrest without a warrant would not be considered to be in the interests of justice if those interests could equally be served by waiting for a warrant.[131] There is no reason to think that "golden rule" will fade as a result of the 2016 Act. Fourth, a constable is permitted to use reasonable force to effect an arrest and convey the arrested

---

[128] 2016 Act s.54. There is one qualification: the power of arrest conferred by s.41(1) of the Terrorism Act 2000 remains.

[129] See, e.g. *McLeod v Shaw (William)*, 1981 S.L.T. (Notes) 93.

[130] *McAughey v HM Advocate* [2013] HCJAC 163; 2-14 SCL 165; *McKenzie v Murphy* [2014] HCJAC 132; 2015 S.C.L. 194. *McKenzie* was endorsed by Lord Malcolm in *Whitehouse v Gormley* [2018] CSOH 93; 2020 S.C.L.R. 27 at [126] (that passage was not criticised on appeal—which was otherwise allowed—2019 S.L.T. 1269).

[131] *Peggie v Clark* (1868) 7 M. 89, per Lord Deas; *Leask v Burt* (1893) 21 R 32; *Somerville v Sutherland* (1899) 2 F 185.

person to any place.[132] Finally, where a constable effects an arrest when they are not in uniform, they must show identification to the arrested person, if asked to do so, as soon as reasonably practicable.[133]

At the point of arrest (or as soon afterwards as is reasonably practicable), a person requires to be provided with certain information, namely: (a) that they are under arrest[134]; (b) the general nature of the offence, if any, for which the person is being arrested; (c) the reason for the arrest[135]; (d) that the person is under no obligation to say anything (other to confirm their name, address, date and place of birth and nationality[136]); and (e) that they have the right to have intimation of their arrest sent to a solicitor and to have access to a solicitor.[137]

Procedure following arrest is prescribed by the 2016 Act. Where a person is arrested outwith a police station, they should ordinarily be taken to a police station as quickly as is reasonably practicable.[138] Once at a police station, the person should again be told they are under no obligation to say anything other than confirming their name, address, date and place of birth and nationality. They must also be informed, as soon as reasonably practicable, that they have a right to have intimation of their arrest sent to another person as well as a solicitor and that they have a right to a consultation with a solicitor.[139] Having arrived at a police station, authorisation is required (from an officer of the rank of sergeant or above) to keep the person in custody.[140] Such authorisation can only be given where there are reasonable grounds for suspecting that the person has committed an offence and keeping the person in custody is necessary and proportionate for the purposes of bringing the person before a court or otherwise dealing with the person in accordance with the law ("the s.14 test").[141] That authorisation (rather than the time of arrest) marks the start of the 12-hour period for which the person can be held.[142] If, by the end of that period, a person has not been charged with an offence, their continued detention requires to be authorised by an officer of the rank of inspector (or, where the detainee is under 18, a chief inspector).[143] In addition to the need to satisfy the s.14 test, continued detention can only be sanctioned where the officer is satisfied that the offence in connection with which the person is in custody is an indictable offence and the investigation is being conducted diligently and expeditiously.[144] Before taking the decision, the detained person should be given a reasonable opportunity to make verbal or **12–17**

[132] 2016 Act s.45.

[133] 2016 Act s.2(3).

[134] It is not necessary to use the word "arrest" but it is preferable to do so: "any form of words will suffice to inform the person that he is being arrested if they bring to his notice the fact that he is under compulsion and the person thereafter submits to that compulsion." (*Alderson v Booth* [1969] 2 Q.B. 216 DC, per Lord Parker CJ.)

[135] It should be the actual reason for arrest: *Forbes (Robin Norman) v HM Advocate*, 1990 J.C. 215.

[136] 2016 Act s.34.

[137] 2016 Act s.3.

[138] 2016 Act s.4.

[139] 2016 Act s.5, read with ss.38, 43 and 44. A person under 18 has a right to consult with a person who is informed of their arrest under s.38.

[140] 2016 Act s.7.

[141] 2016 Act s.14.

[142] 2016 Act s.9. That is a change from the law under s.14 of the 1995 Act, where the (6-hour) time-limit began from the point of detention.

[143] 2016 Act s.11.

[144] 2016 Act s.11(3).

written representation (which can be done through their solicitor).[145] If authorisation is granted, a person can be held for a further 12 hours. At the end of that period, they can only continue to be held in police custody if they have been charged with an offence (or their detention in connection with a breach of bail is permitted).[146] In calculating the 12-hour periods, no account is taken of any time a person is in hospital receiving medical treatment.[147]

12–18 The rights of those arrested are now set out in Ch.5 of Pt 1 of the 2016 Act. There are three general rights: (a) to have the fact of arrest intimated to another person[148]; (b) to have the fact of arrest intimated to a solicitor[149]; and (c) to have a consultation with that solicitor.[150] Persons under 18 have further rights to consult with the person who has been informed for their arrest and to have social work involvement.[151] The right to consult with a solicitor, as we have seen, was introduced so as to comply with the requirements of art.6 of the Convention. A person who is in police custody has the right to a private consultation (which can be by telephone) with a solicitor at any time. Only in exceptional circumstances can the exercise of that right be delayed and then only so far as is necessary in the interests of the investigation or prevention of crime or the apprehension of offenders. Such a delay can only be authorised by an officer hold the rank of sergeant or above and who has not previously been involved in the investigation.

"Citizen's arrest"

12–19 The power of ordinary people to effect a "citizen's arrest" is not expressly abolished by the 2016 Act. It is, however, a power that is strictly circumscribed in Scots law:

> "A private citizen is entitled to arrest without warrant for a serious crime he has witnessed, or where he has a moral certainty that the person he arrests has just committed a crime or perhaps where, being the victim of the crime, he has information equivalent to personal observation, as where the fleeing criminal is pointed out to him by an eyewitness. He has no power to arrest someone who has committed only a breach of the peace, although he may intervene to prevent the occurrence of such a breach… Arrests by private citizens are not encouraged, especially where they involve the use of any force, and the limitations on this right of arrest are strictly enforced by the court."[152]

Beyond this, in other words, the private citizen who purports to arrest a person may render themselves liable to conviction for assault. Given the need for an arresting officer themselves to have sufficient knowledge to justify an arrest, it must be doubtful whether a person detained pursuant to a "citizen's arrest" could necessarily be arrested by a constable if handed over.

---

145 2016 Act s.11(4).

146 2016 Act s.11(7).

147 2016 Act s.15. That, too, is an innovation on detention under the 1995 Act.

148 2016 Act s.38.

149 2016 Act s.43.

150 2016 Act s.44.

151 2016 Act ss.39–41.

152 *Renton and Brown's Criminal Procedure*, 6th edn, para.7–03 (R.7), cited with approval by the High Court of Justiciary in *Codona (Douglas) v Cardle*, 1989 J.C. 99; *Bryans (Peter Herd) v Guild*, 1990 J.C. 51; and *Wightman (David Alexander) v Lees*, 2000 S.L.T. 111.

Detention

One form of detention remains: s.13 of the Criminal Procedure (Scotland) Act 1995. This is best regarded as a power of "quasi-detention". Where a constable has reasonable grounds for suspecting that a person has committed or is committing an offence at any place, s.13(1)(a) of the 1995 Act provides that they may require that person to give their name, address, date of birth, place of birth "in such detail as the constable considers necessary or expedient for the purpose of establishing the person's identity", and nationality, and may additionally ask them for an explanation of the circumstances that have given rise to the constable's suspicion.[153] Provisions that would allow the constable to take the person's fingerprints (only for the purposes of verifying the name and address of the person and whether they are suspected of having committed any other offence) have been passed by the Scottish Parliament but are not yet in force.[154] The constable may require that person to remain with them while they verify the name and address and/or notes the explanation offered, provided that this can be done quickly, and may use reasonable force to ensure that the person remains with them.[155] The constable must inform the person of their suspicion and of the general nature of the offence that they suspect the person has committed or is committing; and if necessary must inform the person why they are being required to remain with them. They must also inform the person that failure to comply with their requirements may constitute an offence for which they may be arrested without warrant.[156] Where the constable believes any other person to have information relating to the offence in question, s.13(1)(b) provides that they may require that person to give their name, address, date and place of birth and nationality. They must inform that person of the general nature of the offence that they suspect has been or is being committed, and that the reason for the requirement is that they believe the person has relevant information. A person who fails to give that information without reasonable excuse is guilty of an offence.[157] Resort to the powers under s.13 is permissible only where the constable has reasonable grounds to suspect an offence has been or is being committed. As to what might constitute reasonable cause, the editors of *Renton and Brown's Criminal Procedure* note that it need not 12–20

> "rest upon personal ocular observation by the officer; [their suspicions] may stem from the observations of other persons, from 'information received' or from prior knowledge of the suspect's habits and background, as well as general knowledge of the area being policed."[158]

---

[153] The information that the person must provide is prescribed by s.13(1A) of the Criminal Procedure (Scotland) Act 1995.

[154] What will be s.13(1B) and (1C) of the 1995 Act, as introduced by the Police, Public Order and Criminal Justice (Scotland) Act 2006 s.82.

[155] Criminal Procedure (Scotland) Act 1995 s.13(2)–(4).

[156] Criminal Procedure (Scotland) Act 1995 s.13(5).

[157] Criminal Procedure (Scotland) Act 1995 s.13(6)(b). A police officer cannot, however, require a person detained under this provision to remain with them while they verify the particulars given.

[158] *Renton and Brown's Criminal Procedure*, 6th edn, (Edinburgh: W. Green), para.A4.27. In *Dryburgh v Galt*, 1981 J.C. 69, Lord Wheatley held that even an ill founded suspicion might constitute reasonable cause to suspect: "... the fact that the information on which the police officer formed his suspicion turns out to be ill-founded does not in itself necessarily establish that the police

But it must, like the suspicion necessary to justify arrest, be founded on facts known, or imparted, to the constable and not the suspicion of someone else: a bald instruction to a constable to detain a suspect will not suffice.[159]

12–21 The status of a person required to "remain" under s.13 while a constable checks their name and address and/or notes their explanation is unclear. While the section must mean something less than arrest, or, under the 1995 Act regime, detention (otherwise there would be no need for s.13 at all), a person can not only be required to remain but can be physically constrained to do so. Moreover, while the constable has the power to require an explanation of the circumstances that have given rise to their suspicion, they are not enjoined to administer a caution at this stage. Presumably if the circumstances were such that a constable felt a caution to be appropriate, the power to arrest should be used instead (although this is not to say that anything volunteered by the person asked to remain would be inadmissible for want of a caution).

SEARCH

12–22 At common law, the police are entitled to search without warrant the person of anyone they have lawfully arrested, and this right of search extends to fingerprinting and photographing the suspect.[160] Section 18(2) of the 1995 Act provides, more specifically, that a constable may take from a person arrested fingerprints, palm prints and other such prints and impressions of an external part of the body as the constable reasonably considers it appropriate to take, having regard to the circumstances of the suspected offence in respect of which the person has been arrested. Section 18(6) provides that the constable may also take, with the authority of an officer of a rank no lower than inspector: a sample of hair; a sample of fingernail or toenail (or of material under the nails); a sample of blood or other body fluid, body tissue or other material from an external part of the body by means of swabbing or rubbing; or a sample of saliva. Reasonable force may be used. Before arrest, however, a person may not be searched at common law.[161] Search before arrest must be justified by reference to some statutory provision,[162] or must be founded on a warrant. It has been held that warrants to search a person prior to arrest:

---

officer's suspicion was unfounded. The circumstances known to the police officer at the time he formed his suspicion constitute the criterion, not the facts as subsequently ascertained."

[159] *HM Advocate v B* [2013] HCJ 71; 2013 S.L.T. 810; *Renton and Brown's Criminal Procedure Legislation* (Edinburgh: W. Green), para.A4-27.

[160] *Adair v McGarry (James Lyon)*, 1933 J.C. 72; and see the Criminal Justice (Scotland) Act 2016 ss.47–48.

[161] Unless they consent to what would otherwise be an assault: see, e.g. *Devlin v Normand*, 1992 S.C.C.R. 875. Searches carried out before arrest in situations of urgency may also be excused in the interests of justice, and the evidence thereby obtained admitted at trial, subject to the overarching test of fairness: see, e.g. *Bell (William Adamson) v Hogg*, 1967 J.C. 49.

[162] e.g. Misuse of Drugs Act 1971 s.23(2), which entitles a constable to detain and search a person whom they have reasonable grounds to believe is in possession of a controlled drug; Civic Government (Scotland) Act 1982 s.60(1)(a), which entitles a constable to search a person whom they have reasonable grounds to suspect is in possession of any stolen property; and Criminal Law (Consolidation) (Scotland) Act 1995 ss.48–50 conferring powers to search for offensive weapons and knives a person is reasonably believed to have about them.

> "will not be lightly granted, and will only be granted where the circumstances are special and where the granting of the warrant will not disturb the delicate balance that must be maintained between the public interest on the one hand and the interest of the accused on the other."[163]

But the requirement of "special circumstances" seems to be met by any intelligible explanation of the need for a warrant.[164] Provided the procurator fiscal applying for the warrant is able to satisfy the court that it is likely to turn up some useful evidence, it will normally be granted: the unusual cases will be those in which the warrant is refused.

In relation to the search of premises, again the ideal form of search is that which is authorised by a warrant. The need to obtain a warrant is removed where a person consents to the search.[165] Arrest warrants normally include warrant to search the arrestee's premises and vehicles for evidence,[166] but warrants to search may be granted in the absence of arrest or charge, either under the numerous statutory provisions that authorise this or at common law. Where the grant of a warrant is conditional, on a constable giving information on oath that they have reasonable cause to suspect, for example the presence of drugs on particular premises, the justice of the peace must inquire into the grounds for that suspicion and satisfy themselves of its reasonableness,[167] and it would seem, in light of the Human Rights Act 1998, that a justice should always so satisfy themselves before granting any warrant to search. Where, however, a warrant is sought for information in the hands of solicitors, and it should be apparent that legal privilege may be asserted, that ought to be made clear to the sheriff at the time the warrant is sought and the fact a warrant is being sought should be intimated to the solicitors so that they have an opportunity to make representations to the sheriff.[168] Where a warrant is granted that may include within its scope material subject to legal privilege, the search should be conducted under the supervision of a court-appointed commissioner or any material that is recovered should be sealed without having been read and delivered to the sheriff to determine what to do with it.[169]

A general warrant to search any premises for any article is incompetent.[170] A search warrant must be specific in its terms and the police must keep within its limits when conducting a search under it. As this implies, "law enforcement officers cannot be treated as acting under and in terms of legal powers of which they are at the time in question ignorant and heedless".[171] Any search conducted in ignorance of the terms of the warrant will, therefore, be a random search and unlawful on that account. The manner of execution of a search warrant may also

---

163 *Morris v MacNeill*, 1991 S.L.T. 607, per Lord Justice Clerk Ross at p.609. See, e.g. *Hay (Gordon) v HM Advocate*, 1968 J.C. 40, where a warrant was granted for the taking of dental impressions.

164 *Renton and Brown's Criminal Procedure*, 6th edn (Edinburgh: W. Green), para.5.08.

165 *Davidson (Heather) v Brown*, 1990 J.C. 324.

166 See, e.g. Criminal Procedure (Scotland) Act 1995 s.135.

167 *Birse (Gordon Dickson) v HM Advocate*, 2000 J.C. 503.

168 *Holman Fenwick Willan LLP v Procurator Fiscal, Glasgow*, 2017 S.L.T. 899 cited with approval (albeit under the name *H, Petitioner*) in *Clyde and Co (Scotland) LLP v Richardson*, 2016 S.L.T. 1200.

169 *Ibid*. See para.12–11, above on the importance of legal privilege.

170 *Bell v Black and Morrison* (1865) 5 Irv. 57.

171 *Hoekstra v HM Advocate*, 2002 S.L.T. 599, per Lord Justice General Cullen at [55]; see also *Leckie v Miln*, 1982 S.L.T. 177.

be relevant to its legality and hence to the admissibility in evidence of items recovered under it. Certainly where a search warrant restricts the class or number of persons who may execute it, any breach of those restrictions will render the search unlawful unless the irregularity is excusable.[172] It may also be the case that the unduly oppressive execution of a search warrant—for example, in the middle of the night, or by an unnecessarily large number of officers—may render the search unlawful as being a disproportionate invasion of the subject's privacy.[173] On the other hand, where police officers engaged on a lawful search of premises stumble across "plainly incriminatory" articles not covered by the warrant, such articles may be removed and will be admissible in evidence.[174]

There are a number of statutory provisions authorising the search without warrant of premises or vehicles, but at common law the power of the police to enter and search private premises is limited. As a starting point, it may be said that the right of a police officer to enter private premises for any purpose without a warrant and without the occupier's consent is no greater than that of any other member of the public, and if the police do so enter, they must be prepared to justify their conduct by reference to special circumstances before any evidence thus obtained may be held admissible:

> "Irregularities require to be excused, and infringements of the formalities of the law in relation to these matters are not lightly to be condoned. Whether any given irregularity ought to be excused depends upon the nature of the irregularity and the circumstances under which it was committed."[175]

An urgent need to obtain evidence, particularly in relation to serious offences, may justify a search without warrant of private property.[176] Other circumstances that may excuse an irregular search are the authority and good faith of those who obtained the evidence.[177] Even where evidence is illegally obtained, it does not necessarily follow, either as a matter of domestic law or under the Convention, that it is inadmissible in subsequent criminal proceedings.[178] Thus, the Convention-proofing of police powers of entry, search and seizure may be less a matter for the police themselves, under reference to art.8 of the Convention, but rather a matter for the court in considering the admissibility of evidence under reference to art.6.

---

[172] *Singh (Manjit) v HM Advocate*, 2001 S.L.T. 812; but cf. *Hepburn (James) v Brown*, 1998 J.C. 63 and *Lord Advocates Reference (No.1 of 2002)*, 2002 S.L.T. 1017.

[173] *Chappell v United Kingdom* (1990) 12 E.H.R.R. 1.

[174] *Pringle v Bremner and Stirling* (1867) 5 M. (H.L.) 55; *HM Advocate v Hepper (Patrick)*, 1958 S.L.T. 160; *Drummond (Thomas) v HM Advocate*, 1992 J.C. 88.

[175] *Lawrie (Jeanie) v Muir*, 1950 S.L.T. 37 at p.42.

[176] *HM Advocate v McGuigan (John)*, 1936 S.L.T. 161.

[177] In addition to *Lawrie v Muir*, see also, e.g. *Wilson (David James) v Brown*, 1996 S.L.T. 686; and *Webley v Ritchie*, 1997 S.L.T. 1241.

[178] *Schenk v Switzerland* (1988) 13 E.H.R.R. 242; *Khan v United Kingdom* (2000) 8 B.H.R.C. 310. Where a warrant has been obtained, if there is a procedural failing (i.e. the validity of the warrant is not subject to question), the admissibility of the evidence recovered falls to be considered in the whole circumstances, one such circumstance being the validity of the warrant: *S(A) v HM Advocate* [2016] HCJAC 126; 2017 J.C. 180.

QUESTIONING

The rules on questioning are, in fact, rules on the admissibility of evidence—there being no point asking questions in a manner that, or in circumstances that, will result in the court refusing to admit the answers as evidence. There are forms of questioning that, whatever the worth of the information they elicit, must be regarded as so offensive to the values of the common law, as well as the Convention, as to render the information inadmissible (or its admission a breach of art.6) and the questioning itself unlawful and a breach of some other Convention right.[179] As a matter of constitutional principle, evidence obtained by torture is inadmissible and torture has, for centuries, been unlawful.[180] Beyond that, the Strasbourg Court has derived a right to silence from the presumption of innocence enshrined in art.6(2) of the Convention, such that a suspect cannot be obliged to answer questions[181] (although this is not to say that adverse inferences cannot be drawn from a suspect's silence).[182] Different issues are raised by compulsory powers of questioning, where the suspect is obliged to answer the questions put by a police officer or other investigative authority on pain of criminal penalty. In *Saunders v United Kingdom*,[183] it was held that the extensive use made by the prosecution at the applicant's trial of answers he had been compelled to give under ss.432 and 442 of the Companies Act 1985 violated the presumption of innocence and rendered his trial unfair. Even so, it does not follow that all compulsory questioning, and any evidence gleaned thereby, is contrary to art.6. As the Judicial Committee of the Privy Council held in *Brown v Stott*,[184] if the right in question is not absolute—and plainly the presumption of innocence is not—the question is whether the restriction or modification of the right pursued a legitimate aim, and whether there is a reasonable relationship of proportionality between the means employed and the aim sought to be realised.[185] The overarching question is always whether the trial viewed as a whole is fair.[186] **12–23**

As a matter of Scots law, a person cannot be questioned further, once they have been formally charged, about the offence with which they are charged.[187] **12–24**

---

179 See, e.g. *Ireland v United Kingdom* (1978) 2 E.H.R.R. 25, where the European Court of Human Rights found the "five techniques" employed in the interrogation of terrorist suspects to constitute inhuman and degrading treatment contrary to art.3.

180 See *A v Home Secretary* [2005] UKHL 71; [2006] 2 A.C. 221, especially per Lord Bingham at [51]. As Lord Rodger notes at [129], it has been unlawful in Scotland since the end of the seventeenth century (which was later than in England).

181 *Funke v France* (1993) 16 E.H.R.R. 297 at 44.

182 See *Murray v United Kingdom* (1996) 22 E.H.R.R. 313, although the court noted that it would be incompatible with art.6(2) of the Convention, to base a conviction wholly or mainly on an accused's silence or failure to answer questions or give evidence.

183 *Saunders v United Kingdom* (1997) 23 E.H.R.R. 313.

184 *Brown v Stott*, 2001 S.C. (P.C.) 43. That case concerned the obligation imposed by the Road Traffic Act 1988 to identify the driver of a car that, in this case, led to her conviction for drink driving.

185 *Brown v Stott*, 2001 S.C. (P.C.) 43, per Lord Hope at [74]–[75].

186 That is not, of course, merely a matter of the fairness of admitting particular items of evidence, but encompasses all the other incidents of a fair trial, such as the right to be tried within a reasonable time (*Dyer v Watson* [2002] UKPC D 1; 2002 S.C. (P.C.) 89), the right to an independent and impartial tribunal (*Starrs v Ruxton*, 2000 J.C. 208) and the right to equality of arms, one aspect of which may be the presence, absence or adequacy of the accused's legal representation (*Buchanan v McLean* [2001] UKPC D 3; 2002 S.C. (P.C.) 1).

187 *Carmichael v Boyd (Ryan)*, 1993 J.C. 219.

Following arrest, the police are entitled to question that person, provided the questioning is not unfair.[188] Whether the court will admit evidence obtained during questioning is ultimately one of fairness, and that is to be assessed in all of the circumstances.[189] Administration of a caution is a factor, but not a decisive factor, in determining fairness and thus admissibility. As Lord Justice General Hope explained in *Pennycuick v Lees*:

> "There is . . . no rule of law which requires that a suspect must always be cautioned before any question can be put to him by the police or by anyone else by whom the inquiries are being conducted. The question in each case is whether what was done was unfair to the accused . . .
>
> [It] is important to note that there is no suggestion in [this] case that any undue pressure, deception or other device was used to obtain the admissions."[190]

A person should ordinarily be cautioned prior to questioning and, to avoid any risk of rendering statements inadmissible, the common law caution should be re-administered as often as necessary during a long period of questioning, and administered afresh after any break in questioning. The "common law" caution requires the person to be told that they are not obliged to say anything, but that anything they do say will be taken down (and recorded) and may be used in evidence. The question of fairness is a question of fact and, accordingly, one that the Appeal Court will only rarely disturb. The fact part of a statement or interview is inadmissible does not necessarily mean that it falls to be excluded in its entirety.[191] Evidence obtained by threat or inducement, or where the questioning amounts to bullying, is inadmissible.[192] Placing two suspects in adjoining cells then stationing a police officer to overhear any conservation between the suspects is also unfair (indeed the court held it amounted to unauthorised intrusive surveillance).[193] The court has come and gone on how strict a line it is prepared to take on what is "unfair" in terms of questioning. In *Codona v HM Advocate*, the Lord Justice General (Hope) held as follows:

> "In order that a statement made by an accused person to the police may be available as evidence against him, it must be truly spontaneous and voluntary. The police may question a suspect, but when they move into the field of cross-examination or interrogation, they move into an area of great difficulty. If the questioning is carried too far, by means of leading or repetitive questioning or by pressure in other ways in an effort to obtain from the suspect what they are seeking to obtain from him, the statement is likely to be excluded on the ground that it was extracted by unfair means. Lord Justice-General Emslie's definition of the words 'interrogation' and

---

[188] *Johnston (Derek) v HM Advocate*, 1993 J.C. 187.

[189] For a general discussion, see *Renton and Brown's Criminal Procedure*, 6th edn (Edinburgh: W. Green), paras 24.39–24.45.

[190] *Pennycuick v Lees*, 1992 S.L.T. 763 at pp.765 and 766. See also, e.g. *Young v Friel*, 1992 S.C.C.R. 567; *HM Advocate v Graham (James)*, 1991 S.L.T. 416. For a recent example, following the approach outlined in *Penncuick*, see: *Logan v HM Advocate* [2020] HCJAC 10.

[191] *Lord Advocate's Reference (No.1 of 1983)*, 1984 J.C. 52.

[192] *Paul (Ross Duncan) v HM Advocate* [2013] HCJAC 13; 2014 S.C.C.R. 119. That includes repetitive or prolonged questioning in the face of the right to silence being exercised, and repeated suggestions that a person should reconsider can amount to undue pressure by undermining the legal advice they have received. Where, in such circumstances, a person does decide to start answering questions, the answers may well be inadmissible: *HM Advocate v H*, 2017 S.L.T. 1328.

[193] *HM Advocate v Higgins* Unreported 11 March 1993 High Court of Justiciary on appeal.

> 'cross-examination' in *Lord Advocates Reference (No.1 of 1983)*, as referring only to improper forms of questioning tainted with an element of bullying or pressure designed to break the will of the suspect or to force from him a confession against his will, should not be understood as implying any weakening of these important principles."[194]

Plainly, the stricter the test of fairness then the easier it is for a trial judge to justify withholding evidence from the jury on the basis that no reasonable jury could conclude that it had been fairly obtained.

FREEDOM OF ASSEMBLY, PUBLIC ORDER AND PROCESSIONS

Introduction

"[One] of the features of a vigorous and healthy democracy [is] . . . that people are allowed to go out onto the streets and demonstrate"[195] and "demonstration and protest and civil disobedience have a long and indeed proud history" in the UK.[196] Despite that, the approach of the common law to freedom of assembly was "hesitant and negative, permitting that which was not prohibited".[197] For Dicey, freedom of assembly was no more than the consequence of the ordinary freedoms enjoyed by the individual: **12–25**

> ". . . it can hardly be said that our constitution knows of such a thing as any specific right of public meeting . . . The right of assembly is nothing more than a result of the view taken by the Courts as to individual liberty of persons."[198]

Whatever view Dicey formed, it is now a matter that is heavily regulated by statute and in this part of the chapter, we are going to consider those regulations. However, this is an area that is heavily influenced by the European Convention on Human Rights and in particular art.10 (freedom of expression), but even more so art.11 (freedom of assembly and association). So it is with art.11 that we begin.

Article 11 of the European Convention on Human Rights

Article 11 of the Convention provides: **12–26**

[194] *Codona v HM Advocate*, 1996 S.L.T. 1100 at p.1105.
[195] *Austin v Metropolitan Police Commissioner* [2009] UKHL 5; [2009] 1 A.C. 564 at [1].
[196] *Lord Advocates Reference (No.1 of 2000)*, 2001 J.C. 143 at [17]. See also *R. (on the application of Catt) v Association of Chief Police Officers* [2015] UKSC 9; [2015] A.C. 1065, per Lord Sumption at [19].
[197] *R. (on the application of Laporte) v Chief Constable of Gloucestershire* [2006] UKHL 55; [2007] 2 A.C. 105, per Lord Bingham at [34].
[198] Albert V. Dicey, *Introduction to the Study of the Law of the Constitution*, 8th edn (London: 1915), pp.169–170. Dicey also wrote (at p.169) that "the police have with us [in England] no special authority to control open-air assemblies". As we will now see, that is certainly no longer the case.

> "Everyone has the right to freedom of peaceful assembly and to freedom of association with others, including the right to form and to join trade unions for the protection of his interests."

Article 11 is important as it provides a vehicle through which other rights, such as freedom of religion (art.9) and freedom of expression (art.10) can be secured.[199] "Assembly" is construed widely, including public and private meetings, marches, public processions and sit-ins. The right is confined to peaceful assemblies, but an assembly does not lose that character merely because it is marred by "incidental" violence or because it attracts a violent response from others:

> "... the possibility of violent counter-demonstrations, or the possibility of extremists with violent intentions, not members of the organising association, joining the demonstration cannot as such take away that right."[200]

Similarly, even where a protest is deliberately intended to cause disruption, it falls within the scope of art.11.[201] As a consequence, art.11 carries with it a positive obligation on the state to provide assistance to those who wish to protest. Simply abstaining from interfering with a person's art.11 right is not sufficient for the state to fulfil its obligations. As the Strasbourg Court has explained:

> "A demonstration may annoy or give offence to persons opposed to the ideas or claims that it is seeking to promote. The participants must, however, be able to hold the demonstration without having to fear that they will be subjected to physical violence by their opponents; such a fear would be liable to deter associations or other groups supporting common ideas or interests from openly expressing their opinions on highly controversial issues affecting the community. In a democracy the right to counter-demonstrate cannot extend to inhibiting the exercise of the right to demonstrate."[202]

Organisers of an assembly, and not just the attendees, fall within the scope of art.11.[203]

Article 11 is, however, a qualified right: it may be restricted where to do so is necessary in a democratic society, pursuant to a legitimate aim and the restriction is prescribed by law. The legitimate aims are set out in art.11(2) and it is normally "public safety" or the "prevention of disorder or crime" that are relied upon to justify an interference with this right. The requirement that an interference is "prescribed by law" is not difficult to satisfy: the law must be sufficiently

---

199 For example, *Metropolitan Church of Bessarabia v Moldova* (2002) 35 E.H.R.R. 13 at [118] where art.9 was required to be interpreted in accordance with art.11; and *Socialist Party v Turkey* (1998) 27 E.H.R.R. 51 at 41.

200 *Christians Against Racism and Fascism v United Kingdom* (1980) 21 D.R. 138 at 4.

201 For example, *Cuadrilla Bowman Ltd v Persons Unknown* [2020] 4 W.L.R. 29.

202 *Plattform "Artze fur das Leben" v Austria* (1985) 13 E.H.R.R. 204 at 32. See also B. Fitzpatrick and N. Taylor, "Trespassers *Might* Be Prosecuted: The European Convention and Restrictions on the Right to Assemble" [1998] E.H.R.L.R. 292; H. Fenwick, "The Right to Protest, the Human Rights Act and the Margin of Appreciation" (1999) 62(4) M.L.R. 491; D. Mead, "The Right to Peaceful Protest under the European Convention on Human Rights—A Content Study of Strasbourg Case Law" [2007] E.H.R.L.R. 345.

203 *Christians Against Racism and Fascism v United Kingdom* (1980) D.R. 21 at 138. A requirement for prior approval does not, on its own, infringe art.11: *Rassemblement Jurassien v Switzerland* (1979) D.R. 17 at 93.

accessible and sufficiently foreseeable.[204] Whether a restriction is "necessary" is normally the most challenging criteria to assess. "Necessary" is not synonymous with "indispensable", but nor does it have the flexibility of words such as "ordinary", "useful", "reasonable" or "desirable". What the use of the word necessary does imply is that there is a "pressing social need".[205] For a measure to be "necessary" it must also be proportionate. The requirements of proportionality have been discussed in Ch.11, above and Ch.15, below.[206] States are normally afforded a generous margin of appreciation is determining what was necessary.[207] We will discuss some of the leading cases where the courts have had to assess the legitimacy of an interference with art.11. Before doing so, however, it is helpful to set out the statutory framework within which public processions and gatherings are now regulated.

Public processions and assemblies

As a general rule, public processions must be notified at least 28 days in advance to the relevant local authority and chief constable.[208] The local authority may, after consulting the chief constable, issue an order either prohibiting the procession or imposing upon it conditions as to its date, time, duration and route.[209] The considerations to which the authority must have regard in deciding whether to make such an order include the risk of damage to property or disruption of the life of the community, and whether the proposed procession would impose a disproportionate burden on the police. Section 64 of the 1982 Act provides a right of appeal to the sheriff against an order made under s.63.[210] The sheriff may only uphold an appeal if they find that the local authority made an error of law or material error of fact, exercised its discretion unreasonably (in the *Wednesbury* sense) or otherwise acted beyond its powers.[211] It is an offence to hold a procession without giving notice as required by s.62 or in contravention of **12–27**

---

204 *Sunday Times v United Kingdom* (1979–80) 2 E.H.R.R. 245 at 49.

205 *Sunday Times v United Kingdom* (1979–80) 2 E.H.R.R. 245 at 59; *Handyside v United Kingdom* (1979–80) 1 E.H.R.R. 737 at 48. In both cases, the court was considering art.10. The court has repeated this formulation in the context of art.8 in *Dudgeon v United Kingdom* (1982) 4 E.H.R.R. 149.

206 For a recent discussion, in the context of whether an interference with art.8 was "necessary", see *Gaughran v Chief Constable of the Police Service of Northern Ireland* [2015] UKSC 29; [2015] 2 W.L.R. 1303.

207 For example, *Kudrevicius v Lithuania* (2016) 62 E.H.R.R. 34.

208 Civic Government (Scotland) Act 1982 s.62, as amended by s.70 of the Police, Public Order and Criminal Justice (Scotland) Act 2006. The Scottish Ministers may designate certain processions as being exempt from these notification requirements, and local authorities may waive the requirement of 28 days' notice in exceptional circumstances.

209 Civic Government (Scotland) Act 1982 s.63, as amended by s.71 of the Police, Public Order and Criminal Justice (Scotland) Act 2006. These conditions may include a prohibition on the entry by the procession into any public place specified in the order.

210 For a recent example, see *Apprentice Boys of Derry, Bridgeton v Glasgow City Council*, 2019 S.L.T. (Sh. Ct) 317.

211 Civic Government (Scotland) Act 1982 s.64(4). Note that in *DPP v Jones* [2002] EWHC 110 (Admin), it was held that the imposition of ultra vires conditions (there, on a public assembly pursuant to the Public Order Act 1986 s.14) did not render the order as a whole invalid, since the unlawful conditions could simply be severed from the notice.

the terms of an order under s.63,[212] and to refuse to desist from taking part in such a procession when required to do so by a uniformed police officer.[213]

Section 12 of the Public Order Act 1986 confers supplementary powers on the police to impose additional (or different) conditions on a public procession should this prove necessary. The power is exercisable only where the senior police officer present at the procession reasonably believes that it may lead to serious public disorder, serious damage to property or serious disruption of the life of the community; or that the purpose of the organisers is to intimidate others with a view to preventing them doing what they have a right to do or compelling them to do something that they have no right to do.[214] The conditions imposed must be those that the police officer believes to be necessary to prevent serious disorder, damage to property, disruption or intimidation. It is an offence to knowingly fail to comply with conditions imposed under s.12, although it is a defence to prove that the failure arose from circumstances beyond one's control.[215] It is also an offence to incite others to commit an offence contrary to s.12.[216]

Powers to regulate and control public assemblies are conferred directly upon the police by s.14 of the 1986 Act. If the senior police officer, having regard to the time, place and circumstances in which any public assembly is being or is intended to be held, reasonably believes that it may lead to serious public disorder, serious damage to property or serious disruption of the life of the community, or that the purpose of the organisers is intimidatory in the sense described above, they may give directions imposing on the organisers and participants such conditions as to the venue, duration and maximum number of persons who may take part as appear necessary to prevent such serious disorder, damage or disruption. These powers apply only to a public assembly, defined by s.16 as meaning "an assembly of twenty or more persons in a public place which is wholly or partly open to the air".[217] A person who organises or takes part in such an assembly, and who knowingly fails to comply with such directions, is guilty of an offence,[218] although it is a defence in either case to prove that failure to comply was due to circumstances beyond one's control. It is also an offence to incite others to commit an offence contrary to s.14.[219]

12–28 The powers of the police in relation to assemblies were augmented by the Criminal Justice and Public Order Act 1994, which inserted new ss.14A–14C into the 1986 Act. Section 14A[220] prohibits "trespassory assemblies", meaning an assembly of 20 or more persons on land wholly in the open air to which the public has no or only limited right of access. If at any time the chief officer of police reasonably believes that a trespassory assembly is intended to be held and

---

[212] Civic Government (Scotland) Act 1982 s.65(1).
[213] Civic Government (Scotland) Act 1982 s.65(2).
[214] The power is exercisable in advance of the procession, but only where people are assembling with a view to taking part in it.
[215] Public Order Act 1986 s.12(4) and (5).
[216] Public Order Act 1986 s.12(6).
[217] "Public place" means "any road within the meaning of the Roads (Scotland) Act 1984" and "any place to which at the material time the public or any section of the public has access, on payment or otherwise, as of right or by virtue of express or implied permission".
[218] Public Order Act 1986 s.14(4) and (5).
[219] Public Order Act 1986 s.14(6).
[220] Criminal Justice and Public Order Act 1994 s.70.

that it is likely to cause serious disruption to the life of the community or significant damage to the land or a building or monument on it (where the land, building or monument are of historical, architectural, archaeological or scientific importance), they may apply to the local authority for an order prohibiting for a specified period not exceeding four days all trespassory assemblies in an area not exceeding the area represented by a circle with a radius of five miles from a specified centre. Section 14B prescribes the offences in connection with trespassory assemblies. Thus, a person who organises or takes part in an assembly that they know to be prohibited by an order made under s.14A is guilty of an offence, as is a person who incites others to take part in a prohibited assembly. Under s.14C, a uniformed police officer may stop a person whom they reasonably believe to be on their way to an assembly prohibited by an order made under s.14A and direct that person not to proceed in the direction of the assembly. This power is only exercisable within the area covered by the order. Failure to comply with the police officer's direction is an offence.

These provisions were considered by the House of Lords in *DPP v Jones*.[221] The defendants were arrested while participating in a peaceful, unobstructive assembly at a roadside near Stonehenge. At the material time, an order made under s.14A prohibiting trespassory assemblies in the vicinity of Stonehenge was in force. The defendants were convicted of offences under s.14B. By a bare majority, the House of Lords quashed the convictions. The critical element in the reasoning of the majority was the finding of fact by the justices of the peace that the defendants' presence at the scene involved no obstruction of the highway. That being so, it fell within the scope of what Lord Irvine LC at least was prepared to recognise as a common law right to use the highway for any reasonable purpose, provided that the activity in question did not amount to a public or private nuisance and did not unreasonably impede the public's primary right to pass and repass.[222] But this was the narrowest of victories for the claims of public protest. Only the Lord Chancellor's speech bore any relation to the analytical pattern established in other cases from the pre-Human Rights Act era involving fundamental rights, in that it identified the scope of the common law right and then insisted that this right was not to be whittled down in the absence of clear statutory words.[223] That apart, one could be forgiven for thinking that the House of Lords discerned no "constitutional issue" in *Jones* at all.

---

221 *DPP v Jones (Margaret)* [1999] 2 A.C. 240.

222 The other members of the majority were rather more equivocal on this point: Lord Hutton, for instance, went no further than saying that the common law right of assembly "is unduly restricted unless it can be exercised in some circumstances on the public highway". For Lord Slynn (dissenting), the common law recognised no common law right to use the highway other than for passage, and "reasonable incidental uses associated with passage".

223 H. Fenwick and G. Phillipson, "Public Protest, the Human Rights Act and Judicial Responses to Political Expression" [2000] P.L. 627, pertinently contrast the decision in *DPP v Jones* with those in the near-contemporaneous cases of *Reynolds v Times Newspapers Ltd* [2001] 2 A.C. 127 and *R. v Secretary of State for the Home Department, Ex p. Simms* [2000] 2 A.C. 115. In both of these, freedom of expression, both as a common law "constitutional right" and as embodied in art.10 of the European Convention, and the values underpinning that freedom, were articulated and formed the starting point for their Lordships' reasoning.

General police powers

12–29 Those specific statutory powers are in addition to the general duty imposed on the police by s.20 of the Police and Fire Reform (Scotland) Act 2012 to maintain order. For example, rallies and assemblies fall outside the scope of the 1986 Act if they are held indoors. In such circumstances, the duty imposed under s.20 of the 2012 Act, coupled with the common law power of the police to prevent or restrain breaches of the peace, provides potentially extensive scope for intruding upon freedom of assembly and expression.[224] The extent of the common law adjunct to statutory police powers was the subject of the decision of the House of Lords in *R. (on the application Laporte) v Chief Constable of Gloucestershire Constabulary*.[225]

The claimant was a passenger on one of three coaches travelling from London to join an anti-war demonstration at RAF Fairford in Gloucestershire. That airbase had become something of a focal point for the expression of opposition to the war in Iraq (it was the base for US B52 bombers that were involved in the conflict), and there had been previous incidents of violent disorder. There was evidence that particular groups were bent on violence at this particular demonstration. The police operation put in place to cover the demonstration was the largest of its kind ever undertaken by the Gloucestershire Constabulary. The day before the demonstration, a senior officer of the force issued a "stop and search" order under s.60 of the Criminal Justice and Public Order Act 1994. Pursuant to that order, the coaches coming from London were intercepted at a village some 5km from the airbase. The vehicles and their passengers were searched. The police found items including wire cutters and baseball bats that led them to conclude that some, but not all, of the people on the coach would commit a breach of the peace when they got to the airbase. Crucially, the chief constable accepted that no breach of the peace was imminent and there were no grounds on which to arrest any of the passengers. Nevertheless, the officer in charge of the operation ordered that the passengers be put back on the coaches and escorted back to London. The claimant subsequently applied for judicial review, contending that the chief constable had acted unlawfully by preventing her from participating in the demonstration and by forcibly returning her to London.

The House of Lords held unanimously that the actions of the chief constable were neither "prescribed by law" nor a proportionate interference with the claimant's rights. The starting point is that a police officer, indeed all citizens, are duty bound to take steps to prevent a breach of the peace occurring in their

[224] See, for example *Thomas v Sawkins* [1935] 2 K.B. 249, in which anticipation of a breach of the peace was held to justify uninvited entry on to private premises; and *McLeod v United Kingdom* (1999) 27 E.H.R.R. 493, in which the existence of this power (or its statutory equivalent under the Police and Criminal Evidence Act 1984) was held not to breach art.8 of the European Convention, but the manner of its exercise in the circumstances of that case (where there was no imminent and immediate threat of disorder) was held to be disproportionate. Equally, the preventive power has been held to permit the imposition of conditions on public meetings otherwise than on a statutory basis: see, for example, *Humphries v Connor* (1864) 17 I.C.L.R. 1; *Duncan v Jones* [1936] 1 K.B. 218; *Piddington v Bates* [1961] 1 W.L.R. 162.

[225] *R. (on the application Laporte) v Chief Constable of Gloucestershire Constabulary* [2006] UKHL 55; [2007] 2 A.C. 105.

presence, whether by arrest or actions short of arrest.[226] Where, however, no breach of the peace had yet occurred a reasonable apprehension of an imminent breach was required before any form of preventative action was permissible.[227] To be imminent the officer concerned must "think that [the breach] is *likely* to happen".[228] Thus, as the chief constable had formed the view that a breach of the peace was *not* imminent when he stopped the coaches he had no power to take preventative action and the decision to send the coaches back to London was unlawful.[229] In any event, four of the five Law Lords held that the police action was premature, was indiscriminate and therefore represented a disproportionate restriction upon the claimant's art.11 right.[230] In dealing with the indiscriminate nature of the chief constable's decision, the House of Lords referred to the Strasbourg decision in *Ziliberberg v Moldova* where the court held:

> "... an individual does not cease to enjoy the right to peaceful assembly as a result of sporadic violence or other punishable acts committed by others in the course of the demonstration, if the individual in question remains peaceful in his or her own intentions or behaviour."[231]

In practice, a "one size fits all" approach to policing public demonstrations may be the only practical option. In *Laporte*, the House of Lords were at pains to emphasise the respect that should be had for the decisions taken by officers who were on the ground.[232] In that case, however, they concluded that the decisions could not be justified and it is clear that the threshold for preventative intervention is a substantial one. It does not, however, follow from *Laporte* that in all circumstances the police are prohibited from taking general and untargeted preventative action.

---

[226] *R. (on the application Laporte) v Chief Constable of Gloucestershire Constabulary* [2006] UKHL 55; [2007] 2 A.C. 105, per Lord Bingham at [29], Lord Rodger at [61] and Lord Brown at [110].

[227] *R. (on the application Laporte) v Chief Constable of Gloucestershire Constabulary* [2006] UKHL 55; [2007] 2 A.C. 105, per Lord Bingham at [30]–[33], Lord Rodger at [62]–[68], per Lord Carswell at [101], Lord Brown at [113]–[114] and Lord Mance at [139]–[142].

[228] *R. (on the application Laporte) v Chief Constable of Gloucestershire Constabulary* [2006] UKHL 55; [2007] 2 A.C. 105, per Lord Rodger at [67] (emphasis in original).

[229] *Moss v McLachlan* [1985] I.R.L.R. 76 DC, upon which the chief constable in *Laporte* placed much reliance, was held, somewhat reluctantly, to be consistent with this analysis. The earlier case arose against the backdrop of the miners' strike of 1984–1985, which was marked by outbreaks of violence between striking and working miners. The claimants in *Moss* were striking miners who were stopped some five minutes' journey time from a colliery on the Nottinghamshire coalfield. Apprehending violence, the police ordered the claimants to turn back. When they refused, they were arrested and charged with obstructing a police officer in the execution of his duty. Skinner J held that the preventive action taken by the police was justified, given the "close proximity in place and time" of the claimants to the colliery and the "imminent and immediate" threat of a breach of the peace occurring there.

[230] *R. (on the application Laporte) v Chief Constable of Gloucestershire Constabulary* [2006] UKHL 55; [2007] 2 A.C. 105, per Lord Bingham at [55], Lord Rodger at [85]–[91], Lord Carswell at [106] and Lord Mance at [152]–[155].

[231] *Ziliberberg v Moldova* (Application No.61821/00) Unreported 4 May 2004 European Court of Human Rights at [2]; see also *R. (on the application Laporte) v Chief Constable of Gloucestershire Constabulary* [2006] UKHL 55; [2007] 2 A.C. 105, per Lord Rodger at [83]: "In the eyes of the law therefore innocent bystanders caught up in a breach of the peace are to be regarded as potentially allies of the police officers who are trying to supress violence."

[232] *R. (on the application Laporte) v Chief Constable of Gloucestershire Constabulary* [2006] UKHL 55; [2007] 2 A.C. 105, per Lord Bingham at [55], Lord Rodger at [90] and Lord Carswell at [106].

12–30 *Austin v Commissioner of Police of the Metropolis* arose out of the 2001 May Day protests in London and concerned the controversial police tactic of "kettling".[233] "Kettling" involves the containment of a group of people by the police on public order grounds. On 1 May 2001, at about 14.00, a large group of protestors arrived in Oxford Circus and took the police by surprise. In 1999 and 2000 there had been a serious breakdown in public order during the May Day demonstrations and the organisers in 2001 had refused to co-operate with the police in relation to the planning of the event. When the group arrived in Oxford Circus, the police took the decision to contain them there and placed an absolute cordon around the group. That group included a number of people that had nothing to do with the demonstration, including at least two that were out on their lunch break. By 14.20 a complete cordon had been put in place by the police. A controlled release was planned but postponed with around 40 per cent of the group actively hostile towards the police. Officers were instructed to identify people that were obviously nothing to do with the protest and 400 such people were released. It was around seven hours before most of the people were released. During that time, they had no access to food, water or toilet facilities. A number of those contained raised proceedings against the police alleging, inter alia, that their art.5 right to liberty had been infringed by the police tactics on 1 May 2001. Founding the claim on art.5 was significant as it is an unqualified right: if it was held that it had been infringed, that could not be justified in the public interest. In the event, the House of Lords held that the people detained within the cordon had not been deprived of their liberty. Lord Neuberger had no difficulty in finding that the police should, in certain circumstances, have the power to detain people to prevent serious public disorder:

> "Any sensible person living in a modern democracy would reasonably expect to be confined, or at least accept that it was proper that she could be confined, within a limited space by the police, in some circumstances."[234]

It was important that any such confinement was proportionate in all the circumstances.[235] That point was emphasised by the Strasbourg Court when it issued its judgment in the case.[236] That court also recognised the challenge facing the police, which made it important that the European Convention on Human Rights was not interpreted in a way that would make it impracticable to maintain public order.[237] This also serves to emphasise the difficult balance that has to be struck, not by lawyers in a courtroom but, in the first instance, by police officers on the ground, in securing both the Convention rights of individuals at the same time as preserving public order.[238]

---

[233] *Austin v Commissioner of Police of the Metropolis* [2009] UKHL 5; [2009] 1 A.C. 564.

[234] *Austin v Commissioner of Police of the Metropolis* [2009] UKHL 5; [2009] 1 A.C. 564 at [58].

[235] *Austin v Commissioner of Police of the Metropolis* [2009] UKHL 5; [2009] 1 A.C. 564, per Lord Hope of Craighead at [34].

[236] *Austin v United Kingdom* (2012) 55 E.H.R.R. 14 at [60].

[237] *Austin v United Kingdom* (2012) 55 E.H.R.R. 14 at [56].

[238] In a similar vein, see *R. (on the application of Catt) v Association of Chief Police Officers* [2015] UKSC 9; [2015] 2 W.L.R. 664 where the blanket retention of information on attendees at political protests was upheld where only an element on the ground were a threat to public order.

Breach of the peace

Finally, a word about the common law offence of breach of the peace. The breadth of the offence gave rise to doubts about its compatibility with the European Convention on Human Rights (being too unspecific so as to not be "prescribed by law"). In *Smith v Donnelly* the High Court reviewed the scope of this offence. S had been protesting at the Faslane Naval Base (home of the UK nuclear submarine fleet). She had lain down on the road to block the entrance to the base. When she refused to move, she was arrested and charged with having committed a breach of the peace. At her trial, S raised a devolution issue and argued that the definition of breach of the peace was too vague to be compatible with the European Convention. The definition, distilled from the existing authorities, of the offence adopted by the court was "conduct which does present as genuinely alarming and disturbing, in its context, to any reasonable person".[239] That formulation has been approved by the Strasbourg Court and an enlarged bench of the High Court.[240] As a consequence, any exercise of the Convention rights of expression, assembly or association must be done in a manner that would not, in that context, present as genuinely alarming or disturbing to a reasonable person. To so is to commit an offence and would justify interference with that person's Convention rights. **12–31**

[239] *Smith v Donnelly*, 2002 J.C. 65 at [17].

[240] *Lucas v United Kingdom* (2003) 37 E.H.R.R. CD 86 and *Jones v Carnegie*, 2004 J.C. 136, respectively.

CHAPTER 13

Terrorism and the Constitution

INTRODUCTION

The scourge of terrorism is not new. The UK has had to contend with the terrorist consequences of the troubles in Northern Ireland (and, prior to that, with terrorist activities associated with the campaign for Irish home rule). Most other western European countries, albeit to lesser extents, have also required to confront domestic terrorism,[1] and Arab terrorism has long been a feature of European life. The nature of the UK's present response to terrorism, however, is relatively new—and is not, as might be thought, merely a reaction to the Al-Qaeda attacks on New York and Washington on 11 September 2001. At one level, it might be thought that the "globalisation" of terror demanded, and demands, unprecedented counter-terrorism measures.[2] At the same time, as the decision of the House of Lords in *A v Secretary of State for the Home Department*[3] makes abundantly clear, certain of those measures, when tested against the precepts of respect for fundamental rights, necessity and proportionality, raise unsettling questions. In refusing the Secretary of State's appeal in *J1 v Home Secretary*, the consequence of which was Abu Qatada's deportation was prevented, Jackson LJ succinctly captured the dilemma that terrorism presents the law: **13–01**

> "I should add that this is a decision which I reach with little enthusiasm. The appellant has been closely associating with Islamist extremists who are involved in terrorism. Such people show scant regard for the rights to life of others. I have no doubt that the Secretary of State was entitled to conclude that the appellant's deportation was conducive to the public interest on national security grounds. The fact remains, however, that the UK is party to the ECHR and has incorporated its provisions into our domestic law. Everyone within our shores is entitled to protection under the ECHR, even those who are involved in or connected with terrorism. The courts are under a duty to uphold those rights and we do so in this case."[4]

---

[1] Basque and Corsican separatists have waged terrorist campaigns against the governments of Spain and France; in Germany, Italy and Greece, extreme left-wing terrorist organisations have engaged in campaigns of terrorist violence, usually involving the kidnapping and/or murder of prominent individuals.

[2] It might equally be thought that it is not merely the globalisation of terror that calls for a heightened response, but also—as witness the perpetrators of the suicide bombings in London on 7 July 2005—its "domestication".

[3] *A v Secretary of State for the Home Department* [2004] UKHL 56; [2005] 2 A.C. 68.

[4] *J1 v Secretary of State for the Home Department* [2013] EWCA Civ 279 at [94].

It is in responding to terrorist threats where many, if not all, of the constitutional ideals discussed earlier come into sharp focus: closed trials; detention without trial; "control orders"; special advocates; reverse burdens of proof; and the need to balance the rights of society with the rights of an individual determined to cause indiscriminate damage to that society. It is an area where there are rarely obviously right answers but selecting the wrong answer can be life threatening. With the stakes (and often emotions) so high it is perhaps unsurprising that it is the response to terrorism that has so often tested our commitment, as a society, to the rule of law and placed the separation of powers under almost unbearable strain.[5] But as Lord Bingham reminded us, "[i]t is, however, when human rights are under pressure that human rights guarantees are most important".[6]

This chapter is split in to two parts. First, we look briefly at some of the main anti-terrorism laws that are currently in place.[7] Second, we look at three different case studies to illustrate the tension that is placed on the constitutional principles discussed elsewhere in this text and to illustrate how difficult the balance is to strike, but also how important it is that in seeking to protect and preserve the state we do not compromise the ideas that define it. But before that, it is helpful to remember that this is not a new problem. The UK has faced many of these questions before and has not always lived up to our modern-day expectations. To illustrate that point, it is helpful to go back to May 1940 and tell the story of a successful Jewish businessman, Jack Perlzweig, who is now more commonly known as Robert Liversidge.[8]

13–02 On 29 May 1940 Mr Liversidge was arrested and taken to Brixton Prison. He was to remain there for nearly 20 months. He did not, however, know why he had been detained and was never charged with any offence. May 1940 was a time of great anxiety: the Second World War was in its second year and a German invasion appeared imminent. The previous year the Home Secretary had made the Defence (General) Regulations 1939. Regulation 18B provided:

> "The Secretary of State, if satisfied with respect to any particular person that with a view to prevent him from acting in any manner prejudicial to the public safety or the defence of the Realm it is necessary to do so, may make an order against that person directing that he be detained."

In May 1940 the Home Secretary signed an order authorising the detention of Mr Liversidge. In the spring of 1941 Mr Liversidge sought to challenge the lawfulness of his detention. At every stage his challenge failed and by September 1941 his appeal to the House of Lords was heard.[9] By then the issue had become a focused one: was it enough for the Home Secretary, acting in good faith, to believe he had reasonable cause to authorise Mr Liversidge's detention? Or did the Home Secretary actually have to have reasonable cause to found that belief?

---

[5] On that point, Sir John Laws second Hamlyn Lecture is commended: J. Laws, *The Common Law Constitution* (CUP; Cambridge: 2014), Lecture II (*The Common Law and Extremism*).

[6] T. Bingham, "The Human Rights Act" [2010] E.H.R.L.R. 568, 575.

[7] As will become apparent in a moment, this is an area where the law changes often. So "current" means in force in early 2020. At the time of writing, the government had committed to further anti-terrorism legislation in response to recent terror-related attacks in the UK.

[8] See also "Mr Perlzweig, Mr Liversidge, and Lord Atkin", in T. Bingham, *The Business of Judging* (Oxford: Oxford University Press, 2000), Ch.3.

[9] *Liversidge v Anderson* [1942] A.C. 206.

If it was the former, there was no role for the courts; if it was the latter, it was for the court to review whether the Home Secretary had reasonable cause for his belief.[10] The House of Lords preferred the former. Lord Macmillan, reflective of the majority view of the House, said:

> "In a matter at once so vital and so urgent in the interests of national safety, I am unable to accept a reading of the regulation which would prescribe that the Secretary of State may not act in accordance with what commends itself to him as a reasonable cause of belief without incurring the risk that a court of law would disagree with him … ."[11]

The majority of the House of Lords was concerned that if the Home Secretary was required to demonstrate the reasonableness of his belief, he would be unable to do so due to the national security consequences of disclosing his sources.[12] In short, the highest court in the land had allowed the executive to claim, through delegated legislation, the power to detain any person without limit of time, without trial and without review by the courts.

Lord Atkin provided the sole dissent and it was a dissent that ensured Mr Liversidge his place in history:

> "I view with apprehension the attitude of judges who on a mere question of construction when face to face with claims involving the liberty of the subject show themselves more executive minded than the executive… In this country, amid the clash of arms, the laws are not silent. They may be changed, but they speak the same language in war as in peace. It has always been one of the pillars of freedom, one of the principles of liberty for which on recent authority we are now fighting, that the judges are no respecters of persons and stand between the subject and any attempted encroachment on his liberty by the executive, alert to see that any coercive action is justified in law. …
>
> I protest, even if I do it alone, against a strained construction put on words with the effect of giving an uncontrolled power of imprisonment to the Minister. …
>
> I know of only one authority which might justify the suggested method of construction: '"When I use a word," Humpty Dumpty said in a rather scornful tone, "it means just what I choose it to mean, neither more nor less."
>
> "The question is," said Alice, "whether you can make words mean so many different things."
>
> "The question is," said Humpty Dumpty, "which is to be master—that's all." …
>
> After all this long discussion the question is whether the words 'If a man has' can mean 'If a man thinks he has'. I am of opinion that they cannot, and that the case should be decided accordingly."[13]

That dissent, not least the reference to Humpty Dumpty, made Lord Atkin deeply unpopular with his colleagues and divided academic opinion at the time.[14]

---

[10] *Liversidge v Anderson* [1942] A.C. 206, per Lord Macmillan at p.248.

[11] *Liversidge v Anderson* [1942] A.C. 206, per Lord Macmillan at p.257.

[12] For example, *Liversidge v Anderson* [1942] A.C. 206, per Lord Macmillan at p.254. As we will see below, this is a problem that the government of today still complains about.

[13] *Liversidge v Anderson* [1942] A.C. 206, per Lord Atkin at p.245.

[14] A. Paterson, *Final Judgment: The Last Law Lords and the Supreme Court* (Oxford: Hart Publishing, 2013), p.150

Although described as a "very peculiar decision",[15] it was not until 1979 that the House of Lords recognised that Lord Atkin had been correct all along:

> "... [T]the time has come to acknowledge openly that the majority of this House in *Liversidge v Anderson* were expediently and, at that time, perhaps, excusably, wrong and the dissenting speech of Lord Atkin was right."[16]

What is the relevance of the case to us today? It serves as a reminder that in times of crisis, it is easy to abridge the rights of those that are perceived to be a threat. In *Liversidge* the executive had claimed, Parliament approved, and the courts endorsed, a power to detain without limit of time on the say so of a government minister. Such an arbitrary power is clearly inconsistent with the rule of law. Yet in the twenty first century, Parliament sought to vest similar powers in the executive, in response to what was said to be a threat to the life of the nation. As we will see, the courts were more vigilant on that occasion. Similarly, the House of Lords in *Liversidge* wrestled with the balance between the accused's right to know the case against him and the need for the security services to protect their sources and their methods. That is a debate that continues today and one that we will examine in the context of closed hearings. Before turning to consider how the courts have addressed those issues in more modern times, it is helpful first to look at the main features of the current anti-terrorism regime.

EMERGENCY POWERS AND TERRORISM[17]

"Civil contingencies"

13–03 Provision has been made for extensive emergency powers in the Civil Contingencies Act 2004. In the event of an "emergency", which includes "war, or terrorism, which threatens serious damage to the security of the United Kingdom",[18] an order conferring emergency powers on the executive may be made.[19] The scope of the emergency powers that can be conferred are listed in s.22 of the Act. No summary can adequately convey the breadth of the powers available, which include provision to confiscate or destroy property (without compensation), restricted movement and assemblies and disapply or modify

---

[15] *Ridge v Baldwin* [1964] A.C. 40, per Lord Reid at p.73.

[16] *R. v Inland Revenue Commissioners, Ex p. Rossminster Ltd* [1980] A.C. 952, per Lord Diplock at p.1011.

[17] L.K. Donohue, *Counter-Terrorist Law and Emergency Powers in the United Kingdom, 1922–2000* (Dublin: Irish Academic Press, 2001); C. Walker, *Terrorism and the Law* (Oxford: Oxford University Press, 2011).

[18] Civil Contingencies Act 2004 s.19(1)(c). It also applies to a situation that threatens serious damage to "human welfare" (s.19(1)(a)) and that includes, inter alia, loss of human life, human illness or injury and disruption of services relating to health (s.19(2)).

[19] Civil Contingencies Act 2004 s.20. Ordinarily this should be done by the Privy Council, but in cases of particularly urgency may be made by the Prime Minister or another "senior Minister of the Crown" (s.20(3)).

almost any other enactment.[20] It is not clear what further powers the executive could require access to.[21] Any such emergency regulations may not last longer than 30 days, but can be remade on or before expiry.[22] Any regulations lapse after seven days unless approved by each House of Parliament.[23] Despite those broad-ranging powers, extensive provision is now made to deal with terrorism in particular.

Terrorism legislation

The hallmark of the contemporary response to the "emergency" of terrorism is the abandonment of any pretence that the powers of the state should be temporary and exceptional in nature.[24] On the contrary, despite provision for regular review of the operation of anti-terrorist legislation and the inclusion of a quasi-judicial layer within the relevant institutional machinery, anti-terrorist powers now have the stamp of something permanent and, indeed, given the frequency with which Parliament now legislates on the matter, routine. There is nothing accidental in this. In 1995, against the backdrop of a diminution of Irish terrorism and the emergence of a new species of radical Islamic terrorism, Lord Lloyd of Berwick was asked to lead an inquiry into whether, in the event of the achievement of permanent peace in Northern Ireland, any need would remain for specific anti-terrorism legislation in the UK. The report of Lord Lloyd's inquiry was published in October 1996.[25] It concluded that there was a need for permanent, UK-wide, legislation (a conclusion no doubt fortified by the bombing in Omagh in August 1998, in which 29 lives were lost). The recommendations of the Lloyd Report were largely implemented by the enactment of the Terrorism Act 2000. **13–04**

That Act remains the basic foundation of counter-terrorism legislation in the UK. It has, however, been supplemented by a number of additional enactments, most of which have been passed by Parliament in remarkably short time scales. In the aftermath of the 9/11 attacks on the US, the Anti-Terrorism, Crime and Security Act 2001 ("surely the most draconian piece of legislation Parliament has passed in peacetime in over a century")[26] was rushed through Parliament, with

[20] Civil Contingencies Act 2004 s.22(3). The Human Rights Act 1998, and s.23 of the 2004 Act (which sets out the limitations of emergency regulations, are the only protected enactments (s.23(5)). Perhaps notably, "constitutional statutes" (other than the 1998 Act) are subject to the 2004 Act powers.

[21] But, despite that wide-ranging list, the Civil Contingencies Act 2004 was not engaged in response to the coronavirus emergency. Instead, bespoke emergency legislation was passed: Coronavirus Act 2020. That Act, given the time it was passed (March 2020) falls outside the scope of this current edition.

[22] Civil Contingencies Act 2004 s.26.

[23] Civil Contingencies Act 2004 s.27.

[24] H. Fenwick, *Civil Rights: New Labour, Freedom and the Human Rights Act* (Harlow: Longman, 2000), Ch.3. As the author notes, counter-terrorism provision following the enactment of the Terrorism Act 2000 is more extensive than anything that obtained, at least on the British mainland, during the worst years of Irish terrorist violence.

[25] Lord Lloyd of Berwick, *Inquiry into Legislation against Terrorism* (The Stationery Office, 1996), Cm.3420. See also the government's consultation document, published in December 1998, Home Office and Northern Ireland Office, *Legislation against Terrorism: a consultation paper* (The Stationery Office, 1998) Cm.4178.

[26] A. Tomkins, "Legislating against terror: the Anti-terrorism, Crime and Security Act 2001" [2002] P.L. 205.

only 16 hours of debate permitted on a Bill that ran to 129 clauses and eight Schedules, many of which contained powers that were a long way removed from what would be necessary to respond to the "emergency" situation. Significant additional powers were conferred on the executive, with resultant inroads made on civil liberties, without any proper scrutiny. This pattern of legislating in response to events has been repeated: the Prevention of Terrorism Act 2005 was passed and came into force within three months of the House of Lords' decision in *A v Secretary of State for the Home Department*,[27] introducing a system of "control orders" to replace the 2001 Act's provisions sanctioning detention of foreign nationals without limit of time; the Terrorism Act 2006 came in response to the 7/7 bombings in London; and the Terrorism Prevention and Investigation Measures Act 2011 abolished control orders (introduced by the 2005 Act) after a series of decisions criticising the system and a change in the political mood in relation to them.[28] In addition to those measures, Parliament has enacted the Counter-Terrorism Act 2008 (introducing, amongst other things, notification requirements for persons convicted of certain terrorism-related offences), the Counter-Terrorism and Security Act 2015 (enacted, it asserts, to help reduce the UK national terrorist threat level) and, most recently, the Counter-Terrorism and Border Security Act 2019 (which updated certain terrorist offences in response to developments in technology and generally increasing sentences for those convicted of terrorist offences). As the Terrorism Act 2000 was designed to be a permanent code responding to a permanent threat, it contains no provision for its periodic review. Subsequent Acts have occasionally included some provision for the review of their operation and continuing need.[29] The annual renewal of counter-terrorism provisions, a feature of the legalisation throughout the 1970s and 1980s, is not now a feature of this type of legislation.

13–05 Just as we talked about the ad hoc approach to constitutional reform in Ch.1, counter-terrorism legislation suffers from the same problem. In a field where the rights and liberties of individuals are inevitably involved, arguably the very worst time to legislate on the matter is in the aftermath of a terrorist attack when emotions are inevitable running high. The 2006 Act provides a good illustration of the concern. First, it created offences that are subject to no geographical limits.[30] That is a remarkable provision: a person of any nationality, who acts in a way that constitutes an offence under the 2006 Act, no matter where in the world, is liable to prosecution in the UK courts under the 2006 Act, even if their acts have no connection whatsoever with this country and they were lawful where they were carried out. Second, it is a mark of just how complacent Parliament had become that it was seen as a triumph for civil liberty that the government's original proposal to permit the detention and interrogation of terrorist suspects for up to 90 days (a proposal that was based on little more than a request from the

[27] *A v Secretary of State for the Home Department* [2004] UKHL 56; [2005] 2 A.C. 68.

[28] The Liberal Democrats went into the 2010 general election with a manifesto commitment to abolish control orders. The coalition agreement that then followed the election promised that control orders would be subject to an "urgent review", which led to their abolition in early 2011.

[29] See Walker, *Terrorism and the Law* (2011), paras 1.77–1.88. For example, ss.13–14 of the Prevention of Terrorism Act 2005.

[30] Terrorism Act 2006 s.17.

police) was reduced to a 28-day period.[31] At the time of enactment, the maximum period of detention under the Criminal Procedure (Scotland) Act 1995 was six hours.[32] It is lamentable that against that background, legislating for a 28-day period of detention was regarded by many as a victory. These, and many other, provisions in the 2006 Act do little to alter the impression that the legislation (not only the 2006 Act, but other counter-terrorism legislation) is a recipe for abuse of civil liberty, mistreatment of innocent people and inevitable confrontation with the courts.

"Terrorism"

An exceptionally broad meaning is given to the word "terrorism" by s.1 of the Terrorism Act 2000: **13–06**

> "(1) In this Act 'terrorism' means the use or threat of action where—
> (a) the action falls within subsection (2);
> (b) the use or threat is designed to influence the government or an international governmental organisation or to intimidate the public or a section of the public, and
> (c) the use or threat is made for the purpose of advancing a political, religious, racial or ideological cause.
> (2) Action falls within subsection if it—
>
> (a) involves serious violence against a person,
> (b) involves serious damage to property,
> (c) endangers a person's life, other than that of a person committing the action,
> (d) creates a serious risk to the health and safety of the public or a section of the public, or
> (e) is designed seriously to interfere with or seriously to disrupt an electronic system."

Any "action" is not limited to one that takes place within the UK (s.1(4)) and an action that involves firearms or explosives is terrorism for the purposes of the 2000 Act, even where s.1(1)(b) is not satisfied (s.1(3)). This definition of terrorism is significantly wider than the previous statutory definition of "terrorism".[33] Whilst the concept of "serious" violence and "serious" damage to property is now contained within the definition, the purposes and motivations that constitute "terrorism" are extended. Whether it is appropriate to use motivation in a definition that creates a criminal offence is controversial: motive is not normally a relevant consideration in the criminal law and requiring the prosecution to prove motive can act as an unnecessary additional hurdle in proving a case.[34] Furthermore, there are fundamental difficulties with any legal definition of terrorism. "One man's terrorist is another man's freedom fighter" is true (Nelson Mandela in South Africa to take probably the best known example)

---

[31] That period has since been reduced further to 14 days: Protection of Freedoms Act 2012. The power itself is found in para.36 of Sch.8 to the Terrorism Act 2000.

[32] That period is now 12 hours: Criminal Justice (Scotland) Act 2016 s.9.

[33] Contained in the Prevention of Terrorism (Temporary Provisions) Act 1989 s.20(1): "… 'terrorism' means the use of violence for political ends and includes any use of violence for the purpose of putting the public or any section of the public in fear."

[34] Walker, *Terrorism and the Law* (2011), para.1.122.

and thus what constitutes terrorism, and who is a terrorist, can change over time.[35] Before moving on, we should pause to note who is, according to the 2000 Act, a "terrorist".

A "terrorist" is defined as a person who has committed any one of a number of offences under the 2000 Act or who is, or has been, concerned in the commission, preparation or instigation of acts of terrorism.[36] Those offences include, for example, membership of proscribed organisations (s.11), assisting the funding of such organisations (ss.15–18) and various acts that are directed at the planning and carrying out of a terrorist attack (ss.56–63). Conviction for many of these offences now brings with it various notification requirements, which are imposed for a period of between 10 and 30 years, requiring an individual to notify the police on an annual basis of various pieces of prescribed information.[37] In addition, an individual subject to the notification requirements must inform the police of any intention to travel abroad.[38]

TERRORISM PREVENTION AND INVESTIGATION MEASURES

13–07 One of the most challenging questions for the government is what to do with people they believe (or possibly know) are terrorists but equally are unable to mount a prosecution against (normally due to a lack of admissible evidence). As already alluded to, and as discussed further below, the original solution (but only when the individual concerned was a foreign national) was to sanction his or her detention without trial and without limit of time. When that was (unsurprisingly) held to be unlawful, the concept of a "control order" was introduced. Under the Prevention of Terrorism Act 2005, the Secretary of State could make an order "against an individual that imposes obligations on him for purposes connected with protecting members of the public from a risk of terrorism".[39] These orders could be made for a (renewable) period of up to one year and allowed significant restrictions to be placed on the activities of an individual.[40] Any obligation imposed had to be one the Secretary of State (or the court) considered "necessary for the purposes connected with preventing or restricting involvement by that individual in terrorism-related activity".[41] Section 1(4) then set out a non-exhaustive list of 16 such obligations, which included restrictions in respect of the individual's work, business or other occupation, restrictions on their association or communications with specified persons or persons generally and restrictions on their residence and movement. They could also be required,

---

[35] C. Walker, "The legal definition of 'terrorism' in United Kingdom law and beyond" [2007] P.L. 331.

[36] Terrorism Act 2000 s.40(1).

[37] Counter-Terrorism Act 2008 Pt 4.

[38] Counter-Terrorism Act 2008 s.52. Counter-Terrorism Act 2008 (Foreign Travel Notification Requirements) Regulations 2009 (SI 2009/2493).

[39] Prevention of Terrorism Act 2005 s.1(1).

[40] There were in fact two forms of order: "non-derogating" orders (which could be made by the Secretary of State) and more restrictive "derogating" orders (which had to be made by the court). See para.12–12 of the third edition of this work.

[41] Prevention of Terrorism Act 2005 s.1(3).

among other things, to surrender their passport and to submit to electronic monitoring. Breach of the conditions of a control order was a criminal offence.[42] Where there was sufficient evidence to prosecute a suspect, that should be done rather than making a control order, but it was not a precondition to making such an order that there be an absence of a realistic prospect of prosecution.[43] It will be obvious that the extent to which the liberty of a person subjected to a control could be restricted was significant. In principle, the conditions imposed could amount to a deprivation of liberty for purposes of art.5 of the Convention (and thus amount to a disproportionate and unlawful interference with the suspect's Convention rights).[44] It was a matter to be determined on the facts and circumstances of each case whether the conditions amounted to a deprivation of liberty.[45] The conditions had, however, to be significant: a 16 hour curfew could only cause a control order to be struck down if accompanied by other conditions that were "unusually destructive of the life the controlee might otherwise have been living".[46]

Politically, however, control orders came to be regarded as unacceptable and the coalition government elected in 2010 legislated to abolish them. In their place came "Terrorism Prevention and Investigation Measures" (TPIMs). Introduced by the Terrorism Prevention and Investigation Measures Act 2011, the Secretary of State may only make a TPIM where five conditions are met:

1) that the Secretary of State reasonably believes that the individual is, or has been, involved in terrorism-related activity (defined as "the relevant activity");
2) some or all of the relevant activity is new terrorism-related activity;
3) that the measure is necessary for purposes connected with protecting members of the public from the risk of terrorism;
4) that the measure is necessary for purposes connected with preventing or restricting the individual's involvement in terrorism-related activity; and
5) either the court gives the Secretary of State permission to make the order or the urgency of the situation leads to the Secretary of State to reasonably conclude that the measure be imposed without obtaining such permission.[47]

The measures that can be imposed are set out in Sch.1 to the 2011 Act and relate to, amongst other things, residence, travel, the ability to transfer property, the use of electronic communication devices and the use of an electronic tag or other

---

[42] Prevention of Terrorism Act 2005 s.9.

[43] *Secretary of State for the Home Department v E* [2007] UKHL 47; [2008] 1 A.C. 499, per Lord Bingham at [15]–[16] and Lord Carswell at [32].

[44] *Secretary of State for the Home Department v JJ* [2007] UKHL 45; [2008] 1 A.C. 385. Lord Hoffmann at [44] dissented, arguing that anything less than actual imprisonment or something that is for practical purposes little different was necessary before the absolute right contained in art.5 of the Convention was engaged: "Otherwise the law would place too great a restriction on the powers of the state to deal with serious terrorist threats to the lives of its citizens."

[45] *Secretary of State for the Home Department v AP* [2010] UKSC 24; [2011] 2 A.C. 1.

[46] *Secretary of State for the Home Department v AP* [2010] UKSC 24; [2011] 2 A.C. 1, per Lord Brown at [4].

[47] Terrorism Prevention and Investigation Measures Act 2011 s.3.

similar device.[48] Failure to comply with any measure imposed by a TPIM, without reasonable excuse, is an offence.[49]

When considering whether to grant permission, the court has to determine whether the Secretary of State's decision that conditions (1)–(4) are satisfied are "obviously flawed".[50] The court can reach its decision without the individual who will be subject to the TPIM being notified of the application, let alone being offered the opportunity to be heard.[51] Once made, a TPIM remains in force for one year and may only be renewed once (for a further year) if conditions (1), (3) and (4) are satisfied.[52] Within seven days of the TPIM being served on an individual, the court must hold a directions hearing at which the individual has the opportunity to attend.[53] A "review hearing", at which the court must review the Secretary of State's decision in relation to conditions (1)–(4) and whether they continue to be met, must be held as soon as reasonably practicable after the directions hearing.[54] The Secretary of State is required to keep under review whether conditions (3) and (4) continue to be met once a TPIM has been made[55] and the relevant police force must keep under review whether sufficient evidence is available to prosecute the individual.[56]

Given the fate of their predecessors, it is noteworthy that the Supreme Court has not yet had the opportunity to consider TPIMs. They are designed to be a much more tailored, and thus proportionate, means of dealing with terrorist suspects for whom there is insufficient admissible evidence to bring a prosecution. Terrorism prevention and investigation measures address the same problem that detention without trial or limit of time was designed to address. It is fairly remarkable that only a decade after Parliament authorised that unpalatable step, it considered the 2011 Act a sufficient response to the same perceived threat.

TERRORISM AND THE RULE OF LAW

Introduction

13–08 Having outlined some of the central features of the legislative response to terrorism, it is now helpful to consider a few case studies where the application of these rules has tested our (or at least the courts') commitment to the rule of law. We start with the issue of detention without trial (a matter that you could have been forgiven for believing had been resolved by Lord Diplock's recognition that Lord Atken's dissent in *Anderson* had been correct all along). Next we consider the right to a fair hearing, in the sense of being entitled to know the case against you and to challenge it. Modern surveillance and intelligence gathering methods often rub up against the rules on admissibility of evidence and can present acute

[48] Terrorism Prevention and Investigation Measures Act 2011 Sch.1.

[49] Terrorism Prevention and Investigation Measures Act 2011 s.23.

[50] Terrorism Prevention and Investigation Measures Act 2011 s.6(3).

[51] Terrorism Prevention and Investigation Measures Act 2011 s.6(4).

[52] Terrorism Prevention and Investigation Measures Act 2011 s.5.

[53] Terrorism Prevention and Investigation Measures Act 2011 s.8.

[54] Terrorism Prevention and Investigation Measures Act 2011 ss.8(5) and 9.

[55] Terrorism Prevention and Investigation Measures Act 2011 s.11.

[56] Terrorism Prevention and Investigation Measures Act 2011 s.10.

dilemmas for the prosecuting authorities. Finally, we consider the right to a fair hearing, in the sense of a public hearing. When can, and should, the court sit in private and on what basis can that be authorised?

Detention without trial

As we saw above, the precursor to TPIMs were "control orders", which were themselves a response to the court objecting to the detention of suspects without trial and without limit of time. That final proposition was established in *A v Secretary of State for the Home Department*: despite it now being almost two decades since it was handed down, it remains one of the most importance decisions to emerge from the UK's highest court this century.[57] In issue was s.23 of the Anti-terrorism, Crime and Security Act 2001 (which provided for the detention of non-nationals if the Home Secretary believed that their presence in the country was a risk to national security and it was not possible to deport them)[58] and the Human Rights Act 1998 (Designated Derogation) Order 2001 (which contained the UK's purported derogation under art.15 of the European Convention on Human Rights from the requirements of art.5(1), the right to liberty).[59] Three issues arose for the House of Lords (which sat as a then unprecedented panel of nine Law Lords) to determine: (a) was there a "threat to the life of the nation" that entitled the UK to derogate from its obligations under the Convention; (b) if so, was the 2001 Order lawfully made; and (c) if not, was s.23 of the 2001 Act nevertheless compatible with the Convention. 13–09

In relation to the first issue, the majority held the question of whether there was a public emergency threatening the life of the nation such as to permit a derogation from the Convention was a pre-eminently political assessment to which the courts should afford great weight.[60] In the circumstances, there was no basis on which to displace the conclusion that such a public emergency justifying a derogation existed. Lord Hoffmann disagreed:

---

[57] *A v Secretary of State for the Home Department* [2004] UKHL 56; [2005] 2 A.C. 68. It appears to have been a closer call than first appeared, with the Law Lords initially split 5:4, a result that would most likely have undermined the authority of the judgment (Lord Hope, *Lord Hope's Diaries, House of Lords 1996–2009* [Edinburgh: Avizandum Press, 2018], p.228).

[58] The bar on deportation arose from the Strasbourg jurisprudence that prohibits the signatories to the Convention returning a person to a country where there was a real risk that his or her rights would be violated in the receiving country (see *Chahal v United Kingdom* (1997) 23 E.H.R.R. 413).

[59] Human Rights Act 1998 (Designated Derogation) Order 2001 (SI 2001/3644). Any derogation pursuant to art.15 is permissible only "to the extent strictly required by the exigencies of the situation [and] provided that such measures are not inconsistent with [the state's] other obligations under international law". The UK remains the only signatory to the European Convention that has considered it necessary to derogate from its obligations under the Convention. That is telling. Not even in the aftermath of the Madrid bombings on 11 March 2003, in which more than 200 lives were lost, did the Spanish Government consider it necessary to adopt measures that would have required it to derogate from its Convention obligations. Against that background, it is perhaps surprising that the Grand Chamber took "as its starting point" in *A v United Kingdom* (2009) 49 E.H.R.R. 625 that "the activities and aims of the Al'Qaeda network had given rise to a 'public emergency threatening the life of the nation' " (at [216]).

[60] *A v Secretary of State for the Home Department* [2004] UKHL 56; [2005] 2 A.C. 68, per Lord Bingham at [27]–[29].

> "This is a nation which has been tested in adversity, which has survived physical destruction and catastrophic loss of life. I do not underestimate the ability of fanatical groups of terrorists to kill and destroy, but they do not threaten the life of the nation. Whether we would survive Hitler hung in the balance, but there is no doubt that we shall survive Al-Qaeda. The Spanish people have not said that what happened in Madrid, hideous crime as it was, threatened the life of their nation. Their legendary pride would not allow it. Terrorist violence, serious as it is, does not threaten our institutions of government or our existence as a civil community."[61]

Those are comments that many would agree with, but equally would be surprised that they emanated from a judge and not the government itself. *A v Secretary of State for the Home Department*, perhaps more than any case that had preceded it, highlighted how the court can now be called upon to adjudicate on questions that a decade or so earlier would have been regarded as clearly non-justiciable.

The majority of the House may have supported the government on the first question, but they found against them on the remaining two. The 2001 Order was quashed, it being held that it was disproportionate to the aim pursued and was unjustifiably discriminatory. As a starting point, it is now generally accepted that internment without trial, more than anything else, plays directly into the hands of terrorists. As Lord Nicholls put it, "... indefinite imprisonment without charge or trial is anathema in any country which observes the rule of law... Wholly exceptional circumstances must exist before this extreme step can be justified".[62]

But the Attorney General, on behalf of the UK Government, objected to the courts undertaking a detailed review of the choices made by the government and by Parliament in response to the perceived terrorist threat. These were matters, argued the Attorney, that properly fell within the discretionary area of judgment that belonged to the "democratic organs of the state", namely Parliament and the government.[63] That argument was firmly rejected by Lord Bingham:

> "I do not in particular accept the distinction which [the Attorney General] drew between democratic institutions and the courts. It is of course true that the judges in this country are not elected and are not answerable to Parliament. It is also true... that Parliament, the executive and the courts have different functions. But the function of independent judges charged to interpret and apply the law is universally recognised as a cardinal feature of the modern democratic state, a cornerstone of the rule of law itself. The Attorney General is fully entitled to insist on the proper limits of judicial authority, but he is wrong to stigmatise judicial decision-making as in some way undemocratic."[64]

That was a particularly strong assertion of the legitimacy of the courts reviewing decisions of the executive (and of Parliament) even in areas concerned with national security. So far as the proportionality of the measure was concerned, the conclusion that it was disproportionate was "irresistible".[65] It was an immigration measure that had been adopted for a national security purpose, the result of which

---

[61] *A v Secretary of State for the Home Department* [2004] UKHL 56; [2005] 2 A.C. 68 at [96].

[62] *A v Secretary of State for the Home Department* [2004] UKHL 56; [2005] 2 A.C. 68 at [74].

[63] *A v Secretary of State for the Home Department* [2004] UKHL 56; [2005] 2 A.C. 68, per Lord Bingham at [37] and p.85 of the report (for the record of the argument).

[64] *A v Secretary of State for the Home Department* [2004] UKHL 56; [2005] 2 A.C. 68 at [42].

[65] *A v Secretary of State for the Home Department* [2004] UKHL 56; [2005] 2 A.C. 68, per Lord Bingham at [43]. Only Lord Walker dissented on that point. Lord Hoffmann, having found there was

was an equally (or even more) dangerous British national could not be deprived of their liberty simply because they were British. That robbed the provisions of any rational connection between the aim pursued and the measure adopted. Furthermore, it was argued by the government that the detention of the appellants was in a prison of three, not four, walls: they were free to leave at any time if they could find a safe country that will take them.[66] That, however, simply served to underscore the disproportionate nature of their detention: as Lord Bingham pointed out, if a detainee was to depart for a country as close as France, there free to pursue their criminal plans, it is hard to reconcile that with the UK Government's assertion that the only proportionate means by which to control the threat they present whilst in the UK was their internment without trial.[67]

In response to the decision, the government were scathing: the decision was, said the then Foreign Secretary, "simply wrong".[68] But *A v Secretary of State for the Home Department* was a test of society's commitment to the rule of law and principles that are said to be fundamental to our way of life. Detention without trial on the whim of the executive has been objected to since the times of Magna Carta. What the decision in *A v Secretary of State for the Home Department* showed beyond doubt, however, was that the courts would be called upon to consider questions that would previously have been the preserve of the executive and that the response to terrorism would require the courts to review, and on occasion alter, the balance struck between the rights of society as a whole and those of a deeply unpopular (and dangerous) minority.

Right to a fair trial: knowing the case

Two other cases serve to illustrate how the court continues to engage with these extremely sensitive issues. Both concern the right to a fair trial, a concept that has long been regarded by the common law as a fundamental right and which is now enshrined in art.6 of the Convention. It is ordinarily uncontroversial to suggest that the right to a fair trial carries with it the right that an accused person know the case against them, know what evidence is founded upon and to test and, if necessary, correct it.[69] So important was the right to a fair hearing, and with it the right of the accused to know the case against them, that "the importance of upholding it far transcends the significance of any particular case".[70] But again the response to terrorism tests our commitment to that seemingly uncontroversial principle. Often evidence against terrorist suspects will be gathered by the **13–10**

no threat to the life of the nation that justified a derogation in the first place, expressed no view on the validity of the purported derogation or the compatibility of s.23 of the 2001 Act.

[66] *A v Secretary of State for the Home Department* [2004] UKHL 56; [2005] 2 A.C. 68, per Lord Hope at [123] and Baroness Hale at [230].

[67] *A v Secretary of State for the Home Department* [2004] UKHL 56; [2005] 2 A.C. 68 at [33]

[68] A comment made by Jack Straw, MP in the course of an interview on the Radio 4, *Today* programme on 17 December 2004. Reported in *The Guardian*, "Law Lords 'simply wrong', says Straw" (17 December 2004) *https://www.theguardian.com/uk/2004/dec/17/terrorism.immigrationpolicy* [Accessed 9 April 2020].

[69] *Kanda v Malaya* [1962] A.C. 322 PC (Federated Malay States), per Lord Denning at p.337. Although inroads, and arguably justifiable inroads, are being made on the right to test evidence with an increasing use of pre-recorded statements in criminal proceedings. See, for example, the Vulnerable Witnesses (Criminal Evidence) (Scotland) Act 2019.

[70] *Ridge v Baldwin* [1964] A.C. 40, per Lord Morris at 113–114.

security and intelligence services using covert measures. Does the right to a fair trial necessitate the disclosure of evidence that would in turn expose the methods used by the security and intelligence services? To what extent does the right to a fair trial have to sit in a balance with the interests of national security? Those questions came before the House of Lords in a series of cases concerning the "control orders" regime that was introduced in the aftermath of the *A v Secretary of State for the Home Department* decision.

Under the (now repealed) Prevention of Terrorism Act 2005, the Secretary of State could make a "non-derogating control order" if they had reasonable grounds for suspecting that an individual was, or had been, involved in terrorism-related activity and they considered it necessary, for purposes connected with protecting members of the public from a risk of terrorism, to make a control order imposing obligations on the individual.[71] Before making such an order, however, the Secretary of State was required to apply to the court for permission to make the order.[72] Only if the grounds for the order were "obviously flawed" could the court refuse permission.[73] In making the application for permission, the question inevitably arose as to how much of the evidence could be provided to the individual concerned. Ordinarily "open" and "closed" evidence was made available to the court with only the former being made available to the individual concerned. The appointment of a "special advocate" ameliorated to some extent the consequences of withholding the "closed" evidence: a "special advocate" was appointed to represent the individual and would be given access to the "closed" material, but they could not discuss that material with the individual and could not take instructions upon it.[74] The special advocate did not, however, remove the concern about withholding part (and often a significant part) of the evidence.[75] In *Secretary of State for the Home Department v MB*, the House of Lords appeared divided on the issue.[76] Lord Bingham held that a person entitled to a fair hearing must have sufficient information, in whatever form, to allow them to challenge or rebut the case against them, with or without the assistance of a special advocate. Whether that had been done in any particular case would have to be determined by looking at the process as a whole.[77] At the other end of the spectrum, Lord Hoffmann concluded that the presence of the special advocate provided a sufficient safeguard to secure a fair hearing and meet the requirements of art.6. The rest of the panel (Lady Hale and Lords Carswell and Brown) took a middle course: the presence of the special advocate would ordinarily provide a sufficient safeguard but in the rare case where the material crucial to determining the

---

[71] Prevention of Terrorism Act 2005 s.2.

[72] Prevention of Terrorism Act 2005 s.3(1).

[73] Prevention of Terrorism Act 2005 s.3(2).

[74] See generally A. Kavanagh, "Special Advocates, Control Orders and the Right to a Fair Trial" (2010) 73 M.L.R. 836.

[75] See Lord Bingham in *Secretary of State for the Home Department v MB* [2007] UKHL 46; [2008] 1 A.C. 440 at [35] and Lord Woolf CJ in *R. (on the application of Roberts) v Parole Board* [2005] UKHL 21; [2005] 2 A.C. 738 at [83].

[76] *Secretary of State for the Home Department v MB* [2007] UKHL 46; [2008] 1 A.C. 440.

[77] *Secretary of State for the Home Department v MB* [2007] UKHL 46; [2008] 1 A.C. 440 at [34]–[35].

reasonable basis of the Secretary of State's suspicions cannot be disclosed in any way, the presence of the special advocate may be insufficient to secure a fair hearing.[78] As Lord Brown concluded:

> "I cannot accept that a suspect's entitlement to an essentially fair hearing is merely a qualified right capable of being outweighed by the public interest in protecting the state against terrorism (vital though, of course, I recognise that public interest to be). On the contrary, it seems to me not merely an absolute right but one of altogether too great importance to be sacrificed on the altar of terrorism control."[79]

Unfortunately, the guidance provided by the House of Lords in *MB* was not easy to apply in practice, with the result that the question (how to balance the individual's right to a fair hearing against the public interest in maintaining the effectiveness of the intelligence and security services) again returned to the House of Lords.[80] In the meantime, the Grand Chamber in Strasbourg had issued its decision in *A v United Kingdom* where it held that a decision "based solely or to a decisive degree on closed material" was inconsistent with the Convention and could not be saved by the presence of a special advocate.[81] Despite Lord Hoffmann expressing serious concerns about the correctness of the decision,[82] the House of Lords held it had no choice but to follow the decision of the Grand Chamber. The rationale for that decision is perhaps best captured by Sedley LJ, during his dissent in the Court of Appeal:

> "There can be few practising lawyers who have not had the experience of resuming their seat in a state of hubristic satisfaction, having called a respectable witness to give apparently cast-iron evidence, only to see it reduced to wreckage by ten minutes of well-informed cross-examination or convincingly explained away by the other side's testimony. Some have appeared in cases in which everybody was sure of the defendant's guilt, only for fresh evidence to emerge which makes it clear that they were wrong. As Mark Twain said, the difference between reality and fiction is that fiction has to be credible. In a system which recruits its judges from practitioners, judges need to carry this kind of sobering experience to the bench. It reminds them that you cannot be sure of anything until all the evidence has been heard, and that even then you may be wrong. It may be, for these reasons, that the answer to Baroness Hale's question—what difference might disclosure have made?—is that you can never know."[83]

---

[78] *Secretary of State for the Home Department v MB* [2007] UKHL 46; [2008] 1 A.C. 440, per Lady Hale at [68]–[74].
[79] *Secretary of State for the Home Department v MB* [2007] UKHL 46; [2008] 1 A.C. 440 at [91].
[80] *Secretary of State for the Home Department v AF (No.3)* [2009] UKHL 28; [2010] 2 A.C. 269.
[81] *A v United Kingdom* (2009) 49 E.H.R.R. 625 at [220].
[82] *Secretary of State for the Home Department v AF (No.3)* [2009] UKHL 28; [2010] 2 A.C. 269 at [70]–[74]: "There are practical limits to the extent to which one can devise a procedure which carries no risk of a wrong decision. It is sometimes said that it is better for ten guilty men to be acquitted than for one innocent man to be convicted. Sometimes it is a hundred guilty men. The figures matter. A system of justice which allowed a thousand guilty men to go free for fear of convicting one innocent man might not adequately protect the public. Likewise, the fact that in theory there is always some chance that the applicant might have been able to contradict closed evidence is not in my opinion a sufficient reason for saying, in effect, that control orders can never be made against dangerous people if the case against them is based 'to a decisive degree' upon material which cannot in the public interest be disclosed. This, however, is what we are now obliged to declare to be the law" (at [74]).
[83] *Secretary of State for the Home Department v AF (No 3)* [2008] EWCA Civ 1148; [2009] 2 W.L.R. 423 at [113] (although paras [110]–[120] deserve to be read in full).

This series of cases illustrates not only the strain that can be placed on hitherto accepted and uncontroversial principles but also the difficulty the court has in striking the balance between the individual interest and the wider public interest. The division of opinion amongst the House of Lords on both occasions shows that there is no clearly correct answer to these questions and again the courts are called upon to rule on matters that have inevitable consequences on the operation of the intelligence and security services.

Right to a fair trial: open justice

13–11 The final example is another subset of the right to a fair trial: a public hearing:

> "Open justice. The words express a principle at the heart of our system of justice and vital to the rule of law. The rule of law is a fine concept but fine words butter no parsnips. How is the rule of law itself to be policed? It is an age old question. *Quis custodiet ipsos custodes*—who will guard the guards themselves? In a democracy, where power depends on the consent of the people governed, the answer must lie in the transparency of the legal process. Open justice lets in the light and allows the public to scrutinise the workings of the law, for better or for worse. Jeremy Bentham said in a well known passage quoted by Lord Shaw of Dunfermline in *Scott v Scott* [1913] A.C. 417, 477: 'Publicity is the very soul of justice. It is the keenest spur to exertion and the surest of all guards against improbity. It keeps the judge himself while trying under trial.'"[84]

But open justice too must admit of some qualification to accommodate the concerns of national security. Again, however, how to balance this core principle of the rule of law with the wider public interest has vexed the Supreme Court. In *Al Rawi v Security Service* the Supreme Court had to consider whether the court, in exercise of its inherent power to regulate its own procedures, could introduce a closed material procedure.[85] A closed material procedure is different from private hearings: in the latter the public are excluded but all parties attend (a procedure frequently used in cases concerning children), whereas in the former not only are the public excluded but so too is at least one of the parties. In *Al Rawi*, the claimants alleged that they had been detained and mistreated at the hands of various foreign authorities. They brought an action claiming damages on various grounds, including false imprisonment, conspiracy to injure and torture. The Security Service denied liability but indicated that they intended to rely upon a substantial amount of material that could not be disclosed without causing a real risk of harm to the public interest. They proposed that the material be withheld from the claimants but made available to special advocates appointed on their behalf. At first instance, the judge held that he could authorise such a procedure under the court's inherent jurisdiction to regulate its own proceedings. That conclusion was reversed by the Court of Appeal. A further appeal by the Security Service to the Supreme Court failed. Although the court was the master of its own procedure, it does not follow that it can do whatever it likes. It must have regard

---

[84] *R. (on the application of Guardian News and Media Ltd) v City of Westminster Magistrates' Court* [2012] EWCA Civ 420; [2013] Q.B. 618, per Toulson LJ at [1].

[85] *Al Rawi v Security Service* [2011] UKSC 34; [2012] 1 A.C. 531. See J. Ip, "Al Rawi, Tariq, and the Future of Closed Material Procedures and Special Advocates" (2012) 75 M.L.R. 606.

to the fundamental principles of open justice and of fairness.[86] Those principles are "extremely important and should not be eroded unless there is a compelling case for doing so" and even then, if it is to be done at all, it should be done by Parliament.[87] Lord Clarke was a sole dissenting voice: " . . . although fundamental, the principles are not absolute and must yield where it is necessary in the interests of justice that they do so".[88] The majority did not necessarily disagree that the principles were not absolute; the disagreement was caused by the majority's insistence that the common law would, in no circumstances, permit a closed material procedure.[89] Following *Al Rawi* the law appeared clear:

> "The basic rule is that (subject to certain established and limited exceptions) the court cannot exercise its power to regulate its own procedures in such a way as will deny parties their fundamental common law right to participate in the proceedings in accordance with the common law principles of natural justice and open justice."[90]

In short, it was for Parliament to authorise such a procedure.

That stance was tested in *Bank Mellat v Her Majesty's Treasury (No.1)*.[91] In that case, the Treasury had imposed various financial restrictions upon Bank Mellat (a major Iranian commercial bank) under the Counter-Terrorism Act 2008. The bank sought to challenge the imposition of those restrictions. Both the judge that heard that application and subsequently the Court of Appeal received closed material from the Treasury and refused the bank's application. On appeal to the Supreme Court, the question arose as to whether that court could consider the closed material. The 2008 Act made specific provision authorising, indeed requiring, the High Court and the Court of Appeal (and the Court of Session in Scotland) to make rules to allow the Treasury to lay before the court material that could not be disclosed to the other party. No provision was made in the 2008 Act allowing (let alone requiring) the Supreme Court to make similar rules nor was any express power conferred by the Constitutional Reform Act 2005 (which had established the Supreme Court) to allow a closed material procedure. A simple application of the majority view in *Al Rawi* would have resulted in the Supreme Court refusing to consider the closed material. Indeed, that was the view of Lords Hope, Kerr and Reed. "Two principles of absolute clarity govern the law in relation to the manner in which trials should be conducted", wrote Lord Kerr: **13–12**

> "The first is that a party to proceedings should be informed of the case against him and should have full opportunity to answer that case in open court. The second principle is that the first principle may not be derogated from except by clear parliamentary authority."[92]

---

[86] *Al Rawi v Security Service* [2011] UKSC 34; [2012] 1 A.C. 531, per Lord Hope of Craighead at [72].
[87] *Al Rawi v Security Service* [2011] UKSC 34; [2012] 1 A.C. 531, per Lord Dyson at [48].
[88] *Al Rawi v Security Service* [2011] UKSC 34; [2012] 1 A.C. 531 at [177].
[89] *Al Rawi v Security Service* [2011] UKSC 34; [2012] 1 A.C. 531, per Lord Dyson at [27].
[90] *Al Rawi v Security Service* [2011] UKSC 34; [2012] 1 A.C. 531, per Lord Dyson at [22].
[91] *Bank Mellat v HM Treasury (No.1)* [2013] UKSC 38; [2014] A.C. 700. See H.J. Hooper, "Crossing the Rubicon: *Bank Mellat v Her Majesty's Treasury (No.1)*" [2014] P.L. 171; P. Scott, "Crossing the Rubicon: closed hearing in the Supreme Court" (2014) 18(1) Edin. L.R. 88.
[92] *Bank Mellat v HM Treasury (No.1)* [2013] UKSC 38; [2014] A.C. 700 at [101]. See also Lord Hope at [81] and Lord Reed at [133].

But the majority took a more nuanced view. As the Constitutional Reform Act 2005 provides for an appeal to the Supreme Court against *any* judgment, that must necessarily include a judgment that is wholly or partly closed. If that is correct, for such an appeal to be effective, the hearing would normally have to include a closed material procedure.[93] Accordingly, it was implicit that the Supreme Court had the authority to conduct a closed material procedure. Having split 6:3 on whether it was competent in principle to conduct such a procedure, the court then split 5:4 on whether, in that particular case, to conduct a closed material procedure.[94] The majority (who all confessed to having had real misgivings about the decision) held that they should examine the closed material.[95] Having crossed the Rubicon, it turned out there was nothing to see:

> "... there was no point in our seeing the closed judgment. There was nothing in it which could have affected our reasoning in relation to the substantive appeal, let alone which could have influenced the outcome of that appeal."[96]

That the Supreme Court was persuaded to embark upon a closed material procedure, in circumstances that had not been expressly authorised by Parliament, for no real benefit is regrettable. Lord Neuberger captures the dilemma for the majority that favoured viewing the material: despite having a strong suspicion that the closed material would have no impact upon the court's judgment, in the absence of the material and without submissions on it they could not be sure. The result of the Supreme Court being led to consider this material in closed session are a set of guidelines placing exacting demands on any party that again asks the Supreme Court to operate a closed material procedure[97] and a strong direction that the Supreme Court should never be placed in a position where it would have to issue a closed judgment.[98] But these steps represent an attempt to shut the stable door after the horse has bolted: almost all agree that the right at stake was a fundamental principle of the common law. It appears to have been compromised, however, for no material gain.

CONCLUSION

13–13 It is in responding to the threat posed by terrorism that our commitment, as a society, to the rule of law is tested. Detention without trial, the restrictions imposed by "control orders" and compromising the common law ideal of a fair trial may be seen by some as an acceptable method by which to interrupt and then punish *actual* terrorists. But that proceeds on the assumption that *only* actual

---

[93] *Bank Mellat v HM Treasury (No.1)* [2013] UKSC 38; [2014] A.C. 700, per Lord Neuberger at [37] (with whom the majority agreed).

[94] Lord Dyson (the author of the leading judgment in *Al Rawi*) joined Lords Hope, Kerr and Reed in dissenting on this point.

[95] *Bank Mellat v HM Treasury (No.1)* [2013] UKSC 38; [2014] A.C. 700, per Lord Neuberger at [64].

[96] *Bank Mellat v HM Treasury (No.1)* [2013] UKSC 38; [2014] A.C. 700, per Lord Neuberger at [66]; see also Lord Dyson at [143].

[97] *Bank Mellat v HM Treasury (No.1)* [2013] UKSC 38; [2014] A.C. 700, per Lord Neuberger at [68]–[74]; see also Lord Hope at [96] and Lord Dyson at [145].

[98] *Bank Mellat v HM Treasury (No.1)* [2013] UKSC 38; [2014] A.C. 700, per Lord Hope at [98]–[100], endorsed by Lord Neuberger at [60].

terrorists will be dealt with by these provisions. Once the possibility that an "ordinary" person, by which we mean a non-terrorist, may be unwittingly subjected to these procedures, their unacceptability should become plain. That is not to suggest that striking the balance is easy. As we have seen, it can present the courts with some exceptionally difficult decisions.

Professor David Feldman cites a remark made by the then Home Secretary, Charles Clarke: "We cannot fight terrorism with one hand tied behind our back."[99] He responds by reference to Israel, a country with "more experience than any other of maintaining a functioning democracy under the rule of law in the face of a pervasive and long-running campaign of terrorist violence aimed at the destruction of the state".

In 1999, the Supreme Court of Israel ruled that the use of torture to combat terrorism was unlawful. It was contended that this disabled the government and security services from effectively combating terrorist threats. The President of the Court answered thus:

> "This is the destiny of a democracy—it does not see all means as acceptable, and the ways of its enemies are not always open before it. A democracy must sometimes fight with one hand tied behind its back. Even so, a democracy has the upper hand. The rule of law and the liberty of an individual constitute important components in its understanding of security. At the end of the day they strengthen its spirit and this strength allows it to overcome its difficulties."[100]

What the Home Secretary failed to appreciate when complaining about having one hand tied behind his back is that is exactly the destiny of a democracy; a point that has been made repeatedly over the years. In his seminal work on the rule of law, Lord Bingham cites the words of Christopher Dawson, penned during the darkest days of the Second World War:

> "As soon as men decide that all means are permitted to fight an evil then their good becomes indistinguishable from the evil that they set out to destroy."[101]

A similar sentiment was expressed by Lord Hoffmann in *A v Secretary of State for the Home Department* when he reminded us that, "the threat to the life of the nation . . . comes not from terrorism but from laws such as these. That is the true measure of what terrorism may achieve."[102]

Despite those warnings from history, the extensive powers, enacted in the name of combatting terrorism, often in the aftermath of a traumatic event, now appear to be a permanent feature of our laws and of our constitution. Every time the response to terrorism comes to be debated in Parliament, it becomes apparent that neither the government nor, to a material extent, Parliament have grasped the

[99] D. Feldman, "Human rights, terrorism and risk: the roles of politicians and judges" [2006] P.L. 364, 370.

[100] *Public Committee against Torture v Israel* (1999) 7 B.H.R.C. 31 at [39]. Lord Hoffmann's remarks in *A v Secretary of State for the Home Department* are a clear echo of the sentiments expressed here.

[101] H.C. Dawson, *The Judgement of the Nations* (London: Sheed and Ward, 1943), p.8, cited by T. Bingham, *The Rule of Law* (London: Allen Lane, 2010), p.159.

[102] *A v Secretary of State for the Home Department* [2004] UKHL 56; [2005] 2 A.C. 68 at [97].

essential truth of these statements that the greatest threat presented by terrorism is the wilful sacrifice of hitherto fundamental civil liberties in the so-called defence of those self same liberties.

CHAPTER 14

Judicial Review: Principles and Procedure

INTRODUCTION

An application for judicial review invokes the supervisory jurisdiction of the Court of Session, meaning that "super-eminent" power of a supreme court to ensure that all those vested with a legal authority exercise that authority in accordance with the law.[1] It is a jurisdiction that can be traced back to the foundation of the Court of Session in 1532.[2] It has been said that the supervisory jurisdiction can be invoked for one reason alone: to ensure that a person to whom a power has been delegated or entrusted does not exceed or abuse that jurisdiction or fail to do what it requires.[3] More recently, it has been suggested that the Court of Session's judicial review jurisdiction can be invoked whenever the rule of law requires it.[4] Either way, it is the means by which the Court of Session, as the supreme civil court of Scotland, can ensure that all other bodies conduct themselves in accordance with the law. As Clyde and Edwards note, while the supervisory jurisdiction has a long history, it is only relatively recently that the term "judicial review" has fallen into normal usage as a way of referring to it. Judicial review is sought by way of petition brought in accordance with Ch.58 of the Rules of the Court of Session.[5] In this chapter, we consider the constitutional basis of judicial review and its development in Scotland. We then turn to consider the circumstances in which the Court of Session's supervisory jurisdiction can be invoked (both the type of decision that can be subject to review and who is 14–01

---

1 Lord Clyde and D.J. Edwards, *Judicial Review* (Edinburgh: W. Green, 2000), para.1.01; also A. O'Neill, *Judicial Review in Scotland: A Practitioner's Guide* (Edinburgh: Butterworths, 1999), paras 1.03–1.05; A.W. Bradley and C.M.G. Himsworth, "Administrative Law", *Stair Memorial Encyclopaedia* (Edinburgh: Butterworths, 1995).

2 *Eba v Advocate General* [2011] CSIH 78; 2010 S.C. 70 at [34].

3 *Ruddy v Chief Constable of Strathclyde* [2012] UKSC 57; 2013 S.C. (U.K.S.C.) 126 at [18] (Lord Hope of Craighead).

4 *Wightman v Secretary of State for Exiting the European Union* [2018] CSIH 62; 2019 S.C. 111 at [67] (Lord Drummond Young).

5 Act of Sederunt (Rules of the Court of Session 1994) (SI 1994/1443) Ch.58, which replaced r.260B as introduced by the Act of Sederunt (Rules of Court Amendment No.2) (Judicial Review) 1985 (SI 1985/500). Rule 260B implemented the recommendations of the Dunpark Working Party on Procedure for Judicial Review of Administrative Action, which was appointed by the Lord President in light of remarks made by Lord Fraser of Tullybelton in *Brown v Hamilton DC*, 1983 S.C. (H.L.) 1 and *Stevenson v Midlothian DC*, 1983 S.C. (H.L.) 50, regretting the lack, in Scotland, of an expedited procedure for judicial review comparable to that established in England by reform of the rules of the court in 1977; see, now, for England, Supreme Court Act 1981 s.31 and CPR r.54.

entitled to seek such review) and the procedural rules that now govern that procedure. In the following chapter we turn to consider the substantive law that the court applies when exercising its judicial review jurisdiction. But we start by considering the place of judicial review within the wider constitution.

CONSTITUTIONAL BASIS OF JUDICIAL REVIEW

14–02 Judicial review is fundamental to, and lies at the very heart of, the rule of law. "There is no principle more basic to our system of law than the maintenance of the rule of law itself and the constitutional protection afforded by judicial review"[6] and it is "[t]he process by which the courts enforce compliance by public authorities with the law".[7] But it is also important to be clear about what judicial review is not. It does not involve the substitution of a judge's decision for an administrative decision they find to be wrong. It is not an appellate process, and the substantive grounds on which it may be sought are limited (if elastic). That distinction is important to understanding the constitutional justification for judicial review, when it is often challenged as "unelected judges" overruling the "democratically elected government".[8] The issue in judicial review proceedings is never[9] whether the "right" or the "wrong" decision has been made, or whether a better decision could have been taken, but whether the decision was taken in accordance with the law.[10] That includes not only the law as enacted by Parliament, but also the fundamental characteristics of the rule of law.[11] That implies, at least in cases involving the review of statutory powers, that the decision maker acted within the four corners of the power conferred upon them, and this basic principle of legality, otherwise known as the ultra vires doctrine, provides a compelling constitutional justification for what the courts do in the context of review. When that is understood, there is no basis for criticising "unelected judges" "overruling" the elected elements of the state: if a judicial review challenge can only succeed if the decision complained of was not taken in accordance with law, and if it is accepted, as it should be, that the state must, like everybody else, act in accordance with the law, the concept of judicial review should be rendered uncontroversial. Where the controversy arises tends to be

---

6 *R (on the application of Alvi) v Secretary of State for the Home Department* [2012] UKSC 33; [2012] 1 W.L.R. 2208 at [38] (Lord Dyson). He said the same thing in *R. (on the application of Cart) v Upper Tribunal* [2011] UKSC 28; [2012] 1 A.C. 663 at [119]–[122], but added: "But the scope of judicial review should be no more (as well as no less) than is proportionate and necessary for the maintaining of the rule of law."

7 T. Bingham, *The Rule of Law* (London: Allen Lane: 2010), p.60.

8 Such a criticism is unfounded for the reasons given by Lord Bingham in *A v Secretary of State for the Home Department* [2004] UKHL 56; [2005] 2 A.C. 68 at [42]; see also Lord Hope at [108].

9 Claims based on Convention Rights under the Human Rights Act 1998 serve to qualify that statement, at least in part. See para.15–11.

10 *Reid v Secretary of State for Scotland*, 1999 S.C. (H.L.) 17 at [41]: "Judicial review involves a challenge to the legal validity of the decision. It does not allow the court of review to examine the evidence with a view to forming its own view about the substantial merits of the case."

11 On those fundamental characteristics, see Bingham, *The Rule of Law* (2010).

where the court, through the vehicle of judicial review, is asked to consider questions that can only loosely be regarded as legal.[12]

Some, however, go further, and insist that the common law provides its own justification for what the courts do on review. This is not to contradict the sovereignty of Parliament, because the "higher order" rights endorsed by the courts in their recent jurisprudence are woven into the very structure of constitutional democracy within which Parliament operates. As Sir John Laws put it, such rights "are not a consequence of the democratic process, but logically prior to it".[13] As will be seen in the discussion concerning standing, the constitutional justification for judicial review is better understood as being grounded in the rule of law.[14] As Lord Reed explained in *AXA General Insurance Co Ltd v Lord Advocate*:

> "Judicial review under the common law is based upon an understanding of the respective constitutional responsibilities of public authorities and the courts. The constitutional function of the courts in the field of public law is to ensure, so far as they can, that public authorities respect the rule of law. The courts therefore have the responsibility of ensuring that the public authority in question does not misuse its powers or exceed their limits."[15]

In a modern constitutional democracy the legislature ought to adhere to the rule of law and the courts ought to presume the legislature has so acted.[16] As we have seen in Ch.3, above, whether Parliament retains the power to legislate in a manner that does not respect a fundamental feature of the rule of law is now regarded by some as unclear: are there some common law rights that are so fundamental to our constitution that not even Parliament can override them?[17] As we saw earlier, in Ch.1, in *Miller (No.1)* the Supreme Court unanimously endorsed the orthodox Diceyian view of the sovereignty, which would result in a resounding "no" to the question. Those comments, as we saw, were not only obiter but, arguably, doubtful.

An alternative complaint, so far as judicial review of the actions and decisions of ministers is concerned, is that it is to Parliament, and not a judge, that a

---

[12] For example, *R (on the application of Nicklinson) v Attorney General* [2014] UKSC 38; [2015] A.C. 657 where the (statutory) law on assisted suicide was challenged but the Supreme Court, by a majority, declined to make the declarators sought, recognising that the issues raised were more properly for the legislature. On the other hand, *R (on the application of Miller) v Secretary of State for Exiting the European Union* [2017] UKSC 5; [2018] A.C. 61 is a reminder that a perfectly legitimate exercise of the court's judicial review jurisdiction can be widely perceived as inappropriate. See paras 3–27—3–33, above for a more general discussion of the separation of powers. For a discussion of the appropriate boundaries between the law and politics, see J. Sumption, *Trials of the State* (Profile Books, London; 2019).

[13] J. Laws, "Law and Democracy" [1995] P.L. 72.

[14] *Eba v Advocate General for Scotland* [2011] UKSC 29; 2012 S.C. (U.K.S.C.) 1, per Lord Hope at [8]: "The rule of law . . . is the basis on which the entire system of judicial review rests."

[15] *AXA General Insurance Co Ltd v Lord Advocate* [2011] UKSC 46; 2012 S.C. (U.K.S.C.) 122 at [142].

[16] *De Smith's Judicial Review* (2018), para.1–023.

[17] *Taylor v New Zealand Poultry Board* [1984] 1 N.Z.L.R. 394, per Sir Robin Cooke at p.398.

minister is answerable.[18] But as Lord Diplock explained in *R v Inland Revenue Commissioners, Ex p. National Federation of Self-Employed and Small Businesses Ltd* that is no answer:

> "It is not, in my view, a sufficient answer to say that judicial review of the actions of officers or departments of central government is unnecessary because they are accountable to Parliament for the way in which they carry out their functions. They are accountable to Parliament for what they do so far as regards efficiency and policy, and of that Parliament is the only judge; they are responsible to a court of justice for the lawfulness of what they do, and of that the court is the only judge."[19]

There are two points to note in relation to that justification for judicial review. First, as we have seen in Ch.7, the success with which Parliament can properly hold central government to account is now, the peculiarities of Brexit apart, questionable (and has certainly changed in the almost 40 years since Lord Diplock's speech).[20] That is coupled with the second point, which we turn to in the next chapter, where we consider the increasing shift to a merits based review of administrative decisions. The rise of proportionality as a self-standing basis of review now requires the court to consider issues that would, in the early 1980s, have been regarded more as "efficiency" and "policy" than questions of law. It, of course, remains correct that in a system that is founded upon the rule of law and a separation of powers that the court, and only the court, can determine the lawfulness of decision. But where the law ends and policy begins is an increasingly grey area.

14–03 It is against that background that attempts to exclude recourse to judicial review must be considered (so called "ouster clauses"). The general rule, which is in fact a constitutional principle and a fundamental component of the rule of law, is that decisions and actions of the executive are, subject to well established but narrow exceptions, reviewable by the courts.[21] The courts have effectively declined to give effect to certain forms of ouster clause,[22] holding that, at most, all they are capable of doing is excluding the possibility of appeal as distinct from review, or that an ouster is effective only to protect intra vires determinations.[23] In principle, any such clause now falls to be tested against the common law canon of statutory interpretation to the effect that the subject's right of access to the court is not to be eroded other than by clear statutory language[24] and the parallel right of access to the courts under art.6 of the Convention.

A distinction must, however, be drawn between attempts to oust the jurisdiction of the courts outright, and those that limit it in some way. One

---

[18] In *R (on the application of Miller) v Secretary of State for Exiting the European Union* [2017] UKSC 5; [2018] A.C. 61, this idea found some favour in Lord Carnwath's dissent: e.g. [251]–[255].

[19] [1982] A.C. 617 at p.644 (Lord Diplock)

[20] That was true even before the events of July 2019 that saw Parliament legislate (by amending the Northern Ireland (Executive Formation) Bill) so as to, in practice, prevent itself being potentially prologued by the Executive so as to avoid it interrupting the United Kingdom's scheduled exit from the European Union.

[21] *R (Evans) v Attorney General* [2015] UKSC 21; [2015] A.C. 1787 at [51]–[54] (Lord Neuberger).

[22] Such as "finality clauses", which provide that the decision of a body shall be final; or "shall not be questioned" clauses, which provide that the decision shall not be questioned in any court of law whatever.

[23] *Anisminic Ltd v Foreign Compensation Commission* [1969] 2 A.C. 147.

[24] *Raymond v Honey* [1983] 1 A.C. 1; *R. v Lord Chancellor, Ex p. Witham* [1998] Q.B. 575.

example of this is to provide that a certificate or statement by the responsible authority stating the existence of a fact shall be "conclusive evidence" thereof, so that it is not open to the aggrieved individual to adduce evidence tending to show that the facts are not as so stated.[25] Another commonplace technique is for statutes conferring a right of appeal on a point of law to provide that the appeal must be taken within a specified, and usually short, period of time.[26] The object of the statutory scheme is to oust the supervisory jurisdiction in favour of an exclusive, and time limited, statutory remedy. In *Smith v East Elloe Rural DC*,[27] the House of Lords held that the applicant was indeed confined to her statutory remedy, and although the speeches in *Anisminic Ltd v Foreign Compensation Commission*[28] appeared to cast doubt on *East Elloe*, its authority has been confirmed on a number of occasions since.[29]

In *R (on the application of Privacy International) v Investigatory Powers Tribunal*,[30] the Supreme Court had occasion to review the jurisprudence on ouster clauses. The Investigatory Powers Tribunal ("the IPT") is a specialist tribunal, established by the Regulation of Investigatory Powers Act 2000 and sitting outside the general tribunals structure, to examine the conduct of the intelligence services. Given the very sensitive nature of the work that they do, and the regular need to protect their methods and their results, the ordinary court system was considered unsuitable for reviewing the work of the intelligence services. Accordingly, Parliament sought to exclude their jurisdiction. It did so by s.67(8) of the 2000 Act:

> "Except to such extent as the Secretary of State may by order otherwise provide, determinations, awards and other decisions of the Tribunal (including decisions as to whether they have jurisdiction) shall not be subject to appeal or be liable to be questioned in any court."[31]

---

[25] In *R. v Registrar of Companies, Ex p. Central Bank of India* [1986] Q.B. 1114 CA (Civ Div), Dillon LJ noted that a computer search had unearthed over 300 instances of "conclusive evidence" clauses. For a home grown example, see the Freedom of Information (Scotland) Act 2002 s.31(2), which provides that a certificate signed by a member of the Scottish Executive stating that information is exempt from the freedom of information regime on national security grounds shall be conclusive of that fact.

[26] Such time limits, even though short, are often construed as absolute (or, at least, admitting of exceptions in only very limited circumstances). See, for example, *Neilly v Nursing and Midwifery Council*, 2019 S.C. 565; *Pomiechowski v District Court of Legnica, Poland* [2012] UKSC 20; [2012] 1 W.L.R. 1604.

[27] *Smith v East Elloe Rural District Council* [1956] A.C. 736.

[28] *Anisminic Ltd v Foreign Compensation Commission* [1969] 2 A.C. 147.

[29] See, e.g. *R. v Secretary of State for the Environment, Ex p. Ostler* [1977] Q.B. 122 CA (Civ Div); *R. v Cornwall CC, Ex p. Huntington* [1994] 1 All E.R. 694 CA (Civ Div). As Simon Brown LJ put it in the latter case: "... the intention of Parliament when it uses an *Anisminic* clause is that questions as to validity are not excluded. When paragraphs such as those in *Ex p. Ostler* are used, then the legislative intention is that questions as to invalidity may be raised on the specified grounds in the prescribed time and in the prescribed manner, but that otherwise the jurisdiction of the court is excluded in the interests of certainty."

[30] [2019] UKSC 22; [2019] 2 W.L.R. 1219.

[31] While the discussion of "ouster clauses" is important, the practical issue for the IPT has been resolved by s.242 of the Investigatory Powers Act 2016, which has conferred a right of appeal, on a point of law, from the IPT to either the Court of Appeal or the Court of Session.

What could be clearer than that? According to the Court of Appeal, that provision excluded judicial review of a decision of the IPT.[32] And, at first blush at least, it is hard to believe Parliament could have meant anything else, especially when put in the context of surrounding provisions providing for a right of appeal, but only if the Minister determined that they should be brought into force. At the relevant time, they had not been brought into force. But that did not render them irrelevant when ascertaining the intention of Parliament.[33] If that were correct, however, s.67(8) had created an enclave, where the law could diverge from that which otherwise applied. If the IPT made, and repeatedly made, an error of law, there was nothing anyone could do to correct it. Whilst it had been established to examine the conduct of the intelligence services, that was not its exclusive function (e.g. CCTV surveillance by a local authority could engage its jurisdiction).[34] Separately, the IPT could be required to engage with some fundamental principles of law. For example, in *Belhaj v Security Services*, the issue concerned the extent to which the security services could intercept communications that were subject to legal professional privilege (which would be regarded as an immutable red line in a society that is faithful to the rule of law).[35] So, there were good arguments why any decision of the IPT, at least on issues of law, ought to be subject to review by the ordinary courts.

Two issues were presented to the Supreme Court: (a) did s.67(8) of the 2000 Act "oust" the supervisory jurisdiction of the High Court; and (b) whether, and, if so, in accordance with what principles, Parliament may by statute "oust" the supervisory jurisdiction of the High Court? The Supreme Court, in answering the first issue "no", divided 4:3. That made it unnecessary to answer the second question, but it did not prevent some members of the court offering a view. It was uncontroversial that if Parliament had created a tribunal of legally limited jurisdiction (as it had in the IPT), then it must have intended that those limits should be enforced. And the courts are the ultimate mechanism for that. So, s.67(8) could not, consistent with Parliament's sovereignty (which requires that its word is given effect to), entirely exclude the court.[36] What, then, was the role of the court? Lord Sumption, who lead the minority, concluded that s.67(8):

> "ousts any kind of merits review of the Tribunal's decision but nothing more than that. This is the narrowest meaning consistent with the language and manifest purpose of the subsection. It does not oust review of those procedural failings which if made our would deprive the Tribunal of its adjudicatory competence."[37]

Viewed like that, and treating the IPT as exercising the role and functions of the High Court, the rule of law is adequately secured by the judicial character of the IPT.[38] All that s.67(8) does is to exclude a judicial review that is tantamount to an appeal (and it is accepted that Parliament can create a judicial body from which

[32] [2017] EWCA Civ 1868; [2018] 1 W.L.R. 2572, upholding an unusually divided Divisional Court: [2017] EWHC 144 (Admin); [2017] 3 All E.R. 1127.
[33] *Bennion on Statutory Interpretation*, 6th edn (2013), p.654 (from p.654 of 6th edn).
[34] See the example cited by Lord Carnwath (from the appellant's submission) at [25].
[35] *Belhaj v Security Services* Unreported, 26 February 2015. See para.12–11, above.
[36] [2019] UKSC 22; [2019] 2 W.L.R. 1219 at [209]–[210] (Lord Sumption, dissenting).
[37] [2019] UKSC 22; [2019] 2 W.L.R. 1219 at [205]. Lord Wilson, also dissenting, reached the same conclusion as Lord Sumption but did not take the same route: [230]–[233].
[38] [2019] UKSC 22; [2019] 2 W.L.R. 1219 at [172].

there is to be no appeal).[39] But for the majority, that was not enough. It is a centuries-old rule that judicial review can only be excluded by the most clear and explicit words and where Parliament has not used such words, it is not for the court to stretch the words used beyond their natural meaning.[40] In s.67(8), Parliament had used language that was in all material respects (so far as the majority were concerned) the same as that which had been ineffective in ousting the court's jurisdiction in *Anisminic*. When that is understood, it follows that s.67(8) is only effective in relation to a legally valid decision and that does not include a decision tainted by an error of law.[41] Nothing in the sensitive information that the IPT had to considered saved s.67(8) from that conclusion.[42]

That conclusion reinforced the difficulty Parliament would face if it wished to protect a statutory decision-maker, no matter its judicial qualities, from judicial review. For the purposes of the appeal, it rendered it unnecessary to answer the second question (whether, and, if so, in accordance with what principles, Parliament may "oust" the supervisory jurisdiction). But Lord Carnwath went on to discuss the point in some detail. For the appellants, the argument ran: a "full" ouster clause cannot be upheld because it would conflict with the rule of law; the rule of law is as fundamental a principle as that of Parliamentary sovereignty; there must be an independent arbiter of the laws enacted by Parliament; and that arbiter must be a court of unlimited jurisdiction (such as the High Court or the Court of Session). Little of that was controversial, but it was argued that it need not be the High Court (or Court of Session) that was the authoritative interpreter of legislation. In short, the rule of law can be satisfied if that interpretative task is given to a body that is not part of, and not subject to review by, the ordinary courts.[43] On that issue, recognising that any comment was obiter, Lord Carnwath concluded:

> "I see a strong case for holding that, consistently with the rule of law, binding effect cannot be given to a clause which purports wholly to exclude the supervisory jurisdiction of the High Court to review a decision of an inferior court or tribunal, whether for excess or abuse of jurisdiction, or error of law. In all cases, regardless of the words used, it should remain ultimately a matter for the court to determine the extent to which such a clause should be upheld, having regard to its purpose and statutory context, and the nature and importance of the legal issue in question; and to determine the level of scrutiny required by the rule of law."[44]

If that comes to be recognised as an accurate statement of the law, then not only can a sovereign Parliament not bind her successors, she cannot shield her

[39] [2019] UKSC 22; [2019] 2 W.L.R. 1219 at [185], under reference to *In re Racal Communications* [1981] A.C. 374. See also: *R (A) v Director of Establishments of the Security Service* [2010] 2 A.C. 1 at [24] (Lord Brown).
[40] [2019] UKSC 22; [2019] 2 W.L.R. 1219 at [111] (Lord Carnwath).
[41] [2019] UKSC 22; [2019] 2 W.L.R. 1219 at [107]–[109] (Lord Carnwath).
[42] [2019] UKSC 22; [2019] 2 W.L.R. 1219 at [112] (Lord Carnwath).
[43] [2019] UKSC 22; [2019] 2 W.L.R. 1219 at [114]–[117] and [127] (Lord Carnwath).
[44] [2019] UKSC 22; [2019] 2 W.L.R. 1219 at [144]. On the second issue, see Lord Sumption at [207]–[211] and Lord Wilson at [237]–[253] (both dissenting on the result) who take a more cautious approach to the second issue. Lord Lloyd-Jones, who was in the majority, did not express a view on the second issue ([168]).

legislation from interpretation by the ordinary courts.[45] But, for now, at the very least *Privacy International* underlines the central role of judicial review in a democracy governed by the rule of law.

DEVELOPMENT OF JUDICIAL REVIEW IN SCOTLAND

Nature of the jurisdiction

14–04 Judicial review proceedings in Scotland, by that name, are often said to have begun with the introduction of Rule of Court of Session 260B in 1985. However, the Court of Session has exercised a supervisory jurisdiction since its very inception.[46] And there was nothing inherently "public" about the supervisory jurisdiction that the court was exercising. Whilst it is apt to capture the actions of public bodies,[47] it was not limited to such bodies.[48] The procedural changes introduced in 1985 did not (and could not) affect the jurisdiction of the Court of Session. But the advantages of the new application for judicial review in terms of expedition and, consequently, economy, were such as to prompt consideration of its proper scope. That exercise was greatly influenced, for a time, by developments in England as to the scope of judicial review there.[49] The principle of "procedural exclusivity" meant that, in England, a person wishing to complain of an infringement of "public law rights" was obliged to proceed by way of judicial review. This made it imperative to identify correctly the nature of one's claim, for a public law claim brought by way of ordinary action risked being struck out, without any inquiry into the merits, as an abuse of the process of the courts. Reliance on this approach in Scotland was criticised as introducing unnecessary technicality at variance with the historical foundations of the supervisory jurisdiction in Scots law.[50] An authoritative statement of the scope of judicial review was finally provided by Lord President Hope in *West v Secretary of State for Scotland*[51]:

> "The Court of Session has power, in the exercise of its supervisory jurisdiction, to regulate the process by which decisions are taken by any person or body to whom a jurisdiction, power or authority has been delegated or entrusted by statute, agreement or any other instrument... The cases in which the supervisory

---

[45] See further: E. Bjorge, "Legislation purporting to oust the High Court's jurisdiction: Privacy International" (2020) 136 L.Q.R. 12; M. Elliott and A.L. Young, "Privacy International in the Supreme Court: jurisdiction, the rule of law and parliamentary sovereignty" [2019] CLJ 490; B.J. Ong, "The ouster of Parliamentary sovereignty?" [2020] PL 41.

[46] See the discussion by the Lord President (Hope) in *West v Secretary of State for Scotland*, 1992 S.C. 385 at pp.394–397.

[47] *Moss Empires Ltd v Assessor for Glasgow*, 1917 S.C. (H.L.) 1 at p.6.

[48] Hence, e.g. the susceptibility of arbiters to judicial review: see *Forbes v Underwood* (1886) 13 R. 465 and, more recently, *Shanks & McEwan (Contractors) Ltd v Mifflin Construction Ltd*, 1993 S.L.T. 1124.

[49] See, e.g. *Connor v Strathclyde RC*, 1986 S.L.T. 530; *Tehrani v Argyll and Clyde Health Board*, 1989 S.C. 342; *Safeway Food Stores Ltd v Scottish Provident Institution*, 1989 S.L.T. 131.

[50] Lord Clyde, "The nature of the supervisory jurisdiction and the public/private distinction in Scots administrative law" in W. Finnie, C.M.G. Himsworth and N. Walker, *Edinburgh Essays in Public Law* (Edinburgh: Edinburgh University Press, 1991), p.281.

[51] *West v Secretary of State for Scotland*, 1992 S.C. 385 at p.413.

> jurisdiction is appropriate involve a tripartite relationship between the person or body to whom the jurisdiction, power or authority has been delegated or entrusted, the person or body by whom it has been delegated or entrusted and the person or persons in respect of or for whose benefit that jurisdiction, power or authority is to be exercised."

Plainly, therefore, judicial review is not confined to the statutory or prerogative powers of public authorities alone. Provided a reviewable jurisdiction exists, the supervisory jurisdiction may also extend to the acts and decisions of bodies that are not obviously "public" at all.[52] By the same token, however, just because a body is a public authority does not mean that all its acts and decisions will be subject to judicial review. In *West* itself, review was incompetent because the dispute between Mr West and the Secretary of State was essentially contractual, relating to the terms and conditions of Mr West's employment as a prison officer.[53] But while there is certainty at the core, uncertainty at the margins remains, and it may be that the Inner House will require at some point to revisit the test prescribed in *West*.[54] As it is, it is possible that, where the court finds difficulty in applying the tripartite relationship criterion to the facts before it,[55] the test collapses into something akin to the public/private divide used to determine the scope of review in England.

Judicial review is normally thought of as a challenge to some sort of act or omission by a public body or tribunal. As a result, invariably reduction of the impugned decision is sought. But the court can also grant the remedy of declarator. Declarator is used to establish a right or to secure the answer to a legal question,[56] and that can be done by judicial review. Such applications are rare and that is because the court will not determine hypothetical or academic questions; it will not issue a declarator that has no purpose: **14–05**

> "The question must be a real and not a theoretical question; the person raising it must have a real interest to raise it; he must be able to secure a proper contradictor, that is to say, some one presently existing who has a true interest to oppose the declaration sought."[57]

---

[52] In addition to the cases on arbiters cited at fn.48, above see also *St Johnstone Football Club v Scottish Football Association Ltd*, 1965 S.L.T. 171 and *Gunstone v Scottish Womens Amateur Athletic Association*, 1987 S.L.T. 611 (sporting bodies); *McDonald v Burns*, 1940 S.C. 376 (religious bodies); *Crocket v Tantallon Golf Club*, 2005 S.L.T. 663; and *Smith v Nairn Golf Club* [2007] CSOH 136; 2007 S.L.T. 909 (disciplinary disputes arising in golf clubs). For a recent example of a football club successfully judicially reviewing a decision of the Scottish Football Association, see *Rangers Football Club Plc, Petitioner* [2012] CSOH 95; 2012 S.L.T. 1156.

[53] But employment matters may in certain circumstances be reviewable, see e.g. *Malloch v Aberdeen Corp*, 1971 S.C. (H.L.) 85; *Rooney v Chief Constable, Strathclyde Police*, 1997 S.L.T. 1261; *Maclean v Glasgow City Council*, 1997 S.C.L.R. 1049.

[54] For discussion of *West*, see W.J. Wolffe, "The Scope of Judicial Review in Scots Law" [1992] P.L. 625 and C.M.G. Himsworth, "Public employment, the supervisory jurisdiction and points West", 1992 S.L.T. (News) 257.

[55] As witness the differing outcomes in *Naik v University of Stirling*, 1994 S.L.T. 449 and *Joobeen v University of Stirling*, 1995 S.L.T. 120.

[56] *Barbour v Grierson* (1827) 5 S 603.

[57] *Russian Commercial and Industrial Bank v British Bank for Foreign Trade Ltd* [1921] 2 A.C. 438, cited with approval by the Lord President in *Law Hospital NHS Trust v Lord Advocate*, 1996 S.C. 301.

In other words, for practical reasons, the court limits the general right to obtain a legal ruling by requiring that the ruling has some practical purpose.[58] In appropriate circumstances, it can still be sought, however. The most recent high-profile example was *Wightman v Secretary of State for Exiting the European Union*. There, the petitioners, who were a group of parliamentarians, sought a declarator that art.50 TEU (the mechanism by which a Member State may leave the European Union) could be unilaterally revoked by the exiting state. That was contrary to the basis on which the Supreme Court had decided *Miller (No.1)*, which had proceeded on a concession that art.50 was irrevocable.[59] But it was argued that knowing the correct position was important to the ongoing deliberations of the House of Commons and a declarator was sought. By the time the case reached the Inner House, review was no longer sought of any particular decision or act. That left a declarator being sought and raised the question as to whether that was within the scope of judicial review. The Lord President explained:

> "[T]he court's jurisdiction in public law matters is not confined to the review of decisions or failures to act. It may be that the case ought to have proceeded simply by way of an action of declarator rather than a petition for judicial review. However, no procedural point in that regard is taken."[60]

That it was described as a procedural point indicates that there was no competence issue (as an issue of competence is *pars judicis*). Accordingly, *Wightman* suggests that even where no act or omission is challenged, but simply a declarator is sought of what the law is on a particular matter, the Court of Session's judicial review jurisdiction can be invoked. The court went on to explain that the declarator sought (on the revocability of art.50) was not academic because:

> "The matter is uncertain in that it is the subject of a dispute … The answer will have the effect of clarifying the options open to MPs in the lead up to what is now an inevitable vote … MPs have an interest in seeing the matter resolved. On that basis the petition is competent at least at the instance of an MP."[61]

The jurisdiction invoked in *Wightman* should not be overstated. That case presented an exceptional set of circumstances. It will likely a need similarly unusual set of circumstances to persuade the court to undertake such an exercise again.[62] But what *Wightman* does demonstrate is that the scope of judicial review is wide (and it may not have yet reached its limits).[63]

58 *Wightman v Secretary of State for Exiting the European Union*, 2019 S.C. 111 at [22].

59 *R (on the application of Miller) v Secretary of State for Exiting the European Union* [2017] UKSC 5; [2018] A.C. 61 at [26].

60 *Wightman v Secretary of State for Exiting the European Union*, 2019 S.C. 111 at [26].

61 *Wightman v Secretary of State for Exiting the European Union*, 2019 S.C. 111 at [27] (Lord President) and [36]–[37] (Lord Menzies). The language of "competence" at this point is interesting given what the Lord President said earlier about limits on responding to hypothetical or academic questions being practical.

62 The obvious inhibiting factor to anyone seeking to invoke that jurisdiction is the cost: litigating is expensive.

63 *Wightman v Secretary of State for Exiting the European Union*, 2018 S.C. 388 at [30].

Territorial scope of the jurisdiction

What of the territorial scope of the Court of Session's jurisdiction? As the supreme civil court for Scotland, the Court of Session obviously has jurisdiction throughout Scotland. But what of an administrative decision that is taken furth of Scotland (for example, in London or Manchester) but the effects of which will be felt by an individual living and working in Scotland? If such an individual wishes to complain about the decision that was made in, say, Manchester, do they have to raise proceedings in the High Court in England? Or can they complain to the Court of Session in Edinburgh? With the spread of tribunals of UK-jurisdiction, the question can be a real one. Can the supervisory jurisdiction of the Court of Session be excluded because a tribunal, for reasons of convenience, chooses to sit in Durham instead of Dundee? **14–06**

That was, in substance, the issue at the root of the case of *Tehrani v Secretary of State for the Home Department*.[64] There an asylum seeker who had entered the UK in London was required by the Secretary of State to move to Glasgow while their application was determined. It was subsequently refused by a tribunal sitting in England. Could the asylum seeker who was living in Glasgow complain to the Court of Session? It was held that the Court of Session had jurisdiction where there was "a sufficient connection with Scotland".[65] In assessing whether such a connection exists, the court should have regard to whether the petitioner is resident in Scotland, whether the "harmful effects" of the decision will be felt in Scotland and whether the decision under challenge was taken in exercise of a UK-wide jurisdiction.[66] That gives rise to the possibility that both the Court of Session and the High Court could have jurisdiction to hear a challenge to the same decision. In the event that both courts were seized of jurisdiction, the rules of forum non conveniens would determine which court decided the issue.[67] Now that Scotland has introduced a time limit and requirement to obtain permission that is in substance the same as England and Wales, there is likely to be little substantive benefit between one jurisdiction and another.

Alternative remedies

Being a discretionary remedy, which is ultimately rooted in equity, judicial review is also a remedy of last resort. Accordingly, the court expects a petitioner to have exhausted any alternative means of appeal or challenge before invoking the Court of Session's supervisory jurisdiction: "the court will not grant redress in the exercise of its supervisory power where all statutory remedies have not been exhausted".[68] That is perfectly sensible: if the scheme under which a decision has been taken allows for an appeal to a particular body, it is to that appellate body **14–07**

---

[64] *Tehrani v Secretary of State for the Home Department* [2006] UKHL 47; 2007 S.C. (H.L.) 1.

[65] *Tehrani v Secretary of State for the Home Department* [2006] UKHL 47; 2007 S.C. (H.L.) 1, per Lord Nicholls of Birkenhead at [23] and Lord Rodger of Earlsferry at [99]–[101].

[66] *Tehrani v Secretary of State for the Home Department* [2006] UKHL 47; 2007 S.C. (H.L.) 1, per Lord Hope of Craighead at [60] and Lord Rodger of Earlsferry at [103].

[67] *Tehrani v Secretary of State for the Home Department* [2006] UKHL 47; 2007 S.C. (H.L.) 1, per Lord Rodger of Earlsferry at [106].

[68] *Tarmac Econowaste Ltd v Assessor for Lothian Region*, 1991 S.L.T. 77 at p.78L (Lord Clyde). Rule of Court r.58.3(1) is now express on the point: "A petition may not be lodged in respect of an

that any complaint about the decision should be directed and not the Court of Session. In other words, where an alternative means of review has been provided, the rule of law does not require that the court intervene. Accordingly, in the normal run of things, if an alternative remedy is available, the Court of Session should not be called upon to provide a remedy and if it is, should refuse to do so. But it appears that the point may have been taken too far. In *McCue v Glasgow City Council*, having undertaken a thorough review of the authorities, the Lord Ordinary determined it was a question of competence.[69] In other words, unless a petitioner has exhausted any alternative remedy, whether statutory or non-statutory, a petition for judicial review is incompetent (that is, the Court of Session has no power to hear and determine it). That view has been subsequently endorsed in the Outer House and is common currency.[70] Framing the issue as one of competence does, however, risk overstating the point. Given many decisions by public authorities now carry with them the right to complain to, for example, an ombudsman, which can result in a protracted process, it would be surprising to find that the doors of the Court of Session were closed to a petitioner unless and until they had exhausted that process, no matter how urgent their complaint.[71] To be fair to the Lord Ordinary, it was recognised that in exceptional circumstances the court may entertain an application to its supervisory jurisdiction where alternative remedies have not been exhausted.[72] That there can be circumstances where an application can be entertained may be thought to point away from the issue being one of fundamental competency. Availability of an alternative remedy should more properly be considered, it is suggested, at the point where the Court of Session considers what, if any, remedy to grant. At that stage, a petitioner who has an alternative, and unutilised, remedy ought to find it difficult to persuade the Court of Session to grant relief (at least, any relief beyond declarator). That would also likely have a consequence for where the expenses of the proceedings fell, and, now that permission is required to proceed with a petition for judicial review, if there is no real prospect of a remedy being granted, permission may be unlikely. But it is more consistent with the fundamental purpose of judicial review (the protection of the rule of law) to allow, subject to the requirement to obtain permission, which is discussed below, a petitioner the opportunity to explain to the court why an alternative remedy has not been utilised (for example, because of some inadequacy in the alternative) and why, instead, a remedy should be granted by the court. At least then, in an appropriate case, the court can provide a remedy, but in any case, it takes an informed decision on the matter.

---

application if that application could be made by appeal or review under or by virtue of any enactment." See also the annotations to the Rules of Court at r.58.3.3.

[69] *McCue v Glasgow City Council* [2014] CSOH 124; 2014 S.L.T. 891 at [60].

[70] For example, *Moore, Petitioner* [2015] CSOH 182 at [95]; *Makombo-Eboma v Glasgow City Council* [2019] CSOH 54 at [20]. *McCue's Guardian v Glasgow City Council* [2019] CSOH 109; 2020 S.L.T. 41 at [13]–[18].

[71] The need to complain to the Scottish Public Services Ombudsman is controversial. Although the Lord Ordinary in *McCue* (both 2014 and 2019) held a failure to complain rendered judicial review incompetent, it is suggested that the correction is that taken by the Lord Ordinary in *O'Neill v Scottish Ministers* [2020] CSOH 28 at [23], where it was held that the Ombudsman's jurisdiction was entirely separate and nothing in the 2002 Act could be construed as ousting the court's jurisdiction. If it were otherwise, the 3-month time limit for judicial review would be easily circumvented given a person has a year to complain to the Ombudsman (s.10 of the Scottish Public Services Ombudsman Act 2002).

[72] *McCue v Glasgow City Council* [2014] CSOH 124; 2014 S.L.T. 891 at [62].

STANDING

Having considered the constitutional function of judicial review and its development in Scotland, the next question is who can invoke that jurisdiction.[73] That threshold is now prescribed by statute. Section 27B(2)(a) of the Court of Session Act 1988, which was introduced by s.89 of the Courts Reform (Scotland) Act 2014, provides that permission to proceed with an application to the supervisory jurisdiction may only be granted where the applicant has, inter alia, "sufficient interest" in the subject matter of the application.[74] As we shall see, the statutory test simply codifies where the common law had already reached. To place the current rules in context, it is helpful to start by understanding how the law previously approached the issue of standing (or, as it was then called, "locus standi"). 14–08

If judicial review is grounded in the rule of law, then access to judicial review is of fundamental importance. For over a century, standing to bring judicial review proceedings was regulated by the two part private law test requiring both "title" and "interest".[75] That required a party to judicial review proceedings be "a party (using the word in its widest sense) to some legal relationship which gives him some right which the person against whom he raises the action either infringes or denies" (the requirement for "title")[76] and to establish that they have some real interest to enforce or protect, involving their "pecuniary rights and status", rather than seeking to resolve some academic point on a hypothetical set of circumstances (the requirement for "interest").[77] Although strictly speaking these were two distinct requirements, situations where there was title but no interest (or vice versa) were rare and in practice the distinction was meaningless. Nevertheless, the formal requirement to show "title and interest" led to increasingly unsatisfactory results. In *Rape Crisis Centre v Secretary of State for the Home Department*,[78] the petitioners (a limited company that provided advice and assistance to rape victims) was held to have no title to challenge the decision of the Home Secretary to allow Mike Tyson, a high profile boxer but convicted rapist, to enter the UK in order to compete in a fight in Glasgow. The Home Secretary's decision was taken under the Immigration Act 1971, and the Immigration Rules promulgated thereunder. Those provisions created no legal nexus between the petitioners and the Home Secretary. In other words, there was no relationship between the Rape Crisis Centre and the Home Secretary and as a consequence the centre had no "title". That conclusion appeared even more unacceptable in light of a similar challenge in England. Permission had been sought from the High Court in London to challenge a decision to allow Tyson to 14–09

[73] For an interesting and historical perspective on the issue of standing see: Sedley, *Lions under the Throne: Essays on the History of English Public Law* (CUP, Cambridge: 2015), Ch.12 ("Standing and 'sitting'").

[74] The test for permission is considered more fully below: see paras 14–21, onwards.

[75] Clyde and Edwards, *Judicial Review* (2000), Ch.10; O'Neill, *Judicial Review in Scotland: A Practitioner's Guide* (1999), paras 6.04–6.11 and A. O'Neill, *Judicial Review in Scotland: A Practitioner's Guide*, 2nd edn (London: LexisNexis, 2007), paras 14.03 and 14.04.

[76] *D & J Nicol v Dundee Harbour Trustees*, 1915 S.C. (H.L.) 7.

[77] *Swanson v Manson*, 1907 S.C. 426; although that phrase should not be regarded as exhaustive: *Scottish Old People's Welfare Council, Petitioners*, 1987 S.L.T. 179.

[78] *Rape Crisis Centre v Secretary of State for the Home Department*, 2000 S.C. 527; *Scottish Old People's Welfare Council, Petitioners*, 1987 S.L.T. 179 provides a similar example.

enter the UK to fight in Manchester. Permission was refused, not because the applicant lacked the necessary standing, but because the court was not satisfied that there were arguable substantive grounds for interfering with the Home Secretary's decision.[79] The Lord Ordinary in the *Rape Crisis Centre* case had reached the same conclusion as the English court with respect to the substantive grounds. But arguably this element of the decision merely papers over the cracks that are apparent in the test for showing title: had the petitioner's complaint on the merits been well founded, Scots law as it then stood would have offered it no form of redress. Given the core function of judicial review is securing the rule of law, that result could be regarded as problematic.

Much was said about the unsatisfactory state of the law following *Rape Crisis Centre v Secretary of State for the Home Department*. Criticism of the rules on standing, grounded as they were in private law, had long been made and calls made for a systematic review of the issue.[80] Those calls were echoed after *Rape Crisis Centre v Secretary of State for the Home Department*, most notably by Lord Hope in a lecture to the Administrative Law Bar Association.[81] Scots law was also becoming increasingly out of step with other common law jurisdictions, most noticeably England and Wales, and set in the context of the purpose of rules on standing (in a public law context) "title and interest" were increasingly seen as unsuitable.[82] The review of the civil justice system in Scotland, chaired by Lord Gill, concluded[83]:

> "... we are persuaded that the current law on standing is too restrictive and that the separate tests of title and interest should be replaced by a single test: whether the petitioner has demonstrated a sufficient interest in the subject matter of the proceedings."

As discussed below, that was one of a number of recommendations made in relation to judicial review, but before the Scottish Parliament could legislate to give effect to Lord Gill's recommendations, the Supreme Court intervened to modernise the rules of standing for judicial review.

14–10 We have already considered the case of *AXA General Insurance Co Ltd v Lord Advocate* in relation to the continuing discussion of the sovereignty of Parliament and in relation to the review of the legislative competence of the Scottish Parliament. For present purposes, however, it is the influence of the case on the rules on standing in judicial review that are important. The case was a challenge to provisions of the Damages (Asbestos-related Conditions) (Scotland) Act 2009, which were said to be beyond the competence of the Scottish Parliament. AXA was an insurance company challenging the competence of legislation that imposed upon it liability to meet claims for damages. Both the Lord Advocate and the Attorney General entered appearance to defend the legislation. Eight respondents were individuals whose pending actions for damages hinged on the

---

[79] *R. v Secretary of State for the Home Department Ex p. Bindel* [2001] Imm. A.R. 1.

[80] C.R. Munro, "Standing in Judicial Review", 1995 S.L.T. (News) 279.

[81] Lord Hope of Criaghead, "Mike Tyson comes to Glasgow—a question of standing" [2001] P.L. 294.

[82] On the latter point, see T. Mullen, "Standing to Seek Judicial Review" in A. McHarg and T. Mullen, *Public Law in Scotland* (Edinburgh: Avizandum: 2006), pp.255–261.

[83] Scottish Civil Courts Review, *Report of the Scottish Civil Courts Review* (The Stationery Office, 2009), Ch.12 at para.25.

competence of the 2009 Act. The Inner House held that these individuals had no title and interest to enter the action to defend its validity, despite being amongst the class of potential beneficiaries of the 2009 Act.[84] As Lord Reed explained in the Supreme Court, that produced a perplexing result: AXA had standing to challenge the validity of the 2009 Act, but the eight respondents—whom AXA might have been required to pay compensation to, as the potential beneficiaries of the Act—had no right to be heard in response.[85] That absurdity sounded the death knell for "title and interest" as the test for standing in the public law sphere:

> "...the time has come when it should be recognised by the courts that Lord Dunedin's dictum [in *D&J Nicol v Dundee Harbour Trustees*] pre-dates the modern development of public law, that it is rooted in private law concepts which are not relevant in the context of applications to the supervisory jurisdiction, and that its continuing influence in that context has had a damaging effect on the development of public law in Scotland. This unsatisfactory situation should not be allowed to persist. The time has come when the courts should cease to use the inappropriate terminology of title and interest in relation to such applications, and should refer instead to standing, based upon a sufficient interest."[86]

Moving to a test based on sufficient interest better allows the court to perform its core function in public law matters of preserving the rule of law, a task that was being inhibited in Scotland by a rights-based approach to standing.[87] What constitutes "sufficient interest" will vary according to the circumstances of a given case, as the rule of law does not require the court to hear and adjudicate upon every allegation of illegality levelled at a public body.[88] It will often require a person to demonstrate a particular interest in the matter, otherwise they may well be regarded as a mere busybody and denied standing.[89] But equally there will be cases where any individual, by mere virtue of the fact that they are a citizen, will have a sufficient interest to draw an alleged unlawful act of a public body to the attention of the court:

> "The rule of law would not be maintained if, because everyone was equally affected by an unlawful act, no one was able to bring proceedings to challenge it."[90]

---

84 *AXA General Insurance Co Ltd v Lord Advocate* [2011] CSIH 31; 2011 S.C. 662 at [56]–[58].

85 *AXA General Insurance Co Ltd v Lord Advocate* [2011] UKSC 46; 2012 S.C. (U.K.S.C.) 122 at [156].

86 *AXA General Insurance Co Ltd v Lord Advocate* [2011] UKSC 46; 2012 S.C. (U.K.S.C.) 122, per Lord Reed at [171]; Lord Hope reached the same conclusion (at [62]): "As for the substantive law, I think that the time has come to recognize that the private law rule that title and interest has to be shown has no place in applications to the court's supervisory jurisdiction that lie in the field of public law. The word 'standing' provides a more appropriate indication of the approach that should be adopted." That suggests that the rules of title and interest remain in what could be called "private law" judicial reviews (for example, those involving golf clubs and their members: see fn.52).

87 *AXA General Insurance Co Ltd v Lord Advocate* [2011] UKSC 46; 2012 S.C. (U.K.S.C.) 122, per Lord Reed at [169].

88 *AXA General Insurance Co Ltd v Lord Advocate* [2011] UKSC 46; 2012 S.C. (U.K.S.C.) 122, per Lord Reed at [170].

89 *Walton v Scottish Ministers* [2012] UKSC 44; 2013 S.C. (U.K.S.C.) 67, per Lord Reed at [94].

90 *AXA General Insurance Co Ltd v Lord Advocate* [2011] UKSC 46; 2012 S.C. (U.K.S.C.) 122, per Lord Reed at [170].

14–11 Two points arise from the Supreme Court's rewriting of the rules on standing. The first is the constitutional justification for doing so. The court, in both *AXA General Insurance Co Ltd v Lord Advocate* and subsequently in *Walton v Scottish Ministers*, repeatedly made the point that the purpose of judicial review was to secure the rule of law and changes to the rules on standing were necessary to ensure that objective was achieved. Lord Reed went so far as to describe the preservation of the rule of law as the "essential function of the courts".[91] That pronouncement appears to signal the end of the ultra vires doctrine as *the* constitutional underpinning of judicial review. Furthermore, the decision in *AXA* ought to be understood as marking a liberalisation of Scots public law. For a short time after the decision in *AXA*, Scotland had the same liberalised approach to standing as England and Wales but not the concomitant limitations or conditions, such as strict time limits for initiating a judicial review and the requirement to obtain permission to commence proceedings. But there was no flood of public law litigation hitting the Scottish courts, and, as we will see in a moment, the strict time-limits and requirement to obtain permission arrived in September 2015.

Following *AXA* the Court of Session continued to take a cautious approach to standing in judicial review matters.[92] Lord Reed reiterated the liberalisation of standing in *Walton*. The Supreme Court had:

> "intended to put an end to an unduly restrictive approach which had too often obstructed the proper administration of justice: an approach which presupposed that the only function of the court's supervisory jurisdiction was to redress individual grievances, and ignored its constitutional function of maintaining the rule of law."[93]

That was necessary to respond to the narrow view taken by the Inner House of Mr Walton's interest in the construction of the new Aberdeen bypass. The distance between Mr Walton's house and the proposed route denied him "sufficient interest", so far as the Inner House was concerned, despite his active role in the campaign against the proposed development. It was that conclusion that Lord Reed was addressing when the case reached the Supreme Court and it was held that Mr Walton did have "sufficient interest" to raise proceedings. In *Christian Institute v Lord Advocate*,[94] a case concerning the provisions of the Children and Young People (Scotland) Act 2014 requiring every child to have a "named individual" appointed to look out for their interests, a narrow view was again taken by the Lord Ordinary at first instance to the question of standing. A number of the petitioners (the Christian Institute, the Family Education Trust and the Young ME Sufferers Trust) were held to have insufficient interest. In reaching that view, the Lord Ordinary had regard to their failure to participate in the pre-legislative consultation and the call for evidence by the relevant parliamentary committee. That, said the Lord Ordinary, left him unconvinced that the petitioners had shown a genuine concern about the legislation before raising

---

91 *AXA General Insurance Co Ltd v Lord Advocate* [2011] UKSC 46; 2012 S.C. (U.K.S.C.) 122 at [169].

92 See C. McCorkindale, "Public Interest Litigants in the Court of Session" (2015) 19 Edin. L.R. 248.

93 *Walton v Scottish Ministers* [2012] UKSC 44; 2013 S.C. (U.K.S.C.) 67 at [90].

94 *Christian Institute v Lord Advocate* [2015] CSOH 7; 2015 S.L.T. 72.

proceedings.[95] Furthermore, the rule of law was secured by the other petitioners who each had children that would be affected by the proposed legislation and accordingly had been found to have standing.[96] Expecting a petitioner to have actively participated in the legislative process as a means of demonstrating "genuine concern" about the legislation, so as to then grant standing, resulted in a substantial barrier being placed in the way of those who sought to raise public interest proceedings and it had the potential to undermine what the Supreme Court sought to achieve in *AXA*. It was, at best, an unfortunate outcome. On appeal, the Inner House reversed the Lord Ordinary's conclusion on standing. The failure to participate in the legislative process was not, in the absence of bad faith, a formal bar to now claiming sufficient interest so as to challenge the legislation.[97] That those petitioners had a genuine interest in family matters was not challenged and, in the circumstances, the Inner House held that they did in fact have sufficient interest to participate in the proceedings. That issue was not pursued in the further appeal to the Supreme Court. Thus, whilst the Scottish courts were initially reluctant to embrace the liberalisation of standing introduced by *AXA*, the new test now appears to have been accepted with the effect that the law on both sides of the Border should, on this matter, be in substance the same.

Before turning to consider the other procedural issues in relation to judicial review, it should be noted that a different test for standing applies to claims alleging a breach of a Convention right. Under the Human Rights Act 1998 a petitioner is required to demonstrate not that they have "sufficient interest", but rather that they are a "victim" within meaning of art.34 of the Convention.[98] A "victim" ordinarily requires that a person be directly affected by a specific act or omission. It is not necessary to show that they suffered damage (though that is relevant for the question of "just satisfaction" under art.41), nor that they suffered no damage under national law. 14–12

PROCEDURAL RULES

Introduction

As a result of the recommendations of the Civil Justice Review, which, so far as judicial review is concerned, were given effect by s.89 of the Courts Reform (Scotland) Act 2014, the procedural rules that govern judicial review changed significantly. There were two main changes: a three-month time limit within which to bring proceedings was introduced, and a requirement to seek the court's permission to proceed with a judicial review application was imposed. Those changes came into force on 22 September 2015. The effect was to bring the procedural aspects of judicial review much closer to the equivalent provisions in 14–13

[95] *Christian Institute v Lord Advocate* [2015] CSOH 7; 2015 S.L.T. 72 at [93].

[96] *Christian Institute v Lord Advocate* [2015] CSOH 7; 2015 S.L.T. 72 at [94].

[97] *Christian Institute v Lord Advocate* [2015] CSIH 64; 2016 S.C. 47 at [41].

[98] Human Rights Act 1998 s.7; see Craig, *Administrative Law* (2016), paras 25–029—25–30; *De Smith's Judicial Review* (2018), paras 2–047—2–063.

England and Wales with a view to giving the court more control over applications to its supervisory jurisdiction and securing a more efficient disposal of such applications.

Time limits

Introduction

14–14 Statute now prescribes the time within which an application for judicial review must be presented to the Court of Session. The Court of Session Act 1988, s.27A provides:

> **"Time Limits**
>
> **27A.**—(1) An application to the supervisory jurisdiction of the Court must be made before the end of—
>
> (a) the period of 3 months beginning with the date on which the grounds giving rise to the application first arise, or
>
> (b) such longer period as the Court considers equitable having regard to all the circumstances.
>
> (2) Subsection (1) does not apply to an application to the supervisory jurisdiction of the Court which, by virtue of any enactment, is to be made before the end of a period ending before the period of 3 months mentioned in that subsection (however that first-ending period may be expressed)."

That provision was introduced by s.89 of the Courts Reform (Scotland) Act 2014, which itself was the implementation of the recommendations of the Civil Justice Review. The Review had concluded that the previous common law plea of *mora*, taciturnity and acquiescence[99] was not well suited to a procedure that was designed to provide a speedy and effective remedy where a challenge was mounted to a decision of a public body. Accordingly:

> "[A] time limit should be introduced within which petitions for judicial review must be presented. If there is good reason for delay in making an application, or where the court is satisfied that injustice would result if a petition presented outwith the time limit was not allowed to proceed, the court should have discretion to allow a petition to proceed."[100]

The Review went on to recommend that, like the rule in England and Wales,[101] the general rule should be that petitions be brought promptly and, in any event, within a period of three months.[102] That overriding duty to bring proceedings "promptly" has been found to lack sufficient certainty so as to be unlawful as a matter of EU law[103] and, separately, incompatible with the Aarhus Convention protecting environmental rights[104] (it did, however, survive a Convention rights

---

99 On which, see para.14–19, below.

100 Civil Justice Review, Ch.12, para.38.

101 Civil Procedure Rules, r.54.5(1).

102 Civil Justice Review, Ch.12, para.39.

103 *R (on the application of Berky) v Newport City Council* [2012] EWCA Civ 378; [2012] 2 C.M.L.R. 44.

104 Final decision ACCC/C/2008/33, determined in September 2010 at para.138.

challenge before the Strasbourg court[105]). In light of those challenges, the "promptly" requirement did not make it into the Scottish legislation.[106] It has been said that that period was selected for reasons of good governance and public policy.[107] Before turning to the three-month period, lest it be lost sight of, the terms of s.27A(2) should be noticed. Read short, it fixes the three-month limit as a long-stop provision. Where a shorter time-limit has been prescribed, that shorter limit applies, but the converse does not appear to be true: where a longer period has been prescribed, it is now cut down by s.27A. For example, on a strict reading of s.27A(2), s.100(3B) of the Scotland Act 1998, which requires proceedings against the Scottish Government alleging a breach of Convention rights be brought within one year of the date on which the act complained of took place (or such longer period as the court considers equitable), must now be read subject to s.27A. It is perhaps noteworthy that a legislative act was excluded from the s.100(3B) time restriction[108] but that would now be undone by s.27A. In other cases, the imposition of three-month period within which to raise judicial review proceedings may draw fresh attention to the issue discussed in *Ruddy v Chief Constable of Strathclyde* (namely, whether a breach of Convention rights could be pursued by way of ordinary action, thus attracting a one-year time limit, rather than by way of judicial review).[109]

Start of the time period

When does the three-month period begin? According to s.27A(1)(a), it begins **14–15**
"with the date on which the grounds giving rise to the application first arise". That ought to be easily ascertainable in the majority of cases. Where a particular decision is subject to challenge, it will be the date on which that decision was taken.[110] In *Obudajo, Petitioner*, the court had to decide whether the three-month period began on the day the decision was taken or the day the petitioner was informed of the decision.[111] Having noted the importance of certainty about the validity of administrative decisions,[112] the Lord Ordinary went on to note that it is "also an important principle, in respect of the rule of law, that the State must accord to individuals the right to know of a decision before their rights can be adversely affected".[113] He then concluded that the s.27A time limit begins to run

---

105 *Hardy v United Kingdom* (2012) 55 E.H.R.R. 28.

106 Policy Memorandum at para.179

107 *Paterson v Scottish Criminal Case Review Commission* [2018] CSOH 106 at [25]. That was not a new idea: "It is recognized that the public interest in good administration requires that public authorities and third parties should not be kept in suspense as to the legal validity of a decision for any longer than is absolutely necessary in fairness to the person affected but it." *King v East Ayrshire Council*, 1998 S.C. 182 at p.196 (Lord President (Rodger)).

108 Scotland Act 1998 s.100(3D).

109 *Ruddy v Chief Constable of Strathclyde* [2012] UKSC 57; 2013 S.C. (U.K.S.C.) 126.

110 In England and Wales, time begins when the "grounds to make the claim" first arise and that is generally taken to be the date on which a public authority does an act with legal effect rather than some preparatory or preliminary step before such an act. See, generally, *De Smith's Judicial Review* (8th edn) at para.16–057.

111 [2020] CSOH 2; 2020 S.L.T. 103.

112 [2020] CSOH 2; 2020 S.L.T. 103 at [16].

113 [2020] CSOH 2; 2020 S.L.T. 103 at [17]. The Lord Ordinary cited *R (on the application of Anufrijeva) v Secretary of State for the Home Department* [2003] UKHL 36; [2004] 1 A.C. 604 at [28] in support of that statement.

on the date on which the decision is made, but the fact that the decision is not received until a later date is relevant to considering whether to extend the time limit.[114] That conclusion provides a clear rule: no matter when the would-be petitioner receives notice of the decision, the three-month time period began to run on the day the decision was made. That clear rule, which accords with the clear words of s.27A, does risk some anomalies. Most obviously, it is, in theory at least, possible for the time period to have expired entirely before a person learns of the decision. In that unlikely event, it would be for the petitioner to explain how that happened and why they should nonetheless be permitted to bring the proceedings.[115] If they were unaware of the decision through no fault of their own, an extension of the time limit (assuming they had raised proceedings promptly[116]) would seem inevitable. But what of a would-be petitioner who learns of the decision some time into the three-month period but before its expiry? Standing the decision in *Obudajo*, there would be little doubt about when the period expired. The practical consequence would be a reduced period within which to raise proceedings.[117] But if, for example, there were still two months before the expiry of the time limit, it is not obvious why, if that date was missed, the delay in issuing the decision would necessarily justify an extension of the period. Unless the delay in issuing the decision caused problems in presenting a petition within time, it is not obvious that it would be relevant. On the other hand, if the petitioner could show practical difficulties (e.g. securing funding or properly instructing solicitors and/or counsel) caused by the delay, the court ought to have some sympathy. The safest course, as ever in relation to time limits, is to act promptly and raise proceedings, if possible, some time before what is believed to be the time limit.

14–16 Identifying the start date when a particular decision is subject to challenge should be straightforward. Similarly, a failure to do something should be straightforward: a petitioner, to complain to the court, will necessarily have to identify by when they say the act should have been done and that would be the start of the time period. What, however, of a continuing act? In the law of prescription, time does not begin to run until a continuing act ceases.[118] That approach is not consistent with the language of s.27A: "the date on which the grounds giving rise to the application *first arise*". Once the grounds have arisen, that they have a continuing effect does not prevent the time period from beginning. That is consistent with the underlying policy objective of achieving certainty about the validity of acts of a public body. And in practice, many decisions by public bodies have continuing consequences, for example a decision

---

114 [2020] CSOH 2; 2020 S.L.T. 103 at [18].

115 The idea of a time limit expiring before a person even knows they have something to complain about is inherently unattractive. Nonetheless, it is the accepted position under the Prescription and Limitation (Scotland) Act 1973 in relation to short-negative prescription. For a fairly stark example, see *Midlothian Council v Raeburn Drilling and Geotechnical Ltd* [2019] CSOH 29; 2019 S.L.T. 1327.

116 At the very least they would have to be raised within three months of learning of the decision. But it would be prudent to raise them as soon as possible as any delay in proceeding once aware of the decision (and knowing any challenge was already late) would likely count against the would-be petitioner.

117 Proceedings are raised, and the time period interrupted, when a petition is lodged with the court: RCS r.58.3(2).

118 Prescription and Limitation (Scotland) Act 1973 s.11(2). See, generally, D. Johnston, *Prescription and Limitation*, 2nd edn (Edinburgh: W. Green), paras 4.64–4.72.

on the security conditions in which a prisoner will be held or the level of benefits that a claimant should receive. As discussed below, that a decision has an ongoing effect is a relevant (and potentially important) factor when considering whether to extend the time period.[119] It is not permissible to "reset" the clock by prompting the public body to restate or re-issue the same decision.[120] Where an appeal against, or review of, a decision has been undertaken, it is ordinarily the appeal or review decision, rather than the original decision, that judicial review should be sought of,[121] but which decision to seek review of it not always clear. In *INEOS Upstream Ltd v Scottish Ministers*,[122] which concerned a challenge to a so-called fracking ban said to have been imposed by the Scottish Government, decisions in 2015 and 2017 were both engaged. For the petitioners it was argued that the earlier decision was so closely related to the 2017 decision that it had to form part of their challenge. On the other hand, the ministers argued that time had long passed to ask the court to review the 2015 decision. The Lord Ordinary granted permission for the challenge in respect of both decisions to proceed, but appeared to anticipate further discussion about timebar.[123]

Challenges to legislative acts throw up other potential complications. Legal certainty is at its most acute when it is the lawfulness of a legislative act of general application that is in issue.[124] Certainty requires that the general population ought to be able to arrange their affairs in accordance with, and in reliance upon, such provisions.[125] That points to encouraging a prompt challenge to any such measure. But that in itself begs a question as to the start date: is it the date of Royal Assent[126] (i.e. when the legislation formally passes on to the statute book) or the date, assuming it to be different, that it is brought into force (i.e. when the allegedly-offending provision takes effect)? The answer is unknown, but again the requirements of certainty (that being the principle concern which underlies the new time limit provisions) would point to any challenge being brought before the provision is brought into force. Accordingly, the prudent view would be that any challenge ought to be presented within three months of the **14–17**

[119] *Wightman v Advocate General*, 2018 S.C. 388 at [33].
[120] *Wightman v Advocate General*, 2018 S.C. 388 at [33].
[121] *Paton v Scottish Ministers* [2019] CSOH 62 at [7]. This is just a variation of the alternative remedies point discussed at para.14–07, above. In other words, to seek review of the initial decision where there was available a right of appeal would likely be held to be incompetent due to the availability of that alternative remedy. However, compare with the decision of the Lord Ordinary in *Lauchlan and O'Neill v Scottish Ministers* [2020] CSOH 28 where it was held that time started from the original decision (and not the end of the subsequent appeal process).
[122] [2018] CSOH 15.
[123] [2018] CSOH 15 at [16]. See also *William Grant & Sons Distilleries Ltd, Petitioner*, 2018 S.L.T. 525, where the court again had to consider the correct date at which grounds had first arisen. In that case, the Lord Ordinary formed the view that matters had "crystallised" at an earlier date and accordingly the petition was out of time.
[124] Acts of the Scottish Parliament, as well as all forms of secondary legislation, are susceptible to judicial review. Acts of the UK Parliament, on a strict Diceyian view of the world, should not be susceptible to judicial review. But as we have seen, the courts have, relying upon the requirements of the rule of law, entertained such challenges (e.g. *R (on the application of Jackson) v Attorney General* [2005] UKHL 56; [2006] 1 A.C. 262).
[125] T. Bingham, *The Rule of Law*, pp.37–39.
[126] Or, in the case of secondary legislation, the date on which it is made.

provision being made.[127] That, however, is not an end to matters. At least so far as Scottish legislation is concerned,[128] lawfulness is not a once and forever question. It is determined at the date of challenge.[129] That necessarily admits of the possibility of legislation that was within competence (and thus lawful) at the time it was made subsequently becoming unlawful. The most obvious possibility is a development in the jurisprudence of the Strasbourg court as to the meaning of the European Convention on Human Rights. When would time begin to run on such a challenge? Adopting the same approach as that taken in *Obudajo*, the date of the judgment of the Strasbourg court would seem the obvious answer. But that cannot be a complete answer. Say, for example, it is a provision of the Criminal Procedure (Scotland) Act 1995 that is rendered unlawful as a result of the evolution of the Strasbourg court's jurisprudence. Any accused person who was subject to that provision would be able to take the point as a compatibility issue. Accordingly, certainty would not be secured by insisting on a strict three-month period from whenever the judgment was issued (or from any other point). Certainty in the statute book cannot be absolute. And an over-zealous application of time limits risks a greater affront to the rule of law because preventing an otherwise well-founded challenge based on a time limit simply leaves in force an otherwise unlawful provision. That, it is suggested, would be a greater afront to the rule of law than the uncertainty (which, in practice, will be fairly limited) that may be caused by hearing a challenge. It is therefore suggested that the prudent course, when considering a challenge to a legislative act, is to take the date on which it first directly affected the actual petitioner, but, in any event, not to delay in raising such proceedings. Where that is done, in order to properly protect the rule of law (which is the core function of judicial review[130]), the court should not be too keen to find that a petition has been presented out of time.

Extending the time period

14–18 Where a petition has been presented out of time, the court has a general discretion to allow it to nonetheless proceed where that is considered "equitable having regard to all the circumstances". There is, as yet, little guidance on how the court will apply the discretion conferred upon it by s.27A. On its face, it bears to confer upon the court a very wide discretion to do what it considers fair in the circumstances.[131] One problem is it ought ordinarily to be dealt with at the very start of the proceedings and possibly before any answers have been lodged.[132] That is because a petitioner is required to state the date on which the grounds giving rise to the application first arose on the face of the petition and where those were more than three months earlier, an application should be made to

[127] Admittedly, this is hard to square with the omission of a legislative action from the scope of s.110(3B) of the Scotland Act 1998 but it is arguably the consequence of s.27A of the 1988 Act.

[128] i.e. both Acts of the Scottish Parliament and secondary legislation made by the Scottish Ministers.

[129] *UK Withdrawal from the European Union (Legal Continuity) (Scotland) Bill Reference* [2018] UKSC 64; 2019 S.C. (U.K.S.C.) 13. See para.6–23, above.

[130] *Wightman v Secretary of State for Exiting the European Union* [2018] CSIH 62 at [67] (Lord Drummond Young); *R (on the application of Privacy International) v Investigatory Powers Tribunal* [2019] UKSC 22; [2019] 2 W.L.R. 1219.

[131] That is consistent with what has been said about the equivalent discretion under the Human Rights Act 1998. See, for example, Lord Kerr in *A v Essex County Council* [2011] 1 A.C. 280 at [167].

[132] RCS r.58.7(1)(b).

extend the time. Despite that, the court has been willing to defer a decision on timebar so as to permit fuller argument.[133] A petitioner seeking an extension of the time limit has to provide a reason for it being extended.[134] If no reason, or no good reason, is proffered, the petition will not be allowed to proceed.[135] Given the lack of Scottish case law on the provision, some assistance may be derived from English authorities.[136] Authorities in relation to the similarly worded s.7(5)(b) of the Human Rights Act 1998 may also provide assistance. In that context, Lord Dyson explained:

> "The relevant principles are not in dispute. The court has a wide discretion in determining whether it is equitable to extend time in the particular circumstances of the case. It will often be appropriate to take into account factors of the type listed in section 33(3) of the Limitation Act 1980 as being relevant when deciding whether to extend time for a domestic law action in respect of personal injury or death. These may include the length of and reasons for the delay in issuing the proceedings; the extent to which, having regard to the delay, the evidence in the case is or is likely to be less cogent than it would have been if the proceedings had been raised within the one-year period; and the conduct of the public authority after the right of claim arose, including the extent (if any) to which it responded to requests reasonably made by the claim for information for the purpose of ascertaining facts which are or might be relevant. However … the words of section 7(5)(b) of the HRA mean what they say and the court should not attempt to rewrite them. There can be no question of interpreting section 7(5)(b) as if it contained the language of section 33(3) of the Limitation Act 1980."[137]

That suggests a very flexible approach to the discretion. As we discussed above, the language of s.27A is not consistent with the concept of a continuing act (in the sense of deferring the start of the time period), but the fact a decision has a continuing consequence is likely to be a relevant factor. If the decision is unlawful, and if it is continuing to adversely impact the petitioner, it could normally be expected to offend the rule of law for the court to shut its eyes to the problem simply because the complaint had come too late. Any continuing impact might be related to how significant the issue raised by the petitioner is (i.e. is it a meaningful interference with their rights or is it a minor nuisance). As a general rule, the more important the point raised (either a general public interest or a cogent reason to have it decided), the more sympathetic the court can be expected to be.[138] That is likely to direct attention at the underlying merits of the claim

---

[133] *INEOS Upstream Ltd v Scottish Ministers* [2018] CSOH 15 at [16]. See para.14–16, above.

[134] *Paterson v Scottish Criminal Cases Review Commission* [2018] CSOH 106 at [24]; *William Grant & Sons Distillers Ltd, Petitioner*, 2018 S.L.T. 525 at [39].

[135] For example, *Lauchlan and O'Neill v Scottish Ministers* [2020] CSOH 28 at [26].

[136] On which, see *De Smith's Judicial Review*, 8th edn (2018), para.16–060 for examples of what have, and have not, constituted good reasons under the equivalent rule in England and Wales.

[137] *Rabone v Pennine Care NHS Trust* [2012] UKSC 2; [2012] 2 A.C. 72 at [75]. Section 33(3) of the Limitation Act 1980 provides a list of circumstances that the court should have particular regard to when considering whether it is "equitable" to extend the period that applies to actions for personal injuries or death. The analogous provision in Scotland is s.19A of the Prescription and Limitation (Scotland) Act 1973, but it contains no list that is the equivalent of s.33(3) of the Limitation Act 1980. The law on the application of s.19A is explained in Johnston, *Prescription and Limitation*, 2nd edn (Edinburgh: W. Green, 2012), Ch.13.

[138] For example, the importance of determining the circumstances in which art.50 TEU could be revoked was significantly important for the court to take a charitable view on both time and

(which may make determining the issue as a preliminary matter challenging).[139] Invariably, the length of any delay will be important: the longer the delay, the more cogent the explanation will be expected to be. If a respondent can point to tangible prejudice as a result of the delay (for example, decisions taken, or expenditure incurred, in reliance upon the decision that is now challenged), a petitioner ought to find it difficult to secure an extension. Where the petitioner is an individual or smaller group, and they face a well-resourced and well-funded respondent, the court has shown itself to be sympathetic.[140] And if the petitioner has engaged in a reasonable alternative course with a view to avoiding judicial review proceedings, the court ought not to come down too harshly if such proceedings prove unavoidable but are late.[141] However, relying on an equitable discretion can be a perilous business so the best advice is always to ensure that any petition for judicial review is brought promptly.

Common law

14–19 The previous common law and the concept of *mora*, taciturnity and acquiescence is not expressly abolished by the 2014 Act.[142] Does that mean a petition could be held to have come too late if it were presented within three months?[143] For a plea of *mora*, taciturnity and acquiescence to be made out, all three aspects of the plea must be established.[144] Delay (*mora*) is not, on its own, sufficient. Acquiescence (that is, inaction that amounts to an implied consent to the changed state of affairs[145]) and taciturnity (a failure to speak out and assert a right) are required. Where a statute requires that a petition be presented earlier than three months after the grounds first arise, that shorter period applies.[146] That suggests there is no principled objection to the time period being shorter. In England and Wales, the overriding requirement to apply "promptly" has come in for criticism (which

---

permission: *Wightman v Advocate General*, 2018 S.C. 388 at [33]. Given the purpose of judicial review is the vindication of the rule of law, it is unsurprising that the courts are generally reluctant to refuse to determine a point of general significance based on a time-limit.

[139] On that, it is interesting to note that in *Lauchlan and O'Neill v Scottish Ministers* [2020] CSOH 28 permission was restricted to the issue of timebar, such that a substantive hearing proceeded in relation to that issue. Permission was reserved in respect of the underlying merits.

[140] *Portobello Park Action Group Association v City of Edinburgh Council*, 2013 S.C. 184.

[141] *R (on the application of Burkett) v Hammersmith and Fulham LBC* [2001] Env. L.R. 684 (CA) at [14].

[142] For details of the previous law, see para.14–09 of the 3rd edn of this book. Whilst the Civil Justice Review agreed that a time-limit should be introduced, nothing is said about what should happen to the existing law. The 2014 Act, and the consultations on the preceding Bill, take the same approach. With hindsight, it may have been preferable if it could have been either expressly abolished or expressly retained.

[143] Conceivably, the previous law could be relevant to an application to extent the time limit. But it is hard to envisage a circumstance where applying the common law as to *mora*, taciturnity and acquiescence would not yield the same result as the new statutory test.

[144] *Somerville v Scottish Ministers*, 2007 S.C. 140.

[145] In *Hanlon v Traffic Commissioner*, 1988 S.L.T. 802, Lord Prosser at p.805 noted that "the length of any delay before implications of acquiescence arise will be almost infinitely variable depending on the circumstances". See also, e.g. *Atherton v Strathclyde RC*, 1995 S.L.T. 557; *McIntosh v Aberdeenshire Council*, 1998 S.L.T. 93.

[146] Court of Session Act 1988 s.27A(2). See also: Clyde and Edwards, *Judicial Review* (2000), para.13.20.

led to it being dropped from the Scottish rule).[147] That may tend to suggest that, absent a specific statutory shortening of the three month period, an application cannot be late if lodged within three months. All that s.27A states, however, is that an application must be made within three months (or such extended period as the court permits); in other words, it fixes an end point.[148] Any finding that a petition had been presented late despite being presented within three months would have to be a result that was consistent with the statutory scheme. As we have seen, s.27A was recommended and introduced to avoid delay and promote certainty in respect of decisions. So, it may not be impossible, but it would require an unusual set of circumstances for a petition that was presented within three months to be barred by the common law. However, take a realistic example: professional disciplinary proceedings are brought against Z and 28 days before the substantive hearing the charges are formally served. Z takes exception to the charges and is advised that she has good grounds to seek judicial review of them. However, Z allows the proceedings to continue and, following the substantive hearing, is found guilty of professional misconduct and sanctioned accordingly. After that decision has been taken, but within three months of the service of the charges, Z presents a petition for judicial review. Under the common law, there is a compelling argument that the petition is too late: she has delayed bringing proceedings, stayed silent about her grounds of complaint and, by participating in the substantive hearing, has acquiesced in the charges. It would be a surprising consequence of the new rules if the price for certainty was that otherwise late applications had (subject to the requirement to obtain permission) to be considered.[149] Such circumstances are likely to be extremely rare. So whether a petition that has been presented within three months can still be late may never fall to be decided, but should such circumstances arise, there is a reasonable argument that the previous common law remains available to prevent such a petition proceeding.[150] Accordingly, Lord Weir's advice remains sound:

---

[147] *R. (on the application of Burkett) v Hammersmith and Fulham LBC* [2002] UKHL 23; [2002] 1 W.L.R. 1593; *Uniplex (UK) Ltd v NHS Business Services Authority* (C-406/08) [2010] 2 C.M.L.R. 47; *R. (on the application of Buglife: The Invertebrate Conservation Trust) v Medway Council* [2011] EWHC 746 (Admin); [2011] 3 C.M.L.R. 39; and *R. (on the application of Berky) v Newport City Council* [2012] EWCA Civ 378; [2012] 2 C.M.L.R. 44. See also: Craig, *Administrative Law* (2012), para.27–036.

[148] The same is true, strictly speaking, of the law of negative prescription: D. Johnston, *Prescription and Limitation*, 2nd edn, para.21.02.

[149] One answer would be for permission to be refused on the basis there was no real prospect of Z obtaining a remedy in the circumstances (the grant of a remedy being inherently a matter of discretion: *King v East Ayrshire Council*, 1998 S.C. 182 at p.196 (Lord President (Rodger)); see para.14–30, below). But if the petition was technically in time, and, for example, the illegality complained of was significant, there may be sufficient prospect of obtaining at least a declarator. It is suggested that the better approach would be to address the timing issue head on and, if appropriate, invoke the common law plea.

[150] It would be possible to frame the argument as one of personal bar, as opposed to founding on *mora*, taciturnity and acquiescence. Indeed, the stronger the element of acquiescence, the easier it may be to characterise the actions of the petitioner as amounting to personal bar.

"Judicial review is a process designed to give speedy consideration to problems which arise and when time is of materiality. In such a situation, potential litigants should lose no time in raising proceedings."[151]

Premature applications

14–20 Finally, the discussion so far has been about delay and the circumstances in which a petition comes too late. Petitions can, however, be brought too soon. There may be a complaint of prematurity where the applicant has failed to resort to an available statutory or other alternative remedy.[152] The rule reflects the underlying character of the supervisory jurisdiction, which exists to correct those wrongs for which no other remedy is provided, but it is not absolute, and in "exceptional circumstances" a failure to exhaust alternative remedies will not bar a petition for review.[153] Where the petitioner has failed to resort to their statutory remedy because of some mistake or procedural irregularity on the part of the respondent,[154] recourse to judicial review will be permitted.[155] Other material factors include: the adequacy of the alternative remedy[156]; the nature of the petitioner's complaint[157]; and, sometimes, considerations of pure practicality.[158] Also, where there is real uncertainty whether the alleged unlawfulness is going to occur, an application may be dismissed as premature. Thus, in *Scottish National Party v Scottish Television Plc*,[159] Lord Eassie remarked that the subject matter of the application (allocation by the companies of broadcasting time for the Scottish

---

[151] *Watt v Secretary of State for Scotland* [1991] 3 C.M.L.R. 429 at p.440. See also, e.g. *Swan v Secretary of State for Scotland*, 1998 S.C. 479, per Lord President Rodger at p.487: "It is, of course, the case that judicial review proceedings ought normally to be raised promptly and it is also undeniable that the petitioners let some months pass without starting these proceedings. None the less, in considering whether the delay was such that the petitioners should not be allowed to proceed, we take into account the situation in which time was allowed to pass.' See also the remarks of Lord Diplock in *O'Reilly v Mackman* [1983] 2 A.C. 237 HL at pp.280–281 to a similar effect: "The public interest in good administration requires that public authorities and third parties should not be kept in suspense as to the legal validity of a decision the authority has reached in purported exercise of decision-making powers for any longer period than is absolutely necessary in fairness to the person affected by the decision."

[152] Clyde and Edwards, *Judicial Review* (2000), Ch.12; O'Neill, *Judicial Review in Scotland: A Practitioner's Guide* (1999), paras 6.12–6.22; and see also RCS r.58.3(2). See para.14–07, above.

[153] *British Railways Board v Glasgow Corp*, 1976 S.C. 224.

[154] As in *Moss Empires Ltd v Assessor for Glasgow*, 1917 S.C. (H.L.) 1 where the assessor omitted to inform the petitioner of its right of appeal.

[155] Where it is the petitioner's agent who fails to advise of a right of appeal, a like leniency is not shown: see, e.g. *R. v Secretary of State for the Home Department, Ex p. Al-Mehdawi* [1990] 1 A.C. 876 HL; *Ouafi v Secretary of State for Home Department*, 1997 S.L.T. 544.

[156] See, e.g. *Accountant in Bankruptcy v Allans of Gillock Ltd*, 1991 S.L.T. 765.

[157] In *British Railways Board v Glasgow Corp*, 1976 S.C. 224, Lord Wheatley held that averments of ultra vires or fraud would constitute "exceptional circumstances" justifying recourse to the supervisory jurisdiction.

[158] As in, e.g. *City Cabs (Edinburgh) Ltd v City of Edinburgh DC*, 1988 S.L.T. 184, where the decision challenged was of general application and one application for judicial review was thought to be a more expeditious way of dealing with the matter than via a large number of statutory appeals.

[159] *Scottish National Party v Scottish Television Plc*, Unreported 15 May 1997 Outer House.

National Party's party political broadcasts prior to the 1997 general election) was premature since neither company had at that point actually taken a decision on the question.[160]

Permission

Introduction

Prior to the coming into force of the 2014 Act, there was no effective means by which the Court of Session filtered applications to its supervisory jurisdiction. Whilst there was a requirement that "first orders" be granted, the threshold for refusing such orders was so high that in practice it never happened.[161] Now, however, s.27B of the Court of Session Act 1988, inserted by s.89 of the 2014 Act, requires that a petition for judicial review be granted permission to proceed.[162] Section 27B, so far as relevant, provides: 14–21

> "(1) No proceedings may be taken in respect of an application to the supervisory jurisdiction of the Court unless the Court has granted permission for the application to proceed.
>
> (2) Subject to subsection (3), the Court may grant permission under subsection (1) for an application to proceed only if it is satisfied that—
>
> (a) the applicant can demonstrate a sufficient interest in the subject matter of the application, and
>
> (b) the application has a real prospect of success.
>
> …
>
> (4) The Court may grant permission under subsection (1) for an application to proceed –
>
> (a) subject to such conditions as the Court thinks fit,
>
> (b) only on such of the grounds specified in the application as the Court thinks fit.
>
> (5) The Court may decide whether or not to grant permission without an oral hearing having been held."

The meaning of the test

For judicial reviews, other than those against a decision of the Upper Tribunal on appeal from the First-Tier Tribunal (which we will come to in a moment), there is a two-part test to satisfy. First, a petitioner must have sufficient interest in the 14–22

---

[160] J. Beatson, "The need to develop principles of prematurity and ripeness for review" in C. Forsyth and I. Hare (eds), *The Golden Metwand and the Crooked Cord: Essays in Honour of Sir William Wade QC* (Oxford: Clarendon, 1998), Ch.4.

[161] In *EY v Secretary of State for the Home Department* [2011] CSIH 3; 2011 S.C. 388, the Inner House confirmed that first orders should only be refused in exceptional circumstances, for example where the court clearly lacks jurisdiction or the averments are incomprehensible or gibberish (at [16]). See also: *Eba v Advocate General for Scotland* [2011] UKSC 29; 2012 S.C. (U.K.S.C.) 1 at [28].

[162] First Orders (for intimation and service of the petition) must still be sought but they are granted automatically. At the point of seeking First Orders, however, a petitioner can seek an acceleration of the process set out below. If good reason is provided, the court has generally shown itself receptive to such requests. See: RCS r.58.4.

subject matter of the petition. In other words, they must have standing (and we have discussed that concept already).[163] In addition to standing, the petition must have a "real prospect of success". What does that mean? "What is says" has been the answer from the court.[164] Developing that slightly, the court in *Wightman* went on to say:

> "The new test is certainly intended to sift out unmeritorious cases, but it is not to be interpreted as creating an unsurmountable barrier which would prevent what might appear to be a weak case being fully argued in due course. Of course the test must eliminate the fanciful, but it is dropping the bar too low to say that every ground of review which is not fanciful passes the test. It is not enough that the petition is not 'manifestly devoid of merit', since that, in essence, reflects the 'manifestly without substance' test adopted in EY. The applicant has to demonstrate a real prospect, which is undoubtedly less than probable success, but the prospect must be real; it must have substance. Arguability or statability, which might be seen as interchangeable terms, is not enough. The substance, or lack of it, is something which the court has to determine as a preliminary issue; not after a full consideration of elaborate pleadings. It is important therefore that those seeking permission are able to plead their cases accurately and, crucially, succinctly both in relation to the facts and the propositions in law."[165]

It is certainly an increase of the height of the bar from refusing first orders under the old rules. But it remains a low hurdle.[166] At the permission stage, the court should not be drawn into substantive argument and if there is a doubt about how good a point it is, permission should be granted.[167] Binding appellate level authority is likely to result in permission being refused, but that is not inevitable.[168] As we will see in a moment, any hearing on permission is restricted to 30 minutes. Accordingly, the question distils to this: based on the papers, failing which a short oral submission, is there an arguable point in the petition? For those drafting a petition, therefore, it is important to be focused in the pleading to ensure that the court does not miss a good point in amongst a series of poor, or poorly expressed, points.[169] Lord Hope's advice on pleading for judicial review remains sound:

> "The factual history should be set out succinctly and the issues of law clearly identified. The aim is to focus the issues so that the court can reach a decision upon them, in the interests of sound administration and in the public interest, as soon as possible."[170]

---

[163] See paras 14–08—14–12, above.

[164] *Wightman v Advocate General*, 2018 S.C. 388 at [9]; *CF (China), Petitioner* [2016] CSOH 28 at [15]; *JOO (Nigeria) v Secretary of State*, 2016 S.L.T. 545.

[165] *Wightman v Advocate General*, 2018 S.C. 388 at [9]. See also: Blair, "Constitutional Importance and Permission for Judicial Review in the Court of Session" [2019] PL 9.

[166] *Carroll v Scottish Borders Council*, 2014 S.L.T. 659 at [26] (albeit in the context of protective expenses orders where the phrase "real prospects of success" also plays a part).

[167] *MIAB v Secretary of State for the Home Department*, 2016 S.C. 871 at [66]. See, for example, the judicial change of heart expressed in *Dinsmore v Scottish Ministers* [2019] CSOH 18.

[168] *Keenan, Petitioner* [2016] CSOH 5.

[169] A point made most forcibly by the Lord President in *Wightman v Advocate General*, 2018 S.C. 388 at [10]–[12].

[170] *Somerville v Scottish Ministers*, 2008 S.C. (HL) 45 at [65].

A petition that follows that advice, and which contains within it an arguable point, should have no difficulty obtaining permission.

Subsection (3) codified the result of *Eba* and applied the second-appeals test to judicial review applications that concerned decisions of the Upper Tribunal on appeal from the First-tier Tribunal.[171] That test requires, in addition to showing sufficient interest and a real prospect of success, that the applicant must also demonstrate that the application would raise a point of principle or practice or there is some other compelling reason to allow it to proceed. That test is a stringent one, designed to permit review in only rare and exceptional cases so as to ensure a compelling injustice cannot occur.[172] An error of law, even a compelling one, is not in itself enough to satisfy the second appeals test.[173] **14–23**

Practicalities of permission

Determination of permission is explained by the Rules of Court. In terms of RCS r.58.7(1), the court must decide whether to grant permission within 14 days of the end of the period for lodging answers. It is important to note that a respondent is not required to lodge answers prior to permission being determined. If a respondent wishes to actively oppose permission, answers are invariable lodged so that the reasons for opposing permission can be articulated. Where answers are lodged, the Lord Ordinary considering permission must assess whether the answers raise points that the petitioner ought to be afforded an opportunity to respond to before permission is determined.[174] Where that is the case, an oral hearing ought to follow.[175] But where a respondent is neutral on permission (or agrees that it should be granted), they can indicate to the court, in writing, that answers will only be lodged in the event permission is granted. It is unusual for permission to be refused in the absence of opposition.[176] In practice, the 14-day period is frequently exceeded by the court. That initial decision is taken on the papers. At the stage of deciding permission, the court has a number of options. It can simply grant permission for the application to proceed. Alternatively, permission can be granted subject to conditions or only on particular grounds of challenge. Where that is done, or where permission is refused, the court must provide reasons.[177] But before taking any decision, the court can order that an oral hearing take place.[178] Such a hearing must take place within 14 days and shall ordinarily last no more than 30 minutes.[179] In terms of Practice Note No.3 of 2017, the court "will ordinarily order an oral hearing" if it is considering refusing **14–24**

[171] para.8–14, above.

[172] *SA v Secretary of State for the Home Department* [2013] CSIH 62; 2014 S.C. 1.

[173] *EP v Secretary of State for the Home Department* [2014] CSIH 30; 2014 S.C. 706 at [31].

[174] *Burns v Scottish Ministers* [2019] CSOH 23; 2019 S.L.T. 337 at [43].

[175] Despite some initial challenge to the competence of amending prior to the grant of permission, it appears clear that it can be done: *Havrila v Secretary of State for the Home Department* [2019] CSOH 108 at [11]; *RA v Secretary of State for the Home Department* [2016] CSOH 182 at [8]. cf. *Wang v Scottish Ministers*, 2017 S.L.T. 1256, where the argument that amendment was incompetent appears to gain some favour with the Lord Ordinary.

[176] But it can, and does, happen, e.g. *Dinsmore v Scottish Ministers* [2019] CSOH 18 at [7].

[177] RCS r.58.7(2)

[178] RCS r.58.7(1)(b).

[179] RCS r.58.7(1)(b); RCS r.58.9.

permission.[180] It has been doubted whether such hearings were ordinarily being held,[181] and, for a spell at least, those doubts accorded with the general experience of many practitioners. Oral hearings are now, however, a regular occurrence.

Where permission is refused without an oral hearing, the petitioner may, within seven days, request a review of that refusal at an oral hearing. That request must be considered by a different Lord Ordinary.[182] At such a review, the question of permission arises de novo for the new Lord Ordinary (in other words, it is not an appeal).[183] Where permission is refused after an oral hearing (or it is granted on conditions or only on particular grounds) a further review, again within seven days, can be sought by the Inner House.[184] Again, the question of permission arises de novo for the Inner House. In practice that means that a petitioner who seeks review of a partial or conditional grant of permission risks having permission refused in its entirety at the review hearing.[185] Where, however, permission is refused without an oral hearing and then the request to review that decision at an oral hearing is also refused, that is the end of an application and no appeal lies to the Inner House. The lawfulness of that provision has been upheld.[186] It is important to note that the seven-day time limits are strict and are not subject to extension by the court.[187]

14–25 There are other practical aspects of the permission system that should be noted. It should be remembered that permission is not an all-or-nothing exercise. Where (as is usually the case) multiple grounds of challenge are advanced, the court can be discriminating on which are permitted to proceed. It inevitably follows that where further grounds are subsequently introduced, whether by way of adjustment or amendment, permission should be sought in relation to them.[188] In relation to adjustment, at least, in practice that is rarely done. Where the means of introducing the new ground is amendment, the existence of a "real prospect of success" is the "minimum requirement" before such an amendment would be allowed but meeting that standard does not mean the amendment will necessarily be allowed.[189] Adjustment is almost always allowed where permission is granted and, unlike amendment, the court does not exercise control over what is pled by

---

[180] Practice Note No.3 of 2017, para.12.

[181] *Dinsmore v Scottish Ministers* [2019] CSOH 18 at [19] (Lord Doherty).

[182] Court of Session Act 1988, s.27C.

[183] *Dinsmore v Scottish Ministers* [2019] CSOH 18 at [16] (Lord Doherty).

[184] Court of Session Act 1988 s.27D; see *PA v Secretary of State for the Home Department* [2020] CSIH 34 at [31]–[33] (Lord President [Carloway]).

[185] Although the point has not been decided, the Inner House (in the form of a single procedural judge) has expressed the view that a respondent does not have any right to appeal a permission decision: *Beggs v Scottish Ministers* [2017] CSOH 62 at [11]. That appears to be the obvious (and sensible) implication from the way in which the relevant provisions have been drafted. Separately, allowing respondents an appeal at the stage of permission does not sit easily with the desire to secure an improvement in the overall efficiency of the judicial review procedure.

[186] *Burns v Scottish Ministers* [2019] CSOH 23; 2019 S.L.T. 337, where at first instance it was held that the refusal of permission without any oral hearing whatsoever was lawful. That decision was upheld by the Inner House: [2020] CSIH 36.

[187] *Beggs v Scottish Ministers* [2017] CSIH 62.

[188] If the point was ever in doubt, it was made clear by the Lord President in *MIAB v Secretary of State for the Home Department* [2016] CSIH 64; 2016 S.L.T. 1220 at [64].

[189] *MIAB v Secretary of State for the Home Department* [2016] CSIH 64; 2016 S.L.T. 1220 at [64] (Lord President (Carloway)).

way of adjustment. In other contexts (for example, limitation periods in respect of personal injury actions), procedural bars can be elided by using adjustment.[190] If that same approach were taken in judicial review, the court could be said to have no power to prevent the addition of new grounds of challenge after the three-month period had expired where they were introduced by adjustment.[191] That was plainly not the intention of the Parliament when introducing the general requirement for permission. A petitioner ought not to be able to elide the requirement to obtain permission by saving more controversial grounds of challenge for the adjustment period. In practice, it is suggested that permission should be sought at the procedural hearing that routinely follows the conclusion of any adjustment period for new grounds of challenge that have been introduced. Where it is not sought, or is not granted, the new grounds ought not to form any part of the discussion at the substantive hearing.[192] But this example perhaps suggests that the traditional rules for adjustment, rooted as they are in private actions, are inappropriate for a modern system of (largely public law) judicial review. Instead, as is the case now in actions appointed to the commercial roll, there is a good argument to end the automatic entitlement to adjust so that the court can keep closer control over the form and content of any judicial review in which it has granted permission to proceed.

Subsequent procedure

Where permission is granted, the court will fix a substantive hearing no more than 12 weeks after permission is granted (unless the Lord Ordinary granting permission is satisfied that a longer period is necessary) and a procedural hearing no more than six weeks after permission is granted (unless the Lord Ordinary granting permission is satisfied a procedural hearing is unnecessary or a longer period is necessary).[193] Otherwise, the Lord Ordinary has a general power (and obligation) to make such orders for further procedure as are appropriate for the speedy determination of the petition.[194] In practice, that usually sees an order allowing for a period of adjustment,[195] a date by which Notes of Argument must be lodged (together with a marked up bundle of authorities and any other documents to be relied upon), a statement of issues and an estimate for the duration of the substantive hearing. At the substantive hearing, factual matters are normally assessed on the basis of documentary evidence that has been produced 14–26

[190] Johnston, *Prescription and Limitation*, 2nd edn (2012), para.22.22

[191] A point that the court was concerned about (albeit in the context of amendment) in *RA v Secretary of State for the Home Department* [2016] CSOH 182 at [13] (Lord Boyd of Duncansby).

[192] It is not clear what would happen if permission were to be refused. Whilst there are very prescriptive rules about challenging a refusal of permission at the start of judicial review proceedings, any appeal would likely have to be a normal reclaiming motion. The time limits for that are more generous and not obviously consistent with the overall goal of reaching a substantive hearing within three months.

[193] RCS r.58.11(1). Where the parties agree that a procedural hearing is unnecessary, it can be dispensed with, but note the comments on the importance of what should be achieved at or before the procedural hearing: *M v Secretary of State for the Home Department*, 2016 S.L.T. 280.

[194] RCS r.58.11(2).

[195] As to whether there should be an automatic entitlement to adjustment, see para.14–25, above.

and, where appropriate, affidavits.[196] Strict proof (for example, an affidavit from someone speaking to the documents) of averments is not appropriate and risks re-opening the underlying decision as opposed to assessing whether recognised grounds of challenge exist.[197] In appropriate cases, the court can be asked to compress the usual timescales.[198] Where there is a reasonable basis for doing so, the court has shown itself to be accommodating of such requests.

FUNDING

14–27 All litigation is expensive and judicial review is no different. In general, the cost of litigation falls on the party that causes it and that party is ordinarily the losing party.[199] In Scotland, the successful party only ever recovers a proportion of the expenses incurred with the result that there is an inevitable "fight and win" cost. Having regard to the fundamental purpose of judicial review (to secure the rule of law), it is important that litigation is not prohibitively expensive with the result that otherwise unlawful decisions are allowed to stand simply because nobody can afford (or is willing to risk the costs associated with) a challenge. As Lord Bingham famously put it, the courts should not be open to everyone in the same sense that anybody (who has the money) can stay at the Ritz. The "expenses follow success" rule has its origins in private law and it appears increasingly ill suited (just as the rules on title and interest had become) to public law litigation. Judicial review differs from ordinary litigation: in the latter the party bringing proceedings invariably has a pecuniary interest in the outcome. That is not always so in judicial review and it would undermine the protection of the rule of law if the only decisions that were in practice susceptible to judicial review were those where someone had a sufficient financial interest in the outcome. In practice, the costs associated with litigation, and in particular the risk of an adverse award of expenses, represents a significant deterrent to anyone considering raising judicial review proceedings.

14–28 That effect can be ameliorated in a number of ways. First, a small (and reducing) category of litigants will be eligible for legal aid.[200] A grant of legal aid has two practical consequences. First, it will fund the petitioner's own costs. Second, and just as importantly, if an adverse award of expenses is made against the petitioner, such an award is normally modified to match the level of any contribution that the petitioner has had to make to their legal aid funding. Invariably that is nil. Where that happens, there is no cost to the petitioner. Given the rules on legal aid funding, it is only those that have very limited means that will qualify.

---

[196] Affidavits may need to be treated with care where they proffer reasons for a decision that are not obvious from the terms of the contemporaneous documentation: *Chief Constable of Lothian and Borders v Lothian and Borders Police Board*, 2005 S.L.T. 315 at [65].

[197] *Gilday v Scottish Ministers* [2019] CSOH 103 at [26]–[28].

[198] RCS r.58.4(4)–(6).

[199] e.g. *Shepherd v Elliot* (1896) 23 R 695; *Ramm v Lothian and Borders Fire Board*, 1994 S.C. 226.

[200] On the practical aspects of applications for legal aid in the context of judicial review, see L. Drummond, F. McCartney and A. Poole, *A Practical Guide to Public Law Litigation in Scotland* (W. Green, Edinburgh, 2020), at paras 2–031—2–057.

Second, the court can be asked to make a "protective expenses order". The effect of a protective expenses order is to limit the applicant's exposure in expenses and thus offer a measure of protection against any adverse award that may be made in the event their claim is unsuccessful. They are relatively new in Scotland.[201] The power to make a protective expenses order exists at common law[202] and is now, in relation to environmental cases at least, regulated by the Rules of Court.[203] So far as the common law power is concerned, it arises from the court's general and wide discretion to regulate all matters of expenses. A consequence of that is any award (being discretionary) will rarely be interfered with on appeal.[204] In exercising that discretion, the Court of Session has had regard to the approach taken by the English courts to similar applications and, in particular, what have become known as the *Corner House* principles.[205] In that case, the Court of Appeal set out the following principles to govern applications for a protective expenses order:

1) the issues raised must be of general public importance;
2) the public interest requires that the issues be resolved;
3) the party seeking the protective expenses order has no private interest in the outcome of the case;
4) having regard to the financial resources of the party seeking the protective expenses order and the likely costs involved, it is fair and just to make the order; and
5) if the protective expenses order is not made the applicant is likely to discontinue proceedings (and would be acting reasonably to do so).[206]

Applications to the Court of Session under the common law power remain rare and have had limited success. Even when granted, the cap on expenses has been fixed at what appeared to be a high level.[207] In practice, few applications for judicial review will benefit from such an order.[208]

Third, the more liberalised rules on standing assist in allowing representative groups to raise proceedings. That does not reduce or avoid the costs associated with litigation, but it does allow those costs to be spread amongst a group of likeminded individuals who have come together to challenge a particular decision. To that extent, it addresses the concerns around funding only in an indirect way. A related development, and one that is a much more recent innovation, is the use of crowdfunding. In short, people are asked to donate to

[201] See *Newton Mearns Residents Flood Prevention Group for Cheviot Drive v East Renfrewshire Council* [2013] CSIH 70 at [26]–[33] for an account of their development in Scotland.

[202] *McArthur v Lord Advocate*, 2006 S.L.T. 170.

[203] RCS r.58A.

[204] *McGinty v Scottish Ministers* [2013] CSIH 78; 2014 S.C. 81 at [62].

[205] *R. (on the application of Corner House Research) v Secretary of State for Trade and Industry* [2005] EWCA Civ 192; [2005] 1 W.L.R. 2600.

[206] *R. (on the application of Corner House Research) v Secretary of State for Trade and Industry* [2005] EWCA Civ 192; [2005] 1 W.L.R. 2600 at [74].

[207] For example, *McGinty v Scottish Ministers* Unreported 28 January 2010 Outer House, where the cap was set at £30,000. In environmental cases, the levels are prescribed and are more reasonable. Exposure to an adverse award is limited to £5,000.

[208] See further: Drummond, McCartney and Poole, *A Practical Guide to Public Law Litigation in Scotland* (2020) at paras 2–078—2–081.

help fund proceedings (including meeting an adverse award of expenses). Various issues can arise with such a model. How well informed are people about what they are funding? What happens if the money is not all used? What if the action is successful and expenses are recovered from the other party? It is an area that will, sooner or later, require some regulation.[209] In the meantime, it has already been used to fund some high-profile litigation in Scotland.[210]

14–29 There is, however, a more radical solution to the problems associated with costs. In personal injury actions, the Scottish Parliament has legislated to introduce "qualified one-way cost shifting".[211] In short, the default rule will, when the provisions are brought into force, be that a defender in a personal injuries action cannot recover their expenses from the pursuers.[212] That general rule is qualified by a requirement that the pursuer must have conducted the proceedings in an appropriate manner.[213] A person conducts civil proceedings in an appropriate manner unless the person (or their legal representative) does one of three things: (a) makes a fraudulent representation or otherwise acts fraudulently; (b) behaves in a way that is manifestly unreasonable; or (c) otherwise conducts the proceedings in a manner that the court considers amounts to an abuse of process.[214] As the provisions are not in force, there is no guidance on how the court will interpret those conditions, but on their face, substantial protection is afforded to the pursuer in a personal injuries action. The main justification advanced in support of that legislation was the need to protect the pursuer (usually an individual with limited means) against an invariably insurance-back defender (with substantial, and in practical terms, unlimited means). Who could argue with the desire to ensure access to justice for those who have sustained personal injuries? But it rather begs the question why those seeking access to the supervisory jurisdiction of the Court of Session do not have a similar benefit? Invariably, a petition for judicial review will be founded upon the alleged unlawful action of a public authority. Given what has been said about the importance of such challenges to securing the rule of law, it might be thought that such litigants are as deserving of protection from an adverse award of expenses as someone pursuing damages for personal injuries. On the other side of the balance, there is a public body that is put to the time and expense of defending a decision it has taken. A petitioner is only exposed to an adverse award of expenses where the claim fails; in other words, the public body did in fact take the decision lawfully. Why, the argument runs, should the public body not recover the costs it has incurred from the party that brought the failed challenge? Given the widespread availability of funding methods that appear to grant fairly ready access to those who seek reparation for personal injuries, as compared to the continuing dearth of public law litigation in Scotland, the 2018 Act does have the feel of being the right solution to the wrong problem.

---

[209] J. Tomlinson, "Crowdfunding public interest judicial reviews: a risky new resource and the case for practical ethics" [2019] PL 166.

[210] A number of Brexit-related challenges were supported by the Good Law Project and its crowdfunding, for example *Wightman v Secretary of State for Exiting the European Union*, 2019 S.C. 111 (Inner House); C-621/18 [2019] QB 199 (CJEU).

[211] Civil Litigation (Expenses and Group Proceedings) (Scotland) Act 2018 Pt.2.

[212] Civil Litigation (Expenses and Group Proceedings) (Scotland) Act 2018 s.8(2).

[213] Civil Litigation (Expenses and Group Proceedings) (Scotland) Act 2018 s.8(1).

[214] Civil Litigation (Expenses and Group Proceedings) (Scotland) Act 2018 s.8(4).

REMEDIES

Although we come to it last, this ought to be the starting point for anyone contemplating raising judicial review proceedings. As Coulson J wryly observed, "[i]t is a not uncommon failing amongst those who practice in public law to believe that, whatever the factual background, and whatever the legal framework, an application for judicial review is a universal panacea for all perceived ills".[215] That alights on the important point that identifying a problem with a decision is easy; formulating the remedy sought from the court can be more difficult. In exercising its supervisory jurisdiction on an application for judicial review, the court may grant or refuse the petition or any part of it, with or without conditions.[216] In particular, the court may, at the substantive hearing, make any of the following orders: reduction; declarator; suspension; interdict; implement; restitution or payment (whether of damages or otherwise).[217] It can make any of those orders whether or not it was sought in the petition. Generous as this is (and the remedies listed are not exhaustive), there are certain limitations on the court's remedial jurisdiction. In deciding whether to grant a particular remedy, it has been said that the court should have regard to the wider interest in good administration.[218] Furthermore, judicial review remains an equitable remedy.[219] Accordingly, whether to grant any particular remedy is a matter for the court's discretion.[220] The court may refused to reduce an impugned decision where there is no realistic prospect of a different decision being taken or where it has caused no substantial prejudice.[221] As Lord Carnwath explained in *Walton*, the court's discretion in relation to granting a remedy is effectively a counter-balance to the widening of the rules of standing.[222] But the onus rests on the respondent to persuade the court why an otherwise unlawful decision should not be reduced. As the Lord Ordinary put it in *McHattie v South Ayrshire Council*, "[a] court should be slow to refuse to quash an illegal decision by a public authority. … The fundamental principle at stake is the rule of law. An illegal decision is an affront to the rule of law."[223] Damages may be awarded only where their award would otherwise be competent[224]; there is no general right to damages for breach of a 14–30

[215] *Carespec Ltd v Wolverhampton City Council* [2016] EWHC 521 (Admin) at [1].
[216] RCS r.58.13(2)(a).
[217] RCS r.58.13(3).
[218] *King v East Ayrshire Council*, 1998 S.C. 182 at p.196 (Lord President (Rodger)). As that case illustrates, the conduct of the petitioner will be an important factor. There, she had changed her line of attack sometime after the petition had been presented and sought a different remedy. Influenced by that, the court refused to reduce the decision challenged despite being satisfied that it had been taken in error.
[219] *Ingle v Ingle's Trustee*, 1999 S.L.T. 650.
[220] To the extent there was any doubt about that in Scots law (cf. *Anderson v Secretary of State for Work and Pensions*, 2002 S.L.T. 68), that was removed by the Supreme Court in *Walton v Scottish Ministers* [2012] UKSC 44; 2013 S.C. (U.K.S.C.) 67.
[221] *Douglas v Perth and Kinross Council* [2017] CSIH 28; 2017 S.C. 523 at [47].
[222] *Walton v Scottish Ministers* [2012] UKSC 44; 2013 S.C. (U.K.S.C.) 67 at [103].
[223] *McHattie v South Ayrshire Council* [2020] CSOH 4 at [51]–[52].
[224] The reference to "payment (whether of damages or otherwise)" in r.58.4(b) appears to countenance the award of monetary redress even absent a cause of action, but if such power exists it appears only to have been exercised twice: *Kelly v Monklands DC*, 1986 S.L.T. 169 and *Mallon v Monklands DC*, 1986 S.L.T. 347.

public law duty.[225] It is now clear, however, that the court is not prevented by s.21 of the Crown Proceedings Act 1947 from granting the remedies of interdict or implement, ad interim or otherwise, against the Crown (including the Scottish Ministers) in the context of an application for judicial review.[226]

[225] *Somerville v Scottish Ministers*, 2008 S.C. (HL) 45 at [182] (Lord Mance); *Poole Borough Council v GN* [2019] UKSC 25; [2019] 2 W.L.R. 1478.

[226] It was established in *R. v Secretary of State for Transport, Ex p. Factortame Ltd (No.2)* [1991] 1 A.C. 603 HL that s.21 did not prevent the grant of injunction or interdict where the Crown was said to have infringed the applicant's rights under community law (see also, in Scotland, *Millar & Bryce Ltd v Keeper of the Registers of Scotland*, 1997 S.L.T. 1000). In *M v Home Office* [1994] 1 A.C. 377, the House of Lords had held that "civil proceedings" did not include proceedings for judicial review in England, so that the equivalent remedies of injunction and specific performance might competently be granted against the Crown in such proceedings even where no community law element existed. In *McDonald v Secretary of State for Scotland*, 1994 S.C. 234, the Second Division held that the plain effect of s.21 had been to exclude interdict and implement in civil proceedings against the Crown and that *M v Home Office*, having turned substantially on aspects of English procedure, was not authoritative as to the meaning of s.21 in Scotland. However, in *Davidson v Scottish Ministers* [2005] UKHL 74; 2006 S.C. (H.L.) 41, the House of Lords held that there was no basis for interpreting the words "civil proceedings" as they appear in s.21 differently north and south of the border.

CHAPTER 15

Judicial Review: Grounds of Review

INTRODUCTION

In the previous chapter we considered the constitutional basis of judicial review along with a number of the procedural rules that surround it. In this chapter, we turn to consider the substantive grounds upon which judicial review can be sought. Here, we are not concerned with the grounds on which the court can review acts of the legislature: judicial review of legislative acts (in the sense of primary legislation, whether emanating from Westminster or one of the devolved legislatures) is a relatively new feature of our constitution that is discussed more fully in Ch.6.[1] We are concerned with other acts that the court can be asked to review. As we have seen, those are not necessarily acts of a public authority but can include acts of "private" bodies where the necessary tri-partite relationship is demonstrated.[2] Whilst caution was advised in relation to English authorities on matters of procedure, so far as the substantive grounds of review are concerned the laws of Scotland and England are in general the same and guidance can normally be found in the decisions of the English courts.[3] **15–01**

The classic statement of the grounds on which judicial review may be sought was, and remains, that of Lord Diplock in *Council of Civil Service Unions v Minister for the Civil Service ("GCHQ")*:

> "Judicial review has I think developed to a stage today when one can conveniently classify under three heads the grounds on which administrative action is subject to control by judicial review. The first ground I would call 'illegality', the second 'irrationality' and the third 'procedural impropriety'."[4]

Lord Diplock went on to acknowledge that that classification was not cast in stone:

> "That is not to say that further development on a case by case basis may not in course of time add further grounds. I have in mind particularly the possible adoption in the future of the principle of 'proportionality' which is recognised in the law of several of our fellow members of the [EU]…."[5]

---

[1] See paras 6–34—6–38, above.

[2] See, for example, the discussion (in the context of disciplinary proceedings in the course of employment) in *Dryburgh, Petitioner* [2016] CSOH 116.

[3] *West v Secretary of State for Scotland*, 1992 S.C. 385 at pp.402 and 405 (Lord President (Hope)); *Somerville v Scottish Ministers* [2006] CSIH 52; 2007 S.C. 140 at [123].

[4] *Council of Civil Service Unions v Minister for the Civil Service* [1985] A.C. 374 at p.410.

[5] *Council of Civil Service Unions v Minister for the Civil Service* [1985] A.C. 374 at p.410.

As we shall see below, proportionality is an increasingly common feature of domestic law, but it has not, despite predictions to the contrary, established itself as a self-standing ground of review.[6] We return to that issue below. Lord Diplock's classification was very quickly adopted in Scotland.[7] It provides a convenient structure in which to consider the various grounds on which the court will exercise its supervisory jurisdiction.

ILLEGALITY

15–02 In one sense, a decision could be said to be illegal whatever the reason for the court's intervention, but as a discrete head of review, illegality means something narrower than this. In *Council of Civil Service Unions v Minister for the Civil Service* Lord Diplock explained what he meant by illegality:

> "By 'illegality' as a ground of judicial review I mean that the decision-maker must understand correctly the law that regulates his decision-making power and must give effect to it."[8]

Judicial review involves the control of powers, and at the most basic level this means ensuring that a given power is only exercised in the circumstances envisaged, and on the conditions imposed by, the donor, whether Parliament or some other body. Where the decision maker misinterprets or fails to apply the conditions of the grant of their power, or jurisdiction, they confer on themselves an authority it was never intended that they should have.[9] Thus, the court on review will, as a matter of principle, ascertain whether the conditions for an exercise of jurisdiction were met, and if it finds that they were not will[10] reduce the decision as being ultra vires. Review on this ground is often discussed in terms of error, whether of law or of fact, on the part of the decision-maker, but review for illegality goes further than this. A grant of power may be more or less prescriptive in the conditions it imposes on the power's exercise. However, even where it apparently imposes no conditions, the courts presume that powers are granted subject to certain implied limitations. Although this is explained in terms of assumed legislative intent, these limitations are very much the product of judicial innovation, and have greatly extended the scope of review for illegality.

---

[6] *R. (on the application of Association of British Civilian Internees (Far East Region)) v Secretary of State for Defence* [2003] EWCA Civ 473; [2003] Q.B. 1397, per Dyson LJ at [34]: "Although we did not hear argument on the point, we have difficulty in seeing what justification there now is for retaining the *Wednesbury* test". See further, paras.15–27, below

[7] *Edinburgh DC v Secretary of State for Scotland*, 1985 S.C. 261.

[8] *Council of Civil Service Unions v Minister for the Civil Service* [1985] A.C. 374 at p.410.

[9] Thus, in *McColl v Strathclyde RC*, 1983 S.L.T. 616, it was held that the local authority's statutory duty to provide "wholesome water" did not entitle it to fluoridate the water in the interests of dental health.

[10] On when the court might decline to reduce a decision that has been held to be flawed, see *King v East Ayrshire Council*, 1998 S.C. 182; *Anderson v Secretary of State for Work and Pensions*, 2002 S.L.T. 68.

Jurisdiction and error

We have seen that the supervisory jurisdiction is to be distinguished from appellate procedures. One of the consequences of this distinction was that, since the supervisory jurisdiction is concerned only with the legal validity of decisions and not with their rightness or wrongness, errors were not reviewable and the only possibility of correcting these depended on the availability of a right of appeal.[11] This was never an absolute rule. An error, whether of law or of fact, that vitiated the power of a body to act or decide might be reviewed because in making such an error the decision-maker stepped outside the four corners of their jurisdiction, conferring on themselves an authority they did not have. Such errors were (and are) described as "jurisdictional" errors, and the scope of review on this basis depended upon where the courts drew the line between such errors and non-jurisdictional errors that the body was at liberty (subject to any appeal) to make. **15–03**

In this area, the decision of the House of Lords in *Anisminic* remains a landmark.[12] That case arose out of the fallout from the Suez crisis in 1956. Anisminic claimed compensation for property lost in Egypt during the crisis. It complained that the Foreign Compensation Commission had erred in determining that the successor in title to its property was required by the relevant Order in Council to be a British national. Anisminic argued that there was no such requirement in the order. Section 4(4) of the Foreign Compensation Act 1950, however, purported to exclude the court's jurisdiction to review any determination by the Foreign Compensation Commission. The core question (was Anisminic entitled to compensation?) was one that fell squarely within the Foreign Compensation Commission's jurisdiction. The question for the House of Lords was whether the court could review the alleged error concerning the subsidiary question (does the successor in title require to be a British national?). By a majority, the House held that it had jurisdiction to review that decision. By asking itself the wrong question, and imposing an erroneous requirement, the Foreign Compensation Commission had, said the House of Lords, exceed its jurisdiction and the decision was a nullity.[13] The significance of the decision in *Anisminic* was explained by Lord Diplock in *Re Racal Communications Ltd*:

> "The break-through made by *Anisminic*... was that, as respects administrative tribunals and authorities, the old distinction between errors of law that went to jurisdiction and errors of law that did not, was for practical purposes abolished. Any error of law that could be shown to have been made by them in the course of

[11] As Lord Reid explained in *Armah v Governor of Ghana* [1968] A.C. 192 at p.234: "If a magistrate or any other tribunal has jurisdiction to enter on the inquiry and to decide a particular issue, and there is no irregularity in the procedure, he does not destroy his jurisdiction by reaching the wrong decision. If he has jurisdiction to go right he has jurisdiction to go wrong."

[12] *Anisminic Ltd v Foreign Compensation Commission* [1969] 2 A.C. 147.

[13] *Anisminic Ltd v Foreign Compensation Commission* [1969] 2 A.C. 147, per Lord Reid at p.171. See Lord Sumption's explanation of the significance of the decision in *R (on the application of Privacy International) v Investigatory Powers Tribunal* [2019] UKSC 22; [2019] 2 W.L.R. 1219 at [176]–[181].

> reaching their decision on matters of fact or of administrative policy would result in their having asked themselves the wrong question with the result that the decision they reached would be a nullity."[14]

That interpretation of *Anisminic* was slow to take hold and it was not until the decision of the House of Lords in *R. v Lord President of the Privy Council, Ex p. Page*[15] that the Lord Diplock view that the distinction between errors of law going to jurisdiction and errors of law within jurisdiction had been abolished was accepted.[16]

It appeared for some time that the law of Scotland was determined to follow a different course from that south of the border. That difference arose from the comments of the Lord President (Emslie) in *Watt v Lord Advocate*.[17] Although strictly speaking his remarks were obiter, the Lord President expressed the view that:

> "[H]owever much this is to be regretted, the Court of Session has never had the power to correct an intra vires error of law made by a statutory tribunal or authority exercising statutory jurisdiction."[18]

That can be seen to be at odds with what the House of Lords held in *Anisminic* as interpreted and applied later by Lord Diplock and then Lord Browne-Wilkinson. That was unfortunate as the Scottish courts have, on numerous occasions, stressed that there was no difference between Scotland and England so far as the substantive grounds of judicial review were concerned.[19] As time went on, the application of the Lord President's comments in *Watt* became increasingly patchy, with some judges simply ignoring it.[20] In *Gillies Ramsay Diamond v PJW Enterprises Ltd*, the argument that *Anisminic* rendered the distinction drawn in *Watt* unnecessary was mentioned, but the court found it unnecessary to decide the point.[21] In *Eba v Advocate General for Scotland*, the Supreme Court accepted the time had finally come to recognise that what was said by the Lord President in *Watt* was irreconcilable with what had been decided in *Anisminic* and it should no longer be followed. Thus, by a somewhat circuitous route, the law of Scotland is now consistent with that of England and Wales: the Court of Session has the power to correct any error of law by an inferior tribunal.

15–04 What, then, is an error of law? The error must affect the decision that was taken and not simply be a subsidiary or incidental matter that was of no

---

[14] *Re Racal Communications Ltd* [1981] A.C. 374 at p.383. See also *O'Reilly v Mackman* [1983] 2 A.C. 237, per Lord Diplock at p.278.

[15] *R. v Lord President of the Privy Council, Ex p. Page* [1993] A.C. 682.

[16] *R. v Lord President of the Privy Council, Ex p. Page* [1993] A.C. 682, in particular Lord Browne-Wilkinson at pp.701–702. Whether they were right to do so has been doubted: *R (on the application of Privacy International) v Investigatory Powers Tribunal* [2019] UKSC 22; [2019] 2 W.L.R. 1219 at [181] (Lord Sumption).

[17] *Watt v Lord Advocate*, 1979 S.C. 120.

[18] *Watt v Lord Advocate*, 1979 S.C. 120 at p.131.

[19] *Brown v Hamilton DC*, 1983 S.C. (H.L.) 1, per Lord Fraser at 42; *West v Secretary of State for Scotland*, 1992 S.C. 385, per Lord President Hope at pp.402 and 405; *Somerville v Scottish Ministers* [2006] CSIH 52; 2007 S.C. 140 at [123].

[20] For example, *Mooney v Secretary of State for Work and Pensions*, 2004 S.L.T. 1141 and *Donnelly v Secretary of State for Work and Pensions* [2007] CSOH 1; 2007 S.C.L.R. 746.

[21] *Gillies Ramsay Diamond v PJW Enterprises Ltd*, 2004 S.C. 430 at [37]–[38].

consequence to the final decision.[22] It must, in other words, be material.[23] In *Wordie Property Ltd v Secretary of State for Scotland*,[24] Lord President Emslie held that a decision of the Secretary of State acting within their statutory remit would be ultra vires if they improperly exercised a discretion confided to them, in particular, "if [their decision] is based upon a material error of law going to the root of the question for determination".[25] In *SS v Secretary of State for the Home Department*, Lord Carloway, giving the Opinion of the Extra Division, summarised what it is that will constitute an error of law:

> "An error of law will occur where a tribunal has: misdirected itself in law; entertained the wrong issue; proceeded upon a misapprehension or misconstruction of the evidence; taken into account irrelevant matters or failed to take account of relevant ones; or has reached a decision so extravagant that no reasonable tribunal, properly directing itself on the law, could have arrived at. An error of law cannot be said to have occurred simply where a tribunal has wrongly assessed the evidence in some way or weighed it in a manner with which a party disagrees. But it will be seen to happen where a tribunal has misunderstood the evidential position."[26]

The language of "error" suggests that legal questions are susceptible only to one, objectively verifiable, answer. That is not (or not always) the case, as is apparent in the decision of the House of Lords in *R. v Monopolies and Mergers Commission, Ex p. South Yorkshire Transport Ltd*.[27] There, the commission had power to take action where it was satisfied that a monopoly situation existed in "a substantial part of the United Kingdom". The commission purported to exercise this power on the basis of a monopoly situation found to exist in an area amounting to only 1.65 per cent of the total area of the UK. The company argued that, in treating so small an area as "substantial", the commission had erred in law and its decision was accordingly ultra vires. The House of Lords disagreed:

> "The courts have repeatedly warned against the dangers of taking an inherently imprecise word and by redefining it thrusting on it a spurious degree of precision... The question is whether the Commission has placed the phrase broadly in the right part of the spectrum of possible meanings [and] within the permissible field of judgment... The statutory criterion of jurisdiction might itself be so imprecise that different decision makers, each acting rationally, might reach differing conclusions when applying it to the facts of a given case. In such a case, the court is entitled to

---

22 Clyde and Edwards, *Judicial Review* (2000), para.22.24.

23 *R (Iran) v Secretary of State for the Home Department* [2005] EWCA Civ 982 at [9]–[10]: "Errors of law of which it can be said that they would have made no difference to the outcome do not matter" (Brooke LJ).

24 *Wordie Property Ltd v Secretary of State for Scotland*, 1984 S.L.T. 345.

25 *Wordie Property Ltd v Secretary of State for Scotland*, 1984 S.L.T. 345 at p.347. See also *R. v Lord President of the Privy Council, Ex p. Page* [1993] A.C. 682 at p.701, where Lord Browne-Wilkinson held that in order to justify intervention the error complained of required to be "relevant and material".

26 [2010] CSIH 72 at [13].

27 *R. v Monopolies and Mergers Commission, Ex p. South Yorkshire Transport Ltd* [1993] 1 W.L.R. 23, followed in Scotland in *Stagecoach Holdings Ltd v Secretary of State for Trade and Industry*, 1997 S.L.T. 940. See also, e.g. *R. v Broadcasting Complaints Commission, Ex p. Granada Television Ltd* [1995] E.M.L.R. 163 CA (Civ Div); *R. v Radio Authority, Ex p. Bull* [1998] Q.B. 294 CA (Civ Div); *R. v Broadcasting Standards Commission, Ex p. BBC* [2000] 3 W.L.R. 1327 CA (Civ Div).

> substitute its own opinion for that of the person to whom the decision has been entrusted only if the decision is so aberrant that it cannot be classed as rational."[28]

This is not to say that the courts will always accord a generous margin of interpretation to the primary decision-maker.[29] In appropriate cases, particularly those involving fundamental rights, they may confine the "spectrum of possible meanings" so closely as to leave only one answer to a given question of statutory interpretation, such that the decision-maker falls into error if they fail to answer that question correctly.[30] Of course, it is *Eba* that highlights the most obvious limit on the court's willingness to correct errors of law. As we have seen, the result of the "second appeals test" that must be satisfied before a challenge to an otherwise unreviewable decision of the Upper Tribunal will be entertained is that an error of law on the part of the tribunal is not sufficient, in and of itself, to justify the court exercising its supervisory jurisdiction.[31] As Wade and Forsyth explain, where, for example, a tribunal has found X liable to pay a certain sum of money to Y, but that decision is marred by an error of law, it is an error that will go uncorrected if the second appeals test cannot be satisfied, but the same error could be pled in defence should Y raise an action for payment against X. At that point, the validity of the decision requires to be determined (in private law proceedings) irrespective of the second appeals test.[32] That sort of anomaly suggests the last word has yet to be written about intra vires errors of law.

15–05 What then of errors of fact? As with errors of law, "jurisdictional" errors of fact have always been reviewable.[33] The circumstances in which the court will entertain a challenge on the basis of a mistake of fact are now most clearly set out by Carnwath LJ in *E v Secretary of State for the Home Department*:

> "[T]he time has now come to accept that a mistake of fact giving rise to unfairness is a separate head of challenge in an appeal on a point of law … Without seeking to lay down a precise code, the ordinary requirements for a finding of unfairness are … First, there must have been a mistake as to an existing fact, including a mistake as to the availability of evidence on a particular matter. Secondly, the fact or evidence must have been 'established', in the sense that it was uncontentious and objectively verifiable. Thirdly, the appellant (or his advisers) must not have been responsible for the mistake. Fourthly, the mistake must have played a material (not necessarily decisive) part in the tribunal's reasoning."[34]

A high hurdle is therefore set for a petitioner that seeks to complain about an error of fact. Such an approach reflects the very nature of judicial review. While a court

---

[28] *R. v Monopolies and Mergers Commission, Ex p. South Yorkshire Transport Ltd* [1993] 1 W.L.R. 23, per Lord Mustill.

[29] But there is a presumption that a specialist tribunal understands the law that it is required to apply such that the court, on an appeal from such a tribunal, should be slow to interfere: *AH (Sudan) v Secretary of State for the Home Department* [2007] UKHL 49; [2008] 1 A.C. 678 at [30] (Lady Hale).

[30] See, e.g. *R. (on the application of Adan) v Secretary of State for the Home Department* [2001] 2 A.C. 477.

[31] See para.14–12, above.

[32] H.W.R. Wade and C. Forsyth, *Administrative Law*, 11th edn (Oxford: Oxford University Press, 2014), p.224.

[33] *R. v Secretary of State for the Home Department, Ex p. Khawaja* [1984] A.C. 74; *Tan Te Lam v Superintendent of Tai A Chau Detention Centre* [1997] A.C. 97 PC (Hong Kong).

[34] [2004] EWCA Civ 49; [2004] QB 1044 at [66]. That passage has been repeatedly endorsed: see *De Smith's Judicial Review*, 8th edn (2019), para.11–046 and cases cited therein.

on review may fairly regard itself as best placed to provide an authoritative interpretation on questions of law (subject to the qualifications noted above), it does not follow that it is best placed to determine questions of fact. The primary decision-maker may have arrived at their findings of fact after a lengthy process of evaluation, possibly hearing witnesses or considering representations, and their function may involve the application of specialist expertise or experience. For a court on review to denominate such findings as erroneous, other than where the error is manifest, involves a substitution of judgment that is less easy to justify or explain. It seems clear, however, that the courts are increasingly willing to intervene on the basis of errors of fact, even where the finding of fact is not a condition precedent to the exercise of jurisdiction. In *R. v Parliamentary Commissioner for Administration, Ex p. Balchin*,[35] where the question was whether the Parliamentary Ombudsman had asked himself the wrong question in deciding whether or not there was maladministration, Sedley J held that "if there is such an error, it does not have to be defined as one of law or of fact (the latter too being reviewable if crucial to the decision)".[36] Further, the courts may now require to be more rigorous in their review of the factual basis of decisions because judicial review might otherwise fail to satisfy the requirements of art.6 of the European Convention on Human Rights. European and domestic case law recognises that breaches of art.6 by a primary decision-maker may be "cured" where there is recourse to a higher court or tribunal having "full jurisdiction" and which does meet the guarantees of art.6.[37] This need not, in all circumstances, involve a full right of appeal,[38] but in certain contexts the restriction of the supervisory jurisdiction to questions of legal validity may deprive it of the fullness of jurisdiction necessary to secure compliance with the fair hearing guarantees.[39] Baroness Hale explained in *R. (on the application of Wright) v Secretary of State for Health*, what was necessary to allow judicial review to amount to full jurisdiction:

> "What amounts to 'full jurisdiction' varies according to the nature of the decision being made. It does not always require access to a court or tribunal even for the determination of disputed issues of fact. Much depends upon the subject matter of the decision and the quality of the initial decision-making process. If there is a 'classic exercise of administrative discretion', even though determinative of civil rights and obligations, and there are a number of safeguards to ensure that the procedure is in fact both fair and impartial, then judicial review may be adequate to supply the necessary access to a court, even if there is no jurisdiction to examine the factual merits of the case."[40]

---

[35] *R. v Parliamentary Commissioner for Administration, Ex p. Balchin* [1998] 1 P.L.R. 1 QBD.

[36] *R. v Parliamentary Commissioner for Administration, Ex p. Balchin* [1998] 1 P.L.R. 1 at p.5. See also *Anderson v Secretary of State for Work and Pensions*, 2002 S.L.T. 68.

[37] *R. (on the application of G) v X School Governors* [2011] UKSC 30; [2012] 1 A.C. 167. See also: Wade and Forsyth, *Administrative Law* (2014), pp.381–383.

[38] *Bryan v United Kingdom* (1995) 21 E.H.R.R. 342.

[39] *Kingsley v United Kingdom* (2001) 33 E.H.R.R. 13.

[40] *R. (on the application of Wright) v Secretary of State for Health* [2009] UKHL 3; [2009] A.C. 739 at [23]; see also the concurring opinion of Mr Bratza of the European Commission of Human Rights in *Bryan v United Kingdom* (1995) 21 E.H.R.R. 342 at p.354.

Wrongful delegation[41]

15–06 "Wrongful delegation" is one of a number of heads of review that arise out of a proper construction of the power that confers a discretion upon a decision-maker. Who is to take the ultimate decision? What factors can the decision-maker have regard to in reaching a decision? For what purposes may the discretion be exercised? Each of these questions is answered by understanding the true scope of the power that has been conferred on the decision-maker. Where the wrong person takes the decision, or irrelevant considerations are taken into account or the power exercised for an illegitimate purpose, review on the ground of illegality is available.

Wrongful delegation arises where it is argued that the decision-maker lacked competence to arrive at the decision complained of as the power to take such decisions was conferred on another. In *Vine v National Dock Labour Board*,[42] for example, the House of Lords granted a declaration that the dismissal of a registered dock worker was invalid because the board, instead of deciding the matter itself, had improperly entrusted the decision to its disciplinary committee. But, although the maxim *delegatus non potest delegare* has been applied at the cost of official convenience,[43] it is not to be regarded as an absolute rule. Rather, it reflects a special canon of statutory construction, which may be displaced by indications of a contrary legislative intent. In any particular case, the question for the court is: does the provision that empowers A to take the decision allow A to delegate that task to B? In general, a statute that authorises one level of delegation does not authorise a further delegation.[44]

The principle applies to powers of all kinds, but is likely to apply with greater rigour to powers classified as "legislative" or "judicial" (bearing in mind that such classifications should be approached with caution). While administrative processes are subject to the rule against wrongful delegation, greater tolerance tends to be shown to large or busy or multi-functional organisations.[45] On occasion, the application of the rule shades explicitly into procedural impropriety, as where decisions have been struck down because of delegation to an outside body or because of participation by non-members in the taking of decisions.[46] Similarly, arrangements characterised as "acting under dictation" have been held to fall foul of the rule,[47] although this might be better described as a species of wrongful fettering of discretion.

A special rule, the *Carltona* principle, applies to central government, whereby officials are treated as the minister's alter ego.[48] Originally conceived in relation

---

41 In relation to both unlawful delegation and the rule against fettering, see generally Wade and Forsyth, *Administrative Law* (2014) Ch.10; Craig, *Administrative Law* (2012), Ch.18.

42 *Vine v National Dock Labour Board* [1957] A.C. 488 HL.

43 *R. v Gateshead Justices, Ex p. Tesco Stores Ltd* [1981] 1 All E.R. 1027 QBD.

44 *Barnard v National Dock Labour Board* [1953] 2 Q.B. 18 CA.

45 *R. v Race Relations Board, Ex p. Selvarajan* [1976] 1 All E.R. 12 CA (Civ Div); *R. v Independent Broadcasting Authority, Ex p. Whitehouse*, *The Times*, 4 April 1985 CA (Civ Div).

46 As in *Leary v National Union of Vehicle Builders* [1971] Ch. 34 ChD.

47 As in *H Lavender and Son Ltd v Minister of Housing and Local Government* [1970] 1 W.L.R. 1231; [1970] 3 All E.R. 871 QBD.

48 *Carltona Ltd v Commissioner of Works* [1943] 2 All E.R. 560 CA; most recently explained by Lord Reed in *R (on the application of Bourgass and others) v Secretary of State for Justice* [2015] UKSC 54; [2016] A.C. 384 at [48]–[52]. For a practical application of the policy, see *R. v Skinner (Edward*

to the UK Government, the same principle also applies to the Scottish Ministers.[49] Exceptionally, statutes may exclude the *Carltona* principle and require a particular minister take a decision,[50] but it was held in *R. v Secretary of State for the Home Department, Ex p. Oladehinde*[51] that the implication of exclusion is not easily to be drawn. Local authorities in Scotland benefit from a general authority to delegate their functions to subcommittees and officers.[52]

The rule against fettering

"[I]t is a well established principle of public law that a policy should not be so rigid as to amount to a fetter on the discretion of decision-makers."[53] That makes perfect sense. There is no point conferring a discretion on a decision-maker only for that decision-maker to adopt a policy that means, in various circumstances, no discretion is exercised and a blanket rule applied. Where a discretion is conferred, the decision-maker is required to properly exercise it when called upon to do so. But the rule against fettering does not prevent a decision-maker adopting a policy that explains how they will ordinarily exercise that discretion. That, too, makes perfect sense. A decision-maker should not have to re-invent the wheel every time and a properly formulated policy provides a predictability in decision-making that helps ensure that like applications have like outcomes. That is all reflective of two competing principles that are engaged when the question of fettering arises. They are best explained by the Court of Appeal in *R (West Berkshire District Council) v Secretary of State for Communities and Local Government*: **15–07**

> "It is important to notice a distinction in this area of the law which is at the core of the debate in this appeal. It is between these two principles. (1) The exercise of public discretionary power requires the decision-maker to bring his mind to bear on every case; he cannot blindly follow a pre-existing policy without considering anything said to persuade him that the case in hand is an exception … But (2): a policy-maker (notably central government) is entitled to express his policy in unqualified terms. He is not required to spell out the legal fact that the application of the policy must allow for the possibility of exceptions."[54]

In relation to the first principle, what the decision-maker is required to do is keep their ears open and be prepared to listen to someone who has something different

---

George) [1968] 2 Q.B. 700 where S challenged his conviction for drink driving on the grounds that the breathalyser used to take the incriminating sample had not been approved (under s.7(1) of the Road Safety Act 1967) by the Minister personally. The appeal was unceremoniously dismissed.

[49] *SHBA Ltd v Scottish Ministers*, 2002 S.L.T. 1321; *Beggs v Scottish Ministers* [2007] UKHL 3; 2007 S.L.T. 235. For a discussion of the limits of the principle, see *Somerville v Scottish Ministers* [2007] UKHL 44; 2008 S.C. (H.L.) 45 (where the actions of a prison governor did not fall to be attributed to the Scottish Ministers).

[50] For example, *H Lavender and Son Ltd v Minister of Housing and Local Government* [1970] 1 W.L.R. 1231; [1970] 3 All E.R. 871. More recently: *R v Adams* [202] UKSC 19; [2020] 1 W.L.R. 2077

[51] *R. v Secretary of State for the Home Department, Ex p. Oladehinde* [1991] 1 A.C. 254 HL.

[52] Local Government (Scotland) Act 1973 s.56.

[53] *R (Lumba) v Secretary of State for the Home Department* [2011] UKSC 12; [2012] 1 A.C. 245 at [21] (Lord Dyson).

[54] [2016] EWCA Civ 441; [2016] 1 W.L.R. 3923 at [16]–[17]. Approved, in a Scottish context, in *Dinsmore v Scottish Ministers* [2019] CSOH 55.

to say.[55] But, that places the onus on the person alleging a fettering of discretion to show that they have something to say that could possibly persuade the decision-maker to depart from a stated policy.[56] In practice, the second point is most important. Often a challenge based on a fettering of discretion is based on a policy that is, on its face, absolute. Again, the Court of Appeal in *West Berkshire* explain the good sense behind the principle:

> "It would surely be idle, and most likely confusing, to require every policy statement to include a health warning in the shape of a reminder that the policy must be applied consistently with the rule against fettering discretion … the law by no means demands that a public policy should incorporate exceptions as part of itself."[57]

In other words, there is no need to state what the law will necessarily imply. The consequence is that the proof of the fettering is in the results: a decision-maker that cannot point to an example of when an exception has been considered, or there being a process for considering exceptions, is likely to find it difficult[58] to persuade the court that the policy has been applied consistent with the common law expectations and not in accordance with the face of its terms.[59]

15–08 It is not only in public law decision-making that a risk of fettering a discretion arises. Public authorities enter into contracts as a matter of routine, but as most contracts fetter freedom of action in some way there may be difficult questions of degree in determining exactly how far the authority may validly bind itself as to the future. In a number of cases, the courts have held that contracts entered into by public authorities were ultra vires and void because they were incompatible with the authority's wider statutory functions.[60] This is not to say that a public authority should in all circumstances be freed from its private law obligations, or that an authority is never competent to limit its discretion by entering into contracts. As Lord Blackburn held in *Attorney General v Great Eastern Railway Co*[61]:

> "The doctrine of ultra vires ought to be reasonably, and not unreasonably, understood and applied, and whatever may fairly be regarded as incidental to, or consequential upon, those things which the legislature has authorised ought not (unless expressly prohibited) be held by judicial construction to be ultra vires."

---

[55] *British Oxygen Co Ltd v Minister of Technology* [1971] A.C. 610 at p.625 (Lord Reid).

[56] *Dinsmore v Scottish Ministers* [2019] CSOH 55 at [18] (Lord Arthurson).

[57] [2016] EWCA Civ 441; [2016] 1 W.L.R. 3923 at [21].

[58] But not impossible: *Belfast City Council v Miss Behavin' Ltd* [2007] UKHL 19; [2007] 1 W.L.R. 1420 where what was effectively a blanket ban on licenced sex shops was upheld by the House of Lords; *Dinsmore v Scottish Ministers* [2019] CSOH 55, where despite the absence of an example of an exceptional case having arisen (in the 10 years the particular scheme had been in operation) a complaint that the statutory discretion had been fettered was rejected. cf. *McDonald v Scottish Ministers* [2019] CSOH 106; 2020 S.L.T. 193 where a similar policy was held to have been applied too rigidly.

[59] *R. v Secretary of State for the Home Department, Ex p. Venables* [1998] A.C. 407 HL at p.433. See also, *De Smith's Judicial Review*, 8th edn (2018), para.9–013.

[60] *Ayr Harbour Trustees v Oswald* (1883) 10 R. (H.L.) 85; (1883) 8 App. Cas. 623; *Birkdale District Electric Supply Co Ltd v Southport Corp* [1926] A.C. 355 HL.

[61] *Attorney General v Great Eastern Railway Co* (1880) 5 App. Cas. 473 HL.

As Viscount Simonds later explained in *British Transport Commission v Westmorland CC*,[62] a public authority cannot by contract sterilise or renounce "part of its statutory birthright". There will require to be a fairly manifest incompatibility between the contract and the authority's statutory functions in order to satisfy this test.[63]

Returning to the public law sphere, and the idea of fettering a discretion inevitably rubs up against the developing jurisprudence on legitimate expectations. That, as we will see, involves asking when can a public authority resile from a representation or assurance it has given members of the public. For now, however, where a decision-maker has adopted a policy to guide the exercise of its discretion, not only must that policy operate in such a way as to preserve the core of the discretion, the policy must be one that is based on relevant considerations and which does not pursue an improper purpose. It is to that we now turn.

Relevant considerations

When exercising a discretion, there are some considerations that a decision-maker must take into account ("relevant considerations") and there are some considerations that a decision-maker must not take into account ("irrelevant considerations"). It is a common misconception that a consideration is either relevant (and must be taken into account) or irrelevant (and must not be taken into account). That dichotomy is misconceived for there is a third category: considerations that a decision-maker may decide to take into account. The underlying principle was explained by the New Zealand Court of Appeal, in a passage that has been approved by the House of Lords more than once,[64] by Cooke J in *CREEDNZ Inc v Governor General*: **15–09**

> "What has to be emphasised is that it is only when the statute expressly or impliedly identifies considerations required to be taken into account by the authority as a matter of legal obligation that the court holds the decision invalid on the ground now invoked. It is not enough that a consideration is one that may properly be taken into account, nor even that it is one which many people, including the court itself, would have taken into account if they had to make the decision. ... there will be some matters so obviously material to a decision on a particular project that anything short of direct consideration of them by the ministers ... would not be in accordance with the intention of the Act."[65]

To found a legitimate complaint that a decision is unlawful for want of considering a relevant consideration, the necessarily prior question is "why is the consideration relevant?" And that question is to be answered by reference to the provision that confers the discretion. Unless that provision expressly, or by necessary implication, requires the decision-maker to take that consideration into

[62] *British Transport Commission v Westmorland CC* [1958] A.C. 126 HL.
[63] See, e.g. *R. v Hammersmith and Fulham LBC, Ex p. Beddowes* [1987] Q.B. 1050 CA (Civ Div).
[64] *In re Findlay* [1985] A.C. 318 at p.334 (Lord Scarman); *R (Hurst) v London Northern District Coroner* [2007] 2 A.C. 189 at [57] (Lord Brown).
[65] [1981] 1 N.Z.L.R. 172 at p.183. The root of the principle is Lord Greene MR's judgment in *Wednesbury* where he said, at p.228: "If, in the statute conferring the discretion, there is to be found expressly or by implication matters which the authority exercising the discretion ought to have regard to, then in exercising the discretion it must have regard to those matters."

account, the decision should not be vitiated simply because it was not considered. In relation to considerations that *may* be taken into account (i.e. the third category identified above), a failure to have regard to such a consideration can only be impeached on the ground that it was unreasonable and irrational (in the *Wednesbury/GCHQ* sense) not to have regard to it. In relation to how the decision-maker balanced the various considerations that they did have regard to (in other words, the weight given to the various factors), the court is very unlikely to intervene:

> "[I]t is entirely for the decision maker to attribute to the relevant considerations such weight as he thinks fit, and the court will not interfere unless he has acted unreasonably in the *Wednesbury* sense."[66]

So far as irrelevant considerations are concerned, a decision-maker must not have regard to them and a decision is liable to reduction if irrelevant considerations are, to a material extent, taken into account. For example, in *Ex p. Venables*,[67] the Home Secretary acted unlawfully in having regard to public petitions and other publicly expressed opinions when he fixed the minimum tariff to be served by two children who had been sentenced to detention at Her Majesty's pleasure for their murder of a small boy. Those public views were irrelevant to the question to be determined by the Home Secretary, namely, the minimum period of imprisonment necessary to satisfy the twin objectives of punishment and deterrence.[68] Irrelevant considerations as a ground of review shade into the pursuit of improper or extraneous purposes, simply because both issues have to be addressed by reference to the policy and purposes of the statute read as a whole when interpreting the exercise of statutory authority. The difficulty is that most statutes do not make explicit which considerations are "relevant" and which purposes "proper". That ultimately becomes a matter for the court. Given the open-textured nature of the exercise, majority decisions are commonplace and the distinctions between the cases often appear rather fine.[69]

---

[66] *Tesco Stores Ltd v Secretary of State for the Environment* [1995] 1 W.L.R. 759 at p.764 (Lord Keith). For a practical illustration, see *Beggs v Scottish Ministers* [2018] CSOH 72.

[67] *R. v Secretary of State for the Home Department, Ex p. Venables* [1998] A.C. 407.

[68] *R. v Secretary of State for the Home Department, Ex p. Venables* [1998] A.C. 407, per Lord Goff of Chieveley at pp.490–491; per Lord Steyn at p.526: "It would be an abdication of the rule of law for a judge to take into account such matters. The same reasoning must apply to the Home Secretary when he is exercising a sentencing function. He ought to concentrate on the facts of the case and balance considerations of public interest against the dictates of justice. Like a judge the Home Secretary ought not to be guided by a disposition to consult how popular a particular decision night be . . . The power given to him requires, above all, a detached approach"; per Lord Hope of Craighead at p.537.

[69] Consider, in this regard, cases raising the question of whether and to what extent a public authority may properly rely on financial or resource considerations in taking discretionary decisions: e.g. *R. v Cambridge DHA, Ex p. B* [1995] 2 All E.R. 129 CA (Civ Div); *R. v Gloucestershire CC Ex p. Barry* [1997] A.C. 584 HL; *R. v Sefton MBC, Ex p. Help the Aged* [1997] 4 All E.R. 532 CA (Civ Div); *R. v East Sussex CC, Ex p. Tandy* [1998] A.C. 714 HL; in Scotland, *MacGregor v South Lanarkshire Council*, 2001 S.C. 502.

Improper purpose

A wide discretion is often conferred on public bodies and it is important that it is exercised for the purpose it was given. Where a discretion is exercised for a purpose other than that for which it was conferred, the resultant decision is liable to be reduced. Ascertaining the purpose of the discretion is ordinarily the result of the court construing the underlying statute. The borderline can, at times, be a fine one. This category of review is best illustrated with some examples.[70] *Congreve v Home Office* concerned TV licences for colour televisions.[71] The Home Secretary announced that, from 1 April the TV licence fee would increase from £12 to £18. C had a licence that was to expire on 31 March and on 26 March he renewed it, paid the existing £12 fee and was issued with a licence until 29 February the following year. Some 24,500 other people also renewed licences after the increase was announced but before it was effective in an attempt to save £6.[72] The Home Office wrote to these individuals demanding the extra £6 or their licence would be revoked (the Home Secretary had a general statutory power to revoke a TV licence).[73] Many paid (the "timid ones" according to Lord Denning)[74] but not C. In November of that year, the Home Office issued a final demand failing which the licence would be revoked and if a new, £18, licence was not purchased, he would be prosecuted should he use his colour TV. C raised an action for a declaration that revocation of his licence would be unlawful. The Court of Appeal accepted that the Home Secretary had a discretion to revoke a TV licence. That discretion was not, however, unlimited and could not be exercised improperly or in a manner that would be considered arbitrary. C had obtained what was then a valid licence. It was not appropriate for the Home Secretary to use the threat of revocation as a means to demand a further payment. 15–10

Highland RC v British Railways Board, the "Glasgow ghost trains" case, provides another example.[75] This case concerned the Fort William to London sleeper train, a nightly service that ran in each direction. After privatisation of the railways in the 1990s[76] British Railways Board retained this service. The board had a statutory obligation to ensure that its revenues met its expenditure, i.e. that it did not run at a loss.[77] The board came under pressure from central government to make cuts in its budget and resolved to cancel the Fort William to London service. Ordinarily that would not be a problem as the board enjoyed a wide discretion to decide what services to run on the rail network. However, the Fort William to London service was the only timetabled passenger service than ran over three small areas of track in and around the Glasgow area. Discontinuing the

---

[70] As Craig notes, the law reports "abound with examples" of decisions being struck down on this basis and a number of further examples are given in Craig, *Administrative Law* (2016), para.19–011.

[71] *Congreve v Home Office* [1976] Q.B. 629 CA (Civ Div). Most readers are now unlikely to realise there were once televisions that only displayed a black and white image and that a separate licence was available for them.

[72] A "bright idea" according to Lord Denning and one that had received considerable promotion in the press in the run up to the increase, with the Minister seemingly happy for that to happen (*Congreve v Home Office* [1976] Q.B. 629 at p.652).

[73] At that point, under the Wireless Telegraphy Act 1949 s.1(4).

[74] *Congreve v Home Office* [1976] Q.B. 629 at p.648.

[75] *Highland RC v British Railways Board*, 1996 S.L.T. 274.

[76] Railways Act 1993.

[77] Transport Act 1968 s.41(2).

service would therefore have the effect of triggering the statutory closure procedures.[78] That would have involved a public consultation and would have delayed the withdrawal of the service by at least three months. In attempt to avoid engaging that process, the board introduced three new services that would run across the affected parts of track once a day, all late in the evening. These were not in fact new services but were existing services re-routed. There was, by the board's own admission, little or no passenger benefit as a result of the changes.[79] Indeed, one service travelled down the affected part of track to a station, simply to reverse it back up and into Glasgow Queen Street station. The question, therefore, was whether the board had the power to exercise their discretion in such a way as to frustrate the closure provisions contained in the Railways Act 1993. The Inner House of the Court of Session was not impressed:

> "We agree with the Lord Ordinary that it is difficult to believe that Parliament could have intended that these procedures could be defeated by the provision of a service for the carriage of passengers on that line which is admitted to be of no benefit to the travelling public."[80]

The board's decision was thus unlawful.

Breach of Convention rights

15–11 In Ch.11, above we considered the provisions of the Human Rights Act 1998 in detail and, in particular, saw that as a result of s.6 of the Act it is now unlawful for a public authority to act in a manner that is incompatible with Convention rights. Any claim founded upon s.6 may[81] be brought by way of judicial review. To the extent that such claims form another ground of "illegality", there are two points that are worthy of note. First, in relation to each of the grounds considered above, the court was asking itself whether the decision-maker had reached their decision in the correct manner. It was not concerned with the substance of the decision. A Convention rights challenge is often different. Whilst some rights, such as art.6, are primarily concerned with procedural guarantees, others, for example arts 8–10, are designed to afford a substantive protection. Accordingly, the court has to concern itself with the merits of the decision and not simply the procedure by which it was made. As Lord Hoffmann explained:

> "In domestic judicial review, the court is usually concerned with whether the decision-maker reached his decision in the right way rather than whether he got

---

[78] Railways Act 1993 ss.37–50, in particular s.37 for present purposes.

[79] *Highland RC v British Railways Board*, 1996 S.L.T. 274 at p.280.

[80] *Highland RC v British Railways Board*, 1996 S.L.T. 274 at p.279; see also p.280 where the Lord President (Hope) also justified the conclusion on the basis of error of law: "The decision was outwith the board's powers because it was based on an error of law which lay at the root of the question which the board had to decide."

[81] But not "must" as it can be raised in an ordinary action: *Ruddy v Chief Constable* [2012] UKSC 57; 2013 S.C. (U.K.S.C.) 126.

> what the court might think to be the right answer. But Article 9 is concerned with substance, not procedure. It confers no right to have a decision made in a particular way. What matters is the result."[82]

It follows that the converse is true: just as defective procedure is not fatal if nevertheless a Convention-compliant decision is reached, an impeccably reasoned decision is of no avail if the decision-maker still reaches the wrong conclusion.[83] The second point to note is a related one and concerns an issue that was raised in *Belfast City Council v Miss Behavin' Ltd.*[84] There the council was criticised for not having even considered whether the decision in question was compatible with art.10 of the Convention. That ground of criticism was rejected by the House of Lords, it again being made clear that in the realm of Convention rights, what matters is the result:

> "Either the refusal infringed the respondent's convention rights or it did not. If it did, no display of human rights learning by the Belfast City Council would have made the decision lawful. If it did not, it would not matter if the councillors had never heard of art.10 or the First Protocol."[85]

PROCEDURAL IMPROPRIETY

As with review for illegality, procedural impropriety covers a variety of more specific grounds of attack. Lord Diplock described this category thus: **15–12**

> "I have described the third head as 'procedural impropriety' rather than failure to observe basic rules of natural justice or failure to act with procedural fairness towards the person who will be affected by the decision. This is because susceptibility to judicial review under this head covers also failure by an administrative tribunal to observe procedural rules that are expressly laid down in the legislative instrument by which its jurisdiction is conferred, even where such failure does not involve any denial of natural justice."[86]

At one level, it may involve nothing more than ensuring that prescribed procedural standards have been observed, but the application of common law standards of natural justice and fairness goes much further than this, even to the extent of "supplying the omission of the legislature"[87] where necessary to ensure that decision-makers act fairly in their dealings with the citizen.

---

82 *R. (on the application of Begum) v Denbigh High School Governors* [2006] UKHL 15; [2007] 1 A.C. 100 at [68]; see Lord Bingham (at [29]) to similar effect: "But the focus at Strasbourg is not and has never been on whether a challenged decision or action is the product of a defective decision-making process, but on whether, in the case under consideration, the applicant's Convention rights have been violated." See also: *R. (on the application of Nasseri) v Secretary of State for the Home Department* [2009] UKHL 23; [2010] 1 A.C. 1, per Lord Hoffmann at [12]–[15].

83 *R. (on the application of Nasseri) v Secretary of State for the Home Department* [2009] UKHL 23; [2010] 1 A.C. 1, per Lord Hoffmann at [14]; *Huang v Secretary of State for the Home Department* [2007] UKHL 11; [2007] 2 A.C. 167 at [11].

84 *Belfast City Council v Miss Behavin' Ltd* [2007] UKHL 19; [2007] 1 W.L.R. 1420.

85 *Belfast City Council v Miss Behavin' Ltd* [2007] UKHL 19; [2007] 1 W.L.R. 1420, per Lord Hoffmann at [13]; see also Lord Neuberger at [90].

86 *Council of Civil Service Unions v Minister for the Civil Service* [1985] A.C. 374 at p.411.

87 *Cooper v Wandsworth Board of Works* (1863) 14 C.B. N.S. 180.

Compliance with prescribed procedural requirements

15–13 Statutes conferring power on public authorities commonly impose procedural conditions, such as the serving of notice, a duty to consult, or a requirement to give reasons for a decision once taken. A distinction is sometimes made in this regard between mandatory and directory procedural requirements: non-compliance with the former, but not the latter, is said to be fatal to the validity of a decision. The utility of the distinction, other than as a very general guide, may be questioned. It has been held, for example, that a condition may be both mandatory and directory: mandatory as to substantial compliance, but directory as to precise compliance.[88] Equally, like many of the distinctions drawn in administrative law, it is far from self-executing. Statutes rarely make clear what the effect of non-compliance with a prescribed procedural requirement is to be, so that it falls to the courts to determine the issue. This is a question of construction to be decided by reference to the whole scheme and purpose of the measure, weighing the importance of the condition, the prejudice to private rights and interests flowing from non-compliance and the claims of the wider public interest.[89] Seen in that light, as Lord Hailsham LC remarked in *London and Clydeside Estates Ltd v Aberdeen DC*,[90] the mandatory/directory distinction presents "not so much a stark choice of alternatives as a spectrum of possibilities in which one compartment or description fades gradually into another". Again in *R. v Secretary of State for the Home Department, Ex p. Jeyeanthan*,[91] Lord Woolf MR held that "it is much more important to focus on the consequences of the non-compliance" than to seek to force procedural requirements into rigid categories.[92]

Even where a statutory procedural code is comprehensive in its coverage, the courts may be called upon to decide whether it has been properly fulfilled. A statutory duty to consult is unlikely to stipulate that the consultation be "genuine" and conducted in a manner that allows interested parties a reasonable opportunity to respond. A duty to give reasons will not insist in terms that the reasons are adequate, intelligible and properly connected to the facts, but the courts will add these glosses to the statutory language as a matter of necessary implication, to ensure that the express requirements operate effectively. A wider question is whether a statutory procedural code is exhaustive or whether the courts may supplement it with further procedural conditions. In the past, the tendency was

---

[88] *R. v Chief Constable of Merseyside Police, Ex p. Calveley* [1986] Q.B. 424 CA (Civ Div).

[89] Instances where non-compliance with a prescribed requirement has been held to render a decision ultra vires include *Moss Empires Ltd v Assessor for Glasgow*, 1917 S.C. (H.L.) 1 and *London and Clydeside Estates Ltd v Aberdeen DC*, 1980 S.C. (H.L.) 1 (failure to notify a party of a right of appeal); *Perfect Swivel Ltd v City of Dundee District Licensing Board (No.1)*, 1993 S.L.T. 109 (failure to notify right of appeal to a sheriff); *Stakis Plc v Boyd*, 1989 S.L.T. 333 (commencement without sworn information of proceedings to condemn unfit food).

[90] *London and Clydeside Estates Ltd v Aberdeen DC*, 1980 S.C. (H.L.) 1.

[91] *R. v Secretary of State for the Home Department, Ex p. Jeyeanthan* [2000] 1 W.L.R. 354 CA (Civ Div).

[92] For a recent example, albeit considered at the stage of interim orders, see *Gair v Dumfries and Galloway Health Board*, 2020 S.L.T. 253.

restrictive.[93] Now, as Lord Bridge held in *Lloyd v McMahon*,[94] it is clear that the courts will "not only require the procedure prescribed by the statute to be followed, but will readily imply so much and no more to be introduced by way of additional procedural safeguards as will ensure the attainment of fairness".

A striking instance of this occurred in *R. v Secretary of State for the Home Department, Ex p. Fayed*.[95] The Fayed brothers had applied for naturalisation as British citizens under s.6(1) and 6(2) respectively of the British Nationality Act 1981. Without reasons, their applications were refused. Prior to giving his decision, however, the Home Secretary had indicated in a press release that the applications were regarded as especially difficult and sensitive. The brothers were not told why this was so. The Court of Appeal therefore held that, even though s.44(2) provides that the Home Secretary is "not required to assign any reason for the grant or refusal of any application", the Home Secretary was nonetheless obliged to act fairly in arriving at his decision. He was therefore required to give the applicants sufficient information as to the nature of his concern so that they would be able to make representations. The refusal was quashed.

NATURAL JUSTICE

Introduction

The twin principles of natural justice—*nemo iudex in sua causa* and *audi alteram partem*—state, first, that no one may be a judge of their own cause (the rule against bias) and, second, that everyone has the right to be fairly heard. Both principles are derived from and rooted in judicial decision-making processes, but have been extended by the courts in the exercise of their supervisory jurisdiction to the proceedings of inferior tribunals, whether statutory or domestic, and to more strictly administrative decision making procedures.[96] Judicial and administrative decision-making processes do, however, differ considerably. To that extent, subjecting administrative officials to standards of procedural fairness crafted for a judicial context may not always be appropriate, for if the right to a fair hearing in an administrative setting meant what it means in a judicial setting, the administrative process would grind to a halt. On the other hand, it is recognised that administrative decisions may affect individuals' rights and interests as much as, if not more than, judicial decisions in the modern administrative state. For that reason, and also because intervention on procedural grounds is perceived as less likely to intrude upon the substance and merits of administrative decisions, the most vigorous development of administrative law has occurred in the context of natural justice. 15–14

[93] See, e.g. *Wiseman v Borneman* [1971] A.C. 297 HL, in which Lord Reid held that the courts could only properly extend statutory procedures where "it is clear that the statutory procedure is insufficient to achieve justice and to require additional steps would not frustrate the apparent purpose of the legislation".

[94] *Lloyd v McMahon* [1987] A.C. 625 HL at p.703.

[95] *R. v Secretary of State for the Home Department, Ex p. Fayed* [1998] 1 W.L.R. 763 CA (Civ Div).

[96] The scope for their application to legislative decision-making processes appears, however, to be limited: see, e.g. *Bates v Lord Hailsham of St Marylebone* [1972] 1 W.L.R. 1373 ChD.

Rule against bias

15–15 We have already examined the application of this rule to judges and judicial decision-makers in the context of judicial independence and impartiality in Ch.8, above, to which reference is made. There it was seen that where a decision-maker has a direct pecuniary or proprietary interest in the outcome of proceedings before them, the consequence is automatic disqualification.[97] The categories of automatic disqualification were extended by the House of Lords in *R. v Bow Street Metropolitan Stipendiary Magistrate, Ex p. Pinochet Ugarte (No.2)*, to include interest in the sense of the promotion of a cause in which the judge is involved together with one of the parties.[98] In either case, the maxim that justice must not only be done but must manifestly and undoubtedly be seen to be done[99] applies with its full force: disqualification is automatic and nothing more than the fact of the interest requires to be proved. If the disqualified judge proceeds nonetheless to decide, their decision cannot stand.[100] The rule against bias also comes into play, even though the judge is not financially interested in the outcome or otherwise acting as a judge of their own cause, where in some other sense their conduct or behaviour gives rise to a doubt about their impartiality. Here the test is whether the circumstances were such as to give a fair-minded and informed observer a reasonable apprehension of partiality or bias on the judge's part.[101]

15–16 As ever, the test can be stated quite easily but its application in practice is another thing. A fixed list of circumstances in which apparent bias will be found is probably impossible to prescribe as the question will always turn on the facts of the particular case. In *Locabail (UK) Ltd v Bayfield Properties Ltd*, the Court of Appeal (which comprised Lord Bingham CJ, Lord Woolf MR and Sir Richard Scott VC) set out circumstances that they could not conceive of founding a valid objection. These included: religion; ethnic or national origin; gender; age; class; means; or sexual orientation.[102] The court also set out circumstances that would ordinarily not found a valid objection: the social, educational, service or employment background of the judge (or their family); previous political associations; extra-curricular utterances; or previous instructions to act for or against any party, solicitor or advocate instructed in the case now before the judge.[103] The case law offers some examples of how the rule has been applied, for example the sheriff who criticised striking miners could not then preside over the summary trial of one such miner[104] or the sheriff who invited one of the parties, who was the local Member of Parliament, into chambers so they could be

---

[97] *Dimes v Proprietors of the Grand Junction Canal* (1852) 3 H.L. Cas. 759; *Wildridge v Anderson* (1897) 25 R. (J.) 27, per Lord Moncreiff at p.34.

[98] *R. v Bow Street Metropolitan Stipendiary Magistrate Ex p. Pinochet Ugarte (No.2)* [2000] 1 A.C. 119.

[99] *R. v Sussex Justices, Ex p. McCarthy* [1924] 1 K.B. 256 KBD, per Lord Hewart CJ at p.262.

[100] Even where the disqualified judge sits as a member of a panel, their participation will suffice to vitiate the decision of the panel as a whole: see *Hoekstra (Lieuwe) v HM Advocate (No.2)*, 2000 J.C. 391 and *Davidson v Scottish Ministers (No.2)* [2004] UKHL 34; 2005 1 S.C. (H.L.) 7.

[101] *Porter v Magill* [2001] UKHL 67; [2002] 2 A.C. 357, per Lord Hope at [103].

[102] *Locabail (UK) Ltd v Bayfield Properties Ltd* [2000] Q.B. 451 CA (Civ Div) at [25].

[103] *Locabail (UK) Ltd v Bayfield Properties Ltd* [2000] Q.B. 451 at [25].

[104] *Bradford v MacLeod*, 1986 S.L.T. 244.

formally introduced failed the test of apparent bias,[105] and when a judge described the European Convention on Human Rights as "a field day for crackpots, a pain in the neck of judges and legislators and a goldmine for lawyers" in a national newspaper an appeal that he had heard and that had turned on Convention law arguments required to be reheard by a fresh bench.[106] But in any given case, the question comes down to whether or not the "fair-minded and informed observer" would have a "reasonable apprehension" of bias on the part of the decision-maker. *Locabail* gives us guidance on what does, and does not, found a "reasonable apprehension" but what are the characteristics of the "fair-minded and informed" observer?

The "fair-minded and informed" observer is not the same as the judge who is considering the question: there would have been no need to create this fictitious character if they were. They have been said to be one that pays attention to the woods, not the trees and who is not to be attributed with a mastery of the minutiae[107] but is someone who is "neither complacent nor unduly sensitive or suspicious".[108] In *Helow v Secretary of State for the Home Department*,[109] Lord Hope explained that the characteristic that they be "fair-minded" required that they be the sort of person that:

> "always reserves judgment on every point until she has seen and fully understood both sides of the argument. She is not unduly sensitive or suspicious . . . But she is not complacent either. She knows that fairness requires that a judge must be, and must be seen to be, unbiased. She knows that judges, like anybody else, have their weaknesses. She will not shrink from the conclusion, if it can be justified objectively, that things that they have said or done or associations that they have formed may make it difficult for them to judge the case before them impartially."[110]

That they be "informed" requires

> "that before she takes a balanced approach to any information she is given, she will take the trouble to inform herself on all matters that are relevant. She is the sort of person who takes the trouble to read the text of an article as well as the headlines. She is able to put whatever she has read or seen into its overall social, political or geographical context. She is fair minded, so she will appreciate that the context forms an important part of the material which she must consider before passing judgment."[111]

Yet even with that guidance, difficulties arise. Is there a single, universal fair-minded and informed observer so that the fair-minded and informed observer on the London Underground will be of the same mind as the fair-minded and informed observer on the Edinburgh tram or, as the case may be, the Queen

---

105 *Doherty v McGlennan*, 1997 S.L.T. 444.

106 *Hoeskstra v HM Advocate (No.2)*, 2000 J.C. 391; this case is also an example of an extra-judicial utterance founding recusal.

107 *Davidson v Scottish Ministers (No.2)* [2004] UKHL 34; 2005 1 S.C. (H.L.) 7, per Lord Bingham at [8].

108 *Johnson v Johnson* (2000) 201 C.L.R. 488, per Kirby J at [53], cited with approval in *Lawal v Northern Spirit Ltd* [2003] UKHL 35; [2004] 1 All E.R. 187, per Lord Steyn at [14].

109 *Helow v Secretary of State for the Home Department* [2008] UKHL 62; 2009 S.C. (H.L.) 1.

110 *Helow v Secretary of State for the Home Department* [2008] UKHL 62; 2009 S.C. (H.L.) 1 at [2].

111 *Helow v Secretary of State for the Home Department* [2008] UKHL 62; 2009 S.C. (H.L.) 1 at [3].

Market Square in Belize? That question divided the Privy Council in *Belize Bank Ltd v Attorney General of Belize*.[112] That case illustrates another difficulty in applying the test: how much knowledge is to be attributed to this "informed" observer? We know from Lord Hope in *Helow* that they will inform themselves of what is relevant. This will include all facts that are capable of being known by members of the public[113] but not the same amount of information as another member of the tribunal under attack.[114] In *Belize Bank* the majority attributed to the reasonably informed observer a fairly detailed knowledge of how a senior civil servant would have gone about recommending members of a commission to the responsible minister[115] and they ended up being endowed with much more knowledge than the ordinary Belizean would have had, yet the purpose of the exercise was to ensure the ordinary Belizean would have faith in the tribunal. So, the risks are clear and the court has to take care to ensure that the "fair-minded and informed observer" is not carved too much in the image of the court itself.

15–17 These rules have been applied readily to the decisions of disciplinary bodies,[116] administrative tribunals[117] and other bodies performing judicial and quasi-judicial functions,[118] but at one time it appeared that different criteria applied in relation to administrative authorities. In some cases, for example, it was held that the test for bias could not apply to policy-based decisions, such as those of planning authorities, since these were "radically different" from the decisions of tribunals, which arrive at objective decisions according to rules.[119] However, as Sedley J pointed out in *R. v Secretary of State for the Environment, Ex p. Kirkstall Valley Campaign Ltd*,[120] this kind of pigeonholing—distinguishing between administrative and judicial functions for the purposes of determining the application of the rules of natural justice—was supposedly done to death by the House of Lords in *Ridge v Baldwin*.[121] In *Kirkstall Valley*, an urban development corporation as local planning authority had granted outline planning permission for a retail development on part of a rugby club's property.

---

[112] *Belize Bank Ltd v Attorney General of Belize* [2011] UKPC 36, comparing Lord Dyson at [75]–[76] and Lord Brown at [113].

[113] *Gillies v Secretary of State for Work and Pensions* [2006] UKHL 2; 2006 S.C. (H.L.) 71, per Lord Hope at [17].

[114] *Gillies v Secretary of State for Work and Pensions* [2006] UKHL 2; 2006 S.C. (H.L.) 71, per Lady Hale at [39].

[115] *Belize Bank Ltd v Attorney General of Belize* [2011] UKPC 36, per Lord Kerr at [42]; Lord Brown dissented, in fairly powerful terms.

[116] *Palmer v Inverness Hospitals Board of Management*, 1963 S.C. 311.

[117] *Barrs v British Wool Marketing Board*, 1957 S.C. 72.

[118] *Brown v Executive Committee of the Edinburgh District Labour Party*, 1995 S.L.T. 985.

[119] *R. v Amber Valley DC, Ex p. Jackson* [1985] 1 W.L.R. 298 QBD; *R. v St Edmundsbury BC, Ex p. Investors in Industry Commercial Properties Ltd* [1985] 1 W.L.R. 1168 DC. In both of these cases, local planning authorities had entered into contracts with developers for the exploitation of land owned by the authorities, and had undertaken to do their best to procure planning permission (to be granted by themselves). In *Investors in Industry*, Stocker LJ considered that the disapplication of the rule against bias in such circumstances was justified because, were it otherwise, "an administrative impasse would occur in any case where a planning authority had, quite properly, become involved in some development within its area". See to similar effect the licensing decisions in *R. v Reading BC, Ex p. Quietlynn Ltd* (1987) 85 L.G.R. 387 and *R. v Chesterfield BC, Ex p. Darker Enterprises Ltd* [1992] C.O.D. 465.

[120] *R. v Secretary of State for the Environment, Ex p. Kirkstall Valley Campaign Ltd* [1996] 3 All E.R. 304 QBD.

[121] *Ridge v Baldwin* [1964] A.C. 40.

The applicant complained that this decision was vitiated by the participation of three members and an officer of the corporation, each of whom had disqualifying pecuniary or personal interests in the development such as to constitute a real danger of bias. Although the application failed on the merits, Sedley J accepted the applicant's argument that the test for bias was a uniform test applicable to all bodies, judicial or administrative, which are subject to control by judicial review. His Lordship explained the *Investors in Industry* line of cases[122] as being concerned not with bias but with a different principle:

> "[The] decision of a body, albeit composed of disinterested individuals, will be struck down if its outcome has been predetermined whether by the adoption of an inflexible policy or by the effective surrender of the body's independent judgment."[123]

It may therefore be said that the distinction between judicial and administrative functions no longer determines the application of the rule against bias, although it may continue to influence the rigour with which the rule is applied in any particular case. As Sedley J observed[124]:

> "[What] will differ from case to case is the significance of the interest and its degree of proximity or remoteness to the issue to be decided and whether, if it is not so insignificant or remote as to be discounted, the disqualified member has violated his disqualification by participating in the decision."

Planning and licensing cases illustrate a particular problem with the application of the rule against bias to administrative decisions. What might be described as "structural bias" is often built into particular statutory schemes, as where a minister or local authority is charged with responsibility both for promoting development or adopting policies and for determining appeals.[125] Viewed from the perspective of the right to a fair hearing in the determination of civil rights and obligations under art.6 of the Convention, none of this is necessarily objectionable, provided the decision-maker is subject to subsequent judicial control by a court or tribunal having sufficiently full jurisdiction to secure compliance with art.6.[126] In practice, such decisions are generally subject to, if not to judicial review, then a statutory right of appeal on a point of law to the Court of Session.[127] Following the entry into force of the Human Rights Act 1998, it was held north and south of the border that neither judicial review nor a statutory appeal on a point of law was sufficient to "cure" the structural bias there complained of.[128] *R. (on the application of Alconbury Developments Ltd) v* **15–18**

---

[122] Which were described as "plainly correct".

[123] *R. v Secretary of State for the Environment, Ex p. Kirkstall Valley Campaign Ltd* [1996] 3 All E.R. 304 at para.321.

[124] *R. v Secretary of State for the Environment, Ex p. Kirkstall Valley Campaign Ltd* [1996] 3 All E.R. 304 at p.325.

[125] See, e.g. *Franklin v Minister of Town and Country Planning* [1948] A.C. 87; *City of Glasgow DC v Secretary of State for Scotland (No.1)*, 1993 S.L.T. 198.

[126] *Bryan v United Kingdom* (1995) 21 E.H.R.R. 342. See para.15–05.

[127] See, e.g. Town and Country Planning (Scotland) Act 1997 s.58.

[128] *County Properties Ltd v The Scottish Ministers*, 2000 S.L.T. 965; *R. (on the application of Alconbury Developments Ltd) v Secretary of State for the Environment, Transport and the Regions* [2001] UKHL 23; [2002] 2 A.C. 295.

Secretary of State for the Environment, Transport and the Regions was appealed to the House of Lords, where it was held that the availability of judicial review and/or statutory appeal on a point of law was sufficient to ensure compliance with art.6, with the consequence that the relevant statutory provisions were compatible with the Convention.[129] It should, however, be noted that this will not invariably be the case. Thus in *Kingsley v United Kingdom*,[130] the European Court held that judicial review proceedings were insufficient to cure the possibility of bias on the part of the Gaming Board of Great Britain in deciding to revoke the applicant's certificate of approval, because all that the court on review could do was quash the revocation and order the decision to be taken afresh by a differently constituted panel. In some circumstances, therefore, only a full rehearing by an appellate body will satisfy the requirements of art.6.

Right to a fair hearing

15–19 In *Board of Education v Rice*,[131] Lord Loreburn remarked that the duty to afford a fair hearing is "a duty lying upon anyone who decides anything". This was in keeping with older authorities,[132] which insisted on the observance of fair procedures by public authorities and private or domestic bodies alike.[133] But in the first half of the twentieth century, during what has been termed the "long sleep" of public law,[134] there was a tendency, perhaps most marked in the English courts,[135] to restrict the application of principles of natural justice to circumstances in which the decision-maker acted judicially or the decision affected actual legal rights or privileges.[136] It is for this reason that the decision of the House of Lords in *Ridge v Baldwin*[137] is so often credited with reawakening public law and establishing the foundations of modern administrative jurisprudence. There, a chief constable who had lately been acquitted of criminal charges was dismissed from office by the local watch committee. He was not invited to attend the committee's meeting but later learned of the resolutions adopted at the meeting, upon which the committee had based their decision. He sought a declaration that the purported termination of his appointment was illegal, ultra vires and void as being in breach of natural justice. By a majority, the House of Lords held that an official such as the chief constable, who was dismissible only for cause, was entitled to notice of the charge against him and to an opportunity

[129] *R. (on the application of Alconbury Developments Ltd) v Secretary of State for the Environment, Transport and the Regions* [2001] UKHL 23; [2003] 2 A.C. 295. Following this decision, the Inner House reversed the first instance decision of Lord Macfadyen in *County Properties*: see *County Properties Ltd v Scottish Ministers*, 2002 S.C. 79.

[130] *Kingsley v United Kingdom* (2001) 33 E.H.R.R. 13.

[131] *Board of Education v Rice* [1911] A.C. 179 HL at p.182.

[132] Perhaps most notably *Cooper v Wandsworth Board of Works* (1863) 14 C.B. N.S. 180.

[133] In the latter case, often on the basis of implied terms, see, e.g. *Enderby Town Football Club v Football Association* [1971] Ch. 591.

[134] S. Sedley, "The Sound of Silence: Constitutional Law without a Constitution" (1994) 110 L.Q.R. 270.

[135] cf. Bradley and Himsworth, "Administrative Law" in *Stair Memorial Encyclopaedia* (1995), para.10.

[136] See, e.g. *Local Government Board v Arlidge* [1915] A.C. 120; *Franklin v Minister of Town and Country Planning* [1948] A.C. 87; *Nakkuda Ali v Jayaratne* [1951] A.C. 66 PC (Ceylon).

[137] *Ridge v Baldwin* [1964] A.C. 40.

to be heard before being dismissed, and quashed the decision of the committee. In doing so, the majority based themselves firmly on the nineteenth century case law and disapproved the impediments to the application of natural justice that had been imported by the more recent decisions.

There are good reasons to insist on a fair hearing. Not only is a fair hearing liable to produce better results, but it is likely to produce an outcome that is more readily accepted by those it affects. "Justice is", Lord Reed explained in *R. (on the application of Osborn) v Parole Board* "intuitively understood to require a procedure which pays due respect to persons whose rights are significantly affected by decisions taken in the exercise of administrative or judicial functions".[138] That requires that a person so affected, provided they have something relevant to contribute, be entitled to participate in the decision-making process.

However, the right to a fair hearing cannot mean the same thing in all contexts **15–20** and it is impossible to lay down rules of universal application.[139] In some situations, as was implicitly acknowledged in *Re HK (An Infant)*[140] by the adoption of the terminology of "fairness" or "a duty to act fairly", it may not involve a hearing as such at all. At its fullest, as seen in the proceedings of the ordinary courts, the right to a fair hearing requires: notice of the case one has to answer; an oral hearing in public, conducted in accordance with the rules of evidence; legal representation; the right to cross-examine; a reasoned decision; and a right of appeal.[141] It is with a fair and open hearing that justice and the rule of law are best secured.[142] But the right to a fair hearing does not equate to the right to an oral hearing. An oral hearing is required where it is necessary to secure

---

[138] *R. (on the application of Osborn) v Parole Board* [2013] UKSC 61; [2014] A.C. 1115 at [68]. See also *Secretary of State for the Home Department v AF (No.3)* [2009] UKHL 28; [2010] 2 A.C. 269, per Lord Phillips at [63]: "... feelings of resentment that will be aroused if a party to legal proceedings is placed in a position where it is impossible for him to influence the result".

[139] For example, see *R (Hassett) v Secretary of State for Justice* [2017] EWCA Civ 311; [2017] 1 W.L.R. 4750, [50]–[62] (Sales LJ).

[140] *Re HK (An Infant)* [1967] 2 Q.B. 617 QBD.

[141] See *Al-Rawi v Security Service* [2011] UKSC 34; [2012] 1 A.C. 531, in particular Lord Dyson at [10]–[15] where the Supreme Court held that only Parliament could abrogate the principles of open and natural justice so the court had no inherent power to authorise a closed material procedure (i.e. where evidence was presented to the court but withheld from one of the parties): "The open justice principle is not a mere procedural rule. It is a fundamental common law principle" (at [11]). That strong position must now be read subject to what was said (and done) by the Supreme Court in *Bank Mellat v HM Treasury (No.2)* [2013] UKSC 38; [2014] A.C. 700, where it was held that the Supreme Court had the implicit authority to hold a closed hearing where the tribunal against whom the appeal was taken had express statutory authority to hold closed hearings. On that question, the dissents of Lords Hope, Kerr and Reed are powerful (and compelling). See H.J. Hooper, "Crossing the Rubicon: *Bank Mellat v Her Majesty's Treasury (No.1)*" [2014] P.L. 171.

[142] "Open justice. The words express a principle at the heart of our system of justice and vital to the rule of law. The rule of law is a fine concept but fine words butter no parsnips. How is the rule of law itself to be policed? It is an age old question. *Quis custodiet ipsos custodes*—who will guard the guards themselves? In a democracy, where power depends on the consent of the people governed, the answer must lie in the transparency of the legal process. Open justice lets in the light and allows the public to scrutinise the workings of the law, for better or for worse. Jeremy Bentham said in a well known passage quoted by Lord Shaw of Dunfermline in *Scott v Scott* [1913] A.C. 417, p.477: 'Publicity is the very soul of justice. It is the keenest spur to exertion and the surest of all guards against improbity. It keeps the judge himself while trying under trial'": *R. (on the application of Guardian News and Media Ltd) v City of Westminster Magistrates' Court* [2012] EWCA Civ 420; [2013] Q.B. 618, per Toulson LJ at [1].

a fair procedure and that will be determined by all the circumstances of the case.[143] Plainly, an oral hearing is not appropriate in the context of much administrative decision-making. Thus while the application of the duty to act fairly does not turn on whether the decision-maker acted judicially or otherwise, the content of the duty will depend on "the character of the decision making body, the kind of decision it has to make and the statutory or other framework in which it operates".[144]

It follows, then, that functional distinctions are not deprived of all vitality: the more nearly "judicial" a decision-making process, then, all other things being equal, the stricter will be the demands for fairness.[145] Clearly, however, this is not the only factor material to determining the scope of the duty to act fairly. In so far as it pertained to the threatened destruction of the pursuer's property, *Errington v Wilson*[146] may be said to also illustrate the relevance of the nature of the right or interest affected by the decision under attack.[147] Another factor relates to the stage that a given decision-making process has reached. Often, a decision is arrived at only on completion of a number of procedural steps, such as a preliminary investigation or a public inquiry or consultation. In some cases, statutory procedural codes applicable to the preliminary stages of a process have been held to be exhaustive of the duty to act fairly.[148] On the other hand, it was held in *Re Pergamon Press Ltd*[149] that a Department of Trade and Industry inspector conducting an inquiry into a company's affairs under the Companies Acts was obliged, before publishing a highly critical report, to communicate the gist of their findings to the persons concerned and accord them an opportunity to respond. But that was the extent of the super-added duty to act fairly.[150] The extent to which the duty to act fairly applies to preliminary or interim stages of a decision-making process will therefore depend on a combination of factors: the terms of the statutory procedural code itself; the impact of the preliminary inquiry upon the individual; the proximity of the challenged decision to the final outcome; and, perhaps also, the nature of the inquiry undertaken. The more "investigative" an inquiry, the less likely are the courts to impose additional procedural safeguards over and above those prescribed by Parliament, in order to avoid hindering what may already be a difficult and delicate task.

---

143 Where a decision is challenged on the basis there ought to have been an oral hearing, it is for the court to determine whether, in the circumstances, a fair procedure was followed and not whether the decision to hold an oral hearing was "reasonable" (in the *Wednesbury* sense): *R. (on the application of Osborn) v Parole Board* [2013] UKSC 61; [2014] A.C. 1115, per Lord Reed at [65].

144 *Lloyd v McMahon* [1987] A.C. 625, per Lord Bridge at p.702. But note the caution by Sales LJ in *Hassett* to avoid judicializing what are essentially administrative (or, in that case, operational) decisions (at [60]).

145 See, e.g. *Errington v Wilson*, 1995 S.L.T. 1193.

146 *Errington v Wilson*, 1995 S.L.T. 1193.

147 See also *McInnes v Onslow-Fane* [1978] 1 W.L.R. 1520 ChD, where Sir Robert Megarry VC distinguished between the levels of procedural protection to which an initial applicant for a benefit, an applicant for renewal of a benefit and the holder of a subsisting benefit, which benefit is revoked, would be entitled.

148 *Wiseman v Borneman* [1971] A.C. 297; *Pearlberg v Varty* [1972] 1 W.L.R. 534 HL; *Bushell v Secretary of State for the Environment* [1981] A.C. 75 HL.

149 *Re Pergamon Press Ltd* [1971] Ch. 388 CA (Civ Div).

150 In *Maxwell v Department of Trade and Industry* [1974] Q.B. 523 CA (Civ Div), it was held that fairness did not oblige the inspector to allow cross-examination of witnesses by the subject of a report.

Lastly, the duty to act fairly may be limited, even excluded, in situations where it would normally otherwise apply by reference to overriding public interests. A clear instance of this is *Council of Civil Service Unions v Minister for the Civil Service*,[151] where the House of Lords held that the applicants' legitimate expectation of consultation prior to changes being made to the terms and conditions of staff at Government Communications Headquarters was defeated by the interests of national security. Again in *R. v Gaming Board for Great Britain, Ex p. Benaim*,[152] the Court of Appeal held that the board was "under a duty to act fairly, but not very fairly" in rejecting applications for gaming licences on the basis of undisclosed information passed to them by the police. The public interest in maintaining the confidentiality of information leading to the detection of crime or wrongdoing outweighed the applicants' claim to be entitled to know the charges against them and to make representations in their own defence.[153] That decision must now be regarded as wrong, or at least unacceptable under art.6 of the European Convention (which applies to the determination of civil rights and obligations as well as criminal proceedings). The Strasbourg Court has held, and the Supreme Court has (reluctantly) accepted, that where a decision is based "solely or to a decisive degree" on material that is withheld from one party, the requirements of a fair hearing can *never* be satisfied.[154]

Duty to give reasons[155]

Often a statute will require a decision-maker to state the reasons for their decision. Where a statute requires reasons to be provided along with notification of the decision, the court will normally interpret such legislation as making the provision of adequate reasons a condition of the validity of the decision.[156] In other words, a lawful decision cannot be made without the provision of adequate reasons. At other times, reasons may follow the decision ,but where that is so, the court will treat with a degree of scepticism reasons that are provided after the **15–21**

[151] *Council of Civil Service Unions v Minister for the Civil Service* [1985] A.C. 374.

[152] *R. v Gaming Board for Great Britain, Ex p. Benaim* [1970] 2 All E.R. 528 CA (Civ Div).

[153] This should be taken as illustrative only. It may be, now, that in such circumstances the courts would hold the applicants entitled at least to know the gist of what had been said against them, bearing in mind the possibility that the information might be false or malicious: *R. v Secretary of State for the Home Department, Ex p. Fayed* [1998] 1 W.L.R. 763 and *Kingsley v United Kingdom* (2002) 33 E.H.R.R. 13.

[154] *A v United Kingdom* (2009) 49 E.H.R.R. 79 Grand Chamber; *Secretary of State for the Home Department v AF (No.3)* [2009] UKHL 28; [2010] 2 A.C. 269. The problem is most acute in relation to counter-terrorism and national security where (it is said) disclosing some evidence to the accused will compromise the work of the security services. This problem is considered in Ch.13, above in more detail. See also J. Jackson, "Justice, security and the right to a fair trial: is the use of secret evidence ever fair?" [2013] P.L. 720; A. Kavanagh, "Special Advocates, Control Orders and the Right to a Fair Trial" (2010) 73(5) M.L.R. 836. But the other point that is made (that the duty is not to act *very* fairly), remains a good one. As Lord Mustill explained in *R v Secretary of State for the Home Department, Ex p. Doody* [1994] 1 A.C. 531 at pp.560–561, the proper question is what the minimum standard of fairness requires. In other words, was what happened *unfair*? It is not enough to show that it could have been fairer.

[155] See *De Smith's Judicial Review* (2018), paras 7–088—7–116; Craig, *Administrative Law* (2016), paras 12–038—12–046.

[156] *Chief Constable of Lothian and Borders v Lothian and Borders Police Board*, 2005 S.L.T. 315 at [70].

event (lest they represent an ex post facto rationalisation of the decision) and where such reasons follow the commencement of proceedings challenging the lawfulness of the decision, they are liable to be rejected by the court.[157] Where no statutory duty is imposed to provide reasons, it has long been asserted that there is no general common law duty to provide reasoned decisions.[158] However, developments in this area have been such that the sum of the exceptions to the general principle probably outweighs the principle itself.[159]

There are a number of rationales for requiring that reasons be provided. Reasons may be required where the effect of their absence is to frustrate a right of appeal or review.[160] Requiring the provision of reasons can also improve the decision-making, by requiring the decision-maker to properly focus their mind. That, in turn, can help maintain public confidence in the process. Alternatively, where all the facts and evidence before the court point in favour of a decision other than that which was actually taken, the court may be entitled to infer, in the absence of reasons to the contrary, that the decision lacks a rational basis.[161] As Lord Keith observed in *R. v Secretary of State for Trade and Industry, Ex p. Lonrho Plc*:

> "... if all other known facts and circumstances appear to point overwhelmingly in favour of a different decision, the decision-maker who has given no reasons cannot complain if the court draws the inference that he had no rational reasons for his decision."[162]

In *R. v Civil Service Appeal Board, Ex p. Cunningham*,[163] the Court of Appeal relied in part on this reasoning. There, the applicant sought judicial review of the board's decision to award him, by way of compensation for unfair dismissal, a sum some two-thirds less than an industrial tribunal would have awarded. But Lord Donaldson MR went further, stating that a "judicialised" tribunal is bound to provide outline reasons for its decisions, sufficient to disclose the matters to which it directed its mind, and that failure to do so is a breach of natural justice. In *R. v Secretary of State for the Home Department, Ex p. Doody*,[164] the House of Lords indicated that the very importance of a decision to the individual affected by it may be such that, in fairness and without more, reasons should be provided for the decision. Accordingly, context, as is so often the case, is important. The

---

157 *R (on the application of Nash) v Chelsea College of Art and Design* [2001] EWHC 538 (Admin) at [34]. See also: *Chief Constable of Lothian and Borders v Lothian and Borders Police Board*, 2005 S.L.T. 315 at [65] (Lord Reed) and *Absalom v Governor of Kilmarnock Prison* [2010] CSOH 109 at [13]–[14] (Lord Tyre).

158 *Stefan v General Medical Council* [1999] 1 W.L.R. 1293 PC, per Lord Clyde at p.1300.

159 M. Elliott, "Has the Common Law Duty to Give Reasons Come of Age Yet?" [2011] P.L. 56.

160 *Minister of National Revenue v Wrights Canadian Ropes Ltd* [1947] A.C. 109 PC (Canada) (appeal); *R. v Secretary of State for the Home Department, Ex p. Dannenberg* [1984] Q.B. 766 CA (Civ Div) (review); *Stefan v General Medical Council* [1999] 1 W.L.R. 1293.

161 *Padfield v Minister of Agriculture, Fisheries and Food* [1968] A.C. 997.

162 *R. v Secretary of State for Trade and Industry, Ex p. Lonrho Plc* [1989] 1 W.L.R. 525 at pp.539–540. Perhaps the most high profile application of that idea came in the Prorogation case, [2019] UKSC 41; [2019] 3 W.L.R. 589; 2019 S.L.T. 1143 where the Supreme Court held that on the evidence available it was unable to conclude that the Prime Minister had any reason, "let alone a good reason", to advise the Queen to prorogue Parliament (at [61]). See further, para.1–22, above.

163 *R. v Civil Service Appeal Board, Ex p. Cunningham* [1992] I.C.R. 817 CA (Civ Div).

164 *R. v Secretary of State for the Home Department, Ex p. Doody* [1994] 1 A.C. 531 HL.

more important the decision, or the more significant the consequences of the decision, the more that will be required of the decision-maker to ensure that the process is fair. Because, ultimately, if it is not clear why one person has lost or has had their rights interfered with or restricted, justice will not have been done.[165]

It is not always appropriate, however, that the courts should impose this obligation on public authorities. In *R. v Higher Education Funding Council, Ex p. Institute of Dental Surgery*,[166] the institute challenged the council's assessment of its research (upon which the level of government funding depended) because it was unsupported by reasons. Sedley J held that the council was not required to recite the reasons for its decision as it depended on an unquantifiable exercise of "pure academic judgment". The courts are also conscious of the resource implications of duties to give reasons, and concede that the interests of the complainant must be balanced against administrative efficiency and convenience.[167] There are numerous dicta scattered through the law reports on what in practice an obligation to give reasons requires.[168] But the numb of the duty is elegantly expressed by the editors of *De Smith's Judicial Review* where they observe:

> "In short, the reasons must show that the decision-maker successfully came to grips with the main contentions advanced by the parties, and must tell the parties in broad terms why they lost or, as the case may be, won. Provided the reasons satisfied these core criteria, they need not be lengthy."[169]

There are therefore two aspects to reasons: to show that the main contentions of the parties have been considered and to explain why a party has won or lost. It is generally said that, where reasons are provided, they must be "proper, adequate and intelligible"[170] in the circumstances of the particular case. And the reasons must be "proper, adequate and intelligible" to a well-informed reader, that is, someone who has a knowledge of the relevant background.[171] Accordingly, it is

---

[165] *English v Emery Reimbold & Strick Ltd* [2002] 1 W.L.R. 2409, Lord Phillips MR at [16].

[166] *R. v Higher Education Funding Council, Ex p. Institute of Dental Surgery* [1994] 1 W.L.R. 242 DC.

[167] A like balance is recognised in the jurisprudence of the European Court of Human Rights. In *Helle v Finland* (1997) 26 E.H.R.R. 159, the court held that "while Article 6(1) obliges the courts to give reasons for their judgments, it cannot be understood as requiring a detailed answer to every argument adduced by a litigant. The extent to which the duty to give reasons applies may vary according to the nature of the decision at issue. It is moreover necessary to take into account, inter alia, the diversity of the submissions that a litigant may bring before the courts and the differences existing in the Contracting States with regard to statutory provisions, customary rules, legal opinion and the presentation and drafting of judgments. That is why the question whether a court has failed to fulfil the obligation to state reasons, deriving from Article 6 of the Convention, can only be determined in the light of the circumstances of the case".

[168] The classic, Scottish, statement as to the form of reasoning is that of Lord President Emslie in *Wordie Properties Co Ltd v Secretary of State for Scotland*, 1984 S.L.T. 345 at p.348: "The decision must, in short, leave the informed reader and the court in no real and substantial doubt as to what the reasons for it were and what were the material considerations which were taken into account in reaching it."

[169] *De Smith's Judicial Review*, 8th edn, para.7–105 (footnotes omitted). That passage was approved by the Lord Ordinary (Ericht) in *Paton v Scottish Ministers* [2019] CSOH 62 at [12].

[170] *Re Poyser and Mills Arbitration* [1964] 2 Q.B. 467 QBD.

[171] *Tesco Stores Ltd, Petitioner* [2014] CSOH 153 at [47].

normally permissible to look beyond the four corners of the written reasons and to have regard to factors that would have been reasonably known of. Context, as with so many things, is key and it is important to maintain a sense of proportion.[172] There are two final points to note. First, if reasons are provided that disclose a failing on the part of the decision-maker (for example, having had regard to an irrelevant consideration) it is no defence to say that there was no duty to give reasons.[173] Second, for a challenge based on reasoning to succeed, the aggrieved party must show that they have been substantially prejudiced by the absence of reasons.[174]

Unfairness as an abuse of power

15–22 It is not always possible to categorise unfairness on the part of a public authority as bias, or a failure to give a hearing, a breach of a legitimate expectation or any other specific head of procedural impropriety. Nevertheless, the unfairness complained of may be of such a degree as to call for redress. In *R. v Inland Revenue Commissioners, Ex p. Preston*, the House of Lords held that such would be appropriate where unfairness in the exercise of statutory powers amounted to an excess or abuse of power.[175] The principle recognised in *Preston* was applied by the Court of Appeal in *R. v Inland Revenue Commissioners, Ex p. Unilever Plc*.[176] There, departing from a well-established practice, the Revenue relied on a statutory time limit as defeating claims for loss relief. The Court of Appeal accepted that there had been no such "clear, unambiguous and unqualified representation"[177] as to generate a legitimate expectation on Unilever's part that the former practice would continue to be followed. Even so, Sir Thomas Bingham MR noted that the categories of unfairness were not closed and that, in all the circumstances "to reject Unilever's claims in reliance on the time limit, without clear and general advance notice, [was] so unfair as to amount to an abuse of power by the Revenue". Again in *R. v National Lottery Commission, Ex p. Camelot Group Plc*,[178] Richards J quashed the decision of the commission to reject two rival bids to run the national lottery but to reopen the bidding process to one of the bidders. It was accepted that the enabling legislation accorded a wide discretion to the commission as to how it would perform its functions, but:

> "such a marked lack of even-handedness between the rival bidders calls for the most compelling justification, which I cannot find in the reasons advanced by the Commission in support of its decision... The Commission's decision to negotiate exclusively with The People's Lottery was, in all the circumstances, so unfair as to amount to an abuse of power."

[172] *Uprichard v Scottish Ministers* [2013] UKSC 21 at [44]–[48] (Lord Reed).

[173] *Rooney v Strathclyde Joint Police Board* [2008] CSIH 54; 2009 S.C. 73, per Lord Reed at [32].

[174] *Tesco Stores Ltd, Petitioner* [2014] CSOH 153 at [46]; *JC v Gordonstoun Schools Ltd*, 2016 S.C. 758 at [63].

[175] *R. v Inland Revenue Commissioners, Ex p. Preston* [1985] A.C. 835, per Lord Scarman at p.851; per Lord Templeman at pp.866–867.

[176] *R. v Inland Revenue Commissioners, Ex p. Unilever Plc* [1996] S.T.C. 681 CA (Civ Div).

[177] As required by the decision of the Court of Appeal in *R. v Inland Revenue Commissioners, Ex p. MFK Underwriting Agents Ltd* [1990] 1 W.L.R. 1545 QBD.

[178] *R. v National Lottery Commission, Ex p. Camelot Group Plc* [2001] E.M.L.R. 3 QBD.

Legitimate expectations[179]

The principle of legitimate expectation has developed to "protect persons from gross unfairness or abuse of power by a public authority".[180] It first appeared in relation to issues of procedural fairness: where a person had a legitimate expectation that a public body would take a decision in a particular way.[181] For example, in *Attorney General of Hong Kong v Ng Yuen Shiu*, the Hong Kong authorities had announced that illegal immigrants would be interviewed and each case determined on its merits. Thus, where the authorities purported to expel the applicant, who had entered Hong Kong illegally from Macau some years previously, the assurance given that all illegal immigrants would be interviewed had given rise to a legitimate expectation that should be enforced.[182] The board described the principle thus: "... that a public authority is bound by its undertakings as to the procedure it will follow, provided they do not conflict with its duty".[183] In that case it was an express statement by the public body that had given rise to the legitimate expectation. Such an expectation can also be implied from a public body's past practice or conduct. For example, where the Inland Revenue consistently accepted claims for a tax refund, despite the claim being submitted after the time limit, the taxpayer had a legitimate expectation that its claim would not be rejected, without good reason, as out of time.[184] That case illustrates another aspect of what can be called procedural legitimate expectations. The consistent practice of accepting such claims late gave rise to a legitimate expectation that the Inland Revenue would not change that policy abruptly and without warning.[185] In such cases it is not the change in policy itself that frustrates a legitimate expectation but the process by which that change was made. 15–23

Implicit in what we have said is that the expectation is legitimate, "... nobody can have a legitimate expectation that he will be entitled to an ultra vires relaxation of a statutory requirement".[186] That rule is long established.[187] Where the expectation is said to be based upon an express promise or statement, the

[179] See *De Smith's Judicial Review* (2018) Ch.12; Craig, *Administrative Law* (2016), Ch.22.

[180] *Rainbow Insurance Co Ltd v Financial Services Commission* [2015] UKPC 15, per Lord Hodge at [51].

[181] The judgment of Lord Denning in *Schmidt v Secretary of State for Home Affairs* [1969] 2 Ch. 149 CA (Civ Div) is believed to be the first reference to the idea of legitimate expectations.

[182] *Attorney General of Hong Kong v Ng Yuen Shiu* [1983] 2 A.C. 629.

[183] *Attorney General of Hong Kong v Ng Yuen Shiu* [1983] 2 A.C. 629 at p.638G.

[184] *R. v Inland Revenue Commissioners, Ex p. Unilever Plc* [1996] S.T.C. 681. See also *Council of Civil Service Unions v Minister for the Civil Service* [1985] A.C. 374, per Lord Fraser at p.401.

[185] *R. (on the application of Niazi) v Secretary of State for the Home Department* [2008] EWCA Civ 755, per Sedley LJ at [70].

[186] *Rainbow Insurance Co Ltd v Financial Services Commission* [2015] UKPC 15, per Lord Hodge at [52]. See also *De Smith's Judicial Review* (2018), paras 12–075—12–083.

[187] *R. v Attorney General, Ex p. ICI Plc* (1986) 60 TC 1 CA (Civ Div), per Lord Oliver at p.64G; *R. v Inland Revenue Commissioners, Ex p. MFK Underwriting Agents Ltd* [1990] 1 W.L.R. 1545, per Bingham LJ at p.1569; *Ali Fayed v Advocate General for Scotland*, 2004 S.L.T. 798, per Lord President Cullen at [115]–[119].

representation must be "clear, unambiguous and devoid of relevant qualification".[188] Whether a representation meets that test is assessed by asking how, on a fair reading of the promise, it would have been reasonably understood by those to whom it was made.[189] Other factors are relevant in determining whether a *legitimate* expectation has arisen. For example, the source of the representation is important. The more specific the representation, the easier it will be to establish a legitimate expectation.[190] A representation contained in a letter specifically addressed to the applicant will found a stronger case than one based on a representation in a general circular addressed to a large group. The knowledge of the applicant is also relevant: could they have foreseen that the public body would be likely to change its policy or decision? If so, a legitimate expectation is unlikely to arise.[191] These factors, not one of which is in itself decisive, are pointers not rules and each case must be judged in the round.[192]

Even where the expectation is legitimate, and is strong, it can still be overridden by a sufficient public interest.[193] It is, however, for the public body to justify its frustration of an otherwise legitimate expectation. As Laws LJ explained in *R. (on the application of Nadarajah) v Secretary of State for the Home Department*:

> "The principle that good administration requires public authorities to be held to their promises would be undermined if the law did not insist that any failure or refusal to comply is objectively justified as a proportionate measure in the circumstances."[194]

Whether the applicant relied upon the representation to their detriment is a relevant consideration at this stage, but it is not determinative of the existence of a legitimate expectation.[195] The ultimate question is whether the frustration of a legitimate expectation is proportionate to the legitimate aim that is pursued. In other words, is what has been done fair?[196]

15–24 Our discussion so far has been of legitimate procedural expectations (the way in which decisions are taken). It is now well established that where a representation by a public body is sufficiently clear, unambiguous and lacking

[188] *R. v Inland Revenue Commissioners, Ex p. MFK Underwriting Agents Ltd* [1990] 1 W.L.R. 1545, per Bingham LJ at p.1569; *R. (on the application of Bancoult) v Secretary of State for Foreign and Commonwealth Affairs (No.2)* [2008] UKHL 61; [2009] 1 A.C. 453, per Lord Hoffmann at [60].

[189] *R. (on the application of Association of British Civilian Internees (Far East Region)) v Secretary of State for Defence* [2003] EWCA Civ 473; [2003] Q.B. 1397, per Dyson LJ at [56].

[190] *R. v Ministry of Agriculture, Fisheries and Food, Ex p. Hamble (Offshore) Fisheries Ltd* [1995] 2 All E.R. 714 QBD; *R. v Secretary of State for Health, Ex p. United States Tobacco International Inc* [1992] Q.B. 353 DC.

[191] *R. v Gaming Board of Great Britain, Ex p. Kingsley (No.2)* [1996] C.O.D. 241.

[192] *R. (on the application of Nadarajah) v Secretary of State for the Home Department* [2005] EWCA Civ 1363, per Laws LJ at [69].

[193] *Council of Civil Service Unions v Minister for the Civil Service* [1985] A.C. 374; *Rainbow Insurance Co Ltd v Financial Services Commission* [2015] UKPC 15, per Lord Hodge at [51].

[194] *R. (on the application of Nadarajah) v Secretary of State for the Home Department* [2005] EWCA Civ 1363 at [68]. That passage has been endorsed by the Privy Council: *Paponette v Attorney General of Trinidad and Tobago* [2010] UKPC 32; [2012] 1 A.C. 1 at [38].

[195] *R. (on the application of Bancoult) v Secretary of State for Foreign and Commonwealth Affairs (No.2)* [2008] UKHL 61; [2009] 1 A.C. 453, per Lord Hoffmann at [60]. See also: *Re Finucane's Application for Judicial Review* [2019] UKSC 7; [2019] 3 All E.R. 191 at [62] (Lord Kerr); see also [55]–[61] for a helpful review of the authorities on legitimate expectations.

[196] *R (Bhatt Murphy) v Independent Assessors* [2008] EWCA Civ 755 at [35] (Laws LJ).

any relevant qualification, it can also produce a legitimate expectation of a *substantive* benefit. The classic example remains the case of *R. v North and East Devon HA, Ex p. Coughlan.*[197] Miss Coughlan had been rendered tetraplegic in a road accident in 1971. She was a resident at the local authority nursing home called Mardon House. When she moved in she had been assured by the local authority that this would be her "home for life". This assurance, albeit the phrase "home for life" had never been used, had been repeated to Miss Coughlan and other residents several times.[198] Time passed and the local authority came to the view that Mardon House was uneconomic and it should be closed with Miss Coughlan, and the other residents, being housed elsewhere. Miss Coughlan sought judicial review of the decision to close Mardon House on the ground she had a legitimate expectation that it would be her "home for life" and to close it would be an abuse of power. The Court of Appeal held the "clear promise" that had been given to Miss Coughlan produced a legitimate expectation that it would be honoured unless there was an overreaching justification for doing otherwise. The representation was such that "strong reasons" were required to resile from the promise that had been given and where to keep the promise would not be inconsistent with any other statutory or common law duties that were incumbent upon the local authority, a decision not to honour the promise would be the equivalent of breach of contract in private law.[199] Having examined the local authority's reasons for breaking their word to Miss Coughlan, the Court of Appeal had "no hesitation" in concluding that the decision was unlawful.[200]

The last word has yet to be written about the doctrine of legitimate expectations (whether procedural or substantive). It is, however, a concept that is "rooted in fairness".[201] Having reviewed the authorities as they then stood, Laws LJ summarised where the law currently stands: 15–25

> "The power of public authorities to change policy is constrained by the legal duty to be fair (and other constraints which the law imposes). A change of policy which would otherwise be legally unexceptionable may be held unfair by reason of prior action, or inaction, by the authority. If it has distinctly promised to consult those affected or potentially affected, then ordinarily it must consult (the paradigm case of procedural expectation). If it has distinctly promised to preserve existing policy for a specific person or group who would be substantially affected by the change, then ordinarily it must keep its promise (substantive expectation). If, without any promise, it has established a policy distinctly and substantially affecting a specific person or group who in the circumstances was in reason entitled to rely on its

---

197 *R. v North and East Devon HA, Ex p. Coughlan* [2001] Q.B. 213 CA (Civ Div). The recent decision of the Court of Session in *McHattie v South Ayrshire Council* [2020] CSOH 4; 2020 S.L.T. 399 is a remarkably similar set of circumstances that, unsurprisingly, gave rise to the same result.

198 *R. v North and East Devon HA, Ex p. Coughlan* [2001] Q.B. 213 at [84].

199 *R. v North and East Devon HA, Ex p. Coughlan* [2001] Q.B. 213 at [86].

200 *R. v North and East Devon HA, Ex p. Coughlan* [2001] Q.B. 213 at [89].

201 *R. v Inland Revenue Commissioners, Ex p. MFK Underwriting Agents Ltd* [1990] 1 W.L.R. 1545, per Bingham LJ at p.1569; *R. v Inland Revenue Commissioners, Ex p. Preston* [1985] A.C. 835, per Lord Scarman at p.851: "I must make clear my view that the principle of fairness has an important place in the law of judicial review, and that in an appropriate case is a ground on which the court can intervene to quash a decision made by a public officer or authority in purported exercise of a power conferred by law"; *R. v North and East Devon HA, Ex p. Coughlan* [2001] Q.B. 213 at [71]; *R. (on the application of Nadarajah) v Secretary of State for the Home Department* [2005] EWCA Civ 1363 at [68], where Laws LJ described the principle as "a requirement of good administration by which public bodies ought to deal straightforwardly and consistently with the public".

> continuance and did so, then ordinarily it must consult before effecting any change (the secondary case of procedural expectation). To do otherwise, in any of these instances, would be to act so unfairly as to perpetrate an abuse of power."[202]

Thus, where a legitimate expectation has arisen, a public body that wishes to frustrate that expectation will have to demonstrate that to do so is proportionate in all the circumstances. That invariably calls upon the court to undertake a substantive review of the underlying decision. Ultimately the question for the court, where it has found that a legitimate expectation properly arises, is whether it is fair for the public authority to depart from the undertaking it has given.

SUBSTANTIVE REVIEW

Introduction

15–26 So far, judicial review has been seen as a procedure by which the court can review the decision-making process. Did the decision-maker act within the limits of their powers? Did they only have regard to relevant considerations? Has the decision-maker provided appropriate reasons for this decision? Did the person affected by the decision have an adequate opportunity to participate in the decision-making process? All of this is consistent with what Lord Hope said in *West* about the function of judicial review, "... there is no jurisdiction to review the judgement of the inferior tribunal or jurisdiction on the merits of the action, which has been entrusted to them alone".[203] But what if the individual still insists that the decision is in some sense legally flawed? Where the decision is "unreasonable" or, increasingly, "disproportionate" the court retains the right to intervene. We will discuss what is meant by "unreasonable" or "disproportionate" in a moment. Before that, however, it is worth pausing to consider the constitutional implications of the court undertaking substantive review of decisions.

First, there is a similar objection to that which is made when a party complains of an unlawful delegation: the discretion or decision-making power has been vested not in the court but in the chosen decision-maker. It is for that chosen decision-maker to exercise the discretion within the limits of their authority. But the answer to that complaint is the answer that underlies the entire system of judicial review: an unreasonable decision is unlawful because the court assumes that Parliament (or the other source of the decision-maker's power) cannot have intended to permit the decision-maker to act unreasonably.[204] That, however, is not to suggest there are no limitations on the courts' ability to undertake substantive review of decisions. There are decisions that the courts, whether on constitutional grounds (namely, respect for the doctrine of the separation of powers) or having regard to the limitations on its institutional competence, should be very slow to interfere in. As to the constitutional grounds, as Lord Bingham explained in *R. (on the application of Countryside Alliance) v Attorney General*:

---

[202] *R. (on the application of Niazi) v Secretary of State for the Home Department* [2008] EWCA Civ 755, per Laws LJ at [51].

[203] *West v Secretary of State for Scotland*, 1992 S.C. 385 at p.397.

[204] Wade and Forsyth, *Administrative Law* (2014), p.287.

> "The democratic process is likely to be subverted if, on a question of moral or political judgment, opponents of the Act achieve through the courts what they could not achieve in Parliament."[205]

Those comments were made in the context of a Convention rights challenge but they apply equally to a case seeking review at common law. The institutional limitations of the court were explained by Lord Carswell in *R. (on the application of Bancoult) v Secretary of State for Foreign and Commonwealth Affairs (No.2)*:

> "Decisions about how far to accommodate such concerns are very much a matter for ministers, who have access to a range of information not available to the courts and are accountable to Parliament for their actions."[206]

Where a decision involves the allocation of finite resources or deciding between competing claims on public finances, the court will rarely be in as good a position as the decision-maker to assess those competing demands.[207]

Reasonableness

The classic formulation of the test of reasonableness remains that of Lord Greene MR in *Associated Provincial Picture Houses Ltd v Wednesbury Corp*: the court may interfere if a decision is "so unreasonable that no reasonable authority could ever have come to it".[208] That is clearly a very difficult test to satisfy. In *Council of Civil Service Unions v Minister for the Civil Service*, Lord Diplock preferred to talk of irrationality rather than unreasonableness: **15–27**

> "By 'irrationality' I mean what can by now be succinctly referred to as '*Wednesbury* unreasonableness'. It applies to a decision which is so outrageous in its defiance of logic or of accepted moral standards that no sensible person who had applied his mind to the question to be decided could have arrived at it."[209]

That language is perhaps unfortunate in that it suggests some sort of extreme behaviour on the part of the decision-maker. But it does present a substantial hurdle for a petitioner.[210] Accordingly, the circumstances in which the test is satisfied ought to be rare.

Wednesbury unreasonableness can take a variety of forms.[211] It may strike at decisions tainted by an element of fraud, dishonesty or bad faith.[212] It may also

---

[205] *R. (on the application of Countryside Alliance) v Attorney General* [2007] UKHL52; [2008] 1 A.C. 719 at [45]. See also, *AXA General Insurance Co Ltd v Lord Advocate* [2011] UKSC 46; 2012 S.C. (U.K.S.C.) 122, per Lord Hope at [49].

[206] *R. (on the application of Bancoult) v Secretary of State for Foreign and Commonwealth Affairs (No.2)* [2008] UKHL 61; [2009] 1 A.C. 453 at [132].

[207] See, for example, L.H. Hoffmann, "The COMBAR Lecture 2001: Separation of Powers" (2002) 7 J.R. 137.

[208] *Associated Provincial Picture Houses Ltd v Wednesbury Corp* [1948] 1 K.B. 223 at p.230.

[209] *Council of Civil Service Unions v Minister for the Civil Service* [1985] A.C. 374 at p.410.

[210] *M v Scottish Ministers*, 2013 S.L.T. 875 at [97]–[98] (Lord Bannatyne).

[211] J. Jowell and A. Lester, "Beyond *Wednesbury*: substantive principles of administrative law" [1987] P.L. 368.

[212] See, e.g. *Roncarelli v Duplessis* (1959) 16 D.L.R. (2d) 689. The "boycott" cases may also fall into this category: see *R. v Ealing LBC, Ex p. Times Newspapers Ltd* (1987) 85 L.G.R. 316 (where the

apply where it is said that a public authority has attributed excessive weight to one factor over others in arriving at a decision.[213] Decisions that are unduly oppressive or onerous in their effect on the citizen may also be struck down as unreasonable. Thus, in *Mixnam's Properties Ltd v Chertsey Urban DC*,[214] the House of Lords quashed conditions attached to caravan site licences as unreasonable, being "a gratuitous interference with the rights of the occupiers". The quasi-penalty cases of *Congreve v Home Office*[215] (where the Home Secretary revoked television licences that had been purchased just in advance of a substantial increase in their cost) and *Wheeler v Leicester City Council*[216] (where the council revoked the licence of a local rugby club to use council-owned recreation grounds because of the club's failure to stop four of its members from joining a tour to South Africa) are other illustrations of judicial intervention to control oppressiveness. Although the respondents had in both cases acted to achieve a legitimate aim, the manner of their actions was excessive in that they punished those who had done no wrong. Arbitrariness, perversity or absurdity is liable to be condemned as unreasonable, not only where it is manifest but also where:

> "there is an absence of logical connection between the evidence and the ostensible reasons for the decision, where the reasons display no adequate justification for the decision, or where there is an absence of evidence in support of the decision."[217]

The demise of *Wednesbury* reasonableness (in favour of a test of proportionality) has been on the horizon for a long time now.[218] Some attempts have been made to soften the language and ask only whether the decision is one that a reasonable decision-maker could reach.[219] *Wednesbury* reasonableness remains, for the time

---

council's ban on Murdoch newspapers, adopted to express councillors' disapproval of a "tyrannical employer", was quashed on *Wednesbury* grounds) and *R. v Derbyshire CC, Ex p. The Times Supplements Ltd* [1991] C.O.D. 129 (where a similar ban based on the publication by *The Times* of articles critical of councillors was struck down). In *R. v Lewisham LBC, Ex p. Shell UK Ltd* [1988] 1 All E.R. 938 DC, however, the council's boycott of Shell's products—motivated by a desire to pressurise the company to sever its links with South Africa—was held illegal but not unreasonable, although "very near the line".

213 See, e.g. *R. v Director of Passenger Rail Franchising, Ex p. Save our Railways*, *The Times*, 18 December 1995 CA.

214 *Mixnam's Properties Ltd v Chertsey Urban DC* [1965] A.C. 735. Such a case would now fall to be dealt with in terms of art.1 of the First Protocol to the European Convention, and accordingly the principle of proportionality would apply.

215 *Congreve v Home Office* [1976] Q.B. 629.

216 *Wheeler v Leicester City Council* [1985] 1 A.C. 1054.

217 *De Smith's Judicial Review* (2018), para.11–033. For a practical illustration of such a complaint, see *Adamczak-Gawrychowska v Common Services Agency*, 2018 S.L.T. 415.

218 *R. (on the application of Association of British Civilian Internees (Far East Region)) v Secretary of State for Defence* [2003] EWCA Civ 473; [2003] Q.B. 1397, per Dyson LJ at [34]: "Although we did not hear argument on the point, we have difficulty in seeing what justification there now is for retaining the *Wednesbury* test."

219 *Boddington v British Transport Police* [1999] 2 A.C. 143; see also *De Smith's Judicial Review* (2018), para.11–021.

being at least, as a ground of review.[220] There is an undoubted overlap between the two and often the same result will be reached whether by "reasonableness" or "proportionality".

Proportionality

In *Council of Civil Service Unions v Minister for the Civil Service*,[221] Lord Diplock alluded to the possible future reception of a free-standing doctrine of proportionality going beyond the traditional grounds of judicial review. In *R. v Secretary of State for the Home Department, Ex p. Brind*,[222] the House of Lords declined to adopt a test of proportionality going beyond that of irrationality or unreasonableness as traditionally understood. But *Brind* did not rule out the reception of proportionality review altogether.[223] It would have been passing strange if it had, since the House of Lords had already accepted that: **15–28**

> "the court... must be entitled to subject an administrative decision to the most rigorous examination, to ensure that it is in no way flawed, according to the gravity of the issue which the decision determines".[224]

Proportionality, in this sense, is now a prominent feature of public law, not only in relation to legitimate expectations, but, as we saw in Ch.11, above, human rights as well. As Lord Drummond Young explained, overall, what proportionality in this sense requires "is consideration of the balance between the public interest in the measure under challenge and the private interest of the person affected by it".[225] That necessarily requires the court to make a value judgment, but, as we have seen, judicial review is not a mechanism by which the court can substitute its own assessment for that of the decision-maker. That has seen the court take a structured and analytical approach to the question. That structured approach of the common law is most often attributed to Lord Clyde's judgment in the Privy Council case of *De Freitas v Permanent Secretary of Ministry of Agriculture, Fisheries, Lands and Housing* where he explained that three questions required to be asked by the court:

> "... whether: (i) the legislative objective is sufficiently important to justify limiting a fundamental right; (ii) the measures designed to meet the legislative objective are rationally connected to it; and (iii) the means used to impair the right or freedom are no more than is necessary to accomplish the objective."[226]

---

220 And it is not without its defenders: J. Goodwin, "The last defence of *Wednesbury*" [2012] P.L. 445.

221 *Council for Civil Service Unions v Minister for the Civil Service* [1985] A.C. 374.

222 *R. v Secretary of State for the Home Department Ex p. Brind* [1991] 1 A.C. 696.

223 Lord Ackner and Lord Lowry were concerned that to adopt such a test would "inevitably involve inquiry into and a decision upon the merits", but the view of the majority was that *Brind* was not an appropriate occasion for applying a stricter standard of scrutiny than *Wednesbury*.

224 *Bugdaycay v Secretary of State for the Home Department* [1987] A.C. 514, per Lord Bridge at p.531.

225 *Main v Scottish Ministers* [2015] CSIH 41; 2015 S.L.T. 349, Lord Drummond Young at [49].

226 *De Freitas v Permanent Secretary of Ministry of Agriculture, Fisheries, Lands and Housing* [1999] A.C. 69 PC (Antigua and Barbuda) at p.80.

That discussion took place in the context of the constitution of Antigua and Barbuda, but was regularly applied by the UK courts when called upon to determine a question of proportionality.[227] That tripartite approach did undergo some modification[228] and in *Bank Mellat v HM Treasury (No.2)*, the Supreme Court explained how the courts should now address the question of proportionality. In a passage that merits repetition in full, Lord Reed explained:

> "As assessment of proportionality inevitably involves a value judgment at the stage at which a balance has to be struck between the importance of the objective pursued and the value of the right intruded upon. The principle does not however entitle the courts simply to substitute their own assessment for that of the decision-maker. As I have noted, the intensity of review under EU law and the Convention varies according to the nature of the right at stake and the context in which the interference occurs. Those are not however the only relevant factors. One important factor in relation to the Convention is that the Strasbourg court recognises that it may be less well placed than a national court to decide whether an appropriate balance has been struck in the particular national context. For that reason, in the Convention case law the principle of proportionality is indissolubly linked to the concept of the margin of appreciation. That concept does not apply in the same way at the national level, where the degree of restraint practised by courts in applying the principle of proportionality, and the extent to which they will respect the judgment of the primary decision maker, will depend on the context, and will in part reflect national traditions and institutional culture. For these reasons, the approach adopted to proportionality at the national level cannot simply mirror that of the Strasbourg court."[229]

Lord Reed went on to set out the structured approach that should be adopted by the court when it is called upon to make an assessment of the proportionality of a particular measure:

> "... it is necessary to determine (1) whether the objective of the measure is sufficiently important to justify the limitation of a protected right, (2) whether the measure is rationally connected to the objective, (3) whether a less intrusive measure could have been used without unacceptably compromising the achievement of the objective, and (4) whether, balancing the severity of the measure's effects on the rights of the person to whom it applies against the importance of the objective, to the extent that the measure will contribute to its achievement, the former outweighs the latter."[230]

---

[227] For example, *R. (on the application of Daly) v Secretary of State for the Home Department* [2001] UKHL 26; [2001] 2 A.C. 532.

[228] See, for example, *R. (on the application of Razgar) v Secretary of State for the Home Department* [2004] UKHL 27; [2004] 2 A.C. 368; *Huang v Secretary of State for the Home Department* [2007] UKHL 11; [2007] 2 A.C. 167; *R. (on the application of Aguilar Quila) v Secretary of State for the Home Department* [2011] UKSC 45; [2012] 1 A.C. 621.

[229] *Bank Mellat v HM Treasury (No.2)* [2013] UKSC 39; [2014] A.C. 700 at [71]. Although Lord Reed was dissenting on the application of the test in that particular case, his analysis of the concept of proportionality was endorsed by the majority: Lord Sumption at [20].

[230] *Bank Mellat v HM Treasury (No.2)* [2013] UKSC 39; [2014] A.C. 700 at [74]; see also Lord Sumption at [20]. In that analysis Lord Reed drew on Lord Clyde's seminal discussion of proportionality in *De Freitas v Permanent Secretary of Ministry of Agriculture, Fisheries, Lands and Housing* [1999] A.C. 69 at p.80 and Dickson CJ's discussion in the Canadian Supreme Court in *R. v Oakes* [1986] 1 S.C.R. 103.

This structured approach to proportionality, requiring the court to address four questions, has been subsequently endorsed by the Supreme Court.[231] In relation to the third question, the courts must not apply that requirement too literally. To do so would permit only a single response and would deny the decision-maker any margin of appreciation.[232] Properly understood, therefore, the third question requires the court to be satisfied that the measure selected by the public body is within the range of measures that can reasonably be considered as required to fulfil the policy objective.[233] In practice, it will normally be the fourth question that proves the most challenging. This question did not feature in Lord Clyde's initial explanation of proportionality in *De Freitas*, but the need to balance the interests of society with those of individuals or groups within society had been recognised by the House of Lords as a part of the proportionality exercise that "should never be overlooked or discounted".[234] By the time this question is reached, the court will already have found that there was no less intrusive measure that could have obtained the desired objective. What is left is a value judgment for the court.

What will now be apparent is that there is a significant overlap between unreasonableness/irrationality and proportionality. Whether a decision-maker has acted reasonably in balancing the competing relevant factors in reaching their decision or whether there is a rational connection between means and ends are two issues that arise in an "unreasonableness" challenge but which have a strong affinity with the concept of proportionality.[235] However, whilst the courts have long been willing to assess the reasonableness of a decision taken by a public body, they continue to deny that proportionality can be relied upon as a self-standing ground of review in the same way. **15–29**

[231] *Gaughran v Chief Constable of the Police Service of Northern Ireland* [2015] UKSC 29; [2016] A.C. 345.

[232] *Bank Mellat v HM Treasury (No.2)* [2013] UKSC 39; [2014] A.C. 700, per Lord Reed at [75]. For a practical application of that approach, see *Main v Scottish Ministers* [2015] CSIH 41; 2015 S.L.T. 349, in particular Lord Justice-Clerk Carloway at [35]–[36].

[233] *Main v Scottish Ministers* [2015] CSIH 41; 2015 S.L.T. 349, per Lord Drummond Young at [48]. For a practical application of that approach, see Lord Justice-Clerk Carloway at [35]–[36].

[234] *Huang v Secretary of State for the Home Department* [2007] UKHL 11; [2007] 2 A.C. 167, per Lord Bingham at [19]. Lord Bingham cited *R. (on the application of Razgar) v Secretary of State for the Home Department* [2004] UKHL 27; [2004] 2 A.C. 368 in support. In that case, Lord Bingham explained that striking a fair balance between the rights of the individual and the interests of the community as a whole was inherent in the entire proportionality exercise (see [17]–[20]).

[235] *De Smith's Judicial Review* (2018), para.11–085.

INDEX

All references are to paragraph number